Analyzing International Business Operations in the Post-Pandemic Era

Bryan Christiansen
The Christiansen Foundation, USA

John D. Branch
University of Michigan, USA

IGI Global
PUBLISHER of TIMELY KNOWLEDGE

A volume in the Advances in Business Strategy and Competitive Advantage (ABSCA) Book Series

Published in the United States of America by
IGI Global
Business Science Reference (an imprint of IGI Global)
701 E. Chocolate Avenue
Hershey PA, USA 17033
Tel: 717-533-8845
Fax: 717-533-8661
E-mail: cust@igi-global.com
Web site: http://www.igi-global.com

Library of Congress Cataloging-in-Publication Data

Names: Christiansen, Bryan, 1960- editor. | Branch, John David, 1967- editor.
Title: Analyzing international business operations in the post-pandemic era / Bryan Christiansen, and John David Branch, editor.
Description: Hershey, PA : Business Science Reference, [2023] | Includes bibliographical references and index. | Summary: "This book investigates how the COVID-19 pandemic has changed many of the rules of the game with regard to issues such as global supply chain management, the continued use of virtual offices, emerging economic and financial models, and international expansion plans, among others"-- Provided by publisher.
Identifiers: LCCN 2022001836 (print) | LCCN 2022001837 (ebook) | ISBN 9781668437490 (hardcover) | ISBN 9781668460269 (softcover) | ISBN 9781668437506 (ebook)
Subjects: LCSH: International business enterprises. | COViD-19 Pandemic, 2020---Economic aspects.
Classification: LCC HD2755.5 .A56 2022 (print) | LCC HD2755.5 (ebook) | DDC 338.8/8--dc23/eng/20220114
LC record available at https://lccn.loc.gov/2022001836
LC ebook record available at https://lccn.loc.gov/2022001837

This book is published in the IGI Global book series Advances in Business Strategy and Competitive Advantage (ABSCA) (ISSN: 2327-3429; eISSN: 2327-3437)

British Cataloguing in Publication Data
A Cataloguing in Publication record for this book is available from the British Library.

Advances in Business Strategy and Competitive Advantage (ABSCA) Book Series

Patricia Ordóñez de Pablos
Universidad de Oviedo, Spain

ISSN:2327-3429
EISSN:2327-3437

Mission

Business entities are constantly seeking new ways through which to gain advantage over their competitors and strengthen their position within the business environment. With competition at an all-time high due to technological advancements allowing for competition on a global scale, firms continue to seek new ways through which to improve and strengthen their business processes, procedures, and profitability.

The **Advances in Business Strategy and Competitive Advantage (ABSCA) Book Series** is a timely series responding to the high demand for state-of-the-art research on how business strategies are created, implemented and re-designed to meet the demands of globalized competitive markets. With a focus on local and global challenges, business opportunities and the needs of society, the **ABSCA** encourages scientific discourse on doing business and managing information technologies for the creation of sustainable competitive advantage.

Coverage

- Resource-Based Competition
- Economies of Scale
- Differentiation Strategy
- Customer-Orientation Strategy
- Competitive Strategy
- Strategic Alliances
- Strategic Management
- Co-operative Strategies
- Cost Leadership Strategy
- Value Chain

IGI Global is currently accepting manuscripts for publication within this series. To submit a proposal for a volume in this series, please contact our Acquisition Editors at Acquisitions@igi-global.com or visit: http://www.igi-global.com/publish/.

The Advances in Business Strategy and Competitive Advantage (ABSCA) Book Series (ISSN 2327-3429) is published by IGI Global, 701 E. Chocolate Avenue, Hershey, PA 17033-1240, USA, www.igi-global.com. This series is composed of titles available for purchase individually; each title is edited to be contextually exclusive from any other title within the series. For pricing and ordering information please visit http://www.igi-global.com/book-series/advances-business-strategy-competitive-advantage/73672. Postmaster: Send all address changes to above address.

Titles in this Series

For a list of additional titles in this series, please visit: http://www.igi-global.com/book-series/advances-business-strategy-competitive-advantage/73672

The Transformation of Global Trade in a New World
Bartolomé Marco-Lajara (University of Alicante, Spain) Ahu Coşkun Özer (Marmara University, Turkey) and Javier Martínez Falcó (University of Alicante, Spain)
Business Science Reference • © 2023 • 308pp • H/C (ISBN: 9781668459508) • US $250.00

Exploring the Economic Opportunities and Impacts of Migrant Entrepreneurship Success Stories and Case Studies
Meena Chavan (Macquarie University, Australia) and Sheba Nandkeolyar (Multiconnexions, Australia)
Business Science Reference • © 2022 • 231pp • H/C (ISBN: 9781668449868) • US $215.00

Analyzing the Relationship Between Corporate Governance, CSR, and Sustainability
Ayberk Soyer (Istanbul Technical University, Turkey) and Umut Asan (Istanbul Technical University, Turkey)
Business Science Reference • © 2022 • 315pp • H/C (ISBN: 9781799842347) • US $215.00

Handbook of Research on Digital Innovation and Networking in Post-COVID-19 Organizations
Ana Pego (Nova University of Lisbon, Portugal)
Business Science Reference • © 2022 • 539pp • H/C (ISBN: 9781668467626) • US $315.00

Antecedents and Outcomes of Employee-Based Brand Equity
Muhammad Waseem Bari (Government College University, Faisalabad, Pakistan) Muhammad Abrar (Government College University, Faisalabad, Pakistan) and Emilia Alaverdov (Tbilisi State University, Georgia)
Business Science Reference • © 2022 • 297pp • H/C (ISBN: 9781668436219) • US $250.00

Cases on Emerging Market Responses to the COVID-19 Pandemic
Raj K. Kovid (Sharda University, India) and Vikas Kumar (Central University of Haryana, India)
Business Science Reference • © 2022 • 332pp • H/C (ISBN: 9781668435045) • US $240.00

Impact of Digital Transformation on the Development of New Business Models and Consumer Experience
Maria Antónia Rodrigues (Polytechnic of Porto, Portugal & CEOS.PP, Portugal & SIIS Porto, Portugal) and João F. Proença (Faculty of Economics, University of Porto, Portugal & Advance/CSG, University of Lisbon, Portugal & ISEG, University of Lisbon, Portugal)
Business Science Reference • © 2022 • 347pp • H/C (ISBN: 9781799891796) • US $240.00

IGI Global
PUBLISHER of TIMELY KNOWLEDGE

701 East Chocolate Avenue, Hershey, PA 17033, USA
Tel: 717-533-8845 x100 • Fax: 717-533-8661
E-Mail: cust@igi-global.com • www.igi-global.com

For Capt. Earle Grace Gardner, Jr. (1913-2005) and Lt. Earle Grace Gardner, Sr. (1885-1960). The former was in the US Navy for 30 years and his father retired from the same after 44 years. Both served abroad for decades and were ardent students of international affairs and business.

Table of Contents

Detailed Table of Contents

The global expansion of supply chains between 1990 and 2010 was characterized by efficiency-seeking through extreme specialization, task fragmentation, and geographical dispersion. Such chains, while offering cost benefits, are vulnerable to damaging disruption when operational conditions shift. The COVID-19 pandemic has initiated a reconsideration of supply chains with calls for enhanced resilience. These calls coincide with a growing fragmentation of global production and supply chains with China's increasing influence in global standards, supply of intermediate inputs, and domestic economic upgrading. This chapter examines the growth and vulnerabilities of lean global supply chains, arguments for greater resilience, and the cost implications of supply chain restructuring at a time of growing uncertainty and possible geographic fracture.

Researchers have studied foreign direct investment (FDI) from various perspectives, and noted the motives of FDI depend predominantly on disadvantages in home countries or advantages in host countries. However, little is known about how investors avail themselves of such advantages. The purpose of this chapter is to offer guidelines to investors to make effective FDI decisions and maintain sustainable international expansions in the post-pandemic era. Via a conceptual review of the extant literature, the authors elaborate on the motives of FDI from the perspective of the capacities of investors and provide a nuanced understanding of how they can make better investment decisions based on both the lacks and capacities. The authors develop a framework elucidating that the motives of FDI can be determined by a firm's level of technology and absorptive capacity. The framework will help investors to find cross-border partners to collaborate with, increase resilience, and deal with post-pandemic recovery.

Whereas firms need to adapt to such changes rapidly, sometimes their efforts remain insufficient in the face of unprecedented environmental changes. The main purpose of this study is to explain the sudden changes to normality that are necessary to overcome the impact of the Covid-19 pandemic on all sectors, enabling competitiveness and value creation. This chapter aims to address the following broad research questions: first, how firms that investigate opportunities can increase their market share in all industries. Second, how firms can ensure sustainability in the new normal. Third, how the change brought about by the pandemic is reflected in the organization and what should be the leaders' role in the adoption of this process. Fourth, how innovation can be implemented that creates value in the new normal. And finally, how the new business model should be designed more competitively and creates more value.

Past studies have attempted to identify the domains of international business over specific periods of time. Most have used data sets for short time periods, providing a snapshot of the field for the period under review. This chapter reviews the research in the area of international business for the past five decades, with the objective of understanding the path that research has taken during that period in terms of research content, relevance, and methodology. While this understanding supports a proposal for a research agenda for the future, from the perspective of both content and methods in international business research, the impact of the pandemic may require a re-look at the trends that have been presented. The chapter addresses some of the potential changes in the trends in the research agenda that could occur due to the pandemic.

The COVID-19 pandemic disrupted international trade networks in 2020. Although worldwide commerce has recovered in the subsequent period, it is anticipated that globalization will make a new turn. The purpose of this study is to review the current research that examines the impact of the pandemic on international business. The methodology encompasses a semi-systematic review, which includes a summary and synthesis of selected empirical papers. The focal content of this review is the implication sections of the articles. By doing so, this study attempts to bridge the research-relevance gap.

The globally mobile workforce of international professionals has been significantly impacted by the COVID-19 pandemic. Closed borders and entry restrictions for foreign residents have left many expatriates separated from partners and family members. Previously held assumptions about the ability to travel whenever needed have been severely challenged, thus leaving some questioning the attractiveness of living and working abroad. The expectations of mobility that individuals as well as organizations used to have are changed. The research aimed to assess the impact of factors like travel and other restrictions on the priorities of expatriates and on their willingness to consider future mobility, as well as how the disruption affected expatriates' concept of family. The research shows that organizations will have to examine if expatriation is a sustainable strategy. Both expatriates and organizations are more than ever subjected to local government regulations concerning the acceptance and conditions of life and travel for expatriates.

As the foreign direct investment (FDI) attractiveness indexes constitute one of the decision tools for governments' politics, it is relevant to assess the Groh and Wich Index (GWI). The main purpose is to verify the capacity of this index to replicate the phenomena of inflow FDI. The index analysis process included reviewing literature and detecting weaknesses on theoretical frameworks and in the selection of basic indicators. Multivariate analysis, applied to a sample of economies, showed evidence that some composite indicators of the GWI have shortages of concordance between simple indicators. Apart from showing that FDI attractiveness index of Groh and Wich does not convey the progress of inflow FDI, the study demonstrates that a FDI attractiveness index built to advanced economies can hardly be employed to developing economies without significant changes to the basic indicators.

In the 21st century, nations are oscillating between globalization, deglobalization, protectionism, and localization. Issues considered while making decisions on what policy to follow include the economic boom, the slump in the economy, and politics. Nations adopt protectionism despite its known negative effects because of political reasons. The size of the economy of the developed countries allows them to implement these policies and withstand any adverse effect arising from isolation or retaliatory actions. The African continent cannot afford to find itself in this war between two elephants. Hence, the chapter reviewed the options available to Africa and recommended the adoption of localization aimed at building size and presenting a common competitive advantage that member states of the local bodies can employ. The chapter recommended certain changes to be made in leadership and mode of operation to avoid localization going the way of globalization.

More than two years have passed since the new type of coronavirus began in Wuhan, China. In addition, it has been more than 22 months since the World Health Organization (WHO) declared a pandemic, and the world continues to struggle with new variants of the virus and cannot return to the old normal. Closures, lockdowns, and restrictions on foreign trade of goods and services have decreased global economic activity. It is seen that two important challenges have emerged due to the pandemic. First, the countries with limited health services capacity in the face of the increasing number of cases and deaths in the world had trouble to combat with the pandemic. Second, low-income countries which have difficulty in accessing medicines and vaccines having an important role in combating the pandemic are more distressed than other countries and need global support. It is seen that the inequality in income distribution between countries in the world also manifests itself in accessing drugs and vaccines.

The COVID-19 pandemic was one of the deadliest pandemics ever encountered by human civilization. However, the unconquerable human resilience and the digital duo of mobile and internet led to a victory over this dreadful pandemic. This chapter initially focuses on India to illustrate the necessity of literacy in a pandemic. Later, the chapter accepts the hypothesis that business and trade is the engine of growth and verifies that in such dire conditions whether digital business and trade acted as a buffer. Both the aforementioned aspects are quantitatively verified. This chapter uses two regression equations with robust standard errors to examine COVID-19 and literacy. Two dependent variables are population recovered to population tested and completely vaccinated to the total population, and both the population density and rate of literacy have been taken as two independent variables. Furthermore, this chapter also has analyzed the relevant data of 137 countries and has emphasized the fact how digitalization has acted as a buffer and kept business and trade going in a "no man's land."

Sustainability is a global need, both for companies and people. It is not only a matter of convenience to achieve more excellent business benefits, but it is also accompanied by the concept of a smart city, which is of fundamental importance since it also goes in parallel with Industry 4.0. This chapter describes the technologies associated with the implementation of smart cities, benefits, limitations, and contribution to sustainability. Different examples of smart cities are described, highlighting the requirements for implementation and the associated risks. The amount and type of specific technologies available in implementing a smart city are striking. Sustainable cities and smart cities undoubtedly share many characteristics, so the interconnection of concepts facilitates implementation, knowing all the technological requirements necessary for development.

Preface

THE DSM

The Diagnostic and Statistical Manual of Mental Disorders (DSM for short) is, as intimated by its appellation, the handbook which is used by most psychologists, psychiatrists, and other clinicians throughout the United States, to diagnose and document psychiatric illnesses. It has been published by the American Psychiatric Association (the APA) since 1952 and is currently in its fifth edition. In summary, the DSM includes descriptions and symptoms of mental disorders, which are needed for clinical diagnosis (the diagnostic part of the manual's title), along with statistics about people who are most afflicted by specific mental disorders, incident rates of these mental disorders, outcomes of treatments for these mental disorders, and so on (the statistical part of the manual's title). The DSM is intended to "help clinicians and researchers define and classify mental disorders, which can improve diagnoses, treatment, and research" ("DSM", 2022).

The United States government made the first coordinated attempt to gather information about the mental health of the American population by recording the frequency of 'idiocy/insanity' in the 1840 census. By the late 1800s, the notion of mental disorder categories began to emerge. But it was not until after World War II that the DSM was published, inspired by the International Classification of Diseases (the ICD) which is published by the World Health Organization (WHO), and whose 6th edition which appeared in 1948 contained, for the first time, a section on mental disorders.

The DSM-2 was published in 1968, its main difference being the elimination of the term reaction, whose use "throughout DSM reflected the influence of Adolf Meyer's psychobiological view that mental disorders represented reactions of the personality to psychological, social, and biological factors." ("DSM History", 2022). The publication of the DSM-3 in 1980 signaled what might be called the modernization of psychiatric diagnosis—"an agnostic approach to the etiology (causes) of mental disorders and instead a focus on explicit diagnostic criteria" ("History of…", 2022). Indeed, for the DSM III, concerted efforts were made to construct and validate specific criteria, and thereby increase the reliability of diagnoses among clinicians.

The DSM-4 arrived in 1994, and with it came: 1. an emphasis on an empirical basis for each entry, 2. modifications to the classification of mental disorders, and 3. closer harmonisation with the 10th edition of the ICD. By emphasising the current state of scholarly research on mental disorders, the DSM-5 which was published in 2013, aimed to stimulate more research in the field of mental health. The most current edition is the DMS-5-TR (TR meaning text revision); it updates and clarifies the text for entries in the manual, includes a new diagnosis for prolonged grief disorder, and reviews the "impact of racism and discrimination on the diagnosis and manifestations of mental disorders" (Diagnostic…", 2022).

TSRD AND THE COVID-19 PANDEMIC

One notable change in the DSM-5 and DSM-5-TR editions is the introduction of a new category of mental disorders which are known collectively as Trauma- and Stressor-Related Disorders (or TSRD), chief among which is post-traumatic stress disorder (or PTSD). Previously, PTSD and other similar mental disorders were categorized along with anxiety- or fear-based mental disorders. But between the publications of DSM 4 and DSM 5, the definition of a trauma was reconsidered, additional stressors were identified, and researchers recognized that trauma- and stressor-related mental disorders were not based on anxiety or fear, thereby necessitating their own category.

Trauma- and stressor-related disorders involve exposure to traumatic or stressful events which cause psychological distress. Traumatic events are often associated with ongoing war, for example, sexual violence, or even a car-accident. Stressors might arise from a toxic relationship, a chronic disease, or the incarceration of a family-member. People who suffer from a traumatic stress-related disorder exhibit "anhedonic symptoms (inability to feel pleasure), dysphoric symptoms (state of unease or dissatisfaction), dissociative symptoms, and an exterernalization of anger and aggressive symptoms" (Trauma &…", 2022).

Now, neither DSM-5 nor DSM-5-TR addressed the COVID-19 pandemic explicitly. Moreover, according to Bridgland *et* al. (2021), "the COVID-19 pandemic does not fit into prevailing Post-traumatic Stress Disorder (PTSD) models, or diagnostic criteria". But there is a growing body of literature which suggests that the COVID-19 pandemic is a traumatic stressor which has led to PTSD and other TSRD symptomology. Indeed,

[d]ifferent groups have met the qualifying criteria for posttraumatic stress disorder (PTSD) according to DSM-5 as a result of the pandemic: those who have themselves suffered from serious COVID-19 illness and potential death; individuals who, as family members and health care workers, have witnessed others' suffering and death; individuals who have learned about the death or risk of death of a family member or friend due to the virus; and individuals who have experienced extreme exposure to aversive details (eg, journalists, first responders, medical examiners, and hospital personnel) (Tucker & Czapla, 2021).

Incidentally, like many people around the world, we both felt the impact of the COVID-19 pandemic. I (John), for example, remember a kind of 'rudderless' feeling which emerged shortly after the March 2020 lockdown. For more than 2 decades, my personal and professional life (for me, the two are inextricably linked) was dominated by two activities: face-to-face classroom teaching and international travel. On 13 March 2020, both activities evaporated, when University of Michigan courses went online, and international travel was suspended. I remember, sometime towards the end of April of the same, awakening one morning and thinking to myself, "I cannot wait to go back to sleep tonight."

THE COVID-19 PANDEMIC AND BUSINESS OPERATIONS

It seems to us that, when it came to the COVID-19 pandemic, companies were not unlike people. Indeed, all companies— from small mom-and-pop shops to large multinational corporations— felt the impact of the COVID-19 pandemic on their business operations. For many companies, supply chains, especially those with an international link, immediately clogged up. Manufactories were shuttered, as product demand dwindled. And access to employees was restricted, due to stay-at-home orders and widespread fear. In short, companies suffered a kind of a trauma- and stressor-related disorder.

An obvious question, however, concerns the ways in which companies have responded to the COVID-19 pandemic. Continuing the TSRD metaphor, which therapies have companies engaged, to address the symptoms of the COVID-19 pandemic? How are they coping with its lingering effects? And what has been implemented to strengthen defences against its recurring (or newly-emerging) symptoms? Voilà, the rationale for this anthology.

We (the editors) sought research on post-pandemic international business operations. Indeed, we aspired to publish an anthology which showcased concrete examples of the ways in which companies responded to the COVID-19 pandemic. We welcomed research of different business functions, with different research perspectives, and in different industrial contexts. We were especially open to research from different geographical regions. Our call for chapter proposals resulted in more than 25 submissions from around the world. The subsequent review and re-submission process, however, whittled these down to the 11 chapters which follow in this anthology. We hope the chapters help you with your response to the COVID-19 pandemic, and that they trigger additional conceptual and theoretical research on post pandemic international business operations.

Chapter 1 examines the global expansion of supply chains between 1990 and 2010 which was characterized by efficiency-seeking through extreme specialization, task fragmentation, and geographical dispersion. Such chains, while offering cost benefits, are vulnerable to damaging disruption when operational conditions shift. The COVID-19 pandemic has initiated a reconsideration of supply chains with calls for enhanced resilience. These calls coincide with a growing fragmentation of global production and supply chains with China's increasing influence in global standards, supply of intermediate inputs, and domestic economic upgrading. This chapter examines the growth and vulnerabilities of lean global supply chains, arguments for greater resilience, and the cost implications of supply chain restructuring at a time of growing uncertainty and possible geographic fracture.

Chapter 2 covers researchers who have studied Foreign Direct Investment (FDI) from various perspectives and noted the motives of FDI depend predominantly on disadvantages in home countries or advantages in host countries. However, little is known about how investors avail themselves of such advantages. The purpose of this chapter is to offer guidelines to investors to make effective FDI decisions and maintain sustainable international expansions in the post-pandemic era. Via a conceptual review of the extant literature, the authors elaborate on the motives of FDI from the perspective of the capacities of investors and provide a nuanced understanding of how they can make better investment decisions based on both the lacks and capacities. The authors develop a framework elucidating that the motives of FDI can be determined by a firm's level of technology and absorptive capacity. The framework will help investors to find cross-border partners to collaborate with, increase resilience, and deal with post-pandemic recovery.

Chapter 3 explains the sudden changes to normality that are necessary to overcome the impact of the Covid-19 pandemic on all international business sectors, thus enabling competitiveness and value creation. Whereas firms need to adapt to such changes rapidly, sometimes their efforts remain insufficient in the face of unprecedented environmental changes. The main purpose of this study addresses the following broad research questions. First, how firms that investigate opportunities can increase their market share in all industries. Second, how firms can ensure sustainability in the new normal. Third, how the change brought about by the pandemic is reflected in the organization and what should be the leaders' role in the adoption of this process. Fourth, how innovation can be implemented that creates value in the new normal. And finally, how the new business model should be designed more competitively and creates more value.

Chapter 4 traces the past of international business research. Past studies have attempted to identify the domains of international business over specific periods of time. Most have used data sets for short time periods, providing a snapshot of the field for the period under review. This chapter reviews the research in the area of international business for the past five decades, with the objective of understanding the path that research has taken over the last five decades in terms of research content, relevance, and methodology. While this understanding supports a proposal for a research agenda for the future, from the perspective of both content and methods in international business research, the impact of the pandemic may require a re-look at the trends that have been presented. The chapter addresses some of the potential changes in the trends in the research agenda that could occur due to the pandemic.

Chapter 5 investigates how the COVID-19 pandemic disrupted international trade networks in 2020. Although worldwide commerce has recovered in the subsequent period, it is anticipated that globalization will make a new turn. The purpose of this study is to review the current research that examines the impact of the pandemic on international business. The methodology encompasses a semi-systematic review, which includes a summary and synthesis of selected empirical papers. The focal content of this review is the implication sections of the articles. By doing so, this study attempts to bridge the research-relevance gap.

Chapter 6 explores why the globally mobile workforce of international professionals has been significantly impacted by the COVID-19 pandemic. Closed borders and entry restrictions for foreign residents have left many expatriates separated from partners and family members. Previously held assumptions about the ability to travel whenever needed have been severely challenged, thus leaving some questioning the attractiveness of living and working abroad. The expectations of mobility that individuals as well as organizations used to have are changed. The research aims to assess the impact of factors like travel and other restrictions on the priorities of expatriates and on their willingness to consider future mobility, as well as how the disruption affected expatriates' concept of family. The research shows that organizations will have to examine if expatriation is a sustainable strategy. Both expatriates and organizations are more than ever subjected to local government regulations concerning the acceptance and conditions of life and travel for expatriates.

Chapter 7 probes Foreign Direct Investment (FDI) indexes and their relevance for emerging economies. As the FDI Attractiveness Indexes constitute one of the decision tools for governments' politics, it is relevant to assess the Groh and Wich (2009) index (GWI). Our main purpose is to verify the capacity of this index to replicate the phenomena of inflow FDI. The index analysis process included reviewing literature and detecting weaknesses on theoretical frameworks and in the selection of basic indicators. The multivariate analysis, applied to a sample of economies, showed evidence that some composite indicators of the GWI have shortages of concordance between simple indicators. Apart from showing that FDI attractiveness index of Groh and Wich (2009) does not convey the progress of inflow FDI, the study demonstrates that a FDI attractiveness index built to advanced economies can hardly be employed to developing economies without significant changes to the basic indicators.

Chapter 8 inspects globalization and deglobalization concerns with regards to the African continent. In the 21st century, nations are oscillating between globalization, deglobalization, protectionism, and localization. Issues considered while making decisions on what policy to follow include the economic boom, the slump in the economy, and politics. Nations adopt protectionism despite its known negative effects because of political reasons. The size of the economy of the developed countries allows them to implement these policies and withstand any adverse effect arising from isolation or retaliatory actions. The African continent cannot afford to find itself in this war between two elephants. Hence, the chapter reviewed the options available to Africa and recommended the adoption of localization aimed at building size and presenting a common competitive advantage that member states of the local bodies can employ. The chapter recommended certain changes to be made in leadership and mode of operation to avoid localization going the way of globalization.

Chapter 9 analyzes the global economy in the post-pandemic recovery. Although more than two years have passed since the new type of corona virus seen in Wuhan and more than 22 months have passed since the World Health Organization (WHO) declared a pandemic, the world continues to struggle with new variants of the virus and cannot return to the old normal. Closures, lockdowns, and restrictions on foreign trade of goods and services have decreased global economic activity. It is seen that two important challenges have emerged due to the pandemic. First, the countries with limited health services capacity in the face of the increasing number of cases and deaths in the world had trouble to combat with the pandemic. Second, low-income countries which have difficulty in accessing medicines and vaccines having an important role in combating the pandemic, are more distressed than other countries and need global support. It is seen that the inequality in income distribution between countries in the world also manifests itself in accessing drugs and vaccines.

Chapter 10 considers the role of literacy and digitalization within international business operations in the post-pandemic era. The COVID-19 pandemic was one of the deadliest pandemics ever encountered by human civilization. However, the unconquerable human resilience and the digital duo of mobile and internet led to a victory over this dreadful pandemic. This chapter initially focuses on India to illustrate the necessity of literacy in a pandemic. Later, the chapter accepts the hypothesis that business and trade is the engine of growth and verifies that in such dire condition whether digital business and trade acted as a buffer. Both the aforementioned aspects are quantitatively verified. This chapter uses two regression equations with robust standard errors to examine COVID-19 and literacy. Two dependent variables are population recovered to population tested and completely vaccinated to the total population and both the population density and rate of literacy have been taken as two independent variables. Further, this chapter also has analyzed the relevant data of 137 countries and has emphasized the fact how digitalization has acted as a buffer and kept business and trade going in a "No Man's Land."

Chapter 11 describes the technologies associated with the implementation of smart cities, benefits, limitations, and contribution to sustainability. Sustainability is a global need, both for companies and people. It is not only a matter of convenience to achieve more excellent business benefits, but it is also accompanied by the concept of a smart city which is of fundamental importance since it also goes in parallel with Industry 4.0. Different examples of smart cities are described, highlighting the requirements for implementation and the associated risks. The amount and type of specific technologies available in implementing a smart city are striking. Sustainable cities and smart cities undoubtedly share many characteristics, so the interconnection of concepts facilitates implementation, knowing all the technological requirements necessary for development.

Bryan Christiansen
The Christiansen Foundation, USA

John D. Branch
University of Michigan, USA

REFERENCES

Bridgland, V., Moeck, E., Green, D., Swain, T., Nayda, D., Matson, L., Hutchinson, N., & Takarangi, M. (2021). Why the COVID-19 Pandemic is a Traumatic Stressor. *PLoS One*, *16*(1), e0240146. doi:10.1371/journal.pone.0240146 PMID:33428630

Diagnostic and Statistical Manual of Mental Disorders (DSM-5-TR). (2022). Retrieved 01 May 2022. https://psychiatry.org/psychiatrists/practice/dsm

DSM. (2022). Retrieved on May 4, 2022, from: https://psychiatry.org/psychiatrists/practice/dsm

DSM history. (2022). Retrieved May 3, 2022, from: https://www.psychiatry.org/psychiatrists/practice/dsm/history-of-the-dsm#section_0

History of the DSM. (2022). Retrieved May 2, 2022, from: https://www.psychdb.com/teaching/1-history-of-dsm

Trauma & Stressor Related Disorders That Are Not PTSD. (2022). Retrieved May 4, 2022, from: https://familypsychnj.com/2020/09/trauma-stressor-related-disorders-that-are-not-ptsd/

Tucker & Czapla. (2021, January 8). Post-COVID Stress Disorder: Another Emerging Consequence of the Global Pandemic. *Psychiatric Times*, *38*(1).

Chapter 1
The Economics of Resilient Global Supply Chains in the Post-COVID-19 Era

Peter Enderwick
AUT University, New Zealand

ABSTRACT

The global expansion of supply chains between 1990 and 2010 was characterized by efficiency-seeking through extreme specialization, task fragmentation, and geographical dispersion. Such chains, while offering cost benefits, are vulnerable to damaging disruption when operational conditions shift. The COVID-19 pandemic has initiated a reconsideration of supply chains with calls for enhanced resilience. These calls coincide with a growing fragmentation of global production and supply chains with China's increasing influence in global standards, supply of intermediate inputs, and domestic economic upgrading. This chapter examines the growth and vulnerabilities of lean global supply chains, arguments for greater resilience, and the cost implications of supply chain restructuring at a time of growing uncertainty and possible geographic fracture.

INTRODUTION

The COVID-19 pandemic provided a stark illustration of the vulnerabilities of international business activities when environmental conditions change. Such vulnerabilities were particularly evident with critical shortages of both essential equipment (PPE and vaccines) (Gereffi, 2020) as well as industrial and consumer products (electronic components, whiteware products). Also clear was an overdependence on China as a global production and supply base with the virus outbreak disrupting manufacturing across significant parts of the country (Evenett, 2020). The negative economic impacts of COVID-19 have been particularly strong in internationally-oriented sectors such as tourism, air travel and shipping. These disruptions have been exacerbated by other underlying concerns including the growing pressures on global infrastructure and resource depletion.

DOI: 10.4018/978-1-6684-3749-0.ch001

The globalization wave initiated in 1990 by the collapse of the Soviet Bloc and rise of large emerging economies saw the value of global exports increase five-fold between 1990 and 2020. The current global infrastructure, much of which is now more than seven decades old, has struggled to deal with this rise in cross-border commerce, as evidenced by the stranding in the Suez Canal of the giant Ever Given container vessel in March 2021. The resource implications of three decades of hyper globalisation have also been immense: huge increases in natural resource and habitat depletion; continuing climate change; and alleged wasteful consumption as product prices fell.

These issues, exacerbated by the global pandemic, have renewed interest in the apparent trade-offs between global supply chain efficiency (but vulnerability) and resilience (Golgeci et al., 2020), how greater resilience might be achieved (Reeves & Varadarajan, 2020), and how any resulting costs could be shared (Fonseca & Azevedo, 2020).

It is useful to distinguish between the security and resilience of a system such as a global supply chain. Security refers to the ability to maintain the integrity of a system, while resilience is concerned with the ability to react and respond to a disruption. While the two characteristics are seen as desirable, they may be incompatible.

For example, while moving to multiple sources of supply may increase resilience through continuity of supply, it is likely to increase the difficulty of achieving security. This chapter examines these questions suggesting that a move away from the efficiency focused supply chains of the recent global wave will require significant geographical and relational restructuring, likely adding to the costs of internationally produced goods.

The arguments underpinning the discussion are developed in eight substantive sections. The first substantive section addresses the economic underpinning of current global supply chains with their efficiency imperative. Section 3 examines the vulnerabilities that such chains contain. This is followed by a discussion of the various resilience strategies that could be adopted and the role of both firms and policy makers in this process. Section 5 examines the costs of supply chain reorganization and the question of whether such costs are likely to be absorbed by producers or passed on to consumers. Section 6 examines possible constraints on supply chain restructuring in an increasingly fractious international business environment defined by trade and investment disputes, techno-nationalism, possible global fracture, and hegemonic competition. The limited evidence on corporate reconfiguration of global supply chains in presented in Section 7. Concluding comments are offered in the final section.

THE DEVELOPMENT OF CONTEMPORARY GLOBAL SUPPLY CHAINS

In the contemporary global economy, the terms global supply chains or global value chains are misnomers. The reality is that such chains, characteristic of linear, integrated and conceptually relatively simple production processes, began to disappear in the 1960s with the decline of large and hierarchically integrated factories such as Ford. Growing competitive pressure, the introduction of new production approaches such as Just-in-Time and increasing recognition of the contribution of specialist external suppliers brought radical change to production systems. These changes were facilitated by revolutions in communications and control technologies (lower cost air travel, digitalisation) and transport (containerisation, inter-modal hubs) that enabled an extension of specialisation or what Baldwin (2016) has termed 'unbundling'.

There are three historical unbundlings that are relevant to our discussion. The first, the geographical separation of production and consumption commenced with the foundations of international trade as consumers outside the country of production became accessible. The second involved the geographical separation of business functions such as research and development (R&D) or marketing as companies sought to exploit locational advantage and differences in factor quality and cost between alternative locations. Such unbundling was made possible by developments in communication technologies but was modest in geographical terms with, for example, US firms shifting assembly to affiliates in Mexico.

The third separation coincided with the Third Global Wave (1990-2010) and involved both spatial and ownership separation. In this stage work tasks were disaggregated (sometimes termed 'fine-slicing') and placed in their desired international location, and in many cases outsourced to specialist local suppliers. This combination resulted in the dominance of offshore outsourcing in the creation of global value (Olsen, 2006). This third stage was made possible by the business environment that prevailed between 1990 and 2010 characterised by strong economic growth, the increasing integration of emerging economies, particularly China and India (Enderwick, 2020), a growing base of specialist suppliers (Liesch et al., 2012), a relatively stable, open, rules-based trading environment, and falling costs of international communication and control.

The result is global value or supply networks, or webs, characterised by task fragmentation, geographical dispersion, and variated ownership arrangements. Such networks are complex, multilayer and subject to competing goals. They are only as strong as the weakest link. Their nature means that they are particularly vulnerable: they operate over considerable spatial distance, feature numerous interconnections and involve participants who may be competing, cooperating or some combination of the two (coopetition). Furthermore, global supply chains involve disparate activities. In addition to the traditional stages of value adding – extraction, harvesting, transport, processing or assembly, and marketing – these must be supported with enabling services including finance, standard setting, insurance, logistics, data protection and effective coordination of network activities.

These complex and fragmented global production systems are underpinned by conventional economic tenets – specialisation, locational advantage and effective reintegration. What is novel is the extent to which these principles have been pursued. Specialisation has enabled brand leaders to differentiate between those tasks that are essential to their operations, those that could be effectively undertaken by outside specialists, and those that form part of an organisation's core competence (Pralahad & Hamel 1990), extending choices between make or buy (Bartel et al., 2012).

Furthermore, while principles such as working collaboratively with suppliers were pioneered by large Japanese firms like Toyota (Iyer et al., 2009), modern businesses have extended these practices beyond local suppliers to access global supply sources. Similarly, requisite services are also increasingly outsourced (Berlingieri, 2013). This has enabled a higher degree of specialisation through the exploitation of locational differences. Differences in resource or skill availability and cost, are likely to be greater between countries than within countries. The development of specialist suppliers has deepened the international division of labour, enabling specialist outsourcers to build scale and experience, while major buyers have been able to focus on those activities in which they enjoy comparative advantage.

Locations such as China have developed globally competitive assembly operations, while India and Hungary for example, provide world-class IT capability. The result is global supply networks that have become more disaggregated, feature more connections, and display greater complexity. Miroudot and Nordstrom (2020) report evidence of an increase in the number of production stages in global value chains (GVCs) from 1995 to 2008, as well as their greater global dispersion. They estimate the average GVC increased in length by 700 kilometres over the period. Technological advances have enabled the efficient reintegration and coordination of these global production systems. Firms enjoy a variety of governance mechanisms encompassing market transactions, contractual arrangements, and hierarchical integration (Gereffi et al., 2005). A range of social mechanisms underpin governance processes (Kano, 2018).

GLOBAL SUPPLY CHAIN VULNERABILITIES

The pursuit of efficiency and lowest cost that characterised the development of global supply chains over the period 1990-2010 brought benefits of higher rates of economic growth, particularly in emerging markets. Several emerging economies made huge strides in poverty reduction and skill development (UNIDO, 2018). However, lean global supply chains are vulnerable to disruption from a variety of sources. Some disruptions such as adverse weather events have long been a concern for international businesses. Other threats, cyber-attacks for example, are more recent in nature. However, for all vulnerabilities two developments are fundamental to understanding. One is in the evolving nature of potential disruptions rendering them uncertainties rather than risks; the second is the increased susceptibility of modern global supply chains.

The potential threats to cross-border commerce are best understood by distinguishing between risk and uncertainty. Since Knight's (1921) analysis, risk is considered as the variation in potential outcomes to which an associated probability can be assigned. In statistical terms, while the distribution of the variable is known, the particular value which will be realised is not. Uncertainty exists when there is no understanding of even the distribution of the variable. For decision-making, uncertainty is a greater problem than risk. Because probabilities can be attached to risk, options to mitigate risks through insurance or hedging are possible.

Because probability cannot be assigned to uncertainty, instruments to reduce uncertainty are not available. This distinction highlights that many of the recent global threats – terrorism, computer hacks and global pandemics -should be seen as uncertainties, not risks. These types of disruptions share a number of characteristics (Enderwick 2006). First, they can be considered as "jolts" that occur randomly. Because such events are not continuous or even regular, it is not possible to assign probabilities to them. Second, the nature of these jolts mean that they "evolve", changing their forms; they do not simply recur.

For example, COVID-19 has demonstrated its ability to rapidly mutate affecting its transmissibility and resistance to vaccines. This makes it difficult to use historical experience as a predictor of future occurrences and impacts. Third, the impact of these uncertainties tends to be concentrated, either by sector or by geographical location. For example, the initial effects of COVID-19 were experienced first in China and the virus has disproportionately affected the transport, tourism and medical industries. The impacts of natural disasters such as extreme weather events, or financial and political problems, appear to be more widely and randomly distributed.

As well as the direct costs of these events, they are also associated with sizeable secondary costs as governments intervene to try to eliminate or reduce their impacts. The secondary costs stemming from new policies are often considerable. The maritime and airline industries faced huge additional costs following the 911 terrorist attacks and the current global pandemic has seen extensive and recurrent lockdowns and travel restrictions. One estimate in the latter part of 2020 suggested the economic cost of COVID-19 might be as much as US$16 trillion (Cutler & Summers, 2020), but any estimate is sensitive to longer term impacts on output levels.

The second consideration affecting global supply chain vulnerability is their efficiency-based, ultra-lean, geographically-dispersed form. As indicated, modern global supply chains have become significantly more complex. Leading multinational enterprises have moved from full internalisation (hierarchical production) to at least partial externalisation (offshore outsourcing), facilitated by continuing technological developments. Multiple stakeholders (lead firms, contract manufacturers, service suppliers, international standard organisations, regional and global trade agreements) present challenges to coordination as the various parties compete and cooperate in the face of disparate goals (Kano, 2018). The global dispersion of production adds to geographical distance, cultural gaps, and time differences. At the same time extreme specialisation encourages geographical concentration with specific localities then potentially subject to adverse weather, medical events, or social unrest. Supply chains are more complex with more network members, more intermediate trade, and product options with frequent changes adding to the likelihood and costs of disruptions. Between 1990 and 2010, the total value of intermediate trade between countries that were neither the origin of the raw material or the destination of the final product, increased more than four-fold.

While more complex, networks are also leaner, making the impact of shocks more immediate. One measure of chain leanness is provided by the ratio of manufacturing inventory to shipments which is available as a time series for the United States (OECD various). This shows a decline from an average of 1.7 in 1980 to 1.3 in 2000 and 1.1 in 2005 before picking up again as a result of the Global Financial Crisis (GFC). In the recent period 2010 to 2018 the ratio averaged 1.3.

Because of their extreme specialisation and geographical dispersion, modern supply chains have put considerable pressure on transport infrastructure, much of which in parts of Europe and the United States is quite aged. The world is currently experiencing a global shortage of shipping containers, particularly refrigerated containers as well as limited air freight capacity. The growing importance of Asia in global production (MGI 2019) is also highlighting the need for significant infrastructure investment in this part of the world, where vulnerability levels are high (Hertel et al., 2014). It is estimated that approximately a quarter of global seaborne trade passes through the restrictive Malacca Strait (Calamur, 2017).

In addition, many network members are likely to have a limited focus on supply chain processes with an emphasis on immediate partners. Self-interest seeking behaviour means that a lead or focal firm must exercise the direction and strategic coherence required to optimise chain operations. This challenge is compounded by the importance of open and transparent information sharing along the chain (Cheung & Myers, 2008). Poor connections between nodes and the need to protect proprietary knowledge impede knowledge sharing, highlighting the appeal of emergent technologies such as blockchain.

Recent changes in the international business environment have also increased uncertainty and vulnerability in global supply chains. Levels of government economic involvement have increased since the GFC and have become more conflictual with trade wars, investment disputes, and sanctions on individual firms. The resulting rise in nationalism, populism (Rodrik, 2018), and possible deglobalisation (Witt 2019) have all contributed to growing uncertainty. While some of these developments predate COVID-19, the pandemic has heightened governmental involvement in economic affairs (Firey, 2020). The rise of large emerging economies such as China based on unique economic systems, sometimes termed State Capitalism 2.0 or Sino-Capitalism (McNally, 2012), adds to supply chain complexities where market processes may be restricted, discrimination by ownership nationality arises, and state-owned or directed firms enjoy ongoing support. What is clear is that it is no longer reasonable to expect a return to the open rules-based global system that prevailed between 1990 and 2010.

BUILDING RESILIENCE IN GLOBAL SUPPLY CHAINS

If it is expected that uncertain events are likely to continue in the future and to disrupt global supply chains, the question that arises is what can be done to ameliorate their negative impacts. Since it is not possible to anticipate all such events, a resilient supply chain would be one that has the ability to manage change, to create new, and possibly erase existing connections, and to encourage flexibility, learning, and adaptation. The literature identifies a number of strategies that firms could adopt (MGI, 2020; Nambar et al., 2018), but governments also have a role in these processes.

Government Policies to Increase Resilience

There are a variety of strategies that governments could adopt that directly or indirectly impact the vulnerability of global supply chains. One is the initiation of home country production or collaborative ventures with other countries to produce critical goods. This occurred during the early stages of the pandemic when a number of engineering companies, including Britain's GKN, Dyson and Airbus, were asked to switch to producing ventilators that were in global short supply. In a number of countries pharmaceutical companies were asked to improve their reporting on stocks and to move to more centralised procurement processes to streamline supply.

In the medium term several governments moved to secure their pharmaceutical supplies by directing companies to supply products to public health facilities, to require producers to prioritise essential medicines (Spain) or to restrict stockpiling (Germany). In the case of Japan, the relevant industry body (Federation of Pharmaceutical Manufacturers' Associations of Japan,) assumed responsibility to prevent drug supply disruptions. Other states, including Colombia and India, introduced controls to prevent the export of key medicines.

Regional initiatives are occurring at the pan-European level, within federated countries such as Canada, and in nations with fragmented procurement structures including Spain and Italy, which have attempted to improve coordination. German officials have supported the development of pan-European drug production capabilities, lessening dependence on China and India for APIs (Active Pharmaceutical Ingredients). Together these two emerging economies account for about 80 percent of all European pharmaceutical ingredients. While together they account for more than 30 percent of the global supply of APIs, India depends on China for around 70 percent of all its pharmaceutical ingredients (Gibson & Singh, 2018; Mullin, 2020). The U.S. authorities, facing similar dependency on China and India, announced plans for a private sector initiative led by Phlow Corp, supported with considerable public funding, to expand manufacturing of APIs within the United States. India is also funding the expansion of domestically produced APIs.

In the longer term governments may identify critical products or services that they wish to source locally, either to complement or replace global sources of supply. While a number of countries, including the U.S., have encouraged firms to consider domestic supply chains, Japan has gone further offering financial incentives to its firms to reshore activities. In April, 2020 the Japanese authorities set aside US$2 billion to attract businesses to shift from mainland China back to Japan, and a further US$218 million to move production facilities to other countries. These incentives cover almost half the costs of relocation.

In addition to such direct interventions' governments can also influence supply chain decisions indirectly. One means is to pursue new trade agreements to encourage geographical diversification. Trade and investment agreements should lower transactions costs by eliminating tariffs and increasing certainty, encouraging firms seeking to invest or outsource tasks to consider alternative locations. Choosing to pursue more regional agreements could discourage continuing global integration of production decisions. Conversely, trade protectionist measures including tariffs, work to raise transaction costs and uncertainty, again prompting a reconsideration of supply chains. In the light of the U.S.- China trade dispute, it is reported that Apple has asked its major contract assembler Foxconn, to establish and expand facilities in Vietnam as an alternative to China. Foxconn is already producing some Air Pods and iPads in Vietnam (Rapoza, 2020).

Governments can also use financial inducements. For example, the French authorities indicated that continuing state support for major vehicle manufacturers PSA and Renault, both of whom produce a majority of their vehicles outside France, could be conditional on increased reshoring (Morgan, 2020). More generally, governments could invest resources in climate proofing critical infrastructure assets such as bridges, ports and harbours.

A more aggressive strategy designed to weaken overseas competitors and overseas supply bases is to restrict access to markets, technology or assets for foreign-owned firms. This is a critical element in the U.S.-China trade dispute that has targeted individual firms including Huawei, restricted access to markets such as 5G for Chinese companies in a number of countries, or rejected planned cross-border acquisitions. A number of countries including the United States, Germany and Australia, have tightened their foreign direct investment screening processes to both protect critical assets and to neutralise the perceived unfair competitive advantages enjoyed by state-owned or -supported firms (Enderwick, 2017).

Firm Strategies to Increase Resilience

There are a variety of strategies available to international businesses seeking to reduce supply chain vulnerabilities. The first is simply geographical diversification. Where suppliers are geographically concentrated, or where localities are prone to adverse events, climatic, geopolitical or social, there may be benefits in pursuing diversification. This is a strategy that has long been advocated for countries such as China which has become indispensable to global supply relations (Enderwick, 2011). Depending on the industry sector there are usually a number of alternative supply bases that could substitute (Javorcik, 2020).

A second strategy is one of supporting suppliers within the global supply network. Identifying and rectifying weak links within the network adds to resilience. During a global crisis such as the COVID pandemic there are likely to be some partners, perhaps smaller specialist suppliers, experiencing difficulties. During the current crisis a number of lead firms including H&M, Marks and Spencer and Boeing have worked closely with network members to ensure their viability and continuity. In the case of Boeing such a move helped protect component supplies essential to future aircraft maintenance and servicing for a product with a likely lifespan of more than two decades.

A third option is the use of innovative technologies to change the economics of locational advantage. For example, digital technologies emphasise higher rates of value adding at the innovation and marketing stages, while commodifying services. Automation is likely to have the opposite effect increasing the productivity of assembly, while additive technologies such as 3D printing reduce the incentive for separation of production and consumption (UNCTAD, 2020). The relative strengths of disparate technologies will impact levels of locational attractiveness.

A fourth and widely discussed strategy is the introduction of spare capacity or 'slack' into global supply chains. While the previous decades have seen a focus on eliminating what is perceived to be waste, in times of uncertainty, such slack can contribute to resilience by reducing the secondary adverse effects of a disruption. Increased slack can be achieved in a number of ways ranging from the adoption of multiple sourcing, increased inventory, to the reservation of spare production capacity that may, or may not, need to be utilised (Christopher & Peck, 2004).

A further option is the development of collaborative or behavioural contracting. Such contracts shift the focus from penalties such as possible termination and damages, to emphasise outcomes. Where outcomes are mutually agreed, the parties are more likely to work collaboratively, to communicate effectively, and to minimize incidences of opportunism (Gilson et al., 2009). The effectiveness of these strategies varies and may need to be utilised in combination. Their success is likely to be enhanced by a reconsideration of supply chain performance measurement with a shift from purely efficiency-based measures (cost, time to market etc.) to those that incorporate resilience (customer satisfaction, business continuity).

THE COST OF INCREASING GLOBAL SUPPLY CHAIN RESILIENCE

A move away from the efficiency-driven supply chains developed over the past three decades is likely to mean higher costs of production and of final products. This, then, raises the question of who, ultimately, will bear these costs. The costs of establishing more regionally- or nationally-focused supply chains would be considerable, particularly in locations that lack supporting services, specialist suppliers or efficient transport and communication links (Enderwick & Buckley, 2020). Even when established, such chains would likely mean higher costs that buyers would have to be willing to assume. Recovery rates between sectors will vary significantly, with air transport and tourism, for example, being slow, meaning that different adjustment rates would be observed. Where there are sectoral interdependencies, these differences add to costs.

Similarly, the creation of regional chains will require significant coordination between members of regional blocs. There are also differences in the costs of creating regional chains that are determined by the nature of the industry involved. Primary industries, particularly those in which resources are locationally bound, will still require global markets and transport links to downstream processors at the regional level. Some regions may seek to reduce their dependence on a limited number of suppliers, as the United States has done with oil.

The new technologies encompassed by Industry 4.0 could help localize some sectors by reducing the labour cost component and generating offsetting cost savings. Regional processing industries such as food and beverages will be easier to establish, as they are often able to source upstream inputs locally and to customize products to meet local consumer preferences (UNCTAD, 2020). Some of the cost disadvantages of regionalism could be partially offset through gains from a lowering of barriers on international labour mobility, the most protectionist of all resources. Smaller economies could benefit where access to supply chain involvement becomes easier because of increased regional specialization and the reduced importance of scale.

A further cost of geographically limiting supply chains is the danger of fragmentation with the growing adoption of incompatible regionally-based standards and technologies. One risk is so-called "technology walls", with irreconcilable technologies being adopted in different regions, particularly between China and the United States. Duplication would be costly, reducing scale economies and production interoperability. There is speculation about the fragmentation of the internet (the "splinternet") which could raise the costs of communication, control and data management. Even in the absence of spatial restructuring, any incorporation of 'redundancy' in supply chains adds to costs.

Many businesses see a clear-cut trade-off: investing in resilience is expensive and reduces efficiency. In terms of costs, firms need to invest in enhanced capabilities to anticipate and respond to disruptive events. In addition, resilience measures such as dual sourcing or increased inventory increase the costs of managing supply chains. In the longer term, fundamental re-engineering may also be required. Given the negative impacts of COVID-19 on corporate earnings, some firms are likely to be unwilling or unable to assume these costs.

Would consumers be willing to carry the expense of increased resilience? They may feel suddenly burdened with new costs they do not consider their responsibility. There are several ways consumers could be persuaded. First, the additional costs of more resilient supply chains could be linked to traits they value. For example, restructuring global supply chains to ensure more ethical production or the enhanced use of locally produced and processed materials could be appealing. An excellent example is provided by the shoe manufacturer Allbirds that sources local (wool) and renewable materials (sugar, recycled bottles, castor bean oil) and offsets carbon emissions through wind energy and regenerative agriculture.

Second, linking resilience to sustainability is attractive – as long as it is authentic. Resilience does not equate to sustainability, except perhaps for a firm's narrow conception of the continuation of its supply links. The danger is that of 'greenwashing', the pretence of being environmentally friendly, as buyers are deluded into seeing a desired trait that is not delivered. The complexity and opacity of many supply chains means that such practices are difficult to detect.

Third, consumers may value a product trait such as quality, novelty or performance that competitors struggle to meet and could justify higher prices. However, the obvious danger is that highlighting such a trait, could attract competitors able to better it. For example, many retailers who have benefitted from the shift to online buying are investing heavily in new technologies to enhance the convenience they offer to customers at a time of product shortages and delays. Attempts to restructure supply chains inevitably means a retreat from the least cost frontier and the need to absorb or pass on higher costs.

SUPPLY CHAIN RESTRUCTURING UNDER HEGEMONIC COMPETITION

Any substantial restructuring of global supply chains must acknowledge the radical changes in the international business operating environment that distinguish the current era. Compared with the period immediately following the collapse of the Cold War in 1989, the period since the GFC has been far more economically challenging. The acceptance and dominance of liberal, market-led economies committed to free and open trading conditions no longer holds. Even more stark is the growing hegemonic challenge that the United States faces from an increasingly powerful China (US Chamber of Commerce, 2021). This evolving context has been described in various ways – technocratic nationalism (Luo, 2021), deglobalisation (Witt, 2019), decoupling (Witt et al., 2021; Williamson, 2021) and hegemonic challenge (Grosse et al., 2021; Norrlof, 2021).

Regardless of the description, these analyses suggest growing divergence between the leading economic powers – the United States and China. Where the analyses differ is in the rationale for division, the likely extent of divergence, and the implications for global supply chains. The costs of any significant decoupling between the world's leading economic powers would be considerable. As discussed earlier, the creation of locationally disparate global supply chains has brought significant cost savings and these economic gains of cost arbitrage and access to specialist skills would be lost.

Similarly, it cannot be assumed that more localised supply chains will automatically result in more robust exchange. A key advantage of globally dispersed production is the risk diversification that geographically distributed operations brings (Miroudot, 2020), and which would be foregone when operations are localised. As well as the loss of production benefits, market exclusion would be a further cost borne by the key parties (Williamson, 2021).

A similar argument applies to innovation which has become an increasingly international and open process. Technology is central to the current decoupling debate as China's challenge has coincided with both the need to dominate emerging technologies within the fourth industrial revolution, and global interdependency in innovation (Luo, 2021). Any significant decoupling would imply costs for companies from both protagonist nations (Roach, 2020). While U.S. detachment may constrain China's advanced technology development, it is likely to strengthen China's advantage in middle- and low-end technologies and to consolidate Factory Asia, favouring substitution of U.S. technologies by leading Asian powers Japan, South Korea and Taiwan (Gang, 2021).

EVIDENCE ON SUPPLY CHAIN RESTRUCTURING

The continuing evolution of the COVID-19 pandemic means that any meaningful assessment of corporate reconfiguring of global supply chains is premature, and that appraisal will require more time. However, even at this early stage there is some evidence, both anecdotal and survey based. All available evidence indicates the elevation of global supply chain thinking within business strategy and the growing dynamism of supply chain management. This is to be expected given that COVID-19 has affected not just supply and demand, but also disrupted logistics with rapid rises in trucking and ocean freight costs, delays and congestion at ports, railheads and trucking centres, and shortages of containers and skilled logistics workers (IFC, 2020).

For example, there is little evidence that multinational businesses are responding to possible decoupling. Despite the significant costs of the trade war, few U.S. companies have disengaged from China (Kennedy & Tan, 2020), rather they appear to be attempting to manage the new risks they face by modifying business models. This is particularly the case for more established U.S. firms in China facing higher exit costs and who are more likely to voice their opposition to the U.S. policies (Zhang & Vortherms, 2021).

Anecdotal evidence suggests the early adoption of easy to implement strategies- increased inventory, some product redesign to eliminate reliance on vulnerable sources of components or materials, and limited nearshoring (Lynch, 2021). For example, Stanley Black and Decker have developed new production sites in Mexico and Fort Worth (Texas) while procuring additional production capacity for lithium-ion battery production with both U.S. and Taiwanese producers. About 40 percent of the company's U.S. sales are also produced in the region and this is a share that the company is keen to increase (Lynch, 2021). While there is evidence of interest in the regionalisation of supply chains, there is little evidence of widespread reshoring.

A similar picture emerges from survey data. Alicke et al. (2021) compared survey evidence from respondent's plans to reform supply chains in 2020, with their actions by 2021. They found that despite diverse reconfiguration plans the majority of respondents had actioned only relatively easy to implement changes such as increased inventories making little progress in diversifying supply bases or nearshoring. Given the short time period for adjustment these findings are not surprising. A large proportion of respondents had formalised risk-management processes but still had limited insight into the risks faced by suppliers beyond tier-one. Longer term, increased regionalisation of supply chains was a goal, while many firms were increasing investment in digital supply chain technologies with the focus on improving chain visibility, but talent shortages were restricting implementation.

CONCLUSION

The expansion of global supply chains over the past three decades has been driven by asset efficiency considerations, extreme specialization, and locational disparities. The result has been long, fragmented, but often geographically concentrated, supply networks. Optimization at each value adding stage is assumed to result in comparable system optimization, with system dynamics an operational constraint. However, extreme fragmentation, multiple connections and growing environmental volatility mean that local disruptions have significant system-wide effects. Digital ties and coordination of such systems simply accelerate the transmission of shocks (Reeves & Varadarajan, 2020).

COVID-19 is likely to affect not just the geography of production, but also the management of supply chains. Outsourcing has minimized margins for many suppliers, making business continuity challenging. Any loss of trusted suppliers may mean a reconsideration of margins and closer supportive relations along supply networks.

There are a variety of operational and strategic options available to improve supply chain resilience, drawing on both firm-level reconfiguration and policy initiatives. However, these are likely to mean higher product prices where cost arbitrage and access to specialist skills are foregone. If consumers are willing to accept higher prices, in the same way that they are prepared to pay a premium for fair trade goods, products may be promoted as being sourced from more resilient supply chains, where slack is incorporated, stockpiling is assured, or higher supplier margins are guaranteed. However, it is unclear as to whether or not consumers will accept such cost impositions.

The early evidence suggests that firms have been tentative in their adjustments focusing on the lower cost and risk options of dual sourcing, stockpiling inventory and modest nearshoring. Reshoring, as predicted under global de-coupling has not been widespread, at least at this relatively early stage. Predictions of deglobalisation and global economic fracture appear to have overlooked the growing role of Chinese businesses in developing highly efficient connected overhead business services in logistics, procurement, technology and industry standards and secure payment systems, essential inputs to global supply chains. This is an area where further work would be valuable in better understanding the nature of global supply chains in the post-COVID-19 era.

REFERENCES

Alicke, K., Barriball, E., & Trautwein, V. (2021, November). *How COVID-19 is Reshaping Supply Chains*. McKinsey and Company.

Baldwin, R. (2016). *The Great Convergence: Information Technology and the New Globalization*. Harvard University Press. doi:10.2307/j.ctv24w655w

Bartel, A. P., Lach, S., & Sicherman, N. (2012). Technological change and the make-or-by decision. *Journal of Law Economics and Organization*, *30*(1), 165–192. doi:10.1093/jleo/ews035

Berlingieri, G. (2013). *Outsourcing and the rise in services.* CEP Discussion Paper DP1199, Centre for Economic Performance, London School of Economics (LSE), London.

Calamur, K. (2017, August 22). High traffic, high risk in the Strait of Malacca. *Atlantic (Boston, Mass.).*

Cheung, M. S., & Myers, M. B. (2008). Managing knowledge sharing networks in global supply chains. *International Journal of Management and Decision Making*, *9*(6), 581–599. doi:10.1504/IJMDM.2008.021216

Christopher, M., & Peck, H. (2004). Building the resilient supply chain. *International Journal of Logistics Management*, *15*(2), 1–13. doi:10.1108/09574090410700275

Cutler, D. M., & Summers, L. H. (2020). The COVID-19 pandemic and the $16 trillion virus. *Journal of the American Medical Association*, *324*(15), 1495–1496. doi:10.1001/jama.2020.19759 PMID:33044484

Enderwick, P. (2006). Managing the new global threats. *University of Auckland Business Review*, *8*(2), 63–72.

Enderwick, P. (2011). A 'China-Plus-One' strategy: The best of both worlds? *Human Systems Management*, *30*(1-2), 85–96. doi:10.3233/HSM-2011-0735

Enderwick, P. (2017). International investment by state-controlled enterprises: A source for concern? *Strategic Change*, *26*(3), 261–271. doi:10.1002/jsc.2127

Enderwick, P. (2020). *The Competitive Challenge of Emerging Markets: China and India*. Cambridge Scholars Publishing.

Enderwick, P., & Buckley, P. J. (2020). Rising regionalization: Will the post-COVID-19 world see a retreat from globalization? *Transnational Corporations*, *27*(2), 99–112. doi:10.18356/8008753a-en

Evenett, S. J. (2020). Chinese whispers: COVID-19, global supply chains in essential goods and public policy. *Journal of International Business Policy*, *3*(4), 408–429. doi:10.105742214-020-00075-5

Firey, T. A. (2020). Government in a Pandemic Policy Analysis 902. CATO Institute.

Fonseca, L., & Azevedo, A. (2020). COVID- 19: Outcomes for global supply chains. *Management and Marketing: Challenges for the Knowledge Society*, *15*(Special Issue), 424–438. doi:10.2478/mmcks-2020-0025

Gang, D. (2021, June 2). Decoupling from China will see US globally detached. *Global Times*.

Gereffi, G. (2020). What does the COVID-19 pandemic teach us about global value chains? The case of medical supplies. *Journal of International Business Policy*, *3*(3), 287–301. doi:10.105742214-020-00062-w

Gereffi, G., Humphrey, J., & Sturgeon, T. (2005). The governance of global value chains. *Review of International Political Economy*, *12*(1), 78–104. doi:10.1080/09692290500049805

Gibson, R., & Singh, J. P. (2018). *China RX: Exposing the Risks of America's Dependence on China for Medicines*. Prometheus Books.

Gilson, R. J., Sabel, C. F., & Scott, R. E. (2009). Contracting for innovation: Vertical disintegration and interfirm collaboration. *Columbia Law Journal, 109*(3), 431–502.

Golgeci, I., Yildiz, H.E., & Andersson, U. (2020). The rising tensions between efficiency and resilience in global value chains in the post-COVID-19 world. *Transnational Corporations, 27*(2), 127-141.

Grosse, R., Gamso, J., & Nelson, R. C. (2021). China's rise, world order, and the implications for international business. *Management International Review, 61*(1), 1–26. doi:10.100711575-020-00433-8 PMID:33679004

Hertel, T., Hummels, D., & Walmsley, T. L. (2014). The vulnerability of the Asian supply chain to localised disasters. In B. Ferrarini & D. Hummels (Eds.), *Asia and Global Production Networks: Implications for Trade, Incomes and Economic Vulnerability* (pp. 81–111). Edward Elgar.

IFC (2020, June). *The Impact of COVID-19 on Logistics*. International Finance Corporation.

Iyer, A. V., Seshandri, S., & Vasher, R. (2009). *Toyota Supply Chain Management: A Strategic Approach to Toyota's Renowned System*. McGraw Hill.

Javorcik, B. (2020). Global supply chains will not be the same in the post-COVID-19 world. In R. Baldwin & S. J. Evenett (Eds.), *COVID-19 and Trade Policy: Why Turning Inward Won't Work* (pp. 111–117). CEPR Press.

Kano, L. (2018). Global value chain governance: A relational perspective. *Journal of International Business Studies, 49*(6), 684–705. doi:10.105741267-017-0086-8

Kennedy, S., & Tan, S. (2020, June 10). *Decoupling between Washington and Western industry*. Center for Strategic and International Studies.

Knight, F. H. (1921). *Risk, Uncertainty and Profit*. University of Chicago Press.

Liesch, P. W., Buckley, P. J., Simonin, B. L., & Knight, G. (2012). Organizing the modern firm in the worldwide market for market transactions. *Management International Review, 52*(1), 3–21. doi:10.100711575-011-0096-x

Luo, Y. (2021). Illustrations of techno-nationalism. *Journal of International Business Studies*. doi:10.105741267-021-00468-5 PMID:34511654

Lynch, D. J. (2021, November 15). As supply lines strain, some corporations rewrite production playbook. *The Washington Post*.

McNally, C. A. (2012). Sino-capitalism: China's re-emergence and the international political economy. *World Politics, 64*(4), 741–776. doi:10.1017/S0043887112000202

MGI. (2019). *The Future of Asia*. McKinsey Global Institute.

MGI. (2020). *Risk, Resilience and Rebalancing in Global Value Chains*. McKinsey Global Institute.

Miroudot, S. (2020). Resilience versus robustness in global value chains: Some policy implications. In R. E. Baldwin & S. J. Evenett (Eds.), *COVID-19 and Trade Policy: Why Turning Inward Won't Work* (pp. 117–130). CEPR Press.

Miroudot, S., & Nordstrom, H. (2020). Made in the world? global value chains in the midst of rising protectionism. *Review of Industrial Organization*, *57*(2), 195–222. doi:10.100711151-020-09781-z

Morgan, S. (2020, May 27.) Macron demands carmakers turn to "Made in France" for €8bn virus aid. *Euractiv*.

Mullins, R. (2020). COVID-19 is reshaping the pharmaceutical supply chain. *Chemical and Engineering News*, *98*(16), 30–45.

Nambar, J., Li, X., Sawhney, R., & Pradhan, N. (2018). Supply chain resilience for single and multiple sourcing in the presence of disruptive risks. *International Journal of Production Research*, *56*(6), 2339–2360. doi:10.1080/00207543.2017.1370149

Norrlof, C. (2021). Is COVID-19 the end of US hegemony? Public bads, leadership failure and monetary hegemony. *International Affairs*, *96*(5), 1281–1303. doi:10.1093/ia/iiaa134 PMID:34191870

Olsen, K. B. (2006). *Productivity Impacts of Offshoring and Outsourcing: A Review*. STI Working Paper 2006/1. Paris: OECD.

Prahalad, C. K., & Hamel, G. (1990). The core competence of the corporation. *Harvard Business Review*, *69*(3), 275–292.

Rapoza, K. (2020). Is Apple slowly moving out of China? Its supplier is. *Forbes*, (August), 14.

Reeves, M., & Varadarajan, R. (2020). *When Resilience is More Important than Efficiency*. BCG/Henderson Institute.

Roach, S. (2020, January 3). The myth of global decoupling. *Project Syndicate*.

Rodrik, D. (2018). Populism and the economics of globalization. *Journal of International Business Policy*, *1*(1), 12–33. doi:10.105742214-018-0001-4

UNCTAD. (2020). *World Investment Report 2020: International Production Beyond the Pandemic*. United Nations.

UNIDO. (2018). *Global Value Chains and Industrial Development: Lessons from China, South-East and South Asia*. UNIDO.

U.S. Chamber of Commerce. (2021). *U.S.-China Decoupling: Macro-Trends and Industry Impacts*. U.S. Chamber of Commerce/Rhodium Group.

Williamson, P. (2021). De-globalisation and decoupling: Post COVID-19 myths versus realities. *Management and Organization Review*, *17*(1), 29–34. doi:10.1017/mor.2020.80

Witt, M., Li, P., Valikangas, L., & Lewin, A. (2021). De-globalisation and decoupling: Game changing consequences? *Management and Organization Review*, *17*(1), 6–15. doi:10.1017/mor.2021.9

Witt, M. A. (2019). De-globalization: Theories, predictions, and opportunities for international business research. *Journal of International Business Studies*, *50*(7), 1053–1077. doi:10.105741267-019-00219-7

Zhang, J., & Vortherms, S. (2021, August 10). Unstoppable force meets an immovable object: US-China supply chains in the age of decoupling. *Asia Dispatches*.

Chapter 2
Internationalization, Sustainability, and Capacity-based Motives of Foreign Direct Investment: A Conceptual Framework

Nasrin Sultana
https://orcid.org/0000-0003-1203-426X
HEC Montreal, Canada

Ekaterina Turkina
HEC Montreal, Canada

ABSTRACT

Researchers have studied foreign direct investment (FDI) from various perspectives, and noted the motives of FDI depend predominantly on disadvantages in home countries or advantages in host countries. However, little is known about how investors avail themselves of such advantages. The purpose of this chapter is to offer guidelines to investors to make effective FDI decisions and maintain sustainable international expansions in the post-pandemic era. Via a conceptual review of the extant literature, the authors elaborate on the motives of FDI from the perspective of the capacities of investors and provide a nuanced understanding of how they can make better investment decisions based on both the lacks and capacities. The authors develop a framework elucidating that the motives of FDI can be determined by a firm's level of technology and absorptive capacity. The framework will help investors to find cross-border partners to collaborate with, increase resilience, and deal with post-pandemic recovery.

DOI: 10.4018/978-1-6684-3749-0.ch002

INTRODUCTION

The COVID-19 pandemic has severely affected the global economy and the flows of FDI. The pandemic is expected to have a negative impact on the global Foreign Direct Investment (FDI) flows, causing a fall of more than 30% even under the most optimistic scenario, as observed by the Organization for Economic Cooperation and Development (OECD). The pandemic is going to affect both the inward and outward flows of FDI (Fang et al., 2021; Fu et al., 2021). However, the extent of the impact will depend not only on the public health and economic policy responses but also on the capacity of the investors. Even though the pandemic has significantly altered the trajectories of economies and altered the strategies of MNEs (Hitt et al., 2021), FDI can play important role in supporting economies during and after the pandemic by creating linkages between local and foreign firms and facilitating the transfer of advanced knowledge and technology.

The literature on FDI focuses predominantly on the investment a country receives. From the recipient's perspective, researchers often link FDI with long-term economic development, attributing it to the knowledge and technology transfer, of a country (Borensztein, 1998; Djulius, 2017; Grossman & Helpman, 1993; Keller, 2010; Lall & Narula, 2004; Ritchie, 2002). When a firm establishes its business activities in a location, it gets into business and establishes different relationships with other local firms. Such intra-industry and inter-industry relationships stimulate knowledge transfer among firms, but the extent may differ depending on the types of relationships of firms. By encouraging foreign investors to invest, host countries hope to catalyze technology transfer in local firms since FDI is associated with the existence of intangible assets of foreign investors (Blomstrom & Kokko, 1999).

At the same time, making FDI can have a beneficial impact on economic development by easing some limitations in the home country such as technological and financial constraints, capability bottlenecks, and resource shortages (Knoerich, 2017). Due to the pandemic, the map of countries' proximity to the global distribution of knowledge, markets, and resources is likely to change (Hitt et al., 2021). In the changing circumstances, FDI can be a strategy to catch up with development in terms of acquiring knowledge and technology, improving production processes, developing managerial skills, and being a part of a business network. The process will eventually foster competitiveness. Similarly, firms have different reasons for investing abroad such as lower cost of production, lower tax rate or no tax, higher profit, access to new markets, access to a new business network, and so on (Caves & Caves, 1996). According to the literature, firms' primary motives to make FDI are to seek natural resources, new markets, efficiency, or strategic assets depending on firms' motives and capabilities (Dunning & Lundan, 2008).

However, researchers, predominantly, focus on the lack of firms to understand the motive of FDI, but they ignore the fact that the capabilities of firms can also play a crucial role in making FDI decisions. For example, the low absorptive capacity of investors can limit the positive effects of FDI in home countries. Therefore, it is important to understand the role of capabilities because the extant literature on FDI points out that firms benefit from making FDI but does not explain how such benefits are realized. For example, firms conduct FDI when they possess unique capabilities, or firms may decide to expand in search of new capabilities that are not available in the home country or market (Cantwell, 1989). A firm can take different measures to protect its unique capabilities while making FDI. However, making FDI does not guarantee that the firm will be able to access new technology available in host countries.

Johanson and Vahlne (1977) explained that a lack of knowledge about the foreign market is an important obstacle to operating in a foreign market, but such knowledge can be obtained mainly through operations abroad. Such a notion indicates the possibility of knowledge transfer between home country firms and host country firms. However, the availability of knowledge and technology in another country does not necessarily mean that a firm will be able to access such knowledge or technology. Firms need to have some prior related knowledge to absorb and utilize the knowledge available in host countries. Therefore, the authors aim to answer the question: *how do the level of technology and absorptive capacity of a firm influence the firm's motive for FDI?*

In any case, a firm will want to ensure the maximum return of its FDI albeit a technologically advanced firm will have different motives for making FDI than a firm that is technologically lagging. However, even a technologically advanced firm's motives can vary according to the firm's absorptive capacity, for instance, whether a firm has enough capacity to absorb knowledge from the environment, or the firm had better focus on protecting its unique capabilities. Similarly, absorptive capacity is also important for technologically lagging firms, for instance, a firm with sufficient absorptive capacity will try to absorb advanced technology from others and will catch up with the technologically advanced firms.

However, it does not mean that firms without sufficient absorptive capacity cannot benefit from the FDI – they can still benefit from the new market and access other opportunities available; such firms can concentrate on increasing efficiency. A nuanced understanding of the phenomenon will help firms to make better strategic decisions regarding FDI by focusing not only on what they lack but also on what they have. The discussion in this chapter will complement the literature on knowledge transfer, technology transfer, absorptive capacity, FDI, and international business.

A BRIEF LOOK BACKWARD: MOTIVES OF FDI

FDI occurs when a firm in one country establishes business operations in another country; it allows the investor to gain access to the resources available in another economy, which might not have been possible to access otherwise. According to the OECD, FDI is "a category of cross-border investment in which an investor resident in one economy establishes a lasting interest in and a significant degree of influence over an enterprise resident in another economy. Ownership of 10 percent or more of the voting power in an enterprise in one economy by an investor in another economy is evidence of such a relationship." Thereby, the motivation of the investor is to establish a strategic long-term relationship with the direct investment enterprise and to ensure a significant degree of influence in the management of the direct investment enterprise.

In this chapter, the authors elaborate on the motives of FDI from investors' technological and absorptive capacity perspectives to provide a nuanced understanding of how a firm can make better investment decisions based on both lacks and capacities. According to OECD, FDI is defined as "transactions that increase the investment that investors in the reporting economy have in enterprises resident abroad less any transactions that decrease the investment that investors in the reporting economy have in enterprises resident abroad, for a specific industry".

According to Buckley (1989), FDI concerns extending firms' activities in foreign markets and controlling activities conducted by intermediate markets, which will reduce the costs related to a transaction. FDI can support the developmental goal of source economies, for instance, FDI can be used to source specialized knowledge that is not present in the home market (Amann & Virmani, 2014), and the effect goes beyond the investing firm (Mani, 2013). Thereby, FDI is becoming a critical tool for firms to maintain and increase competitiveness.

Literature suggests the primary intents of FDI can be natural resource-seeking, market-seeking, efficiency-seeking, or strategic asset seeking depending on firms' motives and capabilities. The market-seeking FDI refers to the type of investment that aims at penetrating the local markets of host countries. Firms that make such investments are usually concerned about market size, per capita income, market growth, access to regional and global markets, consumer preferences, and the structure of the domestic market. In the case of the resource-asset seeking FDI, firms usually seek natural resources, for example, raw materials, the lower unit labor cost of the unskilled labor force and the pool of skilled labor, physical infrastructure such as ports, roads, power, and telecommunication, and the level of technology. The motives behind efficiency-seeking FDI are the possibility of creating new sources of competitiveness for firms, usually in terms of lower costs of production. In the case of strategic asset-seeking FDI, firms aim at advancing their global or regional strategy into foreign networks, improving technology, organizational abilities, and markets (ibid).

The motives of FDI can be explained from other perspectives, too. For instance, firms that have monopolistic advantages such as economies of scale or privileged access to capital and resources will be able to invest abroad and exploit such advantages internationally (Forsgren, 2017). According to Hymer (1960), the decision to invest in foreign countries is a strategy to capitalize on certain capabilities that are not available to competitors in foreign countries. Johansson and Vahlne (1977) explain FDI in the context of learning and contextual distance. In one approach, firms will first invest in neighboring countries before investing in distant markets. In another approach, while investing in foreign markets, firms will start with low-commitment activities such as export and will commit to full-fledged production sites later (ibid). However, this might not always be true, for example, firms with monopolistic advantage can invest in other technologically advanced locations to access the advanced technology (Guillen & Garcia-Canal, 2009).

Dunning explains when and how firms make decisions to invest in a foreign location in the "Eclectic Paradigm" which is known as the OLI paradigm: he classifies the required elements as ownership advantages, location advantages, and internalization advantages (Dunning, 2001). Ownership advantages are firm-specific advantages such as the possession of assets, mainly intangible, that are exclusive to the firms and not available to competitors. Location advantages are determined by the comparative or competitive advantages of specific locations and focus on the benefit of combining the movable assets of the home countries with partially or totally immovable assets of the host countries. Internalization advantages are about deciding whether to produce in-house to avoid market imperfections and are decided by coordination and transaction costs.

This approach assumes that organizations have advantages before investing abroad but does not explain how organizations can obtain or develop such advantages. Dunning also introduced the Investment Development Path (IDP) theory, based on the OLI paradigm, that simultaneously explains inward and outward FDI. According to IDP theory, both inward FDI and outward FDI depend on a country's economic development. Dunning (1982) explains that different structural changes occur as a country develops, which affects a country's inward and outward FDI eventually. Along with these changes, a country's ownership, location, and internalization advantages change, and the country evolves from a recipient of FDI to a direct investor.

Another important theory, which explains the internationalization of firms, is the concept of transaction cost economics (TCE). Coase (1937) and Williamson (1991) explain that different types of costs are involved in the coordination of different activities and risks in a transaction in a foreign country. They emphasize that the lack of properly functioning institutions and perfect markets increases transaction costs and lead MNEs to internalize their production activity. Rugman's (Rugman & Verbeke, 2008) FSA-CSA framework that focuses on the nexus between firm-specific advantages (FSAs) and country-specific advantages (CSAs) is also important in understanding FDI. This framework explains key sources and drivers of competitive advantages of internationalizing firms. The interplay and combination of CSAs and FSAs drive OFDI and is a source of competitive advantages. However, finding the perfect combination following this framework is often difficult.

Later, Luo and Tung (2007) summarized the motives of the FDI in two categories: opportunity seeking and asset seeking. Technology, R&D facilities, know-how, human capita, consumer bases, distribution channels, managerial expertise, and natural resources are usually the types of assets sought in case of asset-seeking FDI. These assets bolster economic and social development and increase the competitive advantage of the firms that are making FDI. Opportunity-seeking FDI mainly aims at reducing costs or increasing revenue by tapping niche opportunities in advanced markets. Other opportunities can be avoiding institutional restrictions in home countries, bypassing trade barriers, or getting preferential treatment in host countries. One unique activity of firms from emerging economies while making FDI is inward internalization (Luo & Tung, 2007).

While making FDI, companies from less advanced countries actively seek assets and advantages such as know-how, resources, and access to foreign markets (Knoerich, 2017; Nelaeva & Nilssen, 2022). A firm can be motivated to make FDI "by current competitive disadvantages that hinder the firm's future growth, and by the potential gain of sustainable competitiveness in the long-term (Cui et al., 2014, p.)". Similarly, firms can make FDI either to exploit factor price differences across countries or to avoid the cost of international trade (Knoerich, 2017; Luo & Tung, 2007).

It is important to note FDI increases both competition and cooperation and is known to contribute to the economic growth and development of a country, for instance, by bringing technology. However, such a benefit might not accrue if foreign firms' intention is to acquire new knowledge or technology. Firms learn new skills by combining their current capabilities, and such cumulative knowledge provides opportunities for them to expand to new and uncertain markets in the future (Kogut & Zander, 1992). Therefore, they will value the knowledge available in a location according to their needs and abilities.

Nonetheless, there are different motives behind firms' decisions to invest abroad. For example, firms looking for access to new markets and access to new knowledge will not necessarily appreciate the advantages in the same way. Chung and Alcacer (2002) found that knowledge-seeking is not prevalent across industries but limited to R&D-intensive industries. Interestingly, contrary to conventional wisdom, both technologically lagging and advanced firms may invest in locations with high Research and Development (R&D) intensity (Cantwell & Janne, 1999).

Some firm-specific knowledge of foreign firms may traverse to local firms when local firms are exposed to products or production processes, marketing techniques, or receiving assistance from upstream and downstream foreign firms. Nonetheless, only making FDI does not guarantee that the investor will access technology or knowledge of the location. In the first place, investors need to have the capacity to absorb available knowledge. If they do not have the capacity to absorb knowledge and diversify the existing knowledge base, they will try their best to maintain their uniqueness. However, it does not mean that firms will not make FDIs if they do not have any technology or special knowledge to protect and diversify. Such firms can still make FDIs, but their motives will be different than those of technologically advanced firms. Therefore, this study aims to provide a nuanced understanding of the firm's motives for FDI from technological and absorptive capacity perspectives and develops a conceptual framework with four propositions.

THINKING FORWARD: A CAPACITY PERSPECTIVE OF FDI MOTIVES

The extant literature shows there are different reasons for engaging in FDI such as the advantage of lower labor costs in other countries, the advantage of proximity to raw materials, avoiding tariff and non-tariff barriers to trade, reduced transportation costs, favorable exchange rate, and access to local knowledge. Firms usually make an investment decision that corresponds to "a combination of current capabilities and expectations regarding future opportunities" (Kogut & Zander, 1992).

Nonetheless, Cantwell and Janne (1999) challenged the conventional understanding of knowledge-seeking behavior and suggested two kinds of knowledge-seeking behavior based on technologically lagging firms and technologically advanced firms: technologically lagging firms may not always find it necessary to expand in a technologically advanced location to catch up latest technology while the technologically advanced firms may find it important to set their operation in such place to increase their diversity. While engaging in FDI, firms want to access advanced knowledge and technology among other advantages available in a location. These observations lead to the argument that the motives of FDI do not depend only on the origin or technology level of firms as traditionally understood. The COVID-19 pandemic has changed the rules of the game in multiple ways, demanding a shift in our thinking of international business operations (Fang et al., 2021; Hitt et al., 2021).

The term "technology" is an inherently abstract concept that is difficult to interpret, observe, and evaluate (Blomstrom & Kokko, 1999). According to Pavitt (1985), technology is mainly differentiated knowledge about the specific application within firms. Based on this argument, technology can be viewed as a firm's intangible or firm-specific asset which forms the basis of the firm's' competitiveness (Dunning, 2001). Technology, in terms of a firm's intangible asset, is rooted in the firm's routine and is not easy to transfer due to the gradual learning process and the higher cost associated with transferring tacit knowledge (Radosevic, 1999).

Therefore, following the extant literature, the authors use technology, technological knowledge, and knowledge interchangeably throughout the chapter to explain firms' motives for FDI and advance the propositions. External knowledge is crucial for firms to maintain competitive advantages and other business activities. The central competitive dimension of a firm, therefore, lies in its ability to create and manage knowledge within the organizational context (Kogut & Zander, 1992).

However, such knowledge may be of tacit nature and highly context-specific, which will require certain capabilities in order to be absorbed. There are two important issues in knowledge transfer: the emitting capability of the source and the receiving capability of the recipient to support the flow of knowledge in a particular situation (Amesse & Cohendet, 2001). Transferring technology involves the transfer of both technical information and the capability to master that specific technology. A successful transfer of technology requires various investments in learning to acquire tacit knowledge. Teece (1977) defines these costs as the costs of transmitting and absorbing relevant disembodied knowledge. Therefore, a firm must have the absorptive capacity to understand and utilize new technologies and knowledge.

The issue of firms' absorptive capacity (Cohen & Levinthal, 1990) within and across sectors has been widely studied in the literature on FDI and spillover effects (Blomstrom & Kokko, 1999; Jordaan, 2012; Mehreen et al., 2021; Saggi, 2002; Volberda et al., 2010). The idea of absorptive capacity is related to firms' prior related knowledge that is important to learn new knowledge. Absorptive capacity is known as a firm's ability to identify, assimilate, and exploit knowledge from the environment (Cohen & Levinthal, 1990). For example, firms in research-intensive industries are more interested to invest in locations with high R&D intensity (Chung, 2012).

Those investors need such capacities to actively integrate into the process of technology diffusion and get the most out of the investment. Investing in basic research increases a firm's ability, on the one hand, to produce new knowledge and to understand external and complementary knowledge on the other hand. According to Cohen and Levinthal (1990), firms, regardless of size, must invest in basic research to develop the ability "to recognize, exploit, and assimilate the knowledge produced elsewhere". Accordingly, whether a firm will be benefited from investing abroad will depend primarily on the firms existing capabilities.

This chapter elaborates on the motives of FDI and develops the following framework (Figure 1) by suggesting that firms' level of technology and absorptive capacity play important roles in making OFDI decisions.

Figure 1. A conceptual framework of the capacity-based FDI motives

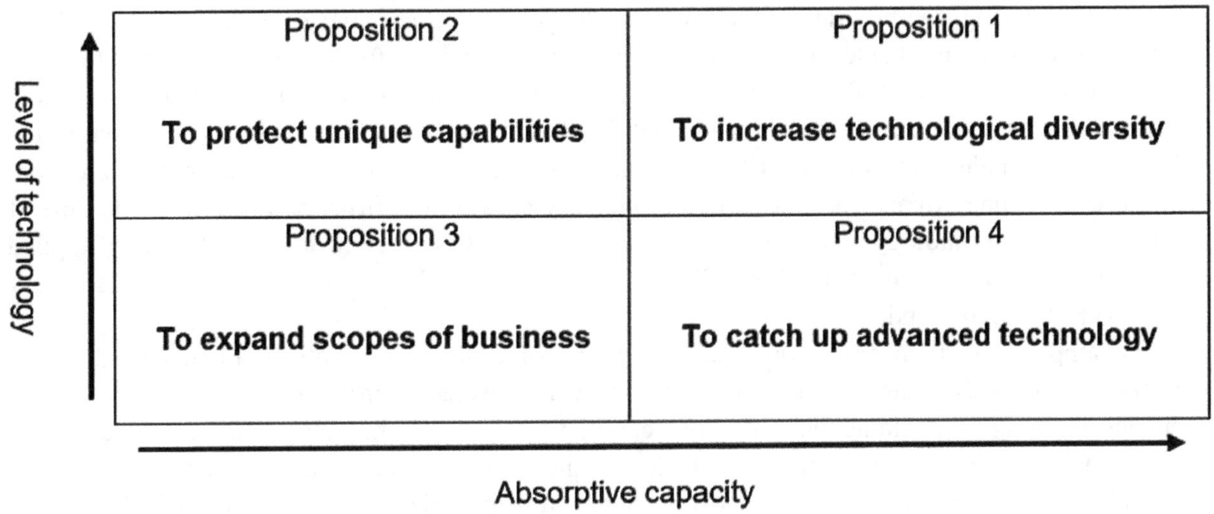

In an industry, some firms are technologically advanced and some firms are technologically lagging. In most cases, firms making FDI need to share experience and knowledge with local firms, which helps them to comprehend local firms' scope of improvement in the production process. Firms will benefit more when the technology gap is large, and the gap can be interpreted as a scope for improvement. However, Jordaan's (2012) findings suggest that it is important to separate the technology gap and absorptive capacity. Both of these concepts can have an independent impact on technology spillover between local firms and foreign firms. For instance, even if a firm is technologically lagging, it cannot get the attendant benefit of making FDI such as new technology or technological knowledge available without having the related capacity to absorb such knowledge. Nonetheless, in the absence of sufficient absorptive capacity firms can, surely, focus on other resources to benefit from.

To Increase Technological Diversity

Proposition 1: Technologically advanced firms with higher absorptive capacity will focus on increasing technological diversity.

Firms that have unique capabilities and want to internalize such capabilities will be interested in using their capabilities as effectively as possible and will be attracted to locations that offer the possibility to reduce costs or increase revenue. According to the knowledge-based view, firms undertake overseas investments for knowledge sourcing (Kogut & Zander, 1992). Mani (2013) noted that two types of knowledge transfer can take place in FDI: soft and hard technological knowledge. Soft knowledge refers to information about markets, consumer preferences, labor market conditions, institutional information, norms of business behavior, and such that are required to do business in a host country. Hard technological knowledge refers to detailed knowledge about machinery, plant layout, details of raw materials, and other relevant information required to carry out production. The knowledge transfer can be bi-directional and depends on the mode of FDI. In the case of greenfield FDI, the knowledge is likely to flow "from the acquirer to the target" firm (Mani, 2013). But it is also possible that with a sufficient amount of absorptive capacity, the acquirer can also absorb knowledge from the target firm. Although the literature on FDI is getting attention recently, the role of absorptive capacity in knowledge flow is relatively unexplored.

FDI firms are engaged in different types of knowledge transfer activities of both technological and organizational nature, but the level of absorptive capacity is important for the spillover benefit to materialize. Firms with monopolistic advantage can invest in technologically advanced locations to access the advanced technology (Guillen & Garcia-Canal, 2009). Often, positive intra-industry spillover occurs only in high-tech industries (Jordan, 2012). The benefits of technology and knowledge transfer are more likely to occur among firms within a particular industry because the firms produce the same type of products, and the technology and management knowledge used by foreign firms can be easily applied to local firms in the same industry (Liu, 2008). At the same time, knowledge spillover can also occur across firms in different industries.

For example, when firms from a different industry become clients or suppliers of firms in a different industry, they need to exchange some knowledge to meet their expectations. However, although strategic decisions play a role in deciding the quality of technology transferred, the capabilities of recipient firms are also important. In summary, a technologically advanced firm with more absorptive capacity will be able to absorb complementary knowledge from other local firms and increase its technological diversity.

To Protect Unique Capabilities

Proposition 2: Technologically advanced firms with lower absorptive capacity will focus on protecting their unique capabilities.

In the case of FDI, technology transfer can occur in both directions: on the one hand, local firms can absorb technology from the direct investor firms, and on the other hand, direct investor firms absorb technology from host firms and transfer it to the home country (Keller, 2004). In developing countries, firms in more technology-intensive industries show a higher propensity to adopt digital technologies (Mani, 2013). Therefore, technologically advanced firms will try to enhance their safeguards to protect their proprietary knowledge. For instance, Zhao (2006) argues that MNEs with alternative mechanisms such as possession of specialized & complementary assets, bargaining position, connection to related products and services, and the sheer complexity of strategies may choose to do R&D activities in countries that have weak intellectual property rights. By doing so, MNEs can retain control over the technology for a relatively long time.

According to Hymer (1960), the decision to invest in foreign countries is a strategy to capitalize on certain capabilities that are not available to competitors in foreign countries. Therefore, the priority of a technologically advanced firm will be to maintain its uniqueness than to access different opportunities available in a location by making FDI. As Pedersen and Dobbin (2006) explain, from an institutional and cultural perspective, new entrants in a market will choose a unique identity in relation to the existing market participants. Protecting unique technological capabilities can be a way to maintain a unique identity in a new location. A firm will usually make FDI in a place where similar firms are operating; however, it will also claim to be a distinct member (ibid).

Technologically advanced firms, therefore, prefer making a direct investment in developing countries to imparting the technology because of uncertainty in those countries. Managerial knowledge and advanced technologies are firm-specific advantages that are developed over time and are unique to each firm. Because of the firm-specific nature of technology, developers invest to preserve their technological capabilities, and recipients invest to learn those capabilities. This circumstance suggests the notion of technological distance or technology gap which influences the cost and magnitude of technology transfer even if the technology is a matured one and general characteristics of that technology are publicly known (Radosevic, 1999).

Such knowledge and technologies provide the direct investor firms the ownership advantages that local firms cannot emulate without complementary resources. For the same reason, the investor will not be able to access the technology of host firms if it does not have the capacity to absorb the technology. In that case, the direct investor firm's priority will be to protect its unique capabilities. In summary, a technologically advanced firm with less absorptive capacity will be not able to absorb complementary knowledge from other local firms, and therefore, will focus on protecting its unique capabilities.

To Expand the Scope of Business

Proposition 3: Technologically lagging firms with lower absorptive capacity will focus on expanding scopes of business.

The extant literature on FDI explains the motives of FDI mainly from two perspectives: direct investors invest either to exploit price differences across countries or to avoid the cost of international trade. In other words, direct investors can benefit either from the advantages available in other locations to obtain competitive advantages or from avoiding competitive disadvantages in the home country location. Examples of different location advantages include the availability of natural resources, different sizes, and structures of the market, prospects of market growth and levels of development, different cultural, legal, and political environments, favorable government policies and regulations, etc. Therefore, firms that have monopolistic advantages such as economies of scale or privileged access to capital and resources will be able to invest abroad and exploit such advantages internationally (Forsgren, 2017).

Firms in this category are motivated to make FDI mainly by "pull factors" such as the desire to acquire critical resources, obtain managerial expertise, and gain access to consumers in key foreign markets (Luo & Tung, 2007). However, a firm will have no competitive advantage in a new market without having any complementary knowledge or capability required for that market. For the same reason, a firm will not get any benefit from the complementary knowledge or advanced technology available in the new location if the firm does not have the absorptive capacity to absorb knowledge from the environment.

Firms in this category will make FDI to increase the market share in a foreign market and serve the consumers directly in an effort to become global. FDI is a form of counterattack to global rivals since those global rivals are also penetrating the home market (Luo & Tung, 2007). For example, market-seeking FDI refers to the type of investment that aims at penetrating the local markets of host countries. Firms that make such investments are usually concerned about market size, per capita income, market growth, access to regional and global markets, consumer preferences, and the structure of the domestic market. By making FDI, firms also want to bypass direct and indirect trade barriers such as quota restrictions and obtain benefits offered by home countries such as tax benefits.

Therefore, FDI is also a convenient means to take advantage of preferential agreements and take opportunities to enter advanced markets, increase company size, establish brand and reputation, and leverage cost-effective manufacturing capacities. The above-mentioned advantages are rewarding enough for a firm to make FDI, and these advantages are not necessarily related to firms' technological capability or absorptive capacity. In the end, a firm can be motivated to make FDI in order to explore opportunities in unrelated and new areas of business. To sum up, a technologically lagging firm with less absorptive capacity will not be able to absorb complementary knowledge from other local firms and will focus on expanding the scope of business.

To Catch Up on Advanced Technology

Proposition 4: Technologically lagging firms with higher absorptive capacity will focus on catching up with advanced technology.

FDI can be a strategy to catch up with development in terms of acquiring knowledge and technology, improving production processes, developing managerial skills, and being a part of a business network. As Hofmann (2013) points out, an investor's motive for investing abroad is to gain access to foreign firms' knowledge and technology. When investing in developed countries, firms usually seek sophisticated technology or advanced managerial know-how by acquiring or entering into a joint venture with such firms that have advanced technology and know-how (Djulius, 2017; Luo & Tung, 2007; Nelaeva & Nilssen, 2022). According to the classic knowledge-seeking point of view, technologically lagging firms are more inclined to seek new technology and invest in technologically advanced locations. By investing abroad, such firms try to minimize the gap and acquire needed technology from foreign sources.

For example, emerging multinationals invest abroad to acquire the resources they need to compete successfully (Barney, 1991; Deng, 2008). FDI can be used to source specialized knowledge that is not present in the home market (Amann & Virmani, 2014). Though the firms that have the latest technology will, surely, have enough incentives to protect the technology as long as possible to obtain maximum benefit compared to their peers in the industry, they might also be willing to exchange technology with firms in different industries while doing business.

An investor's motive for investing abroad is to gain access to foreign firms' knowledge and technology (Hofmann, 2013). Therefore, FDI can be used to source specialized knowledge that is not present in the home market (Amann & Virmani, 2014), but it requires a substantial amount of investment from the recipients to understand a piece of new knowledge, and they will not get the benefit of such knowledge unless they have the required absorptive capacities (Teece, 1997). An investor will naturally be interested to operate business activities from such a location of knowledge hotspot.

However, a research report in a particular area of study may not be understood by someone who is not familiar with the subject (Amesse & Cohendet, 2001). Therefore, the circulation of knowledge is not only about the form of knowledge or the codification of knowledge but also about the capacity of the user. Even though a location offers the same knowledge to all firms, it is often difficult to understand and utilize such knowledge because of the inherent and complex nature of technical knowledge (Iammarino & McCann, 2006). The net impact of foreign direct investment, therefore, depends on the absorptive capacity of firms; positive externalities happen only when the firms have some competitiveness (Ferragina & Mazzotta, 2014; Volberda et al., 2010).

In the end, the authors theorize the decision to make FDI is motivated by the capabilities a firm has and the advantages a location offers. To be specific, though there are different advantages and resources available in a location, a firm will evaluate such resources and advantages based on its capability; a firm will have different motives to make FDI based on its level of technology and absorptive capacity. The value of a resource is the function of both internal and external factors, and one firm can value the same resource differently than another firm even after having the same information about the resource (Schmidt & Keil, 2013). Schmidt and Keil (2013) identified four factors that influence how a firm values a resource ex-ante - before taking the decision on whether to acquire to build it: the firm's ex-ante market position; its ex-ante resource base that allows for complementarities; its position in the inter-organizational network that gives it access to relevant knowledge and information; it's managers knowledge and experience that allow superior judgment about how to use the resources. Accordingly, the framework proposed in this chapter will offer a comprehensive view of the strategic behavior of firms. To sum up, a technologically advanced firm with more absorptive capacity will be able to absorb complementary knowledge from other local firms and catch up with advanced technology.

DISCUSSION

FDI is a form of investment in which an investor expands business operations in another country, which increases the volume of transactions and potential for profit. At the same time, the international expansion of operations also increases the risks and liability of investors (Marjanovic, & Domazet, 2021). According to the observations by global economic bodies including United Nations Conference on Trade and Development (UNCTAD), World Economic Forum (WEF), and Organization for Economic Cooperation and Development (OECD), the COVID-19 pandemic is going to influence the global flows of FDI. As a result, investors are highly likely to rethink the costs and benefits of the internationalization of their business (Moosa & Merza, 2022). The pandemic might cause MNEs to reorganize their geographic and sectoral activities and diversify in order to deal with post-pandemic recovery and obtain sustainability in their cross-border activities. Under the changed circumstance, the framework will help investors to reflect on and find effective ways to deal with post-pandemic recovery and remain sustainable.

Therefore, an investor needs to understand its capacity to manage its operation in a foreign country before deciding to invest. It is important to understand how heterogeneous entrepreneurial firms develop unique knowledge and apply relevant strategies to deal with competition in the market; in the presence of uncertainties in the business environment, managers must evaluate the environment from different points of view. Therefore, they take different strategies and allocate resources based on distinct organizational capabilities inside the firm (Teece, 2019). Depending on capabilities, firms will decide whether to emphasize exploitation or exploration, which in turn, will affect the nature of relationships with other firms (Parmigiani et al., 2011). At the same time, such decisions will affect firms' competitive advantages in the market.

Therefore, different forms of inter-organizational relationships will tell us different stories behind such relationships. For example, FDI can be thought of as a source of inimitable and non-substitutable resources and capabilities. Keller (2010) finds that foreign sources of technology can account for 90% or more domestic productivity growth and finds evidence of technology spillover in the case of both inward FDI and outward FDI. FDI literature mainly emphasizes either the benefits available to recipients through inward FDI or the benefits available to investors in the host country based on what is not available in the home countries.

In this chapter, the authors propose that the motives of FDI can also be considered from a different perspective – that of the technology level and absorptive capacity of the investor firms. The conceptual framework developed in this chapter explains that a technologically advanced firm will aim either to diversify its existing technologies by absorbing technology and knowledge available in the host country or to protect its existing technology if it does not have absorptive capacity. Similarly, a technologically lagging firm will try to catch up with the advanced technology available in a host country if it has the required absorptive capacity or will focus on availing itself of other advantages available that do not require the absorptive capacity.

In the end, a firm's level of technology and absorptive capacity, therefore, will influence its FDI strategy and how firms' resources are coordinated and managed. These capabilities are crucial for both competitive success and survival. Thereby, the conceptual framework proposed in this chapter offers different implications for strategic decision-making as discussed below.

To Increase Technological Diversity

Technology is fundamentally changing the way firms produce and market products and services across borders. The investors are eager to establish a research facility closer to the foreign cluster to acquire knowledge of the research status quo (Djulius, 2017). The technical and managerial competence of the investors is an important determinant to understand the extent of advantages such as advanced technology and knowledge available in a host country.

For example, a critical factor in transferring technology is the extent to which the technology is understood by the parties involved because the older the technology, ceteris paribus, the better understood the technology, which facilitates the transmission and absorption (Tallman et al., 2004). For the same reason, obtaining new knowledge is costly and requires time in most cases, but a firm can obtain such knowledge from external sources with a sufficient level of absorptive capacity.

Therefore, firms from technologically advanced locations will invest in similarly and technologically advanced locations to increase their technological diversity. To increase technological diversity, firms will focus on both ownership and internalization advantages. Such firms will be willing to engage in joint R&D programs and knowledge and technology-intensive activities with other technologically advanced local firms.

To Protect Unique Capabilities

Business strategies concern both power and efficiency. To make appropriate strategies, firms consider the technology to be employed, the price under which a good or service will be transferred, and the governance structure within which a transaction is located (Williamson, 1991). For example, while making FDI, firms often transfer older technologies to subsidiaries and other partners in the host countries to maintain the upper hand in future competitions (Saggi, 2002). To protect unique capabilities, firms will be concerned about ownership advantages because technology spillover occurs when activities of one firm lead to an improvement in technology and production of other firms such that the first firm cannot capture all benefits created by its technology (Sinani & Meyers, 2004).

Such FDI can be directed from technologically advanced locations to both technologically advanced and technologically not advanced locations. A firm with the motive to protect its unique capabilities will be interested to obtain other advantages in the host country such as access to larger markets and business networks, the opportunity to avoid direct and indirect trade barriers, lower tax rates, etc. Such firms will incur R&D expenditure, but they will try to internalize the advantages as long as possible.

To Expand the Scope of Business

Resources are heterogeneously distributed across firms, and a firm's sustained competitive advantage derives from its resources and capabilities (Barney, 1991). Such resources and capabilities can be viewed as bundles of tangible and intangible assets such as a firm's management skills, organizational processes and routines, and information and knowledge. For example, organizations facing resource scarcity will seek alternative resources to be more competitive without any clear indication of the process (Sherer & Lee, 2002). Similarly, international trade need not always result from the differences in technologies or factor endowments among countries. Krugman (1979) develops a model showing that trade may simply be a way of expanding markets to exploit scale economics, and such effects are similar to labor force growth and regional agglomeration.

Labor will move to places with higher wages inducing more immigration, more populous regions will offer more variety of goods, and eventually, a cluster will form with skilled labor in specific industries (ibid). MNCs as agents of FDI not only transfer the "hard" - patentable form of technologies but also create positive externalities by transferring "soft" technologies such as marketing and managerial skills (Thompson, 2002). FDI in this category will usually occur from technologically not advanced locations to other similar locations. The main concern of firms will be to benefit from the location advantages and other resources and opportunities available in a location.

To Catch Up on Advanced Technology

While engaging in FDI, companies from less advanced countries actively seek assets and advantages such as know-how, resources, and access to foreign markets (Djulius, 2017; Knoerich, 2017). Partnership with firms in host countries provides valuable opportunities to emulate capabilities since the internal knowledge and assets of the firms involved become accessible to partner firms (Ahuja & Katila, 2001). Often, the investors need to assist the host firms in capacity building by transferring technologies and giving advice. However, firms in high-technology sectors do not benefit from the horizontal FDI while firms in low and medium-technology sectors do (Ferragina & Mazzotta, 2014).

Depending on their location, challenges in the external ecosystems can either enhance or erode a firm's competitive advantage in terms of technology leadership. The magnitude of the learning opportunity depends both on the extent to which innovating firms need to change their current approach to problem-solving and on the scope the firm has for doing so (Adner & Kapoor, 2010). Unless the body of knowledge produced internally is not understood, such knowledge cannot be translated for external use. The net impact of foreign firms depends on the absorptive capacity of the domestic firms; positive externalities arise only when the domestic firms have the required competitiveness (Mehreen et al., 2021). Therefore, such FDI will, usually, take place from technologically not advanced locations to technologically advanced locations. Firms will emphasize the location advantages such as strategic resources and advanced technologies available in a location.

Future Research Directions

The applicability of this framework can be well understood through an observational study – by studying firms that are making FDI in different industries. For example, semi-structured interviews with strategic decision-makers in firms can be done to understand the motives of FDI. A firm's level of technology can be measured by using the definition discussed in this chapter or as defined by a particular industry and by using a scale. The age of technology should be considered. A firm's absorptive capacity can be measured by using the firm's human capital and R&D expenditure (Cohen & Levinthal, 1990). It is also important to understand the complexity of the knowledge and technology of the firm, the home country, and the host country (Hausmann et al. 2007). Relevant information such as the firms' monopolistic capability such as access to resources and capital, the host country's economic condition, the firm's age, size, etc. should also be considered.

This framework is also in line with the 5Ps suggested by noted by Mintzberg (1998): plan, position, perspective, pattern, and ploy. Following this framework will help strategists to plan where to make FDI or position their firm from the perspective of both firms' needs and abilities. Eventually, strategists will understand the pattern of relationships with other actors in the new locations and will ploy the opportunities available. As the framework suggests, depending on whether a firm is technologically advanced or technologically lagging and its absorptive capacity, the firm can either look for opportunities to diversify its technology or emphasize protecting the technology it has on the one hand, and look for opportunities to catch up advanced technology or focus on other opportunities to exploit on the other hand.

CONCLUSION

FDI is an opportunity for firms to obtain additional knowledge, skills, technological upgrading, managerial expertise, and a brand's goodwill (Knoerich, 2017). When FDI takes place in equal or more advanced economies, the returns include increasing return, knowledge transfer, improvement in processes or inputs, etc., and when FDI takes place in less advanced economies, the returns include increasing income, savings, upgrading technology or systems, input, etc. (Knoerich, 2017). The benefits of FDI depend on motives, but such benefits are not necessarily limited to the original expectations. For instance, a firm's original motive may be to seek access to advanced knowledge in the home country, but the total benefit comprises other benefits such as access to foreign markets or an increase in profit. Therefore, for sustainable development, an organization needs to sense the environmental threats, opportunities, and customer needs, seize the opportunities, and transform itself as and when needed (Teece, 2019).

Ultimately, it is a firm's self-interest and capabilities that regulate the decision to make FDIs in a particular location. Besides, firm and industry-specific characteristics are also important to explain the course of action regarding a firm's FDI decisions (Iammarino & McCann, 2006). On the one hand, firms conduct foreign direct investment when they possess unique capabilities because either they do not want to share such capabilities with others or sharing such capabilities is difficult/costly. On the other hand, instead of utilizing their capabilities, firms may decide to expand in search of new capabilities that are not available in the home country or market (Cantwell, 1989). However, engaging in FDI does not guarantee that a firm will be able to avail itself of the opportunities in foreign countries. The authors theorize that, based on absorptive capacity, technologically advanced and technologically lagging firms will have different motives for FDI.

In the end, it is important to take the capacities of investors into account while making FDI decisions because cross-border partnerships can facilitate finding long-term solutions not only to deal with post-pandemic recovery but also to obtain sustainability of their international business operations. The conceptual framework proposed in this chapter can be generalized to all industries since the framework points out the importance of considering both capabilities and lacks in a firm while making the FDI. However, this study is not without limitations.

Though the role of FDI in technology transfer, knowledge transfer, and technology spillover has received enough attention from researchers, technology has rarely been studied as a capacity of investors that can influence FDI decisions. Therefore, technology, technological knowledge, and knowledge have been used interchangeably in this chapter. Further studies are needed to understand the role of technology and absorptive capacity in both inward and outward FDI. It will also be possible to categorize the existing theories of the internationalization of firms and motives of outward FDI by using this framework.

REFERENCES

Adner, R., & Kapoor, R. (2010). Value creation in innovation ecosystems: How the structure of technological interdependence affects firm performance in new technology generations. *Strategic Management Journal*, *31*(3), 306–333. doi:10.1002mj.821

Ahuja, G., & Katila, R. (2001). Technological acquisitions and the innovation performance of acquiring firms: A longitudinal study. *Strategic Management Journal*, *22*(3), 197–220. doi:10.1002mj.157

Amann, E., & Virmani, S. (2015). Foreign direct investment and reverse technology spillovers. *OECD Journal: Economic Studies*, *2014*(1), 129–153.

Amesse, F., & Cohendet, P. (2001). Technology transfer revisited from the perspective of the knowledge-based economy. *Research Policy*, *30*(9), 1459–1478. doi:10.1016/S0048-7333(01)00162-7

Barney, B. (1991). Firm resources and sustained competitive advantage. *Journal of Management*, *17*(1), 99–120. doi:10.1177/014920639101700108

Blomström, M., & Kokko, A. (1999). *How Foreingn Investment Affects Hose Countries*. World Bank Publications. doi:10.1596/1813-9450-1745

Borensztein, E., De Gregorio, J., & Lee, J. W. (1998). How does foreign direct investment affect economic growth? *Journal of International Economics*, *45*(1), 115–135. doi:10.1016/S0022-1996(97)00033-0

Buckley, P. J. (1989). Foreign direct investment by small-and medium-sized enterprises: the theoretical background. In *The multinational enterprise* (pp. 24–45). Palgrave Macmillan. doi:10.1007/978-1-349-11026-1_2

Cantwell, J. (1989). *Technological innovation and multinational corporations*. Blackwell.

Cantwell, J., & Janne, O. (1999). Technological globalisation and innovative centres: The role of corporate technological leadership and locational hierarchy. *Research Policy*, *28*(2-3), 119–144. doi:10.1016/S0048-7333(98)00118-8

Caves, R. E., & Caves, R. E. (1996). *Multinational enterprise and economic analysis*. Cambridge University Press.

Chung, W., & Alcácer, J. (2002). Knowledge seeking and location choice of foreign direct investment in the United States. *Management Science*, *48*(12), 1534–1554. doi:10.1287/mnsc.48.12.1534.440

Coase, R. H. (1937). The nature of the firm. *Economica*, *4*(16), 386–405. doi:10.1111/j.1468-0335.1937.tb00002.x

Cohen, W. M., & Levinthal, D. A. (1990). Absorptive capacity: A new perspective on learning and innovation. *Administrative Science Quarterly*, *35*(1), 128–152. doi:10.2307/2393553

Cui, L., Meyer, K. E., & Hu, H. W. (2014). What drives firms' intent to seek strategic assets by foreign direct investment? A study of emerging economy firms. *Journal of World Business*, *49*(4), 488–501. doi:10.1016/j.jwb.2013.12.003

Deng, P. (2008). Resources, capability, and outbound FDI from Chinese companies. *Globalization of Chinese Enterprises*, 17-30.

Djulius, H. (2017). Foreign Direct Investment and Technology Transfer: Knowledge Spillover in the Manufacturing Sector in Indonesia. *Global Business Review*, *18*(1), 57–70. doi:10.1177/0972150916666878

Dunning, J. H. (1982). Explaining the international direct investment position of countries: towards a dynamic or developmental approach. In *International Capital Movements* (pp. 84–121). Palgrave Macmillan. doi:10.1007/978-1-349-05989-8_4

Dunning, J. H. (2001). The eclectic (OLI) paradigm of international production: Past, present and future. *International Journal of the Economics of Business*, *8*(2), 173–190. doi:10.1080/13571510110051441

Dunning, J. H., & Lundan, S. M. (2008). *Multinational enterprises and the global economy*. Edward Elgar Publishing.

Fang, J., Collins, A., & Yao, S. (2021). On the global COVID-19 pandemic and China's FDI. *Journal of Asian Economics*, *74*, 101300. doi:10.1016/j.asieco.2021.101300 PMID:35702564

Ferragina, A. M., & Mazzotta, F. (2014). FDI spillovers on firm survival in Italy: Absorptive capacity matters! *The Journal of Technology Transfer*, *39*(6), 859–897. doi:10.100710961-013-9321-z

Forsgren, M. (2017). *Theories of the multinational firm: A multidimensional creature in the global economy*. Edward Elgar Publishing.

Fu, Y., Alleyne, A., & Mu, Y. (2021). Does lockdown bring shutdown? Impact of the COVID-19 pandemic on foreign direct investment. *Emerging Markets Finance & Trade*, *57*(10), 2792–2811. doi:10.1080/1540496X.2020.1865150

Grossman, G. M., & Helpman, E. (1993). *Innovation and growth in the global economy*. MIT press.

Guillén, M. F., & García-Canal, E. (2009). The American model of the multinational firm and the "new" multinationals from emerging economies. *The Academy of Management Perspectives*, *23*(2), 23–35. doi:10.5465/amp.2009.39985538

Hausmann, R., Hidalgo, C. A., Bustos, S., Coscia, M., Simoes, A., & Yildirim, M. A. (2014). *The atlas of economic complexity: Mapping paths to prosperity*. MIT Press. doi:10.7551/mitpress/9647.001.0001

Hitt, M. A., Holmes, R. M. Jr, & Arregle, J. L. (2021). The (COVID-19) pandemic and the new world (dis) order. *Journal of World Business*, *56*(4), 101210. doi:10.1016/j.jwb.2021.101210

Hofmann, P. (2013). *The impact of international trade and FDI on economic growth and technological change*. Springer Science & Business Media. doi:10.1007/978-3-642-34581-4

Hymer, S. H. (1960). The international operations of national firms: A study of direct foreign investment.

Iammarino, S., & McCann, P. (2006). The structure and evolution of industrial clusters: Transactions, technology and knowledge spillovers. *Research Policy*, *35*(7), 1018–1036. doi:10.1016/j.respol.2006.05.004

Johanson, J., & Vahlne, J. E. (1977). The internationalization process of the firm—A model of knowledge development and increasing foreign market commitments. *Journal of International Business Studies*, *8*(1), 23–32. doi:10.1057/palgrave.jibs.8490676

Jordaan, J. A. (2012). Foreign Direct Investment and Technology Transfers to Local Suppliers: Identifying the effects of type of ownership and the technology gap.

Keller, W. (2004). International technology diffusion. *Journal of Economic Literature*, *42*(3), 752–782. doi:10.1257/0022051042177685

Keller, W. (2010). International trade, foreign direct investment, and technology spillovers. Handbook of the Economics of Innovation, 2, 793-829.

Knoerich, J. (2017). How does outward foreign direct investment contribute to economic development in less advanced home countries? *Oxford Development Studies*, *45*(4), 443–459. doi:10.1080/13600818.2017.1283009

Kogut, B., & Zander, U. (1992). Knowledge of the firm, combinative capabilities, and the replication of technology. *Organization Science*, *3*(3), 383–397. doi:10.1287/orsc.3.3.383

Krugman, P. R. (1979). Increasing returns, monopolistic competition, and international trade. *Journal of International Economics*, *9*(4), 469–479. doi:10.1016/0022-1996(79)90017-5

Lall, S., & Narula, R. (2004). Foreign direct investment and its role in economic development: Do we need a new agenda? *European Journal of Development Research*, *16*(3), 447–464. doi:10.1080/0957881042000266589

Liu, Z. (2008). Foreign direct investment and technology spillovers: Theory and evidence. *Journal of Development Economics*, *85*(1-2), 176–193. doi:10.1016/j.jdeveco.2006.07.001

Luo, Y., & Tung, R. L. (2007). International expansion of emerging market enterprises: A springboard perspective.

Mani, S. (2013). Outward foreign direct investment from India and knowledge flows, the case of three automotive firms. *Asian Journal of Technology Innovation, 21*(supl), 25-38.

Marjanović, D., & Domazet, I. S. (2021). Foreign Direct Investments: A Key Factor for Business Globalization. In *Handbook of Research on Institutional, Economic, and Social Impacts of Globalization and Liberalization* (pp. 96–116). IGI Global. doi:10.4018/978-1-7998-4459-4.ch006

Mehreen, H., Rammal, H. G., Pereira, V., & Del Giudice, M. (2021). Investigating the influence of absorptive capacity of recipients within cross-border transfer of knowledge: Evidence from emerging markets. *International Marketing Review*.

Mintzberg, H., Ahlstrand, B., & Lampel, J. (1998). Chapter 1, And over here, ladies and gentlemen: the strategic management beast, pp 1-21. In Strategy Safari. The Free Press.

Moosa, I. A., & Merza, E. (2022). The effect of COVID-19 on foreign direct investment inflows: Stylised facts and some explanations. *Future Business Journal*, *8*(1), 1–12. doi:10.118643093-022-00129-5

Nelaeva, A., & Nilssen, F. (2022). Contrasting knowledge development for internationalization among emerging and advanced economy firms: A review and future research. *Journal of Business Research*, *139*, 232–256. doi:10.1016/j.jbusres.2021.09.053

Parmigiani, A., & Rivera-Santos, M. (2011). Clearing a path through the forest: A meta-review of interorganizational relationships. *Journal of Management*, *37*(4), 1108–1136. doi:10.1177/0149206311407507

Pavitt, K. (1985). Patent statistics as indicators of innovative activities: Possibilities and problems. *Scientometrics*, *7*(1-2), 77–99. doi:10.1007/BF02020142

Pedersen, J., & Dobbin, F. (2006). In search of identity and legitimation. *The American Behavioral Scientist*, *49*(7), 897–907. doi:10.1177/0002764205284798

Radosevic, S. (1999). *International technology transfer and catch-up in economic development*. Edward Elgar Publishing.

Ritchie, B. K. (2002). Foreign direct investment and intellectual capital formation in Southeast Asia.

Rugman, A. M., & Verbeke, A. (2008). Internalization theory and its impact on the field of international business. In *International business scholarship: AIB fellows on the first 50 years and beyond*. Emerald Group Publishing Limited. doi:10.1016/S1064-4857(08)00003-X

Saggi, K. (2002). Trade, foreign direct investment, and international technology transfer: A survey. *The World Bank Research Observer*, *17*(2), 191–235. doi:10.1093/wbro/17.2.191

Schmidt, J., & Keil, T. (2013). What makes a resource valuable? Identifying the drivers of firm-idiosyncratic resource value. *Academy of Management Review*, *38*(2), 206–228. doi:10.5465/amr.2010.0404

Sherer, P., & Lee, K. (2002). Institutional change in large law firms: A resource dependency and institutional perspective. *Academy of Management Journal, 45*(1), 102–120. doi:10.2307/3069287

Sinani, E., & Meyer, K. E. (2004). Spillovers of technology transfer from FDI: The case of Estonia. *Journal of Comparative Economics, 32*(3), 445–466. doi:10.1016/j.jce.2004.03.002

Teece, D. (2019). A capability theory of the firm: An exonomics and (Strategic) management perspective. *New Zealand Economic Papers., 53*(1), 1–43. doi:10.1080/00779954.2017.1371208

Teece, D. J. (1977). Technology transfer by multinational firms: The resource cost of transferring technological know-how. *Economic Journal (London), 87*(346), 242–261. doi:10.2307/2232084

Thompson, E. R. (2002). Clustering of foreign direct investment and enhanced technology transfer: Evidence from Hong Kong garment firms in China. *World Development, 30*(5), 873–889. doi:10.1016/S0305-750X(02)00009-8

Volberda, H. W., Foss, N. J., & Lyles, M. A. (2010). Perspective—Absorbing the concept of absorptive capacity: How to realize its potential in the organization field. *Organization Science, 21*(4), 931–951. doi:10.1287/orsc.1090.0503

Williamson, O. (1991). Strategizing, economizing and economic organization. *Strategic Management Journal, 12*(Special issue), 75–94. doi:10.1002mj.4250121007

Zhao, M. (2006). Conducting R&D in countries with weak intellectual property rights protection. *Management Science, 52*(8), 1185–1199. doi:10.1287/mnsc.1060.0516

Chapter 3
Competitiveness and Value Creation in the "New Normal"

Rukiye Sönmez
Canakkale Onsekiz Mart University, Turkey

ABSTRACT

Whereas firms need to adapt to such changes rapidly, sometimes their efforts remain insufficient in the face of unprecedented environmental changes. The main purpose of this study is to explain the sudden changes to normality that are necessary to overcome the impact of the Covid-19 pandemic on all sectors, enabling competitiveness and value creation. This chapter aims to address the following broad research questions: first, how firms that investigate opportunities can increase their market share in all industries. Second, how firms can ensure sustainability in the new normal. Third, how the change brought about by the pandemic is reflected in the organization and what should be the leaders' role in the adoption of this process. Fourth, how innovation can be implemented that creates value in the new normal. And finally, how the new business model should be designed more competitively and creates more value.

INTRODUCTION

The boundaries between the industries disappear in the new normal; therefore, one cannot clearly distinguish between them. Radical innovation that works in a specific industry may undermine another industry. On the one hand, the new normal has allowed some sectors to be more attractive and developed, doubling their profitability (e.g., logistics, finance, and technology). On the other hand, it has created devastating impacts on some other industries. This chapter touches upon how firms survive, how competition changes, and how the rules of the game are reshaped in new normal periods, such as pandemics, concerning current examples.

The Concept of New Normal

The pandemic has unfortunately brought dramatic changes and boosted uncertainty. The pandemic has not only caused health problems and deaths, but it has also had a deleterious influence on businesses

DOI: 10.4018/978-1-6684-3749-0.ch003

and business environments (Zou et al., 2020). This emerging new normal situation has prompted the researchers to investigate diverse solutions to struggle against future pandemics (Agarwal et al., 2022).

The new normal concept refers to that aggressive growth, high earnings, and overvaluation are replaced by normal growth, normal earnings, and normal valuation. In the aftermath of the 2008 financial crisis, many changes to the business world brought about a new normal business environment changing the core practices of managers, strategists, and entrepreneurs (Ahlstrom et al., 2020, p. 411).

Initially, it is needed to explore the concept of competition and the evolution of competitive advantage to be able to mention competitive advantage in the new normal. Porter (1985) defined the concept of competition as the competitive strategies adopted to gain sustainable competitive advantage and initiated the discussions on competition in the strategic management literature. Besides, Kogut (1988) defined competition as an institution-specific superiority. What is noteworthy here is to ensure the continuity of such superiority and make it sustainable. According to Hoffman (2000, p. 1), it is the implementation of some strategies creating value.

Considering the change in competitive strategy in its historical course, the focus was on corporate strategy to gain competitive advantage in the 1970s. These years popularized corporate strategy (Belohlav, 1996, p. 12). Firms adopted a holistic perspective, identified their corporate strategies on which areas they should continue their activities and from which areas they should withdraw, and created various matrices to do this. The essential concepts of this period, where strategic planning was emphasized, are the terms of the matrices, such as market share, growth rate, industry attractiveness, and competitive position. Early research in industry analysis considered both external factors (opportunities and threats) and internal factors (strengths and weaknesses). In this period, successful organizations were shown as those matching their external environment with their internal capabilities and deciding on the appropriate strategy.

In the following years, it was questioned why some firms were always superior to others in competition. In this context, Porter emphasized the structure of the industry in gaining competitive advantage in his books "Competitive Strategy: Techniques for Analyzing Industries and Competitors" (1980) and "Competitive Advantage: Creating and Sustaining Superior Performance" (1985). These studies, introducing the Industrial-Organization Theory, focus on the industry where the firms compete, develop strategies for industries, and explain the performance differences between firms by industry. Although a firm has many advantages and weaknesses compared to its competitors, Porter identifies the strategies that will enable that firm to gain competitive advantage as cost leadership, diversification, and focus strategies (Porter, 1985).

Afterward, focusing on internal factors, the competitive strategy was started to be determined within the framework that the advantage depends on resources and capabilities (Barney, 1991). Then, Barney's focus on internal resources led to the formation of the Resource-Based Theory; this period emphasizes the significance of internal resources of organizations and managing the firm's capabilities (Liu & Chan-Olmsted, 2002, p. 48). The theory, which was introduced to complement the Industrial-Organization Theory, turned into a rival for the latter over time. This theory proposes that firms need to focus on their internal factors and compete with them.

On the other hand, it has become even more difficult to gain a competitive advantage in the "new normal." As firms experience collapses in economic crises, some managers realize the need to change their business cycles, which will lead to the restructuring of the economic order. Some call this period the "new normal" (Chui et al., 2009). In this period, the strategy becomes more complex, each planning stage gets narrower, and it becomes more challenging to reach the expected growth in the future. In this respect, it is a period where business assumptions, having seemed uncontroversial, are now being questioned (Webb, 2009). To be successful in the new normal, organizations must focus on what has fundamentally remained the same and what has changed for consumers, firms, and industries (Davis, 2009).

Firms need to seek value from their consumers and collaborators. In addition, the importance of efficiency is likely to increase in this period. Together with their business partners, managers may seek technology-based innovation to provide their firms with a long-term competitive advantage (Chui et al., 2009). Besides, since innovation and brand-specific competition play an important role in international trade, organizations prioritizing innovation, creativity, brand, R&D, and marketing are likely to emerge stronger from a global crisis (Yılmam, 2011, p. 188). Some analysts assert that the deeper one goes, the faster they come back. However, this applies to the "old normal" (Rogoff, 2009). For some organizations, surviving in the short term is just the agenda item.

Some, on the other hand, look at the fog and blur of uncertainty and think about what position they need to take when the crisis evolves to normal (Davis, 2009). Nevertheless, the new normal that emerged from the impacts of financial crises has brought about significant changes, and the old normal strategy and structure may not yield returns for organizations. The changes brought by the new normal involve a regression in the trend of economic growth, constantly high unemployment in industrial countries, reduction in the risks of both balance sheets and assets of banks, and from free-market activities to government interventions (El-Erian, 2010).

Regarding the issue based on countries by consumer behavior, most of such discussions originated from around North America. If one looks at other geographies from a global perspective, one may realize that the new normal in North America is actually "normal." What is seen before more mature markets is a more normalization of the American consumer (Webb, 2009). Firms seeking high income and consumption are gravitating towards Asia and will head even more. Yet, the growth of Asia is not a result of the 1997 Asian crisis. It stemmed from the achievement of efficiency, adaptation to technology, and cultural and institutional change. In the new normal, technological innovation and the value of human knowledge will continue (Davis, 2009).

Firms engage in intense competition with their competitors concerning price, quality, speed, and cost to gain a competitive advantage. In this competition, all competitors continue their activities with diverse losses. The concept of the Red Ocean Strategy is used to describe the strategy generated in this contentious and highly competitive environment. The opposite of this concept is the Blue Ocean Strategy, referring to getting out of the current competitive conflicts and making the competition meaningless (Ağraş et al., 2017). Accordingly, the only way to win in competition is to stop trying to win in competition (Kim & Mauborgne, 2005).

The term **Blue Ocean Strategy** was first introduced by W. Chan Kim and Renee Mauborgne in their book published in 2005. In the book, The Blue Ocean Strategy, the market areas are divided into red oceans and blue oceans. On the one hand, the boundaries of the industry and the competitive rules of the game are well-defined in red oceans. Competitors in the industry often strive to gain market share from each other and to surpass their competitors. Yet, the probability of profit and growth decreases as the market becomes crowded. Blue oceans, on the other hand, correspond to industries that do not exist yet. Besides, the rules of the game have not been designed yet, and there is no competition (Kim & Mauborgne, 2005).

Blue ocean strategy refers to a method to neutralize competition through new values for a firm and its customers. This strategy proposes that the firm should raise their operating standards over the industry standards and offer greater value to their customers than their competitors. In short, it should differentiate in products/services and the market compared to its competitors, which should not be imitated by competitors in a short time. In addition, it is needed to reduce or eliminate other activities to provide value at a low cost (Emiroğlu, 2017). Table 1 presents the prominent characteristics of the red ocean and blue ocean strategies (Kim & Mauborgne, 2005).

Table 1. Characteristics of the Red Ocean and Blue Ocean Strategies

RED OCEAN STRATEGY	BLUE OCEAN STRATEGY
Compete in existing market space	Compete in existing market space
Beat the competition	Beat the competition
Exploit existing demand	Exploit existing demand
Make the value-cost trade-off	Make the value-cost trade-off
Align the whole system of a firm's activities with its strategic choice of differentiation or low cost	Align the whole system of a firm's activities with its strategic choice of differentiation or low cost

Source: Kim and Mauborgne, 2005

In the new normal, staying out of competition mandates firms to create new markets where they can offer unique value to consumers. However, customer focus is of little use in this regard since how new markets will be created is often not imagined by customers. Therefore, it is necessary to consider non-customers more than customers in a market. The fundamental principle of creating a new market is to stay out of competition and restructure the boundaries of the market (Kıyan & Özer, 2011). Here, a new perspective is needed other than the wishes and needs of the existing customers or the markets that may create needs.

GETTING MARKET SHARE IN THE NEW NORMAL COMPETITIVENESS

A competitive strategy has improved the competitive position in a particular industry, market, or business unit (Wheelen & Hunger, 2011). The source of enhancing the competitive position or the competitive advantage is characterized by the industry-market characteristics (Mason 1939; Bain 1964; Porter 1980; 1981; 1985; 1991; 2007; Bartol & Martin 1994) and the characteristics of the firm's resources and capabilities (Wernerfelt 1984; Barney 1991; 1995; Barney & Clark 2007; Dierickx & Cool 1989; Collis 1994; Mata et.al., 1995; Collis & Montgomery 1999).

The way to gain a competitive advantage is to increase the market share, which may happen in three different situations, as in the figure below. In Figure 1, there are five firms A, B, C, D, and E, and each circle represents the market or industry where firms operate. It is assumed that E has the highest market share, and the shares of other firms are almost close to each other.

Increasing the market share of the firms operating in such a market is realized in three ways: getting a share from the existing market, expanding the market, and creating a new market.

Getting a Share From the Existing Market

In the case of getting a share from the existing market, that is, from competitors, firms with similar resources and capabilities are in fierce competition. Each firm designs its strategy to get the market share of the others or protect its shares from the competitors. In such industries with intense competition, competitors are constantly surveilling each other's moves. A firm should act by considering the retaliation of the competitors when deciding to make a new move. However, competing in these industries may cost high to firms.

Figure 1. Getting a Share from the Existing Market

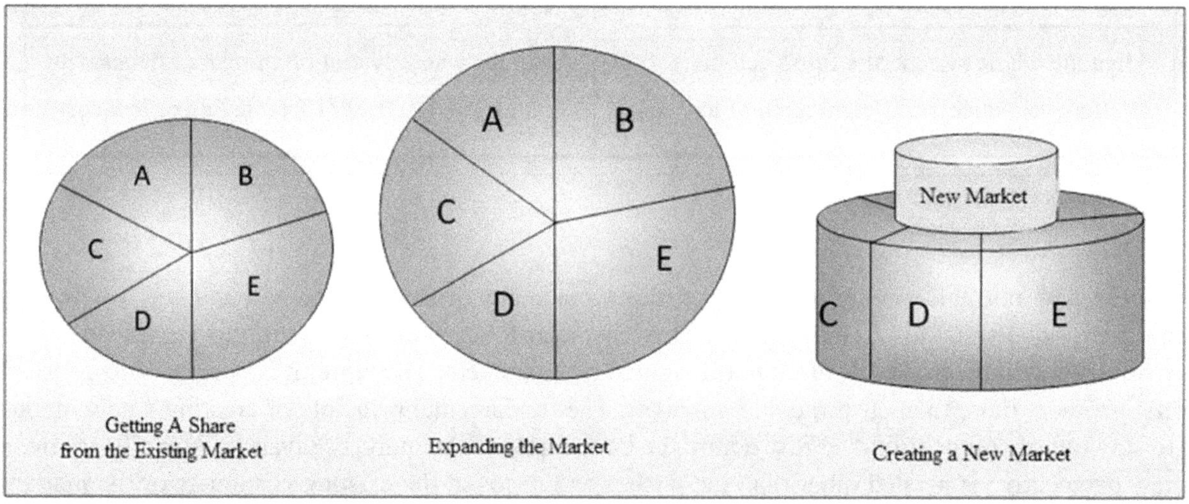

Expanding the Market

In the case of expanding the market, the market area is expanded with radical innovation and creativity activities adopted by one or more firms. A proactive strategy is adopted, and industry standards are modified thanks to such innovation and creativity activities. The industry can also be expanded by adding new customers to the portfolio and differentiating offered products or services. For instance, fast food restaurants may offer healthy foods like salads, or bus firms may schedule non-stop trips to attract time-sensitive customers.

The growth potential of mature and stagnating industries is "zero." Firms operating in such industries can accelerate their industries with innovative activities, which may ensure the industry's growth. In the cases of getting a share from the existing market and expanding the market in Figure 1, the fact that the market shares are equally increased between the two indicates industrial expansion. However, a firm that makes a radical innovation in expanding the market will further increase its market share, and the expansion of the market will, in turn, ensure an increase in the sales volumes and profitability ratios.

Creating a New Market

Creating a new market, on the other hand, is to create a new market that appeals to an entirely new customer base by focusing on non-customers instead of the existing customer base. Yet, there will be no competition in this new market unless capturing the customers of competitors. While the firm is operating alone in the newly created market, after a while, there may be those desiring to enter the market, or even those who do, as the competitors see it as profitable. While most strategies are concerned with being more competitive, the focus is on creating a non-competitive area. Such an area can be realized by creating a new market or business model or introducing a new value.

Creating a new market does not mean creating a new market from scratch but finding novel solutions to the needs of the existing market with existing products or services. As an instance, Nintendo Wii, the creator of popular games such as Super Mario, has generated such a market in the gaming industry. Compared to those of its competitors, the game console of Nintendo has features demanding less operating power, lower resolution game graphics, and less storage. Besides, while traditional video games are aimed at the young and children, Nintendo extends the target audience of the Wii to all family members. It has a wide variety of games from karaoke to mind gym to adventure games and has also redesigned the popular games of the arcade era for adults. It also targets to reach middle-aged people and retirees in the gaming market thanks to its DS models (Tetris-like gaming devices) (Bessant & Tidd, 2018, p. 172).

Another example is the MittiCool refrigerator with a ceramic crucible, introduced to solve the problem of 500 million people who must live with constant power cuts in India and cannot use their refrigerators. This non-electric refrigerator produced to solve the electricity problem has gone beyond the relevant market and started to be sold to the whole world (Radjou et al., 2012). As in these two examples, it should be highlighted that reverse innovation is rather practical in creating a new market. Reverse innovation involves using old technology instead of state-of-art technology and presenting it to consumers with low costs. Various products and services offered to the emerging markets lacking a rich population may initiate to create of new markets.

Akash Computer has launched a mobile phone for $20 and a computer for US$35 for the Indian market, with a target audience of 110 million students and planning to include higher education students in the future. With open office software and open-source Linux operating system, its computers that do not require super hardware appeal to low-income groups. Tablet-like versions compete with Apple's iPad (Bessant & Tidd, 2018, p. 172).

SUSTAINABILITY IN THE NEW NORMAL

Today, we are faced with a rapid change in science, technology, ways of doing business, and competition. The pandemic has not only had a critical role in accelerating and shaping such changing conditions but also has nourished uncertainty and unpredictability. Firms have responded to such changes in three different ways: 1) trying to adapt to the changes quickly or continuing activities despite being a little bit late to adapt to the changes, 2) stopping being a follower of changing conditions, showing proactive behavior, and shaping the industry, and 3) terminating activities with structural rigidity in the face of changes.

Recent changes have also led all the phenomena perceived as normal to be replaced by new phenomena. Therefore, it has become almost impossible for businesses, which cannot manage change well and adapt quickly to the new normal, to survive within the fierce competition in every field today. For firms affected by unprecedented changes to survive for a longer period, executive bodies should be informed of how to adapt the changing competitive strategy to the changing conditions and the industry in the new normal and rearrange their "game board." In this respect, a firm adopting proactive or reactive strategies becomes sustainable in its activities.

The term sustainability is perceived in two different senses in the management literature. First, as mentioned at the beginning of the study, sustainable competitive advantage refers to that firms maintain the continuity of their competitive advantages and increase their competitiveness. The other is corporate sustainability.

Sustainability is becoming an increasingly seminal issue for managers in both senses. In the first sense, the underlying assumption of sustainability is that it is a part of growth (Coombs, 2011). In other words, organizations make productions by using materials and energy and cause waste and emissions as a result of their operations. This fact, however, was realized after many years, and it was aired that organizations would not be sustainable in this way (Holliday, 2001).

Although the concept of sustainability is not new, what is new is that this concept is a robust alternative in guiding existing management approaches. The economic, social, and ecological sustainability of businesses has become one of the key discussion topics of this century. Sustainability-related issues, such as population growth, resource consumption, and environmental destruction, have been on the agenda since the 1950s. Yet, the traditional management approach does not consider these issues among the responsibilities of businesses because their primary responsibility is toward their shareholders and focuses on profit and growth. The neo-classical economic theory, on which the traditional management approach is built, is interested in maximizing social benefit by analyzing the benefits and costs of alternative operation models under controlled conditions (Tokgöz & Erken, 2009).

Firms have a wide range of stakeholders and responsibilities. The management styles adopting the input-output model of the past and not transcending beyond relations with a few stakeholder groups have inevitably become unable to satisfy the needs emerging in this age (Sarıkaya et al., 2010). Although corporate sustainability is considered environmental responsibility, it is accepted as a set of ecological, economic, and social responsibilities that all individuals and organizations should bear (Sarıkaya & Kara 2007). The social, technological, and environmental risks of the industrial society have further increased its threat power (Tokgöz & Erken, 2009). Just like in environmental conditions, the functioning of organizations is also governed by the uncertain behavior of these systems (Öge, 2005). Firms that do not attempt to solve a social problem and compensate for the damage they cause to the environment are warned and then boycotted by consumers. In such a case, it is not prudent to mention sustainability.

ORGANIZATIONAL CHANGE AND LEADERSHIP IN THE NEW NORMAL

Today, no organization is immune to change; leaders must fundamentally change the way their organizations run their business to overcome new technology, competition, and demographic forces (Şirin & Yetim, 2009). However, the process of adaptation to change will be painful since the change is likely to bring about uncertainty and the deterioration of the old order. Situations of comprehensive change such as radical innovation and competence-destroying innovation bring strong resistance.

It is necessary to prevent resistance to change as it will disrupt organizational dynamics. Therefore, top management needs to prioritize raising employees' awareness of the necessity for change and reach a consensus on the reasons for such a necessity (Kim & Mauborgne, 2005).

Leadership plays a vital role in organizational change, and organizational leadership requires two competencies. The first is to deal with continuous change. It requires the manager to embrace change, construct the organizational chart by defining the strategic intent, and redesign the organization to keep up with the opportunities and change demands. The second is to gain management skills to cope with the problems through continuous change. Therefore, organizational leadership develops a vision for employees' overtime, guides them, and improves the future leadership and organizational culture of the organization (Pearce & Robinson, 2015).

Organizational culture is a set of important - often unspecified - assumptions shared by the members of an organization. Leaders primarily have a passion for changing or shaping the current organizational culture and use tools such as reward systems, symbols, and plans (Pearce & Robinson, 2015). To do so, the organization should facilitate access to information and ensure the continuity of information sharing.

Thus, the organizational learning process will be initiated. This is a step towards the transformation of the firm into a learning organization. Based on the learning organization phenomenon, there are activities to obtain, share, and disseminate information within the organization. However, this phenomenon becomes functional only thanks to both vertical and horizontal communication channels within the organization and the elimination of structures restraining individuals within specific roles and boundaries (Altuntuğ, 2007).

VALUE CREATION AND INNOVATION IN THE NEW NORMAL

To be able to offer a value proposition to its consumers, the organization must find a solution to a problem, satisfy the expectations of consumers, and differentiate by doing more than other firms do. Realizing all these is only possible by integrating innovative and creative thinking into the organizational structure.

Craig Wynett, Director of Growth at Procter & Gamble, states the company does not separate innovation from the rest of the firm, that is, not making it front-page news. Innovation needs to be dealt with systematically. The creative process is assumed to be a self-limiting process, not related to ordinary people's sound management of their efforts but to the light bulbs burning above the heads of inspired geniuses (Peeples, 2003).

Establishing a separate unit in the firm for innovation or creativity will make the whole organization think that invention is only the task of that unit and will keep others away from being innovative. Innovative thinking alone is not enough, but the key to market leadership is consistent innovation (Pearson, 2003). The ability to consciously and purposefully see opportunities and disciplined work is required for the essence of making an invention. Influential inventions start with small steps and focus on one thing. For example, such a focus was on ensuring that a moving vehicle could receive electricity while traveling on rails, which made possible the invention of electric trams. Or focusing on providing the same number of matches placed in the matchbox; such simple thinking enabled the automatic filling of matchboxes, ensuring a Swiss monopoly for half a century (Drucker, 2000).

The most innovative organizations seem to exhibit five key behaviors: 1) believing there is always a way to do things better, 2) focusing on customers' aired and unaired needs and desires, 3) collaborating heavily inside and outside the firm, 4) believing that success requires experimentation, rapid iterations, and frequent mistakes, and 5) encouraging and empowering people to take reasonable risks, express their opinions, and seek necessary resources (Scott et al., 2019).

It is needed to put forward a well-established analysis of the element(s) creating value within a firm. The owner of McDonald's, Ray Kroc, realized in the 1960s that selling hamburgers with low margins would not achieve the desired return. Instead, according to him, what creates the real value was the real estate value of the restaurants. It was a turning point to realize where the real value lies (Kadaster, 2017).

Every firm creates value with its product(s) or service(s). However, the value created by production may remain insufficient in today's conditions. Instead, a combination of several values or the value proposition offered by a specific business model may be required. For example, LG Electronics and Hyundai Motors have collaborated and introduced the IONIQ Concept Cab offering a personalized in-car experience by combining the idea of feeling at home on the road with many value-creating activities. As elements that create value, this cabin is featured with a capsule coffee machine that makes coffee on the morning commute, a compartment under the seat that dries and freshens wet or old shoes before reaching the destination, a wardrobe manager that keeps clothes clean and wrinkle-free while driving, and a mini-fridge that keeps drinks cold.

In addition, there is a flexible OLED screen whose optimum viewing angle for the rear passengers and degree of curvature can be adjusted with intuitive hand movements. It also covers most of the vehicle's roof, allowing two passengers to watch different content simultaneously. The headrest speakers create a personal sound zone that does not disturb the other passenger. When out of the vehicle, a sliding stick cleans the floor, picking up the crumbs and wiping the floor. To destroy all germs and other microorganisms, overhead UV LED lights constantly disinfect the interior (lg.com, 2022). In this example, two firms combine their capabilities and bring many value-creating factors together to create a differentiated product.

The collaboration of Carlo Ratti Associati, a design and innovation firm, and famous architect Italo Rota have given birth to an umbrella Sammontana, the Italian ice cream, and frozen dessert brand. The project is called "Cool Under the Sun," which cools or keeps food and drinks cold. Adopting a sustainable approach, this umbrella has been developed to cool food and drinks with clean energy on hot summer days in coastal areas. The umbrella acts like origami, and foldable photovoltaic panels at the top absorb sunlight and convert it into electricity, powering coolers and nebulizers at the bottom. Thus, it turns into a mini-fridge allowing users to keep their food and drinks fresh. Nebulizers also refresh the user with cold water vapor. Furthermore, electrical power from one or more umbrellas can be pooled together to power a large ice cream refrigerator. If desired, electronic devices can be charged with an umbrella. Thus, the design and function of the umbrella offer a multi-faceted value proposition with an environmentalist approach (girisimhaberleri, 2022).

The "Feel the Peel" project has been launched by Carlo Ratti Associati for Eni to find a solution to the plastic waste threat to the environment. In this project, a 2.74 m long machine can store approximately 1,500 oranges on its dome-shaped roof. It also collects the peels of the oranges squeezed in a closet at the bottom. It dries and grinds the peels and mixes them with polylactic acid to form bioplastics. It then heats and melts this mixture and sends it as filament to an internal 3D printer to print recyclable cups. Furthermore, the firm anticipates producing even clothes from orange peels thanks to the improvements in this technology (ekolojist.net).

There are many similar applications regarding the recycling of waste. Biohm, a London-based biotechnology and biomanufacturing startup, has designed lighting from coffee waste and orange peels to reduce plastic use. Rens Original has produced waterproof shoes from coffee waste and recycled plastic. Singapore-based sustainable footwear brand Ccilu has introduced the first rain boots made of coffee grounds. Even coffee waste can be converted into many products, from coffee cups to fuel, and these products are planned to be used in double-decker buses in London.

BUSINESS MODEL INNOVATION IN THE NEW NORMAL

Firms producing and marketing new products or services for the first time are called pioneers of the industry. Among the most important benefits of being a pioneer may be the reputation as an industry leader, the cost leadership provided by the lowering of the learning curve, the temporary high profits (market skimming) since the product or service is valuable to the buyers (Wheelen & Hunger, 2011). Yet, being a pioneer in the industry is not enough because a profitable market also attracts competitors. In this case, the resources and capabilities of the firm should be evaluated compared to the competitor. For example, General Electric's resources and capabilities in transistor manufacturing became less valuable as its competitors discovered semiconductors. Likewise, the resources and capabilities of IBM became less useful with the decrease in prices of personal computers, their prevalence, and the increase in their quality (Barney, 1995). Value propositions offered by firms can be imitated by their competitors in a short time. Therefore, besides presenting a value proposition, transforming it into a business model, that is, realizing business model innovation, is of great importance.

A business model is a short story that tells how a proven business has been done and how value has been created. While any business, product, or service can be copied in a short time, it is even more difficult to copy a business model since the whole way of doing business needs to be changed, which may take time.

Business model innovation is deemed critical for firms to improve their performance in the new normal. It enables collaboration with competitors, diversification when the local market is saturated, meeting new customers' demands and needs, and rapid seizure of new opportunities. Besides, understanding the creation of new and innovative business models in the new normal has become a must for researchers and managers (Loon et al., 2020).

When an innovative product or service that creates value in more than one area is introduced to the market, it is always at the risk of being copied by competitors. Although it is more difficult compared to high-tech products and other types of innovative products, even radical and competence-destroying innovation can be copied in a few days. Yet, replicating business model innovation takes more time, even years. Besides, if the business model is positioned within a wide collaborative network, copying the synergy and value created within this network becomes much more difficult or even impossible. There must be strong collaboration management behind value creation through the business model so that the value created cannot be copied even if the business model is replicated. To do so, it is needed to go beyond traditional ways of doing business.

Nest is a venture firm that develops products on smart home technology and has two products: "Nest Learning Thermostat," launched in 2011, and "Nest Protect," a smoke and carbon monoxide detector released in 2013. The combination of these two products creates a distinct synergy. Unlike its competitors, Nest has designed a thermostat in such a way that the consumer can install it in thirty minutes without the need for any assistance and completed the necessary infrastructure with a 24/7 hotline and easy installation videos.

Then, it has sold its product in technology markets that consumers can easily access. Therefore, this has dramatically reduced the time spent buying and installing a thermostat. Equipped with the Internet of Things (IoT) and machine learning technology, the new generation thermostat learns the user's heating/cooling need within a week and satisfies this need automatically. It also adapts quickly to changes in heating needs. In addition, it is equipped with a speech notification and voice warning system. It also creates value by saving energy by up to 20 percent and showing how more energy can be saved through monthly statistics.

While Nest creates value with its undebatable innovative and technological features, it also offers many value propositions with its collaborations. For example, in partnership with Mercedes-Benz, the thermostat connects to the car navigation to lower the temperature when the car leaves the house and increase it when approaching the house. In cooperation with LIFX, it makes the lights in the house flash automatically within specific time intervals when you are on vacation or not at home for a long time. It allows Whirlpool brand devices to work only when total energy consumption is decreased. Overall, Nest's business model innovation has been reinforced by many similar collaborations. Even if other firms attempt to copy its business model, not only will it take time, but Nest will also improve its value proposition day by day thanks to new collaborations. Meanwhile, realizing its potential in 2014, Google acquired the firm for 3.2 billion dollars (teknolo.com).

A year later, a German firm called Tado entered the industry as a competitor with a similar business model. Like Nest's, Tado's thermostat works compatible with iOS and Android operating systems. It can automatically adjust the temperature in different time zones, weather changes, or when you are not at home. The smartphone application provided with the device monitors your daily behavior and physical condition. The device also checks the weather conditions online and adjusts the temperature according to unexpected changes. Tado's thermostat had no screen when it first came out; all controls were performed via smartphones or tablets. However, the versions with a screen are currently available. Recently, the firm has received investment from Amazon and Siemens and continues its activities with strong cooperation management, like Nest.

Over time, the current business model may also be far from encouraging innovation and creativity. In this case, the business model that fails to create value, compete with competitors, and provide benefits in strengthening or completing the core business can be replaced with a new business model that will change the game for the industry or market (Sönmez et. al., 2019). A business model may need to be revised or even radically changed over time. If Quibi had changed its business model on time, it would still be operating profitably now. Quibi, a short form streaming platform, was founded by Jeffrey Katzenberg in August 2018. It broadcasted 5-6-minute episodes that can be followed between meetings or on public transport.

These episodes were called "quick bites," from which the name "QUI-ck BI-tes" comes. The firm achieved exceptional success thanks to its business model and received a high amount of investment. Nevertheless, the pandemic has dramatically hit the firm since closures have led consumers to spend more time in front of the screen. Six months after starting operations, the firm officially announced the permanent termination of its activities.

The transformation of the business model powered by digital technology is one of the strategies to respond to disruptive environmental changes (Richter, 2020). Firms should rapidly react to increasing competition and environmental changes in the new normal by extending innovation and, especially, developing a new business model (Loon et al., 2020).

CONCLUSION

The most crucial factor that brings dynamism to competitiveness is that firms are prepared for possible changes that may occur by uncertainties and the degree of certainty of these uncertainties. On the other hand, the factor that can eliminate differences between current strategies and changes and prevent the interruption of competitiveness is the talent and skill portfolio of the employees (Altuntuğ, 2007). Employees, members of the organization are the initiators, carriers, and sharers of concepts woven with innovation, talent, creativity, and invention. Such values are brought by the employees and prepare the way to success by being shared and multiplied following the motivation of the current environment (Altuntuğ, 2007).

REFERENCES

Agarwal, P., Swami, S., & Malhotra, S. K. (2022). Artificial Intelligence Adoption in the Post COVID-19 New-Normal and Role of Smart Technologies in Transforming Business: a Review. *Journal of Science and Technology Policy Management.*

Ağraş, S., Atba, F., & Şeyba, E. (2017). Mavi Okyanus Stratejisi: Dünyadan ve Türkiye'den Örnekler. [Blue Ocean Strategy: Examples from the World and Turkey.]. *Yönetim, Ekonomi, Edebiyat, İslami ve Politik Bilimler Dergisi, 2*(2), 126–144.

Ahlstrom, D., Arregle, J., Hitt, M. A., Qian, G., Ma, X., & Faems, D. (2020). Managing Technological, Sociopolitical, and Institutional Change in the New Normal. *Journal of Management Studies, 57*(3), 411–437. doi:10.1111/joms.12569

Altuntuğ, N. (2007). Rekabet Sürecinin Dinamik Boyutu, Bileşenleri ve Dinamizmi Sürdürebilme Yolları. [The Dynamic Dimension of the Competitive Process, Its Components and Ways of Sustaining Dynamism.]. *Süleyman Demirel Üniversitesi Sosyal Bilimler Enstitüsü Dergisi, 5*, 29–15.

Bain, J. S. (1964). The impact on industrial organization. *The American Economic Review, 54*(3), 28–32.

Barney, J. B. (1991). Firm Resources and Sustained Competitive Advantage. *Journal of Management, 17*(1), 99–120. doi:10.1177/014920639101700108

Barney, J. B. (1995). Looking inside for Competitive Advantage. *The Academy of Management Executive, 9*(4), 49–61. doi:10.5465/ame.1995.9512032192

Barney, J. B., & Clark, D. N. (2007). *Resource-based Theory: Creating and Sustaining Competitive Advantage*. Oxford University Press.

Bartol, K. M., & David, C. M. (1994). Management, Second Edition. New York.

Belohlav, J. A. (1996). The Evolving Competitive Paradigm. *Business Horizons, 39*(2), 11–19. doi:10.1016/S0007-6813(96)90018-X

Bessant, J., & Tidd, J. (2007). *Innovation and Entrepreneurship*. John Wiley & Sons.

Chui, M., Edin, P., & Manyika, J. (2009). Time to Raise the CIO's Game. *McKinsey on Business Technology, 17*, (4-9).

Collis, D. J. (1994). Research Note: How Valuable Are Organizational Capabilities? *Strategic Management Journal, 15,* 143-152.

Collis, D. J., & Montgomery, C. A. (1999). Competing on Resources: Strategy in the 1990s. *Harvard Business Review*, 33–62. doi:10.1016/B978-0-7506-7088-3.50005-X

Coombs, W. T. (2010). Sustainability: a new and complex 'challenge' for crisis managers. *International Journal Sustainable Strategic Management, 2*(1), 4-17.

Davis, I. (2009, March). The New Normal. *The McKinsey Quarterly*.

Dierickx, I., & Cool, K. (1989). Asset Stock Accumulation and Sustainability of Competitive Advantage. *Management Science, 35*(12), 1504–1511. doi:10.1287/mnsc.35.12.1504

Drucker, P. (2000). Buluşçuluk Disiplini. [The Discipline of Inventiveness.] [Çığır Açıcı Düşünme,] [Çev. Ahmet Gürsel] [MESS Yayınları, İstanbul.]. *Harvard Business Review*, 143–158.

El-Erian, M. A. (2010). Sovereign Wealth Funds in the New Normal. *Finance & Development*, 44–48.

Emiroğlu, A. (2017). *Çekişmesiz Pazar Alanı Yaratmak: Mavi Okyanus Stratejisi ve Uygulama Örnekleri. [Creating a Non-Contentious Market Area: Blue Ocean Strategy and Implementation Examples.]* Uluslararası Yönetim İktisat ve İşletme Kongresi, Zonguldak, Türkiye.

Hoffman, P. N. (2000). An Examination of the "Sustainable Competitive Advantage Concept: Past, Present, and Future. *Academy of Marketing Science Review*, 4.

Holliday, C. (2001, September). Sustainable Growth, the DuPont. *Harvard Business Review*, 129–136. PMID:11550629

Kadaster, P. (2017). The Founder: Patates Kızartmasından Franchise Restoranlara Uzanan Dönüşüm. *Harvard Business Review*.

Kim, W. C., & Mauborgne, R. (2005). Mavi Okyanus Stratejisi, 9. Baskı. [Blue Ocean Strategy, 9. Printing.] CSA Global Publishing.

Kıyan, Ş. S., & Özer, A. (2011). İşletme Sınırlarının Girişimci Faaliyetle Yeniden Yapılandırılması: Yeni Pazar Oluşturma. [Restructuring Business Boundaries Through Entrepreneurial Activity: Creating a New Market.]. *Ankara Üniversitesi SBF Dergisi, 66*(2), 93–120. doi:10.1501/SBFder_0000002205

Kogut, B. (1988). Joint Ventures: Theoretical and Empirical Perspectives. *Strategic Management Journal, 9*(4), 319–332. doi:10.1002mj.4250090403

Liu, F., & Chan-Olmsted, S. M. (2002). Partnerships Between the Old and the New: Examining the Strategic Alliances Between Broadcast Television Networks and Internet Firms in the Context of Convergence. *The International Journal on Media Management*, *5*(1), 47–56. doi:10.1080/14241270309390018

Mason, E. S. (1939). Price and Production Policies of Large-Scale Enterprise. Papers and Proceedings of the Fifty-first Annual Meeting of the American Economic Association. *The American Economic Review*, *29*(1), Supplement,, 61-74.

Mata, F. J., Fuerst, W. L., & Barney, J. B. (1995). Information Technology and Sustained Competitive Advantage: A Resource-Based Analysis. *Management Information Systems Quarterly*, *19*(4), 487–505. doi:10.2307/249630

Öge, S. (2005). Düzen mi Düzensizlik (Kaos) mi? Örgütsel Varlığın Sürdürülebilirliği Açısından Bir Değerlendirme. [Order or Chaos? An Assessment in terms of the Sustainability of Organizational Existence.]. *Selçuk Üniversitesi Sosyal Bilimler Enstitüsü Dergisi*, *13*, 285–303.

Pearce, J. A., & Robinson, R. B. (2015). Stratejik Yönetim: Geliştirme, Uygulama ve Kontrol. [Strategic Management: Development, Implementation and Control.] (Çev: M. Barca), Nobel Yayınları, Ankara.

Pearson, A. E. (2003). Yenilikçilikte Kararlı Olma Yolları. [Ways to Be Committed to Innovate.] [Yenilikçilik,] [Çev. Ahmet Kardam] [MESS Yayınları, İstanbul.]. *Harvard Business Review*, 37–58.

Peeples, E. (2003). Yeniliği Esinlendirmek. [Inspiring Innovation.] [Yenilikçilik,] [Çev. Ahmet Kardam] [, MESS Yayınları, İstanbul.]. *Harvard Business Review*, 97–118.

Porter, M. E. (1980). *Competitive Strategy: Techniques for Analyzing Industries and Competitors*. Free Press.

Porter, M. E. (1981). The Contributions of Industrial Organization To Strategic Management. *Academy of Management Review*, *6*(4), 609–620. doi:10.2307/257639

Porter, M. E. (1985). *Competitive Advantage: Creating and Sustaining Superior Performance*. Free Press.

Porter, M. E. (1991). Competitive Advantage and Global Trade in the 1990's. *Harvard International Review*, *13*(4), 12–15.

Porter, M. E. (2007). Rekabet Stratejisi: Sektör ve Rakip Analizi Teknikleri. [Competitive Strategy: Sector and Competitor Analysis Techniques.] (Çev. Gülen Ulubilgen), Sistem Yayıncılık, İzmir.

Radjou, N., Prabhu, J., & Ahuja, S. (2012). Jugaad innovation: Think frugal, be flexible, generate breakthrough growth. In J. Bessant & J. Tidd (Eds.), *Innovation and Entrepreneurship*. John Wiley & Sons.

Richter, A. (2020). Locked-down digital work. *International Journal of Information Management*, *55*, 102–157. doi:10.1016/j.ijinfomgt.2020.102157 PMID:32836629

Rogoff, K. (2009). The "New Normal" for Growth. *Project Syndicate*, 1-2.

Sarıkaya, M., Erdoğan, M., & Kara, F.Z. (2010). Internet Ekonomisi ve Kurumsal Sürdürülebilirlik. [Internet Economics and Corporate Sustainability.] Eskişehir Osmangazi Üniversitesi *İİBF Dergisi*, *5*(2), (31-50).

Sarıkaya, M., & Kara, F.Z. (2007). Sürdürülebilir Kalkınmada İşletmenin Rolü: Kurumsal Vatandaşlık. [The Role of Business in Sustainable Development: Corporate Citizenship.] *Yönetim ve Ekonomi*, *14*(2), (221-233).

Scott, A. D., Cobban, P., Nair, R., & Painchaud, N. (2019). İnovasyonun Önündeki Engelleri Kaldırmak. [Removing Barriers to Innovation.]. *Harvard Business Review*.

Şirin, E. F., & Yetim, A. A. (2009). Beden Eğitimi Ve Spor Yüksekokulu Yöneticilerinin Dönüşümcü Liderlik Stiline İlişkin Yönetici Algıları. [Executive Perceptions of School of Physical Education and Sports Administrators on Transformational Leadership Style.]. *Niğde Üniversitesi Beden Eğitimi ve Spor Bilimleri Dergisi*, *3*(1), 69–85.

Sönmez, R., Düzgün, A., & Öz, E. (2019). Firmanın İş Modeli Değişiminin Rekabetçiliğine Etkisi: Atlasjet'ten Atlasglobal'e", 27. [The Impact of Business Model Change on Competitiveness: From Atlasjet to Atlasglobal", 27.] Ulusal Yönetim ve Organizasyon Kongresi, İstanbul Üniversitesi, 18-20 Nisan, Antalya.

Tokgöz, N., & Önce, S. (2009). Şirket Sürdürülebilirliği: Geleneksel Yönetim Anlayışına Alternatif. [Company Sustainability: Alternative to Traditional Management Approach.] Afyon Kocatepe Üniversitesi *İ.İ.B.F. Dergisi*.

Webb, A. (2009). Navigating the New Normal: A Conversation with Four Chief Strategy Officers. *The McKinsey Quarterly*, 1–6.

Wernerfelt, B. (1984). A Resource-Based View of the Firm. *Strategic Management Journal*, *5*(2), 171–180. doi:10.1002mj.4250050207

Wheelen, T. L., & Hunger, J. D. (2011). Strategic Management and Business Policy, (5th ed.). Addison – Wesley Publishing Firm.

Yılmam, M. (2011). *Yeni Normal"de Rekabet II* [Competition in the New Normal II.]. KobiEfor, Nisan.

Zou, C., Zhao, W., & Siau, K. (2020), COVID-19 calls for remote reskilling and retraining. Cutter Business Technology, 33(7).

Chapter 4
Tracing the Path of International Business Research

Etayankara Muralidharan
https://orcid.org/0000-0001-7985-3089
MacEwan University, Canada

Sejal Tiwari
University of Ottawa, Canada

ABSTRACT

Past studies have attempted to identify the domains of international business over specific periods of time. Most have used data sets for short time periods, providing a snapshot of the field for the period under review. This chapter reviews the research in the area of international business for the past five decades, with the objective of understanding the path that research has taken during that period in terms of research content, relevance, and methodology. While this understanding supports a proposal for a research agenda for the future, from the perspective of both content and methods in international business research, the impact of the pandemic may require a re-look at the trends that have been presented. The chapter addresses some of the potential changes in the trends in the research agenda that could occur due to the pandemic.

INTRODUCTION

As a field of inquiry, international business (IB) has shown tremendous growth in the past five decades. The attention that practitioners and academics alike give to the field of international business has increased in step with the pace of globalization. Since the field is growing, many scholars have conducted reviews to define the field and its trends over the past five decades, in terms of content and the outlets where the articles have appeared. Some of the reviews with their broad objectives are shown in Table 1.

DOI: 10.4018/978-1-6684-3749-0.ch004

Table 1.

Year	Author/s	Journal	Period of Review	Broad Objectives
2002	Werner & Brouthers	JIBS	1976-80 & 1996-2000	Amount & Type of international research
2002	Werner	JOM	1996-2000	Trends in IM research based on 12 areas
2003	Lu	JIM	1991-2000	Breadth & contribution of International Strategic Management research
2005	Acedo & Casilla	IBR	1997-2000	Trends most relevant in the field
2009	Pisani	JOM	2002-2006	Comprehensive picture of the field

Most of the review objectives shown in the table above serve to define the domain of this research by identifying key areas of study and looking at trends during the periods reviewed. The initial studies look at defining the field of international business (IB) research in terms of the domain, and clearly distinguish it from pure management studies (Boddewyn, 1999; Contractor, 2000; Martinez & Toyne, 2000). Only 1.6% of articles belonging to the area of IB research were published during 1976-1980 (Werner & Brouthers, 2002); in 1996-2000 this increased to 5.5% (Werner, 2002), and in 2002-2006 it reached 7%. These findings confirm that research in the IB field is steadily increasing and is becoming an important field of inquiry in the area of management. While the overall studies have mainly addressed the areas of research during the time periods reviewed, none has studied how IB research has evolved. Examining the evolution of the research and reporting findings in the area will enable scholars to identify gaps both in the content of research and its methods. This will also help to describe the relevance of IB research.

With the current changes in global business environments due to the increasing influence of developing economies, changing strategies of multinational enterprises, progress in telecommunications, and challenges in the transfer of knowledge across subsidiaries, it is important to understand whether certain categories will become more relevant than others in the development of the IB field (Pisani, 2009). This is more so with the external shock of the COVID pandemic. It is also important for any field of study to take an occasional step back to reflect on the composition of the research area and to evaluate the relevance of its content (Daniels, 1991). International business views itself as an applied discipline (Oesterle & Laudien, 2007). Therefore, the importance of the practical relevance of IB research is as Dunning (1989) stated:

. . . the effectiveness of our scholastic efforts to study and teach international business is entirely dependent on our capability to marshal and organize the necessary human and other assets so as to supply a range of end products which are acceptable to the academic community of which we are part, our paymasters and the main purchasers of our products, viz, the business community.

Thus, tracing the path that academic research in the area has taken can be one of the ways to evaluate the current and future relevance of the categories that constitute the domain of IB research. The objectives of this study, which is essentially a literature review, are threefold. The first is to understand the path that IB research has taken over the past five decades in terms of content and methodologies for conducting research. The second is to understand the relevance of IB research—in other words, to see whether research has kept pace with the evolution of the practice of international business. The final objective, based on the gaps identified, is to propose an agenda for future IB research.

In line with these objectives, this paper is organized as follows. The next section provides detail on the methodology used, including sample selection, coding, and other protocols applied in the analysis of the literature. Thereafter, a detailed analysis of the patterns that emerge from the review is presented, followed by discussion of the findings, the potential influence of the COVID pandemic, and the proposed research agenda. The last section will offer conclusions, limitations of the study, and the way forward.

METHODOLOGY

The basic methodology used is a systematic literature review. Research articles that have appeared over the past five decades in the area of IB are reviewed using the protocols of content analysis. These research articles will illustrate the content of IB inquiry in terms of the motivation behind the research, and the relevant methodological rigor employed.

Sample Selection and Time Frame

The study follows key principles of review, including inclusiveness and reproducibility (Pittaway et al., 2004). Selection of journals for samples is difficult, due to the fact that the field is an open one with numerous and relevant exchanges with other disciplines such as economics, organizational behavior, strategic management, and marketing (Chandy & Williams, 1994). Therefore, rankings offered to date in the work of scholars in the area is followed. The process here is to analyze the path of IB research, independent of other areas of management. Works aimed at creating a ranking of journals within the IB field (DuBois & Reeb, 2000; Lu, 2003) is studied. Going by data-summary and impact-factor criteria used by DuBois and Reeb (2000), *Journal of International Business Studies* (JIBS) is ranked the highest for IB impact. The IB impact factor for JIBS was a high 11.38, compared to the next publication, *Management International Review* (MIR) at 4.32 (Dubois & Reeb, 2000).

Ranking of JIBS among the top 20 management journals (Werner, 2002) for the number and percentage of IB articles per journal is also considered. JIBS (Pisani, 2009) is ranked the highest with 71%, followed by *Strategic Management Journal* (SMJ) (16.6%), *Journal of Management Studies* (JMS) (11.5%), *Academy of Management Review* (AMR) (8%), and *Academy of Management Journal* (AMJ) (7.8%). Therefore, JIBS was selected as the primary source of the data set required for the review. The JIBS Decade Award is designed to recognize the most influential paper published in the JIBS volume one decade ago, and the award is presented at the Academy of International Business (AIB) conference.

One major measure of influence is the degree to which the candidate article has been cited in the ten years following its publication. Citation-count data from Web of Science is used to determine the pool of candidates and forms the basis for selection of possible award winners. From discussions with the editor of JIB it is understood that the AIB committee selects the manuscript that has made (or is making) the most "insightful and influential" contribution to international business studies. That may or may not be the paper with the highest citation count.

The following criteria was therefore considered for this analysis. First, the top five articles in JIBS by citation count were considered, to ascertain the research areas that have been pursued by IB scholars over the past five decades. The award-winning articles from the year 1970 (the year when the Decade

Award was instituted) through the 2016 announcement of the 2015 Decade Award were considered to identify the most influential areas in IB research. IB research articles which are the top five most cited articles of the top management journals (Pisani, 2009) along with JIBS were also considered.

The classification of articles is shown in Table 2, which clearly indicates that JIBS (10.55%) have the highest number of IB articles from among the top five most cited. The distribution of IB research areas from 1970 to 2016 in these journals was also considered for comparative purposes. The five broad time periods considered for analysis of the articles were 1970-1976, 1977-1986, 1987-1996, 1997-2006 and 2007-2016. The number of articles selected based on the criteria above is 355 [215 articles from JIBS and 140 articles from the other journals (see Table 2].

Table 2.

Journal	Year From- To	Total No of Articles	Total IB Articles in Top 5 Cited Each Year	Percentage
Journal of International Business Research (JIBS)	1976-2016	2037	215	10.55%
Strategic Management Journal (SMJ)	1980-2016	2302	54	2.35%
Journal of Management Studies (JMS)	1970-2016	2629	36	1.37%
Academy of Management Journal (AMJ)	1970-2016	2975	34	1.14%
Academy of Management Review (AMR)	1983-2016	2211	15	0.68%
	Total	**12,154**	**355**	**2.92%**

Coding

In this study, content-analysis protocols were used to generate inferences from text, including categories both quantitative (e.g., frequency counts, trends, patterns, and differences over time) and qualitative (e.g., theme identification, pattern recognition, and elaboration). After the basic coding, the content is classified into the 12 categories used by Werner (2002) and Werner & Brouthers (2002) for examining IB research. Two additional categories (13 and 14) called Research Methods and Entrepreneurship respectively were added, which were found to be distinct categories in themselves. Each of the 14 categories, adapted from Werner (2002), is briefly defined as follows:

- Global Business Environment (GBE): Studies on the global economy, market structure, political and regulatory risks, and international risk.
- Internationalization (INT): Studies on the descriptions and measurement of internationalization, antecedents (level, motivations, speed), and consequences (performance) of internationalization.
- Entry Mode Decisions (EMD): Studies on the predictors of entry mode choices, international equity ownership levels, and consequences of entry mode decisions.
- International Joint Ventures (IJV): Studies on motivations of international joint ventures, partner selection, partner relations, and consequences of IJVs.
- Foreign Direct Investment (FDI): Studies on timing, motivations, location, and firm and host consequences of FDI.

- International Exchange (IEX): Studies on exchange overviews, determinants of exporting, export intermediaries, and consequences of exporting.
- Transfer of Knowledge (TOK): Studies on antecedents (firm, partner, and venture factors), processes, and consequences (performance) of knowledge transfer.
- Strategic Alliances and Networks (SAN): Studies on strategic alliance networks, business networks, and outcomes of strategic alliances.
- Multinational Enterprises (MNE): Studies on policies (relationship between environment and firm performance), strategies (strategic processes like flexibility, change, and performance), and models and descriptions (classifications, flexibility, legitimacy, and structural changes) of MNEs.
- Subsidiary-Headquarters Relations (SHQ): Studies on the role, control, and performance of subsidiaries.
- Subsidiary and Multinational Team Management (SMTM): Studies on subsidiary human resource management practices, subsidiary behaviours, multinational negotiations, and multinational team management.
- Expatriate Management (EMN): Studies on expatriate HRM issues, and expatriate and repatriate reactions.
- Research Methods (RMT): Studies on journals, research agendas, research methodologies, constructs, and measures used in IB research.
- Entrepreneurship (ETP): Studies on international entrepreneurship orientation toward new ventures, opportunity recognition, national culture, born-global firms, description and measurement, and social entrepreneurship.

RESULTS

Descriptive Statistics

As discussed earlier, the total number of papers selected from JIBS for the review from 1970 to 2016 is 215. The articles were categorized as Empirical, Theoretical, and Others. The breakdown by decade of the articles (Empirical 169, Theoretical 38, and Others 8) is shown in Table 3. Theoretical articles increased over the decades, indicating the importance of IB as an independent field. Other articles include commentaries on the field of IB research and have appeared more recently.

Table 3.

Decade-wise Publication Type Distribution (JIBS)						
	1970-76	**1977-86**	**1987-96**	**1997-06**	**2007-16**	**Total**
Empirical	11	45	42	40	31	**169**
Theoretical	0	4	8	6	20	**38**
Others	0	1	0	4	3	**8**
Total	**11**	**50**	**50**	**50**	**54**	**215**

ANALYSIS

Consistent with Werner's (2002) methodology, each of the 215 articles from JIBS has been classified into one of the 14 categories and their subthemes that Werner described in detail. In order to determine those that most influenced the field of IB over the last five decades, the study examined the top five most cited articles in each of Werner's broad themes and compared the articles in each theme that won awards to calculate the success percentage, which indicates the relevance accorded to the theme by the academic community.

While the top five most cited themes in JIBS will show the area of research that IB scholars addressed, the award-winning themes will be considered the most relevant in view of their highly insightful and influential nature as decided by the JIBS editorial committee. One assumption made at this point is that the relevance accorded by the academic community to the categories will align with their relevance to the practice of IB. The success percentage of themes that won the award will also indicate the mismatch between the relevance of each and the extent of research done on the theme.

In other words, the higher the success percentage, the higher is the relevance of the theme. To evaluate the top five most cited articles, the Web of Science Database was used. For comparison purposes, the citations of award-winning JIBS articles were compared with the citations as recorded by Google Scholar, and both databases show a similar trend for all the years from 1970 until 2016 in which the awards were given (Figure 1).

Figure 1.

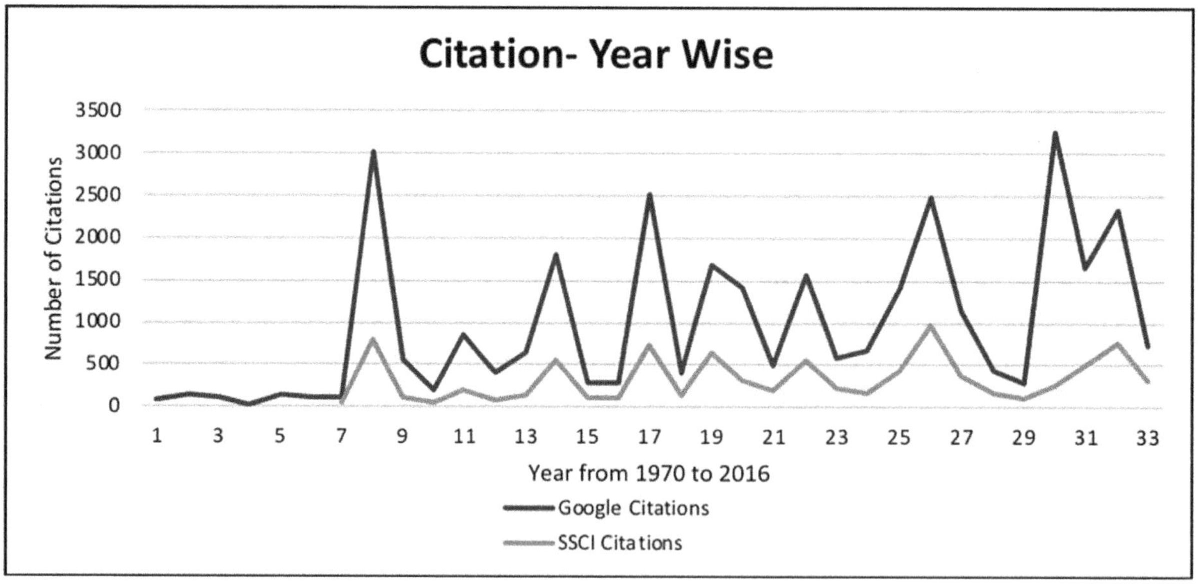

The calculation of success percentage—and therefore relevance—for both Empirical and Theoretical papers appear in Tables 4 and 5. Comparing findings on articles that appear in the top five and their percentage of success (i.e., awards won) shows about 22% of Empirical papers and 27% of Theoretical papers meet the criteria for higher relevance among the academic community. The key themes that emerge as the most influential among the Empirical articles are Transfer of Knowledge (67%), Entry Mode Decisions (44%), International Joint Venture (33%), Subsidiary and Multinational Team Management (30%), Strategic Alliance and Networks (29%), Internationalization (27%), and Global Business Environment (20%).

The most influential among Theoretical papers are those on Entry Mode Decisions (56%), Strategic Alliances and Networks (50%), Foreign Direct Investment (50%), and Internationalization (40%). Combining both the Empirical and Theoretical papers' success percentages results in the ranking of relevant areas in JIBS as shown in Table 6. The top seven categories by relevance are Transfer of Knowledge (67%), Entry Mode Decisions (48%), International Joint Ventures (33%), Strategic Alliances and Networks (33%), Internationalization (31%), Subsidiary and Multinational Team Management (27%), and Global Business Environment (18%).

Table 4.

Research vs. Recognition-Empirical Papers				
	Category	**Most Cited**	**Awarded**	**Success**
1	Global Business Environment	10	2	20%
2	Internationalization	11	3	27%
3	*Entry Mode decisions*	*16*	*7*	*44%*
4	*International Joint Ventures*	*6*	*2*	*33%*
5	Foreign Direct Investment	22	2	9%
6	International Exchange	20	3	15%
7	*Transfer of knowledge*	*9*	*6*	*67%*
8	*Strategic alliances and networks*	*7*	*2*	*29%*
9	Multinational enterprises	11	1	9%
10	Subsidiary-headquarters relations	8	1	13%
11	*Subsidiary & multinational team management*	*10*	*3*	*30%*
12	Expatriate Management.	5	0	0%
13	Research Methods	12	0	0%
14	Entrepreneurship	6	1	17%
	TOTAL EMPIRICAL	**153**	**33**	**22%**

Table 5.

Research vs. Recognition-Theoretical Papers				
	Category	Most Cited	Awarded	Success
1	Global Business Environment	1	0	0%
2	*Internationalization*	*5*	*2*	*40%*
3	*Entry Mode decisions*	*9*	*5*	*56%*
4	International Joint Ventures	0	0	-
5	*Foreign Direct Investment*	*2*	*1*	*50%*
6	International Exchange	0	0	-
7	Transfer of knowledge	0	0	-
8	*Strategic alliances and networks*	*2*	*1*	*50%*
9	Multinational enterprises	8	0	0%
10	Subsidiary-headquarters relations	1	0	0%
11	Subsidiary & multinational team management	1	0	0%
12	Expatriate Management.	0	0	-
13	*Research Methods*	*8*	*1*	*13%*
14	Entrepreneurship	0	0	0%
	TOTAL Theoretical	**37**	**10**	**27%**

Table 6.

Top Relevant Categories					
No	Category	Code	Most Cited	Number That Won Awards	Success
1	Transfer of knowledge	TOK	9	6	67%
2	Entry Mode decisions	EMD	25	12	48%
3	International Joint Ventures	IJV	6	2	33%
4	Strategic alliances and networks	SAN	9	3	33%
5	Internationalization	INT	16	5	31%
6	Subsidiary & multinational team management	SMTM	11	3	27%
7	Global Business Environment	GBE	11	2	18%
8	Entrepreneurship	ETP	6	1	17%
9	International Exchange	IEX	20	3	15%
10	Foreign Direct Investment	FDI	24	3	13%
11	Subsidiary-headquarters relations	SHQ	9	1	11%
12	Multinational enterprises	MNE	19	1	6%
13	Research Methods	RMT	20	1	5%
14	Expatriate Management.	EMN	5	0	0%
	TOTAL		**190**	**43**	**23%**

Table 7.

Article Distribution Category Wise /Publication Wise																
Journal	**Year**	**GBE**	**INT**	**EMD**	**IJV**	**FDI**	**IEX**	**TOK**	**SAN**	**MNE**	**SHQ**	**SMTM**	**EMN**	**RMT**	**ETP**	**Total**
JIBS	1970-2016	11	21	32	6	26	19	8	9	23	8	11	5	27	9	**215**
SMJ	1980-2016	6	10	5	5	5	0	2	4	8	5	4	0	0	0	**54**
JMS	1970-2016	6	5	1	2	2	1	2	3	4	0	6	1	0	3	**36**
AMJ	1970-2016	5	9	0	2	3	0	0	1	2	4	2	6	0	0	**34**
AMR	1983-2016	1	1	0	1	0	0	2	0	7	0	0	2	2	0	**16**
Total		**29**	**46**	**38**	**16**	**36**	**20**	**14**	**17**	**44**	**17**	**23**	**14**	**29**	**12**	**355**

For comparison purposes, the study also examined the top five management journals and coded the available IB articles that appeared among the top five most cited articles (from Web of Science) from 1970 through 2016 for the four management journals; namely, *Strategic Management Journal* (SMJ), *Journal of Management Studies* (JMS), *Academy of Management Journal* (AMJ), and *Academy of Management Review* (AMR). The 140 articles from these four journals were coded and content analyzed in the same way as the JIBS articles. The total 355 articles (215 from JIBS and 140 from the other four journals) are classified according to Werner's (2002) categories and shown by journal in Table 7. Eight of the articles in JIBS were narratives and did not fall into any of the 14 categories under discussion.

On comparing the rankings of categories in the top five management journals (including JIBS) with those of JIBS alone, similarity in the rankings was found (Table 8). Although the order may not be same, in the composition of the top five categories, four of the categories are the same (i.e., MNE, EMD, FDI, and RMT). This observation suggests that the top researched areas over the years have been inquiries on Multinational Enterprises, Entry Mode Decisions, Foreign Direct Investment, and Research Methods in international business.

This ranking may, however, not align with relevance (in terms of influence) as discussed earlier. On examining the award success as per the 'JIBS Award Success' (Table 8), the top relevant categories are TOK, EMD, IJV, SAN, and INT. Comparing relevance with top researched areas suggests that research on Entry Mode Decisions is the category that appears in the top rankings of all top management publications (including JIBS), rankings of JIBS alone, and is also relevant (as shown in the top rankings of the ones that have won the JIBS Award as shown in table 8). In the next sections literature on each of the key categories are summarized in order to develop an agenda for future research.

Table 8. Rankings – Comparison of Categories.

Rank	All Top Publications	JIBS Alone	JIBS Award Success
1	**INT**	**EMD**	**TOK**
2	**MNE**	**FDI**	**EMD**
3	**EMD**	**IEX**	**IJV**
4	**FDI**	**RMT**	**SAN**
5	**RMT**	**MNE**	**INT**
6	GBE	INT	SMTM
7	SMTM	SMTM	GBE
8	IJV	GBE	ETP
9	IEX	TOK	IEX
10	SAN	SAN	FDI
11	SHQ	SHQ	SHQ
12	TOK	IJV	MNE
13	EMN	ENT	RMT
14	ETP	EMN	EMN

DISCUSSION

Key inputs from all the categories analyzed are discussed in this section.

Entry Mode Decisions (EMD)

This category has been constantly influential over the five-time periods reviewed in this study. Articles in this category have won the maximum number of awards during the period analyzed (i.e., 12 awards out of the 25 presented in the last five decades). Theoretical articles that won the JIBS award also fall into this category. Out of the 10 theoretical papers that qualified for the award, five were from this area. In 1988, Dunning's article on the Eclectic paradigm was a joint winner, along with an empirical article by Kogut and Singh (1988) on cultural distance.

The winners in this category were empirical pieces testing the predictors of entry mode decisions made by firms, and their consequences. The key subthemes in this section fall into two areas. First, covers the predictors of entry mode in the destination country (Buckley & Casson, 1998). Most entry mode decisions, be they related to marketing or setting up facilities in foreign countries, were influenced largely by bias or stereotypes toward foreign products (Schooler,1971), channel integration in foreign markets (Aulakh & Kotabe, 1997), country of origin, influence of national culture and transaction cost (Bilkey, 1982; Anderson & Gatingnon, 1986), cultural distance between host country and home country (Kogut & Singh, 1988), and managerial perceptions of the foreign country (Agrawal & Ramaswami, 1992).

The eclectic model of production' uses the tripod of ownership, location, and internalization dimensions for entry mode decisions, and forms the intellectual foundation of IB research (Dunning, 1988). The second, covers the predictors of entry ownership levels in destination countries, where the degree of control, the extent of control (Goodnow & Hansz, 1972), and trust (Madhok, 1995) are key factors that decide ownership levels.

Internationalization (INT)

The various themes that form this category are antecedents, consequences, and description and measurement of the internationalization process. Risk reduction (Rugman, 1976), knowledge development, innovation, and experiential knowledge (Johnson & Vahlne, 1977; Eriksson et al., 1997; Lewin et al., 2009) are some of the reasons that organizations decide to internationalize (antecedents). Internationalization has been redefined and distinguished from the traditional paradigm of the emergence of global firms, with empirical and theoretical work on born-global firms and the paradigm of international new ventures through entrepreneurial orientation (Knight & Cavusgil, 2004; Zahra, 2005).

The articles that discuss consequences mainly deal with the performance of the firms as a result of their internationalization decisions (Luo & Peng, 1999, Contractor et al., 2003, Zhou et al., 2007). The important area in this section is the study of the dynamics involving the early stages of internationalization of new companies or born-global companies (Zahra, 2005) and cultural influences (Zaheer et al., 2012). Oviatt and McDougall (1994), whose attempt to theorize the phenomenon of international new ventures by describing the phenomenon and developing a framework for explaining how international new ventures fit within the theory of the MNE, won the JIBS Decade Award.

Transfer of Knowledge (TOK)

The articles covering this category can be classified into two broad areas—antecedents to knowledge transfer and process of knowledge transfer. Determinants of technology transfer modes (Davidson & McFetridge, 1985), types of knowledge (in terms of its ability to be codified) (Kogut & Zander, 1993) and its transfer, characteristics of IJVs and their influence in the transfer of knowledge, consequences (Lyles & Salk, 1996), and subsidiary absorptive capacities are the key attributes that influence the effectiveness of knowledge transfer.

Process of knowledge transfer involving multiple methods of knowledge transfer, such as visits, meetings, and other modes that emphasize relationships between international partners, are expected to facilitate better transfer of knowledge (Bresman et al., 1999). Particularly important here is the role of trust and shared values in the transfer of tacit knowledge in mature IJVs (Dhanaraj et al., 2004). Also, organizational socialization and dense intra and inter unit communication facilitates better contribution to innovation tasks by an MNC's subsidiary (Ghoshal & Bartlett, 1988).

Multinational Enterprises (MNE)

The articles that fall in this category revolve around MNE strategies, policies, and models and descriptions that can fit the workings of a multinational enterprise. MNE strategies discuss bargaining power of firms with respect to host governments (Fagre & Wells, 1982; Lecraw, 1984), MNE global branding initiatives (Steenkamp et al., 2003), and the myth behind globalization versus regionalization (Rugman & Verbeke, 2004). Models and descriptions revolve around studies on the evolving theory of multinational firms (Cantwell et al., 2010), service multinationals (Calvet, 1981; Boddewyn et al., 1986), performance of multinationals (Grant, 1987; Roth & Morrison, 1990; Banalieva & Dhanaraj, 2013), and spillover effects of multinationals in emerging economies (Meyer, 2004).

Another especially important area of work in this category are the articles on MNE policies that revolve around a corporate code of conduct and ethical behaviour (Langlois & Schlegelmilch, 1990), environmental issues and globalization (Christmann & Taylor, 2001), cross-cultural differences in corporate social responsibility (Maignan & Ralston, 2002), and international expansion of emerging market multinationals (Luo & Tung, 2007). This category had only one award winner in the JIBS Decade Award list, and this article studies the bargaining power of MNEs and ownership patterns in less developed countries (Lecraw, 1984)

Strategic Alliance Networks (SAN)

The articles on strategic alliances mainly discussed the essentials for building relationships and networks within alliances, which are basically the strategies, culture, and trust involved (Adler & Graham, 1989; Kim & Hwang, 1992; Dyer & Chu, 2000; Johanson & Vahlne, 2009). Like the articles on the transfer of knowledge, these articles appeared in the second half of the time period reviewed.

International Joint Ventures (IJV)

The articles in this area revolve around the performance of IJVs and the factors that affect their performance. IJVs have been suggested to be the optimal mode of investment for international operations (Beamish & Banks, 1987). Especially key areas of research on trust (Aulakh et al., 1996) and research focusing on the differences between task and partner characteristics (Geringer, 1991) in the selection of partners drive scholarship in this domain. Cultural background (Barkema & Vermeulen, 1998) is the other influence on partner selection in IJVs.

International Exchange (IEX)

Studies in this category mainly address the determinants and consequences of exporting. Articles analyze the determinants of export behaviour of firms (Bilkey & Tesar, 1977; Bilkey, 1978; Cavusgil et al., 1979; Cassiman & Golovko, 2011), international marketing of firms (Boddewyn, 1981), and export performance and profitability (Rosson & Ford, 1982; Bilkey, 1982; Cooper & Kleinschmidt, 1985; Christensen et al., 1987). Studies in this category occurred mainly in the 1970s, with topics revolving around determinants of exporting, the relevant theme at that time.

Foreign Direct Investment (FDI)

Along with "International Exchange" and "Entry Mode Decision," FDI was another category widely written about during the 1970s and 1980s. All the articles revolved around motivations for FDI, location of FDI, and the consequences of FDI. Studies on the motivations for FDI focused on investor profile and decision processes (Daniels, 1970), country policies on attracting investment (Root & Ahmed, 1978), market size and strength (Kuemmerle, 1999), and spillover effects in the context (Meyer & Sinani, 2009).

Location-specific studies related to environmental determinants (Kobrin, 1976; Flowers, 1976), host-country influences (Davidson, 1980; Nigh, 1985), and service-industry investments and other areas such as R&D and sourcing (Weinstein, 1977; Ronstadt, 1978; Buckley & Pearce, 1979; Terpstra & Yu, 1988). There has been an increase in studying China's state ownership and FDI policies (Buckley et al., 2007; Yiu et al., 2007; Cui & Jiang, 2012). In summary, the key discussions in this section relate to profiling the investor and the decision processes followed in making FDI-related decisions.

Global Business Environment (GBE)

The key areas in this section are discussions on environmental risks related to exchange rate fluctuations (Giddy & Dufey, 1975), and the political and regulatory risks involved in operating in global environments (Korbin, 1979). As there have not been many articles in this area in the recent past, the JIBS award winners in this area were for work in the 1970s.

Subsidiary Headquarters Relationship (SHQ)

All the articles in the area of subsidiary control of MNEs appeared in the 1980s and 1990s. They mainly discuss the types and levels of control (Jaeger, 1983; Egelhoff, 1984), degree of centralization of control (Martinez & Jarillo, 1989), structural characteristics supporting control mechanisms (Birkinshaw & Morrison, 1995), and heterogeneity of subsidiaries (Ma et al., 2013). The sole article winning the JIBS award was about subsidiary control and ownership structures (Casseres, 1990).

Subsidiary and Multinational Team Management (SMTM)

The discussions in this category revolved around behaviour of subsidiaries and multinational management, including the differences in work values among managers (Ralston et al., 1993) and the influence of human-resource practices on subsidiaries (Rosenzweig & Nohria, 1994). The articles on multinational management deal with the impact of national culture, economic ideologies, and language distance on managerial work values (Kelley et al., 1987; Newman & Nollen, 1997; Ralston et al., 1997; Tenzer et al., 2014).

Expatriate Management (EMN)

The articles on expatriate management mainly deal with issues on career management, personnel problems in adjusting to international work environments (Peterson & Schwind, 1977; Feldman & Thomas, 1992), and expatriate reaction on work-role transitions and adjustments (Black, 1988; Shaffer et al., 1999). As yet, there has been no JIBS Decade Award in this category.

Research Methodology (RMT)

Articles on research methodology seem to be increasing. Articles in this area comprise over 9% of the total articles that have appeared in IB research and show a rising trend. These articles can be divided into two main groups, Research Methodology and Measures. The articles that study research methodology focus primarily on cross-cultural or cross-national research, or culture clusters (Green & White, 1977; Sekaran, 1983; Ronen & Shenkar, 2013; Stahl et al., 2009; Stahl & Tung, 2015). The other set of articles looks at methods and measures beyond Hofstede's cultural framework.

In addition, new methods have been suggested (Kirkman et al., 2006; Javidan et al., 2006; Dow & Karunaratna, 2006). Measurement issues in international marketing research, international consumer research and national culture, the suggestion of new measures in cross-cultural issues, and internationalizing research have also been addressed in the literature in this area, including research interests in emerging economies (Parameswaran & Yaprak, 1987; Sullivan, 1994; Mullen, 1995; Singh, 1995; Shenkar, 2001; Hofstede, 2006; Meyer & Peng, 2016).

Entrepreneurship

A total of six articles can be classified in the category of International Entrepreneurship. Knight & Cavusgil's (2004) article received the Decade Award and looks at early internationalization as a result of entrepreneurial orientation. Various other articles cover topics from different angles of entrepreneurship. These subthemes include entrepreneurial orientation for born-global firms (Cavusgil & Knight, 2015), the influence of national culture (Autio et al., 2013), international new ventures (Zahra, 2005), models and descriptions of international entrepreneurship (Jones & Coviello, 2005), and social entrepreneurship (Stephan et al., 2015).

IMPLICATIONS OF THE COVID PANDEMIC

Scholars have written that the global economy will be affected by the COVID 19 pandemic resulting in changes in patterns of international trade and the way MNEs conduct their operations (Baldwin & Tomiura, 2020). Specifically, is the reconfiguration of global supply chains (Ivanov & Dolgui, 2020; Verbeke, 2020) since the pandemic was reported. It is estimated that close to 94% of Fortune 1000 experienced global supply chain interruptions (Sherman, 2020). As per UNCTAD, 60% of global trade consisted of intermediate goods and services and around a quarter of them crossed international borders at least twice before final processing (UNCTAD, 2013). In a world after the pandemic, it is envisaged that there will be a shift in MNE strategies in they being more inclined to risk aversion, nationalism, and protectionism (Fontaine, 2020).

The outbreak of the COVID 19 pandemic, therefore, has created challenges to globalization and international business as a field (Alon, 2020). The need for increased social distancing has resulted in the generation of new habits and behavior patterns such as increased telework, reduction in car traffic, reduction in the consumption of services and travel demand etc. (De Vos, 2020). As a consequence, some of changes in the environment that will affect international business as highlighted by scholars are as follows:

1. Growing nationalism will lead to increased protectionism and pose strategic challenges to MNEs (Curran et al., 2021).
2. Increased restriction on international travel.
3. Access to information could also be a concern during the pandemic. While democracies communicate available information, authoritarian ones hide, manipulate, and control the flow of information (Alon, 2020).
4. Economic problems as a result of the pandemic could lead to increasing value fluctuations and internationalization of capital.

5. Recession due to the pandemic could lead to reduction in cross border investments or increasing regionalization of MNEs (Rugman & Oh, 2008).
6. Challenges of the pandemic has led to strains in the global value chains which has made MNEs to relook at their sourcing policies.
7. Trade in goods and services will be affected with spillover effects on the supply chains affecting highly trade dependent countries (Fernandes, 2020).
8. International strategy will also need to be revisited. As per Verbeke and Yuan (2021), the 'new normal' which has resulted due to the pandemic suggest that the notions of FSAs (Firm specific advantages), CSAs (Country specific advantages), advantages of subsidiary integration, and the tradeoff between product and international diversification may need to be revisited. The embedded international business research designs and methodology may also need to be revisited in view of the above.

In comparing with the effects post the Global Financial Crisis (GFC) of 2010, the above shift is seen a little over a decade since the GFC. Indications are that the effect of COVID-19 on global flows may be more pronounced both in trade (WTO, 2020a) and global investments (UNCTAD, 2020). Potential reasons for the above could be the following. First, COVID 19 is both a demand and a supply shock, whereas the collapse after the GFC was mainly due to a shock or drop in demand (Baldwin & Tomiura, 2020). As a result, global trade in both goods and services will be affected (WTO, 2020a).

The pandemic will also have spillover effects throughout global supply chains, and typically trade-reliant countries will be adversely affected (WTO, 2020b). Evidence exists to show that firms and various sectors of the economy that are highly integrated into Global Value Chains (GVCs) are particularly sensitive to such trade shocks (WTO, 2020a). Second, protectionist measures in countries in response to the COVID-19 pandemic are more widespread than those related to the GFC (Curran et al., 2021) and these measures have been seen to be increase since the GFC (UNCTAD, 2020).

The way the above changes would affect the broad areas of future IB research that have been identified in this study are as follows. The topmost categories of research from this study EMD (entry mode decisions) and INT (internationalization) would be affected as these which are decided by international strategy need to be relooked in view of the changes that have happened due to the pandemic. Second, is research on MNEs (multinational enterprises). Research on MNEs would be more inclined to be regionalized as they relook at their global value chains. Changes in technology, reduced travel, and increasing virtual interface would lead to changes in the way TOK (transfer of knowledge) happens among global partners.

From the next set of categories (i.e., FDI, IJV, GBE, and SAN), the importance of GBE (global business environment) would be significantly high since this category addresses the risks in the global environment. The challenges of the pandemic would require future research to explore proactive measures that firms can adopt to address such challenges. The remaining categories of SHQ (subsidiary-headquarters relations) and IEX (international exchanges/exports) may need to be examined from the point of view of the changes that can be seen in the trade of goods and services as well as regionalization both being consequences of the pandemic. Finally, from the point of view of RMTs (Research methods), the need to deploy more complex configurational approaches that would integrate micro and macro level parameters in IB research is suggested (Verbeke &Yuan, 2021).

CONCLUSION

In line with the objectives of this study to trace the path of international business research, understand the relevance of research, and identify a broad agenda for the future, content analyses of the literature in the five management journals (JIBS, SMJ, AMJ, AMR, and JMS) in the area of IB was done. JIBS was studied in detail since it had the highest content of IB research, and the remaining four journals were used for comparative purposes. The time period from 1970 to 2016 was divided into five periods, starting from the first year (1970) when the JIBS instituted the Decade Award for the most influential article. Using the categorization by Werner (2002), all the articles were content analyzed for the most researched categories, categories that showed an increasing trend for focus among IB scholars, and the most influential categories for relevance as identified by the JIBS award. To a large extent, classification of the articles in these three broad areas helped to meet the objectives as identified at the beginning of this study.

A rising trend in research among IB scholars clearly emerged for topics in the categories INT (Internationalization), EMD (Entry Mode Decisions), TOK (Transfer of Knowledge) and, MNE (Multinational Enterprises). MNE, EMD, and INT have been among the most researched among IB scholars, along with FDI (Foreign Direct Investment) and IJV (International Joint Venture). The categories that have remained relevant are TOK (Transfer of Knowledge), EMD (Entry Mode Decisions), IJV (International Joint Venture), SAN (Strategic Alliances and Networks), and INT (Internationalization). Clearly the areas that emerge as frontrunners in the future will be EMD (Entry Mode Decisions), INT (Internationalization), MNE (Multinational Enterprises), and TOK (Transfer of Knowledge), the categories that will drive research in the future. Methodological rigor will need to be enhanced by focusing on various levels of research in IB (Toyne & Nigh, 1998) and advancing multidisciplinary research (Cheng et al., 2009).

Given the changing landscape of IB research and the inputs it draws from various disciplines, scholarly work must focus on generating theories to broadly base the phenomena that fall in the domain of IB. The fact that over 50% of the most cited theoretical papers have won the JIBS Decade Awards is ample indication of the importance of generating theoretical insights to explain the various phenomena covered and explained by IB research. Finally, the pandemic has the potential to affect research in all the above categories given that the pandemic affects the way firms look at globalization i.e., the move to regionalization, restrictions in travel and access of information, move to virtual means of doing business, changes in the way products and services are traded etc.

Future IB research may need to consider different research methodologies to factor the changes in the context caused by the pandemic that have changed the way globalization is now viewed. Furthermore, areas that can fall within the purview of IB research, over and above the broad categories discussed in the preceding sections are as follows.

Global Business Environment

Simply defined, this involves the study of the environments in which international transactions occur. Globalization has magnified the conflicting interests of MNEs, regions, and nation states, leading to a wide array of rarely harmonized policy initiatives by states. Key questions must be explored, such as how these policy initiatives can be harmonized in order to simplify the environments in which MNEs operate. Emerging economies, their influence, and associated political risks are some of the key business-environment issues that require further focus. Besides the study of the national cultural environment, its changing nature, and its influence on IB needs further attention.

Multinational Enterprises

MNEs can be defined as the governance mechanisms that carry out transactions in international environments. Studies on MNE policies, strategies, and the general model of MNE operations must increase. The role of innovation in MNE operations to create high value-added activities in the locations in which they operate needs special attention. Globalization tends to bring MNEs into contact with a variety of business environments. Internationalization of service enterprises is another area that can be explored (Roberts et al., 2020). At the micro level, the host-country environment influences management practices, organizational structures, and modes of operation.

How MNEs will continue to adapt organizational forms and management practices to diverse institutional contexts is another key question on which IB research will especially need to focus. Finally, whether perspectives on multinationals from emerging markets be different from the ones from developed economies (Muralidharan et al., 2017).

Network Alliances

Attention in this area will be on alliance structures among MNE firms across national borders. Globalization has changed the relative merits of alternative organizational firms. Is the concept of internationalization as relevant as it was in the 1970s and the 1980s, and sufficient to explain cross-border exchanges or activities now? IB research must answer questions about whether new business concepts such as outsourcing, alliances, and global production networks make the concept of the monolithic MNE obsolete.

Sustainable Development

Looking at the consequences of increasing globalization and internationalization, including increasing global warming, corporate scandals, economic crises, and the growing North-South divide, what role can the agents of globalization (MNEs) play in mitigating such negative consequences? MNEs and their role through policies and strategies in covering the three fundamentals of sustainable development—i.e., social responsibility, environmental responsibility, and value creation—must be at the top of the IB research agenda.

Macro and Supra-level Institutions of Capitalism and the Role of Informal Institutions

The watch guards of international exchanges—the IMF, World Bank, WTO, regulating and rating agencies such as BIS and Moody's, and international agreements such as double-tax treaties, bilateral-investment treaties, and their roles—require IB research attention. These macro institutions of global capitalism affect all actors party to international transactions. So, the study of the role of these institutions and their "moral upgradation" (in the words of Dunning) must be on the agenda of IB scholars. The role of informal institutions (Muralidharan & Pathak, 2017; Pathak & Muralidharan, 2020a; Pathak & Muralidharan, 2020b) and their interface with formal institutions (Muralidharan & Pathak, 2020; Pathak et al., 2014; Stephan et al., 2015) in driving international business are other areas that can be explored by future research.

LIMITATIONS AND FUTURE RESEARCH

This study has some limitations. First, the coding must be done by multiple sources in order to increase validity. Further, the JIBS Decade Awards may not be sufficient to evaluate relevance. The editorial policy statement of JIBS in 2004, which states that 'the policy does not require or expect that papers being published in JIBS be judged by their relevance to the practice of management' (Lewin, 2004), may not be encouraging enough to support our assumption that JIBS awards indicate relevance to the practice of IB. Something similar to the Delphi Study involving interviews with leading scholars and practitioners in the area of IB research and practice, must be conducted in order to strengthen the findings of the current study.

Interviews with CEOs, consultants, and academic scholars on the possible research questions that must be addressed under the purview of IB research can substantiate relevant findings. The greater the deviation between practitioners (CEOs and consultants) and academic scholars in their responses to this question, the less relevant IB research becomes (Gopinath & Hoffman, 1995; Oesterle & Laudien, 2007). Furthermore, the basis for identifying the time periods needs to be clarified further.

While the period of review starts from 1970, the first phase is only 1970-1975 (since data for JIBS most cited articles were not available on the Web of Science Database) compared to the other periods, which are each 10 year long. The starting year for some other leading management journals also differs, and this can be a limitation. The time periods will also need to be standardized across all the journals used. Finally, at the time that this study was conducted, the period considered for published IB research was till 2016. While the authors do not anticipate major changes in the trends thereafter till the pre-COVID year in the categories that have been identified, future research may update the above study with insights from articles published in the years from 2017 till date.

Keeping in view the above limitations, future work in order to strengthen this study needs to comprise several components. First, the possibility of extending the sample base to include articles beyond the top five most cited in each of the top five management journals should be examined. The possibility of including other international business journals such as *Management of International Review* (MIR) and *Journal of World Business* (JWB) would also require evaluation. Second, IB articles from practitioner journals such as *Harvard Business Review*, *Sloan Management Review*, and *California Management Review* should be included to further strengthen insights on the relevance of IB research. Third, structured interviews with CEOs, consultants, and academic scholars should be considered, in order to identify important IB research areas as perceived by these stakeholders. These interviews can substantiate the deviation between academicians and practitioners on the relevance of IB research.

Three key scholars in the area of IB—i.e., Buckley (2002), Peng (2004), and Shenkar (2004) have debated the future of international business studies. Each had his own perspective on debating the future of IB. Buckley (2002) talked about the need for a big question to drive the agenda of IB research. Peng (2004) suggested that the big question already exists in how to explain the success of IB activities. Shenkar's (2004) perspective was that IB's main mission is to integrate knowledge created by related disciplines of business administration, within an applicable theoretical and empirical framework. While Peng's (2004) argument will perhaps represent more of a strategic perspective, and Shenkar's (2004) will be more applicable to business administration in general (Oesterle & Laudien, 2007), Buckley's perspective on the 'big question' will guide the future of IB research.

International business is running out of steam for want of any big question to guide its research. Close interaction between theoretical development and empirical reality is important, in order that the field does not become just another area of application for concepts from other disciplines (Buckley, 2002). Based on current developments globally (pandemic, financial crisis, emerging markets, geopolitics etc.), one of the key questions that can drive IB research, given the impact of the pandemic on the global economy and multinational operations, could be 'Will external shocks such as the pandemic change the nature of global business models and how should scholars factor such changes in IB research'?

In summary, it is especially important to review the status of research in IB on a regular basis for updated agendas. As Peng (2004) commented, keeping alive in all the research agendas the question of what determines international success and failure of firms will enable scholars to leverage IB's comparative advantage, and generate sufficient theories and insights as the field progresses. This will entail regular reflection on the content of the field and where it is heading.

REFERENCES

Acedo, F. J., & Casillas, J. C. (2005). Current paradigms in the international management field: An author co-citation analysis. *International Business Review*, *14*(5), 619–639. doi:10.1016/j.ibusrev.2005.05.003

Adler, N. J., & Graham, J. L. (1989). Cross-Cultural Interaction: The International Comparison Fallacy? *Journal of International Business Studies*, *20*(3), 515–537. doi:10.1057/palgrave.jibs.8490367

Agarwal, S., & Ramaswami, S. (1992). Choice of Foreign Market Entry Mode: Impact of Ownership, Location and Internalization Factors. *Journal of International Business Studies*, *23*(1), 1–27. doi:10.1057/palgrave.jibs.8490257

Alon, I. (2020). COVID-19 and international business: A viewpoint. *FIIB Business Review*, *9*(2), 75–77. doi:10.1177/2319714520923579

Anderson, E., & Gatignon, H. (1986). Modes of Foreign Entry: A Transaction Cost Analysis and Propositions. *Journal of International Business Studies*, *17*(3), 1–26. doi:10.1057/palgrave.jibs.8490432

Aulakh, P. S., & Kotabe, M. (1997). Antecedents and Performance Implications of Channel Integration in Foreign Markets. *Journal of International Business Studies*, *28*(1), 145–175. doi:10.1057/palgrave.jibs.8490096

Aulakh, P. S., Kotabe, M., & Sahay, A. (1996). Trust and Performance in Cross-Border Marketing Partnerships: A Behavioral Approach. *Journal of International Business Studies*, *27*(5), 1005–1032. doi:10.1057/palgrave.jibs.8490161

Autio, E., Pathak, S., & Wennberg, K. (2013). Consequences of cultural practices for entrepreneurial behaviors. *Journal of International Business Studies*, *44*(4), 334–362. doi:10.1057/jibs.2013.15

Baldwin, R., & Tomiura, E. (2020). Thinking ahead about the trade impact of COVID-19. *Economics in the Time of COVID*, *19*(59), 59–71.

Banalieva, E. R., & Dhanaraj, C. (2013). Home-region orientation in international expansion strategies. *Journal of International Business Studies*, *44*(2), 89–116. doi:10.1057/jibs.2012.33

Barkema, H. G., & Vemeulen, F. (1998). International Expansion through Start up or Acquistion: A Learning Perspective. *Academy of Management Journal*, *41*(1), 7–26. doi:10.2307/256894

Beamish, P. W., & Banks, J. C. (1987). Equity Joint Ventures and the Theory of the Multinational Enterprise. *Journal of International Business Studies*, *18*(2), 1–16. doi:10.1057/palgrave.jibs.8490403

Bilkey, W. J. (1978). An Attempted Integration of the Literature on the Export Behavior of Firms. *Journal of International Business Studies*, *9*(1), 33–46. doi:10.1057/palgrave.jibs.8490649

Bilkey, W. J. (1982). Variables Associated with Export Profitability. *Journal of International Business Studies*, *13*(2), 39–55. doi:10.1057/palgrave.jibs.8490549

Bilkey, W. J., & Tesar, G. (1977). The Export Behavior of Smaller-Sized Wisconsin Manufacturing Firms. *Journal of International Business Studies*, *8*(1), 93–98. doi:10.1057/palgrave.jibs.8490783

Birkinshaw, J. M., & Morrison, A. J. (1995). Configurations of Strategy and Structure in Subsidiaries of Multinational Corporations. *Journal of International Business Studies*, *26*(4), 729–753. doi:10.1057/palgrave.jibs.8490818

Black, J. S. (1988). Work Role Transitions: A Study of American Expatriate Managers in Japan. *Journal of International Business Studies*, *19*(2), 277–294. doi:10.1057/palgrave.jibs.8490383

Boddewyn, J. J. (1981). B Comparative Marketing: The First Twenty-Five Years. *Journal of International Business Studies*, *12*(1), 61–79. doi:10.1057/palgrave.jibs.8490571

Boddewyn, J. J. (1999). The domain of international management. *Journal of International Management*, *5*(1), 3–14. doi:10.1016/S1075-4253(99)00003-4

Boddewyn, J. J., Halbrich, M. B., & Perry, A. C. (1986). Service Multinationals: Conceptualization, Measurement and Theory. *Journal of International Business Studies*, *17*(3), 41–57. doi:10.1057/palgrave.jibs.8490860

Bresman, H., Birkinshaw, J., & Nobel, R. (1999). Knowledge Transfer in International Acquisitions. *Journal of International Business Studies*, *30*(3), 439–462. doi:10.1057/palgrave.jibs.8490078

Buckley, P. J. (2002). Is the International Business Research Agenda Running out of Steam? *Journal of International Business Studies*, *33*(2), 365–373. doi:10.1057/palgrave.jibs.8491021

Buckley, P. J., & Casson, M. C. (1998). Analyzing Foreign Market Entry Strategies: Extending the Internalization Approach. *Journal of International Business Studies*, *29*(3), 539–561. doi:10.1057/palgrave.jibs.8490006

Buckley, P. J., Clegg, L. J., Cross, A. R., Liu, X., Voss, H., & Zheng, P. (2007). The determinants of Chinese outward foreign direct investment. *Journal of International Business Studies*, *38*(4), 499–518. doi:10.1057/palgrave.jibs.8400277

Buckley, P. J., & Pearce, R. D. (1979). Overseas Production and Exporting by the World's Largest Enterprises: A Study in Sourcing Policy. *Journal of International Business Studies, 10*(1), 9–20. doi:10.1057/palgrave.jibs.8490626

Calvet, A. L. (1981). A Synthesis of Foreign Direct Investment Theories and Theories of the Multinational Firm. *Journal of International Business Studies, 12*(1), 43–59. doi:10.1057/palgrave.jibs.8490570

Cantwell, J., Dunning, J. H., & Lundan, S. M. (2010). An evolutionary approach to understanding international business activity: The co-evolution of MNEs and the institutional environment. *Journal of International Business Studies, 41*(4), 567–586. doi:10.1057/jibs.2009.95

Casseres, B. G. (1990). Firm Ownership Preferences and Host Government Restrictions: An Integrated Approach. *Journal of International Business Studies, 21*(1), 1–22. doi:10.1057/palgrave.jibs.8490324

Cassiman, B., & Golovko, E. (2011). Innovation and internationalization through exports. *Journal of International Business Studies, 42*(1), 56–75. doi:10.1057/jibs.2010.36

Cavusgil, S. T., & Knight, G. (2015). The born global firm: An entrepreneurial and capabilities perspective on early and rapid internationalization. *Journal of International Business Studies, 46*(1), 3–16. doi:10.1057/jibs.2014.62

Cavusgil, T., Bilkey, W. J., & Tesar, G. (1979). A Note on the Export Behavior of Firms: Exporter Profiles. *Journal of International Business Studies, 10*(1), 91–97. doi:10.1057/palgrave.jibs.8490633

Chandy, P. R., & Williams, T. G. E. (1994). The impact of journals and authors on international business research: A citation analysis of JIBS articles. *Journal of International Business Studies, 25*(4), 715–728. doi:10.1057/palgrave.jibs.8490221

Cheng, J. L., Henisz, W. J., Roth, K., & Swaminathan, A. (2009). From the Editors: Advancing interdisciplinary research in the field of international business: Prospects, issues and challenges. Journal of International Business Studies, 40(7), 1070-1074.

Christensen, C. H., Rocha, A., & Gertner, R. K. (1987). An Empirical Investigation of the Factors Influencing Exporting Success of Brazilian Firms. *Journal of International Business Studies, 18*(3), 61–77. doi:10.1057/palgrave.jibs.8490412

Christmann, P., & Taylor, G. (2001). Globalization and the Environment: Determinants of Firm Self-Regulation in China. *Journal of International Business Studies, 32*(3), 439–458. doi:10.1057/palgrave.jibs.8490976

Contractor, F. J. (2000). The raisons d'être for international management as a field of study. *Journal of International Management, 6*(1), 3–10. doi:10.1016/S1075-4253(00)00017-X

Contractor, F. J., Kundu, S. K., & Hsu, C. C. (2003). A Three-Stage Theory of International Expansion: The Link between Multinationality and Performance in the Service Sector. *Journal of International Business Studies, 34*(1), 5–18. doi:10.1057/palgrave.jibs.8400003

Cooper, R. G., & Kleinschmidt, E. J. (1985). The Impact of Export Strategy on Export Sales Performance. *Journal of International Business Studies, 16*(1), 37–55. doi:10.1057/palgrave.jibs.8490441

Cui, L., & Jiang, F. (2012). State ownership effect on firms' FDI ownership decisions under institutional pressure: A study of Chinese outward-investing firms. *Journal of International Business Studies*, *43*(3), 264–284. doi:10.1057/jibs.2012.1

Curran, L., Eckhardt, J., & Lee, J. (2021). The trade policy response to COVID-19 and its implications for international business. *Critical Perspectives on International Business*, *17*(2), 252–320. doi:10.1108/cpoib-05-2020-0041

Daniels, J. D. (1970). Recent Foreign Direct Manufacturing Investment in the United States. *Journal of International Business Studies*, *1*(1), 125–132. doi:10.1057/palgrave.jibs.8490725

Daniels, J. D. (1991). Relevance in international business research: A need for more linkages. *Journal of International Business Studies*, *22*(2), 177–186. doi:10.1057/palgrave.jibs.8490298

Davidson, W. H. (1980). The location of foreign direct investment activity: Country characteristics and experience effects. *Journal of International Business Studies*, *11*(2), 9–22. doi:10.1057/palgrave.jibs.8490602

Davidson, W. H., & McFetridge, D. G. (1985). Key characteristics in the choice of international technology transfer mode. *Journal of International Business Studies*, *16*(2), 5–21. doi:10.1057/palgrave.jibs.8490448

De Vos, J. (2020). The effect of COVID-19 and subsequent social distancing on travel behavior. *Transportation Research Interdisciplinary Perspectives*, *5*, 100121. doi:10.1016/j.trip.2020.100121 PMID:34171016

Dhanaraj, C., Lyles, M. A., Steensma, H. K., & Tihanyi, L. (2004). Managing Tacit and Explicit Knowledge Transfer in IJVs: The Role of Relational Embeddedness and the Impact on Performance. *Journal of International Business Studies*, *35*(5), 428–442. doi:10.1057/palgrave.jibs.8400098

Dow, D., & Karunaratna, A. (2006). Developing a multidimensional instrument to measure psychic distance stimuli. *Journal of International Business Studies*, *37*(5), 578–602. doi:10.1057/palgrave.jibs.8400221

DuBois, F. L., & Reeb, D. (2000). Ranking the international business journals. *Journal of International Business Studies*, *31*(4), 689–704. doi:10.1057/palgrave.jibs.8490929

Dunning, J. H. (1988). The Eclectic Paradigm of International Production: A Restatement and Some Possible Extensions. *Journal of International Business Studies*, *19*(1), 1–31. doi:10.1057/palgrave.jibs.8490372

Dunning, J. H. (1989). The study of international business: A plea for a more interdisciplinary approach. *Journal of International Business Studies*, *20*(3), 411–436. doi:10.1057/palgrave.jibs.8490371

Dyer, J. H., & Chu, W. (2000). The Determinants of Trust in Supplier-Automaker Relationships in the U.S., Japan, and Korea. *Journal of International Business Studies*, *31*(2), 259–285. doi:10.1057/palgrave.jibs.8490905

Egelhoff, W. G. (1984). Patterns of Control in U. S., UK, and European Multinational Corporations. *Journal of International Business Studies*, *15*(2), 73–83. doi:10.1057/palgrave.jibs.8490866

Eriksson, K., Johanson, J., Majkgard, A., & Sharma, D. D. (1997). Experiential Knowledge and Cost in the Internationalization Process. *Journal of International Business Studies, 28*(2), 337–360. doi:10.1057/palgrave.jibs.8490104

Fagre, N., & Wells, L. T. Jr. (1982). Bargaining power of multinationals and host governments. *Journal of International Business Studies, 13*(2), 9–23. doi:10.1057/palgrave.jibs.8490547

Feldman, D. C., & Thomas, D. C. (1992). Career Management Issues Facing Expatriates. *Journal of International Business Studies, 23*(2), 271–293. doi:10.1057/palgrave.jibs.8490268

Fernandes, N. (2020). Economic effects of coronavirus outbreak (COVID-19) on the world economy. Retrieved on August 22, 2021, from: https://papers.ssrn.com/sol3/papers.cfm?abstract_id=3557504

Flowers, E. B. (1976). Oligopolistic Reactions in European and Canadian Direct Investment in the United States. *Journal of International Business Studies, 7*(2), 43–55. doi:10.1057/palgrave.jibs.8490700

Fontaine, R. (2020, April 17). Globalization will look very different after the coronavirus pandemic. In: *Foreign policy*. Retrieved on June 2, 2021, from: https://foreignpolicy.com/2020/04/17/globalization-trade-war-after-coronavirus-pandemic/

Geringer, J. M. (1991). Strategic Determinants of Partner Selection Criteria in International Joint Ventures. *Journal of International Business Studies, 22*(1), 41–62. doi:10.1057/palgrave.jibs.8490291

Ghoshal, S., & Bartlett, C. A. (1988). Creation, Adoption, and Diffusion of Innovations by Subsidiaries of Multinational Corporations. *Journal of International Business Studies, 19*(3), 365–388. doi:10.1057/palgrave.jibs.8490388

Giddy, I. H., & Dufey, G. (1975). The Random Behavior of Flexible Exchange Rates Implications for Forecasting. *Journal of International Business Studies, 6*(1), 1–32. doi:10.1057/palgrave.jibs.8490765

Goodnow, J. D., & Hansz, J. E. (1972). Environmental Determinants of Overseas Market Entry Strategies. *Journal of International Business Studies, 3*(1), 33–50. doi:10.1057/palgrave.jibs.8490740

Gopinath, C., & Hoffman, R. C. (1995). The relevance of strategy research; practitioners and academic viewpoints. *Journal of Management Studies, 32*(5), 575–594. doi:10.1111/j.1467-6486.1995.tb00789.x

Grant, R. M. (1987). Multinationality and Performance among British Manufacturing Companies. *Journal of International Business Studies, 18*(3), 79–89. doi:10.1057/palgrave.jibs.8490413

Green, R. T., & White, P. D. (1976). Methodological Considerations in Cross-National Consumer Research. *Journal of International Business Studies, 7*(2), 81–87. doi:10.1057/palgrave.jibs.8490703

Hofstede, G. (2006). What did GLOB really measure? Researchers' minds versus respondents' minds. *Journal of International Business Studies, 37*(6), 882–896. doi:10.1057/palgrave.jibs.8400233

Ivanov, D., & Dolgui, A. (2020). Viability of intertwined supply networks: Extending the supply chain resilience angles towards survivability. A position paper motivated by COVID-19 outbreak. *International Journal of Production Research, 58*(10), 2904–2915. doi:10.1080/00207543.2020.1750727

Jaeger, A. M. (1983). The Transfer of Organizational Culture Overseas: An Approach to Control in the Multinational Corporation. *Journal of International Business Studies, 14*(2), 91–114. doi:10.1057/palgrave.jibs.8490520

Javidan, M., House, R. J., Dorfman, P. W., Hanges, P. J., & Luque, M. S. (2006). Conceptualizing and measuring cultures and their consequences: A comparative view of GLOBE's and Hofstede's approaches. *Journal of International Business Studies, 37*(6), 897–914. doi:10.1057/palgrave.jibs.8400234

Johanson, J., & Vahlne, J.E. (1977). The Internationalization Process of the Firm-A Model of Knowledge Development and Increasing Foreign Market Commitments. *Journal of International Business Studies, 8*(1).23-32.

Johanson, J., & Vahlne, J. E. (2009). The Uppsala internationalization process model revisited: From liability of foreignness to liability of outsidership. *Journal of International Business Studies, 40*(9), 1411–1431. doi:10.1057/jibs.2009.24

Jones, M. V., & Coviello, N. E. (2005). Internationalisation: Conceptualising an Entrepreneurial Process of Behaviour in Time. *Journal of International Business Studies, 36*(3), 284–303. doi:10.1057/palgrave.jibs.8400138

Kelley, L., Whatley, A., & Worthley, R. (1987). Assessing the Effects of Culture on Managerial Attitudes: A Three-Culture Test. *Journal of International Business Studies, 18*(2), 17–31. doi:10.1057/palgrave.jibs.8490404

Kim, W. C., & Hwang, P. (1992). Global strategy and multinationals' entry mode choice. *Journal of International Business Studies, 23*(1), 29–53. doi:10.1057/palgrave.jibs.8490258

Kirkman, B. L., Lowe, K. B., & Gibson, C. B. (2006). A quarter century of culture's consequences: A review of empirical research incorporating Hofstede's cultural values framework. *Journal of International Business Studies, 37*(3), 285–320. doi:10.1057/palgrave.jibs.8400202

Knight, G., & Cavusgil, S. (2004). Innovation, Organizational Capabilities, and the Born-Global Firm. *Journal of International Business Studies, 35*(2), 124–141. doi:10.1057/palgrave.jibs.8400071

Kobrin, S. J. (1976). The Environmental Determinants of Foreign Direct Manufacturing Investment: An Ex-Post Empirical Analysis. *Journal of International Business Studies, 7*(2), 29–42. doi:10.1057/palgrave.jibs.8490699

Kobrin, S. J. (1979). Political Risk: A Review and Reconsideration. *Journal of International Business Studies, 10*(1), 67–80. doi:10.1057/palgrave.jibs.8490631

Kogut, B., & Singh, H. (1988). The Effect of National Culture on the Choice of Entry Mode. *Journal of International Business Studies, 19*(3), 411–432. doi:10.1057/palgrave.jibs.8490394

Kogut, B., & Zander, U. (1993). Knowledge of the Firm and the Evolutionary Theory of the Multinational Corporation. *Journal of International Business Studies, 24*(4), 625–645. doi:10.1057/palgrave.jibs.8490248

Kuemmerle, W. (1999). The Drivers of Foreign Direct Investment into Research and Development: An Empirical Investigation. *Journal of International Business Studies, 30*(1), 1–24. doi:10.1057/palgrave.jibs.8490058

Langlois, C. C., & Schlegelmilch, B. B. (1990). Do Corporate Codes of Ethics Reflect National Character? Evidence from Europe and the United States. *Journal of International Business Studies, 21*(4), 519–539. doi:10.1057/palgrave.jibs.8490340

Lecraw, D. J. (1984). Bargaining Power, Ownership, and Profitability of Transnational Corporations in Developing Countries. *Journal of International Business Studies, 15*(1), 27–43. doi:10.1057/palgrave.jibs.8490469

Lewin, A. Y. (2004). Letter from the Editor. *Journal of International Business Studies, 35*(1), 79–80. doi:10.1057/palgrave.jibs.8400079

Lewin, A. Y., Massini, S., & Peeters, C. (2009). Why are companies offshoring innovation? The emerging global race for talent. *Journal of International Business Studies, 40*(6), 901–925. doi:10.1057/jibs.2008.92

Lu, J. W. (2003). The evolving contributions in international strategic management research. *Journal of International Management, 9*(2), 193–213. doi:10.1016/S1075-4253(03)00006-1

Luo, Y., & Peng, M. W. (1999). Learning to Compete in a Transition Economy: Experience, Environment, and Performance. *Journal of International Business Studies, 30*(2), 269–295. doi:10.1057/palgrave.jibs.8490070

Luo, Y., & Tung, R. L. (2007). International expansion of emerging market enterprises: A springboard perspective. *Journal of International Business Studies, 38*(4), 481–498. doi:10.1057/palgrave.jibs.8400275

Lyles, M. A., & Salk, J. E. (1996). Knowledge Acquisition from Foreign Parents in International Joint Ventures: An Empirical Examination in the Hungarian Context. *Journal of International Business Studies, 27*(5), 877–903. doi:10.1057/palgrave.jibs.8490155

Ma, X., Tong, T. W., & Fitza, M. (2013). How much does subnational region matter to foreign subsidiary performance? Evidence from Fortune Global 500 Corporations' investment in China. *Journal of International Business Studies, 44*(1), 66–87. doi:10.1057/jibs.2012.32

Madhok, A. (1995). Revisiting Multinational Firms' Tolerance for Joint Ventures: A Trust-Based Approach. *Journal of International Business Studies, 26*(1), 117–137. doi:10.1057/palgrave.jibs.8490168

Maignan, I., & Ralston, D. A. (2002). Corporate Social Responsibility in Europe and the U.S.: Insights from Businesses' Self- Presentations. *Journal of International Business Studies, 33*(3), 497–514. doi:10.1057/palgrave.jibs.8491028

Martinez, J. I., & Jarillo, J. C. (1989). The Evolution of Research on Coordination Mechanisms in Multinational Corporations. *Journal of International Business Studies, 20*(3), 489–514. doi:10.1057/palgrave.jibs.8490370

Martínez, Z. L., & Toyne, B. (2000). What is international management, and what is its domain? *Journal of International Management, 6*(1), 11–28. doi:10.1016/S1075-4253(00)00018-1

Meyer, K. E. (2004). Perspectives on Multinational Enterprises in Emerging Economies. *Journal of International Business Studies*, *35*(4), 259–276. doi:10.1057/palgrave.jibs.8400084

Meyer, K. E., & Peng, M. W. (2016). Theoretical foundations of emerging economy business research. *Journal of International Business Studies*, *47*(1), 3–22. doi:10.1057/jibs.2015.34

Meyer, K. E., & Sinani, E. (2009). When and where does foreign direct investment generate positive spillovers? A meta-analysis. *Journal of International Business Studies*, *40*(7), 1075–1094. doi:10.1057/jibs.2008.111

Mullen, M. R. (1995). Diagnosing Measurement Equivalence in Cross-National Research. *Journal of International Business Studies*, *26*(3), 573–596. doi:10.1057/palgrave.jibs.8490187

Muralidharan, E., & Pathak, S. (2017). Informal institutions and international entrepreneurship. *International Business Review*, *26*(2), 288–302. doi:10.1016/j.ibusrev.2016.07.006

Muralidharan, E., & Pathak, S. (2020). Home Country Institutions and International Entrepreneurship: A Multi-Level Framework–Institutions and International Entrepreneurship. In J. G. L. Dantas & L. G. Carvalho (Eds.), *Handbook of Research on Approaches to Alternative Entrepreneurship Opportunities: 291-314*. IGI Global. doi:10.4018/978-1-7998-1981-3.ch014

Muralidharan, E., Wei, W., & Liu, X. (2017). Integration by emerging economy multinationals: Perspectives from Chinese mergers and acquisitions. *Thunderbird International Business Review*, *59*(4), 503–518. doi:10.1002/tie.21850

Newman, K. L., & Nollen, S. D. (1996). Culture and Congruence: The Fit between Management Practices and National Culture. *Journal of International Business Studies*, *27*(4), 753–779. doi:10.1057/palgrave.jibs.8490152

Nigh, D. (1985). The Effect of Political Events on United States Direct Foreign Investment: A Pooled Time-Series Cross-Sectional Analysis. *Journal of International Business Studies*, *16*(1), 1–17. doi:10.1057/palgrave.jibs.8490439

Oesterle, M. J., & Laudien, S. (2007). The future of international business research and the relevance gap: A German perspective. *European Journal of International Management*, *1*(1/2), 39–55. doi:10.1504/EJIM.2007.012916

Oviatt, B. M., & McDougall, P. P. (1994). Toward a Theory of International New Ventures. *Journal of International Business Studies*, *25*(1), 45–64. doi:10.1057/palgrave.jibs.8490193

Parameswaran, R., & Yaprak, A. (1987). A Cross-National Comparison of Consumer Research Measures. *Journal of International Business Studies*, *18*(1), 35–49. doi:10.1057/palgrave.jibs.8490398

Pathak, S., & Muralidharan, E. (2020a). The Role of Emotional Intelligence in the Culture-Entrepreneurship Fit Perspective. In *Cultural Factors and Performance in 21st Century Businesses* (pp. 90–120). IGI Global. doi:10.4018/978-1-7998-3744-2.ch005

Pathak, S., & Muralidharan, E. (2020b). Implications of culturally implicit perspective of emotional intelligence. *Cross-Cultural Research*, *54*(5), 502–533. doi:10.1177/1069397120938690

Pathak, S., Muralidharan, E., & Laplume, A. (2014). Home country factors and the decision to internationalize technology-based new ventures: A multi-level study of early-stage entrepreneurs. *Frontiers of Entrepreneurship Research, 34*(19), 1.

Peng, M. W. (2004). Identifying the big question in international business research. *Journal of International Business Research, 35*(2), 99–18. doi:10.1057/palgrave.jibs.8400077

Peterson, R. B., & Schwind, H. F. (1977). A Comparative Study of Personnel Problems in International Companies and Joint Ventures in Japan. *Journal of International Business Studies, 8*(1), 45–55. doi:10.1057/palgrave.jibs.8490678

Pisani, N. (2009). International management research: Investigating its recent diffusion in top management journals. *Journal of Management, 35*(2), 199–218. doi:10.1177/0149206308321552

Pittaway, L., Robertson, M., Munir, K., Denyer, D., & Neely, A. (2004). Networking and innovation: A systematic review of the evidence. *International Journal of Management Reviews, 5/6*(3&4), 137–168. doi:10.1111/j.1460-8545.2004.00101.x

Ralston, D. A., Gustason, D. J., Cheung, F. M., & Terpstra, R. H. (1993). Differences in Managerial Values: A Study of U.S., Hong Kong and PRC Managers. *Journal of International Business Studies, 24*(2), 249–275. doi:10.1057/palgrave.jibs.8490232

Ralston, D. A., Holt, D. H., Terpstra, R. H., & Cheng, Y. K. (1997). The Impact of National Culture and Economic Ideology on Managerial Work Values: A Study of the United States, Russia, Japan, and China. *Journal of International Business Studies, 28*(1), 177–207. doi:10.1057/palgrave.jibs.8490097

Roberts, M. J., & Muralidharan, E. (2022). Internationalization of service SMEs: Perspectives from Canadian SMEs internationalizing in Asia. *Global Business Review, 23*(4), 890–910. doi:10.1177/0972150919887250

Ronen, S., & Shenkar, O. (2013). Mapping world cultures: Cluster formation, sources and implications. *Journal of International Business Studies, 44*(9), 867–897. doi:10.1057/jibs.2013.42

Ronstadt, R. C. (1978). International R&D: The Establishment and Evolution of Research and Development Abroad by Seven U. S. Multinationals. *Journal of International Business Studies, 9*(1), 7–24. doi:10.1057/palgrave.jibs.8490647

Root, F. R., & Ahmed, A. A. (1978). The Influence of Policy Instruments on Manufacturing Direct Foreign Investment in Developing Countries. *Journal of International Business Studies, 9*(3), 81–93. doi:10.1057/palgrave.jibs.8490670

Rosenzweig, P. M., & Nohria, N. (1994). Influences on Human Resource Management Practices in Multinational Corporations. *Journal of International Business Studies, 25*(2), 229–251. doi:10.1057/palgrave.jibs.8490199

Rosson, P. J., & Ford, D. (1982). Manufacturer-Overseas Distributor Relations and Export Performance. *Journal of International Business Studies, 13*(2), 57–72. doi:10.1057/palgrave.jibs.8490550

Roth, K., & Morrison, A. J. (1990). An Empirical Analysis of the Integration-Responsiveness Framework in Global Industries. *Journal of International Business Studies, 21*(4), 541–564. doi:10.1057/palgrave.jibs.8490341

Rugman, A., & Oh, C. H. (2008). Friedman's follies: Insights on the globalization/regionalization debate. *Business and Politics*, *10*(2), 1–14. doi:10.2202/1469-3569.1222

Rugman, A. M. (1976). Risk Reduction by International Diversification. *Journal of International Business Studies*, *7*(2), 75–80. doi:10.1057/palgrave.jibs.8490702

Rugman, A. M., & Verbeke, A. (2004). A Perspective on Regional and Global Strategies of Multinational Enterprises. *Journal of International Business Studies*, *35*(1), 3–18. doi:10.1057/palgrave.jibs.8400073

Schooler, R. (1971). Bias Phenomena Attendant to the Marketing of Foreign Goods in the U. S. *Journal of International Business Studies*, *2*(1), 71–80. doi:10.1057/palgrave.jibs.8490732

Sekaran, U. (1983). Methodological and Theoretical Issues and Advancements in Cross-Cultural Research. *Journal of International Business Studies*, *14*(2), 61–73. doi:10.1057/palgrave.jibs.8490519

Shaffer, M. A., Harrison, D. A., & Gilley, K. M. (1999). Dimensions, Determinants, and Differences in the Expatriate Adjustment Process. *Journal of International Business Studies*, *30*(3), 557–581. doi:10.1057/palgrave.jibs.8490083

Shenkar, O. (2001). Cultural Distance Revisited: Towards a More Rigorous Conceptualization and Measurement of Cultural Differences. *Journal of International Business Studies*, *32*(3), 519–535. doi:10.1057/palgrave.jibs.8490982

Shenkar, O. (2004). One more time: International business in a global economy. *Journal of International Business Studies*, *35*(2), 161–171. doi:10.1057/palgrave.jibs.8400074

Sherman, E. (2020). 94% of the Fortune 1000 are seeing coronavirus supply chain disruptions. *Fortune*. https://fortune.com/2020/02/21/fortune-1000-coronavirus-china-supply-chain-impact/

Singh, J. (1995). Measurement Issues in Cross-National Research. *Journal of International Business Studies*, *26*(3), 597–619. doi:10.1057/palgrave.jibs.8490188

Stahl, G. K., Maznevski, M. L., Voigt, A., & Jonsen, K. (2009). Unraveling the effects of cultural diversity in teams: A meta-analysis of research on multicultural work groups. *Journal of International Business Studies*, *41*(4), 690–709. doi:10.1057/jibs.2009.85

Stahl, G. K., & Tung, R. L. (2015). Towards a more balanced treatment of culture in international business studies: The need for positive cross-cultural scholarship. *Journal of International Business Studies*, *46*(4), 391–414. doi:10.1057/jibs.2014.68

Steenkamp, J. E. M., Batra, R., & Alden, D. L. (2003). How Perceived Brand Globalness Creates Brand Value. *Journal of International Business Studies*, *34*(1), 53–65. doi:10.1057/palgrave.jibs.8400002

Stephan, U., Uhlaner, L. M., & Stride, C. (2015). Institutions and social entrepreneurship: The role of institutional voids, institutional support, and institutional configurations. *Journal of International Business Studies*, *46*(3), 308–331. doi:10.1057/jibs.2014.38

Sullivan, D. (1994). Measuring the Degree of Internationalization of a Firm. *Journal of International Business Studies*, *25*(2), 325–342. doi:10.1057/palgrave.jibs.8490203

Tenzer, H., Pudelko, M., & Harzing, A. (2014). The impact of language barriers on trust formation in multinational teams. *Journal of International Business Studies, 45*(5), 508–535. doi:10.1057/jibs.2013.64

Terpstra, V., & Yu, C. M. (1988). Determinants of Foreign Investment of U.S. Advertising Agencies. *Journal of International Business Studies, 19*(1), 33–46. doi:10.1057/palgrave.jibs.8490373

Toyne, B., & Nigh, D. (1998). A more expansive view of international business. *Journal of International Business Studies, 29*(4), 863–876. doi:10.1057/palgrave.jibs.8490056

UNCTAD. (2013). *World investment report 207 3: Global value chains: Investment and trade for development*. United Nations.

UNCTAD. (2020). *World investment report 2020: International production beyond the pandemic*. United Nations.

Verbeke, A. (2020). Will the COVID-19 pandemic really change the governance of global value chains? *British Journal of Management, 31*(3), 444–446. doi:10.1111/1467-8551.12422

Verbeke, A., & Yuan, W. (2021). A few implications of the COVID-19 pandemic for international business strategy research. *Journal of Management Studies, 58*(2), 597–601. doi:10.1111/joms.12665

Weinstein, A. K. (1977). Foreign Investments by Service Firms: The Case of Multinational Advertising Agencies. *Journal of International Business Studies, 8*(1), 83–91. doi:10.1057/palgrave.jibs.8490681

Werner, S. (2002). Recent Developments in International Management Research: A Review of 20 Top Management Journals. *Journal of Management, 28*(3), 277–305. doi:10.1177/014920630202800303

Werner, S., & Brouthers, L. E. (2002). How International is Management? *Journal of International Business Studies, 33*(3), 583–591. doi:10.1057/palgrave.jibs.8491033

WTO. (2020a). Trade set to plunge as COVID-19 pandemic upends global economy. *WTO*. www.wto.org/english/news_e/pres20_e/pr855_e.pdf

WTO. (2020b). The Covid-19 pandemic and trade-related developments in LDCS. *WTO*. www.wto.org/english/tratop_e/covid19_e/ldcs_report_e.pdf

Yiu, D. W., Lau, C., & Bruton, G. D. (2007). International venturing by emerging economy firms: The effects of firm capabilities, home country networks, and corporate entrepreneurship. *Journal of International Business Studies, 38*(4), 519–540. doi:10.1057/palgrave.jibs.8400278

Zaheer, S., Schomaker, M. S., & Nachum, L. (2012). Distance without direction: Restoring credibility to a much-loved construct. *Journal of International Business Studies, 43*(1), 18–27. doi:10.1057/jibs.2011.43

Zahra, S. A. (2005). A Theory of International New Ventures: A Decade of Research. *Journal of International Business Studies, 36*(1), 20–28. doi:10.1057/palgrave.jibs.8400118

Zhou, L., Wu, W., & Luo, X. (2007). Internationalization and the performance of born-global SMEs: The mediating role of social networks. *Journal of International Business Studies, 38*(4), 673–690. doi:10.1057/palgrave.jibs.8400282

Chapter 5
Research on International Business and the COVID-19 Pandemic:
A Review of the Managerial and Policy Implications

Aytug Sozuer
https://orcid.org/0000-0003-2680-2071
Yalova University, Turkey

ABSTRACT

The COVID-19 pandemic disrupted international trade networks in 2020. Although worldwide commerce has recovered in the subsequent period, it is anticipated that globalization will make a new turn. The purpose of this study is to review the current research that examines the impact of the pandemic on international business. The methodology encompasses a semi-systematic review, which includes a summary and synthesis of selected empirical papers. The focal content of this review is the implication sections of the articles. By doing so, this study attempts to bridge the research-relevance gap.

INTRODUCTION

COVID-19 was a global shock. In the first phase, lockdowns were implemented all around the world to avoid infection. That affected the world economy. The manufacturing sector came to a halt in an interlinked trade network at a global scale. According to World Trade Organization's (WTO) estimate, the volume of world merchandise trade slumped by 5% annually in 2020. Although there has been a recovery in international commerce aftermath, challenging times persist. The world's major players must carefully consider their next actions in the context of increasing commodity prices, rising inflation, struggling supply networks, and conflicting global political interests.

DOI: 10.4018/978-1-6684-3749-0.ch005

In terms of government-industry interactions, the debate on the evolution of globalization is ongoing. Petricevic and Teece (2019) emphasize the necessity for the reconfiguration of global value chains orchestrated by multinational enterprises (MNEs). They point out increasing volatile, uncertain, complex, and ambiguous conditions (VUCA) for businesses due to new forms of government interventions in both Western and Chinese markets. As a solution, they address the dynamic capabilities approach (Teece, 2007; 2014). While acknowledging the VUCA environment, Buckley (2020) on the other hand, suggests the internalization theory is quite applicable to dealing with the new context and also references the COVID-19 situation. In another agenda, Callaghan (2021) questions whether deindustrialization -defined as declining shares of manufacturing output in countries' gross domestic product- has contributed to the slowdown of globalization. His analysis finds statistical evidence for such a relationship. He warns the political sentiment against globalization may prevail if state policies are regarded as unbalanced in the post-COVID-19 order, and he sees orchestration theory as a useful framework to evaluate the MNEs' activities. Referring to the post-pandemic era, Contractor (2022) argues that further globalization is needed because the interdependencies of global value chains are so strong and the advances in information and communication technologies are so substantial that MNEs would pave the way for operational efficiencies.

Even though it is early to assess the true consequences of the pandemic crisis, there may be valuable lessons to take from the various experience so far. The body of literature on international business activities under pandemic conditions is expanding. For instance, a research stream examining global manufacturing argues that reshoring cannot be a sustainable solution against acute drops in trade or protectionist trade policy measures as seen in 2020. Instead, a viable balance should be achieved between efficiency and resilience such as considering regional structures for the value chains (Kersan-Skabic, 2022). This requires the improvement of liberal trade policies as well. In parallel, the objective of this study is to review the managerial and policy implications identified in recent literature in order to gather further valuable insights that may be useful in real-life decision-making.

The expected value of this study stems from the rigor-relevance discussion as in Rynes et al. (2001), Gulati (2007), Carter (2008), and Geuens (2011). The perspective urges business management researchers to focus more on the transferability of created knowledge to reduce the research-practice gap. This notion is being recognized since the publications are placing greater emphasis on managerial and policy implications. In addition, the knowledge fragmented across separate papers is compiled and synthesized from time to time as in literature reviews and meta-analyses. Recently, van Hoek (2020) and Verbeke and Yuan (2021) remarked on this necessity in the international business domain. Therefore, this timely overview can be considered as a step toward the realm of decision-makers.

METHODOLOGY

This study includes a semi-systematic review method which is developed for issues that have been conceptualized differently and investigated by numerous groups of researchers from distinct fields. This form of study is beneficial for discovering themes, viewpoints, or common concerns within a certain research discipline or approach, as well as for identifying the elements of a theoretical approach (Snyder, 2019). For this analysis, a list of academic journal articles is compiled from the EBSCO database containing "international business" or "international trade" and "COVID-19" terms in their titles, abstracts, or subject terms. After selecting the empirical studies for review, their managerial and/or policy implications sections are studied thoroughly.

FINDINGS

The search included publications released between June 2020 and June 2022. There would be more research available soon on the topic but for the scope of this study, 25 empirical (quantitative/qualitative) papers are identified for review. According to their areas of interest, papers could be grouped under four themes in research related to international trade, global value chains, multinational enterprises, and resilience. The themes and cited research are shown in Table 1.

Table 1. Reviewed articles according to their area of interest

Theme	Studies
International Trade	Barbero et al. (2021), Bekkers & Coopman (2022), Belu (2021), Coquide et al. (2022), Hayakawa & Mukunoki (2021), Kumari & Bharti (2021), Nitsch (2022), Vidya & Prabheesh (2020)
Global Value Chains	Castaneda-Navarrete et al. (2021), Dallas et al. (2021), Handfield et al. (2020), Hava (2020), Qin et al. (2020), Zeshan (2021)
Multinational Enterprises	Ajide & Osinubi (2020), Ar & Abbas (2021), Bait et al. (2021), Hong et al. (2022), Lorenzen et al. (2020), Peerally et al. (2022)
Resilience	Arita et al. (2022), Mena et al. (2022), Santos et al. (2021), Song et al. (2020), Uminski & Borowicz (2021)

In the following sections, each study will be described with a focus on its implications.

Implications for International Trade

There are eight papers in this category, three of which make investigations on a particular region or country whereas others examine a broader range of countries' trade networks. Regarding COVID-19's implications for international trade in a global scope; Barbero et al. (2021) analyze the impact of COVID-19 on bilateral trade flows using the monthly trade data of 68 exporting countries. They find that countries having regional trade agreements are more negatively impacted by COVID-19 on trade flows.

Furthermore, their findings demonstrate that the COVID-19 consequences on trade were only detrimental when the income levels of exporting and importing nations with regional trade agreements are equal, particularly in the case of high-income nations. In terms of policy implications, they emphasize the trade effects can be viewed as less negative than in the first wave from March to May 2020. The explanation depends on how well a nation can adjust to the various crisis stages. Countries may need to establish public expenditure programs and promote private investment to lessen the impact of this trade shock. Given the significance of these institutional initiatives' significant effects on trade flows, such governmental acts may necessitate other institutional initiatives.

However, the focus on vaccinations may influence the formation of future laws that concentrate vaccine production on a small number of producers. The majority of countries' immunization programs are projected to have a significant impact on the transition to a non-COVID-19 environment. Authors emphasize that, throughout the COVID-19 epidemic, nations must maintain their competitiveness while, if practical, reestablishing their economic links. Similarly, Hayakawa and Mukunoki (2021) examine the exports of 34 countries to 173 countries in 2019 and 2020. They show COVID-19 has a considerable detrimental impact on both exporting and importing countries' international trade.

Since July 2020, these consequences, particularly the effects of COVID-19 in importing countries, have tended to become minor. Although the negative effects of COVID-19 in exporting countries continued until August 2020, the scale of those effects diminished over time. These findings demonstrate that the negative effects of COVID-19 on foreign trade were mitigated to some extent following the first wave of the epidemic. A further in-depth examination of particular sectors indicated diverse effects across industries. Labor-intensive businesses, for example, were found to be more vulnerable to the negative effects of COVID-19 in exporting countries. Furthermore, Coquide et al. (2022) conduct a Google matrix analysis of the multiproduct world trade network between 2018 and 2020. Their findings show that COVID-19 has a significant impact on foreign trade. They propose that this negative impact has numerous social and economic causes.

The pandemic reduced the cross-country mobility of people and products, lowering the demand for petroleum and gas. Because of people's illnesses, the output of specific items was curtailed, resulting in a negative product balance for the United States and practically all European countries; only China was unaffected in the context of these product groups. Indeed, the majority of these products were manufactured in Asia and were not available in Europe. They propose that the impact of COVID-19 demonstrated that industrial production in the United States and the European Union should be enhanced to become more self-sufficient and independent -a fact that policymakers should address.

There are also two estimation studies within this vein. First, Vidya and Prabheesh (2020) use network analysis to estimate the future course of commerce and quantify the degree of trade connectivity between nations before and after the COVID-19 outbreak. Their results show that: (1) After the COVID-19 breakout, there has been a significant decrease in trade connectivity and density among nations, (2) The trade network's structure has changed significantly, (3) The pandemic had no impact on China's "center" status in the world trade, and (4) Up until December 2020, most economies' trading would experience a severe drop.

Second, Bekkers and Coopman (2022) examine the expected impact of the COVID-19 pandemic on international trade by building three scenarios (dubbed V-shaped, U-shaped, and L-shaped recovery) to project the economic effects with a quantitative trade model. There are two policy implications in their analysis: First, the predicted economic losses between the various recovery scenarios range significantly. The Gross Domestic Product (GDP) decline in the L-shaped recovery scenario would be greater than it would be in the U-shaped recovery scenario. This suggests that creating effective methods of social isolation and effectively putting the economy on hold to limit long-term consequences both have very significant economic payoffs. Third, when the initial epidemic peak has passed, it is essential for international trade that nations coordinate their social exclusionary policies. According to the simulations presented in the research, long-lasting travel restrictions would have significant negative effects on international trade, especially trade in services, specialized equipment, and air-transported goods.

In terms of region or country-specific studies; Kumari and Bharti's (2021) study finds a negative impact of COVID-19 on exports for the South Asian economies where Nepal is the most and India is the least affected. The study suggests that all South Asian nations modify their trade facilitation (TF) policies in order to increase exports and make up for their declining levels. For instance, the report recommends that the governments of Nepal, Bangladesh, Sri Lanka, and Pakistan enhance their TF performance. There is a lot of room to undertake policy measures to decrease the trade time and costs in order to minimize the negative impact of COVID-19 because costs and time to export have always remained high in South Asian countries.

The study's conclusions advise the governments of Pakistan, Sri Lanka, and Nepal to lower export costs. To lessen the impact of the pandemic on their country's trade, the governments and policymakers of Pakistan, Sri Lanka, and Nepal are advised to be more cautious while lowering the time to export. Bangladesh and India require the least effort compared to others. Therefore, the study suggests that governments and policymakers should focus resources on prudently and seriously adopting TF changes. Such changes can make up for the trade losses incurred as a result of the pandemic. Belu (2021) describes the effects of the COVID-19 crisis on foreign trade operations as well as the development of Romania's export-import activities in 2020–2021.

The author addresses three challenges that companies need to solve with managing international trade operations. The first one is the reconfiguration of global supply chains as regional supply chains by locating contractors and suppliers in the same region. The diversification of export markets and the range of exported goods is the second challenge. For businesses to grow sustainably over the long run, diversification is a crucial component. The continuation of digitization is another challenge facing businesses. New technologies have made it possible to set up smart logistics, which have lowered inventory costs and diverted investments toward more rapid and dependable deliveries. To improve port and intermodal connectivity, port administrations and terminal operators have teamed up. Shippers and other interested parties have backed a maritime logistics discussion to promote information sharing and teamwork across international supply chains.

Authors posit that, in a post-COVID environment, the key obstacles will be the supply chain's main issues such as interoperability, agility, and transparency. Nitsch (2022) analyzes data from New Zealand and suggests that during pandemic lockdowns, the value of seaborne exports and imports rises in comparison to shipments by air. This conclusion supports the significance of trade frictions on the supply side, even if it is consistent with several explanations, from trade financing limitations to infrastructural shortcomings. Furthermore, given the partial substitutability of transportation modes in trade, shocks whose impact differs depending on the mode of shipment may motivate specific policy responses.

Implications for Global Value Chains (GVCs)

There are six papers under this theme. One of them is a qualitative case study and two of them examine specific product groups. Qin et al. (2020) analyze cross-border trade ties between China and other nations. It is demonstrated that many countries or regions experience the COVID-19-related production shock from China, and the severity of the impact is largely determined by how closely a specific nation or territory is connected to China through global value chains. Downstream nations/regions and industry sectors are generally more influenced than upstream ones. Given the breadth of effect and the magnitude of damage, it is obvious that China plays such a significant role in GVCs and cannot be replaced currently.

With a broader look, Hava (2020) examines two international trade networks in the early stage of the pandemic showing that the supply chain issues restrict both production and trading of goods. In light of the results, it was determined that flexible new supply chain networks should be developed that enable quick and practical decisions to be made when the flow of supply chain networks that function is disrupted due to crises or other reasons, and how much enterprises should have just-in-time production plans and stocks as well as the importance of putting the reshaping of international trade to the forefront as the problems that evolved after the beginning of normalization.

On the other hand, Zeshan (2021) presents a simulation of how a second pandemic outbreak would disrupt the global value chains. Results indicate that manufacturing export industries are affected the most. The transportation and communication sectors suffer significant losses as export-supporting enterprises as well. The study offers the following policy recommendations: (1) A coherent fiscal stimulus; (2) Allocation of public funds to both the economic and healthcare sectors; (3) Providing liquidity for small and medium labor-intensive firms; and (4) Short-, medium-, and long-term measures for market stability and economic stimulation that are specific to each country.

In one of the two papers focusing on the trade of important product groups, Dallas et al. (2021) study the linkages between the type of state intervention across the US, Europe, China, and Malaysia with the geographic distribution of production and technological characteristics of personal protective equipment. They discuss that although state policies have an impact on GVCs, the fundamental structures of GVCs, which had been built up over decades, remained important even during emergency interventions. In many cases, activist state policy was rendered ineffective by geographic and technological structures. Such restrictions were even openly acknowledged in policy reshaping, such as the reversal of self-defeating EU trade policies.

Beyond medical industries, close attention should be paid to how and when different states shape but are also shaped by GVCs. The research identifies the geographic extent and technological complexity as essential aspects of GVCs that shape state policy choices. In another study, Castaneda-Navarrete et al. (2021) examine the COVID-19 pandemic's effects on the global apparel value chain with an emphasis on how they have affected developing nations. They report that the pandemic has severely disrupted the global apparel value chain, due to the direct effects of disease on factory workers, the lower output of materials used to manufacture clothing, and decreased demand for apparel in high-income countries. Profits, wages, job stability, and employee safety are all suffering disproportionately in developing countries.

Women in the garment industry have been impacted particularly hard, not only because the majority of workers in the industry are women, but also because they have encountered more unpaid care work and a heightened risk of gender-based harassment. In the policy agenda, they suggest the following five themes: (1) Providing emergency assistance to ensure business survival and the protection of workers' livelihoods; (2) redefining FDI attraction and market diversification strategies to take advantage of opportunities from the reconfiguration of the apparel global value chain; (3) encouraging technology adoption and skills development to upgrade in the value chain; (4) implementing labor standards to improve workers' conditions and strengthen social protection systems; and (5) implementing gender-sensitive measures to address systemic inequalities.

At the micro level, Handfield et al. (2020) describe how the pandemic would impact the design of future global supply chains through case studies. They underline that supply chain managers frequently aim to optimize costs or negotiate better supplier contracts. They are known for being iterative and focused on making modest, subtle adjustments to their current system and way of thinking.

However, in the current climate, these operations have shown to be of minor importance when contrasted to the powerful forces of economic disruption of the previous years. Businesses that have more responsive and compressed supply chains are benefiting greatly from the COVID-19 crisis and are no longer at the mercy of the outcomes of foreign governments' political actions. Authors believe that rapid disruptions in the supply chains may occur again in the future and supply chains would be less cost-driven and more intelligently impacted by considerations like sustainability, low emissions, and superior risk-recovery procedures. The effects of pandemics on the economy, society, and people can then be addressed more skillfully in the short- and long-term.

Implications for Multinational Enterprises (MNEs)

There are six papers in this domain. Three of them are related to functional, while the remaining are associated with the strategical behavior of firms. With respect to corporate-level strategy issues, Lorenzen et al. (2020) discuss the interdependencies of MNEs and city-regions and strategy shifts during disruptions like the COVID-19 pandemic. International connectivity's propensity to disrupt local connectivity exemplifies the hazards of regional high-tech innovation strategies and incentive schemes designed to encourage MNE entry. They demonstrate that, for city-regions, innovation-based development may concentrate in core cities and has the potential to disengage and disenfranchise portions of the other regions.

Consequently, it becomes difficult for policymakers to engage in local upskilling and knowledge-intensive enterprises that benefit the entire city region, including the catchment districts. Moreover, while MNEs have the ability to connect city-regions internationally, those following a traditional strategy centered on global orchestration may worsen the difficulties of local disconnection that are intrinsic to the knowledge economy. Therefore, they suggest that regional governments must engage with new MNEs to incentivize them to pursue complementing local spawning activities for the benefit of the domestic entrepreneurship ecosystem.

In a prescriptive type of study, Bait et al. (2021) propose a multi-criteria decision-making model that MNEs can use to evaluate the best nations in Africa for establishing new manufacturing settlements, with additional criteria of COVID-19 factor. The research provides an outline of the primary criteria used to select the appropriate land for the development of a plant. They presume this guide could be valuable for investors who wish to quantitatively compare countries to determine the optimal location. The method could assist in excluding places whose conditions are too far from the sector-specific needs, hence decreasing investment risk. In addition, the paper proposes a methodology for identifying those regions most affected by COVID-19, from an industrial perspective, in order to assist local governments in identifying the most relevant mitigation actions to be adopted.

In another study regarding direct investments, Ajide and Osinubi (2020) investigate the influence of the COVID-19 pandemic on foreign direct investment (FDI) outflows using first-quarter data for 43 countries in 2020. They provide evidence for a correlation between COVID-19 confirmed cases and FDI outflows. The COVID-19 pandemic impairs the desirability of many economies, causing multinational enterprises to shift their assets during the initial phases of the pandemic. The study demonstrates that the COVID-19 pandemic fuels foreign direct investment outflows in the economies because of a shortage of labor caused by governments' social distancing policies, a decline in corporate profits, and an increase in the cost of financing on the financial market.

In addition, the investment propensities of most economies have been adversely affected. These factors also become apparent because economies are currently experiencing a high level of risk perception in the financial markets, which has significantly curtailed the investment programs of foreign investors to maintain resilience in the face of any additional destruction in their home countries. A further policy implication of this report is that there is a need to improve public policies in wooing the confidence of foreign investors during economic challenges and that the government should ensure a conducive international business environment to attract a substantial amount of FDI in any future crisis period.

There are several studies with the sustainability perspective in MNEs. Hong et al. (2022) examine four case studies to understand the role of leadership in determining the course of action in the crisis context. The paper indicates that Indian MNEs implemented their business plans to provide many individuals with stable work possibilities during the COVID-19 pandemic. MNEs are incorporated into their domestic and international network.

When a crisis occurs, they are not left in isolation. They are considerably more knowledgeable about the prospects and limitations of a pandemic situation. MNEs, therefore, made an extra effort to support their suppliers, engage with their consumers, and think about their staff in addition to trying to save themselves. These MNEs were put to the test when it came to carrying out their CSR for their stakeholders during the epidemic. By doing this, they could reduce bigger hazards brought on by the pandemic. The behaviors of major MNEs show that they aspire to do what is appropriate in meeting their requirements while taking their part of the responsibility for the wider stakeholders as the world continues to fight to sustain economic progress following each wave of the epidemic.

The paper posits that the COVID-19 crisis presents MNEs with chances to introduce CSR and sustainability practices in their countries and the global community. Peerally et al. (2022) illustrate several MNE pandemic-induced social innovation approaches to argue whether they are transitory or can and should be sustained long-term. The MNEs' responses demonstrate their executives' abilities to quickly react or pivot in a global crisis and harness their knowledge on optimizing their operations to change business models and adapt supply chains to solve a great societal health concern. MNE practitioners can nurture and refine this ability, especially through scholar-practitioner engagement, to develop innovative and socially conscious mindsets and corporate culture, which allows future business models to evolve and become fluid in their resource allocation and utilization, and respond harmoniously to the opposing demands of financial sustainability and contributing to sustainable development.

This needs managers to create internal skills, resources, knowledge, and experiences for tackling social and sustainability concerns and fostering external partnerships and collaborations for social impact. On the other hand, the study suggests policymakers from developed countries, especially those who allocate pandemic-relief loans to enterprises, should focus on understanding this emerging and possibly reversible trend in the business model shift so they can support MNEs in sustaining these social innovation efforts post-pandemic in a way that is beneficial to society and financially sustainable for enterprises. Furthermore, developing countries well behind the technical frontier should focus on incentives and systems that encourage MNEs to tackle social and other major concerns and work with domestic players.

This point is deemed important since their domestic firms lack the resources, competencies, and capacities to achieve economic goals and tackle major challenges. Ar & Abbas (2021) discuss Ford-Otosan's—an international joint venture (IJV) in Turkey—an attempt to design a corporate social responsibility (CSR) project to assist Turkish civilians during COVID-19. It reveals how far a firm would go to carry out a CSR project in the event of an exceptional disaster. It demonstrates how an IJV's shifting of a production strategy in multiple iterations ensures a true solution to a critical social problem.

Another significant conclusion drawn from this situation is the link between dynamic capabilities and CSR. The study demonstrates that corporations do not solely rely on pre-existing skill sets to carry out CSR projects. They are constantly looking for new talents to help them adapt to society's ever-changing needs and external market conditions. Furthermore, the Ford-Otosan instance highlights how businesses can gain public legitimacy and improve their reputation in domestic and international business chambers.

Implications From Research on Resilience

In this area, five studies are reviewed. Three of them are multi-factor country comparisons to see whether nations are vulnerable or resilient to shocks. One of the remaining papers is country-specific and the other is sector-specific. Among country comparisons, Mena et al. (2022) investigate country-level trade resilience during the pandemic based on country profiles as in their global connectedness, logistics performance, healthcare preparedness, governmental actions, and national income. They emphasize the significance of important characteristics that might enhance the resilience of export economies, hence guiding the investment priorities of host governments in support of national economic growth objectives.

Their findings highlight the connection between a sustainable international trading system, equal access to health care, and the safeguarding of livelihoods. Consequently, the development of a healthcare capability and a smart logistics infrastructure become essential elements of a credible and resilient export-oriented national development strategy. Furthermore, policymakers can assess the factors influencing trade resilience and attempt to improve their predictions of the likelihood of disruptions originating from specific sourcing locations. Appropriate mitigation measures can be devised based on country profiles comprising national GDP, globalization levels, and infrastructural capabilities. In addition, they underline that low-income nations lacking the required trade robustness and responsiveness during an international trade disruption of this magnitude must inform global attempts to assure more equitable access to health-related resources during future pandemics.

Moreover, Santos et al. (2021) compare nations with similar populations to determine what factors may explain the COVID-19 pandemic figures. According to social and economic indices, the conditions of the nine countries studied were positive until the new coronavirus appeared. Countries with a higher security index and tourism infrastructure test their populations more. Innovation, competitiveness, and GDP per capita boost population testing. Low-birth-rate countries are more likely to test. The study suggests international business practitioners focus on how countries handled the COVID-19 crisis. This means grouping countries by their daily infection rate. The report includes countries with low, moderate, and high infection rates. As international business managers face severe challenges during the crisis, they can use these categories to analyze countries. The study proposes comparing crisis management tactics by countries.

International business managers are supposed to use that strategy to group countries to better manage the change. In another study covering emerging markets, Song et al. (2020) examine the performance of industrial structures in response to external shocks during COVID-19 by using simulation models. They report that the ability of a country to absorb shocks is not proportional to the amount of the shock, but rather to its industrial structure and the type of shock. It is challenging to alter the industrial structure in the near term; thus, when exogenous shocks occur, governments should identify the types of shocks and develop appropriate policies. Different industrial structures have varying capacities for stress absorption. China has more shock absorption capacity than Vietnam, for example. Governments should strengthen domestic industrial ties to withstand exogenous shocks. They also suggest that governments must develop a variety of solutions to address various shocks.

For instantaneous shocks (e.g., restrictions on entertainment), the economy can absorb shocks gradually. The government must prioritize the entertainment business and encourage the consumption of internet entertainment. For continuous shocks (e.g., trade control), the economy cannot absorb these shocks to their full capacity. Since the government's attempts to increase imports are ineffectual, trade restraints must be eliminated. Finally, they propose governments should avoid trade restrictions since they are detrimental to their own economy.

In a country-specific paper, Uminski and Borowicz (2021) estimate the involvement of foreign-owned enterprises in Poland's post-pandemic recovery. They believe that rebuilding resilience through FDI in the context of post-pandemic recovery for Poland should include (1) maintaining openness to incoming FDI in order to secure membership among post-pandemic winners and using the opportunity to reallocate investments to the country, and (2) attracting greenfield and knowledge-intensive business services investments in particular. In a sector-specific study, on the other hand, Arita et al. (2022) assess the consequences of COVID-19 incidence rates, regulatory constraints imposed by states to contain the epidemic, and the de facto reduction in human mobility/lockdown effect on global agricultural commerce. Their calculations indicate that COVID-19 lowered global agricultural trade by 5-10 percent.

The most obvious mechanisms via which the pandemic has affected agricultural trade are the decline in human mobility and government policy restrictions. Several international organizations, including the WTO and the United Nations, were concerned that the epidemic might have a disproportionate impact on low-income developing nations because these nations may not be as integrated into global supply networks. However, there is minimal and contradictory evidence indicating the trade flows of low-income and least-developed countries were more susceptible to the COVID-19 shock. In conclusion, their results indicated small but statistically significant negative effects of the pandemic, which may be regarded as the resilience of agricultural commerce, at least in aggregate.

In the next section, the implications and the lessons learned from those studies will be summarized.

DISCUSSION

The COVID-19 pandemic impaired international trade networks, especially in mid-2020. On the other hand, there has been a rebound in the following terms as seen in the volume of world merchandise trade. Furthermore, China appears to preserve its central position in global value chains despite of severe disruptions. Among the reviewed studies above, the context and research methods varied to a large extent. Table 2 summarizes the studies by their research goal, geographical scope, and whether they are focused on a specific industry.

Table 2. Frequency of studies according to their goal, scope, and sectoral focus

Research goal		
Description	Prediction	Causation
11	8	6
Geographical scope		
Worldwide	Regional	Local
17	2	6
Specific sectoral focus		
	Yes	No
	4	21

In this table, descriptive research under the first heading reflects the number of studies that apply the qualitative case study method as well as quantitative analyses based on ratios, rates of change, and simple correlations. Predictive studies include methods such as simulation models and multi-criteria decision analysis. Causal studies are those which mainly examine panel data to explain the effects of independent variables on dependent variables. In the geographical scope heading, *worldwide* refers to the number of studies using data from multiple countries across several parts of the world. *Regional* shows the studies within a particular world region such as South Asia and Africa. *Local* refers to analyses conducted only in one country.

Lastly, studies are grouped into two categories based on whether they are sector-specific or not. Based on this review, the issues that *international business managers* should consider when dealing with exogenous shocks like the pandemic include the following:

- Reconfiguring the supply chain to make it compact, agile, and not-so-distant
- Investing in digitization and smart technologies
- Advocating sustainability and social responsibility
- Diversifying the markets and the products further
- Observing government policies and actions to identify lucrative investment opportunities

The major concerns that *policymakers* should take into account are as follows:

- Utilizing public budget for trade stimulation and surviving small and medium-sized labor-intensive businesses
- Implementing social restrictions moderately to avoid the sudden slowdown in the economy
- Ensuring the Improvement of labor standards and working conditions
- Reinforcing governance to attract foreign direct investments
- Cooperating with other nations to enable healthcare and financial accessibility for low-income countries

The aforementioned points are the pragmatic insights drawn from empirical studies. Moreover, they coincide with the conceptual perspectives explained in Alon (2020), Contractor (2022), Dörrenbacher et al. (2021), Ghauri et al. (2021), and Soundararajan et al. (2021). However, the review is limited to the author's selected list of articles. Obviously, the research on international business during the pandemic conditions is growing. Further studies can elaborate on the other aspects of international business such as trade policy (e.g., Curran et al., 2021; Mariani, 2021; Torsello & Winkler, 2020) or entrepreneurship (e.g., Mihaylova, 2021; Ratten, 2020; Pilloni et al., 2022).

CONCLUSION

International business scholars and policymakers anticipate that COVID-19 will speed up the restructuring of global trade. It is plausible to think that companies will be more risk-averse and governments will be more protectionist. The new normal in business appears as being challenged by unstable commodity prices, cost of logistics, cost of semi-finished goods, consumer demand, market valuation, and so on. In order to understand the necessity for adaptation, this study has reviewed the preliminary estimations of the impacts of the pandemic on international business. In light of the implications in current literature, state and business can have separate roles. Here, a reference would be made to the exploration-exploitation conundrum. Based on the evidence, it can be argued that governments should exploit the merits of the social state, whereas businesses should explore the opportunities by establishing deeper relationships with the stakeholders in the post-pandemic era.

REFERENCES

Ajide, F. M., & Osinubi, T. T. (2020). Covid-19 pandemic and outward foreign direct investment: A preliminary note. *ECONOMICS, 8*(2), 79–88. doi:10.2478/eoik-2020-0019

Alon, I. (2020). COVID-19 and international business: A viewpoint. *FIIB Business Review, 9*(2), 75–77. doi:10.1177/2319714520923579

Ar, A. Y., & Abbas, A. (2021). Corporate response against COVID-19: Manufacturing shift by Ford-Otosan. *Annals of Global Health, 87*(1), 1–5. doi:10.5334/aogh.3434 PMID:34277362

Arita, S., Grant, J., Sydow, S., & Beckman, J. (2022). Has global agricultural trade been resilient under coronavirus (COVID-19)? Findings from an econometric assessment of 2020. *Food Policy, 107*, 102204. doi:10.1016/j.foodpol.2021.102204 PMID:34903907

Bait, S., Lauria, S. M., & Schiraldi, M. M. (2021). Multi-criteria decision-making model for supporting manufacturing settlements location in Africa after COVID-19. *International Journal of Engineering Business Management, 13*, 1–15. doi:10.1177/18479790211023348

Barbero, J., de Lucio, J. J., & Rodríguez-Crespo, E. (2021). Effects of COVID-19 on trade flows: Measuring their impact through government policy responses. *PLoS One, 16*(10), 1–20. doi:10.1371/journal.pone.0258356 PMID:34644312

Bekkers, E., & Koopman, R. B. (2020). Simulating the trade effects of the COVID-19 pandemic. *World Economy, 45*(2), 445–467. doi:10.1111/twec.13063 PMID:33362334

Belu, M. G. (2021). COVID-19 Pandemic Impact on the Exports and Imports. *The Romanian Economic Journal, 82*(82), 31–46. doi:10.24818/REJ/2021/82/03

Buckley, P. J. (2020). The theory and empirics of the structural reshaping of globalization. *Journal of International Business Studies, 51*(9), 1580–1592. doi:10.105741267-020-00355-5 PMID:32836503

Callaghan, C. W. (2021). Consequences of deindustrialisation for globalisation: Insights for international business. *International Business Review, 30*(3), 101804. doi:10.1016/j.ibusrev.2021.101804

Carter, C. R. (2008). Knowledge production and knowledge transfer: Closing the research – practice gap. *The Journal of Supply Chain Management, 44*(2), 78–82. doi:10.1111/j.1745-493X.2008.00059.x

Castaneda-Navarrete, J., Hauge, J., & López-Gómez, C. (2021). COVID-19's impacts on global value chains, as seen in the apparel industry. *Development Policy Review, 39*(6), 953–970. doi:10.1111/dpr.12539

Contractor, F. J. (2022). The world economy will need even more globalization in the post-pandemic 2021 decade. *Journal of International Business Studies*, *53*(1), 156–171. doi:10.105741267-020-00394-y PMID:33551513

Coquidé, C., Lages, J., Ermann, L., & Shepelyansky, D. L. (2022). COVID-19's impact on international trade. *Entropy (Basel, Switzerland)*, *24*(3), 327. doi:10.3390/e24030327 PMID:35327838

Curran, L., Eckhardt, J., & Lee, J. (2021). The trade policy response to COVID-19 and its implications for international business. *Critical Perspectives on International Business*, *17*(2), 252–320. doi:10.1108/cpoib-05-2020-0041

Dallas, M. P., Horner, R., & Li, L. (2021). The mutual constraints of states and global value chains during COVID-19: The case of personal protective equipment. *World Development*, *139*, 105324. doi:10.1016/j.worlddev.2020.105324 PMID:33293754

Dörrenbacher, C., Sinkovics, R. R., Becker-Ritterspach, F., Boussebaa, M., Curran, L., de Jonge, A., & Khan, Z. (2021). The Covid-19 pandemic: Towards a societally engaged IB perspective. *Critical Perspectives on International Business*, *17*(2), 149–164. doi:10.1108/cpoib-02-2021-0021

Geuens, M. (2011). Where does business research go from here? Food-for-thought on academic papers in business research. *Journal of Business Research*, *64*(10), 1104–1107. doi:10.1016/j.jbusres.2010.11.005

Ghauri, P., Strange, R., & Cooke, F. L. (2021). Research on international business: The new realities. *International Business Review*, *30*(2), 101794. doi:10.1016/j.ibusrev.2021.101794

Gulati, R. (2007). Tent poles, tribalism, and boundary spanning: The rigor-relevance debate in management research. *Academy of Management Journal*, *50*(4), 775–782. doi:10.5465/amj.2007.26279170

Handfield, R. B., Graham, G., & Burns, L. (2020). Corona virus, tariffs, trade wars and supply chain evolutionary design. *International Journal of Operations & Production Management*, *40*(10), 1649–1660. doi:10.1108/IJOPM-03-2020-0171

Hava, H. T. (2020). An analysis of the effects of Covid-19 Outbreak on global supply chain and international trade. *Turkish Studies-Economics, Finance. Politics*, *15*(4), 2083–2100.

Hayakawa, K., & Mukunoki, H. (2021). The impact of COVID-19 on international trade: Evidence from the first shock. *Journal of the Japanese and International Economies*, *60*, 101135. doi:10.1016/j.jjie.2021.101135

Hong, P. C., Singh, N. P., Elangovan, N., & Yeon, G. (2022). Responding to pandemic challenges: Leadership lessons from multinational enterprises (MNEs) in India. *Journal of Management Development*, *41*(4), 205–222. doi:10.1108/JMD-11-2021-0309

Kersan-Škabić, I. (2021). The COVID-19 pandemic and the internationalization of production: A review of the literature. *Development Policy Review*, *40*(2), 12560. PMID:34219988

Kumari, M., & Bharti, N. (2021). Estimating the impact of COVID-19 on South Asia's exports: Does trade facilitation matter now more than ever? *Transnational Corporations Review*, *13*(4), 406–421. doi:10.1080/19186444.2021.1911280

Lorenzen, M., Mudambi, R., & Schotter, A. (2020). International connectedness and local disconnectedness: MNE strategy, city-regions and disruption. *Journal of International Business Studies*, *51*(8), 1199–1222. doi:10.105741267-020-00339-5 PMID:32836501

Mariani, P. (2021). The EU market in times of a global state of emergency: Internal and external trade barriers in the age of pandemics. *Legal Issues of Economic Integration*, *48*(1), 5–18. doi:10.54648/LEIE2021002

Mena, C., Karatzas, A., & Hansen, C. (2022). International trade resilience and the Covid-19 pandemic. *Journal of Business Research*, *138*, 77–91. doi:10.1016/j.jbusres.2021.08.064 PMID:34538982

Mihaylova, M. (2021). The impact of global trends and Covid-19 on international new ventures. *Economic Archive*, *3*, 46–58.

Nitsch, V. (2022). Covid-19 and international trade: Evidence from New Zealand. *Economics Letters*, *217*, 110627. doi:10.1016/j.econlet.2022.110627 PMID:35645436

Peerally, J. A., De Fuentes, C., Santiago, F., & Zhao, S. (2022). The sustainability of multinational enterprises' pandemic-induced social innovation approaches. *Thunderbird International Business Review*, *64*(2), 115–124. doi:10.1002/tie.22256

Petricevic, O., & Teece, D. J. (2019). The structural reshaping of globalization: Implications for strategic sectors, profiting from innovation, and the multinational enterprise. *Journal of International Business Studies*, *50*(9), 1487–1512. doi:10.105741267-019-00269-x

Pilloni, M., Kádár, J., & Abu Hamed, T. (2022). The impact of COVID-19 on energy start-up companies: The use of global financial crisis (GFC) as a lesson for future recovery. *Energies*, *15*(10), 3530. doi:10.3390/en15103530

Qin, M., Liu, X., & Zhou, X. (2020). COVID-19 shock and global value chains: Is there a substitute for China? *Emerging Markets Finance & Trade*, *56*(15), 3588–3598. doi:10.1080/1540496X.2020.1855137

Ratten, V. (2020). Coronavirus and international business: An entrepreneurial ecosystem perspective. *Thunderbird International Business Review*, *62*(5), 629–634. doi:10.1002/tie.22161

Rynes, S. L., Bartunek, J. M., & Daft, R. L. (2001). Across the great divide: Knowledge creation and transfer between practitioners and academics. *Academy of Management Journal*, *44*(2), 340–355. doi:10.2307/3069460

Santos, E., Oliveira, M., Ratten, V., Tavares, F. O., & Tavares, V. C. (2020). A reflection on explanatory factors for Covid -19: A comparative study between countries. *Thunderbird International Business Review*, *63*(3), 285–301. doi:10.1002/tie.22188

Snyder, H. (2019). Literature review as a research methodology: An overview and guidelines. *Journal of Business Research*, *104*, 333–339. doi:10.1016/j.jbusres.2019.07.039

Song, P., Zhang, X., Zhao, Y., & Xu, L. (2020). Exogenous shocks on the dual-country industrial network: A simulation based on the policies during the COVID-19 pandemic. *Emerging Markets Finance & Trade*, *56*(15), 3554–3561. doi:10.1080/1540496X.2020.1854723

Soundararajan, V., Sahasranamam, S., Khan, Z., & Jain, T. (2021). Multinational enterprises and the governance of sustainability practices in emerging market supply chains: An agile governance perspective. *Journal of World Business, 56*(2), 101149. doi:10.1016/j.jwb.2020.101149

Teece, D. J. (2007). Explicating dynamic capabilities: The nature and microfoundations of (sustainable) enterprise performance. *Strategic Management Journal, 28*(13), 1319–1350. doi:10.1002mj.640

Teece, D. J. (2014). A dynamic capabilities-based entrepreneurial theory of the multinational enterprise. *Journal of International Business Studies, 45*(1), 8–37. doi:10.1057/jibs.2013.54

Torsello, M., & Winkler, M. M. (2020). Coronavirus-infected international business transactions: A preliminary diagnosis. *European Journal of Risk Regulation, 11*(2), 396–401. doi:10.1017/err.2020.30

Umiński, S., & Borowicz, A. (2021). Will multinational enterprises contribute to Poland's economic resilience and recovery during and post COVID-19 pandemic. *Transnational Corporations Review, 13*(1), 74–87. doi:10.1080/19186444.2021.1888638

van Hoek, R. (2020). Research opportunities for a more resilient post-COVID-19 supply chain – closing the gap between research findings and industry practice. *International Journal of Operations & Production Management, 40*(4), 341–355. doi:10.1108/IJOPM-03-2020-0165

Verbeke, A., & Yuan, W. (2020). A few implications of the COVID-19 pandemic for international business strategy research. *Journal of Management Studies, 58*(2), 597–601. doi:10.1111/joms.12665

Vidya, C. T., & Prabheesh, K. P. (2020). Implications of COVID-19 pandemic on the global trade networks. *Emerging Markets Finance & Trade, 56*(10), 2408–2421. doi:10.1080/1540496X.2020.1785426

Zeshan, M. (2020). Double-hit scenario of Covid-19 and global value chains. *Environment, Development and Sustainability, 23*(6), 8559–8572. doi:10.100710668-020-00982-w PMID:32982574

KEY TERMS AND DEFINITIONS

Global Value Chains: A phenomenon characterized by the division of production into activities and tasks performed in different nations.

International Joint Venture: Two or more enterprises based in different countries create a partnership with a separate legal entity.

Multinational Enterprise: An organization that conducts at least some of its business in countries other than those in which it is headquartered.

Pandemic: An infectious disease that spread across multiple nations rapidly.

Policymaker: A member of the legislature, a government department, or another body in charge of enacting new legislation

Practitioner: a person engaged in a skilled occupation, that is business management in this text.

Rigor-relevance Gap: The practical applicability of the knowledge produced with methodological and analytical validity.

Chapter 6
The Future of Mobility:
Key Areas That Play a Significant Role in Expatriates' Future Decisions

Judit Vegh
Eötvös Loránd University, Hungary

Joyce Jenkins
Expert Humans, Singapore

Marie-Therese Claes
Vienna University of Economics and Business, Austria

ABSTRACT

The globally mobile workforce of international professionals has been significantly impacted by the COVID-19 pandemic. Closed borders and entry restrictions for foreign residents have left many expatriates separated from partners and family members. Previously held assumptions about the ability to travel whenever needed have been severely challenged, thus leaving some questioning the attractiveness of living and working abroad. The expectations of mobility that individuals as well as organizations used to have are changed. The research aimed to assess the impact of factors like travel and other restrictions on the priorities of expatriates and on their willingness to consider future mobility, as well as how the disruption affected expatriates' concept of family. The research shows that organizations will have to examine if expatriation is a sustainable strategy. Both expatriates and organizations are more than ever subjected to local government regulations concerning the acceptance and conditions of life and travel for expatriates.

INTRODUCTION

The COVID-19 pandemic has brought previously unimaginable changes in people's lives and ways of working around the globe. As new variants and new waves continue to cause disruption and hardship, the world is also experiencing a period of social, racial, environmental and economic upheaval which looks

DOI: 10.4018/978-1-6684-3749-0.ch006

like it will continue to be felt for some time. This research concentrates on just one group of people: the globally mobile workforce of international professionals and their families - or expatriates - and on the particular challenges and complications which have affected them.

This group has been significantly impacted by the pandemic's effects on travel. Closed borders, canceled flights and the introduction of new visa, quarantine and entry restrictions for foreign residents have resulted in many expatriates being separated for long periods of time from partners, family members and friends and unable to return to the countries where they have homes and jobs. Previously held assumptions about the ability to travel to see relatives in case of emergency or whenever needed have been severely challenged at this time and for the foreseeable future, leaving some questioning the attractiveness of living and working abroad.

BACKGROUND

This chapter identifies the terms relevant to the study. It defines the globally mobile workforce of international professionals and their families and the different kinds of expatriates that participated in the study. It explores the changes in the concept of global mobility, as well as the requirements of the global talent pool of which expatriates are a part. It also briefly describes the background of the study, including the global pandemic.

Definition of Terms

Expatriates

Expatriates are people who live and work outside of their home country. This common definition of the expatriate can be discussed and questioned, because it offers many possible interpretations. In international management literature, the term 'expatriate' is used in reference to the people who are moved across borders to work, more particularly in multinational corporations (Berry & Bell, 2012). The reasons for expatriate employees are diverse, from career development for young potentials to control or implementation of changes in host countries' subsidiaries. Especially in career advancement, foreign experience is seen as an imperative. Even in education, there seems to be a "mobility imperative" for educators and students (Cairns, 2014, p. 46; Cairns et al., 2017).

Others undertake assignments abroad independently as self-initiated expatriates. Self-initiated expatriates usually relocate to a country of their choice for personal, cultural or development reasons, without a definite period in mind (Suutari & Brewster, 2000). In contrast, company-assigned expatriates represent the organization that sends them for a clearly defined assignment and time horizon.

Another category of expatriates are older people who retire to places with favorable characteristics such as climate or the cost of living (Balkir & Kirkulak, 2007, Gibler et al., 2009). Recently, a new trend in expatriation reflecting the changing global economy, seems to point to the use of home-grown expertise rather than relying on foreign experts to drive their economy (Groves & O'Connor, 2018), meaning that the hegemony of Western expatriates will be questioned (Farrer, 2010; Fechter & Walsh, 2010; Leonard, 2010). Even so, these local or regional employees are expected to have some international experience and global expertise. The sample of the study comprises expatriates from the different categories.

Global Mobility

One focus of research is the impact of the transformation and digitalization of expatriation in the adaptation of expatriation to the new normal (Bucher & Deller, 2021). However, according to the Ernst & Young survey of 500 board members and chief executive officers (CEOs) globally in 2019, only 20% of the executives surveyed believed their companies were prepared to respond to a large adverse risk (EY, 2020). Simultaneously, globalization seems to be slowing down in trade, capital, and FDI flows (IMF, 2020; WIR, 2020), and may possibly descend if the current trend towards a more nationalistic view over technology continues (Farrell & Newman, 2020; Garcia-Herrero, 2020; Luo, 2021).

The pandemic may have aggravated the trend of techno-nationalism and regionalization. Indeed, the trend of deglobalization, heightened regionalization and value chain configuration seem to point that way (Devinney & Hartwell, 2020; Enderwick & Buckley, 2020). The pandemic has placed additional strain on the globalization thesis, while nations and firms compete for leadership (Segal, 2020; Delios et al., 2021).

During the pandemic, mobility for work, leisure and study was severely impeded, and simultaneously, citizens of the host country have become less open and tolerant, as we also found in our survey. It can be declared that the us-versus-them mentality became stronger, which in turn leads to a lack of the intercultural, social support system that is needed for international business. Social isolation and working from home have further affected expatriates' integration into the local communities as well as their organizations, while most organizations want their assignees to acquire local cultural and business skills (Anderson & Kelliher, 2020; Bebenroth, 2022).

In addition, new assignments have not been able to start, and more companies are expecting decreases in the number of assignments. It remains to be seen if the pandemic will have an impact on the willingness to relocate. (ECA 2021; Milani & Dickmann, 2021; Deloitte, 2020). People experienced a different life working from home, and the challenges to manage professional and personal life became visible (Schieman et al., 2021; Mello & Tomei, 2021; AETNA, 2020). At the same time, organizations had to rethink the use of international assignments (Caligiuri et al., 2020). For many organizations, the pandemic meant more work and cost, as they had to ensure health coverage for their workers, stress management and in some repatriation to their own countries (Tripathy & Singh, 2021; Cooper, 2022).

Deloitte (2020) concludes that the pandemic is acting as a catalyst for change: organizations may reconsider the role of expatriation, and expatriates might need to be encouraged to relocate. In the months ahead, the emotional impact of the crisis may be seen with employees re-thinking their pre COVID-19 work pattern. There is the potential to see those who have been globally minded feel stronger ties to home and family, potentially considering the practicalities of the distance between them, perhaps looking for an assignment back home or a permanent transfer.

Even before the pandemic, a 2018 survey of FTSE 100 organizations (Santa Fe Relocations, 2018) showed that 61 percent said they were actively redesigning jobs around artificial intelligence, robotics and new business models. Organizations need to demonstrate the benefits of different types of assignments (Worbey, 2020). However, traditional physical mobility is unlikely to disappear, as past recessions have shown. Organizations will develop a balance between virtual assignments and the need to be physically present.

In his 2021 article on the "Change of Geography of Work", Choudhury summarizes the advantages of geographic mobility:

geographic mobility creates value by facilitating the transfer and recombination of knowledge, transfer of social capital, organizational norms, and financial capital, as well as by creating opportunities for individuals to develop skills, seek resources, and experience wage increases (p. 1).

International living and working experience is highly valued by organizations and human resource and talent recruiters as a predictor of ability to work effectively across cultures. Living abroad has been linked to increased creativity and problem-solving ability even when compared to the experience of traveling abroad. (Aytug et al., 2018; Maddux & Galinsky, 2009). Although new forms of workforce mobility are emerging and actively supported by a majority of employees as reported by BGRS (2021), physical mobility remains strong. As the context is changing, virtual mobility has become an important issue for organizations. Costs of time and money for quarantine and other safety measures are seen as a barrier to business trips and expatriation.

Global Talent

Today's world is one of rapid change, volatile economies, technical revolutions and increasing globalization. With more people living outside their 'countries of origin' than ever before, the world today is becoming increasingly global, and yet simultaneously increasingly divided. To succeed therefore, businesses and societies need more people who are able to bridge cultural divides and bring a global perspective. Organizations are seeking to find and develop talent and leaders with a global mindset/ cultural intelligence/ global competence (Grandin & Hedderich, 2009).

Businesses now can be 'born global' (Johanson & Vahlne, 2002) leading to almost instant global markets and customer bases even for the smallest of companies, which in the past would have taken years to develop internationally. With advances in technology, the internet, social media and artificial intelligence (AI), staff and workforces can be working virtually with global teams and clients around the world, without even leaving their home office. Whether you are a global nomad, grasping the opportunities presented by non-location specific work and of AI and technology to travel and work wherever you feel like spending some time, or are taking advantage of being able to work with the rest of the world from the comfort of your own front room, the chances are that you will be in communication and contact with people from all over the world on a regular basis. Most people in today's global workforce will probably be dealing with and leading people from other countries and cultures, whether that be colleagues, line managers, customers, suppliers or direct reports.

This creates both huge opportunities as well as great challenges for society, for communities, for business and organizations – as well as for the individuals themselves. On the one hand, these individuals are a potential talent pool as well as a new and expanding consumer market for businesses and organizations. On the other hand, to maximize this potential requires a range of cross-cultural and intercultural knowledge and skills along with a 'global mindset' (Hitt et al., 2007; Dorfman et al., 2012) to lead and facilitate effective work and communication.

Universities and schools offer 'year abroad' and other opportunities to seek international experience. Pre-COVID-19, young people crossed borders to broaden their horizons and increase their work prospects, becoming 'self-initiated expats'. Parents taking on international assignments often cite 'giving children international experience and the chance to learn a foreign language' as a key reason for choosing to live and work abroad (HSBC Global Expat Report, 2019).

At the same time, even before the global pandemic, there has been evidence of growing aversion to immigration in some communities and societies who feel threatened by the volume of incomers. At government levels nationalist and protectionist policies and political rhetoric, such as “Brexit” and “America First” have increased tensions and a rise in economic and political nationalism (Horak et al., 2019). Successive waves of COVID-19 have exacerbated this, with many countries closing their borders to foreign nationals and suspending immigration to protect jobs for their own citizens (BBC, 2020).

According to the United Nations (UN), the pandemic and the consequent economic slowdown has put nearly half of the global workforce at risk of job losses as governments struggle to balance the safe opening of their economies with managing the risks of containing the pandemic. (Marinov & Marinova, 2020). ‘Working from Home’ suddenly became the “new normal as many organizations and workers try to keep operating under the social distancing restrictions needed to stamp out the spread of the COVID-19 virus,” (Dockery & Bawa, 2020, p. 1) For knowledge workers, in particular this often led to “a radical shift from on-site to virtual collaboration,” (Waizenegger et al., 2020, p. 429).

For global professionals, and, often of necessity for expatriates who found themselves ‘locked out’ of the countries they were hired to work in, this presented opportunities to ‘work from anywhere’. Initially this concept was seen as a short-term quick-fix solution to the problem presented by COVID-19 lockdowns. However, as time goes on and the uncertainty of the ongoing pandemic continues, HR departments and global mobility professionals find themselves under pressure to implement the option for both existing and new hires. According to Olivier Meier of Mercer (Meier, 2021) some HR professionals dismissed it as a fad at the beginning of the pandemic but now realize that the debate is not going away and are trying to manage the expectations of ‘CEOs promising the option to work from anywhere and employees envisioning every possibility of anywhere.’

Intercultural competencies are therefore seen as increasingly vital for success in the global workplace. Around the world, organizations are under increasing pressure to reduce costs while simultaneously increasing their success and building up global leadership talent resources. More than that, the goal of many organizations when hiring and developing global talent is to go beyond simply ‘functioning effectively’ which is felt to imply a minimum level of requirement, simply avoiding cultural errors. Global success should be about “not only preventing calamities” Rather, the aim is; “the leveraging of cultural diversity to realize its potential in creativity, problem-solving and so on.” (Spencer-Oatey & Franklin, 2009, p. 204)

It is widely recognized that multicultural teams, when they work well together, outperform their equivalent monocultural teams (Adler, Brody & Osland, 2001). However, with cultural and communication style differences the potential to not work well together is higher than with monocultural teams and in such cases they could significantly underperform in comparison. The intercultural competence of the managers and team members is a big differentiator. (Hampden-Turner & Trompenaars, 2020).

Beechler and Javidan (2007) describe ‘a global mindset’ as a set of attributes that enhance a manager’s ability to influence and build trust with others who are different from them. According to Javidan (2013), global organizations require their managers to work with diverse groups of people, whereas societies typically develop their children into adults who are capable of working effectively with people who are like them. Javidan (2010) states that having a global mindset requires: ‘Intellectual capital: Global business savvy, cognitive complexity, cosmopolitan outlook; Psychological capital: Passion for diversity, quest for adventure, self-assurance; Social capital: Intercultural empathy, interpersonal impact, diplomacy’.

Various scholars suggest that a global mindset is a critical success factor for global managers (Levy et al., 2007) while both researchers and practitioners argue that managers who have a global-mindset are better equipped to deal with the complexity and volatility of today's global workplaces, with their 'transnational cultures'. (Levy et al., 2019). Earley and Peterson describe Cultural intelligence (CQ) as the "ability to gather, interpret, and act upon radically different cues to function effectively across cultural settings or in a multi-cultural situation,"(Earley & Peterson, 2004, p.105).

Earley and Ang identified three facets of cultural intelligence (CQ): comprising mental, motivational, and behavioral components focused specifically on resolving cross-cultural problems (Earley & Ang, 2003) while the current CQ model consists of four sets of capabilities; CQ Drive, CQ Knowledge, CQ Action and CQ Strategy, which are all aspects of the overall capability to function effectively in culturally diverse settings. (Ang et al., 2007).

Thomas and Inkson (2005, p. 5) refer to "the need for effective interactions with people from different cultures which is no longer limited to expatriates or jet-setting corporate troubleshooters. It has become a fundamental management skill involving what people term cultural intelligence." They describe a culturally intelligent person as someone who is skilled and flexible about understanding a culture, who learns more about it from interactions with it, and gradually reshapes their thinking to be 'more sympathetic' to the culture.

According to their definition, the culturally intelligent person draws on a breadth of experience and can make fine distinctions among subtly different behaviors that perfectly fit the situation. Cultural intelligence (CQ) has also been described as an 'elusive' 'chameleon' like quality (Earley & Peterson, 2004).

Global Pandemic

This global pandemic has changed the experience of work for most employees, forcing organizations globally to adapt to new ways of work, and to evaluate employee risk (Collings et al., 2021) and personal health and safety considerations associated with COVID-19 (Collings & Sheeran, 2020). The PwC Global Mobility Pulse Survey (2020) looked at the actions companies were taking in relation to their globally mobile workforce during the pandemic. They identified three main potential strategies, (1) keeping up to date with regulatory changes, (2) work on communications and planning and (3) understanding who their mobile employees are and where they are. The pandemic has added to the current geopolitical changes, advances in technology, communication, and global travel and organizational and demographic trends in the business population (Cascio & Aguinis, 2008) that have affected the way expatriates are managed and supported.

In any disaster or crisis, such as a pandemic, the importance of maintaining family and social cohesion is stressed, along with re-enforcement of support and self-help networks.

According to Choudhury (2021, p.18),"regulatory frictions entail legal limitations to mobility at the global, national, or local level, occupational/organizational frictions include occupation-specific and firm-specific limitations, personal frictions consist of individual, and family-level limitations, and economic/environmental frictions combine financial barriers with other macro-level effects."

This study identifies and illustrates the frictions that Choudhury mentions in his 2021 article. The legal limitations have become more complex and changing, the organizational financial risks and costs have increased, family issues have become prioritized, and the environmental friction due to the pandemic creates clear impediments to geographic mobility.

MAIN FOCUS OF THE CHAPTER

Method

Research Questions

The main objective of the current research was to explore the experiences of expatriates at the start and at different stages during the global disruption caused by the COVID-19 pandemic. The aim was to assess the impact of factors like travel and other restrictions on the motivation and priorities of expatriates and on their willingness to consider future mobility, as well as how the disruption affected expatriates' concepts of 'family', 'home' and 'belonging'. The research questions were formulated as follows:

1. What impact did travel restriction have on expatriates and how did they react?
2. Did the willingness for mobility change? If so, how?
3. Did the expatriates' meaning of family change? If so, how?
4. Did the priorities and motivation of the expatriates change? If so, how?

Research Design

Drawing on the nature of a pandemic, the research design has evolved over time. The intention was to follow up the experience of expatriates during a pandemic. This led the researchers to create a longitudinal research plan adapting to the current situation from time to time. The research was based on a mixed method which includes qualitative and quantitative approaches (Teddlie & Tashakkori, 2011). It follows a sequential explanatory research design, which is typically used to help to explain and interpret quantitative results by collecting and analyzing follow-up qualitative data (Creswell & Creswell, 2003, Creswell et al., 2011), where interviews are linked to the quantitative database with an identifier.

At the beginning of the data collection a snowball sampling as a non-probability sampling technique was applied. 'Snowball sampling consists of identifying respondents who are then used to refer researchers on to other respondents' (Atkinson & Flint, 2001, p.1.). This sampling method enabled the collection of large amounts of data from diverse samples. (Wilson & Dewaele, 2010).

At the start of the pandemic, the researchers sent out a questionnaire to expatriates in different parts of the world about their expectations before the pandemic struck, and their expectations immediately after. The first two questionnaires were created based on a literature review and the personal expatriate pandemic experience of the researchers. To establish content validity, two external experts on the topic were involved in the questionnaire design process. The five experts (researchers and external experts) live and work in four different countries and they all have different nationalities.

In the first two phases of the study researchers utilized a quantitative method using questionnaires which included some open-ended questions, while in the third phase of the data collection a qualitative method was applied conducting semi-structured interviews. The second questionnaire was sent out after four months and after more than one year interviews were conducted.

Research Group

The definition of expatriates that authors applied throughout the research was clearly defined to the participants as 'those who live 'abroad' (in a country other than your/passport or citizenship country)'. The study included self-initiated expats, as well as those who had been expatriated by their employers and spouses, partners, or adult family members. Participants had to be adults (over the age of 18). The first phase of the research intended to explore the immediate experience of expatriates, who at the beginning of the COVID-19 pandemic, lived and worked in a country other than their home or citizenship country.

The study group included 589 participants, from 55 countries with 48 nationalities. The next quantitative phase of the research consisted of a follow up questionnaire sent out to all the participants of the first phase, who had indicated their willingness to provide further information. Reaching the end of 2020 without a major change in the pandemic situation, the authors decided to follow up with the participants in a different manner.

For the final phase of the data collection, the study utilized a qualitative research method aiming to gather more elaborated data which can explore deeper the overall experience of expatriates during the first nine months of the pandemic as well as to examine their concept of the future.

Table 1. Distribution of demographic variables of expatriates

Demographic Variables (n=583)		F (%)
Gender	Male	29%
	Female	71%
Age in years	18-20	1.1%
	21-29	6.4%
	30-39	26.5%
	40-49	30.2%
	50-59	27.2%
	60 or older	8.6%
Reason for living abroad	Expatriated by company/organisation	25.1%
	Self-initiated expatriate (own choice to move abroad)	45%
	Accompanying spouse or partner of expatriate	28.9%
	Adult (over 18) child of expatriate	1%
Type of employment in the country	Full-time employee	48.51%
	Part-time employee	5.98%
	Self-employed, freelance or own business	19.54%
	Voluntary work	3.45%
	Student	3.45%
	Stay at home spouse/parent	19.08%
Total length of time lived abroad	Under a year	4.50%
	1-5 years	23.20%
	6-10 years	18.24%
	10 years or more	54.05%

Research Method

As the COVID-19 global pandemic situation remains ongoing, the authors aim to keep continuing the research. Thus, a descriptive statistical data analysis process has been chosen in order to leave space for further research phases and to allow for a final analysis of the process once the pandemic situation is deemed to have ended. During the research process in both the interpretation of the researchers and the conducting of interviews personal reflexivity is important. The researchers have a bias/biases in that they share the same transnational experience that the interviewees have, which affects their interpretation. At the same time, it also gives them a deeper view and understanding of the participants' experience.

As part of the qualitative method, semi structured interviews were conducted online with 20 participants who were willing to share their experience as an expatriate during the COVID-19 pandemic. For the qualitative data analysis process authors applied thematic analysis which is a useful method for examining the different perspectives of research participants, exploring similarities and differences, and identifying insights (Braun & Clarke, 2006, King, 2004). The interview transcripts were managed using Quirkos computer assisted qualitative data analysis software (CAQDAS).

Although for most research using thematic analysis, conducted with relatively homogenous individuals, 12 interviews should be a sufficient sample size (Ando et al. 2014; Guest et al., 2006) the authors decided to use all 20 interviews for the data analysis. Generating initial themes is based on the idea of a central organizing concept. (Braun & Clarke, 2013; Braun, Clarke & Rance, 2014). Thematic analysis is a useful method for examining the different perspectives of research participants, exploring similarities and differences, and identifying insights (Braun & Clarke, 2006; King, 2004). In the process of data analysis researchers followed an inductive approach.

Results

Throughout the longitudinal study responding to the research questions, the researchers followed the four key areas: (1) travel restrictions, (2) willingness for mobility, (3) family and (4) priorities and motivation during the data analysis process as well as in data presentation. These areas play a significant role in expatriates' decisions related to future mobility in the post-pandemic world and tend to be crucial and must be examined in future international business HR strategy. Following the research questions, data are presented in linear order. Each research question is answered first by the quantitative data that has been collected in the first two quantitative phases of the study, followed by the qualitative data presentation, collected in the last phase of the research.

Travel Restrictions

One of the consequences of globalization has been an increase in the number of international business trips. A business trip can be described as a dual experience of hassles and uplifts, losses and gains, all impacting the well-being of the travelers (Westman et al., 2009).

The COVID-19 global pandemic is not the first external condition that has created additional stress on international business. Previous research investigated the effect of external events such as the H1N1 influenza outbreak and the September 11 attacks that have made international travel more stressful (Herjanto, 2017), however in neither situation was travel completely restricted for such an extended period and on such a global scale.

International travel acts as an important tool. Besides its role for international business, in the case of global families, international travel also means the opportunity to stay in personal contact with their extended family. Until the beginning of the pandemic, the opportunity to travel freely was taken for granted. The restriction of international travel was a very new experience for expatriates. Despite the general and logistical difficulties associated with international travel even before the pandemic, the assumption of the possibility of travel if needed had always been there for expatriates. Thus, travel restrictions to the extent brought about by the pandemic had never been experienced before (with the possible exception of World War II.).

Restriction of travels was one of the first and most significant impacts of the pandemic on global professionals and their families. Based on the travel limitations, the future is considered to be more challenging, thus requiring expatriates to be more cautious and reserved.

What Impact Did Travel Restriction Have on Expatriates During the Pandemic and How Did They React?

The significance of international travel to those who live, and work abroad is about much more than business trips or holiday tourism. Travel restrictions on personal contacts and family members (including children who are studying in their 'home' or other countries outside the country of residence) also had a big impact on those surveyed.

Based on the quantitative results of the study, data shows that international travel (for work, leisure and personal visits) was very or completely impacted for most participants in the survey (92%). Like most of the world, the pandemic grounded most survey participants, reporting zero international trips during the first wave of the pandemic in 2020. This was a stark contrast to their travel habits before the COVID-19 situation, where 73% of those surveyed traveled internationally for work at least 1-2 times per year, with 36% traveling more than six times per year. 74% of those surveyed indicated that before the COVID-19 situation they traveled at least 1-2 times per year for personal/family visits.

A total of 23% indicated they traveled internationally for family visits 3-5 times per year, 6% traveled 6-10 times per year and 3% more than 10 times per year for family visits alone. With 'seeing new places' and 'new experiences' being key attractions for those choosing to work abroad, survey participants also reported high levels of frequent travel for tourism/leisure prior to the COVID-19 situation, with 28% reporting international travel 1-2 times per year, 40% reporting 3-5 times per year, 19% reporting 6-10 times per year and 9% reporting more than 10 times per year.

Since COVID-19, between March and June 2020, a total of 99% of those surveyed said their travel plans had been impacted, with most having made no international trips during that period. Most also predicted that their travel from June to August 2020 would be very (34%) or completely (52%) impacted, with 49% predicting that even beyond September, travel would be very (49%) or completely (13%) impacted. Others indicated that even when travel restrictions eased, they would think twice about

Hopping on a plane for a business meeting or discussion which could just as easily be conducted on Zoom.

However, the significance of international travel to those who live and work abroad is about much more than business trips or holiday tourism. As one survey respondent said:

As an expat, maintaining relationships depends on international travel.

Limitation of travels indicated a change in expatriates‘ plans, as they constantly questioned their opportunities for traveling.

God forbid, if anything happens to our family, being able to jump on a plane tomorrow and see them tomorrow.

The fact that again, they can't jump in a plane here, or we can't jump on a plane to go back there.

As a result of the qualitative phase of the study, focusing on the impact of travel restrictions, three themes were generated. The first theme was the desire to travel again. In their narratives participants constantly emphasized their high hopes for being able to travel again

And hopefully, we might be able to do our own travel, personal travel soon.

Life won't go back to being fully normal, but at least to have some, some elements of that, like being able to travel.

Being able to jump on a plane tomorrow and see them tomorrow.

The second theme was the redefinition of travel. Exploring the extended meaning of travel and its implication was a recurring theme as well.

Well, the whole concept of living abroad, I guess, is based on the fact that you're able to travel. And if you can't travel, then you have to start questioning, is it possible to live abroad?

So that international lifestyle was something that we had both just taken for granted. I think once the pandemic hit, that's where things became interesting, because we suddenly realized that, you know, getting on a plane and going to visit relatives in the way that we had done before was no longer possible.

It's really strange, not being able to hop on a plane and go to my home country.

Getting stuck outside of the country not being able to go where we want to not knowing what's going to happen next. Nobody to blame for a lot of that, but no control has been very challenging.

The third theme of the travel restriction was assumptions of the future. In many cases, research participants stepped out from their subjective experience and assumed a future concept based on changes.

In the markets, given the cost and difficulties traveling these days, they will see how they can manage their global operations in a different fashion.

I mean, I think the ban on travel or the inability to travel as an expat, that's one of the benefits is that we, we get on a plane and we go places, and part of why, you know, we don't mind living in Singapore is that we can travel a lot from here, because and when we get tired a lot, whether we can go somewhere cool.

Do it but when that opportunity is taken away, it certainly does make you wonder quite a lot about what the benefits are, because Singapore itself is very, very small.

Willingness for Mobility

The willingness for future global mobility is strongly related to the travel restrictions. This second theme of the research reflects on the change caused by these restrictions.

Did the Willingness for Mobility Change? If So, How?

Despite the raft of difficulties experienced by many who took part in the first questionnaire at the beginning of the pandemic, the majority of respondents (74%) indicated that they were 'likely' or 'very likely' to continue living and working abroad or to go abroad again to live and work.

Some were sanguine and saw the COVID-19 situation as 'just another challenge' of living abroad. For others, living abroad has become a way of life or they are settled in the countries they are living in. The research indicated that the borderless, international lifestyle which many global professionals and their families have taken for granted over past decades has been drastically affected by the COVID-19 pandemic.

Over 75% of those surveyed indicated that the situation had impacted their attitude to living and working abroad, with 20% indicating it had 'very impacted' and 6% indicating it had 'completely impacted' their attitude. International travel (for work, leisure and family visits) was very or completely impacted for most participants in the survey (92%). Like most of the world, since COVID-19, from March to the end of June 2020, most survey participants were grounded, reporting zero international trips during this time.

As a result of the qualitative phase of the study, the first theme connected to the willingness for mobility was 'towards more local direction'. A different way of looking at the concept of global has been described as moving towards a less diverse, less global and more local direction.

It will make it more difficult to find people that are willing to freely move about on a global basis and that's before we get to the discrimination issues.

I think the understanding, the respect that people pay to those that are different by nationality, age, gender, sexual orientation, religion, political beliefs, I think that will also suffer going forward.

In a cross cultural context.... I worry about the world not being as diverse spread across....the pendulum swinging back to so I don't know how many hundreds... have returned home, and we used to be quite spread around the world, and I'm going so what's that mean for our general global reach as a country?

I worry about the tensions between us and them in countries when countries' governments are clearly looking after their national citizens, and what that's doing for the broader global fabric of the world, and longer term relationships across countries and nationalities.

I really get worried for you know, the broader collective, and a lot of the cross cultural tapestry of the web and networks and people.

So I think at some point that the mobility is going to return, maybe not in the same way as it was before in terms of what it looks like. But I think it is going to, there is going to be a demand for that.

The second generated theme was ambiguity. Besides uncertainty there was also a wide range of ambiguity expressed towards expatriate life and as a concept referring to a potential end of this type of transnational life.

So there's no mopping up after the crisis, because we're still navigating. And I don't think we know the depth of the tolls yet. So I think the importance of good people around and putting people into personal and colleagues, making sure you've got that in use is critical.

I see an even greater reluctance of our families to relocate than I saw in the past, taking children out of school. If you have children at that age, it has always been traumatic, and it's even more of a risk.

Family

Throughout the entire research, the theme of family was a continuously recurring and strongly determining topic. The possibility of being able to visit the family whenever is needed or planned has a key role to play in all aspects of global mobility. It is an interesting approach to what culturally different definitions of the nuclear family might be applied to an expatriate family. Perhaps it is more appropriate to talk about a conceptual unit of "household" than a nuclear family, as the definition of the family can be interpreted differently from a cultural point of view.

The definition of a household stated by Baldassar et al. (2016) is a group of people who are in the same place of residence and participate collectively and cooperatively in the basic tasks of reproduction and consumption. McNulty (2014, p. 5) defined expatriate family as "married, de-facto, live-in, or long-term partners of the opposite or same sex, with or without children, with family members that reside in one or many locations; and legally separated or divorced (single) adults with children, with family members that reside in one or many locations."

For expatriate families, there are constant changes in family circumstances which can generate a range of choices in their family life in general. This could be the case, for example, when a child goes to university / college in another country or the family is expanding. Even the long-term presence of parents could lead to permanent change. These changes already require continuous adaptation from expatriate families.

Expatriate family adjustment indicates that career decisions of expatriate workers are influenced by their family and understanding the challenges and adjustment processes of family members is crucial (McNulty & Selmer, 2017). Long-distance family support is crucial during an assignment (Richardson, 2006), and electronic communication allows family members to stay connected with their extended family and friends (Rosenbusch & Cseh, 2012).

Did the Meaning of Family Change for Expatriates? If So, How?

After the onset of the pandemic, an extra burden was placed on expatriate families. Based on the research results, it seems that this notion of family has changed and expanded. The extended family came to the fore, and the possibility of simply being together physically with the extended family members, gained an extra importance which has never been seen before. The earlier forms of connections such as electronic communication, were no longer enough.

The current research findings suggest that in future it won't be sufficient to consider only nuclear families in global mobility decisions, but the ability for expanded family relationships will have a significant role hereafter in successful global employment.

During the pandemic thousands of international professionals around the world have been separated for extended periods-sometimes months - from their spouses, partners, and children. Many have lost their jobs and livelihoods along with their rights of residence in the countries where they work and have set up home.

One of the first decisions expats had to make was whether they would stay or go back to their home country. Not an easy decision, as work, children, pets and the concept of 'home' all had to be taken into consideration. According to the quantitative phase of the research, as borders started to close and flights were grounded in response to the COVID-19 pandemic, the majority (over 75%) of those surveyed stayed in the country in which they were living and working. This is despite the fact that nearly 30% of the respondents found themselves separated from partners or immediate family members, some for several months when borders closed and flights stopped.

At the beginning of summer in 2020, as border and travel restrictions eased around the world, reports indicated there were still tens of thousands of foreign residents waiting to get government permission to enter the countries they consider home and where they could be reunited with their family members. For many, this was an extremely stressful experience with a profound impact on their wellbeing and finances. Some respondents have given birth during this period without the presence or support of their partners and have newborns who have not yet been able to see their fathers. Numerous social-media groups with thousands of members world-wide were set up and provide mutual support and advice for those separated in this situation.

Some saw the advantages of being unable to travel especially if they were able to continue working from home.

Unable to travel for my job, which is good for family life.

While I love traveling, it was also okay to have a break from the logistics of constant travel.

I always stayed abroad on condition that I could jump on a plane in case I needed to attend to urgent family matters. Being unable to do this has made me reconsider the net benefit of staying overseas.'

Travel restrictions on personal contacts and family members (including children who are studying in their 'home' or other countries outside the country of residence) also had a big impact on those surveyed. Some reported that their children could not come 'home' when their educational institutions closed down because of COVID-19 and that it was difficult for them to find somewhere to go. Those whose children did make it 'home' before borders closed and flights were grounded were concerned about what to do when their visas expired, as this respondent commented:

My oldest child does not have a residence permit, so can only stay 90 days, then an extension of 20 days. Not sure what to do next.

Drawing on the qualitative research phase, the first theme of the family concept was choosing a location which is safe and easily reachable by family and close friends. Priority towards family appeared in the process of planning and choosing future locations, where being safe and being easy to visit by family members was a crucial point.

When that opportunity is taken away, it certainly does make you wonder quite a lot about what the benefits are.

I would say this uncertainty about the possibility to travel that's definitely the most difficult because it gives me uncertainty about the possibility to meet my family.

So that's my biggest preoccupation, my biggest. It's the capacity of giving myself and my children quality time with their grandparents… and often enough.

The second theme is the separation. It also refers to moments that are not present or included when expected or supposed to be, such as constantly missing family, social life as well as face to face meetings.

Because expats, maybe I'm wrong, but I feel like expats travel more than local people do, right? Because we've got to visit family and things like that. But because, I think, as an expat, we don't just travel for tourism, we travel for love, and family, things like that, right?

Missing of course going to the office and seeing the people in real.

I miss the traveling and the excitement and the adrenaline of traveling.

I'm missing that whole fabric of the social life and the trips, so people who'd visit me, you'd spend a day with them, and that's rich, as they're passing through, or you, you go back to your home country, and you spend a couple of days with a really good girlfriend, and, you know, that's not happening.

I think it's also kind of stressful for us, because we're so far away, and we don't know when they will be able to see their grandkids.

You can't bring the kids in for Christmas. And obviously you can't bring them back. I'm not even allowed back even if I wanted to at the moment now.

Sense of being separated from their loved ones and not being able to plan in the near future were mentioned many times throughout the research.

I think it's also kind of stressful for us, because we're so far away, and we don't know when they will be able to see their grandkids.

I have a partner who lives overseas. So I haven't seen him for nine and a half months now. And so the fact that the Singapore government controls, if I leave, they control whether I can come back or not. And that's very, very difficult.

The third theme is the stress and worries caused by missing family connections. Participants consistently experienced stressful, emotionally burdensome situations. Being away from families and constant restrictions and uncertainty brought different worries into the expatriates‘ life. They also mentioned potential changes related to families.

Well here in the pandemic, my husband and I don't see each other. It has been quite stressful in a bizarre and wonderful way.

I got to the point where I'm a little bit angry about the way that my family life has ended.

They also emphasized the hardship of physical distance from their family and friends.

But it's not the same thing and the physical separation from your immediate family.

The physical separation from people that you grew up with in the organization where I would have my pre formal meeting with the board member in a very casual atmosphere with a cup of coffee.

I think that's going to be even more difficult and the many empirical evidence that you have of the hardship of family separation of taking people out of school, losing a school year, etc.

So again, I'm feeling that sense of detachment because my experience is different from what my closest loved ones are experiencing.

I think it was more, it was, while we were in Mexico, I think it was more a case of us providing support for family back home. It was more about us reassuring them that we were okay. So that was one less thing for them to worry about.

Because my father died. My mother is on her own. And I've been putting off, you know, trying to get there -but while I've been trying to get back there, I'm also concerned about not being able to come back here.

And this is kind of how we've expected our lives to be, you know, we live far away from our families. But if something goes wrong, we can, at relatively short notice, get on a plane and go to them.

So we're more concerned about our relatives and parents especially because, you know, they're in a more vulnerable age group. And of course, we're far away and we cannot see them.

Priorities and Motivation

Ultimately all the previously mentioned key areas; the travel restrictions, the willingness for future mobility and the importance of the family led to changes in expatriates' priorities and motivation. These changes may determine the future decision making process of global professionals and their families.

Did the Priorities and Motivation of the Expatriates Change? If So, How?

As shown in the research, before the COVID-19 situation, the top motivation factors for living and working abroad were: 'seeing the world (58%) 'new skills and experiences' (57%) and 'career development' and 'new opportunities' (48%). Only 25% chose 'family reasons' and 19% 'health, safety and security'.

After the arrival of COVID-19 'health, safety and security' has become the top priority with 37% reporting it as 'very important' slightly above 'financial reasons' while 'family reasons' was rated 'very important' by 32%. 'Career development', 'new skills and experiences', 'seeing the world' and 'new opportunities for self' were still rated as 'very important' by 34-35% of participants.

In the second phase of the research the biggest impact they reported on their life was being unable to leave their country of residence (42%) followed by quarantine (35%), income reduction or loss (33%), disruption of children's education and separation from immediate family/household member/s for long period (both 30%). Participants reported the impact on international travels as one of the highest at over 70%. The COVID-19 impact on their life was labeled as mostly negative at over 50%.

However, when asked. 'Given the ongoing COVID-19 situation and other global disruption, how valuable do you think living and working abroad is?' over 82% indicated they thought it was valuable, very valuable or extremely valuable for themselves and their families. While over 90% indicated they felt that it was valuable, very valuable or extremely valuable in general, in terms of having a global workforce. Reasons given for this included the following:

Diversity of ideas and inputs.

We have to keep building relationships.

So you can see different perspectives. How else can you think global, act local?

A global perspective is an adaptive and necessary one. The pandemic has shown we are a global community, but it has increased xenophobia, so travel and global community is more important than ever now.

Did the priorities of the expatriates change? At the outset of the pandemic, there was a shift in motivation and priorities for expatriation. Before the COVID-19 situation, the top motivation factors were: 'seeing the world', 'new skills and experiences' and 'career development' and 'new opportunities'. After the arrival of COVID-19 'health, safety and security', 'financial reasons' and 'family reasons' have become the top priorities though 'career development', 'new skills and experiences' and 'seeing the world' and 'new opportunities for self' were still rated as 'very important'.

They also reported that they experienced a high level of impact on their work life – with the effects including job losses, salary cuts and working from home. For those who lost their jobs during the pandemic, many found they also lost their right to live in their country of residence.

The research reveals that over time priorities have changed. If before the pandemic a great amount of importance was given to the job, career, position or location, the priorities immediately shifted to two different aspects of family. On the one hand, family life at home changed as much as it did for everyone during the pandemic: working from home changed the family structure, what with spending more time together, home-schooling children and facilities for example. On the other hand, expatriates had to devise ways of connecting with their extended family, in their "home countries" or elsewhere in different ways, as traveling had become impossible. For some families it meant being separated from parents or children, not being able to be present for birth, sickness, or death.

In the third phase of the research COVID-19 has also shown a big impact on the future priorities of expatriates. Previous leading vocational priorities became secondary motivation and family emerged in the character of a pivotal motivation factor as the first theme.

I think that there will still be a few premium locations where people will be willing to relocate to with their families, but otherwise, it will become progressively more difficult.

It's most probably changed what's important in considering how and when and where I do it.

But it's not, it's not the same, you can't get the physical touch. And I think it's important for both the kids and the grandparents to see each other because of that growing and changing.

No, I think we will have more individuals, male and female, parachuted into more short term jobs for perhaps two years, one year and two years for project work rather than long term expected assignments.

It's not as exciting anymore. I don't want to be here. It's just driven home the point that I want to be back in my home country now. I don't want to be here anymore.

Reframing things has been really very much what this year for me has been about what is family? What is home? What is travel?

The second theme was their post-pandemic desire for social life and close connections (family and friends). Participants expressed their desire to be able to visit children, family, and friends and simply to resume everything that has been interrupted. They expressed their wish for their familiar, joyful social life.

I was looking for things like choirs, I was looking for music groups, I was looking for dance classes, because I used to dance a lot. And those kinds of things, I'm really itching to get back into, not only because they are activities that I enjoy, but because I want that social connection.

So there's light at the end of the tunnel, and it is getting easier. Thank goodness.

We tell one another that we need to meet in person and drink a glass of wine and do some food, walk or take a walk in the Georgian mountains, which are beautiful. And we sort of keep pushing that forward.

I think that hopefully on the other side of COVID, we can return to more personal interactions.

I anticipate that once things are back under control, there'll be a lot of pent up desire, so to speak, for people to go out and experience even more of the world than perhaps they had thought that they wanted to do before.

DISCUSSION

An epidemic makes a useful lens through which fundamental patterns of social value and institutional practice can be examined. Social structural and attitudinal factors create patterns of social response to disease constructed by a particular society. (Rosenberg, 1992). The case of expatriate society during the COVID-19 pandemic is no different. Exploring the special patterns of response can support better responses at individual, family. and institutional levels in a post-pandemic world.

It appears from this survey that the global pandemic has had a huge impact on expatriates. The travel restrictions created deep distress, influencing their priorities and motivation. Although the willingness to be mobile in the future remains strong, they will be looking for more local postings. Certainly the strongest changes can be seen in priorities and motivation. The concept of family seems to move from the nuclear family to the extended family: not being able to join family members in case of illness or decease was traumatic and being separated from close family members for an unknown period of time was equally difficult. But international businesspeople also discovered the ease with which one can move to online communication and the comfort this brings. Motivation to relocate has also changed: career and international experience are still important, but trumped by concerns for health, safety and security.

With the disruption of the ongoing pandemic situation looking set to continue for some time, along with the discovery by many individuals and organizations of the benefits and possibilities offered by online arrangements, the prospect of international remote working and virtual assignments continues. Another factor to consider is how multinational enterprises (MNEs) are changing and the concept of the global factory; a structure through which multinational enterprises aim to boost their global value creation (GVQ) by integrating their global strategies through a combination of innovation, distribution and production of both goods and services.

Although there are compliance issues which make international remote working difficult to implement, solutions such as combining remote and onsite working (hybrid working), redefining and even splitting jobs are being explored. Organizations are looking at versions of offshoring and outsourcing as possible solutions to the compliance issues they face in engaging global professionals to work remotely in locations which, because of border or other restrictions they cannot physically move to.

One solution is working with an Employer of Record (EOR). EORs serve as the legal employer and ensure compliance with local employment laws and other regulations, enabling companies to hire anywhere in the world. Unsurprisingly, their business has boomed during the COVID-19 pandemic. While it is possible to overcome the legal, regulatory and compliance constraints of remote international working and virtual teams, it is more difficult and

Something every business leader with global ambition should prioritize,' according to Charles Ferguson, GM for Asia-Pacific of one EOR, *'understanding the challenges and opportunities of building teams across rich and varied cultures.' (Modgil, 2021)*

Two streams of research which attempt to address these societal challenges and the challenges faced by global businesses are: global mindset (Beechler & Javidan, 2007; Hitt et al., 2007; Javidan et al., 2010) and cultural intelligence (Livermore, 2011; Earley & Peterson, 2004; Ang et al., 2007) both figuring prominently within research in the international business and management fields. (Cohen, 2010; Andresen & Bergdolt, 2017). According to management and social-science literature, one of the most pressing issues of the 21st Century is the need to "hire, develop and retain 'borderless leaders' who can function effectively in complex global environments and manage global business teams" (Cumberland et al., 2016 p.302)

The future of mobility will be influenced by these frictions. The expectations of mobility that individuals as well as organizations used to have are changed. This study shows that ultimately organizations will have to examine if expatriation is a sustainable strategy, given the financial risks and costs of for instance quarantine, travel and test expenses, as well as the changing trend in globalization. Both expatriates and organizations are more than ever subjected to local government regulations concerning the acceptance and conditions of life and travel for expatriates.

The pandemic changed the future of work, but equally so the future of mobility. In his article on the future of work, Kropp (2021) mentions that the pandemic has enabled managers to become aware of the personal and professional challenges and struggles of their employees. He asserts that in the future employers will give their employees more support in their personal lives, for example their mental health. He also states that the rate of disruption will potentially accelerate.

To overcome the barriers, organizations will consider flexible work arrangements in location and in time. This will no doubt support mobile workers and alleviate some of the friction mentioned earlier, but the questions remain as to the impact of these work arrangements on the values widely attributed to geographical mobility for individuals and organizations in the international business world.

SOLUTIONS AND RECOMMENDATIONS

What is a new norm for expatriates, for global mobility? Can we define a clear direction based on the current experience? 'None of us are safe, until all of us are safe' said UN Secretary-General Antonio Guterres (UN News, 2020). The COVID-19 pandemic has highlighted the interconnectedness of the world and the need for global collaboration across borders. Successive waves and new variants of COVID-19 show that the outlook is still uncertain, with restrictions to cross-border movement likely to continue impacting the global workforce for the foreseeable future. New models for global talent management are emerging and there have been innovations and technology which have facilitated continuity of virtual work.

However, according to this research, the biggest challenge facing expatriates and skilled global professionals is not directly work-related but is the impact of border closures and mobility restrictions on families and relations. Ensuring that individuals will not be separated indefinitely or long-term from their immediate and extended family members is the key concern for the majority of participants taking part in the research.

Why does this matter? Resolving the current disruption and dealing with the looming economic and environmental crises will require the collaboration across borders of the world's best talent. At the same time, maximizing the potential of the complex and volatile global marketplace of the 21st Century also requires a range of international skills, a global perspective and intercultural competence, along with a 'global mindset' to lead and facilitate effective work and communication. The development of these skills and characteristics is shown to be enhanced by 'living and working abroad' and is one of the key reasons that individuals choose and HR departments encourage international assignments.

So what happens now? With the disruption of the ongoing pandemic situation looking set to continue for some time, along with the discovery by many individuals and organizations of the benefits and possibilities offered by such arrangements, the prospect of international remote working and virtual assignments continues. (Meier & Traber, 2021) Solutions such as combining remote and onsite working (hybrid working), redefining and even splitting jobs are being explored (Alexander et al., 2021; Jesuthasan et al., 2021)

CONCLUSION

Organizations are considering versions of offshoring and outsourcing as possible solutions to the compliance issues they face in engaging global professionals to work remotely in locations which, because of border or other restrictions they cannot physically move to (see ILO, 2020). In light of the current uncertain situation, even as vaccines are rolled out, borders begin to reopen and the world takes cautious steps towards an uncertain future that is shaped around living with the pandemic, it is likely that the four key areas (1) travel restrictions, (2) willingness for mobility, (3) family and (4) priorities and motivation will continue to play a significant role in expatriates' decisions related to future mobility in the post-pandemic world and must be examined in future international business HR strategy.

REFERENCES

Adler, N. J., Brody, L. W., & Osland, J. S. (2001). Going beyond twentieth century leadership: A CEO develops his company's global competitiveness. *Cross Cultural Management, 8*(3/4), 11–34. doi:10.1108/13527600110797263

AETNA. (2020). Expat Family Wellness Survey. *AETNA*. https://www.aetnainternational.com/en/about-us/explore/living-abroad/expatriate-life/expat-family-wellness-survey-2020.html

Alexander, A., Mysore, M., Cracknell, R., De Smet, A., Langstaff, A., & Ravid, D. (2021). What executives are saying about the future of hybrid work. *McKinsey*. https://www.mckinsey.com/business-functions/organization/our-insights/what-executives-are-saying-about-the-future-of-hybrid- work

Anderson, D., & Kelliher, C. (2020). Enforced remote working and the work-life interface during lockdown. *Gender in Management, 35*(7), 677–683. doi:10.1108/GM-07-2020-0224

Andresen, M., & Bergdolt, F. (2017). A systematic literature review on the definitions of global mindset and cultural intelligence–merging two different research streams. *International Journal of Human Resource Management, 28*(1), 170–195. doi:10.1080/09585192.2016.1243568

Ang, S., Van Dyne, L., Koh, C., Ng, K. Y., Templer, K. J., Tay, C., & Chandrasekar, N. A. (2007). Cultural intelligence: Its measurement and effects on cultural judgment and decision making, cultural adaptation and task performance. *Management and Organization Review, 3*(3), 335–371. doi:10.1111/j.1740-8784.2007.00082.x

Atkinson, R., & Flint, J. (2001). Accessing hidden and hard-to-reach populations: Snowball research strategies. *Social Research Update, 33*(1), 1–4. doi:10.4135/9780857020024.n94

Aytug, Z. G., Kern, M. C., & Dilchert, S. (2018). Multicultural experience: Development and validation of a multidimensional scale. *International Journal of Intercultural Relations, 65*, 1–16. doi:10.1016/j.ijintrel.2018.04.004

Baldassar, L. (2016). De-demonizing distance in mobile family lives: Co-presence, care circulation and polymedia as vibrant matter. *Global Networks*, *16*(2), 145–163. doi:10.1111/glob.12109

Balkir, C., & Kirkulak, B. (2007). Turkey as a new destination for retirement migration. *International migration, multi-local livelihoods and human security: perspectives from Europe, Asia and Africa.* doi:10.4337/9781849802017.00015

BBC. (2020). Coronavirus: Immigration to US to be suspended amid pandemic, Trump says. 21 April. *BBC.* .https://www.bbc.com/news/world-us-canada-52363852

Bebenroth, R. (2022). *Adjustment of Expatriates' Work Practices during the Covid-19 Pandemic.* Discussion paper Series. Research Institute for Economics & Business Administration (RIEB)

Beechler. S., & Javidan, M. (2007). Leading with a global mindset. In The global mindset. Emerald Group Publishing Limited. doi:10.10161571-5027(07)19006-9

Berry, D. P., & Bell, M. P. (2012). 'Expatriates': Gender, race and class distinctions in international management. *Gender, Work and Organization*, *19*(1), 10–28. doi:10.1111/j.1468-0432.2011.00577.x

BGRS. (2021) Virtual mobility. Evolving mobility for the future of work. *BGRS.* https://www.bgrs.com/tmts_article/virtual-mobility-evolving-mobility-for-the-future-of-work/

BGRS. (2021) Growth opportunity for employee mobility in the next normal. *BGRS.* https://www.bgrs.com/tmts_article/growth-opportunity-for-employee-mobility-in-the-next-normal/

Braun, V., & Clarke, V. (2006). Using thematic analysis in psychology. *Qualitative Research in Psychology*, *3*(2), 77–101. doi:10.1191/1478088706qp063oa

Bucher, J., & Deller, J. (2021). *Digital Technologies and Expatriation.* A systematic literature review. *Academy of Management Proceedings*, (1), 11027

Cairns, D. (2014). Becoming Mobile. In Youth Transitions, International Student Mobility and Spatial Reflexivity (pp. 41-93). London: Palgrave Macmillan. doi:10.1057/9781137388513_3

Cairns, D., Cuzzocrea, V., Briggs, D., & Veloso, L. (2017). *The consequences of mobility: Reflexivity, social inequality and the reproduction of precariousness in highly qualified migration.* Springer., doi:10.1007/978-3-319-46741-2

Caligiuri, P., De Cieri, H., Minbaeva, D., Verbeke, A., & Zimmermann, A. (2020). International HRM insights for navigating the COVID-19 pandemic: Implications for future research and practice. *Journal of International Business Studies*, *51*(5), 697–713. doi:10.105741267-020-00335-9 PMID:32836500

Cascio, W. F., & Aguinis, H. (2008). 3 Staffing Twenty-first-century Organizations. *The Academy of Management Annals*, *2*(1), 133–165. doi:10.5465/19416520802211461

Choudhury, P. (2021). Geographic Mobility, Immobility, and Geographic Flexibility–A Review and Agenda for Research on the Changing Geography of Work. *Academy of Management Annals*, (ja). https://journals.aom.org/doi/pdf/10.5465/annals.2020.0242?casa_token=BFsejbgQCzgAAAAA:BmKRU-N8Ep9uItdgqem0bN8eMj-bBZ1hTGvr0Wb01s4ChPoGAC1TWkPBH7Iuh_0OgCiq7Ku_doM

Cohen, W. M. (2010). Fifty years of empirical studies of innovative activity and performance. Handbook of the Economics of Innovation, 1, 129-213. doi:10.10160169-7218(10)01004-x

Collings, D. G., McMackin, J., Nyberg, A. J., & Wright, P. M. (2021). Strategic human resource management and COVID-19: Emerging challenges and research opportunities. *Journal of Management Studies, 58*(5), 1378–1382. doi:10.1111/joms.12695

Collings, D. G., & Sheeran, R. (2020). Research insights: Global mobility in a post-covid world1. *Irish Journal of Management, 39*(2), 77–84. doi:10.2478/ijm-2020-0002

Cooper, W. (2022). COVID-19 & Mental Health For Expats Research. *William Russell.* https://www.william-russell.com/blog/how-has-covid-affected-mental-health-awareness-for-expats-research/

Cumberland, D. M., Herd, A., Alagaraja, M., & Kerrick, S. A. (2016). Assessment and development of global leadership competencies in the workplace: A review of literature. *Advances in Developing Human Resources, 18*(3), 301–317. doi:10.1177/1523422316645883

Delios, A., Perchtold, G., & Capri, A. (2021). Cohesion, COVID-19 and contemporary challenges to globalization. (2021). *Journal of World Business, 56*(3), 101197. doi:10.1016/j.jwb.2021.101197

Deloitte. (2020). *Understanding the COVID-19 impact for Global Mobility*. Turning the dial towards recovery https://www2.deloitte.com/content/dam/Deloitte/uk/Documents/energy-resources/deloitte-uk-er-covid-19-global-mobility.pdf

Devinney, T. M., & Hartwell, C. A. (2020). Varieties of populism. *Global Strategy Journal, 10*(1), 32–66. doi:10.1002/gsj.1373

Dickmann, M., & Oleškevičiūtė, E. (August 2021). Do expatriates want this new normal? Covid, flexible work and embeddedness. *GLOMO.* https://www.relocatemagazine.com/articles/do-expatriates-want-this-new-normal-covid-flexible-work-and-embeddedness-health-wellbeing-dickmann-olekeviit-0821

Dockery, M., & Bawa, S. (2020). Working from Home in the COVID-19 Lockdown. Bentley: Bankwest Curtin Economics Centre.

Dorfman, P., Javidan, M., Hanges, P., Dastmalchian, A., & House, R. (2012). GLOBE: A twenty year journey into the intriguing world of culture and leadership. *Journal of World Business, 47*(4), 504–518. doi:10.1016/j.jwb.2012.01.004

Earley, P. C., & Ang, S. (2003). *Cultural intelligence: Individual interactions across cultures.*

Earley, P. C., & Peterson, R. S. (2004). The elusive cultural chameleon: Cultural intelligence as a new approach to intercultural training for the global manager. *Academy of Management Learning & Education, 3*(1), 100–115. doi:10.5465/amle.2004.12436826

ECA. (2020). How Covid-19 has affected Global Mobility. Retrieved on October 4, 2021, from: https://www.forum-expat-management.com/posts/how-covid-19-has-affected-global-mobility

Enderwick, P., & Buckley, P. J. (2020). Rising regionalization: will the post-COVID-19 world see a retreat from globalization? *Transnational Corporations Journal, 27*(2).

EY. (2020). Global board risk survey, EY. https://www.ey.com/en_us/news/2020/04/nearly-80-percent-of-board-members-felt-unprepared-for-a-major-risk-event-like-covid-19-ey-survey (April 20, 2020)

Farrell, H., & Newman, A. L. (2020). *Chained to globalization*: Why it's too late to decouple. *Foreign Affairs, 99*, 70–80.

Farrer, J. (2010). New Shanghailanders or New Shanghainese? Narratives of emplacement of Western expatriate settlers in shanghai. *Journal of Ethnic and Migration Studies, 36*(8), 1211–1228. doi:10.1080/13691831003687675

Fechter, A. M., & Walsh, K. (2010). Examining 'expatriate' continuities: Postcolonial approaches to mobile professionals. *Journal of Ethnic and Migration Studies, 36*(8), 1197–1210. doi:10.1080/13691831003687667

Fee, A., McGrath-Champ, S., & Liu, H. (2013). Human resources and expatriate evacuation: A conceptual model. *Journal of Global Mobility, 1*(3), 246–263. doi:10.1108/JGM-01-2013-0007

Finaccord (2017). *Global Expatriates: Size, Segmentation and Forecast for the Worldwide Market.* https://www.finaccord.com/Home/About-Us/Press-Releases/Global-Expatriates-Size,-Segmentation-and-Forecast

Garcia-Herrero, A. (2020, February 3) From globalization to deglobalization: Zooming into trade. *Bruegel Report.* https://www.bruegel.org/2020/02/from-globalization-to-deglobalization-zooming-into-trade

Gibler, K. M., Casado-Díaz, J. M., Casado-Díaz, M. A., Rodríguez, V., & Taltavull, P. (2009). *Late life second move housing choices of international retiree migrants.* International Journal of Housing Markets and Analysis., doi:10.1108/17538270910963117

Grandin, J. M., & Hedderich, N. (2009). Global competence for engineers. The SAGE handbook of intercultural competence, 362-373. doi:10.4135/9781452218397.n16

Groves, J. M., & O'Connor, P. (2018). Negotiating global citizenship, protecting privilege: Western expatriates choosing local schools in Hong Kong. *British Journal of Sociology of Education, 39*(3), 381–395. doi:10.1080/01425692.2017.1351866

Hampden-Turner, C., & Trompenaars, F. (2020). Riding the waves of culture: Understanding diversity in global business. Hachette UK.

Herjanto, H., Erickson, E., & Calleja, N. F. (2017). Antecedents of business travelers' satisfaction. *Journal of Hospitality Marketing & Management, 26*(3), 259–275. doi:10.1080/19368623.2017.1234954

Hitt, M. A., Javidan, M., & Steers, R. M. (2007). *The global mindset: An introduction*. Emerald Group Publishing Limited. doi:10.10161571-5027(07)19001-x

Horak, S., Farndale, E., Brannen, M. Y., & Collings, D. G. (2019). International human resource management in an era of political nationalism. *Thunderbird International Business Review, 61*(3), 471–480. doi:10.1002/tie.21959

IMF. (2020). IMF annual report 2020: a crisis like no other. Washington DC, USA.

Javidan, M. (2007). Forward-thinking cultures. *Harvard Business Review, 85*(7-8), 20.

Javidan, M. (May 19, 2010) *Bringing the Global Mindset to Leadership* https://hbr.org/2010/05/bringing-the-global-mindset-to.html

Javidan, M. (2013). Comments on the interview: Competencies required for working across borders and managing multicultural teams. *Academy of Management Learning & Education, 12*(3), 506–508. doi:10.5465/amle.2012.0246b

Javidan, M., Teagarden, M., & Bowen, D. (2010). Making it overseas. *Harvard Business Review, 88*(4), 109–113.

Jenkins, J. (2019). *Is living abroad the key to developing a global mindset and skillset?* If so-is there a 'golden age' at which to do so? [Unpublished master's thesis, Birkbeck, University of London, England].

Jenkins, J. (2020, September 21) The Future of Global Work. *People Matters Global*. https://www.peoplematters.in/article/life-at-work/the-future-of-global-work-27026

Jesuthasan, R., Malcolm, T., & Cantrel, S. (2020). How the Coronavirus Crisis Is Redefining Jobs. *Harvard Business Review, 2020*(4). https://hbr.org/2020/04/how-the-coronavirus-crisis-is-redefining-jobs

Johanson, J., & Vahlne, J. E. (2002). The internationalization process of the firm. *International Business: Theory of the multinational enterprise, 1*(1), 47.

King, N. (2004). *Using Templates in the Thematic Analysis of Text*. Essential guide to qualitative methods in organizational research, 256. doi:10.4135/9781446280119.n21

Kropp, B. (2021). Trends that will shape work in 2021 and beyond. *Harvard Business Review*. https://hbr. org/2021/01/9-trends-that-will-shape-work-in-2021-and-beyond. https://hbr.org/2021/01/9-trends-that-will-shape-work-in-2021-and-beyond

Leonard, P. (2010). Work, identity and change? Post/colonial encounters in Hong Kong. *Journal of Ethnic and Migration Studies, 36*(8), 1247–1263. doi:10.1080/13691831003687691

Levy, O., Beechler, S., Taylor, S., & Boyacigiller, N. A. (2007). What we talk about when we talk about 'global mindset': Managerial cognition in multinational corporations. *Journal of International Business Studies*, *38*(2), 231–258. doi:10.1057/palgrave.jibs.8400265

Levy, O., Lee, H. J., Jonsen, K., & Peiperl, M. A. (2019). Transcultural brokerage: The role of cosmopolitans in bridging structural and cultural holes. *Journal of Management*, *45*(2), 417–450. doi:10.1177/0149206318773404

Livermore, D. (2011). The cultural intelligence difference-special eBook edition: Master the one skill you can't do without in today's global economy. *Amacom.*

Luo, Y. (2021). Illusions of techno-nationalism. *Journal of International Business Studies*, 1–18. doi:10.105741267-021-00468-5 PMID:34511654

Maddux, W. W., & Galinsky, A. D. (2009). Cultural borders and mental barriers: The relationship between living abroad and creativity. *Journal of Personality and Social Psychology*, *96*(5), 1047–1061. doi:10.1037/a0014861 PMID:19379035

Marinov, T. T., & Marinova, R. S. (2020). Dynamics of COVID-19 using inverse problem for coefficient identification in SIR epidemic models. Chaos. *Solitons & Fractals: X*, *5*, 100041. doi:10.1016/j.csfx.2020.100041

McNulty, Y. (2014). *Women as female breadwinners in non-traditional expatriate families*: Status-reversal marriages, single parents, split families, and lesbian partnerships. In *Research Handbook on Women in International Management*. Edward Elgar Publishing. doi:10.4337/9781781955031.00025

McNulty, Y., & Selmer, J. (Eds.). (2017). *Research handbook of expatriates*. Edward Elgar Publishing. doi:10.4337/9781784718183

McWilliam, S. E., Kim, J. K., Mudambi, R., & Nielsen, B. B. (2020). Global value chain governance: Intersections with international business. *Journal of World Business*, *55*(4), 101067. doi:10.1016/j.jwb.2019.101067

Meier, O. (2021) *Managing international employees working from anywhere, part 1: Redefining mobility*.

Meier, O., & Traber, Y. (2021). The impact of the COVID-19 crisis on talent mobility. *Mercer.* https://www.mercer.com/events/webcasts/the-impact-of-the-covid-19-crisis-on-talent-mobility-cost-of-living-survey.html

Mello, S. F., & Tomei, P. A. (2021). The impact of the COVID-19 pandemic on expatriates: A pathway to work-life harmony? *Global Business and Organizational Excellence*, *40*(5), 6–22. doi:10.1002/joe.22088

Milani, G. S., & Dickman, M. (2021). *Is global work losing its attractiveness?* https://www.relocatemagazine.com/articles/international-assignments-is-global-work-losing-its-attractiveness-giovanna-silveira-milani-michael-dickmann-glomo-su21

Modgil, S. (2021, April 08) With a distributed workforce, companies need to be even more aware of compliances: Charles Ferguson, Globalization Partners. *People Matters Global*. https://www.peoplemattersglobal.com/article/strategic-hr/with-a-distributed-workforce-companies-need-to-be-even-more-aware-of-compliances-charles-ferguson-globalization-partners-28956

Montano, S., & Savitt, A. (2020) *Not All Disasters Are Disasters: Pandemic Categorization and Its Consequences*. https://items.ssrc.org/covid-19-and-the-social-sciences/disaster-studies/not-all-disasters-are-disasters-pandemic-categorization-and-its-consequences/

News, U. N. (2020, May 4). None of us is safe until we all are, says UN chief at EU push to end COVID-19 pandemic. https://news.un.org/en/story/2020/05/1063132

Richardson, J. (2006). Self-directed expatriation: Family matters. *Personnel Review*, *35*(4), 469–486. doi:10.1108/00483480610670616

Rosenberg, C. E. (1992). *Explaining epidemics*. Cambridge University Press. doi:10.1017/CBO9780511666865.015

Rosenbusch, K., & Cseh, M. (2012). The cross-cultural adjustment process of expatriate families in a multinational organization: A family system theory perspective. *Human Resource Development International*, *15*(1), 61–77. doi:10.1080/13678868.2011.646895

Santa Fe Relocations. (2018). *Transformation in The Age of Uncertainty: The Global Mobility Survey 2018*. https://www.aon.es/site/ipm-club/2018/11/15/santafe-survey/

Schieman, S., Badawy, P. J. A., Milkie, M., & Bierman, A. (2021). Work-life conflict during the COVID-19 pandemic. *Socius*, *7*, 2378023120982856. doi:10.1177/2378023120982856

Segal, A. (2020). The coming tech cold war with China. *Foreign Affairs*, 99.

Spencer-Oatey, H., & Franklin, P. (2009). *Intercultural interaction: A multidisciplinary approach to intercultural communication*. Springer. doi:10.1057/9780230244511

Suutari, V., & Brewster, C. (2000). Making their own way: International experience through self-initiated foreign assignments. *Journal of World Business*, *35*(4), 417–436. doi:10.1016/S1090-9516(00)00046-8

Teddlie, C., & Tashakkori, A. (2011). Mixed methods research. The Sage Handbook of Qualitative Research, 4, 285-300.

The PwC Global Mobility Pulse Survey (2020, April). What does COVID-19 mean for global mobility. *PWC*. https://www.pwc.com/gx/en/services/tax/publications/covid-19-mean-for-globalmobility.html

Thomas, D. C., & Inkson, K. (2005). People skills for a global workplace. *Consulting to Management*, *16*(1), 5.

Tripathi, C. M., & Singh, T. (2021). Sailing through the COVID-19 pandemic: managing expatriates' psychological well-being and performance during natural crises. *Journal of Global Mobility: The Home of Expatriate Management Research.*

Waizenegger, L., McKenna, B., Cai, W., & Bendz, T. (2020). An affordance perspective of team collaboration and enforced working from home during COVID-19. *European Journal of Information Systems, 29*(4), 429–442. doi:10.1080/0960085X.2020.1800417

Westman, M., Etzion, D., & Chen, S. (2009). Crossover of positive experiences from business travelers to their spouses. *Journal of Managerial Psychology, 24*(3), 269–284. doi:10.1108/02683940910939340

Wilson, R., & Dewaele, J. M. (2010). The use of web questionnaires in second language acquisition and bilingualism research. *Second Language Research, 26*(1), 103–123. doi:10.1177/0267658309337640

WIR (World Investment Report). (2020). International Production beyond the Pandemic. *UNCTAD.*

Worbey, L. (2020) *Flexibility and agility post COVID-19.* KPMG Insights. https://home.kpmg/xx/en/home/insights/2020/08/flexibility-and-agiliity-post-covid-19.html

Zaman, U., Barnes, S. J., Abbasi, S., Anjam, M., Aktan, M., & Khwaja, M. G. (2022). The Bridge at the End of the World: Linking Expat's Pandemic Fatigue, Travel FOMO, Destination Crisis Marketing, and Vaxication for "Greatest of All Trips". *Sustainability, 14*(4), 2312. doi:10.3390u14042312

Chapter 7
Foreign Direct Investment (FDI) Indexes:
Relevance for Emerging Economies

J. Zambujal-Oliveira
University of Madeira, Portugal

José Pestana-Amaral
Instituto Superior Técnico, Portugal

ABSTRACT

As the foreign direct investment (FDI) attractiveness indexes constitute one of the decision tools for governments' politics, it is relevant to assess the Groh and Wich Index (GWI). The main purpose is to verify the capacity of this index to replicate the phenomena of inflow FDI. The index analysis process included reviewing literature and detecting weaknesses on theoretical frameworks and in the selection of basic indicators. Multivariate analysis, applied to a sample of economies, showed evidence that some composite indicators of the GWI have shortages of concordance between simple indicators. Apart from showing that FDI attractiveness index of Groh and Wich does not convey the progress of inflow FDI, the study demonstrates that a FDI attractiveness index built to advanced economies can hardly be employed to developing economies without significant changes to the basic indicators.

INTRODUCTION

The study of Foreign Direct Investment (FDI) has been assuming a relevant important role in the sustainable development of the countries, in result of being one of the least volatile sources of international investment for host countries and the most dependable source of foreign investment for developing countries. The relevant issue for policy makers in countries starving capital concerns the determinants of FDI attraction (Moosa & Cardak, 2006). To make this task easier, there has been created some knowledge aggregators that includes composite indicators. One of those aggregators is the one authored by Groh and Wich (2009), who constructed an FDI attractiveness index that captures the business attractiveness

DOI: 10.4018/978-1-6684-3749-0.ch007

of more than 100 countries. The task of this chapter corresponds to appraise the consistency of Groh and Wich's (2009) index on describing the phenomenon of business attractiveness.

Some of the benefits of the positive impact of FDI correspond to technology transfer, introduction of new production processes and productivity gains (Barros, 2009). Despite the profuse literature there is a need to rationalise the knowledge about the factors of FDI attraction. Until now, there has been an inability to determine, based on complete data collected, the FDI attractiveness in a given country (Teixeira & Tavares-Lehmann, 2007). To improve this scenario, some authors, as Groh and Wich (2009) developed FDI attractiveness indexes able to rank 127 countries. Therefore, it is very useful evaluating the consistency of the Groh and Wich (2009) to formally describe the FDI attractiveness phenomenon.

Our study should consider the Organization for Economic Cooperation and Development (2008) considering its operational knowledge on how FDI should be measured and its global standards for FDI statistics. FDI is a key element for quick engagement and international economic integration and provides the means to create direct links, stable and long-lasting between two economies. A right policy environment can serve as an important vehicle for local development and can also help to improve the competitiveness of both sides (country of origin and the host country of FDI). FDI particularly encourages the transfer of technology and know-how between economies and provides an opportunity for the economy of the country of origin to promote its products more broadly in the international market (Amaral, 2013).

The global flow of FDI has grown over the last 30 years and continues to play a primary role in production activities of developed countries which captured roughly 75% in 2008 of the global FDI flows (UNCTAD, 2008). Recently, UNCTAD (2012) revealed that the percentage of total FDI incoming flow absorbed by the developing countries has improved by then. The evidence of a substantial FDI growth in recent years reflect an intensification in the number of transactions, and in its value, and can be interpreted as an entrepreneurial purpose to diversify businesses across economies and industrial sectors OECD (2005, 2008). Multinational enterprises (MNE) are traditionally the major players in each FDI transaction. This development has coincided with the increasing of the MNE's propensity to participate in the international market. The MNEs appear to be the main players in FDI transactions, resulting this role from the growing propensity of the MNEs to act as global market players (Amaral, 2013).

The creation of composite indicators that associate several factors is a frequently solution employed to integrate these factors. Extensively used indexes are the Global Competitiveness Index of World Economic Forum, the Ease of Doing Business Index (EDBI) and the Worldwide Governance Indicators, both coming from the World Bank. The basic assembly of these indexes is often done recurring to methodologies with weighted indicators, adopting often an equal weight for all the indicators (Amaral, 2013).

To create that kind of index, Nardo et al. (2005) explains all the steps that should be taken during the process, as the assortment of sub-indicators, the treatment of missing values, the selection of the integration model and the indicators' weights. Even the fulfilment of all the steps, along with a diligent process of information's recovery can origin distorted or fragile policy conclusions. In that sense, the considerations made by Pinheiro-Alves and Zambujal-Oliveira (2012) on the consistency and validity of Ease of Doing Business Index (EDBI) are an excellent example how the choice of the data sets that represent sub-indicators and the index structure remain questionable.

Groh and Wich (2009) grounded its index structure on a set of literature that describe the FDI attractiveness relationship with their determinants. Our main propose consists in validating this the quality of the relationship implemented between the determinants the FDI, considering the possibility of existing missing relevant indicators. For that reason, our task is trying to replicate (in an initial phase and as much as possible) the Groh and Wich (2009) process, employing the same or similar databases worked by the authors to follow the attractiveness of a countries set, which derives from one defined by the International Monetary Fund (IMF) (2012) as Advanced Economies (AE), over a number of years as wide as the available data (2006 to 2011).

FOREIGN DIRECT INVESTMENT AND ATTRACTIVENESS INDEXES

Our analysis has the main purposes of verifying the robustness of the Groh and Wich (2009) index in replicating the FDI evolution in countries under study and qualifying its use as a tool for decision support. According to the OECD (2008), FDI represents the investments' category whose key objective is establishing a lasting entrepreneurial interest in another economy that implies the presence of a long-term relationship between the investor and the host country. The foreign direct investor should be originated from one economy and acquires (directly or indirectly) at least 10% of the voting rights in a company established in another economy.

Therefore, a foreign direct investor may come from any sector of the economy and can be one of the following entities or any combination of them: an individual, a group of related individuals, a company incorporated or unincorporated, a public or private company, a group of related companies; organ government, a fund or other social organization. In the particular case in which two, or more, companies hold at least 10% of the voting rights of one over the other, each company can be considered as a direct investor. Thus, IMF's (2012) categorization seems even more relevant, after knowing that Portes and Smith (2010) performed several empirical tests over reputational indexes that consider countries as analysis units and concluded by the existence on the FDI literature of conflicting definitions about the concept of institution.

To clearly identify the type of FDI, the OECD (2008) states that should be known its direction. Inward Direct Investment is the investment made by a foreign entity in the origin country and Outward Direct Investment describes the investment made abroad by an entity registered in the origin country. The approach to FDI can have multiple perspectives, among others we highlight the study of bilateral flows between countries, the development of the theory of internationalization based on eclectic paradigm, which was published and developed by Dunning (1980, 1988, 1993, 1995), and the impact of FDI in the host country that defines the approach taken.

Recent search of Nee and Opper (2009) on the development of financial markets have focused on the nature of the legal system. It is possible to study the FDI from multiple perspectives. Among others, it can be analysed the bilateral flows between countries, the evolution of internalization theory under the eclectic paradigm Dunning (1980, 1988, 1993, 1995), and the FDI effect in the host country. For instance, Nee and Opper (2009) have been centering their work on the nature of the legal system, collecting evidence of the existence of correlation between the bureaucratic quality of public administration of countries and the progress level of their financial markets and subsequent aptitude to attract foreigner investments. The work conducted by Bénassy-Quéré et al. (2007) about the performance of public institutions concluded that it corresponds to the main determinant for FDI attractiveness.

More broadly, Nasser (2007) verified the relationship between investment and economic and social factors (such as market size, growth of GDP, macroeconomic stability, trade openness, education level, and infrastructure availability). Particularly, Shatz and Venables (2000) even concluded that market size and productivity of a country show a close relationship to FDI development, and Fung et al. (2002) found evidence in developed countries of the relevance of GDP as decision variable for FDI. The relationship between economic activity and FDI has been confirmed by many studies.

Helpman et al. (2004) and Brainard (1997) demonstrated that economic and political factors as transportation costs, barriers to trade, the dimension of economies of scale, the linguistic similarity and political risk contribute to increase bilateral FDI. Borensztein et al. (1998) concluded that in countries with greater availability of human capital, the FDI inflow has a significant positive impact on economic growth.

The positive relationship between bilateral FDI flows and economic growth was, once more, confirmed by Addison and Heshmati (2003), Noorbakhsh et al. (2001) and Saggi (2002). Studying the countries' openness to international trade, Asiedu (2002) concluded by its positive influence on FDI flows. For Alesina et al. (2005), foreigner investment is a function of market regulation level. Makki and Somwaru (2004) and Borensztein et al. (1998) went further on the analysis about the impact of FDI on economic growth and found evidence that it can often constituted the principal way for technology transfer, leaving a legacy of human capital quality. The negative impact on exports of Germany, the UK, Sweden, and France, as a result of investments abroad, seems to confirm FDI as a channel for spreading ideas and innovation among developed economies (Barrell & Pain, 1997).

FDI benefits the host country giving resources and access to markets and, consequently, promoting development and modernization of native resources. However, there is some concern with this special vehicle of importation for intermediate products. First, having a high bargaining power, the investing foreigner company will be able to capture an uncomfortably share of the value created by its subsidiary company in the host country, and second, decisions about the volume, type and usage of resources transferred, may bring lower benefits to the recipient country than the ones that would result from standard resource allocation (Dunning, 1988). Apart from the relationship's authentication of FDI with determinants, our paper verifies also its compliance with the general index purposes. Among several examples of distinct purposes, we can enumerate the necessity to simplify the analysis of complex issues, inform and reveal changes of position in the rankings over time, and the concern to evaluate the progress of a country to international commitments as tools for enhancing decision policies and improving investors' information (Bandura, 2005).

To verify, Saisana and Tarantola (2002) and Pellegrini (2006) compared a variety of techniques employed in the index construction as aggregation techniques, multiple linear regression analysis, principal component analysis and factor analysis, Cronbach's alpha, neutralizing the effect of correlation, expert's opinion, target distance, public opinion and the analytic hierarchy process.

ANALYSIS OF GROH AND WICH (2009)'S INDEX

Among several authors that usually analyze indexes, Pellegrini (2006) evaluated various competitiveness indexes, concluding by their weak adherence to literature. A common problem criticized by him is the equal weight's structure because conveys a meaningless perception to the indicators. Some authors as Cracolici and Nijkamp (2008) dedicated their work to the study of sectorial indexes. In this case, they analyzed the competitiveness and attractiveness of tourist destinations in the south of Italy and created an index for that purpose, not forgetting to compare its outcomes with the results obtained from polls among tourists.

A frequent but difficult to realize characteristic of the indexes' creators, consists in the assumption of a structure with appropriate weights to all indicators. Examples of this practice are Afonso et al. (2005), Gwartney et al. (2012), World Economic Outlook (IMF, 2012) and Global Competitiveness Report (WEF, 2012). Nardo et al. (2008) provides a guide to the construction and use of composite indicators for developing indexes for policy makers, academics, the media and other stakeholders. Knowing the existence of different types of composite indexes, these authors created a manual focused exclusively on building indexes that compare and rank countries in areas such as industrial competitiveness, sustainable development, globalization and innovation. Therefore, they have contributed to a better understanding of the complexity of composite indexes, to improve techniques currently used to build them, and to enhance the quality of data.

The revision of the works of the referred authors creates conditions to analyze carefully the Groh and Wich (2009)'s index. Thus, GWI distinguishes 20 different data sets as representations of the key factors of the phenomenon of the FDI attractiveness. These data sets, units, sources and indexing structures are presented in the table in attachment, which shows the integration of diverse sources of information. The index structure of FDI is based on three levels, where the first level represents the aggregation of simple indicators into four subthemes: *Economic Activity*, *Political and Legal Systems*, *Business Environment*, and *Infrastructure*. The second level consists of data series (simple indicators) or intermediate composite indicators that are themselves aggregations from data series at level three.

With a pyramidal index structure, the data series at lowers levels have reduced weight in the overall composite indicators, benefiting from the free readjustment of the weight of middle level composite indicators and thus, contributing to improve the robustness of the structure (Amaral, 2013).

Following the methodology of Nardo et al. (2008), our study began its tests to the GWI, making the comparison between the data sets that represent the FDI evolution and development of the GWI between the years 2006 and 2011, for each one of the countries selected. The comparing process requires normalizing the FDI, which was serious problems because of the lack of data. In that sense, our study recurred to the various techniques employed by Buuren (2012) to fill in the data gaps with plausible values. It became evident, the major challenge corresponds to the selection of the adequate method to fill the voids.

The aggregation of the low-level indicators involves the normalisation of the data. Ebert and Welsch (2004) suggest the z-scores and min-max methods to complete that task. Besides from this standardisation, the aggregation process requires the estimation of the weights of the items.

Knowing from Nardo et al. (2008) that the majority of composite indexes allocate equal weights to all their inner indicators, Groh and Wich (2009) decided to follow the methodology of Nicoletti et al. (2000) and suggested by Nardo et al. (2008) of assigning diverse weights to the CI's by using the analysis of variance factors (AVF). Not forgetting Land et al. (2012) who showed the existence of suitable alternative methods, our study followed the AVF because we intend, in a first analysis, ascertain if the index built by Groh and Wich (2009) responds according to the evolution of FDI of the countries being study.

Therefore, chosen the same relative weights used in the GWI, Amaral (2013) considers the nature of the data needs to be carefully considered before building the composite indicator in order to understand on the consequences of the methodological choices during the construction phase of the composite indicator.

There are a set of multivariate techniques adequate to collect knowledge about the data set's structure of composite indicators. The principal component analysis (PCA) exposes the relationship between correlated variables through its transformation, employing a covariance matrix, into a new set of uncorrelated variables. One of the interesting characteristics of PCA consists in its capacity to reduce the data set dimensionality. The factor analysis (FA) is similar to PCA but is based on a particular statistical model. The most common approach to analyse internal consistency is done through the calculation of Cronbach's alpha coefficient that explores the correlation between a variable set (Nardo et al., 2008).

Cronbach's alpha coefficient is therefore an estimation of the correlation between random samples of variables from a universe of variables and it's found to be an appropriate coefficient of equivalence and of relevance of the first-factor concentration in the internal structure tests (Cronbach, 1951). As Groh and Wich (2009) did, our study employed the Cronbach's alpha coefficient to assess the internal consistency of intermediate composite indicators and simple indicators of each group.

But our study went further, using Cronbach's approach for various periods (2006-2011), not forgetting to check before the suitable number of clusters and the adequacy of the index structure and weights associated to the composite indicators. This test uses factor analysis based on a linear model of y factors represented by observable variables ϕ_i (corresponding to the sub-indicators) that are function x factors Ψ_j (corresponding to the indicators) where typify the factor loadings associated with factors and residuals.

First, our study considers a trivial linear model of y factors represented by its observable variables ϕ_i (sub-indicators) that are functions of x factors Ψ_j (indicators) characterized by having factor loadings $\kappa_{i,j}$ associated with factors and residuals.

$$\phi_j = \kappa_{i1}\Psi_1 + \kappa_{i2}\Psi_2 + \ldots + \kappa_{ix}\Psi_x + \varepsilon_j;\ \left(i = 1..x; j = 1..y\right)$$

κ_{ij}, ε_i: factor loadings Ψ_j: factors

Our analysis assumes factors Ψ_j and residuals ε_i not correlated and residuals with null mean. The variance of factors is unitary, and the variance of the residuals does not have any restrictions. Furthermore, factor analysis explains the covariance and correlation between the variables that comprise the index. Its application serves for estimating a factorial model using principal components. With common factors, this approach is used to explain portions of variance and covariance. To know the percentage of variance of the sub-indicators explained by two or more common factors used to calculate the commonalities (Pinheiro-Alves & Zambujal-Oliveira, 2012).

For ensuring the inexistence of correlation between the variables and verifying the adequacy of the sample for the application of factor analysis approach there are available two tests: the sphericity test of Bartlett (Snedecor & Cochran, 1967) and the measure of Kaiser-Meyer-Olkin (KMO). Measuring the correlation between answers by their profile analysis, Cronbach (1954) created its alpha coefficient to examine the reliability of a survey, given by the following expression:

$$\alpha = \frac{n\bar{R}}{1 + \left(n - 1\right)\bar{R}}$$

n = number of components on idex;
$\bar{R}$ = mean correlation of items.

The Cronbach's coefficient estimates (on a scale ranging from 0 to 1) how consistently the indicators do not contribute to the weighted sum of the index. As this property is known for assessing internal consistency of the scales, the Cronbach coefficient can be understood as the weighted average of the estimated internal consistency of all the indicators that would be obtained, if all the possible divisions of the scale were made (Cronbach, 1954).

Figure 1. Distribution value of two basic indicators
(Yu, 2014)

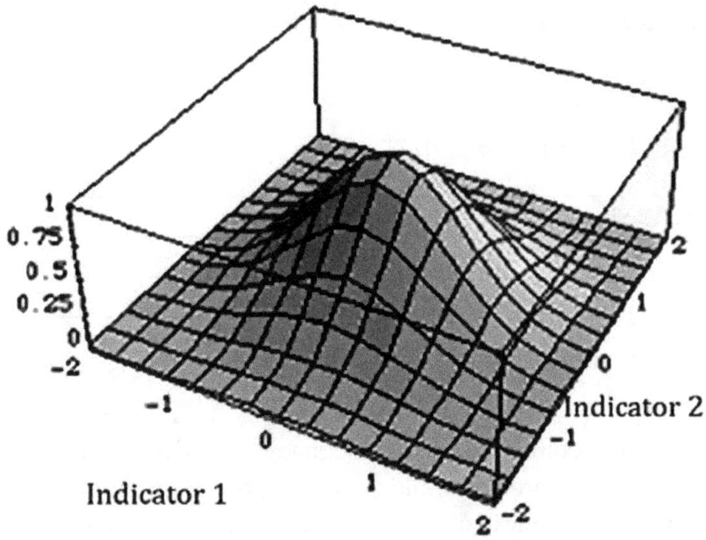

In the above example, indicators 1 and 2 have means equal to zero because its covariance value comes from standardized z-scores. The mountain shape illustrated by the graph can give information whether the response patterns to indicators 1 and 2 are consistent. Slopes of all directions spread out evenly and a mountain peak near zero indicates that indicators can be considered consistent (Yu, 2014).

There are known, other useful interpretations for the Cronbach's coefficient. Cortina (1993) supports its usage, stating that the variability resulting from the process need to divide the index to calculate the split-half reliability, produces a measure of reliability. It seems clear that higher covariances (or correlation between indicators) mean greater indicators homogeneity and higher consistency of each one to measure the same size or theoretical construct (Maroco & Garcia-Marques 2006).

The Cronbach's alpha assumes a unitary value. Therefore, a high value of the coefficient indicates that underlying indicators constitute relevant proxies of the composite indicator (Amaral, 2013). Nardo et al. (2008) assume a benchmark value of 0.7 to the Cronbach's coefficient, previously suggested by Nunnally (1978), as an acceptable cut-off limit of acceptance, and widely accepted in the index's literature.

The completely diverse multidimensional living conditions index (LCI) presented by (Krishnan, 2014) also accepts it as an adequate cut-off value. With these considerations, we are prepared to begin testing the internal consistency of GWI and compare with the results obtained by Groh and Wich (2009).

We are waiting the existence of some discrepancies. There are several reasons for explaining them. As our study works with less countries, one of the reasons to potential discrepancies may be the fact of existing, in our study, different boundaries scales to normalize. One possible result of these tests is the detection of limitations in the construction index. In that case, the study will proceed with the analysis by the paired sample t-test to draw more objective conclusions.

RESULTS

Our study initiates the index analysis with the Bartlett's test of sphericity (Snedecor & Cochran, 1967) and the extent of Kaiser-Meyer-Olkin (KMO). These tests will allow us to assess the potential lack of correlation between indicators and check the adequacy of the sample for the application of factor analysis approach.

Table 1. KMO and Bartlett's Test (Amaral, 2013)

Kaiser-Meyer-Olkin Measure of Sampling Adequacy.		.786
Bartlett's Test of Sphericity	Approx. Chi-Square	2837.921
	df	190
	Sig.	.000

Table 1 contains values that confirm the data adequacy. The KMO value can be considered comfortable because is above the standard threshold (0.5). To proceed with the process of estimating the number of factors relevant to the index, our study followed the subsequent steps (Pinheiro-Alves & Zambujal-Oliveira, 2012)

1. Analyze the proportion of the overall variance associated with each eigenvalue, maintaining the indicators whose eigenvalues contribute proportionally more to the explanation of overall variance. The last indicator should contribute to exceed 75% of explanation of cumulative variance (Nunnally, 1978; Nardo et al., 2005).
2. Retain indicators with eigenvalues superior to 1.00 (Mingoti, 2005). The acceptance of that boundary intends to include in the factor analysis, the indicators that represent, at least, the variance of one original variable.
3. Analyse the slope of the factor analysis graph, identifying the eigenvalues distribution. It is necessary to find the number of factors to extract from the point at which the curve begins to flatten (Hair Jr et al., 2005).

After normalizing the data to obtain indicators with unit variance, there were created the conditions to build the correlation matrix. Subsequently, we determined the eigenvalues for the significant indicators. The number of composite indicators (4) came from applying the criteria of latent value (Kaiser, 1958) and corresponds to the number of composite indicators with significant explanatory power (Table 2). This criterion was applied with success by Najmi et al. (2010) in a business intelligence project for helping managers and organizations to manage information and make factual decisions as part of a process of turning data into information and then into knowledge.

Table 2. Eigenvalues and cumulative variance of main factors (Amaral, 2013)

Component	Initial Eigenvalues			Rotation Sums of Squared Loadings		
	Total	% of Variance	Cumulative %	Total	% of Variance	Cumulative %
1	9.248	46.241	46.241	5.748	28.738	28.738
2	2.750	13.751	59.992	5.225	26.125	54.863
3	1.773	8.866	68.859	2.169	10.846	65.709
4	1.202	6.010	74.869	1.832	9.159	74.869
5	.988	4.939	79.808			
6	.849	4.246	84.054			
7	.771	3.854	87.908			
8	.587	2.936	90.843			
9	.400	2.001	92.845			
10	.353	1.765	94.609			
11	.259	1.293	95.902			
12	.181	.904	96.806			
13	.166	.831	97.638			
14	.153	.766	98.404			
15	.093	.463	98.867			
16	.080	.402	99.269			
17	.060	.298	99.567			
18	.039	.195	99.763			
19	.029	.143	99.906			
20	.019	.094	100.000			

The column "Cumulative%" from Table 2 indicates the existence of four composite indicators (components) that cover 74.87% of the global cumulative variance. Considering the GWI also contains four main composite indicators, it seems to be adequately structured to the available data. Observing Figure 1, we detected an abrupt slope among the composite indicators 1 and 2, followed by a slowdown in the succeeding composite indicators. Arriving at indicator 4, there is evidence of a slope's attenuation. Meaning a relevant decrease on the marginal contribution to the variance explanation and supporting the elimination of the remaining composite indicators from the point where the cumulative variance is above 75% (Table 2).

Figure 2. Eigenvalue to main aggregated of the index

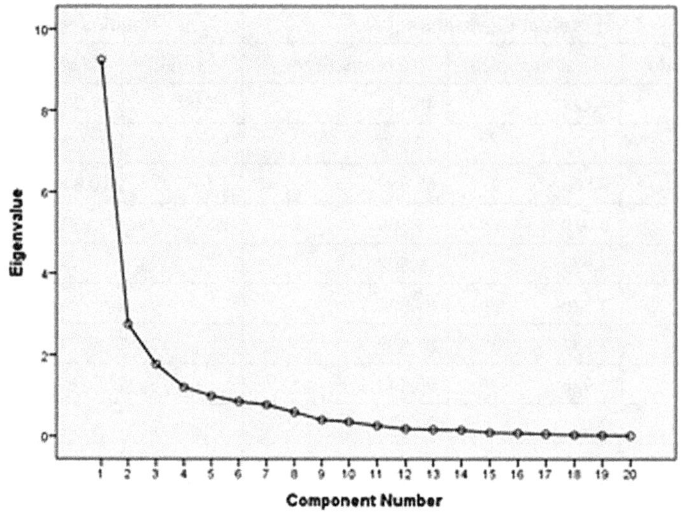

For the examination of the matrix components, we analysed the correlation between simple indicators.

Table 3. Rotated component matrix (Amaral, 2013)

	Indicator	Component			
		1	2	3	4
1.1.1	(GDP PPP per capita)	.703	.182	-.420	-.048
1.1.2	(real GDP Grow yoy)	.030	.060	.127	.591
1.2	(Prevalence of Trade Barriers)	-.013	-.017	.923	.045
1.3	(Central Gross Government Surplus / Deficit)	.577	.029	.619	.005
2.1.1	(Rule of Law)	.766	.493	.188	.258
2.1.2	(Regulatory Quality)	.798	.293	.333	.191
2.1.3	(Legal Enforcement of Contracts)	.338	.454	.147	.116
2.1.4	(Business Impact on FDI)	.474	.151	.471	.427
2.2.1	(Stability and Absence of Violence / Terrorism)	.614	.166	.083	.361
2.2.2	(Government Effectiveness)	.743	.556	.133	.259
3.1	(Pay and Productivity)	.446	.266	-.227	.591
3.2	(Profit and Capital Gains Tax)	.836	-.081	.046	-.024
3.3	(Administrative Requirements)	.585	.258	-.078	.518
3.4	(Control of Corruption)	.722	.523	.217	.281
4.1.1	(Quality of Roads)	-.152	.857	.003	.286
4.1.2	(Quality of Railroad Infrastructure)	-.071	.891	-.202	.285
4.1.3	(Quality of Port Infrastructure)	.288	.848	.167	-.053
4.1.4	(Quality of Air Transport Infrastructure)	.427	.752	.217	.009
4.2	(Quality of Electricity Supply)	.348	.803	-.182	.163
4.3	(Fixed Line and Mobile Phone Subscribers)	.502	.646	-.268	-.304

Assuming the indicators with the areas of fulfilled with grey show evidence of agreement, Amaral (2013) added all the values contained in each of the shaded groups to determine the explanatory power and calculate the relative weights of each composite indicator.

Table 4. Concordance matrix of composite indicators (Amaral, 2013)

	Composite Indicator	Component			
		1	2	3	4
1	Economic Activity	1.297	.254	1.250	.593
2	Legal and Political System	3.733	2.113	1.355	1.610
3	Business Environment	2.590	.965	-.042	1.367
4	Infrastructure	1.342	4.797	-.265	.387
	Weights	33.5%	43.0%	11.2%	12.3%

Table 3 shows the Composite Index Infrastructure represents 43.0% agreement, followed by the IC Legal and Political System with 33.5% of representativeness. Therefore, it was found that those two IC's agreement represent more than 75%. On the other hand, since higher values are predominantly in the first factor and therefore, we do not detect clouds of high values for each of the other factors leads us to conclude that the aggregate made by Grow and Wich (2009) is not statistically consistent. Values marked with dark grey (Table 3) are the highest among the indicators. A reconstruction of the index could go through a regression of indicators.

Table 4 shows that composite indicator *Infrastructure* explains 43.0% of the attractiveness phenomena, followed by *Legal and Political System* representing 33.5%. Therefore, there is evidence these two composite indicators contain more than 75% of the indicators relevant to explicate the phenomena of business attractiveness.

On the other hand, since higher eigenvalues are mostly concentrated in the first component that is associated with the composite indicator *Legal and Political System*, the cross analysis shows evidence of some structural inconsistency on the GWI. Considering that cells with values marked with dark grey (Table 4) represent the highest eigenvalues among the indicators, a potential index reconstruction could imply to run a regression process which include the indicators.

The process of index analysis proceeded with check of the internal consistency (simple compositors and composite indicators) of GWI. We know that any kind of improvement in the index structure will cause the change of the weights of composite indicators for compliance matrix presented (Table 5). Thus, after examining the internal consistency of the four composite indicators and its internal indicators, we applied the weights model of GWI to data of the year 2006 and replicated in subsequent years to certify the results. Table 6 shows the Cronbach's alpha values for each year of study.

Table 5. Cronbach's alfa for composite indicator "Economic Activity"

Year	2006	2007	2008	2009	2010	2011
Alfa Value	0.772	0.819	0.833	0.842	0.870	0.882

The analysis of Table 5 shows, in all the years and in especially 2006, Cronbach's alphas above the acceptable consistency boundary (0.7) defined by Nunnally, (1978) and generally accepted by other authors. This proves the correlation between CI's and ensures the approval in the test of internal consistency. The next step of the analysis process consisted in the determination of the Cronbach's alpha associated to the simple indicators that make up each composite indicator. Table 6 illustrates the results of internal consistency test for the 4 composite indicators inside the period between the years 2006 and 2011:

Table 6. Alfa value applied to simple indicators (Amaral, 2013)

Year	2006	2007	2008	2009	2010	2011
1. Economic Activity	0.148	0.338	0.289	0.299	0.263	0.538
2. Legal and Political System	0.900	0.902	0.903	0.903	0.905	0.912
3. Business Environment	0.805	0.819	0.809	0.821	0.845	0.857
4. Infrastructures	0.935	0.944	0.933	0.920	0.902	0.893

The outcomes from our Cronbach's test applied to our set of countries revealed a compositor indicator *Economic activity* composed by internal indicators weakly correlated (0.148). We can thus anticipate that for advanced economies, the indicators do not correlate underlying simple. Confronting the CAs achieved by Groh and Wich (2009) in their sample of 127 countries for the year 2009 (Table 7), it seems possible to improve the understanding over our results.

Table 7. Cronbach's alpha

Composite Indicators	Groh & Wich (2009)	Amaral & Zambujal-Oliveira (2014)	% Difference
1. Economic Activity	0.617	0.299	-52%
2. Legal and Political System	0.908	0.903	-1%
3. Business Environment	0.522	0.821	57%
4. Infrastructures	0.894	0.92	3%

Analysing Table 7 with some outcomes originated by Groh and Wich (2009) permit to notice that the composite indicators *Economic Activity* and *Business Environment* present Cronbach levels below the minimal cut-off value suggested by Nunally (1978) on the first version of the GWI. Therefore, Groh and Wich, making use of a more detailed analysis, concluded that they should discard the indicator "Growth rate of GDP" (indicator 1.1.2) to increase the Cronbach's alpha of composite indicator *Economic Activity*. For the composite indicator *Business Environment*, Groh and Wich (2009) state that the indicator for "*Taxes*" (indicator 3.2) has little correlation to the remaining internal indicators and therefore they considered that it should be discarded to increase the statistical consistency of the index.

However, even knowing this aspect, the authors decided to keep these low correlated indicators in the index because the literature on these topics considers them relevant for the FDI attractiveness. As expected, comparing the two tables presented above, the results of Amaral (2013) tests in internal consistency diverge from the ones presented by Groh and Wich (2009). One of the reasons for this discrepancy may be the fact that boundaries of the scales to normalize the data sets from the indicators differ due to the lower size of the sample of the countries. These discrepancies can support some additional limitations of GWI.

The results of experiments done by Groh and Wich (2009) over the composite indicators *Economic Activity* and *Business Environment* and our results in the case of composite indicator *Business Environment* can constitute evidence of existing different FDI attractiveness indexes according to the evolution level (advanced or emerging) of the economies. Even recognizing the relevance of conclusion drawn in the previous paragraph, the process of analysis and improvement of the GWI must go on. Therefore, after the exclusion of the two internal indicators with lower eigenvalues (1.1.1: "*GDP PPP per capita*"; 1.1.2: "*Real GDP Growth y-o-y*") of the composite indicator *Economic Activity*, the CA associated to this composite indicator presented a positive enhancement (max: 279%, min: 5%; average: 115%), increasing the variance explanatory power of the composite indicator (Table 8).

Table 8. Cronbach's alpha impact from basic indicators removal (Amaral, 2013)

Year	2006	2007	2008	2009	2010	2011
1. Economic activity	0.148	0.338	0.289	0.299	0.263	0.538
1. Economic activity (excluding 1.1.1 and 1.1.2)	0.561	0.604	0.651	0.619	0.504	0.565
Percentage variation	279%	79%	125%	107%	92%	5%

However, since the CAs of both composite indicators remain below the cut-off, additional analysis work should be done. In that sense, Table 6 shows that indicator 3.2 (*Profit and Capital Gains Tax*) had an insufficient contribution to the consistency of the composite indicator *Infrastructure*. Having similar problems with indicators about *Infrastructure*, Merz et al. (2013) determined industry-specific determinants and developed two-stage methodology to explain the underlying regional industrial vulnerability, combining a composite indicator model to evaluate sector-specific indicators with a new regionalization method.

As we previous referred, Groh and Wich (2009) characterizes the indicator *Profit and Capital Gains Tax* as little related with the others internal indicators integrated on the same composite indicator but intentionally preferred not to discard it. The outcomes contained in Table 9 shows the change in the Cronbach's alpha in result of the exclusion of indicator 3.2 (see attachment).

Table 9. Cronbach's alpha variation (adapted from Amaral (2013))

Year	2006	2007	2008	2009	2010	2011
3. Business Environment	0.805	0.819	0.809	0.821	0.845	0.857
3. Business Environment (excluding 3.2)	0.776	0.822	0.828	0.853	0.854	0.852
Percentage variation	-4%	0%	2%	4%	1%	-1%

Examination of Table 9 allowed us to notice the inexistence of significate enhancements or disadvantages CAs over the years with the exclusion of indicator 3.2. Therefore, considering the incapacity of the basic indicator of the composite indicator *Business Environment* to add variance explanatory power to the index, we considered that the indicator should be removed from the index. The first phase of the index analysis process consists in standardizing and normalizing the data series to calculate the relative weights and managing some simple indicators to check their internal consistency. The second phase purpose corresponds to compare the behaviour of the GWI with the real evolution of the inflow of FDI to assess its ability to represent the phenomena.

Intuitively, the inflow of FDI should represent an adequate indicator of a country's attractiveness to foreign investors (Groh & Wich, 2009). Thus, the behaviour of GWI should present a strong similarity with the evolution of FDI. Otherwise, we should conclude by its not solid adherence to phenomena of business attractiveness and question its use as political decision tool. There are some steps that we must complete in order to compare the GWI and IFDI. The process begins normalizing the values of FDI. In each period, we divided the IFDI (Annex - Table 43) by the GDP of the country (Annex - Table 44) and then we applied the rescaling method with z-scores.

To smooth out high variations of the inflows of FDI, we followed the approach defined by Groh and Wich (2009) and employed an average value of three years. Besides, Groh and Wich (2009) analyze the data series and remove very odd values or strong fluctuations. As in our study, there was no necessity to do it as we compared the values by paired sample t-test (Table 10).

Table 10. Paired Sample t-test (Amaral, 2013)

Country	Paired Differences					t	df	Sig. (2-tailed)
	Mean	Std. Deviation	Std. Error Mean	95% Confidence Interval of the Difference				
				Lower	Upper			
Australia	.11229	.08341	.03405	.02476	.19982	3.298	5	.022
Austria	.19056	.72053	.29416	-.56559	.94671	.648	5	.546
Belgium	2.21891	.56979	.23262	1.62096	2.81687	9.539	5	.000
Canada	.07853	.24090	.09835	-.17428	.33134	.798	5	.461
Denmark	-.69677	.11411	.04658	-.81651	-.57702	-14.957	5	.000
Finland	-.41502	.26821	.10950	-.69649	-.13355	-3.790	5	.013
France	.13507	.11673	.04765	.01257	.25756	2.834	5	.036
Germany	-.21959	.11146	.04550	-.33655	-.10262	-4.826	5	.005
Greece	1.54582	.19461	.07945	1.34159	1.75006	19.456	5	.000
Ireland	1.63241	.49393	.20165	1.11406	2.15076	8.095	5	.000
Italy	1.54523	.04779	.01951	1.49508	1.59538	79.203	5	.000
Japan	.37512	.17073	.06970	.19595	.55429	5.382	5	.003
Netherlands	.00918	.48991	.20000	-.50494	.52331	.046	5	.965
New Zealand	-.13286	.17977	.07339	-.32152	.05579	-1.810	5	.130
Norway	.05470	.10131	.04136	-.05161	.16102	1.323	5	.243
Portugal	.85873	.12746	.05204	.72496	.99249	16.502	5	.000
Spain	1.02475	.13877	.05665	.87911	1.17038	18.088	5	.000
Sweden	-.13168	.44622	.18217	-.59996	.33660	-.723	5	.502
Switzerland	-.05811	.31984	.13057	-.39375	.27754	-.445	5	.675
United Kingdom	.34673	.36565	.14928	-.03700	.73045	2.323	5	.068
United States	.08982	.11090	.04528	-.02656	.20621	1.984	5	.104

The observation of Table 10 allows to verify that in only 9 of the 21 countries sample showed values of significance (two-tail Sig.) superior to 0.05. Therefore, as expected, the GWI seems not being reliable to assess the FDI attractiveness of the other 11 countries. We can proceed our index analysis using other tests that compared more explicitly the relationship between the GWI and the actual evolution of the inflows of FDI, however it is clear that the GWI have shown successively weak scores in the different phases of our index analysis process. Throughout the text, there were pointed out some shortcomings, first with some deficient theoretical framework and after with deficient selection of adequate indicators.

CONCLUSION

The present study shows relevant some weaknesses of FDI attractiveness index of Groh and Wich (2009) - GWI. The index analysis process followed, step by step, the index construction methodology stated by Nardo et al. (2008). In the sequence of a detailed literature review, there were check out some of the main determinants of FDI that permitted to detect relevant weaknesses on the theoretical framework that contributed to the subsequent deficient selection of individual indicators. Maybe the most relevant problems are not considering different indicators according to the economy level of development (advanced or in development), not making the differentiation between horizontal FDI and vertical FDI and finally, as Amaral (2013) underlines, including indicators with little theoretical support to the "*Quality of port infrastructure*".

It is known that Noorbakhsh et al. (2001), Johnson (2006), Makki and Somwaru (2004), Borensztein et al. (1998) Barrell and Pain (1997) and Benacek et al. (2000), had already found evidence of significant differences between determinants of the FDI attractiveness in the advanced economies and in the developing economies. In that sense, our analysis process included the examination of the GWI in a countries sample that included both advanced and emerging economies. That index examination revealed a better suitability of the GWI to replicate the inflow FDI in advanced economies environments than in emerging ones.

In what concern to the selection of the indicators' selection, the index analysis process include the fine revision of the data source, showing that many base indicators are actually aggregates of other indicators. As many of these basic indicators result from opinion surveys, consequently built with ordinal scales, (Amaral, 2013) alerts to its deficient information quality, aggravated by the potential distortion of their contents after the normalization process. The subsequent multivariate analysis found evidence of composite indicators built without the optimal concordance between simple indicators. Our study improve the consistency (internal and global) suggesting the removal of some indicators and the change of the weighting structure.

For a period between 2006 and 2011, our study assesses the relation between the behaviour of the inflows of the FDI and the progress of the GWI. After reducing to a common denominator, the data series that represents the evolution of the inflows of FDI, the index analysis revealed weak adherence of the GWI to the inflows of FDI on 12 of the 21 countries that constitutes the sample. Therefore, for each one of these 12 countries, the progression of the country attractiveness in the GWI seems to have no conditions to become a proxy of the real evolution of the inflows of FDI.

Our study produced two main contributions. The evaluation over the Groh & Wich (2009) attractiveness index, similar to other indexes and often used as political decision tools, revealed some serious problems over its consistency and ability to represent adequately the FDI phenomena. Therefore, defining public politic strategies and monitoring them through the GWI can cause severe distortions in terms of public budget definition. Even though, our study leaves some pertinent suggestions that may help a possible reconstruction of the GWI, contributing to enhance its adherence to the performance of inflows of the FDI. The most relevant is the one that considers that an unbiased FDI attractiveness index should contain different indicators in function of the economic development level of each country. However, it does not mean that some new indicators like the one proposed by Archibugi and Coco (2004) to represent the technological capabilities cannot be allocate for both indexes. The first one associates with developed countries and the other is linked to the developing countries.

REFERENCES

Addison, T., & Heshmati, A. (2003). *The New Global Determinants of FDI Flows to Developing Countries: he Importance of ICT and Democratization*. World Institute for Development Economics Research.

Amaral, J. (2013). Index of Foreign Direct Investment Attractiveness of Groh & Wich: Robustness Analysis and Reconstruction [Master's thesis]. Instituto Superior Técnico, Lisboa.

Archibugi, D., & Coco, A. (2004). A New Indicator of Technological Capabilities for Developed and Developing Countries (ArCo). *World Development, 32*(4), 629–654. doi:10.1016/j.worlddev.2003.10.008

Bandura, R. (2005). *Measuring Country Performance and State Behavior: A Survey of Composite Indices*. Office of Development Studies United Nations Development Programme.

Barrell, R., & Pain, N. (1997). *Foreign Direct Investment, Technological Change, and Economic Growth within Europe* (107th ed.). The Economic Journal. doi:10.1111/j.1468-0297.1997.tb00081.x

Benacek, V., Miroslaw, G., & Holland, D. (2000). The Determinants and Impact of Foreign Direct Investment in Central and Eastern Europe: A comparison of survey and econometric evidence. *Journal of United Nations, 9*, 163–212.

Bénassy-Quéré, A., Coupet, M., & Mayer, T. (2007). *Institutional Determinants of Foreign Direct Investment* (35th ed., Vol. 30). World Economy.

Borensztein, E., De Gregorio, J., & Lee, J.-W. (1998). How does foreign direct investement affect economic growth? *Journal of International Economics, 45*(1), 115–135. doi:10.1016/S0022-1996(97)00033-0

Brainard, S. L. (1997). An Empirical Assessment of the Proximity-Concentration Trade-off Between Multinational Sales and Trade. *The American Economic Review, 87*, 520–544.

Buuren, S. V. (2012). *Flexible Imputation of Missing Data*. CRC Press. doi:10.1201/b11826

Cortina, J. (1993). What is coefficient alpha? An examination of theory and applications. *Journal of Applied Psychology, 78*(1), 98-104.

Cronbach, L. J. (1954). Coefficient Alpha and the Internal Structure of Tests. Psychometrik, 16(3).

Dunning, J. H. (1980). Toward an ecletic Theory of International Production: Some Empirical Tests. *Journal of International Business Studies, 11*(1), 9–31. doi:10.1057/palgrave.jibs.8490593

Dunning, J. H. (1988). The Eclectic Paradigm of International Production: A Restatement and some Possibel Extensions. *Journal of International Business Studies, 19*(1), 1–31. doi:10.1057/palgrave.jibs.8490372

Dunning, J. H. (1993). *Multinational Enterprises and the Global Economy*. Addison-Wesley.

Dunning, J. H. (1995). Reaprising the Eclectic Paradigm in an Age of Alliance Capitalism. *Journal of International Business Studies, 26*(3), 461–491. doi:10.1057/palgrave.jibs.8490183

Ebert, U., & Welsch, H. (2004). Meaningful environmental indices: A social choice approach. *Journal of Environmental Economics and Management, 47*(2), 270–283. doi:10.1016/j.jeem.2003.09.001

Fung, K. C., Iizaka, H., Lee, J., & Parker, S. (2002). Determinants of U.S. and Japanese Foreign Direct Investment in China. *Journal of Comparative Economics, 30-3*(3), 567–578. doi:10.1006/jcec.2002.1788

Groh, A. P., & Wich, M. (2009). *A Composite Measure to Determine a Host Country's Attractivenessfor Foreign Direct Investement.* IESE Business School.

Hair, J., Anderson, R., Tatham, R., & Black, W. (1998). Multivariate Data Analysis. Academic Press.

Helpman, E., Melitz, M. J., & Yeaple, S. R. (2004). Export Versus FDI with Heterogeneous Firms. *The American Economic Review, 94*(1), 300–316. doi:10.1257/000282804322970814

Hora, H., Monteiro, G., & Arica, J. (2010). Confiabilidade em Questionários para Qualidade: Um Estudo com o Coeficiente Alfa de Cronbach. *Produto & Produção, 11*(2), 85–103. doi:10.22456/1983-8026.9321

IMF. (2012). World Economic Outlook. *Coping with High Debt and Sluggish Growth*, p. 151.

Johnson, A. (2006). The Effects of FDI Inflows on Host Country Economic Growth. *CESIS Working Paper Series in Economics and Institutions of Innovation, 58*, 1-57.

Kaiser, H. (1958). The varimax criterion for analytic rotation in factor analysis. *Psychometrika, 23*(3), 187–200. doi:10.1007/BF02289233

Land, K. C., Michalos, A. C., & Sirgy, M. J. (2012). *Handbook of Social Indicators and Quality-Of-Life Research.* Springer. doi:10.1007/978-94-007-2421-1

Makki, S., & Somwaru, A. (2004). Impact of Foreign Direct Investment and Trade on Economic Growth. *American Journal of Agricultural Economics, 86*(3), 795–801. doi:10.1111/j.0002-9092.2004.00627.x

Maroco, J., & Garcia-Marques, T. (2006). *Qual a fiabilidade do alfa de Cronbach? Questões antigas e soluções modernas?* (Vol. 4-1). ISPA Laboratório de Psicologia.

Merz, M., Hiete, M., Comes, T., & Schultmann, F. (2013). A composite indicator model to assess natural disaster risks in industry on a spatial level. *Journal of Risk Research, 16*(9), 1077–1099. doi:10.1080/13669877.2012.737820

Mingoti, S. (2005). *Análise de dados através de métodos de estatística multivariada.* Ed. UFMG.

Moosa, I. A., & Cardak, B. A. (2006). The Determinants of Foreign Direct Investment: An Extrexeme Bounds Analysis. *Journal of Multinational Financial Management, 16*(2), 199–211. doi:10.1016/j.mulfin.2005.07.002

Najmi, M., Sepehri, M., & Hashemi, S. (2010). *The evaluation of Business Intelligence maturity level in Iranian banking industry.* Paper presented at the Industrial Engineering and Engineering Management (IE&EM), 2010 IEEE 17Th International Conference.

Nardo, M., Saisana, M., Saltelli, A., & Tarantola, S. (2005). *Tools for Composite Indicators Building.* European Commission Joint Research Centre.

Nardo, M., Saisana, M., Saltelli, A., Tarantola, S., Hoffmann, A., & Giovannini, E. (2008). *Handbook on Constructing Composite Indicators: Methodology and User Guide.* OECD Publications.

Nasser, O. M. (2007). The Determinants of the U.S. Foreign Direct Investment: Does the Region Matter? *Global Economic Review*, *36*(1), 37–51. doi:10.1080/12265080701217181

Nee, V., & Opper, L. (2009). *Bureaucracy and Financial Markets*. Academic Press.

Nicoletti, G., Scarpetta, S., & Boylaud, O. (2000). Summary Indicators of Product market Regulation With an Extension to Employment Protection Legislation. *OECD, Economic Department Working Papers 226*.

Noorbakhsh, F., Paloni, A., & Youssef, A. (2001). Human Capital and FDI Inflows to Developing Countries: New Empirical Evidence. *World Development*, *29*(9), 1593–1610. doi:10.1016/S0305-750X(01)00054-7

Nunnally, J. C. (1978). *Psychometric theory*. McGraw Hill.

Pellegrini, G. (2006). Measures of Competitiveness and Attractiveness: a Critical appraisal focused on Italy. *Proceedings of the Scientific Meeting of the Italian Statistical Society*, 1, 355-364.

Pinheiro-Alves, R., & Zambujal-Oliveira, J. (2012). The Ease of Doing Business Index as a tool for investment location decicions. *Economics Letters*, *117*(1), 66–70. doi:10.1016/j.econlet.2012.04.026

Portes, A., & Smith, L. D. (2010). Institutions and national development in Latin America: A comparative study. *Socio-economic Review*, *8*(4), mwq018. doi:10.1093er/mwq018 PMID:26543407

Saggi, K. (2002). Trade, Foreign Direct Investment, and International Technology Transfer: A Survey. *The World Bank Observer*, *17*(2), 191–235. doi:10.1093/wbro/17.2.191

Saisana, M., & Tarantola, S. (2002). *State-of-the-art Report on Current Methodologies and Practices for Composite Indicator Development*. European Commission-JRC.

Shatz, H. J., & Venables, A. J. (2000). The Geography of International Investment. *The World Bank, Policy Research Working Paper 2338*.

Snedecor, G., & Cochran, W. (1967). *Statistical Methods* (6th ed.). Iowa State University Press.

Yu, C.-h. (2014). *Using SAS for Item Analysis and Test Construction*. Retrieved on August 22, 2021, from: http://www.creative-wisdom.com/teaching/assessment/alpha.htm l

APPENDIX

Table 11. Index structure and data series

Identifier	Data Series (Simple Indicator)	Units	Source
1. Economic Activity			
1.1	Market dimension and potential		
1.1.1	(GDP PPP per capita)	[Per capita]	IMF, World Economic Outlook Database
1.1.2	(real GDP y-o-y Growth)	[%]	World Bank, Data Catalog (em substituição do Euromonitor International, IMF).
1.2	(Prevalence of Trade Barriers)	[#]	World Economic Forum, The Global Competitiveness Index 2012-2013 data platform
1.3	(Central Gross Government Surplus / Deficit)	[%]	IMF, World Economic Outlook Database
2. Legal and Political System			
2.1	Legal System		
2.1.1	(Rule of Law)	[#]	World Bank, WGI (Worldwide Governance Indicator)
2.1.2	(Regulatory Quality)	[#]	World Bank, WGI (Worldwide Governance Indicator)
2.1.3	(Legal Enforcement of Contracts)	[#]	World Bank, IFC (International Finance Corporation) – Doing Business (em substituição do Fraser Institute)
2.1.4	(Business Impact on FDI)	[#]	World Economic Forum, The Global Competitiveness Index 2012-2013 data platform
2.2	Political System		
2.2.1	(Stability and Absence of Violence / Terrorism)	[#]	World Bank, WGI (Worldwide Governance Indicator)
2.2.2	(Government Effectiveness)	[#]	World Bank, WGI (Worldwide Governance Indicator)
3. Business Environment			
3.1	(Pay and Productivity)	[#]	World Economic Forum, The Global Competitiveness Index 2012-2013 data platform
3.2	(Profit and Capital Gains Tax)	[%]	World Bank, IFC (International Finance Corporation) - Doing Business
3.3	(Administrative Requirements)	[#]	World Economic Forum, The Global Competitiveness Index 2012-2013 data platform (em substituição de Fraser Institute)
3.4	(Control of Corruption)	[#]	World Bank, WGI (Worldwide Governance Indicator)
4. Infrastructures			
4.1	Transportation		
4.1.1	(Quality of Roads)	[#]	World Economic Forum, The Global Competitiveness Index 2012-2013 data platform
4.1.2	(Quality of Railroad Infrastructure)	[#]	World Economic Forum, The Global Competitiveness Index 2012-2013 data platform
4.1.3	(Quality of Port Infrastructure)	[#]	World Economic Forum, The Global Competitiveness Index 2012-2013 data platform
4.1.4	(Quality of Air Transport Infrastructure)	[#]	World Economic Forum, The Global Competitiveness Index 2012-2013 data platform
4.2	Energy (Quality of Electricity Supply)	[#]	World Economic Forum, The Global Competitiveness Index 2012-2013 data platform
4.3	Telecommunications (Fixed Line and Mobile Phone Subscribers)	[Per capita]	World Bank, Data Catalog

Chapter 8
Deglobalization and Globalization Concerns:
Which Way for the African Continent?

Okechukwu Ethelbert Amah
Lagos Business School, Pan Atlantic University, Nigeria

ABSTRACT

In the 21st century, nations are oscillating between globalization, deglobalization, protectionism, and localization. Issues considered while making decisions on what policy to follow include the economic boom, the slump in the economy, and politics. Nations adopt protectionism despite its known negative effects because of political reasons. The size of the economy of the developed countries allows them to implement these policies and withstand any adverse effect arising from isolation or retaliatory actions. The African continent cannot afford to find itself in this war between two elephants. Hence, the chapter reviewed the options available to Africa and recommended the adoption of localization aimed at building size and presenting a common competitive advantage that member states of the local bodies can employ. The chapter recommended certain changes to be made in leadership and mode of operation to avoid localization going the way of globalization.

INTRODUCTION

Globalization was initiated to create a single village with the free movement of people, goods, and knowledge across borders. Past authors have questioned the effectiveness of globalization across nations (Prah, 2000; Ngwane, 2001). This has led to various forms of integration, such as deglobalization, protectionism, localization, and individualism (Leblang & Peters, 2022; Kim et al., 2020; Vargas-Hernandez, 2022). Africa has two challenges: globalization has performed poorly in the continent (Prah, 2000; Ngwane, 2001) and has not articulated actions to compete in the various forms of world integration. Africa needs to define how it integrates with the rest of the world in the future of world integration.

DOI: 10.4018/978-1-6684-3749-0.ch008

Africa can no longer stay aloof and watch a repetition of what happened to its economy during and after the current cold war. Africa must find answers to some critical questions. The big questions this chapter addressed include:

- What is the actual state of Globalization in Africa?
- Did globalization deliver the expected benefit in Africa?
- Where is the world heading?
- What should the African continent do to get better results in any future form of world integration? Are there structural changes the continent should make to prepare for the next wave of globalization?

This chapter addressed these questions to help policymakers position the continent for what happens in the game of chess to determine the future of globalization. Answers obtained led to the recommendation of what form of future world integration Africa should adopt.

The origin of globalization is as controversial as its definition (Amah, 2019). Since people of old depended on each other to certain levels, perhaps globalization is as old as human history. For example, the concept of the community came up in Africa when people lived together for the mutual benefit of each member of the community (Michalopoulos & Papaioannou, 2013). The historical perspective of globalization divided it into three eras: globalization of countries, companies, and individuals (Friedman, 2005). The ultimate goal of globalization was to make the world a single village in which there is no barrier to the movement of goods, people, and technology.

Based on this, globalization is defined as "The free flow of goods and services, human resources, and capital across national borders that is facilitated by the free flow of technology in such a way as to affect the economic development of nations and well-being of societies" (Amah, 2019, p.12). This definition is robust enough to include all aspects of the integration of nations and people to enhance the economic and other parts of national development. The level at which globalization has led to the single village as envisaged by the original concept of the term is questionable. Globalization made progress in some aspects of globalization and some countries before Covid-19.

Authors have questioned the importance of globalization in situations where the African continent does not have a competitive advantage in producing any finished goods (Amah, 2019; Bodomo, 2017). This belief has led to the polarization of researchers into two blocks. In the first block, the anti-globalists think that globalization was a plot by the western world to enslave the continent, knowing there is nothing the continent will benefit from globalization (Prah, 2000; Ngwane, 2001). In the second block, the pro-globalists state that globalization was beneficial to the continent, but environmental and leadership issues prevented the realization of the expected benefit (Amah, 2019). The pro-globalists listed factors specific to the continent that worked against globalization, such as leadership effectiveness. This debate may not end because of the constant changes in people's beliefs in Africa and the Western world.

Some powerful western countries, by their policies, have leaned towards total or selective protectionism irrespective of what the world bodies advocate. This action has incapacitated world bodies, such as the World Trade Organization (WTO), World Bank (WB), and International Monetary Fund (IMF). These independent world bodies now operate based on the boundary placed by the western countries. Thus, the world is witnessing a continuum with globalization on one end, protectionism on the other, and both deglobalization and localization between the two.

Political and emotional issues complicate the decisions on this continuum. For example, The New York Times quoted the USA President stating the war between the USA and China is "a battle between the utility of democracies in the twenty-first century and autocracies". This battle is not suitable for the economy of the fighting elephants. It is worse for Africa and other blocks that are the proverbial grass at the battleground between two big elephants.

WHERE IS AFRICA ON THE GLOBALIZATION SCALE?

The definition of globalization adopted in this book chapter shows that globalization is a multi-dimensional concept that covers the economic, social, cultural, political, and legal sectors. Two conditions must be satisfied for globalization to be considered successful. The first is it must cover the entire dimensions listed in its definition. The second is that it must be successful in all the countries and continents of the world. Social Globalization aims to achieve interconnectedness among the people of the world to achieve a reasonable level of quality of life, work, and family. The political and legal dimensions of globalization enhance this. The amount of barriers countries put in place to restrict the movement of people from one country to the other attest to the failure of social globalization. The world bodies, such as the World Bank, were put in place to guarantee these movements. However, the existence of regional bodies with varying degrees of restriction hampered the activity of these world bodies. Hence, considering the social, legal, political dimensions of globalization, world integration is a dream that is yet to be realized, and this places globalization in its infancy. Thus, globalization's social, political, and legal dimensions are dreams yet to be actualized.

The level of Foreign Direct Investments (FDI), Human Development Index (HDI), Industrial Production Rate (IPR), and Gross Domestic Product (GDP) per capita (Aalto-yliopisto, 2011; Zhang & Houghlin, 2006) can gauge the success of economic globalization. The FDI, HDI, IPR, and GDP per capita growth show that economic globalization was a success (Kim, 2013; Sharma & Gani, 2004; UNCTAD World Investment Report, 2016). Considering the economic growth in Africa, Globalization is a failure because the continent did not have the economic growth associated with globalization (UNCTAD World Investment Report 2016 and International Monetary Fund World Economic Outlook Database 2016). Other parts of the world had gained from economic integration, but existing data does not show that the African continent realized the same benefit in the economic dimension of globalization.

The globalization index measures the level of gain countries receive from the integration of nations. Amah (2019) carried out a regression analysis involving the globalization index and FDI on economic development parameters to find out the contribution of Globalization to African countries. The results are reproduced in Tables 1 to 3. Table 1 shows that while the globalization index improved the economic indicators for combined African countries, the FDI did not. However, when the nations were separated into those with high HDI and low HDI, regression analysis showed that globalization and FDI did not improve the economic indicators for low HDI countries but marginally for high HDI countries.

Table 1. Regression: Globalization and economic development for all African countries (Amah, 2019, p.20)

Globalization Indicators	Economic Development Indicators	β	R^2(%)
Globalization index	GDP per capita	.275*	7.5
	GDP	.163*	2.7
	HDI	.587**	34.5
FDI	GDP per capita	.04	
	GDP	-.01	
	HDI	.23*	5.3

*p<.05; p<.01

Table 2. Regression: Globalization and economic development for low HDI African countries (Amah, 2019, p. 20)

Globalization Indicators	Economic Development Indicators	β	R^2(%)
Globalization index	GDP per capita	.09	
	GDP	.18	
	HDI	.23	
FDI	GDP per capita	.55**	30.5
	GDP	-.05	
	HDI	.27	

*p<.05; p<.01

Table 3. Regression: Globalization and economic development for high HDI African countries (Amah, 2019, p. 21)

Globalization Indicators	Economic Development Indicators	β	R^2(%)
Globalization index	GDP per capita	.07	29.7
	GDP	.41*	
	HDI	.55**	34.5
FDI	GDP per capita	.36	
	GDP	.17	
	HDI	-.02	5.3

*p<.05; p<.01

Two factors have been recognized as responsible for the poor performance of FDI in African countries. These are the sectors where FDI is invested and the failed leadership in Africa that did not create appropriate foundational factors for the effectiveness of FDI (Bodomo, 2017). As the world debates the future and nature of globalization, this book chapter advocates that the African continent must take advantage of this to position itself on the path of competitiveness in any future form of world integration.

GLOBALIZATION, DEGLOBALIZATION, AND LOCALIZATION

Issues in the drive for world integration question the likelihood that globalization, as envisioned, will survive in the next century. When considering world integration, terms such as deglobalization, localization, and protectionism are mentioned. Deglobalization can mean the pulling down of some structures in globalization by nations to make globalization fit into their internal conditions. The systems pulled down are open to debate because they depend on the judgment of the countries that are advocating the pulling down. For example, Huang (2021) stated that what began as a trade war between China and USA has degenerated into a "bitter war", with issues outside trade taking center stage in the conflict. Introducing arbitrary tariffs based on the perception of unfairness is a significant component of this pulling down.

Similarly, the exit of Britain from the European Union has some elements of the pulling down of globalization. The pulling down has metamorphosed into two primary groups. The first is that nations are alone in this pulling down, so they take control of how they compete in the globalized world. The second is that nations form localized bodies to assume the authority of member countries and initiate or negotiate the pulling down with other blocks in the world. For example, the West African single currency is an attempt to surrender the authority of the member states to the body. The same is happening in all the blocks in the world.

Protectionist policies aim to completely pull down globalization or allow it to function only according to countries' desires. Nations who pursue this policy give the impression that they still subscribe to the ideals of globalization, but their stance shows the fallacy in their statements. Protectionism negates globalization's aims that allow the free flow of goods and services worldwide and tries to dismantle it completely. Deglobalization and localization question the ideals of globalization and demand the repositioning of the same to give more powers to local governance and individual countries. Localization is the basis of forming some local bodies, such as the African Union, the European Union, the Economic Community of West African States (ECOWAS), and others. Globalization, protectionism, deglobalization, and localization fall into a continuum, as shown in Figure 1.

Figure 1. Globalization and Protectionism Continuum

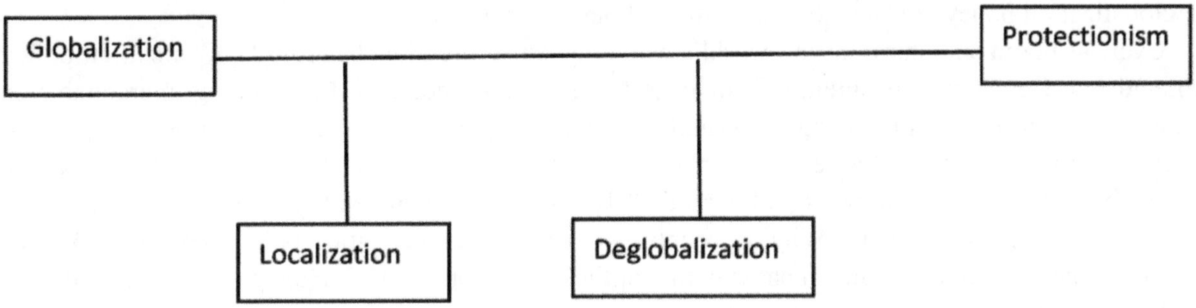

Nations and continents can decide on their location on the extremes or any point along the continuum. In reality, the world may not go back to the end of protectionism. This is because even the most powerful nations need some integration to have an advantage in the political chess game. For example, China and the USA are in a cold trade war, but with a political undertone (Huang, 2021), they are forming alliances with other countries or blocks to enhance their position in the chess game.

OPTIONS OPEN TO THE AFRICAN CONTINENT

The options to be considered will depend on understanding the basis of world integration advocated for globalization. Globalization is premised that nations will develop competitive advantage and compete in areas they have competencies and trade in areas they do not (Porter, 1990). Competitive advantage is created and not inherited. Hence, leaders consciously behave in ways that make it. The critical questions to address are how do African countries create competitive advantage? Do they compete as individual countries, or do they form blocks to compete with other blocks? In answering these questions, leaders must be able to balance national interest with global interest. Below are the analyses of the various options highlighting their advantages and disadvantages and concluding with what the African continent should do.

Deglobalization

Deglobalization is "the process of diminishing interdependence and integration between nations" (Kim et al., 2020, p.84). The history of deglobalization dates back to the 1930s but has gained momentum because of recent events in the world. Countries justify deglobalization because of the perceived lopsided achievement of globalization in the world. These include uneven reduction of poverty and income inequality (Klein, 2009; Salvatore, 2004; Shah, 2008) and low FDI growth (UNCTAD World Investment Report 2016 and International Monetary Fund World Economic Outlook Database, 2016). For example, these reports show that the African share of world FDI is 3.1% compared to other regions, such as 30.7% for Asian countries. This occurred despite the high GDP growth in Africa.

Deglobalization is more prevalent in the developed countries where globalization delivered great dividends; hence attributing deglobalization to the failure of globalization is questionable (Kim et al., 2020). The drivers of deglobalization are "trade imbalance, political pressure, high unemployment rate and trade tension between countries" (Kim et al., 2020, p. 84). Even in the countries that pursued a deglobalization policy, it is not consistent throughout the years.

Cyclical boom and slump in the world's economy cause the globalization-deglobalization policy conundrum. Hence, nations attempt to manage the economic recession by reducing interconnection with other countries by introducing tariffs and import quotas (Karunaratne, 2012). Nations that pursued deglobalization experienced a decline in major economic parameters such as GDP, GDP per capita, annual wage for unskilled workers (Hillebrand, 2010), decreased merchandise capital, and people flow across nations (Herrero, 2020). Why do countries pursue a deglobalization policy despite the known disadvantages? There is a political chess gain that the nations play, which Huang (2021) referred to as policy, but with a political undertone.

Among the features of deglobalization, the following are relevant in deciding if it is a policy that African countries should consider in future dealing with other nations (Bellow, 2008):

- Producing for the domestic market
- Provision of subsidies at the national level
- Low-income inequity
- Deemphasize growth, but emphasize development in the quality of life
- Transformed and decentralized power and transportation system
- Gender equality
- Civil society has the power to monitor the public sector

African countries are not in the position to guarantee any of these features. For example, there is income and gender inequality in most African countries and ineffective power and transportation system, which have defiled attempts to decentralize (Adesina, 2016; African Development Bank Group). African countries did not get the gains of globalization because of their inability to set up foundation structures necessary for effective participation in Globalization (Amah, 2019). The author posited that:

There are intervening variables consisting of people, structures, and policies which can jointly create the comparative advantage needed to compete effectively in a globalized world. Only countries that mobilize leaders who can create the suitable environment, policy, and rally people, can develop the comparative advantage needed to drive cooperation with the outside world (p. 8).

It is not likely that African countries can succeed with deglobalization as a policy based on the above. The continent does not have a sustainable structure to guarantee that it can be independent of other regions. The African continent has consistent potential growth in GDP and natural resources, but it has not positioned its economy to attract FDI in areas that develop it (Bodomo, 2017).

Protectionism

Protectionism is defined as "a defensive, often politically-motivated policy intended to shield a country's business, industries, and workers from foreign competition through the imposition of trade barriers" (Longley, 2018, p. 1). Developed countries use protectionism to shield infant industries, but it ultimately harms consumers who pay high prices for essential imported goods. There is no structure to enable the infant industry to increase its output, leading to shortage and inevitable importation to fill the gap. For example, the *Premium Times* (December, 2021) reported that the ban on imported rice in Nigeria had increased the cost of locally produced rice.

The problem was that plan was not implemented to enhance the capacity of local producers to make up for the shortfall arising from the ban on the importation of rice. The following are the expected advantage of protectionism for developing countries: protection of the new industry from competition from foreign firms, creating jobs for local workers, lower imports, and high foreign reserves. The downsides are lack of innovation by the local business, economic isolation, and the entire economy will suffer (Hufbauer & Elliot, 1994; Irwin, 2005).

The protectionist policy introduced by the USA in 2018 led to a total loss of US$51 billion to consumers and firms and spiral effects arising from retaliatory policies from other nations (Fajgelbaum et al., 2020). Melgar et al. (2013) reviewed the support for protectionism by various sections of a nation's population and found that the level of support varies among multiple categories. The workforce's opinion toward trade liberalization depends on the condition of the labor force. When skilled laborers are more mobile than unskilled laborers, the former would support trade liberalization and oppose protectionism while the opposite holds for unskilled laborers. In the same manner, those with higher education will embrace trade liberalization more than those with low education (Doyle & Fidrmuc, 2006; Gabel, 1998). Daniels and van der Ruhr (2005) identified social status, relative income, and values as determinants of preference for protectionism.

Certain foundations must be established for protectionism to succeed. For example, protecting the rice industry in Nigeria failed because the local producers did not adequately prepare to make up for the total demand for rice and people's preference. Hence, the gap created drove up the price of the local products while preference for foreign rice led to illegal importation. The overall consequence was the non-realization of the benefits expected. The growing number of skilled workforces in Africa and the inability to employ them because of rising unemployment makes protectionist policy not adoptable in Africa. Lastly, one disadvantage of protectionism is the isolation of the economy.

The African economy heavily depends on the foreign economy, and protectionist policy will isolate the continent and create scarcity and other economic problems. For example, Nigeria imported petrol worth $687 billion despite being a top producer of crude oil (Varrela, 2021) because of the ineffective refineries in the country. Hence, protectionism does not appear to be a path to be pursued by African governments.

Localization

Globalization places much responsibility on national leaders to manage their resources to create a competitive advantage, the basis for integration with other nations. This means that the national leaders must exercise their authority in a way that is beneficial to their economy and the growth of well-being of their people. Most African leaders had failed to perform this role, leading to the situation that Nwoke (2019) described as "failed leadership". In failed leadership, national leaders cannot play the role mandated by globalization, and hence the nations do not have the proper structure to compete. Localization is an attempt by national leaders to cede some of their powers to sub-regional bodies and regional bodies. Hence, these bodies become the basis for integration with other parts of the world.

For example, the newly formed African Continental Free Trade Area (AfCFTA) is an attempt by African countries to form one of the most extensive trade areas as a basis for competing with other parts of the world. It creates a single market of goods and services in Africa, and the body becomes a single contact point for all member countries. This can only happen if the member countries cede some of their authority to be exercised by the new body. Therefore, member states must ratify the treaty and state their conditions for participation.

Hines (2003) recommended localization as an alternate integration option in place of globalization. The author posited that localization allows "nations, local government, and communities to reclaim control of their local economy, to make it as diverse as possible and build stability into the community life" (p. 1). Localization does not support protectionist policy by participating countries under any disguise; however, it allows nations to pull their economies together to create the size needed to compete with bigger economies (Hines, 2003).

This will ultimately enhance the economic development of the collaborating nations and build the well-being of the citizens. It does not take full responsibility for the actions of the national government. It only helps to form a large block that can effectively compete with other regional bodies and vast economies of the world. For example, with about 1.3 billion people and 54 countries, AfFCTA will be better positioned to negotiate with the USA than any participating member.

Localization appears to be a viable option for consideration by the African continent. This will help balance the current view of countries like the USA and Britain for more nationalism and the call to review globalization to allow more powers to countries through regional bodies. What happened in the procurement of Covid-19 vaccines is a pointer to the control of localization and regionalization. For example, the African Union partnered with the World Bank in the Africa Vaccine Acquisition Task Team (AVATT) initiative to buy many vaccines for African countries (World Bank, 2021). Before this, the African countries found it difficult to purchase as a nation.

STRUCTURAL CHANGES TO BE MADE IN AFRICA TO BENEFIT FROM FUTURE WORLD INTEGRATION

This chapter aligns with the concept of the pro-globalists that globalization failed in Africa because the continent did not adequately prepare to compete in an integrated world. This is the position of some other African writers (Amah, 2017; Hoch et al., 2018). Like Africa, India and Singapore were disadvantaged early in Globalization (Mukherji, 2009; Yew, 2000). However, the national leaders put in place structures that eventually led to an increase in the economy of the nations. These are the foundational changes African leaders must make to take advantage of the regional bodies.

The first change expected is mindset change needed to reposition leadership and leadership achievement. For example, Yew (2000) increased Singapore's GDP per capita from US$400 in 1959 to US $22,000 in 1999 by making specific mindset changes. He articulated the changes in these words: "only if we changed people's thinking and attitude could we raise a large army like Switzerland's or Israeli's. We gave ourselves a decade to accomplish this" (p.18). His actions were more locally developed and adapted to local conditions instead of copying ideas that had no local relevance.

Hence, Africa's development path does not need to follow developed economies. The first mindset to be developed is what is the purpose of leadership? Should people be in leadership to earn status and prestige or to serve to build people and nations? The mentality that has governed African leadership for a long time and left us undeveloped and with long-serving leaders is that leadership is to earn status and power (Amah, 2019). African leaders must see leadership as an opportunity to serve to develop people and the nation. This calls for a review of the process of electing and replacing leaders.

The second change is deciding what level of power to keep at the national level and cede to the regional body. If the localized bodies are to act on behalf of member states and represent them in world integration, each member state must cede a certain level of power to the bodies. For example, the ECOWAS was set to enhance the economic development of member states through cooperation between them. This cooperation is to be at the economic and political levels. The decision-making process in this body occurs at two levels. The ministerial level formulates policies, and the head of government of each member state approves the policies.

Only a few members states have ratified the resolutions made by the body. Despite the success recorded by the body, Cernicky (ND) stated that "ECOWAS does not define or even influence any national political decision of its member states. That the leaders of the states ascribe little importance to the community is obvious" (P. 3). The reluctance of the member states to cede a certain level of their power to the body caused the incapacitation of ECOWAS to act and speak on behalf of members in the world integration.

The location of the units that coordinate the affairs of ECOWAS in each member state showed this. For example, Nigeria located the team in the Ministry of External Affairs and not the economic development.

AfFCTA envisaged that inter-Africa trade would increase at a higher rate than trade with the rest of the world and that tariffs between African states would decrease to -9% by 2045. This cannot be achieved unless the member states ratify the treaty and cede some level of power to the body to achieve the goals. Secondly, while there are many potential benefits of AfFCTA, the wide variation in the level of development in the member states can become an obstacle to achieving these benefits. This will happen if the more developed member states are unwilling to make some concessions to accommodate the less developed member states.

Ceding the power of the member states to the body is central to the performance of any localized body. The authorities are those of the heads of government, and unless these national leaders have the overall interest of the African continent, ceding such power will be challenging. The paradox that may become difficult to overcome is retaining some authority to be relevant in your country and ceding some control for the advancement of the localized body. Where the dividing line falls is something that will challenge the patriotism of each head of state of member states.

The third issue is the ethical standard of member states and the level of corruption in each country. The aim of the lower tariff is defeated if the corrupt practices of those at the border hamper the free movement of goods and services. For example, Adekoya (2020) reported that the average global rank in the Corruption Perception Index (CPI) in the Sub-Saharan African region is 32 out of 100. The author puts the loss due to corruption in Africa at $140 billion. This level of corruption increases the cost of doing business in Africa since the money lost to corruption is reflected as the cost of doing business. Political instability is another issue to be addressed in achieving localization. Political instability arises from the process of achieving change in governance in Africa. Only a few African states have reached a stable method of changing government that does not lead to instability. There may be a need to review the entire process of regime change in Africa to ensure that the process is corruption-free and elections are free and fair. Localization is the way to go for Africa. Still, African countries must make specific foundational changes for the local bodies to function effectively and drive the desire of African states to integrate with the rest of the world.

CONCLUSION

Boom, slump, and politics have dictated the choice of globalization, deglobalization, and protectionism. The movement has also been attributed to the failure of globalization to achieve what it promised. However, pro-globalists and anti-globalists have different reasons for the failure of globalization. Globalization is premised on the fact that nations would develop competitive advantage and would use this as a basis for world integration. This is what African countries could not achieve, hence the failure of globalization on the continent.

Thus, this chapter argues, along with other authors, that the failed leadership in Africa is the foundation of the failure of globalization. This is because African leaders could not prepare their country for competition in world integration (Amah, 2019; Bodomo, 2017; Nwoke, 2019). The book chapter advocates that the African continent cannot practice deglobalization and protectionism since more negative consequences would arise from adopting these principles (Fajgelbaum et al., 2020; Melgar et al., 2013; Varrela, 2021). Globalization is still the best form of integration globally, but the African continent needs to build size and power to compete globally. Hence, localization becomes an option that should be considered. This is because localization creates local bodies such as AfFCTA that act on behalf of members on the broader world integration.

Like globalization, localization will also fail unless the leaders in Africa are willing to carry out specific structural and behavioral changes aimed at positioning their countries to cede power to the local bodies to act on their behalf in the world's integration. Cooperation at the local bodies will create a collective competitive advantage that will form the basis of integration in the world. To achieve these goals, African leaders must rethink their mindset and understanding of leadership to a type that sees leadership as an opportunity to serve and not to gain power. In this way, the leaders would cede some levels of power to the local bodies to act on behalf of the nations involved in the collaboration.

This mindset will also enable the leaders to handle the paradox in need to keep some levels of power and cede to the local bodies. The last role of the mindset is that Africa will take responsibility for what happens to the continent instead of shifting blame to external factors outside the continent's control and the leaders.

REFERENCES

Aalto-yliopisto, A. (2011). *Investigating the relationship of inward foreign direct investment and poverty in developing countries* [Master's dissertation]. Aalto University School of Economics.

Adekoya, F. (2020, Dec. 8). $140bn yearly loss to corruption can address Africa's power challenge. *The Guardian*. Retrieved on May 4, 2021, from: https://guardian.ng/business-services/140bn-yearly-loss-to-corruption-can-address-africas-power-challenge/

Adesina, J. O. (2016). *Inequality in Sub-Saharan Africa: Dimensions & drivers. World Social Science Report, 2016*. Retrieved on September 22, 2021, from: https://en.unesco.org/inclusivepolicylab/sites/default/files/analytics/document/2019/7/Adesina_wssr_2016_chap_18.pdf

African Development Bank Group. (2021). Retrieved on December 22, 2021, from: https://www.afdb.org/en/topics-and-sectors/topics/quality-assurance-results/gender-equality-index

Amah, O. E. (2017). Leadership styles and relational energy in high quality mentoring Relationship. *Indian Journal of Industrial Relations*, *53*(1), 59–71.

Amah, O. E. (2019). *Globalization and leadership in Africa: Developments and challenges for the future*. New York Palgrave Macmillan. doi:10.1007/978-3-319-98764-4

Bellow, W. (2008). *Deglobalization: Ideas for a New World Economy*. Zed Books.

Bodomo, A. (2017). The globalization of foreign investment in Africa: The Role of Europe, China, and India. Emerald Publishing. doi:10.1108/9781787433571

Cernicky, J. (n.d.). *What is the good of ECOWAS?* Retrieved on January 3, 2022, from: https://www.kas.de/documents/252038/253252/7_dokument_dok_pdf_11781_2.pdf/75ef6c30-4f45-bd72-73f3-19b78fec8cf9?version=1.0&t=1539664207887

Daniels, J. P., & von der Ruhr, M. (2005). God and the global economy: Religion and attitudes towards trade and immigration in the United States. *Socio-economic Review*, *3*(3), 467–489. doi:10.1093/SER/mwi020

Doyle, O., & Fidrmuc, J. (2006). Who favors enlargement?: Determinants of support for EU membership referenda. *European Journal of Political Economy*, *22*, 520–543. doi:10.1016/j.ejpoleco.2005.09.008

Fajgelbaum, P. D., Goldberg, P. K., Kennedy, P. J., & Khandelwal, A. K. (2020). The return of protectionism. *The Quarterly Journal of Economics*, 1–55. https://doi. doi:10.1093/qje/qjz036

Friedman, T. L. (2005, Apr. 3). It is a Flat World, After All. *NY Times Magazine*.

Gabel, M. (1998). *Interests and Integration: Market Liberalization, Public Opinion, and the European Union*. University of Michigan Press. doi:10.3998/mpub.15828

Herrero, A. C. (2020). *From globalization to deglobalization: Zooming into trade*. Retrieved on November 11, 2021, from: https://www.bruegel.org/2020/02/from-globalization-to-deglobalization-zooming-into-trade/

Hillebrand, E. E. (2010). Deglobalization scenarios: Who wins? who loses? *Global Economy Journal*, *10*(2), 1850197. doi:10.2202/1524-5861.1611

Hoch, J. E., Bommer, W. H., Dulebohn, J. H., & Wu, D. (2018). Do ethical, authentic, and servant leadership explain variance above and beyond transformational leadership? *Journal of Management*, *44*(2), 501–529. doi:10.1177/0149206316665461

Hofbauer, G. C., & Elliot, K. A. (1994). *Measuring the costs of protectionism in the United States*. Institute of International Economic.

Huang, Y. (2021). *The U.S.-China Trade War Has Become a Cold War*. Retrieved on December 2, 2021, from: https://carnegieendowment.org/2021/09/16/u.s.-china-trade-war-has-become-cold-war-pub-85352

International Monetary Fund World Economic Outlook Database. (2016). Retrieved on December 22, 2021, from: https://www.imf.org/external/pubs/2016

Irwin, D. A. (2005). *Free trade is under fire*. Princeton University Press.

Karunaratne, N. D. (2012). The globalization-deglobalization policy conundrum. *Modern Economy*, *3*, 373-383. https://doi. doi:10.4236/me.2012.34048

Kim, H. (2013). Regionalism, globalization, and economic development of the world. *Journal of Globalization Studies*, *4*(2), 21–31.

Kim, H., Li, P., & Lee, Y. R. (2020). Observations of deglobalization against globalization and impacts on global business. *International Trade, Politics and Development*, *4*(2), 83–103.

Klein, L. K. (2009). Measurement of Shift in the World's Canter of Economic Gravity. *Journal of Policy Modelling*, *31*(4), 489-492. https://doi. doi:10.1016/j.jpolmod.2009.05.005

Leblang, D., & Peters, M. E. (2022). Immigration and Globalization (and Deglobalization). *Annual Review of Political Science*, *25*(1), 377–399. doi:10.1146/annurev-polisci-051120-105059

Longley, R. (2018). *Understanding the pros and cons of protectionism.* https://www.thoughtco.com/protectionism-definition-and-examples-4571027?print

Melgar, N., Milgram-Baleix, J., & Rossi, M. (2013). *Explaining protectionism support: The role of economic factors.* Hindawi Publishing Corporation. . doi:10.1155/2013/954071

Michalopoulos, S., & Papaioannou, E. (2013). Pre-colonial ethnic institutions and contemporary African development. *Econometrica*, *81*(1), 113–152. doi:10.3982/ECTA9613 PMID:25089052

Mukherji, R. (2009). The state, economic growth, and development in India. *India Review*, *8*(1), 81–106. doi:10.1080/14736480802665238

Ngwane, M. G. (2001). *Going Global.* Retrieved on December 3, 2021, from: https://www.accord.org.za/publications/ct-2001/global.htm

Nwoke, N. (2019). (In)Effective business responsibility engagements in areas of limited statehood: Nigeria's oil sector as a case study. *Business & Society*, 1–37.

Porter, M. E. (1990, March-April). The competitive advantage of nations. *Harvard Business Review.*

Prah, K. K. (2000). *African Unity, Pan-Africanism and the Dilemmas of Regional Integration.* Paper presented to the Southern African Regional Institute for Policy Studies (SARIPS) Annual Colloquium, Harare.

Premium Times. (2021, December). *Nigerian govt says ban on rice import stays.* Retrieved on May 3, 2022, from: https://www.premiumtimesng.com/news/more-news/435082-nigerian-govt-says-ban-on-rice-import-stays.html

Salvatore, D. (2004). Growth and Poverty in a Globalizing World. *Journal of Policy Modeling*, *26*(4), 543-551. https://doi. doi:10.1016/j.jpolmod.2004.04.009

Shah, A. (2008). Poverty Facts and Stats. *Global Issues.*

Sharma, B., & Gani, A. (2004). The effects of foreign direct investment on human Development. *Global Economy Journal*, *4*(2), 1–18. doi:10.2202/1524-5861.1049

UNCTAD World Investment Report. (2016). Retrieved on August 14, 2021, from: https://www.unctad,org,en/pages

Vargas-Hernández, J. G. (2022). Sustainable Green Resilience and Globalization or De-Globalization in a Post-COVID World. In *Economic and Societal Transformation in Pandemic-Trapped India* (pp. 33–51). Springer. doi:10.1007/978-981-16-5755-9_2

Varrela, S. (2021). Petrol import in Nigeria 2018-2021. *Statista.* Retrieved on October 7, 2021, from: https://www.statista.com/statistics/1165962/petrol-import-in-nigeria/

World Bank. (2021). *World Bank and African Union team up to support rapid vaccination for up to 400 million people in Africa.* Retrieved on June 2, 2022, from: https://www.worldbank.org/en/news/press-release/2021/06/21/world-bank-and-african-union-team-up-to-support-rapid-vaccination-for-up-to-400-million-people-in-africa

Yew, L. K. (2000). *From third world to first world: The Singapore story:1965-2000.* HarperCollins Publishers.

Zhang, C., & Houghlin, K. (2006). Does international investment help poverty reduction in China. *Chinese Economy, 34*(3), 79–70. doi:10.2753/CES1097-1475390306

Chapter 9
Analyzing the Global Economy in the Post-Pandemic Recovery:
Is the Recovery Near or Not?

Özlem Özsoy
https://orcid.org/0000-0003-4438-5734
Izmir Ekol Hospital, Turkey

Metin Gürler
https://orcid.org/0000-0002-9263-0258
Istanbul Medipol University, Turkey

ABSTRACT

More than two years have passed since the new type of coronavirus began in Wuhan, China. In addition, it has been more than 22 months since the World Health Organization (WHO) declared a pandemic, and the world continues to struggle with new variants of the virus and cannot return to the old normal. Closures, lockdowns, and restrictions on foreign trade of goods and services have decreased global economic activity. It is seen that two important challenges have emerged due to the pandemic. First, the countries with limited health services capacity in the face of the increasing number of cases and deaths in the world had trouble to combat with the pandemic. Second, low-income countries which have difficulty in accessing medicines and vaccines having an important role in combating the pandemic are more distressed than other countries and need global support. It is seen that the inequality in income distribution between countries in the world also manifests itself in accessing drugs and vaccines.

INTRODUCTION

At the end of 2019, a novel coronavirus emerged and spread very fast worldwide. COVID-19 (coronavirus disease 2019) has not only become a global epidemic, but the World Health Organization also (WHO) declared it as a pandemic on March 11, 2020 (Gürler & Özsoy 2020). Closures, lockdowns, and restrictions on mobility and foreign trade of goods and services have decreased economic activities in

DOI: 10.4018/978-1-6684-3749-0.ch009

the countries. COVID-19 not only shook up the health systems in countries and tested their capabilities by pushing their limits, but also caused a decline in economic growth, foreign direct investment (FDI), employment, foreign trade, social life and an increase in price levels, unemployment, external debt, poverty, and loss in working hours.

The global economy has faced the deepest recession since World War II due to the pandemic. Gross Domestic Product (GDP) per capita has experienced the highest decline since 1870 and fell in more than 90% of countries by 2020 (World Bank, 2020). The pandemic may leave lasting damage to human capital and economies, causing declines in investment, disruptions in global trade, global supply and value chains, and an increase in unemployment and loss of schooling. These effects can also reduce productivity and limit the ability of economies to increase real incomes in the long run. Developing a resilient supply chain strategy can help the Micro Small and Medium Enterprises (MSMEs) which plays a crucial role contributing to GDP and foreign trade of the countries can handle any kind of disruption such as pandemic (Mukherjee, Baral, & Venkataiah, 2022).

Declining economic activities have further deteriorated the inequality of income distribution both among citizens within the country and between countries. The negative effects of the pandemic have further affected the fragile parts of the society, especially the elder population who need care. It is also noteworthy that deaths from the pandemic are higher among the elderly population who are more in need of care and often have chronic diseases. One of the main areas of interest of social states is public health. States aim to ensure that every member of the society is healthy by trying to provide health services to their citizens, especially to the elderly population who need support. Facing lower physical and mental capacity otherwise causes older people to live more negatively in additional life years (Özsoy & Gürler, 2021a).

Inequality in income distribution also manifested itself in access to vaccines, and high-income countries transitioned to the new normal more quickly than low-income countries, with the increase in vaccination rate. With the COVID-19 pandemic, inequalities have emerged in the response of countries to the pandemic, thus necessitating countries to take global cooperation and concerted action together to better respond to global health threats.

Main Focus of the Chapter

This chapter aims to investigate the COVID-19 effects on health systems and economies. The study also aims to analyze COVID-19 related health indicators such cases, deaths, Case Fatality Rate (CFR), vaccination and health system infrastructure with the negative effects of the pandemic on global economy, FDI, foreign trade, external debt, poverty, tourism, unemployment, interest rates, and inflation.

METHODS AND MATERIALS

In the study, some basic pandemic indicators such as confirmed global COVID-19 related cases, deaths, Case Fatality Rate (CFR) and fully vaccinated people data were taken into consideration to analyze the pandemic effect on health systems in the countries. Global data were analyzed for regional both for geographical and WHO classification and the World Bank's income classification. For the analysis of the health system capacity, data for hospital beds, number of nurses, and medical doctors were examined.

GDP per capita is also a main economic indicator for a person to access diagnostics and treatments in the countries. As the income increases in a country, health expenditure, Research and Development (R&D) in health system also increase so that citizens will have a better and longer life. Higher health expenditure, health system capacity and health workforce are good estimators of the fight with the pandemic so that indicators related with these topics are analyzed in the study. To see the effect of pandemic on global economy, some basic economy related indicators such as economic growth, FDI, foreign trade, external debt, poverty, labor force and inflation were also analyzed in the study.

Tables and figures were used to investigate the relationships, flow, and changes in time series between the data. Growth convergence approach was applied to understand the success in closing the gap between countries in a time-period. Determining the normality of the data is important whether to use non-parametric or parametric correlation tests to use for investigating the relationship between the indicators.

H_0: Data for the indicator is normally distributed.
H_1: Data for the indicator is not normally distributed.

The Kolmogorov-Smirnov and Shapiro-Wilk normality tests were applied to the health-related indicators and income per capita. All of the indicators are not normally distributed as a result of the test statistics (all p values are smaller than the critical value 0.05 so that we reject the null hypothesis) (Table 1).

Table 1. Normality tests of the data set

	Kolmogorov-Smirnov			Shapiro-Wilk		
	Statistic	**df**	**Sig.**	**Statistic**	**df**	**Sig.**
vaccination	.089	188	.001	.954	188	.000
cases	.179	188	.000	.846	188	.000
deaths	.192	188	.000	.823	188	.000
beds	.130	188	.000	.843	188	.000
nurses	.147	188	.000	.858	188	.000
doctors	.149	188	.000	.884	188	.000
GDP per capita	.267	188	.000	.609	188	.000

Source: Our World in Data (2022a), IBM-SPSS (2022)

Since the data for all indicators are not normally distributed, Spearman's rho non-parametric correlation test is appropriate to test the relationship between the indicators. All indicators are correlated positively with each other (Table 2).

As the GDP and income per capita is high in a country, the health system capacity is also sufficient so that the countries have higher health personnel such as nurses and medical doctors, and higher hospital beds. Of course, the higher economic activity causes higher mobility in the population so that the cases and deaths are also high in these countries.

Table 2. Bilateral correlation coefficients between the data (Spearman's rho)

		Vaccination	Cases	Deaths	Doctors	Beds	Nurses	GDP per Capita
vaccination	Correlation Coeff.	1.000	.537**	.341**	.661**	.483**	.663**	.726**
	Sig. (2-tailed)		0.000	0.000	0.000	0.000	0.000	0.000
cases	Correlation Coeff.	.537**	1.000	.854**	.770**	.575**	.672**	.720**
	Sig. (2-tailed)	0.000		0.000	0.000	0.000	0.000	0.000
deaths	Correlation Coeff.	.341**	.854**	1.000	.675**	.477**	.493**	.529**
	Sig. (2-tailed)	0.000	0.000		0.000	0.000	0.000	0.000
doctors	Correlation Coeff.	.661**	.770**	.675**	1.000	.720**	.811**	.799**
	Sig. (2-tailed)	0.000	0.000	0.000		0.000	0.000	0.000
beds	Correlation Coeff.	.483**	.575**	.477**	.720**	1.000	.756**	.633**
	Sig. (2-tailed)	0.000	0.000	0.000	0.000		0.000	0.000
nurses	Correlation Coeff.	.663**	.672**	.493**	.811**	.756**	1.000	.818**
	Sig. (2-tailed)	0.000	0.000	0.000	0.000	0.000		0.000
GDP per capita	Correlation Coeff.	.726**	.720**	.529**	.799**	.633**	.818**	1.000
	Sig. (2-tailed)	0.000	0.000	0.000	0.000	0.000	0.000	

Source Our World in Data (2022a), IBM-SPSS (2022) **. Correlation is significant at the 0.01 level (2-tailed)

COVID-19 CASES, DEATHS, AND VACCINATIONS

In the first days of 2022, COVID-19 related cases reached 289 million and deaths passed 5.4 million with a 1.88 Case Fatality Rate (CFR) and 3.8 billion fully vaccinated people. As the end of 2021, the number of cases per thousand population was 37.3 and for the deaths per thousand population was 0.70, the average number of fully vaccinated people per hundred population was 49.5 in the world (WHO 2022a). The pandemic has affected not only the human life but also total economy and social life altering the expectations and increasing anxiety for the future as well. Pandemic has also showed there is inequality in vaccination as well as inequality in income distribution in the world.

COVID-19 has disrupted global supply chains and value chains. This disruption has also affected the economies negatively and contracted the GDP. Lockdowns, closures, and social distances have caused new attitudes in economic and social life. Increasing price levels and unemployment have also negative effect on consumers and households. Due to the pandemic, governments and international organizations have taken responses and strict protective decisions to decrease the negative effect of the pandemic on economy and social life. Governments and international institutions have tried to support the vulnerable economies and citizens. As the demand for both internal and external markets decreased and the flow in supply chain was halted the countries faced decreases in GDP, foreign trade, tax revenues and employment where individuals lost their jobs and income (Gürler & Özsoy, 2021a).

Both the number of cumulative global COVID-19 related cases and deaths move together (Figure 1), which means that as the number of the cases increase the number of the deaths increase too. The correlation between these indicators was 0.854, which indicates a very high positive correlation. The figure shows a bell-shaped data. New variants have occurred in November 2021, so the curve gained speed and had upward slope again. Regardless of the new variant effect, the number of cases has reached the highest level in April 2021 as 22.5 million and the number of deaths has reached the highest level in January 2021 as 417.4 thousand.

Figure 1. Monthly total cases and deaths
Source: Our World in Data (2022)

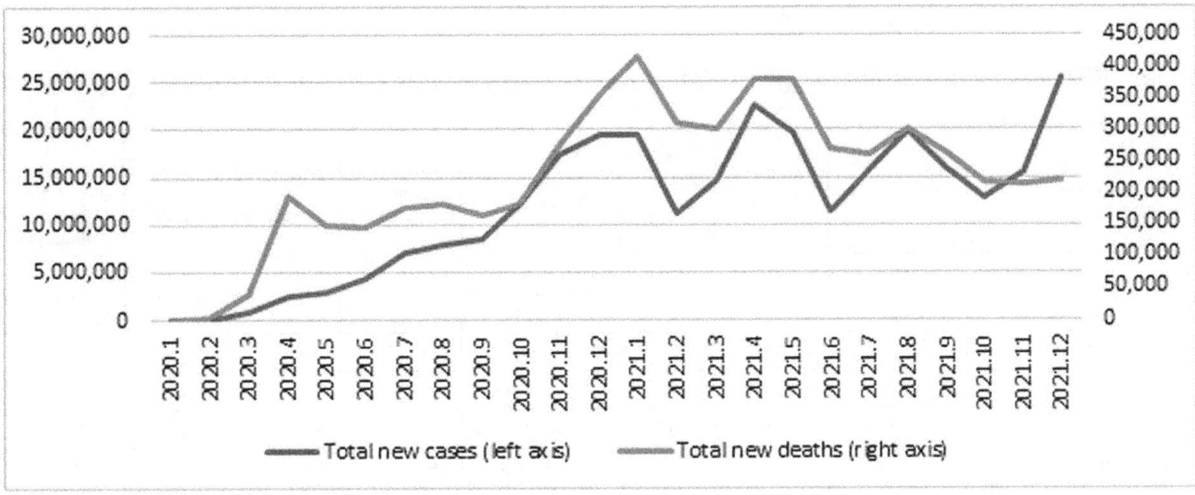

The data of COVID-19 for related cases, deaths, Case Fatality Rate (CFR) and vaccination can be seen according to the WHO regional distribution in Table 3. Africa has 2.5% of total cases as 7.35 million, the Americas has 36.2% of total cases as 104.7 million, the Eastern Mediterranean area has 6% of total cases as 17.2 million, Europe has 35.7% of total cases as 103.2 million, South-East Asia has 15.6% of total cases as 45 million and Western Pacific region has 3.8% of total cases as 11.4 million. Africa has 2.9% of total deaths as 156.5 thousand, the Americas has 44.4% of total deaths as 2.4 million, Eastern Mediterranean has 5.8% of total deaths as 316.1 thousand, Europe has 30.8% of total deaths as 1.7 million, South-East Asia has 13.3% of total deaths as 721.9 thousand and the Western Pacific region has 2.9% of total deaths as 156.5 thousand. Africa has CFR as 2.13, Americas has CFR as 2.30, Eastern Mediterranean has CFR as 1.84, Europe has CFR as 1.62, South-East Asia has CFR as 1.60 and Western Pacific region has CFR as 1.37.

Africa has 2% of total fully vaccinated people as 74.4 million, Americas has 16.4% of total fully vaccinated people as 625 million, and Eastern Mediterranean has 6.1% of total fully vaccinated people as 233.9 million. On the other hand, Europe has 14.4% of total fully vaccinated people as 547.8 million, South-East Asia has 20.2% of total fully vaccinated people as 768.3 million and Western Pacific region has 41% of total fully vaccinated people as 1.56 billon.

The number of cases per thousand population was 6.63 cases in Africa, 103 cases in the Americas, 23.7 cases in the Eastern Mediterranean, 110.9 cases in Europe, 22.3 cases in Southeast Asia and 6 cases in the Western Pacific region. COVID-19 mostly affects Europe and America as of the end of 2021 according to the cases considering the population size. The number of deaths per thousand population was 0.14 deaths in Africa, 2.37 deaths in the Americas, 0.44 deaths in the Eastern Mediterranean, 1.80 deaths in Europe, 0.36 deaths in Southeast Asia and 0.08 deaths in the Western Pacific region. COVID-19 mostly affects Europe and Americas as of the end of 2021 according to the deaths considering the population size. The higher mobility and the economic activity made these regions mostly affected by the pandemic.

The number of fully vaccinated people per hundred population was 6.71 in Africa, 61.52 in the Americas, 32.23 in Eastern Mediterranean, 58.85 in Europe, 38 in Southeast Asia and 82.14 in the Western Pacific region. It is seen that vaccination against COVID-19 was higher in the Western-Pacific, the Americas, and Europe, respectively, as of the end of 2021.

Table 3. WHO regional distribution of COVID-19 related cases, deaths, case fatality rate and vaccination

Region	Total Cases	Total Deaths	Case Fatality Rate (CFR)	People Fully Vaccinated	Cases per Thousand Population	Deaths per Thousand Population	Case Fatality Rate	Fully Vaccinated People per Hundred Population
Africa	7,350,001	156,451	2.13%	74,421,289	6.63	0.14	2.13%	6.71
Americas	104,698,449	2,411,818	2.30%	625,037,928	103.05	2.37	2.30%	61.52
Eastern Mediterranean	17,201,367	316,141	1.84%	233,853,062	23.71	0.44	1.84%	32.23
Europe	103,190,471	1,674,758	1.62%	547,837,914	110.85	1.80	1.62%	58.85
South-East Asia	45,034,821	721,940	1.60%	768,331,322	22.26	0.36	1.60%	37.99
Western Pacific	11,391,761	156,515	1.37%	1,563,246,978	5.99	0.08	1.37%	82.14
World	288,866,870	5,437,623	1.88%	3,812,728,493	37.48	0.71	1.88%	49.47

Source: Our World in Data (2022), WHO (2022a), the World Bank (2022a)

In Table 4, we can see the COVID-19 related cases, deaths, the Case Fatality Rate (CFR) and vaccination data according to the continental distribution. Africa has 3.4% of total cases as 9.7 million, America has 36.4% of total cases as 104.6 million, Asia has 29.1% of total cases as 83.8 million, Europe has 30.9% of total cases as 89 million and Oceania region has 0.2% of total cases as 566.3 thousand. Africa has 4.2% of total deaths as 227.9 thousand, America has 44.3% of total deaths as 2.4 million, Asia has 23.1% of total deaths as 1.25 million, Europe has 28.3% of total deaths as 1.53 million and Oceania region has 0.1% of total deaths as 4.5 thousand.

Africa has CFR as 2.35, America has CFR as 2.29, Asia has CFR as 1.49, Europe has CFR as 1.72, and Oceania region has CFR as 0.80. Africa has 3.3% of total fully vaccinated people as 126.9 million, America has 16.4% of total fully vaccinated people as 625 million, Asia has 67.6% of total fully vaccinated people as 2.58 billion, Europe has 12% of total fully vaccinated people as 458.9 million and Oceania region has 0.7% of total fully vaccinated people as 25.6 million.

The number of cases per thousand population was 7.30 cases in Africa, 102.9 cases in the America, 18.75 cases in Asia, 104.4 cases in Europe, 13.4 cases in Oceania. COVID-19 mostly affected Europe and America at the end of 2021, according to the cases considering the population size. The number of deaths per thousand population was 0.17 in Africa, 2.36 deaths in the America, 0.28 deaths in Asia, 1.79 deaths in Europe, 0.11 deaths in Oceania region. COVID-19 mostly affected Europe and America according to the deaths per thousand population.

The higher mobility and the economic activity made America and Europe regions mostly affected by the pandemic. The number of fully vaccinated people per hundred population was 9.56 in Africa, 61.52 in America, 57.65 in Asia, 53.83 in Europe and 60.5 in Oceania region. The vaccination rate against the COVID-19 was quite high in all regions except Africa, and more than 50% of the population were vaccinated in these regions on the last day of 2021.

Table 4. Continental distribution of COVID-19 related cases, deaths, case fatality rate and vaccination

Region	Total Cases	Total Deaths	Case Fatality Rate (CFR)	People Fully Vaccinated	Cases per Thousand Population	Deaths per Thousand Population	Case Fatality Rate	Fully Vaccinated People per Hundred Population
Africa	9,692,595.00	227,907.00	2.35%	126,930,251.00	7.30	0.17	2.35%	9.56
America	104,586,952.00	2,398,284.00	2.29%	625,037,928.00	102.94	2.36	2.29%	61.52
Asia	83,798,635.00	1,252,273.00	1.49%	2,576,227,495.00	18.75	0.28	1.49%	57.65
Europe	89,012,863.00	1,529,865.00	1.72%	458,938,239.00	104.41	1.79	1.72%	53.83
Oceania	566,271.00	4,512.00	0.80%	25,594,580.00	13.40	0.11	0.80%	60.55
World	287,657,316.00	5,412,841.00	1.88%	3,812,728,493.00	37.32	0.70	1.88%	49.47

Source: Our World in Data (2022), the World Bank (2022a)

The data of COVID-19 for related cases, deaths, the Case Fatality Rate (CFR) and vaccination can be seen according to the World Bank's income distribution classification of the countries in Table 5. Low-income countries have 0.54% of total cases as 1.56 million, lower-middle countries have 22.7% of total cases as 65.4 million, upper-middle income countries have 29.7% of total cases as 85.3 million and high-income countries have 47.1% of total cases as 135.4 million.

Low-income countries have 0.71% of total deaths as 38.4 thousand, lower-middle countries have 21.94% of total deaths as 1.19 million, upper-middle income countries have 41.5% of total deaths as 1.94 million and high-income countries have 35.9% of total deaths as 1.94 million. Low-income countries have CFR as 2.47, lower-middle countries have CFR as 1.82, upper-middle income countries have CFR as 2.63 and high-income countries have CFR as 1.43.

The Low-income countries have 0.75% of total fully vaccinated people as 28.7 million, lower-middle countries have 29.2% of total fully vaccinated people as 1.11 billion, upper-middle income countries have 47.7% of total fully vaccinated people as 1.82 billion and high-income countries have 22.4% of total fully vaccinated people as 852.5 million.

Low-income countries have total cases per hundred people as 2.4, lower-middle countries have total cases per hundred people as 19.6, upper-middle income countries have total cases per hundred people as 33.5 and high-income countries have total cases per hundred people as 115.

Low-income countries have total deaths per hundred people as 0.06, lower-middle countries have total deaths per hundred people as 0.36, upper-middle income countries have total deaths per hundred people as 0.88 and high-income countries have total deaths per hundred people as 1.65. COVID-19 mostly affects high-income countries as of the end of 2021 according to the cases and deaths considering the population size. The higher mobility and the economic activity made higher-income countries mostly affected by the pandemic.

The number of fully vaccinated people per hundred population was 4.38 in low-income countries, 33.5 in lower-middle income countries, 71.3 in upper-middle income countries and 72.4 in high-income countries. The vaccination rate of COVID-19 in the population was quite high in upper-middle income and high-income countries, and more than 50% of the population were vaccinated in these countries. Low-income and lower-income countries have difficulties in vaccination. As the world became global village with borderless, the vaccination should be done all over the world to minimize the negative effects of the pandemic on the global supply chains, FDI, and global trade.

Table 5. COVID-19 related cases, deaths, case fatality rate and vaccination considering the World Bank's income distribution regions

Income Group	Total Cases	Total Deaths	Case Fatality Rate (CFR)	People Fully Vaccinated	Cases per Thousand Population	Deaths per Thousand Population	Case Fatality Rate	Fully Vaccinated People per Hundred Population
Low income	1,557,370	38,409	2.47%	28,665,151	2.4	0.06	2.47%	4.38
Lower middle income	65,350,998	1,187,622	1.82%	1,113,407,211	19.6	0.36	1.82%	33.47
Upper middle income	85,345,345	2,245,493	2.63%	1,818,126,248	33.5	0.88	2.63%	71.34
High income	135,397,086	1,941,266	1.43%	852,529,883	115.0	1.65	1.43%	72.38
World	287,650,799	5,412,790	1.88%	3,812,728,493	37.3	0.70	1.88%	49.47

Source: Our World in Data (2022), the World Bank (2022a)

It is clear the mobility which emerges as a result of economic activity can cause the virus to be transmitted from person to person due to close working, especially in industrialized and industrializing countries. As the income per capita increases mobility, economic activity, and cases per hundred people increase as well. There is a positive correlation between GDP per capita and number of cases in the world (Figure 2).

Figure 2. Cases per hundred people and income per capita
Source: Our World in Data, SPSS (2022)

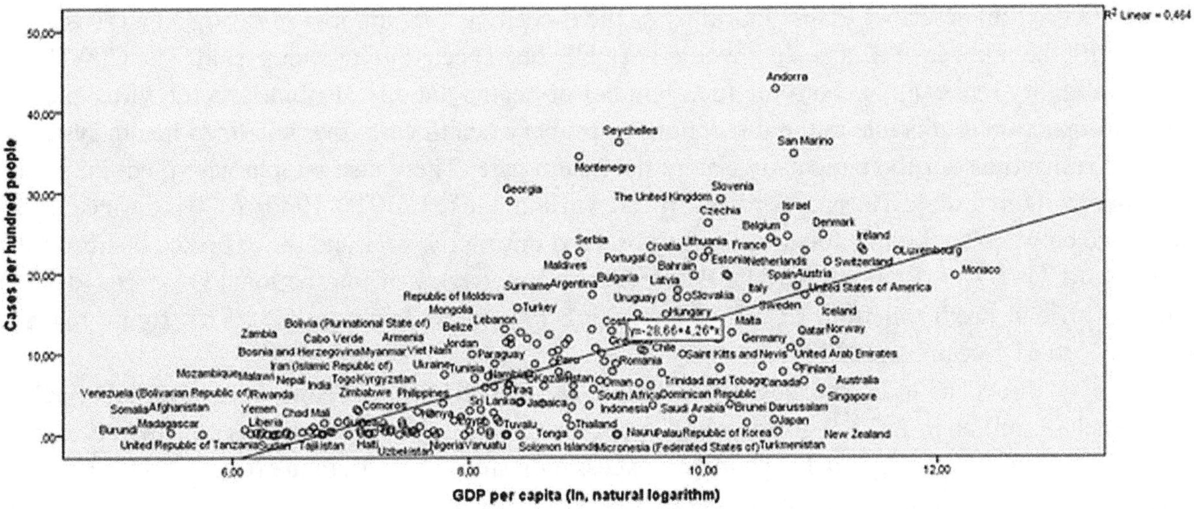

Higher income per capita is a driven force to access better health care service in a country. As income per capita increases, the number of fully vaccinated people per hundred population in the world also increases (Figure 3).

Figure 3. Vaccination and income per capita
Source: Our World in Data, SPSS (2022)

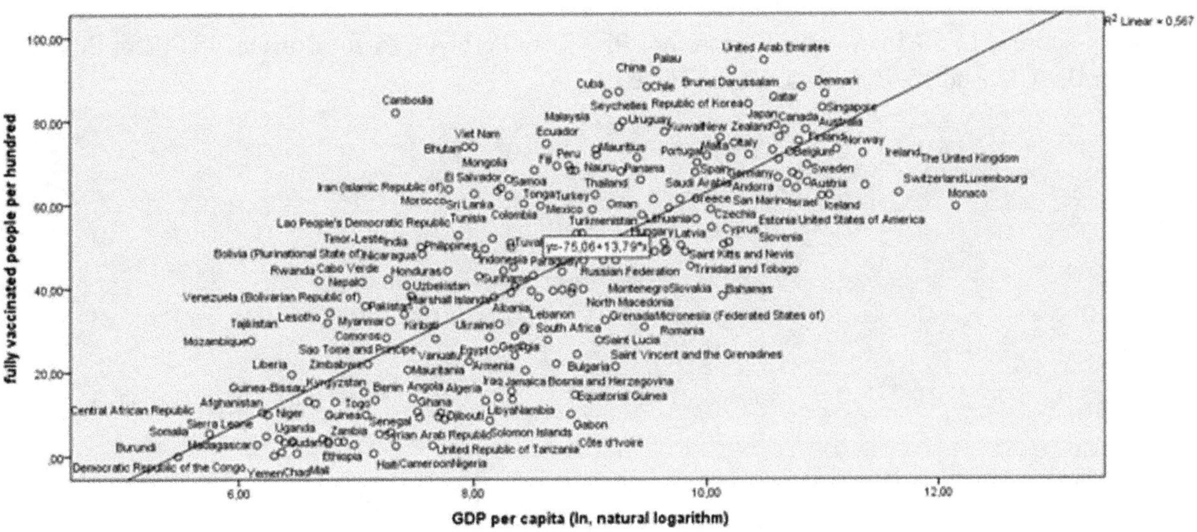

Excess Mortality

The WHO (2022b) describes excess mortality as the exceeding total number of deaths in a crisis comparing with the number of deaths what would normally be expected in a given period. The COVID-19 excess mortality rate explains both the total number of deaths directly attributed to the virus and the indirect impact on deaths due to the disruptions to primary health care (overwhelmed health systems) or travel restrictions for the patients to access the health care. There also people who died due to the pandemic without testing. The excess mortality rate attributable to COVID-19 for 2020 is defined as the difference between the total number of deaths observed during the year and the expected deaths in the absence of COVID-19. WHO declared a Public Health Emergency of International Concern (PHEIC) with the official death toll from COVID-19 reaching 171 on 30 January 2020. This figure reached 1,901,767 on 31 December 2020.

While the direct and indirect excess deaths due to the COVID-19 pandemic were reported to be approximately 3 million in 2020, it corresponds to approximately 1.1 million more deaths than officially reported. In the Americas region, the pandemic excess mortality estimates range from 1.34-1.46 million whereas 1.11-1.21 million in the Europe Region in 2020. This means that excess mortality is approximately 60% and 50% more than reported COVID-19 deaths, respectively. In OECD countries, COVID-19 has caused 2.5 million excess deaths (OECD 2021a).

The formula to measure the excess mortality (P-score) which is the percentage difference between the reported and projected number of deaths is as below (Our World in Data 2022b).

$$P\text{-}score = \frac{\left(Number\ of\ reported\ deaths - Number\ of\ expected\ deaths\right)}{Number\ of\ expected\ deaths} * 100$$

Total p-score is 14.5% in average. P-score was 95.4% for Peru, 49.9% for Bolivia, 48.3% for Ecuador, 10.4% for the UK, and 15.7% for the USA (Table 6).

Table 6. Average excess mortality rates (P-scores, 2020-2021)

Country	Average P-Score (2020-2021)	Rank
Peru	95.4	1
Bolivia	49.9	2
Ecuador	48.3	3
Kuwait	45.7	4
Armenia	40.6	5
Nicaragua	40.1	6
Mexico	40.0	7
North Macedonia	36.0	8
Colombia	34.4	9
Iran	33.8	10
Canada	3.5	84
Germany	2.8	87
United Kingdom (UK)	10.4	63
United States (USA)	15.7	44
Total	14.5	

Source: Our World İn Data (2022b)

HEALTH SYSTEM INFRASTRUCATURE

Globally at the beginning of 2022, there were more than 288.9 million confirmed COVID-19 cases and 5.44 million deaths all over the world with a 1.88 Case Fatality Rate (CFR) (WHO 2022a). With COVID-19, it has been seen that the health system and health personnel are indispensable in the fight against the virus, even during the pandemic period. Increasing demand and need for a strong healthcare workforce including doctors and nurses have been emerged. The lack of equal distribution of health personnel around the world for a resilience health system, which was already a very important problem before the pandemic, has become more evident with the pandemic (Özsoy, 2021).

The COVID-19 pandemic is no longer an individual nation's problem; it is a global problem even for the human development and a collaborated partnership is needed (Özsoy & Gürler 2021b). Apart from limited capacity of the health system in the countries, skilled health personnel has very crucial importance. Health workforce including nurses is the other main input of the health system in the countries (Özsoy, 2021). Abi-Rached (2021), in his five book review study, has not only argued that after the pandemic, everything should be rediscovered and that we need a more "flexible" health system, but also stated that human health has a priority over profits, and that more investment should do be done in prevention and preparedness against epidemics.

A skilled health workforce and good working conditions are indispensable to have a strong health system in a country. The healthcare personnel including medical doctors and nurses are responsible for both daily healthcare needs and emergencies. By 2030, according to the Sustainable Development Goal 3c (SDG 3c), mostly in low-income countries and lower-middle income countries, the world needs 18 million more healthcare staff and nine million of them are the nurses and midwives (WHO, 2020a; WHO, 2020b).

According to the WHO, a total of 59% of the global health professions are nursing workforce. There are 27.9 million nurses and 19.3 million of them are professional nurses. The associate professional nurses are 22% of total nurses as 6.0 million. There was a global shortage of nurses before the pandemic and need for them has increased during pandemic (WHO, 2020a). The distribution of the human resources in health care are not equal across the world. The capacity and competence of the health systems and the skills of the health personnel in the countries play a very important role in the fight against the pandemic.

While the countries that have sufficient levels of health system and health personnel have achieved success in the fight against the pandemic. The pandemic also showed that countries should review their policies regarding the education and training of health personnel, their continuing professional development, and the equal geographical distribution of personnel in the country. It has become clear that countries need to plan how they will meet the future demand for health professionals and how they will manage the supply of health professionals. Countries should encourage healthcare professionals to follow the technological developments and innovations in the field of health in the world and ensure they meet these technologies as soon as possible and have innovative devices and methods (Özsoy & Gürler 2021b).

There is a total of 28.4 million nurses, 13.2 million medical doctors, and 19.7 million hospital beds in the world as of 2019 (Table 7). Africa has 3.2% of total nurses as 902.1 thousand, Americas has 29.2% of total nurses as 8.3 million, Eastern Mediterranean has 3.8% of total nurses as 1.1 million, Europe has 24.2% of total nurses as 6.9 million, South-East Asia has 15.4% of total nurses as 4.4 million and Western Pacific region has 24.3% of total nurses as 6.9 million.

Africa has 2.1% of total medical doctors as 277.9 thousand, Americas has 21.5% of total medical doctors as 2.8 million, and Eastern Mediterranean has 5.8% of total medical doctors as 763 thousand. On the other hand, Europe has 30.2% of total medical doctors as 4 million, South-East Asia has 13.2% of total medical doctors as 1.75 million and Western Pacific region has 27.2% of total medical doctors as 3.6 million.

Africa has 4.7% of total hospital beds as 923.8 thousand, the Americas has 11.4% of total hospital beds as 2.24 million, and Eastern Mediterranean has 4.1% of total hospital beds as 810.8 thousand. On the other hand, Europe has 24.7% of total hospital beds as 4.9 million, South-East Asia has 9.3% of total hospital beds as 1.8 million and Western Pacific region has 45.8% of total hospital beds as nine million.

It seems the Americas, Europe and Western-Pacific regions have more resilient health system against pandemic. The Americas, Europe, and Western-Pacific regions have most of the health personnel and Europe and Western-Pacific regions have most of the hospital beds. The number of nurses per thousand population was 0.81 nurses in Africa, 8.16 nurses in the Americas, 1.49 nurses in the Eastern Mediterranean, 7.38 nurses in Europe, 2.16 nurses in Southeast Asia and 3.62 nurses in the Western Pacific region.

The number of medical doctors per thousand population was 0.25 medical doctors in Africa, 2.80 medical doctors in the Americas, 1.05 medical doctors in the Eastern Mediterranean, 4.28 medical doctors in Europe, 0.86 medical doctors in Southeast Asia and 1.89 medical doctors in the Western Pacific region. Africa and Eastern Mediterranean regions have the least nurses per thousand population and Africa and South-East Asia regions have the minimum number of medical doctors per thousand population considering population size.

The number of hospital beds per thousand population was 0.83 hospital beds in Africa, 2.21 hospital beds in the Americas, 1.12 hospital beds in the Eastern Mediterranean, 5.22 hospital beds in Europe, 0.90 hospital beds in Southeast Asia and 4.74 hospital beds in the Western Pacific region. Africa and

Southeast Asia regions have the least hospital beds per thousand population whereas Europe and Western Pacific regions have the most considering the population size.

Table 7. WHO regional distribution of health personnel (2019 and most recent year)

Region	Number of Nurses	Number of Medical Doctors	Number of Hospital Beds	Region's Share in Nurses	Region's Share in Medical Doctors	Region's Share in Hospital Beds	Number of Nurses per Thousand Population	Number of Medical Doctors per Thousand Population	Number of Hospital Beds per Thousand Population
Africa	902,067	277,902	923,775	3.2%	2.1%	4.7%	0.81	0.25	0.83
Americas	8,292,336	2,843,682	2,241,005	29.2%	21.5%	11.4%	8.16	2.80	2.21
Eastern Mediterranean	1,079,676	763,039	810,849	3.8%	5.8%	4.1%	1.49	1.05	1.12
Europe	6,869,080	3,984,157	4,861,693	24.2%	30.2%	24.7%	7.38	4.28	5.22
South-East Asia	4,366,307	1,745,287	1,829,966	15.4%	13.2%	9.3%	2.16	0.86	0.90
Western Pacific	6,889,097	3,597,788	9,019,309	24.3%	27.2%	45.8%	3.62	1.89	4.74
World	28,398,563	13,211,855	19,686,597	100.0%	100.0%	100.0%	3.68	1.71	2.55

Source: WHO (2022c), the World Bank (2022a)

The number of nurses, medical doctors and hospital beds can be seen according to the continental distribution in Table 8.

Africa has 4.4% of total nurses as 1.26 million, America has 29.2% of total nurses as 8.3 million, Asia has 42.8% of total nurses as 12.2 million, Europe has 22.2% of total nurses as 6.3 million and Oceania has 1.3% of total nurses as 371.3 thousand. Africa has 3.2% of total medical doctors as 418.7 thousand, America has 21.5% of total medical doctors as 2.8 million, Asia has 45.9% of total medical doctors as 6.1 million, Europe has 28.5% of total medical doctors as 3.8 million, and Oceania has 0.84% of total medical doctors as 111.6 thousand.

Africa has 6.11% of total hospital beds as 1.2 million, America has 11.4% of total hospital beds as 2.24 million, Asia has 59% of total hospital beds as 11.6 million, Europe has 22.9% of total hospital beds as 4.5 million, and Oceania has 0.58% of total hospital beds as 114.9 thousand. It seems that America, Asia, and Europe have more resilient health systems against pandemic. America, Asia, and Europe have most of the health personnel and Europe and Asia regions have most of the hospital beds.

The number of nurses per thousand population was 0.95 nurse population in Africa, 8.16 in the Americas, 2.72 nurses in Asia, 7.40 nurses in Europe, and 8.8 nurses in Oceania. The number of medical doctors per thousand population was 0.32 medical doctors in Africa, 2.80 medical doctors in the America, 1.36 medical doctors in the Asia, 4.42 medical doctors in Europe, and 2.64 medical doctors in Oceania. Africa and Asia regions have the least nurses per thousand population and Africa and Oceania regions have the least doctors per thousand population considering the population size.

The number of hospital beds per thousand population was 0.91 hospital beds in Africa, 2.21 hospital beds in the America, 2.60 hospital beds in Asia, 5.29 hospital beds in Europe, 2.72 hospital beds in Oceania. Africa has the least hospital beds per thousand population whereas Europe has the most considering the population size.

Table 8. Continental distribution of health personnel (2019 and most recent year)

Region	Number of Nurses	Number of Medical Doctors	Number of Hospital Beds	Region's Share in Nurses	Region's Share in Medical Doctors	Region's Share in Hospital Beds	Number of Nurses per Thousand Population	Number of Medical Doctors per Thousand Population	Number of Hospital Beds per Thousand Population
Africa	1,256,840	418,670	1,202,435	0.04	3.17%	6.11%	0.95	0.32	0.91
America	8,292,336	2,843,682	2,241,005	0.29	21.52%	11.38%	8.16	2.80	2.21
Asia	12,168,151	6,068,587	11,617,424	0.43	45.93%	59.01%	2.72	1.36	2.60
Europe	6,309,922	3,769,330	4,510,855	0.22	28.53%	22.91%	7.40	4.42	5.29
Oceania	371,314	111,586	114,878	0.01	0.84%	0.58%	8.78	2.64	2.72
World	28,398,563	13,211,855	19,686,597	1.00	100.00%	100.00%	3.68	1.71	2.55

Source: WHO (2022c), the World Bank (2022a)

The number of nurses, medical doctors and hospital beds can be seen according to the World Bank's income distribution classification of the countries in Table 9.

Low-income countries have 1.8% of total nurses as 501.8 thousand, lower-middle countries have 22.6% of total nurses as 6.4 million, upper-middle income countries have 28.9% of total nurses as 8.2 million and high-income countries have 46.7% of total nurses as 13.3 million. Low-income countries have 1.5% of total medical doctors as 191.8 thousand, lower-middle countries have 20.4% of total medical doctors as 2.7 million, upper-middle income countries have 45% of total medical doctors as 5.95 million and high-income countries have 33.1% of total medical doctors as 4.4 million. Low-income countries have 3.8% of total hospital beds as 746 thousand, lower-middle countries have 17% of total hospital beds as 3.3 million, upper-middle income countries have 48.3% of total hospital beds as 9.5 million and high-income countries have 30.9% of total hospital beds as 6.1 million. Low-income countries seem as the most vulnerable countries considering the health personnel and hospital beds.

Low-income countries have total nurses per thousand people as 0.77, lower-middle countries have total nurses per thousand people as 1.93, upper-middle income countries have total nurses per thousand people as 3.22 and high-income countries have total nurses per thousand people as 11.27. Low-income countries have total medical doctors per thousand people as 0.29, lower-middle countries have total medical doctors per thousand people as 0.81, upper-middle income countries have total medical doctors per thousand people as 2.33 and high-income countries have total medical doctors per thousand people as 3.71.

Low-income countries have total hospital beds per thousand people as 1.14, lower-middle countries have total hospital beds per thousand people as 1.0, upper-middle income countries have total hospital beds per thousand people as 3.73 and high-income countries have total hospital beds per thousand people as 5.17. Low-income countries have the least number of nurses per thousand population; low income and lower middle-income countries have the least number of medical doctors and hospital beds per thousand population considering the population size.

Table 9. Health personnel considering the World Bank's income distribution regions (2019 and most recent year)

Income Group	Number of Nurses	Number of Medical Doctors	Number of Hospital Beds	Region's Share in Nurses	Region's Share in Medical Doctors	Region's Share in Hospital Beds	Number of Nurses per Thousand Population	Number of Medical Doctors per Thousand Population	Number of Hospital Beds per Thousand Population
Low income	501,840	191,832	746,034	1.77%	1.45%	3.79%	0.77	0.29	1.14
Lower middle income	6,413,979	2,697,578	3,343,141	22.59%	20.42%	16.98%	1.93	0.81	1.00
Upper middle income	8,208,394	5,950,577	9,506,187	28.90%	45.04%	48.29%	3.22	2.33	3.73
High income	13,274,350	4,371,868	6,091,235	46.74%	33.09%	30.94%	11.27	3.71	5.17
World	28,398,563	13,211,855	19,686,597	100.00%	100.00%	100.00%	3.68	1.71	2.55

Source: WHO (2022c), the World Bank (2022a)

HEALTH EXPENDITURE AND LIFE EXPECTANCY DUE TO COVID-19

A better health service in a country, which lowers the mortality rates, also promotes a long with a higher life expectancy and healthy labor force (Gürler & Özsoy, 2019).

The Effect of COVID-19 on Health Expenditures

In the traditional economic growth model, labor constitutes another main factor of production with capital input. Productivity has a great importance on the economic growth of a country. The increase in health expenditures also increases the provision of good health services to citizens. People who benefit from good health care make themselves more productive and well-being. Increased productivity in the workforce and working hours from productivity leads to economic growth.

Gross Domestic Product (GDP) and per capita income will increase continuously in the country. In addition, higher per capita income means better access to health services provided by the public and private sectors in a country. Thus, positive feedback occurs between the increase in health expenditures and the per capita income (Özsoy & Gürler, 2020). Health expenditure which includes not only health consumption expenditures such as salaries, medicine and treatments but investment for infrastructures, equipment and research and development (R&D) are very important to fight the pandemic (Özsoy, 2021).

As per capita income in countries increases, health expenditures also increase, and as a result, while the growth rate at birth decreases, life expectancy at birth increases. Developments in health innovations and the increase in health expenditures cause people to live longer, especially in high-income countries. The decreasing birth rate also causes an increase in the share of the elderly population in the total population. The elderly population is increasing much faster than the total population, especially in high-income countries.

One of the main purposes of social states is to improve public health, so governments try to provide health services to their citizens (Özsoy & Gürler, 2021a). As the healthcare system is preoccupied with the pandemic and the government's budget revenues have contracted, COVID-19 has disrupted the provision of services and care to the elderly population. Older people and socially disadvantaged groups are more likely to be severely ill or die from the virus (OECD, 2021a).

While global healthcare expenditures have more than doubled in real terms over the past two decades, reaching to 9.8% of global GDP as US$8.5 trillion in 2019, there is an uneven distribution between the countries. As the high-income countries have made for approximately 80% of global health expenditures, in low-income countries health expenditures are primarily financed by out-of-pocket (WHO, 2021a).

For 25 countries, total health expenditure was US$5.9 trillion in 2019 and increased 8.8% to US$6.4 trillion dollars in 2020. In average health expenditure per capita was US$5,567 in 2019 and US$6,029 in 2020 (Table 10). Citizens in some countries such as USA, the UK, Sweden, Estonia, Ireland, Czechia, and Lithuania are blessed to have higher health expenditure and to access the health care against pandemic while citizens in Canada, Mexico, Norway, and Turkey are not happy due to the contraction in health expenditures.

The USA has the highest health expenditure per capita with US$11,449 in 2019 and US$12,517 in 2020. Turkey has the lowest health expenditure per capita with US$428.7 in 2019 and US$427 in 2020. Chile has the lowest growth rate in health expenditure per capita as 9.9% and United Kingdom has the highest growth rate as 19.9%.

Table 10. The effect of COVID-19 on health expenditure per capita

Country	Health Expenditure per Capita (2019, $)	Health Expenditure per Capita (2020, $)	Change (2019-2020)
Austria	5,228.9	5,586.5	6.8%
Canada	5,023.7	4,999.3	-0.5%
Chile	1,375.8	1,239.1	-9.9%
Czech Republic (Czechia)	1,853.8	2,079.5	12.2%
Denmark	5,951.3	6,480.0	8.9%
Estonia	1,574.6	1,854.1	17.8%
Finland	4,455.5	4,657.8	4.5%
France	4,509.1	4,830.8	7.1%
Germany	5,473.6	5,789.9	5.8%
Iceland	5,905.5	5,816.2	-1.5%
Ireland	5,402.4	6,134.2	13.5%
Italy	2,916.4	3,081.4	5.7%
Korea, Rep.	2,607.3	2,658.6	2.0%
Lithuania	1,371.5	1,530.7	11.6%
Mexico	540.6	517.3	-4.3%
Netherlands	5,334.2	5,877.9	10.2%
Norway	7,977.7	7,644.7	-4.2%
Poland	1,016.6	1,124.1	10.6%
Portugal	2,223.7	2,243.4	0.9%
Slovak Republic	1,343.3	1,489.7	10.9%
Slovenia	2,211.4	2,479.0	12.1%
Sweden	5,672.3	5,983.9	5.5%
Turkey	428.7	426.8	-0.4%
United Kingdom (the UK)	4,373.4	5,245.0	19.9%
United States (USA)	11,449.2	12,516.6	9.3%
Average	5,567.0	6,028.7	8.3%

Sources: OECD (2022a), the U.S.CMS (2021), TURKSTAT (2021)

The amount of health expenditure in GDP (as a share of GDP) may vary due to both the growth of health spending and overall economic growth (OECD 2021a). In 2019, low-income countries have 6.01% health expenditure share, lower-middle-income countries have 5.08%, upper-middle-income countries have 6.9% and high-income countries have 7.69%. Africa region has 5.33% health expenditure share, the Americas has 7.2%, South-East Asia has 4.42%, Europe has 7.63%, Eastern Mediterranean has 5.52%, and Western Pacific has 7.32% (WHO, 2022c).

For 25 countries average health expenditure as a share of GDP was 13.54% in 2019 and increased to 15.20% in 2020. USA has the highest health expenditure as a share of GDP with 17.54% in 2019 and 19.74 in 2020. Turkey has the lowest health expenditure as a share of GDP with 4.70% in 2019 and 5.00% in 2020 (Table 11).

Table 11. The effect of COVID-19 on health expenditure as a share of GDP

Country	Health Expenditure as a Share of GDP (2019, %)	Health Expenditure as a Share of GDP (2020, %)	Change (%)
Austria	10.43	11.50	1.06
Canada	10.84	11.56	0.71
Chile	9.33	9.37	0.03
Czech Republic	7.84	9.07	1.23
Denmark	9.96	10.61	0.66
Estonia	6.73	8.05	1.32
Finland	9.15	9.55	0.40
France	11.11	12.38	1.27
Germany	11.70	12.53	0.83
Iceland	8.57	9.81	1.25
Ireland	6.68	7.19	0.52
Italy	8.67	9.72	1.05
Korea, Rep.	8.16	8.41	0.24
Lithuania	7.01	7.57	0.56
Mexico	5.43	6.21	0.78
Netherlands	10.17	11.22	1.05
Norway	10.52	11.34	0.82
Poland	6.46	7.15	0.69
Portugal	9.53	10.12	0.58
Slovak Republic	6.96	7.73	0.77
Slovenia	8.52	9.72	1.19
Sweden	10.92	11.45	0.53
Turkey	4.70	5.00	0.30
United Kingdom	10.15	12.75	2.60
United States	17.54	19.74	2.20
Average	13.54	15.20	0.09

Sources: OECD (2022a), the U.S.CMS (2021), TURKSTAT (2021)

The Effect of COVID-19 on Life Expectancy on Birth

Due to COVID-19, excess mortality rates showed that increase in life expectancy has slowed or even declined in the majority of the world. WHO (2021b) states that investing in stronger health systems could increase life at expectancy as 8.4 years. For 40 countries total life expectancy at birth has decreased 0.66 years in average in 2020 comparing with 2019. The highest decrease in life expectancy was seen in Liechtenstein with 2.4 years. In South Africa it was 2.2 years, in the USA it was 1.60 years, and in Bulgaria the decrease was 1.5 years. The highest increase in life expectancy was in Costa Rica as 0.2 years and in New Zealand 0.66 years (Table 12).

Table 12. COVID-19 effect on life expectancy at birth

Country	2019	2020	Change	Country	2019	2020	Change
Austria	82.00	81.30	-0.70	Japan	84.40	84.70	0.30
Belgium	82.10	80.90	-1.20	Latvia	75.50	75.50	0.00
Bulgaria	75.10	73.60	-1.50	Liechtenstein	84.30	81.90	-2.40
Canada	82.10	81.70	-0.40	Lithuania	76.40	75.10	-1.30
Colombia	76.70	76.80	0.10	Luxembourg	82.70	81.80	-0.90
Costa Rica	80.50	80.70	0.20	Malta	82.90	82.60	-0.30
Croatia	78.60	77.80	-0.80	Netherlands	82.20	81.50	-0.70
Cyprus	82.30	82.30	0.00	New Zealand	82.10	82.76	0.66
Czechia	79.30	78.30	-1.00	Norway	83.00	83.30	0.30
Denmark	81.50	81.60	0.10	Poland	78.00	76.70	-1.30
Estonia	78.80	78.50	-0.30	Portugal	81.80	81.10	-0.70
Finland	82.10	82.20	0.10	Romania	75.60	74.20	-1.40
France	83.00	82.30	-0.70	Slovakia	77.80	77.00	-0.80
Germany	81.30	81.10	-0.20	Slovenia	81.60	80.60	-1.00
Greece	81.70	81.20	-0.50	South Africa	64.20	62.00	-2.20
Hungary	76.50	75.70	-0.80	Spain	83.90	82.40	-1.50
Iceland	83.20	83.10	-0.10	Sweden	83.20	82.50	-0.70
Ireland	82.80	82.55	-0.25	Switzerland	84.00	83.20	-0.80
Israel	82.90	82.80	-0.10	United Kingdom	81.40	80.40	-1.00
Italy	83.60	82.40	-1.20	United States	78.90	77.30	-1.60

Sources: OECD (2022b), EUROSTAT 2022a)

THE EFFECTS OF COVID-19 ON GLOBAL ECEONOMY

COVID-19 has caused many negative effects on people, especially health, and caused contractions and in national economies and global trade and disruptions in global supply chains and foreign direct investments.

The Effect of COVID-19 on Foreign Direct Investments (FDI)

The coronavirus pandemic has speeded up the fragilities of the structurally weak economies by affecting the investment in various sectors. Besides, global fluctuations in economy, trade war, national protectionism in foreign trade, sanctions, and geopolitical instability in some regions, slow economic growth due to the pandemic will negatively affect the inflow and outflow of FDI which was searching new appropriate target markets to make investment because of the COVID-19 related restrictions of the governments. Global FDI, which was US$1.53 trillion in 2019, has contracted 35% to US$1 trillion in 2020 even below the level in the global financial crisis by pandemic (Table 13).

COVID-19 caused a decrease in FDI by 8.4% in developing countries and by 58.3% in developed countries especially due to the oscillations in the activities of multinational enterprises (MNEs). This has also altered the global supply chains in many products and caused a decrease in global value chains.

For this reason, especially western countries with high purchasing power have started to turn to alternative producer and supplier countries rather than being dependent on a few countries in the global supply chain. As a result, the increasing global demand in the new normal period created an opportunity in exports for some countries.

These negative developments have also affected Greenfield investments, which has been an important driving force in the fight against climate change in recent years. Greenfield investments decreased by 42% in developing countries and by 19% in developed countries. International project financing for infrastructure also decreased by 14% in developing countries, while it decreased by 8% in developed countries (UNCTAD, 2021a).

Table 13. Global FDI inflows by development region (million $)

Region/Economy	1990	2000	2010	2015	2019	2020	Change (2019-2020)
World	*204,888*	*1,356,645*	*1,393,729*	*2,032,298*	*1,530,228*	*998,891*	*-34.7%*
A. Developed economies	*170,167*	*1,118,415*	*707,368*	*1,267,808*	*748,999*	*312,170*	*-58.3%*
Europe	*102,630*	*706,728*	*438,221*	*712,907*	*362,644*	*72,537*	*-80.0%*
European Union	*65,099*	*564,990*	*335,881*	*591,208*	*380,281*	*103,190*	*-72.9%*
B. Developing economies	*34,650*	*232,306*	*622,537*	*730,434*	*723,385*	*662,562*	*-8.4%*
Least developed countries (LDCs)	*542*	*4,598*	*23,213*	*37,790*	*23,294*	*23,610*	*1.4%*
BRIICS	*5,726*	*76,070*	*268,912*	*259,831*	*318,253*	*269,545*	*-15.3%*
C. Transition economies	*71*	*5,924*	*63,825*	*34,056*	*57,844*	*24,160*	*-58.2%*

Source: UNCTAD (2021a)

At the country level, the USA leads FDI inflows with US$156.3 billion in 2020 and a decrease of 40.2% comparison with 2019. China followed the USA with US$149.3 billion in FDI value in 2020 and an increase of 5.75% comparison with 2019. Hong Kong was the third country after the USA and China with US$119.2 billion in FDI value in 2020 and an increase of 61.75% comparison with 2019 (Table 14).

Table 14. Global FDI inflows by countries (million $)

Rank	Country	FDI Inflow (2019, million $)	FDI Inflow (2020, million $)	Growth (2019-2020, %)
1	United States	261.412	156.321	-40,20%
2	China	141.225	149.342	5,75%
3	Hong Kong, China	73.714	119.229	61,75%
4	Singapore	114.162	90.562	-20,67%
5	India	50.558	64.062	26,71%
6	Luxembourg	14.792	62.145	320,13%
7	British Virgin Islands	39.103	39.620	1,32%
8	Germany	54.063	35.651	-34,06%
9	Ireland	81.104	33.424	-58,79%
10	Mexico	34.097	29.079	-14,72%
11	Sweden	10.112	26.109	158,19%
12	Brazil	65.386	24.778	-62,11%
13	Israel	19.047	24.758	29,98%
14	Canada	47.837	23.823	-50,20%
15	Cayman Islands	28.165	23.621	-16,13%
16	Australia	39.224	20.146	-48,64%
17	United Arab Emirates	17.875	19.884	11,24%
18	United Kingdom	45.454	19.724	-56,61%
19	Indonesia	23.883	18.581	-22,20%
20	France	33.965	17.932	-47,20%
	Other countries	335.049	99	-99,97%
	World	1.530.228	998.891	-34,72%

Source: UNCTAD (2021a)

Even the pandemic started to affect the global economy and FDI in the second quarter of 2020, it seems the decrease started for G20 countries with the first quarter of 2019. Both G20 countries and the world have faced with the contraction in FDI in the second quarter of 2020 where lockdowns and closures were mostly applied (Figure 4).

Figure 4. Global FDI in G20 (2013-Q1=100)
Source: OECD (2022c)

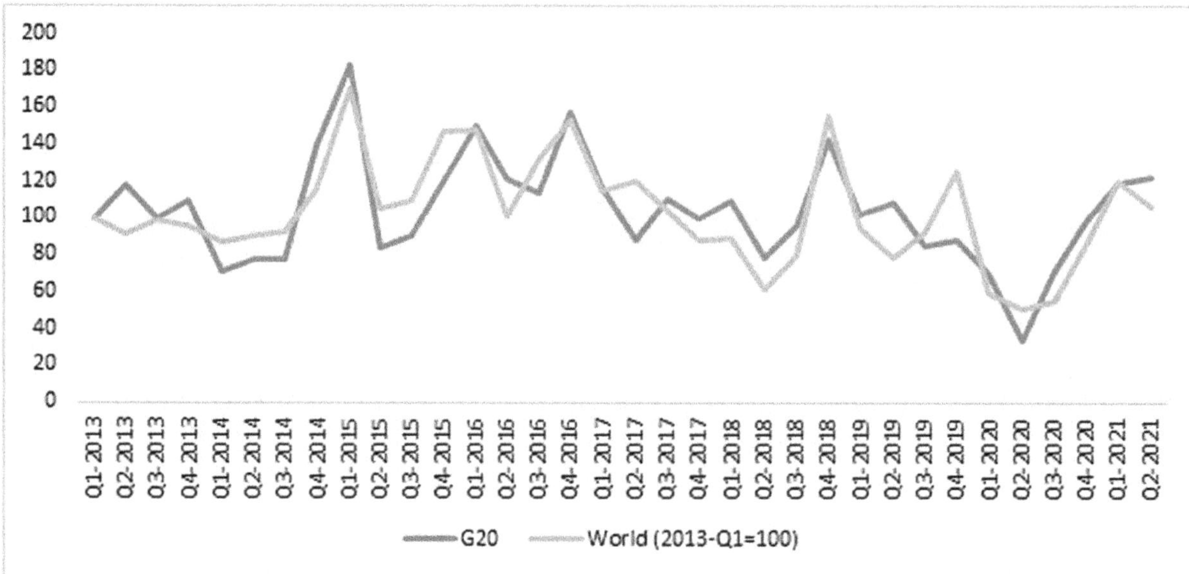

The Effect of COVID-19 on Production (Gross Domestic Product "GDP" and Manufacturing Value Added "MVA")

Global output (GDP) was US$87.6 trillion in 2019 and contracted 3.3% to US$84.7 trillion in 2020 in current prices. It amounted to US$84.6 trillion in 2019 and contracted 3.4% to US$81.7 trillion in 2020 in constant prices of 2015. The decrease was even greater than the global financial crisis level. According to the World Bank country classification, the growth rate of output for high-income countries decreased 4.601%, whereas it decreased 3.416% for lower middle-income countries and 0.713% for upper middle-income countries.

The GDP increased only for Low-income countries by 0.613% in 2020 compared to 2019 (World Bank, 2022b). It seems that COVID-19 mostly affected the high income and lower middle-income countries and due to the lower economic activity low-income countries has succeeded to increase their production.

According to the International Monetary Fund (IMF) country classification, the growth rate of output contracted 4.5% for advanced countries and 2.1% for emerging market and developing economies (EMDE) (IMF, 2021). The IMF predicts the world income will recover in 2021 and will increase 5.88% to US$95 trillion. Global growth is expected to be 4.4% in 2022 and 3.8% in 2023. Due to rising inflation, ongoing supply chain disruptions and higher energy prices expected to continue in 2022 (IMF, 2022). The OECD predicts the highest optimistic growth recovery in global output as 4.5% in 2022 and the IMF predicts it as 3.8% in 2023 (Table 15).

Table 15. Global output (GDP) projections

Institution	2020	2021	2022	2023	2024	2025	2026
UNCTAD	-3.5	5.3	3.6				
The World Bank	-3.4	5.5	4.1	3.2			
IMF	-3.1	5.9	4.4	3.8			
OECD	-3.4	5.6	4.5	3.2			
WTO	-4.0	5.3	4.1				

Source: WTO (2021), the IMF (2021), the World Bank (2022b), UNCTAD (2021b), OECD (2021b)

Due to the breakdowns in global supply chains and value chains in manufacturing, global total value added (MVA) has also decreased 6.6% in constant prices in 2020 comparing to 2019 (UNIDO 2022). The decrease was higher in advanced countries such as USA with 10%, Japan with 14%, Germany with 16.9% and the United Kingdom with 13.9%. Taiwan with 21% increase in MVA and Macao with 30% increase were the gainers in 2020 (Table 16).

Table 16. Manufacturing Value Added (2019, 2020, MVA, constant 2015 $)

Country	Manufacturing Value Added (2019, MVA, Constant 2015 $)	Manufacturing Value Added (2020, MVA, Constant 2015 $)	Change (2019-2020)	Rank in 2019	Rank in 2020	Rank in change
China	4,090,000,000,000	4,062,391,900,000	-0.7%	1	1	62
United States of America	2,300,000,000,000	2,071,060,300,000	-10.0%	2	2	154
Japan	992,000,000,000	853,118,104,240	-14.0%	3	3	179
Germany	714,000,000,000	593,436,760,767	-16.9%	4	4	190
Republic of Korea	433,000,000,000	423,174,399,426	-2.3%	6	5	87
India	441,000,000,000	392,987,755,496	-10.9%	5	6	162
Italy	284,000,000,000	250,709,545,087	-11.7%	7	7	164
United Kingdom	280,000,000,000	241,165,852,304	-13.9%	8	8	177
China, Taiwan Province	191,112,127,406	231,257,963,928	21.0%	12	9	3
France	263,000,000,000	225,664,675,118	-14.2%	9	10	180
Other countries	8,001,509,413,847	7,702,870,766,192	-3.7%			
World	13,899,621,541,253	12,985,446,122,558	-6.6%			

Source: UNIDO (2022)

The Effect of COVID-19 on Foreign Trade of Goods

COVID-19 has negatively affected global supply chains and global value chains by disrupting the goods flow cross-border. Due to the pandemic, many governments has taken temporary trade measures aiming to restrict the export of vital medical supplies and liberalize the import of vital medical supplies as well as other essential products related with health. As January 12, 2022, there were 98 countries which have export restrictions, two countries have export liberalizations, and three countries have both for COVID-19.

There were 13 countries, which have, import restrictions, 110 countries have import liberalizations and 22 countries have both for COVID-19 (ITC, 2022a).

Global exports in merchandised goods contracted 7.8% in 2020 compared with 2019. China is the country, which has the best performance in merchandised goods exports both in 2019 and 2020 with US$2.5 trillion and US$2.6 trillion, respectively. China has made the 13.3% of total global goods export in 2019 and 15% in 2020. China's global goods export has increased 2.7% in 2020 despite of COVID-19. The USA followed China with US$1.64 trillion goods export value in 2019 and US$1.42 trillion goods export value in 2020 and a decrease of 13.3% compared with 2019.

The USA has made 8.8% of total global goods export in 2019 and 8.3% in 2020. Germany was the third country after China and the USA with US$1.49 trillion goods export value in 2019, and US$1.38 trillion goods export value in 2020 and a decrease of 7.3% compared with 2019. Germany has made the 7.9% of total global goods export in 2019 and 8% in 2020 (Table 17).

Table 17. Global exports in merchandised goods (FOB, 2019, 2020, 1,000 $)

Country	Export (2019)	Export (2020)	Export Growth (2019-2020)	Rank (Export, 2019)	Rank (Export, 2020)
China	2,498,569,866	2,590,607,686	3.7%	1	1
United States of America	1,642,820,352	1,424,934,919	-13.3%	2	2
Germany	1,486,877,250	1,378,030,840	-7.3%	3	3
Japan	705,842,013	640,953,137	-9.2%	4	4
Netherlands	576,784,455	551,820,270	-4.3%	5	5
Hong Kong, China	535,711,019	551,515,756	3.0%	9	6
Korea, Republic of	542,333,337	512,788,606	-5.4%	7	7
Italy	537,748,429	495,976,960	-7.8%	8	8
France	556,550,374	476,082,181	-14.5%	6	9
Belgium	446,876,870	419,478,288	-6.1%	12	10
Other countries	9,206,109,998	8,228,829,105	-10.6%		
World	18,736,223,963	17,271,017,748	-7.8%		

Source: ITC (2022b)

Global imports in merchandised goods contracted 8% in 2020 compared with 2019. USA is the country, which has the highest import value in merchandised goods in both 2019 and 2020 with US$2.56 trillion and US$2.41 trillion, respectively. The USA's global import value increased to US$2.94 trillion in 2021. The USA has produced 13.4% of total global goods import in 2019 and 13.7% in 2020. The USA's global goods export has contracted 6.1% in 2020. China followed the USA with US$2.07 trillion goods import value in 2019 and US$2.07 trillion goods import value in 2020 and a decrease of 0.6% compared with 2019.

China has made the 10.8% of total global goods import in 2019 and 11.7% in 2020. Germany was the third country after the USA and China with US$1.24 trillion goods import value in 2019 and US$1.27

trillion goods import value in 2020 and a decrease of 5.2% compared with 2019. Germany has produced 6.5% of total global goods import in 2019 and 6.7% in 2020 (Table 18).

Table 18. Global imports in merchandised goods (CIF, 2019, 2020, 1,000 $)

Country	Import (2019)	Import (2020)	Import Growth (2019-2020)	Rank (Import, 2019)	Rank (Import, 2020)
United States of America	2,563,536,173	2,406,931,650	-6.1%	1	1
China	2,068,950,255	2,055,590,612	-0.6%	2	2
Germany	1,236,217,435	1,171,580,759	-5.2%	3	3
Japan	720,964,445	634,678,167	-12.0%	4	4
United Kingdom	692,494,170	634,174,870	-8.4%	5	5
Hong Kong, China	578,590,151	573,061,310	-1.0%	7	6
France	643,953,084	569,325,016	-11.6%	6	7
Netherlands	514,857,688	485,489,156	-5.7%	8	8
Korea, Republic of	503,259,397	467,540,264	-7.1%	9	9
Italy	474,957,328	422,648,102	-11.0%	11	10
Other countries	9,082,305,310	8,130,445,921	-10.5%		
World	19,080,085,436	17,551,465,827	-8.0%		

Source: ITC (2022b)

In 2021, the negative impact of the pandemic on global trade started to decrease and there was an increase in global foreign trade and in global demand with the recovery in the global economy. According to the WTO (2022) data, global quarterly import has exceeded US$5 trillion in 2021 for the first time. Global imports amounted to US$5.08 trillion in the first quarter, increasing to US$5.52 trillion in the second quarter, then US$5.65 trillion in the third quarter, and finally up to US$5.8 trillion in the fourth quarter of 2021 (Figure 5).

Figure 5. Quarterly global imports (2005.Q1-2021.Q3, billion $)
Source: WTO (2022)

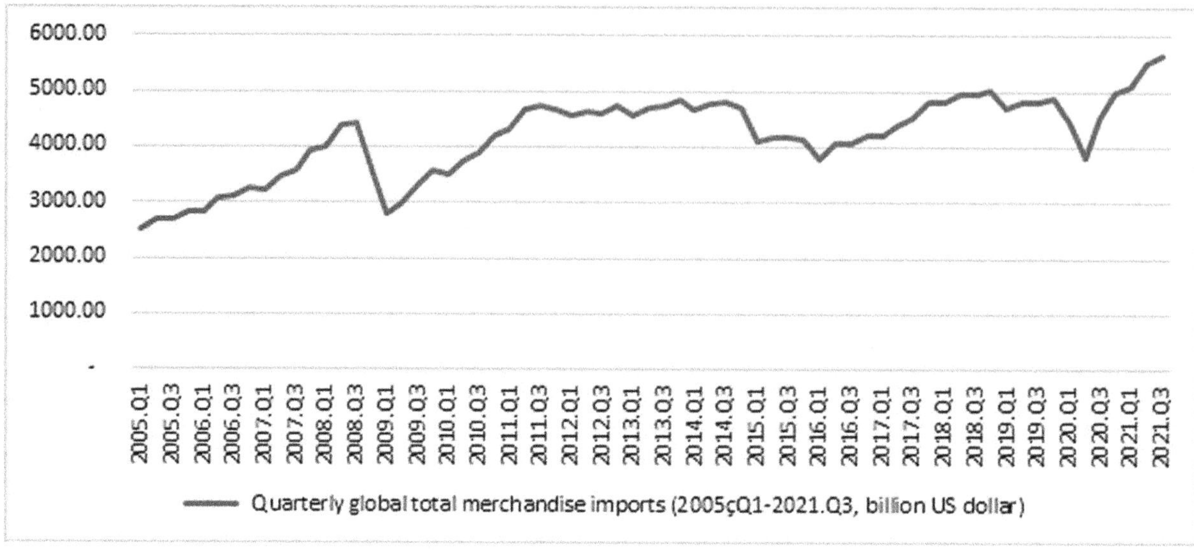

Both global import growth rates compared with previous quarter and same quarter in last year showed that the recovery started in global foreign trade. Global import has contracted 29.6% in 2009.Q1 and 32.4% in 2009.Q2 and 26% in 2009.Q3 in financial crisis era then the recovery has started in 2010.Q1 with a 24.91% growth rate in global demand. The "V"-shaped recovery in global trade after the pandemic started in the fourth quarter of 2020 and global imports grew by 2.2%, and in the second quarter of 2021, the growth in global imports reached 44.4%, even surpassing the recovery performance after the financial crisis (Figure 6).

Figure 6. Quarterly growth rates in global import
Source: WTO (2022)

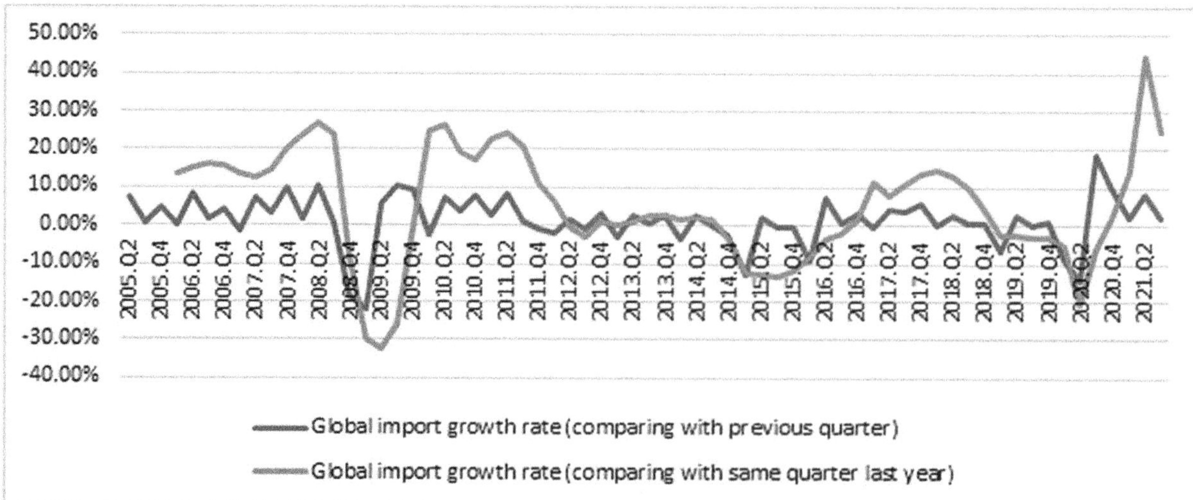

The pandemic has mostly affected the African and Europen regions. Africa's global import share was 1.77% in the last quarter of 2019 and the first quarter of 2020. It suddenly decreased to 1.50% in second quarter of 2020 due to the pandemic. The global export share of Africa was 1.40% in the last quarter of 2019, 1.43% in the first quarter of 2020 and decreased to 1.15% in the second quarter of 2020 due to the pandemic.

The global import share of the Europe region was 39.09% in the last quarter of 2019 and 42.02% in the first quarter of 2020. It suddenly decreased to 39.68% in the second quarter of 2020 due to the pandemic. Europe's global export share was 41.67% in the last quarter of 2019 and 45.30% in the first quarter of 2020. It suddenly decreased to 41.10% in the second quarter of 2020 due to the pandemic (Table 19).

Table 19. Regional foreign trade shares (2010.Q1-2021.Q2, 1,000$)

Period	Africa	Asia	America	Oceania	Europe	Global Import
2019.1	1.70%	35.94%	20.05%	1.48%	40.82%	4,263,503,560
2019.2	1.74%	36.80%	20.68%	1.46%	39.31%	4,361,107,003
2019.3	1.72%	37.27%	20.96%	1.50%	38.55%	4,366,634,833
2019.4	1.77%	37.62%	20.04%	1.53%	39.09%	4,397,185,089
2020.1	1.77%	36.89%	20.78%	1.45%	42.02%	3,991,317,714
2020.2	1.50%	38.36%	20.75%	1.57%	39.68%	3,441,397,432
2020.3	1.49%	37.12%	21.10%	1.57%	41.07%	4,065,071,655
2020.4	1.53%	36.88%	20.85%	1.61%	41.77%	4,434,584,658
2021.1	1.08%	38.17%	20.35%	1.60%	42.33%	4,465,845,161
2021.2	1.04%	35.34%	21.80%	1.66%	44.90%	4,594,264,688
2019.1	1.38%	37.56%	15.51%	1.78%	43.76%	4,133,185,189
2019.2	1.37%	38.50%	15.84%	1.90%	42.39%	4,236,143,672
2019.3	1.41%	39.98%	15.60%	1.88%	41.14%	4,209,228,620
2019.4	1.40%	39.79%	15.33%	1.81%	41.67%	4,321,360,074
2020.1	1.43%	37.11%	16.30%	1.88%	45.30%	3,843,991,082
2020.2	1.15%	42.79%	14.41%	2.12%	41.10%	3,385,704,074
2020.3	1.25%	42.10%	14.55%	1.78%	42.23%	4,030,012,182
2020.4	1.25%	41.56%	14.29%	1.84%	42.83%	4,446,137,248
2021.1	1.01%	40.39%	14.69%	2.03%	44.34%	4,429,818,236
2021.2	1.11%	38.59%	15.94%	2.31%	46.26%	4,587,241,843

Source: ITC (2022b)

China broke a foreign trade surplus record in 2021. During the pandemic period, contrary to 2020, with the increasing global demand in 2021, China's export increased by 30% to US$3.3 trillion, while its imports increased by 30.1% to US$2.7 trillion and experienced a foreign trade surplus of US$676.4 billion in 2021. This has risen despite the lack of processor chips for smartphones (despite the shortage of semiconductors) and other goods as global demand is recovering (McDonald, 2022).

According to the data from World Trade Organization for 207 countries, the convergence analysis indicates that global import has diverged 0.44% from 2019 to 2020 (Table 20). This means the import gap between the countries has increased so that import for some countries have increased or decreased more than the other countries. As global imports have decreased, the low and middle-income countries were more affected.

$$\ln\left(y_{it}\right) = \propto + \left(1-\beta\right) * \ln\left(y_{it-1}\right) + u_t$$

Y: global import, *ln*: natural logarithm *t:* 2020, *t-1*: 2019, *i*=1,2,3…207 (*i,* number of the countries)

$$\ln\left(y_{it}\right) - \ln\left(y_{it-1}\right) = \propto - \beta * \ln\left(y_{it-1}\right) + u_t$$

The regression above shows Growth Convergence Equation[1]. The import of the country *i* at time *t* is a positive function of the import of the country *i* at time *t-1*. Alternatively, the growth rate of import of the country *i* is a negative function of the import of the country *i* at time *t-1*. Left side of the equation is growth rate in global import.

The estimated equation for global import in 2019 and 2020 is as:

$\ln\left(y_{it}\right) = -0.174 + 1.0044 * \ln\left(y_{it-1}\right) + u_t$; α=-0.174, (1-β) =1.044, β=-0.0044=-0.44%

Table 20. Divergence in global import

Dependent Variable: LNIMP2020 Method: Least Squares Date: 01/24/22 Time: 10:22 Sample: 1 207 Included observations: 207				
Variable	**Coefficient**	**Std. Error**	**t-Statistic**	**Prob.**
C	-0.173564	0.042332	-4.100104	0.0001
LNIMP2019	1.004449	0.004470	224.7105	0.0000
R-squared	0.995957	Mean dependent var		9.030286
Adjusted R-squared	0.995937	S.D. dependent var		2.413658
S.E. of regression	0.153853	Akaike info criterion		-0.896022
Sum squared resid	4.852509	Schwarz criterion		-0.863822
Log likelihood	94.73829	Hannan-Quinn criter.		-0.883001
F-statistic	50494.80	Durbin-Watson stat		2.035480
Prob(F-statistic)	0.000000			

Source: WTO (2022)

According to the data from World Trade Organization for 205 countries, the convergence analysis indicates that global export has diverged 0.70% from 2019 to 2020 (Table 21). It means that the export gap between the countries has increased so that export for some countries have increased or decreased more than the other countries. As the global export has decreased, the low and middle-income countries were more affected.

$$\ln\left(y_{it}\right) = \propto + \left(1 - \beta\right) * \ln\left(y_{it-1}\right) + u_t$$

Y: global export, *ln*: natural logarithm *t:* 2020, *t-1*: 2019, *i*=1,2,3…205 (*i,* number of the countries)

$$\ln\left(y_{it}\right) - \ln\left(y_{it-1}\right) = \propto - \beta * \ln\left(y_{it-1}\right) + u_t$$

The export of the country *i* at time *t* is a positive function of the export of the country *i* at time *t-1*. Or, the growth rate of import of the country *i* is a negative function of the import of the country *i* at time *t-1*. Left side of the equation is growth rate in global export.

The estimated equation for global export in 2019 and 2020 is as:

$\ln\left(y_{it}\right) = -0.193 + 1.007 * \ln\left(y_{it-1}\right) + u_t$; α=-0.193, (1-β) =1.007, β=-0.007=-0.7%

Table 21. Divergence in global export

Dependent Variable: LNEXP2020
Method: Least Squares
Date: 01/24/22 Time: 10:52
Sample: 1 205
Included observations: 205

Variable	Coefficient	Std. Error	t-Statistic	Prob.
C	-0.193062	0.052563	-3.672948	0.0003
LNEXP2019	1.007014	0.005779	174.2662	0.0000
R-squared	0.993360	Mean dependent var		8.413734
Adjusted R-squared	0.993327	S.D. dependent var		3.153183
S.E. of regression	0.257575	Akaike info criterion		0.134700
Sum squared resid	13.46806	Schwarz criterion		0.167120
Log likelihood	-11.80675	Hannan-Quinn criter.		0.147813
F-statistic	30368.70	Durbin-Watson stat		2.000084
Prob(F-statistic)	0.000000			

Source: WTO (2022), Eviews (2022)

The Effect of COVID-19 on Foreign Trade of Services

Due to the pandemic, global trade in services has also been affected negatively much like global goods exports. Global exports in service have declined more than global goods trade in 2020 compared with 2019 as 20% in which the USA is the country with the best performance in exports of service in both 2019 and 2020 with US$876.3 billion and US$705.6 billion, respectively.

The USA produced 14.1% of total global service exports in 2019 and 14.2% in 2020. The USA's global service export decreased 19.5% in 2020. The UK followed the USA with US$405.5 billion in service export value in 2019 and US$342.4 billion in service export value in 2020 and a decrease of 15.5% compared to 2019. The UK has made the 6.5% of total global service export in 2019 and 6.9% in 2020. Germany was the third country after the USA and the UK with US$346.7 billion in service export value in 2019 andUS$310.7 billion in service export value in 2020 and a decrease of 10.4% compared to 2019. Germany produced 5.6% of total global service exports in 2019 and 6.2% in 2020 (Table 22).

Table 22. Global exports in service (million dollars)

Country	Export (2019)	Export (2020)	Export Growth (2019-2020)	Rank (Export, 2019)	Rank (Export, 2020)
United States of America	876,295	705,643	-19.5%	1	1
United Kingdom	405,483	342,439	-15.5%	2	2
Germany	346,660	310,661	-10.4%	3	3
China	283,192	280,629	-0.9%	5	4
Ireland	247,818	262,704	6.0%	7	5
France	294,122	245,578	-16.5%	4	6
India	214,762	203,253	-5.4%	9	7
Singapore	217,187	187,564	-13.6%	8	8
Netherlands	275,799	186,644	-32.3%	6	9
Japan	207,421	160,287	-22.7%	10	10
Other countries	2,859,935	2,099,927	-26.6%		
World	6,228,674	4,985,329	-20.0%		

Source: WTO (2022)

Global imports in services have declined more than global goods imports in 2020 compared to 2019 as 21.3%. The USA has the best performance in imports of service as export of service in both 2019 and 2020 with US$591.1 billion and US$460.3 billion, respectively. The USA produced 9.9% of total global service imports in 2019 and 9.8% in 2020. The USA's global services imports decreased by 22.1% in 2020. China followed the USA with US$500.7 billion in service import value in 2019 and US$381.1 billion in service import value in 2020 with a decrease of 23.9% compared to 2019.

China produced 8.4% of total global service imports in 2019 and 8.1% in 2020. In line with the increase in per capita income, China has started to play an important role in global tourism industry as well, causing it to have a high share in service sector imports. Germany was the third country after the

USA and China with US$371 billion in service import value in 2019 and US$308.8 billion in service import value in 2020, which is a decrease of 16.8% compared to 2019. Germany produced 6.2% of total global service imports in 2019 and 6.6% in 2020 (Table 23).

Table 23. Global imports in service (million dollars)

Country	Import (2019)	Import (2020)	Import Growth (2019-2020)	Rank (Import, 2019)	Rank (Import, 2020)
United States of America	591,121	460,301	-22.1%	1	1
China	500,680	381,088	-23.9%	2	2
Germany	370,956	308,800	-16.8%	3	3
Ireland	332,150	295,745	-11.0%	4	4
France	269,951	231,664	-14.2%	6	5
United Kingdom	277,360	204,748	-26.2%	5	6
Japan	206,276	184,531	-10.5%	9	7
Singapore	208,198	172,689	-17.1%	8	8
Netherlands	265,502	169,252	-36.3%	7	9
India	179,430	153,925	-14.2%	10	10
Other countries	2,746,187	2,118,792	-22.8%		
World	5,947,811	4,681,535	-21.3%		

Source: WTO (2022)

The Effect of COVID-19 on Tourism

COVID-19 has also negatively affected global tourism as it caused a decrease in tourist arrivals and tourism receipts due to the restrictions, closures, and banned travel. Many people work in tourism industry or related industries. The tourism industry not only supports national income directly and indirectly, but also protects nature, cultural heritage, and biodiversity. There is a hope that vaccinations have removed barriers against tourism and tourism has gained speed again even it is still below pre-pandemic period.

However, the new variants still pose a risk to the free travel and tourism industry. Flight bans hit especially the transportation and the tourism sectors. This unfavorable situation negatively affected the balance of payments by disrupting both the export of goods and tourism revenues in many countries, especially in countries whose income is mainly from tourism (Gürler & Özsoy, 2020).

The total number of international tourist arrivals amounted to 1.47 billion in 2019. It suddenly decreased by 72.6% to 399 million in 2020. Total tourism receipts were US$1.47 billion in 2019 but suddenly decreased by 63.4% to US$536 million in 2020 due to COVID-19. The change in tourist arrivals is 72.5% for advanced countries and 72.7% for emerging countries. The change in tourism receipts is 61.3% for advanced countries and 67.1% for emerging countries. It seems tourism in emerging countries is more affected than in advanced countries by the pandemic (Table 24).

Table 24. COVID-19 effect on tourist arrivals and tourism receipts

		Advanced Countries	Emerging Countries	World
International tourist arrivals	2019	777	689	1,466
	%	53.0%	47.0%	100%
	2020	214	188	402
	%	53.2%	46.8%	100%
International tourism receipts	2019	922	544	1,466
	%	62.9%	37.1%	100%
	2020	357	179	536
	%	66.6%	33.4%	100%
	Change in international tourist arrivals (2019-2020)	-72.5%	-72.7%	-72.6%
	Change in international tourism receipts (2019-2020)	-61.3%	-67.1%	-63.4%
	Tourism receipts per tourist (2019)	1,186.6	789.6	1,000.0
	Tourism receipts per tourist (2020)	1,668.2	952.1	1,333.3

Source: UNWTO (2021)

As mentioned above, international tourist arrivals have decreased by 72.6%. According to the latest UNWTO data, international tourist arrivals are expected to remain nearly at 2020 value in 2021 so it will be 70% to 75% below 2019 levels. Export revenues from international tourism was US$1.7 trillion in 2019, and it could be more than 2020 values but less than 2019 value in 2021.

Export revenues are predicted to reach US$700-800 billion in 2021. The direct economic contribution of tourism to global economy was estimated at US$1.9 trillion in 2021, which was still below the pre-pandemic value of US$3.5 trillion dollars (UNWTO 2021).

Tourism is one of the world's major economic sectors so that after fuels and chemicals it ranks as the third largest exporting industry.

In 2019, tourism export revenues were accounted for 7% of global trade. Its contribution to national GDP is more than 20% for some countries. Tourism industry is one of the sectors which was most affected by the COVID-19 pandemic. Decrease in export revenues from tourism reduced global GDP by 1.5% to 2.8% in 2020. Tourism supports one in 10 jobs, so due to the pandemic 100-120 million direct tourism jobs were at risk. Besides this, an additional 144 million workers worldwide are in sectors associated with tourism such as labor-intensive accommodation and food services industries (UNWTO 2022a). For the July-September period, number of international tourist arrivals who are overnight visitors has increased by 58% in 2021 compared to the same period of 2020; however, this is below 2019 levels which stood at 64% (Table 25).

Table 25. Monthly change in international tourist arrivals

Period	% Change in International Tourist Arrivals in 2020 Comparing to 2019						% Change in International Tourist Arrivals in 2021 Comparing to 2019					
	Africa	Americas	Asia and the Pacific	Europe	Middle East	World	Africa	Americas	Asia and the Pacific	Europe	Middle East	World
Jan	0%	1%	-3%	4%	9%	1%	-81%	-76%	-95%	-85%	-80%	-86%
Feb	0%	4%	-49%	2%	4%	-14%	-82%	-78%	-97%	-87%	-84%	-88%
Mar	-39%	-49%	-82%	-61%	-73%	-65%	-81%	-72%	-95%	-87%	-83%	-86%
Apr	-91%	-94%	-99%	-97%	-99%	-97%	-81%	-67%	-94%	-87%	-84%	-85%
May	-89%	-93%	-99%	-95%	-99%	-95%	-78%	-59%	-94%	-82%	-84%	-81%
Jun	-90%	-91%	-98%	-88%	-98%	-91%	-72%	-58%	-95%	-75%	-81%	-77%
Jul	-87%	-88%	-98%	-69%	-96%	-79%	-71%	-60%	-94%	-58%	-82%	-67%
Aug	-87%	-87%	-97%	-65%	-94%	-76%	-77%	-61%	-96%	-50%	-86%	-63%
Sep	-85%	-82%	-96%	-68%	-85%	-77%	-74%	-59%	-94%	-51%	-74%	-63%
Oct	-81%	-78%	-95%	-76%	-83%	-82%						
Nov	-80%	-75%	-95%	-84%	-82%	-85%						
Dec	-75%	-73%	-95%	-84%	-82%	-84%						
YTD (%)	-69%	-68%	-84%	-69%	-74%	-73%	-77%	-65%	-95%	-69%	-82%	-76%

Source. UNWTO (2022b)

The destinations most affected by COVID-19 by the tourism receipts share in GDP were as follows: Macao (China) 48%; Fiji 13%; Jordan 12%; Spain 12%; Croatia 11%; Montenegro 10%; Mauritius 10%; Panama 9%; Jamaica 9%; and Mexico 9%. The impact of COVID-19 on world scheduled passenger traffic in 2020 compared to 2019 (estimated actual results):

- Seats offered by airlines have decreased by 50% overall
- A 2,703 million decrease in the number of passengers (-60%)
- Approximately US$372 billion loss in gross passenger operating income of airlines

Impact of COVID-19 on world scheduled passenger traffic in 2021 compared to 2019 (preliminary estimates):

- Seats offered by airlines decreased by 40% overall
- A 2.203 million decrease in the number of passengers (-49%)
- Approximately US$372 billion loss in gross passenger operating income of airlines

The negative impact of the pandemic decreased in 2021 compared to 2020. The COVID-19 impact on world scheduled passenger traffic for year 2022 (estimated actual results), compared to 2019 levels:

- Overall reduction of 20% to 23% of seats offered by airlines
- Overall reduction of 1,195 to 1,420 million passengers (-27% to -32%)

- Approx. USD 190 to 220 billion loss of gross passenger operating revenues of airlines (ICAO 2022).

It is not expected to return to pre-COVID tourist arrival levels until 2023 or later, and some experts expected the return in 2024 or later. Travel restrictions, slow containment of the virus, low traveler confidence and a poor economic environment are main the main barriers for tourism. Tourism industry contributes about 5% of the GDP in Turkey. The number tourist arrivals has fallen by 69% in 2020. Tourism revenues were expected to decrease US$33 billion and this will affect the food, beverages, retail trade, communications and transport sector who supply to tourism sector. The total fall in output is US$93 billion and contributes to a real GDP loss of about 9% (UNCTAD, 2021c).

The Effect of COVID-19 on Unemployment

In the early stages of industrialization, labor is the main determinant of the economic growth for developing countries. A skilled and healthy workforce increases productivity resulting in economic growth and increased per capita income in a country (Gürler & Özsoy, 2021b). Closures, lockdowns, and restrictions on foreign trade of goods and services have decreased economic activities in the countries. Low economic activity has led to the closure of workplaces and the dismissal of workers from workplaces in the countries.

As a result, working hours and participation in the labor force have decreased and the unemployment rate has increased in many countries. Many industries such as tourism for contactless services started to use robots instead of human labor due to the pandemic. It may be a good solution for running the business but will also increase unemployment (Mukherjee et al., 2021).

According to International Labour Organization (ILO) statistics, global unemployment rate has increased from 5.35% in 2019 to 6.57% in 2020. The unemployment rate has mostly increased in upper-middle income countries and high-income countries as 6.74% and 6.48% respectively in 2020. The ILO predicts a decrease in unemployment in 2022 in middle and high-income countries but an increase in low-income countries. Low-income countries will make a recovery in 2023 (Table 26).

Table 26. COVID-19 effect on unemployment rate by income group (ILO modelled estimates, Nov. 2021, %)

Year	World	Low Income	Lower-Middle Income	Upper-Middle Income	High Income
2010	5.90	4.95	5.11	5.69	8.22
2011	5.76	4.94	5.05	5.56	7.89
2012	5.74	4.95	5.03	5.50	7.93
2013	5.73	4.82	5.05	5.52	7.83
2014	5.60	4.82	5.03	5.51	7.23
2015	5.62	4.90	5.19	5.67	6.63
2016	5.65	4.91	5.29	5.89	6.16
2017	5.56	4.90	5.28	5.91	5.60
2018	5.39	4.89	5.24	5.75	5.08
2019	5.35	4.89	5.07	5.97	4.78
2020	6.57	5.62	6.61	6.74	6.48
2021	6.17	5.85	5.89	6.75	5.64
2022	5.87	6.00	5.57	6.55	4.94
2023	5.67	5.69	5.41	6.34	4.74

Source: ILO (2022a)

Lower-middle income countries have the highest working hours lost due to the COVID-19 crisis. Global working hours lost was 4.9% in first quarter of 2020 in average and has increased to 18.7% in second quarter. In high-income countries, working hours lost was 2.8% in first quarter of 2020 in average and has increased to 15.6% in second quarter. In low-income countries, working hours lost was 1.8% in first quarter of 2020 in average and has increased to 13.6% in second quarter. In lower-middle income countries working hours lost was 2.3% in first quarter of 2020 in average and has increased to 27.5% in second quarter.

In upper-middle income countries working hours lost was 8.8% in first quarter of 2020 in average and has increased to 11.8% in second quarter. Due to the pandemic high income and lower-middle income countries have the highest working hours lost. All income groups have recovery in working hours lost in the last quarter of 2021 (Figure 7).

The pandemic mostly affected the Central America, South America, Southern Asia and Western Asia regions in the second quarter of 2020. These regions have the highest working hours lost due to the COVID-19.

Figure 7. Working hours lost due to the COVID-19 crisis -- ILO modelled estimates (%)
Source: ILO (2022b)

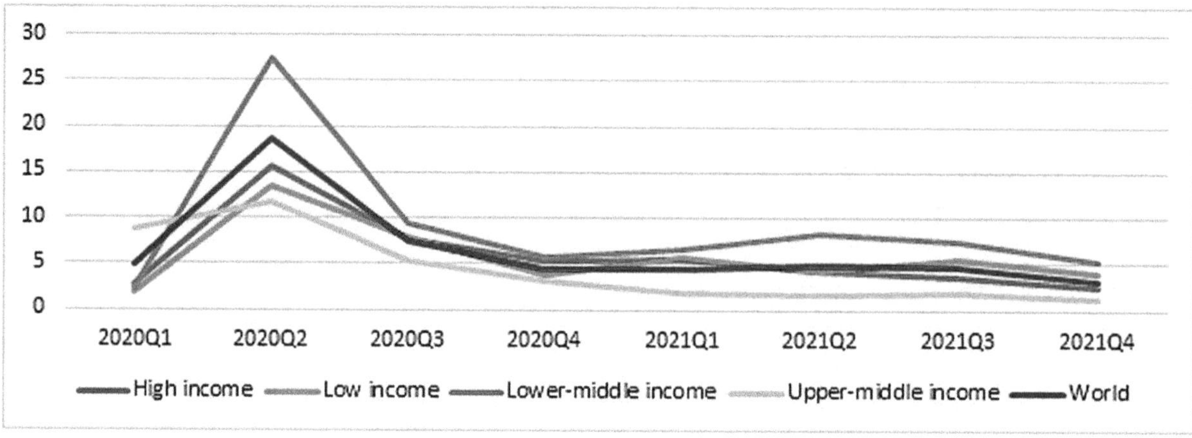

Lower-middle income countries have the lowest labor force participation rate due to the COVID-19 crisis. Global labor force participation rate was 60.5% in 2019 in average and decreased to 58.6% in 2020. In high-income countries, labor force participation rate was 61% in 2019 in average and decreased to 60.2% in 2020. In low-income countries, labor force participation rate was 67.3% in 2019 in average and has decreased to 65.4% in 2020. In lower-middle income countries, labour force participation rate was 54.8% in 2019 in average and has decreased to 52.8% in 2020. In upper-middle income countries, labor force participation rate was 65.5% in 2019 in average and has decreased to 63.6% in 2020.

Lower-middle income countries have the lowest labor force participation rate as 2.3% decrease in labor force participation rate compared with 2019 due to the pandemic. All income groups have recovery in labor force participation rate in 2021 (Figure 8). The pandemic mostly affected the South America, Latin America and the Caribbean, Central America, Southern Africa, Western Asia, and Southern Asia the regions in 2020. These regions had a higher decrease in the labor force participation rate.

Figure 8. COVID-19 effect on labor force participation rate by income group (ILO modelled estimates, Nov. 2021, %)
Source: ILO (2022c)

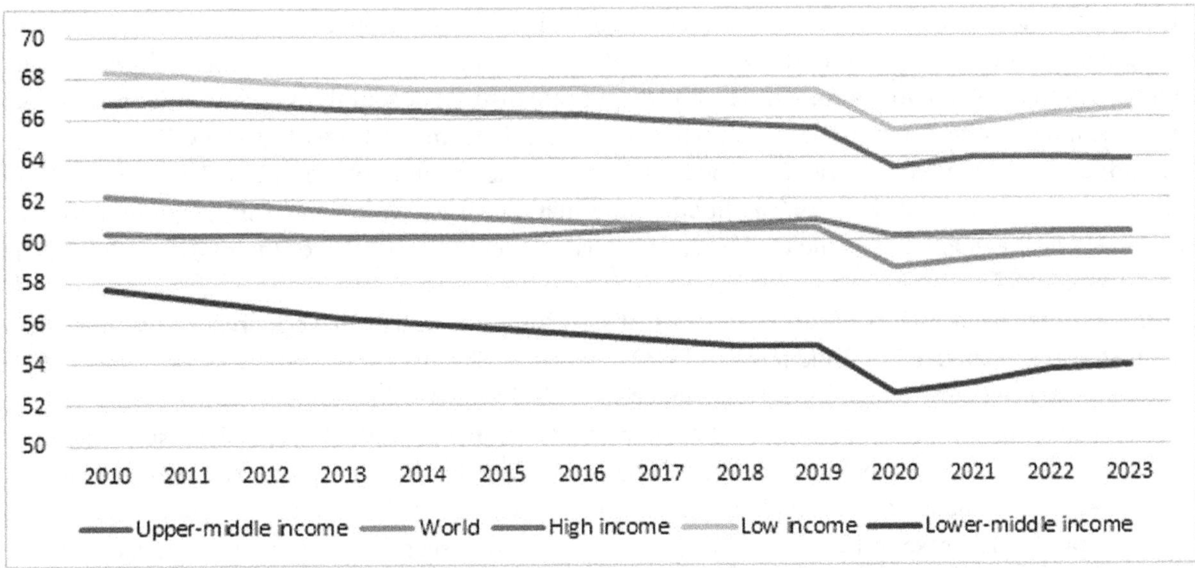

The Effect of COVID-19 on Poverty

The pandemic has caused income inequality to rise not only between the countries but within-countries such as emerging markets and developing economies (EMDEs) as a result of particularly severe job and income losses among lower-income population groups (World Bank, 2022a). Contracted global output and increasing unemployment have caused decrease in income and purchasing power from lockdown, closures, and broken supply chains due to the pandemic.

The World Bank (2021a) estimated that between 119 and 124 million people will fell into the extreme poverty due to the pandemic in the world in January 2021 report. The World Bank issued an update report in June 2021 and stated that the pandemic has caused 97 million more people to become poor in 2020. Even if it is below 20 million from the January estimation, this represents a historically unprecedented increase in global poverty.

There were 655 million poor people in the world in 2019 and it was predicted to rise to 635 million in 2020 and 613 million in 2021 before the pandemic. Due to the pandemic, the number of the people in poverty is projected to decline from 732 million to 711 million in 2021.

The Effect of COVID-19 on External Debt

Countries had difficulties securing foreign financing and in rolling over their debts due to the falling economic activity because of closures, restrictions, and disruptions in global supply chains, and decreasing the interest rates to revive the domestic market. It was the largest 1-year global debt increase since World War II in 2020, so the global total debt rose to US$226 trillion as the world was hit by a deep economic recession due to COVID-19. Debt was high prior to the pandemic, but now governments must navigate a world of record high public and private debt levels, new virus mutations, and rising inflation (Gapar et al., 2021).

Because of the slowdown in economic activities due to the closures and restrictions in the pandemic era, countries have gone to borrow from international markets, and global debt levels have increased. Total global debt reached its highest level by 263.3% of GDP in 2020 as US$223 trillion. Today, many countries, especially low-income countries, are now in debt distress or at high risk of debt distress. Global government debt is 98.7% of global GDP, whereas private debt was 164.6% of global GDP.

In advanced countries, total debt reached 302% and government debt was 122.8% of their GDP in 2020 whereas private debt was 179.2%. In emerging markets and developing countries, total debt was 205.2% and government debt is the 63.1% whereas private debt was 142.1% of their GDP in 2020 (The World Bank, 2022).

On the other hand, the external debt stocks of developing countries have increased by more than 4.6% in 2020 compared to 2019 and reached US$11.3 trillion. This figure is 2.5 times more than US$4.5 trillion, the amount during the global financial crisis in 2009 (UNCTAD, 2021a).

Public debt now accounts for almost 40 percent of total global debt, the highest share since the mid-1960s. The accumulation of public debt since 2007 can be largely attributed to the two major economic crises facing governments: first the global financial crisis and then the COVID-19 pandemic. In advanced countries, public debt rose to 124% of GDP, an increase like that seen during the global financial crisis, on the other hand, private debt rose to 178% of GDP in 2020(Gaspar et al., 2021).

The USA, United Kingdom, France, Germany, Japan, Netherlands, Luxembourg, Ireland, Italy, and Spain are at the top of the list of the countries with external debts. These countries are all high-income countries and there is no problem in rolling over their debts. The total external debt stocks of low- and middle-income countries were 8.7 trillion dollars at the end of 2020 (Table 27).

The Top-10 low and middle-income borrowers, defined as those with the largest external debt stock, are Argentina, Brazil, China, India, Indonesia, Mexico, the Russian Federation, South Africa, Thailand, and Turkey by the end of 2020. Even before the onset of the crisis, rising public debt levels and rising debt vulnerabilities were already a concern in many countries; the COVID-19 pandemic has brought unprecedented challenges and vulnerabilities to low- and middle-income countries in 2020. While the crisis increased financing needs and thus public borrowing, it weakened the economic fundamentals and capacity of individual countries to pay their public debt. The current risk is that too many countries will emerge from the COVID-19 crisis with a huge debt burden that could take years to manage. The average ratio of external debt stock to GDP for low-income countries is 36.3%, whereas it is 3-digits for some countries (World Bank, 2021).

Table 27. Global external debt by income group

Income Group	External Debt Stocks (Current Billion $)	Population (Million)	GDP (Billion $)	External Debt Stocks Per Capita ($)	Ratio of External Debt Stocks to GDP (%)
Low income	166.3	665.1	457.6	0.25	36.3
Lower middle income	2,399.9	3,330.7	7,384.8	0.72	32.5
Upper middle income	6,123.3	2,522.5	23,150.7	2.43	26.4
Middle income	8,523.2	5,853.1	30,535.4	1.46	27.9
Low & middle income	8,689.4	6,518.3	30,993.1	1.33	28.0
High income	82,793.0	1,214.9	53,396.3	68.15	155.1
World	91,482.4	7,733.2	84,389.4	11.83	108.4

Source: The World Bank (2021b) and the World Bank (2022b)

According to data from the World Bank for 123 countries, the convergence analysis indicates that countries' total external debt has converged 1.3% from 2019 to 2020 (Table 28). It means the debt gap between the countries has decreased. Low and middle-income countries' external debt has increased during the pandemic.

$$\ln\left(y_{it}\right) = \propto + \left(1-\beta\right) * \ln\left(y_{it-1}\right) + u_t$$

Y: external debt stock, *ln*: natural logarithm *t:* 2020, *t-1*: 2019, *i*=1,2,3…123 (*i,* number of the low and middle income countries which have external debt stock data)

$$\ln\left(y_{it}\right) - \ln\left(y_{it-1}\right) = \propto - \beta * \ln\left(y_{it-1}\right) + u_t$$

The regression above shows Growth Convergence Equation. The external debt stock of the country *i* at time *t* is a positive function of external debt stock of the country *i* at time *t-1*. Alternatively, the growth rate of external debt stock of the country *i* is a negative function of external debt of the country *i* at time *t-1*. Left side of the equation is growth rate in external debt stock.

The estimated equation is:

$\ln\left(y_{it}\right) = 0.402 + 0,987 * \ln\left(y_{it-1}\right) + u_t$ where α=0.402, (1-β)=0,987, β=0,013=1.3%

Table 28. Convergence in global external debt of low and middle-income countries

Dependent Variable: EXTERNALDEBT2020 Method: Least Squares Date: 01/24/22 Time: 09:05 Sample: 1 123 Included observations: 123				
Variable	**Coefficient**	**Std. Error**	**t-Statistic**	**Prob.**
C	0.402587	0.092796	4.338403	0.0000
EXTERNALDEBT2019	0.986568	0.004003	246.4810	0.0000
R-squared	0.998012	Mean dependent var		23.19023
Adjusted R-squared	0.997996	S.D. dependent var		1.978605
S.E. of regression	0.088578	Akaike info criterion		-1.993751
Sum squared resid	0.949363	Schwarz criterion		-1.948025
Log likelihood	124.6157	Hannan-Quinn criter.		-1.975177
F-statistic	60752.89	Durbin-Watson stat		2.028032
Prob(F-statistic)	0.000000			

Source: The World Bank (2021b), the World Bank (2022b), Eviews (2022)

In Table 29 according to the gross debt position (as a percentage of GDP) by analytical group advanced economies debt ratio increased from 103.8% to 122.7%. For emerging market and middle-income economies, the ratio was 54.7% in 2019 and increased to 64.0% in 2020. For low-income developing countries, the ratio was 44.3% in 2019 and increased to 49.9% in 2020. It seems that advanced countries have more gross debt position than emerging market and developing countries. Debt position has increased for all countries by COVID-19.

Table 29. Gross debt position by analytical group (as a percentage of GDP)

Analytical Group	2019	2020	2021	2022	2023	2024	2025
Advanced economies	103.8	122.7	121.6	119.3	119.3	119.1	118.8
Major advanced economies (G7)	118.0	140.2	139.0	135.7	135.8	135.8	135.8
Euro area	83.7	97.5	98.9	96.3	95.4	94.5	93.4
Advanced G-20	112.8	133.8	132.8	130.2	130.4	130.5	130.5
Emerging Market and Middle-Income Economies	54.7	64.0	64.3	65.8	67.1	68.2	69.0
Emerging and Middle-Income Asia	57.3	67.3	70.1	72.4	74.2	75.7	77.0
Emerging and Middle-Income Europe	29.2	38.0	36.6	36.7	36.8	37.1	37.2
Emerging and Middle-Income Latin America	68.3	78.1	73.0	73.6	74.2	74.2	73.8
Emerging and Middle-Income Middle East and North Africa and Pakistan	45.7	52.6	48.4	47.1	47.5	47.9	48.2
Low-Income Developing Countries	44.2	49.9	50.2	49.8	49.0	48.5	48.0

Source: The IMF (2022)

The Effect of COVID-19 on Central Bank Policy Interest Rates

The Bank for International Settlements (BIS), which was established in 1930, is owned by 63 central banks from the countries all over the world. The country group represents together account for about 95% of world GDP. According to the BIS data, central bank policy interest rates decreased for 30 countries in the first quarter of 2020 comparing with the last quarter of 2019 to support economic activities and domestic consumption.

Denmark and Sweden have increased their policy rates whereas Hungary, Israel, Japan, Switzerland and the Euro zone has kept constant in same period. In the second quarter of 2020, the COVID-19 was called as pandemic and has spread all over the world. Twenty-five countries decreased policy interest rates in this period comparing with the first quarter of 2020 while Australia, Argentina, Canada, Denmark, Japan, New Zealand, Saudi Arabia, Sweden, Switzerland, United Kingdom, the USA, and the Euro zone did not change.

In the first and second quarters of 2020, Argentina, Turkey, and Mexico have the highest policy rates and Switzerland, Denmark and Japan have the lowest rates in order. Argentina has kept the policy rate as 38% and Mexico has decreased to first quarter of 2021 and then increased to 4.5% in third quarter of 2021. Turkey has started to decrease policy interest rates in the third quarter of 2021 (Table 30). In 2021-Q3 Denmark, Japan, Sweden, Switzerland, and Euro zone policy interest rates were still zero or below zero.

Table 30. Central Bank Policy rates during pandemic (end of period)

Country	Central Bank Policy Rates								Rank	
	Q4 2019	Q1 2020	Q2 2020	Q3 2020	Q4 2020	Q1 2021	Q2 2021	Q3 2021	Rank in (Q1 2020)	Rank in (Q2 2020)
Switzerland	-0.75	-0.75	-0.75	-0.75	-0.75	-0.75	-0.75	-0.75	37	37
Denmark	-0.75	-0.60	-0.60	-0.60	-0.60	-0.50	-0.50	-0.50	36	36
Japan	-0.10	-0.10	-0.10	-0.10	-0.10	-0.10	-0.10	-0.10	35	35
Mexico	7.25	6.50	5.00	4.25	4.25	4.00	4.25	4.50	3	3
Turkey	12.00	9.75	8.25	10.25	17.00	19.00	19.00	18.00	2	2
Argentina	55.00	38.00	38.00	38.00	38.00	38.00	38.00	38.00	1	1

Source: BIS (2022)

Compared to the last quarter of 2019, Argentina was the country whose policy interest rate decreased the most from 55% to 38% in first quarter of 2020. Turkey's policy interest rate was 12% in 2019-Q4 and decreased to 9.75% in 2020-Q1 and 8.25% in 2020-Q2. However, because of the economy's need for foreign financing, Turkey had to increase interest rates to attract foreign capital to the country in 2020-Q3 and this increase continued to 2021-Q2. Denmark and Sweden have increased their policy interest rates in 2020-Q1 and Switzerland has kept constant as -0.75% 8 (Table 31).

Table 31. Central Bank Policy rates during pandemic (end of period)

Country	Central Bank Policy Rates Changes (%)							Rank	
	Q1 2020	Q2 2020	Q3 2020	Q4 2020	Q1 2021	Q2 2021	Q3 2021	Rank in Change (Q1 2020)	Rank in Change (Q2 2020)
Argentina	-17.00	-17.00	-17.00	-17.00	-17.00	-17.00	-17.00	37	37
Turkey	-2.25	-3.75	-1.75	5.00	7.00	7.00	6.00	36	36
Canada	-1.50	-1.50	-1.50	-1.50	-1.50	-1.50	-1.50	34	23
United States	-1.50	-1.50	-1.50	-1.50	-1.50	-1.50	-1.50	34	23
Iceland	-1.25	-2.00	-2.00	-2.25	-2.25	-2.00	-1.75	30	31
Norway	-1.25	-1.50	-1.50	-1.50	-1.50	-1.50	-1.25	30	23
Saudi Arabia	-1.25	-1.25	-1.25	-1.25	-1.25	-1.25	-1.25	30	20
South Africa	-1.25	-2.75	-3.00	-3.00	-3.00	-3.00	-3.00	30	35
Czech Republic	-1.00	-1.75	-1.75	-1.75	-1.75	-1.50	-1.25	28	27
Peru	-1.00	-2.00	-2.00	-2.00	-2.00	-2.00	-1.25	28	31
Hong Kong SAR	-0.84	-1.99	-1.99	-1.99	-1.99	-1.99	-1.99	27	30
Brazil	-0.75	-2.25	-2.50	-2.50	-1.75	-0.25	1.75	21	33
Mexico	-0.75	-2.25	-3.00	-3.00	-3.25	-3.00	-2.75	21	33
Philippines	-0.75	-1.75	-1.75	-2.00	-2.00	-2.00	-2.00	21	27
Russia	-0.25	-1.75	-2.00	-2.00	-1.75	-0.75	0.50	9	27
Euro area	0.00	0.00	0.00	0.00	0.00	0.00	0.00	3	3
Hungary	0.00	-0.15	-0.30	-0.30	-0.30	0.00	0.75	3	7
Israel	0.00	-0.15	-0.15	-0.15	-0.15	-0.15	-0.15	3	6
Japan	0.00	0.00	0.00	0.00	0.00	0.00	0.00	3	3
Switzerland	0.00	0.00	0.00	0.00	0.00	0.00	0.00	3	3
Denmark	0.15	0.15	0.15	0.15	0.25	0.25	0.25	2	2
Sweden	0.25	0.25	0.25	0.25	0.25	0.25	0.25	1	1

Source: BIS (2022)

Although falling policy rates stimulated domestic demand, they resulted with the higher price levels; in other words eventually inflation. Additionally, emerging markets struggled with a dilemma by decreasing the policy interest rates: suffering from decreasing foreign capital inflows and inflation.

The Effect of COVID-19 on Prices (Inflation)

Countries' record levels of debt and rising inflation are limiting the ability of many countries to address new problems as they arise. In addition, supply chain disruptions, energy price volatility and localized wage pressures mean inflation. Uncertainty regarding policy pathways are also so high. As the beginning of 2022, the global economy started in a weaker position than previously anticipated. The new COVID-19 variant spreads so countries have begun re-imposing mobility restrictions. Rising energy prices and falling supply have resulted in higher and broader-based inflation than expected in many emerging market and emerging economies, particularly in the United States (IMF, 2022). Government investment programs that stimulate the economy and the market through resource allocation because of fiscal incentives or public debt may distort the prices of products and services necessary to achieve balanced economic growth (Reyes & Rajagopal, 2022).

As a result of the disruptions in the supply chain caused by the global pandemic, increasing energy and input prices, and the decrease in global supply as a result of the expansionary monetary policy implemented by the countries to revive the falling demand, both cost and demand inflation pressures have increased on a global scale. These developments have caused many international organizations to revise their global growth forecasts for 2022.

Primary commodities price index (All Commodity Price Index, 2016 = 100, includes both Fuel and Non-Fuel Price Indices, 1992-2021) has suddenly increased in 2021. The price index, which was 116.9 in the year of the 2009 financial crisis, became 105.9 in 2020 due to the pandemic and took a value close to the crisis value. The index value increased to 162.3 in 2021 and very close to 163.1 in 2008 (Figure 9).

Figure 9. Primary commodities price index (All Commodity Price Index, 2016 = 100, includes both Fuel and Non-Fuel Price Indices, 1992-2021)
Source: IMF (2022)

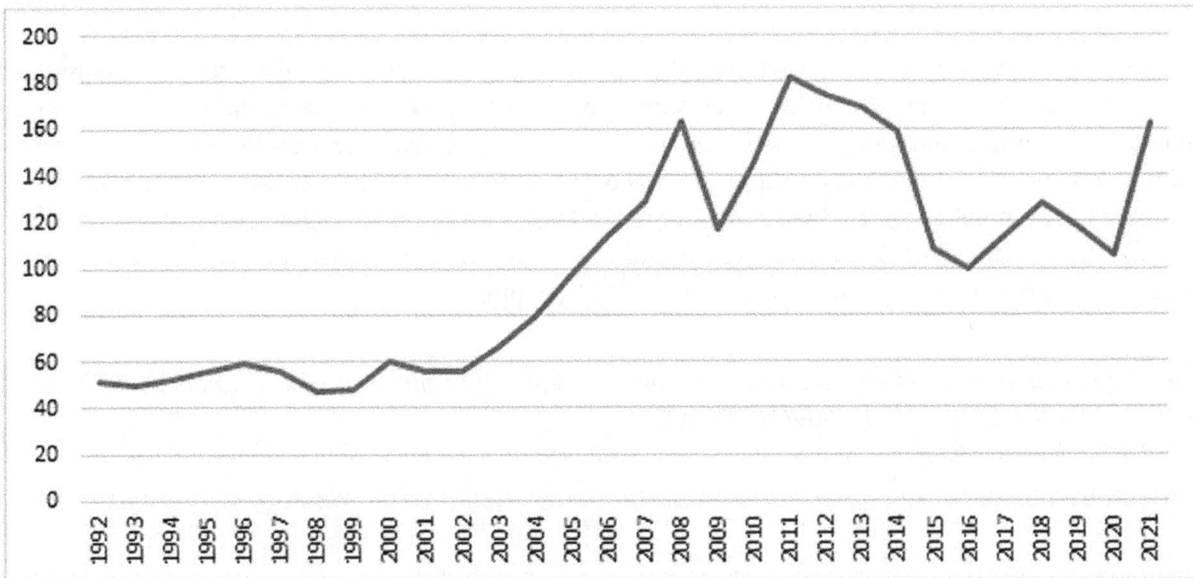

When the quarterly values of the price index are analyzed, the index value, which was 116.7 in the fourth quarter of 2019, decreased to 108.1 in the second quarter of 2020, and this decline continued until the third quarter of 2020. The index value, which saw the lowest level of recent years with 91.7 in the second quarter of 2020, started to increase after this period and reached its highest value with an increase 71 index value to 187.7 in the last quarter of 2021 (Figure 10).

Figure 10. Primary commodities price index (All Commodity Price Index, 2016 = 100, includes both Fuel and Non-Fuel Price Indices, 2009Q1-2021Q4)
Source: IMF (2022)

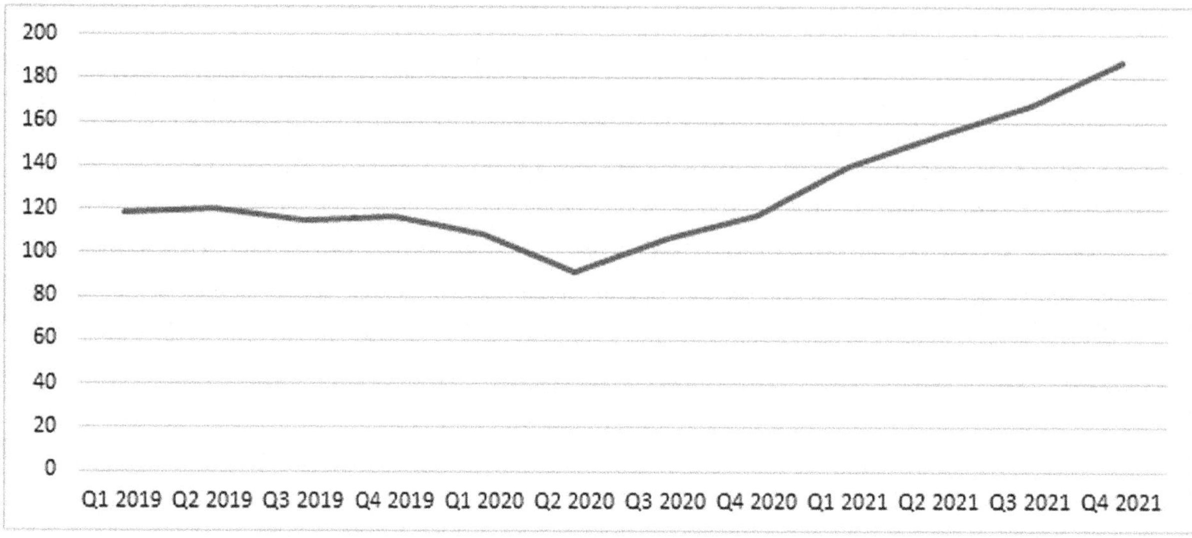

Not only "Energy index" but "Coal index" and "Natural gas index" have also increased more than all commodity price index level in 2021. This inflationary pressure causes an increase in both producer and consumer prices and reduces purchasing power with its negative effect on incomes. The "energy index" value was 127.3 in the last quarter of 2019 before pandemic and rose to 245.4 in the last quarter of 2021. The "natural gas index" value was 89 in the last quarter of 2019 before pandemic and rose to 461.3 in the last quarter of 2021. The "coal index" value was 108.9 in the last quarter of 2019 before the pandemic and rose to 269.9 in the last quarter of 2021 (Figure 11).

Figure 11. Primary commodities and energy price index (All Commodity, Coal, Energy and Natural Gas Price Index, 2016 = 100, 2009Q1-2021Q4)
Source: IMF (2022)

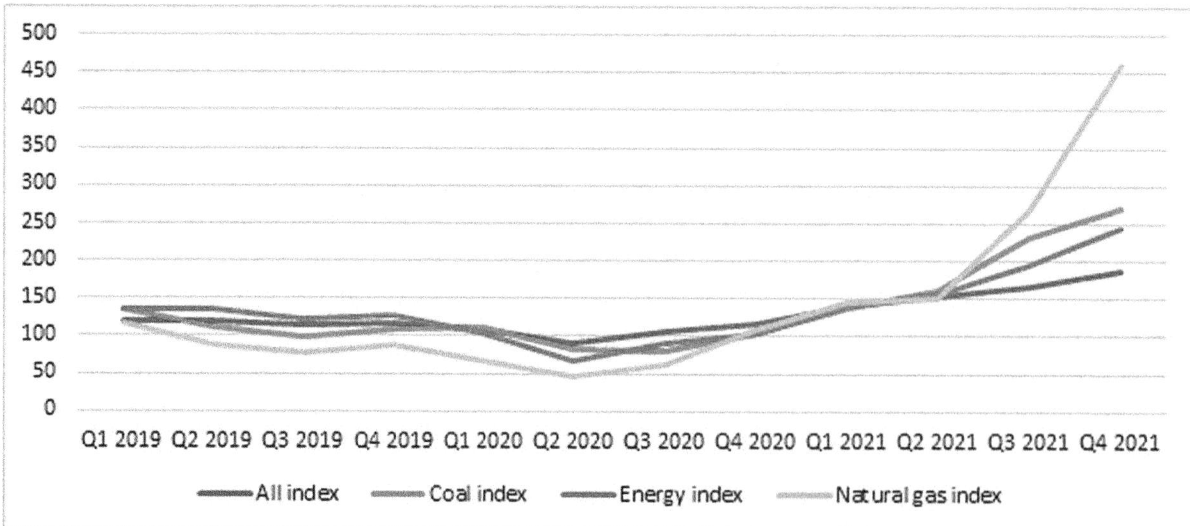

The global annual inflation (Consumer Price Index, "CPI") has increased 1.94% in 2020 compared to 2019. According to the income group, low-income countries have the highest inflation rate with 6.63% in 2020. The heavily indebted poor countries (HIPC) have the second highest inflation rate with 3.58% in 2020. "High income" and "upper middle income" countries have the lowest inflation rates with 0.51% and 2.05%, respectively (Table 32).

Table 32. Inflation, change in consumer prices (annual %)

Income Group	2015	2016	2017	2018	2019	2020
High income	0.37	0.39	1.59	1.83	1.53	0.51
Heavily indebted poor countries (HIPC)	3.77	4.66	4.98	3.05	2.69	3.58
Low income	4.89	5.80	8.28	3.91	2.83	6.63
Lower middle income	3.88	3.37	3.63	3.95	3.17	3.26
Low & middle income	3.14	2.82	3.56	3.21	2.74	2.95
Middle income	2.89	2.46	3.32	3.20	2.70	2.68
Upper middle income	1.49	1.69	3.21	2.61	2.12	2.05
World	1.43	1.55	2.19	2.44	2.17	1.94

Source: the World Bank (2022)

Turkey has the highest inflation rate with 19.3% quarterly (year-over-year, "YOY") price changes in third quarter of 2021. The price level was 10.3% in the last period of 2019 (pre-pandemic). It has increased 9% in the third quarter of 2021 to 19.3%. In Algeria, the inflation was 1.8% in the last period of 2019 and increased 6.7% to 8.5% in third quarter of 2021. In USA, the price level was 2% in the last period of 2019 and increased 3.3% to 5.3% in third quarter of 2021 (Table 33).

Over the last 12 months, the CPI has increased 7% in December 2021, 6.7% in the fourth quarter of 2021 and 4.7% annually in 2021. For Turkey, the CPI has increased 36.1% in December 2021, 25.8% in fourth quarter of 2021 and 19.6% annually in 2021. In OECD countries, the CPI has increased 6.6% in December 2021, 5.9% in fourth quarter of 2021 and 4% annually in 2021 (OECD 2022d).

Table 33. Consumer Price Index (Changes over one year, in percent, not seasonally adjusted)

Rank	Country	Q4 2019	Q1 2020	Q2 2020	Q3 2020	Q4 2020	Q1 2021	Q2 2021	Q3 2021	Difference (Q4 2019-Q3 2021)
1	Turkey	10.3	12.1	11.6	11.8	13.5	15.6	17.1	19.3	9
2	Algeria	1.8	2	2.5	1.8	3.4	5.1	6.2	8.5	6.7
3	Brazil	3.4	3.8	2.1	2.6	4.2	5.3	7.7	9.6	6.2
4	Cyprus	-0.2	1.1	-1.6	-1.2	-0.8	-1.4	2.4	4.4	4.6
5	Estonia	1.7	1.5	-1.2	-0.9	-1.1	0.6	3.1	5.5	3.8
6	North Macedonia	0.1	0.6	0.4	1.5	2.2	1.9	2.8	3.6	3.5
7	Lithuania	2	2.5	0.8	1	0.5	0.8	3.2	5.4	3.4
8	Russia	3.4	2.4	3.1	3.5	4.4	5.5	6	6.8	3.4
9	United States	2	2.1	0.4	1.2	1.2	1.9	4.8	5.3	3.3
10	Philippines	1.5	2.7	2.3	2.5	3.1	4.5	4.4	4.6	3.1

Source: BIS (2022)

CONCLUSION

People realized that health is very important for humanity after losing many of relatives and friends due to the pandemic. Nothing will be the same after the pandemic and new normal will change known attitudes. Disruption in global supply chains caused the countries to search for alternative supplier countries. The importance of health and food sectors raised during the pandemic. Some countries have lost in international trade whereas some have won.

Decreasing income has mostly affected the vulnerable population in the countries and vulnerable countries with low income and high debts in the world. Because of expansionary monetary policies, citizens and countries became even more indebted than before. The distribution of income between regions is not equal so that the countries should work in a global collaboration to minimize the negative effects of the pandemic. The pandemic demonstrated that the health system capacity and health workforce in a country have crucial roles in fighting against the pandemic.

Many governments and international institutions have implemented quick responses against pandemic to support the vulnerable citizens and firms by credits (Özsoy & Gürler, 2021a). Crises such as the pandemic are not the problem of a single country, but the world must act together in the face of such problems. A new global social contract consisting of structural reform, new technology and re-integration starting at national level is the solution for the recovery in the post-pandemic era (Song & Zhou, 2020).

Highlights

- At the end of 2021, COVID-19 related cases reached to 289 million and deaths passed 5.4 million with a 1.88 Case Fatality Rate (CFR) and 3.8 billion fully vaccinated people. The number of cases per thousand population was 37.3 and was 0.70 for the deaths per thousand population. The average number of fully vaccinated people per hundred population was 49.5 in the world.
- COVID-19 related cases, deaths, vaccination, hospital beds, nurses, medical doctors, and income (GDP) per capita are not distributed normally (even) between the countries in the world.
- All indicators are correlated with each other positively. As the GDP and income per capita is high in a country, the health system capacity is also sufficient so that the countries have higher health personnel such as nurses and medical doctors, and higher hospital beds. Of course, the higher economic activity causes higher mobility in the population so that the cases and deaths are also high in these countries.
- New variants occurred in November 2021, so the curve became upward sloped again. Regardless of the new variant effect, the number of cases has reached the highest level in April 2021 as 22.5 million and the number of deaths has reached the highest level in January 2021 as 417.4 thousand.
- COVID-19 mostly affects Europe and the Americas according to the deaths considering the population size. The higher mobility and the economic activity made these regions mostly affected by the pandemic.
- COVID-19 was higher in the Western-Pacific, the Americas, and Europe, respectively as of the end of 2021.
- COVID-19 mostly affects high-income countries according to the cases and deaths considering the population size.
- Low-income and lower-income countries have difficulties in vaccination. As the world became global village with borderless, the vaccination should be done all over the world to minimize the

negative effects of the pandemic on the global supply chains, Foreign Direct Investment (FDI) and global trade.

- As the income per capita increases, mobility, economic activity, and cases per hundred people increase as well. There is a positive correlation between GDP per capita and the number of cases in the world.
- As income per capita increases, the number of fully vaccinated people per hundred population in the world also increases.
- The excess mortality is approximately 60% and 50% more than reported COVID-19 deaths in the Americas and Europe, respectively. In the OECD countries, COVID-19 has caused around 2.5 million excess deaths.
- According to the WHO, a total of 59% of the global health professions are nursing workforce. There are 27.9 million nurses and 19.3 million of them are professional nurses. The associate professional nurses are 22% of total nurses as 6.0 million. There was a global shortage of nurses before the pandemic and need for them has increased during the pandemic.
- There are totally 28.4 million nurses, 13.2 million medical doctor and 19.7 million hospital beds in the world in 2019 and the most recent year.
- Africa and the Eastern Mediterranean regions have the least nurses per thousand population and Africa and South-East Asia regions have the least doctors per thousand population considering the population size.
- The African and Southeast Asia regions have the least hospital beds per thousand population whereas Europe and Western Pacific regions have the most considering the population.
- Low-income countries have the least number of nurses per thousand population; low income and lower middle-income countries have the least number of medical doctors and hospital beds per thousand population considering the population size.
- For 25 countries, total health expenditures amounted to US$5.9 trillion in 2019 and increased by 8.8% to US$6.4 trillion in 2020. In average health expenditure per capita was US$5,567 in 2019 and US$6,029 in 2020.
- For 25 countries, average health expenditures as a share of GDP was 13.54% in 2019 and increased to 15.20% in 2020. The USA has the highest health expenditure as a share of GDP with 17.54% in 2019 and 19.74 in 2020. Turkey has the lowest health expenditure as a share of GDP with 4.70% in 2019 and 5.00% in 2020.
- For 40 countries the total life expectancy at birth has decreased 0.66 years in average in 2020 comparing with 2019. Liechtenstein has the highest decrease in life expectancy with 2.4 years.
- As a result of the disruptions in the supply chain caused by the global pandemic, increasing energy and input prices, and the decrease in global supply as a result of the expansionary monetary policy implemented by the countries to revive the falling demand, both cost and demand inflation pressures have increased on a global scale.
- COVID-19 caused a contract in global FDI, which was US$1.53 trillion in 2019, as 35% to US$1 trillion in 2020 even below the level in the global financial crisis.
- COVID-19 caused a decrease in FDI by 8.4% in developing countries and by 58.3% in developed countries especially due to the oscillations in the activities of multinational enterprises (MNEs).
- Greenfield investments decreased by 42% in developing countries and by 19% in developed countries.

- Global output (GDP) was US$87.6 trillion in 2019 and contracted 3.3% to US$84.7 trillion in 2020 in current prices. Output was US$84.6 trillion in 2019 and contracted 3.4% to US$81.7 trillion in 2020 by 2015-year constant prices. The decrease was even greater than the global financial crisis level.
- The growth rate of output for high-income countries decreased 4.601%, whereas it decreased 3.416% for lower middle-income countries, 0.713% for upper middle-income countries and increased for low-income countries by 0.613% in 2020 comparing with 2019. The growth rate of output contracted 4.5% for advanced countries and 2.1% for emerging market and developing economies.
- The global growth is expected to be 4.4% in 2022 and 3.8% in 2023 due to rising inflation, ongoing supply chain disruptions and higher energy prices expected to continue in 2022. In 2022, the OECD is the international institution with the highest optimistic growth recovery in global output at 4.5% and in 2023, it is the IMF with 3.8%.
- Due to the breakdowns in global supply chains and value chains in manufacturing global total value added (MVA) has also decreased 6.6% in constant prices in 2020 comparing to 2019. The decrease was higher in advanced countries such as USA with 10%, Japan with 14%, Germany with 16.9% and the United Kingdom with 13.9%.
- As of January 12, 2022, there were 98 countries which have export restrictions, two countries have export liberalizations, and three countries have both for COVID-19. There were 13 countries, which have import restrictions, 110 countries have import liberalizations and 22 countries have both for COVID-19.
- Global exports in merchandised goods contracted 7.8% in 2020 compared with 2019. China is the country, which has the best performance in merchandised goods exports in both 2019 and 2020 with US$2.5 trillion and US$2.6 trillion, respectively.
- Global imports in merchandised goods contracted 8% in 2020 compared with 2019. USA is the country, which has the highest import value in merchandised goods in both 2019 and 2020 with 2.56 trillion dollars and 2.41 trillion dollars respectively.
- The "V"-shaped recovery in global trade after the pandemic started in the fourth quarter of 2020 and global imports grew by 2.2%, and in the second quarter of 2021, the growth in global imports reached 44.4%, even surpassing the recovery performance after the financial crisis.
- Global quarterly import has exceeded US$5 trillion in 2021 for the first time. Global imports amounted to US$5.08 trillion in the first quarter, a total of US$5.52 trillion in the second quarter, a total of US$5.65 trillion in the third quarter, and US$5.8 trillion in the fourth quarter of 2021.
- The pandemic has mostly affected the African and European regions. Africa's global import share was 1.77% in the last quarter of 2019 and the first quarter of 2020. It suddenly decreased to 1.50% in the second quarter of 2020 due to the pandemic.
- Europe region's global import share was 39.09% in the last quarter of 2019 and 42.02 in the first quarter of 2020. It has suddenly decreased to 39.68% in second quarter of 2020 due to the pandemic.
- During the pandemic, contrary to 2020 with the increasing global demand in 2021, China's export increased by 30% to US$3.3 trillion dollars, while its import has increased by 30.1% to US$2.7 trillion and the country's foreign trade surplus was US$676.4 billion in 2021.
- The convergence analysis indicates that global import has diverged 0.44% from 2019 to 2020.
- The convergence analysis indicates that global export has diverged 0.70% from 2019 to 2020.

- Global exports in service have declined more than global goods trade in 2020 compared with 2019 as 20% which.
- USA is the country which has the best performance in exports of service in both 2019 and 2020 with US$876.3 billion and US$705.6 billion, respectively.
- Global imports in service have declined more than global goods import in 2020 compared with 2019 as 21.3%.
- USA is the country which has the best performance in imports of service as export of service in both 2019 and 2020 with US$591.1 billion and US$460.3 billion, respectively.
- COVID-19 also negatively affected global tourism as it has caused a decrease in tourist arrivals and tourism receipts due to the restrictions, closures, and banned air flights and travel. The total number of international tourist arrivals was 1.47 billion in 2019 but decreased by 72.6% to 399 million in 2020 due to COVID-19. Total tourism receipts were US$1.47 billion in 2019 but decreased by 63.4% to US$536 million in 2020 due to the pandemic.
- The direct economic contribution of tourism to global economy is estimated at US$1.9 trillion in 2021, which was still below the pre-pandemic value of US$3.5 trillion.
- Global unemployment rate has increased from 5.35% in 2019 to 6.57% in 2020. The unemployment rate has mostly increased in upper-middle income countries and high-income countries as 6.74% and 6.48%, respectively in 2020.
- Lower-middle income countries have the highest working hours lost due to the COVID-19 crisis. Global working hours lost was 4.9% in first quarter of 2020 in average and has increased to 18.7% in second quarter. Due to the pandemic high income and lower-middle income countries have the highest working hours lost. All income groups have recovery in working hours lost in the last quarter of 2021.
- The pandemic mostly affected the Central American, South American, Southern Asian, and Western Asia regions in the second quarter of 2020. These regions have the highest working hours lost due to COVID-19.
- Lower-middle income countries have the lowest labor force participation rate due to the COVID-19 crisis. Global labor force participation rate was 60.5% in 2019 in average and decreased to 58.6% in 2020. Due to the pandemic lower-middle income countries have the lowest labor force participation rate as 2.3% decrease in labor force participation rate compared with 2019. All income groups have recovery in labour force participation rate in 2021.
- Pandemic mostly affected the South America, Latin America and the Caribbean, Central America, Southern Africa, Western Asia, and Southern Asia regions in 2020 and these regions have higher decrease in labor force participation rate.
- The pandemic has caused income inequality to rise not only between the countries but within-countries such as emerging markets and developing economies (EMDEs) from particularly severe job and income losses among lower-income population groups. The pandemic has caused 97 million more people to become poor in 2020.
- In 2020, it was the largest one-year global debt increase since World War II so that it rose to US$226 trillion as the world was hit by a deep economic recession due to COVID-19. Total global debt reached 263.3% of GDP in 2020.
- The Top-10 low and middle-income borrowers, defined as those with the largest external debt stock were Argentina, Brazil, China, India, Indonesia, Mexico, the Russian Federation, South Africa, Thailand, and Turkey by the end of 2020.

- The convergence analysis indicates that countries' total external debt has converged 1.3% from 2019 to 2020.
- Advanced economies debt ratio increased from 103.8% to 122.7%, for emerging market and middle-income economies, the ratio was 54.7% in 2019, and increased to 64.0% in 2020.
- According to BIS data, central bank policy interest rates decreased for 30 countries in the first quarter of 2020 comparing with the last quarter of 2019 to support economic activities and domestic consumption.
- The price index, which was 116.9 in the year of the 2009 financial crisis, became 105.9 in 2020 due to the pandemic and took a value close to the crisis value. The index value increased to 162.3 in 2021 and very close to 163.1 in 2008.
- Not only "Energy index" but "Coal index" and "Natural gas index" have also increased more than all commodity price index level in 2021.
- The "energy index" value was 127.3 in the last quarter of 2019 before pandemic and rose to 245.4 in the last quarter of 2021.
- The "coal index" value was 108.9 in the last quarter of 2019 before pandemic and rose to 269.9 in the last quarter of 2021.
- The annual inflation (Consumer Price Index, "CPI") has increased 1.94% in 2020 compared to 2019.
- According to the income group, low-income countries have the highest inflation rate with 6.63% in 2020. The heavily indebted poor countries (HIPC) have the second highest inflation rate with 3.58% in 2020. "High income" and "upper middle income" countries have the lowest inflation rates with 0.51% and 2.05%, respectively.

ACKNOWLEDGEMENT

Ethical Approval

Ethics approval and consent to participate: Since the submitted manuscript do not include any studies involving human participants, human data or human tissue, any individual person's data in any form (including individual details, images or videos) no ethical approval and consent are needed for the study.

Consent to Participate

The research did not involve human subjects as participants, not describing human transplantation studies and reporting studies involving vulnerable groups.

Consent to Publish

The research did not involve any human subjects as participants so nobody can object to having their data published.

Authors' Contributions

Both authors analyzed and interpreted the data and wrote the manuscript together. All authors read and approved the final manuscript.

Funding

This research received no specific grant from any funding agency in the public, commercial, or not-for-profit sectors.

Competing Interests

The authors declare they have no competing interests.

Availability of Data and Materials

Data sources are indicated in the study and data can be provided if needed. The datasets used and/or analyzed during the current study are available from the corresponding author on reasonable request.

REFERENCES

Abi-Rached, J. M. (2021). The Covid-19 caesura and the post-pandemic future. *Biosocieties*, *16*(1), 142–156. doi:10.105741292-020-00212-6

Eurostat. (2022a). *Health Main Tables.* Retrieved on January 31, 2022, from: https://ec.europa.eu/eurostat/web/health/data/main-tables

Eurostat. (2022b). *Glossary: Free on board (FOB).* Retrieved on January 29, 2022, from: https://ec.europa.eu/eurostat/statistics-explained/index.php?title=Category:International_trade_glossary

EViews. (2022). *Innovative Solutions for econometric analysis, forecasting & simulation.* Retrieved on December 19, 2021, from: https://www.eviews.com/home.html

Gapar, V., Medas, P., & Perrelli, R. (2021). *IMFBlog: Global Economy/ Global Debt Reaches a Record $226 Trillion.* Retrieved on January 23, 2022, from: https://blogs.imf.org/2021/12/15/global-debt-reaches-a-record-226-trillion/#:~:text=Policymakers%20must%20strike%20the%20right,crisis%20and%20a%20deep%20recession

Gürler, M., & Özsoy, Ö. (2019). Exploring the relationship between life expectancy at birth and economic growth in 56 developing countries. *Journal of Global Health Reports*, *3*, e2019001. doi:10.29392/joghr.3.e2019001

Gürler, M., & Özsoy, Ö. (2020). Benchmarking the Devastating Effects of COVID-19 on Economies and Social Life in the EU and In Selected Countries Mostly Affected By the Pandemic. *Diversity and Equality in Health and Care*, *17*(4), 136–145. doi:10.36648/2049-5471.17.4.204

Gürler, M., & Özsoy, Ö. (2021a). The Health System Infrastructure and Economic Effects of COVID-19 in OECD Countries, the Policy Responses of Nations and international Organizations against Pandemic. *Diversity and Equality in Health and Care*, *18*(4), 258–275.

Gürler, M., & Özsoy, Ö. (2021b). Schooling Effect in Economic Growth: Benchmarking Turkey vs High Income Countries. *Acta Scientific Nutritional Health*, *5*(2), 67–79. doi:10.31080/ASNH.2020.05.0812

IBM-SPSS. (2022). *IBM SPSS Statistics.* Retrieved on January 30, 2022, from: https://www.ibm.com/products/spss-statistics

ILO. (2022a). *ILOSTAT data: Unemployment rate by sex and age -- ILO modelled estimates, Nov. 2021 (%).* Retrieved on January 25, 2022, from: https://www.ilo.org/ilostat-files/WEB_bulk_download/indicator/UNE_2UNE_SEX_AGE_NB_A.csv.gz

ILO. (2022b). *ILOSTAT data: Working hours lost due to the COVID-19 crisis -- ILO modelled estimates (%).* Retrieved on January 25, 2022, from: https://www.ilo.org/shinyapps/bulkexplorer30/?lang=en&segment=indicator&id=HOW_2LSS_NOC_RT_A

ILO. (2022c). *ILOSTAT data: Labour force participation rate by sex and age -- ILO modelled estimates, Nov. 2021 (%).* Retrieved on January 25, 2022, from: https://www.ilo.org/shinyapps/bulkexplorer3/?lang=en&segment=indicator&id=EAP_2WAP_SEX_AGE_RT_A

International Trade Centre (ITC). (2022a). *COVID-19 Temporary Trade Measures.* Retrieved on January 25, 2022, from: https://www.macmap.org/covid19

International Trade Centre (ITC). (2022b). *TradeMap.* Retrieved on January 29, 2022, from: https://www.trademap.org/Country_SelProduct_TS.aspx?nvpm=1%7c%7c%7c%7c%7c%7cTOTAL%7c%7c%7c2%7c1%7c1%7c1%7c2%7c1%7c2%7c1%7c1%7c1

McDonald, J. (2022). *China's Trade Surplus Hit Record in 2021—With Exports Jumping 30% Amid Pandemic Demand.* Retrieved on January 23, 2022, from: https://time.com/6139334/china-record-trade-surplus-2021/

Mukherjee, S., Baral, M. M., & Venkataiah, C. (2022). Supply Chain Strategies for Achieving Resilience in the MSMEs: An Empirical Study. In H. Webb & H. Al Numairy (Eds.), *External Events and Crises That Impact Firms and Other Entities* (pp. 158–183). IGI Global. doi:10.4018/978-1-7998-8346-3.ch004

Mukherjee, S., Baral, M. M., Venkataiah, C., Pal, S. K., & Nagariya, R. (2021). Service robots are an option for contactless services due to the COVID-19 pandemic in the hotels. *Decision (Washington, D.C.), 48*, 445–460. doi:10.100740622-021-00300-x

OECD. (2021a). *Health at a Glance 2021: OECD Indicators.* OECD Publishing. doi:10.1787/ae3016b9-en

OECD. (2021b). *Economic Outlook, 2021.* Retrieved January 23, 2022, from https://www.oecd-ilibrary.org/sites/66c5ac2c-en/index.html?itemId=/content/publication/66c5ac2c-en

OECD. (2022c). *Statistics/Globalisation: FDI main aggregates – Summary.* Retrieved on January 23, 2022, from: https://stats.oecd.org/

OECD. (2022d). *Definition of Inflation (CPI).* Retrieved on January 29, 2022, from: https://data.oecd.org/price/inflation-cpi.htm/

OECD Statistics. (2022a). *Health expenditure and financing.* Retrieved on January 31, 2022, from: https://stats.oecd.org/

OECD Statistics. (2022b). *Health Status: Life expectancy.* Retrieved on January 31, 2022, from: https://stats.oecd.org/

Our World in Data. (2022a). *Dataset.* Retrieved on January 7, 2022, from: https://covid.ourworldindata.org/data/owid-covid-data.csv

Our World in Data. (2022b). *Excess mortality during the Coronavirus pandemic (COVID-19).* Retrieved on January 23, 2022, from: https://ourworldindata.org/excess-mortality-covid

Özlem, Ö., & Gürler, M. (2020). The Analysis of Health Expenditure as a Determinant of Economic Growth in 37 High Income Countries. *Acta Scientific Nutritional Health*, *4*(9), 19–33.

Özsoy, Ö. (2021). Dilemma in Health during Pandemic in OECD Countries: Increasing Health Expenditures for Preventing against the Pandemic Will Cause a Crowding-out in Increasing the Employment in Nursing Service or not? *European Journal of Science and Technology*, (32), 1094-1102.

Özsoy, Ö., & Gürler, M. (2021a). *Poverty and social exclusion of older people in ageing European Union and Turkey. J Public Health.* doi:10.100710389-021-01525-x

Özsoy, Ö., & Gürler, M. (2021b). The Negative Effects of COVID-19 on the Sustainable Development Goals, Economic Growth, Foreign Trade, and Social Life. *Advances in Human Services and Public Health*, 105–155. doi:10.4018/978-1-7998-8202-2.CH007

Reyes, J. A. P., & Rajagopal, A. (2022). The Secondary Economic Sector's Role in Post-pandemic Recovery: Analysis in the Neoliberal Capitalism Context. In A. M. López-Fernández & A. Terán-Bustamante (Eds.), *Business Recovery in Emerging Markets. Palgrave Studies in Democracy, Innovation, and Entrepreneurship for Growth.* Palgrave Macmillan. doi:10.1007/978-3-030-91532-2_2

Song, L., & Zhou, Y. (2020). The COVID-19 pandemic and its impact on the global economy: What does it take to turn crisis into opportunity? *China & World Economy*, *28*(4), 1–25. doi:10.1111/cwe.12349

The Bank for International Settlements (BIS). (2022). *Central Bank Policy rates (End of period).* Retrieved on January 25, 202, from: https://stats.bis.org/statx/srs/table/l1

The International Civil Aviation Organization (ICAO). (2022). *Economic Impacts of COVID-19 on Civil Aviation.* Retrieved on January 25, 2022, from: https://www.icao.int/sustainability/Documents/COVID-19/ICAO_Coronavirus_Econ_Impact.pdf

The International Monetary Fund (IMF). (2020). *Gross Domestic Product: An Economy's All.* Retrieved on January 29, 2022, from: https://www.imf.org/external/pubs/ft/fandd/basics/gdp.htm

The International Monetary Fund (IMF). (2021a). *World Economic Outlook databases.* Retrieved on January 23, 2022, from: https://www.imf.org/en/Publications/WEO/weo-database/2021/October

The International Monetary Fund (IMF). (2021b). *Datasets. Fiscal Monitor October 2021. Gross Debt Position.* Retrieved on January 25, 2022, from: https://www.imf.org/external/datamapper/G_XWDG_G01_GDP_PT@FM/ADVEC/FM_EMG/FM_LIDC

The International Monetary Fund (IMF). (2022). *World Economic Outlook International Monetary Fund: Rising Caseloads, a Disrupted Recovery, and Higher Inflation.* Retrieved on January 27, 2022, from: https://www.imf.org/-/media/Files/Publications/WEO/2022/Update/January/English/text.ashx

The U.S. Centers for Medicare & Medicaid Services. (n.d.). *The National Health Expenditure Accounts (NHEA) data*. Retrieved on January 31, 2022, from: https://www.cms.gov/Research-Statistics-Data-and-Systems/Statistics-Trends-and-Reports/NationalHealthExpendData/National HealthAccountsHistorical#:~:text=U.S.%20health%20care%20spending%20grew,spending%20accounted%20for%2019.7%20percent

The World Bank. (2020). *Global Economic Prospects June 2020: HIGHLIGHTS from Box 1.1: How Deep Will the COVID-19 Recession Be?* Retrieved on January 31, 2022, from: https://thedocs.worldbank.org/en/doc/395721588788243295-0050022020/original/GlobalEconomicProspectsJune2020TopicalIssue3 highlights.pdf

The World Bank. (2021a). *Updated estimates of the impact of COVID-19 on global poverty: Turning the corner on the pandemic in 2021?* Retrieved on March 24, 2022, from: https://blogs.worldbank.org/opendata/updated-estimates-impact-covid-19-global-poverty-turning-corner-pandemic-2021#:~:text=In%20January%202021%2C%20we%20estimated,around%20the%20globe%20in%202020

The World Bank. (2021b). *International Debt Statistics 2022.* Retrieved on January 24, 2022, from: https://openknowledge.worldbank.org/bitstream/handle/10986/36289/9781464818004.pdf?sequence=4&isAllowed=y

The World Bank. (2022a). *Dataset.* Retrieved on January 24, 2022, from: https://data.worldbank.org

The World Bank. (2022b). *Global Economic Prospects.* Retrieved on January 23, 2022, from: https://openknowledge.worldbank.org/bitstream/handle/10986/36519/9781464817601.pdf

The World Bank. (2022c). *Metadata Glossary.* Retrieved on January 29, 2022, from: https://databank.worldbank.org/metadataglossary/jobs/series/BX.KLT.DINV.WD.GD.ZS

TURKSTAT. (2021). *Health Expenditure Statistics, 2020.* Retrieved on January 31, 2022, from: https://data.tuik.gov.tr/Bulten/Index?p=Health-Expenditure-Statistics-2020-37192

UNCTAD. (2021c). *COVID-19 and Tourism an Update.* Retrieved on January 25, 2022, from: https://unctad.org/system/files/official-document/ditcinf2021d3_en_0.pdf

United Nations Conference on Trade and Development. (2021a). *World Investment Report 2021.* Retrieved on January 24, 2022, from: https://unctad.org/system/files/non-official-document/WIR2021_tab01.xlsx

United Nations Conference on Trade and Development. (2021b). *Trade and Development Report 2021.* Retrieved on January 23, 2022, from: https://unctad.org/system/files/official-document/tdr2021_en.pdf

United Nations Industrial Development Organization (UNIDO). (2022). Retrieved on January 25, 2022, from: https://stat.unido.org/database/MVA%202021,%20Manufacturing

United States Census Bureau. (2022). Census.gov/ *Business & Industry/ Foreign Trade/ Definitions.* Retrieved on January 29, 2022, from: https://www.census.gov/foreign-trade/reference/definitions/index.html

WHO. (2020a). *State of the world's nursing 2020: investing in education, jobs and leadership.* Retrieved on January 19, 2021, from: https://apps.who.int/iris/rest/bitstreams/1274201/retrieve

WHO. (2020b). *Home/Newsroom/Fact sheets/Detail/Nursing and midwifery/ Key facts.* Retrieved on January https://www.who.int/news-room/fact-sheets/detail/nursing-and-midwifery

WHO. (2021a). *Global expenditure on health: public spending on the rise?* World Health Organization. https://apps.who.int/iris/bitstream/handle/10665/350560/9789240041219-eng.pdf

WHO. (2021b). *Home/Multimedia/Multimedia item/Extending Life Expectancy.* https://www.who.int/multi-media/details/extending-life-expectancy-SDGs

WHO. (2021c). *Home/Newsroom/Questions and answers/Global excess deaths associated with the COVID-19 pandemic.* https://www.who.int/news-room/questions-and-answers/item/global-excess-deaths-associated-with-the-COVID-19-pandemic

WHO. (2022a). *COVID-19 Weekly Epidemiological Update. Edition 73, published 6 January 2022* https://www.who.int/docs/default-source/coronaviruse/situation-reports/20220106_weekly_epi_update_73.pdf?sfvrsn=c731e59b_3&download=true

WHO. (2022b). *The true death toll of COVID-19: Estimating global excess mortality.* https://www.who.int/data/stories/the-true-death-toll-of-covid-19-estimating-global-excess-mortality

WHO. (2022c). *The Global Health Observatory Data:* https://www.who.int/data/gho/data/indicators

WHO. (2022d). *The Global Health Observatory: Indicator Metadata Registry List.* https://www.who.int/data/gho/indicator-metadata-registry

World Economic Forum (WEF). (2014). *The Global Competitiveness Report 2014–2015.* Retrieved on January 24, 2022, from: https://www3.weforum.org/docs/WEF_GlobalCompetitivenessReport_2014-15.pdf

World Tourism Organization. (2021, November). *UNWTO World Tourism Barometer and Statistical Annex, November 2021.* Retrieved on January 25, 2022, from: https://www.e-unwto.org/doi/epdf/10.18111/wtobarometereng.2021.19.1.6

World Tourism Organization. (2022a). *Secretary-General's Policy Brief on Tourism and COVID-19: Tourism and Covid-19 – Unprecedented Economic Impacts*. Retrieved on January 25, 2022, from: https://www.e- https://www.unwto.org/tourism-and-covid-19-unprecedented-economic-impacts

World Tourism Organization. (2022b). *UNWTO Tourism Data Dashboard*. Retrieved on January 25, 2022, from: https://www.unwto.org/unwto-tourism-dashboard

WTO. (2021). *World Trade Statistical Review 2021*. https://www.wto.org/english/res_e/statis_e/wts2021_e/wts2021_e.pdf

WTO. (2022). *Documents, data and resources/WTO data portal*. https://data.wto.org/

KEY TERMS AND DEFINITIONS

CIF: CIF (Cost, Insurance, and Freight) import value represents the landed value of the merchandise at the first port of arrival in the country (US Census Bureau 2022). The CIF price is the price of a good delivered at the frontier of the importing country, or the price of a service delivered to a resident, before the payment of any import duties or other taxes on imports or trade and transport margins within the country (Eurostat, 2022b).

Current Health Expenditure (CHE) per Capita in US$: This indicator calculates the average expenditure on health per person. It contributes to understand the health expenditure relative to the population size facilitating international comparison. Per capita current expenditures on health expressed in respective currency - US dollar (WHO, 2022d).

Excess Mortality: Excess mortality is defined as the difference between the total number of deaths estimated for a specific place and given time period due to a crisis or pandemic as COVID-19 and the number that would have been expected in the absence of the crisis and pandemic (no-COVID-19 scenario) (WHO, 2021c).

Export: To send or transport goods and/or services out of a country to the other countries. Exports measure the total physical movement of merchandise goods and/or services out of the country to the foreign countries (US Census Bureau 2022). An export of a good or service occurs when there is a change of ownership from a resident to a non-resident (Eurostat, 2022b).

FDI: Foreign direct investment (FDI) are the net inflows of investment to acquire a lasting management interest (10 percent or more of voting stock) in an enterprise operating in an economy other than that of the investor (World Bank, 2022c).

FOB: The FOB (free on board) value of exports and imports of goods is the value of the goods at the exporter's customs frontier. Foreign transport and insurance services between the exporter's and importer's frontiers are not included in the value (but are recorded under services) (Eurostat, 2022).

GDP: GDP measures the monetary value of final goods and services—that is, those that are bought by the final user—produced in a country in a given period of time (say a quarter or a year). It counts all output generated within the borders of a country (IMF, 2020).

Imports: All goods and/or services physically brought into the country from other countries. Imports measure the total physical arrivals of merchandise goods and/or services into the country from the foreign countries (US Census Bureau, 2022).

Inflation (CPI): Inflation measured by consumer price index (CPI) is defined as the change in the prices of a basket of goods and services that are typically purchased by specific groups of households (OECD, 2022d).

Life Expectancy at Birth (Years): The average number of years that a new-born could expect to live, if he or she were to pass through life exposed to the sex- and age-specific death rates prevailing at the time of his or her birth, for a specific year, in a given country, territory, or geographic area (WHO, 2022d).

Pandemic: A pandemic is defined as "an epidemic occurring worldwide, or over a very wide area, crossing international boundaries and usually affecting a large number of people". The classical definition includes nothing about population immunity, virology, or disease severity (WHO, 2022d).

ENDNOTE

1 WEF, The Global Competitiveness Report, 2014-2015, p.48.

Chapter 10
International Business Paradigm in the Post-Pandemic Era:
The Role of Literacy and Digitalization

Subhanil Banerjee
https://orcid.org/0000-0001-7485-9967
School of Humanities, K.R. Mangalam University, Gurgaon, India

Souren Koner
Amity University, Raipur, India

Shilpi Gupta
https://orcid.org/0000-0003-4382-3616
Amity University, Raipur, India

ABSTRACT

The COVID-19 pandemic was one of the deadliest pandemics ever encountered by human civilization. However, the unconquerable human resilience and the digital duo of mobile and internet led to a victory over this dreadful pandemic. This chapter initially focuses on India to illustrate the necessity of literacy in a pandemic. Later, the chapter accepts the hypothesis that business and trade is the engine of growth and verifies that in such dire conditions whether digital business and trade acted as a buffer. Both the aforementioned aspects are quantitatively verified. This chapter uses two regression equations with robust standard errors to examine COVID-19 and literacy. Two dependent variables are population recovered to population tested and completely vaccinated to the total population, and both the population density and rate of literacy have been taken as two independent variables. Furthermore, this chapter also has analyzed the relevant data of 137 countries and has emphasized the fact how digitalization has acted as a buffer and kept business and trade going in a "no man's land."

DOI: 10.4018/978-1-6684-3749-0.ch010

INTRODUCTION

With the worldwide acceptance of the capitalist construct, especially following Liberalization, Privatization, and Globalization (LPG), international trade has emerged as the fulcrum for further growth. The dawn of the Internet, followed by smart phones and their conjugation, gave international trade a digital platform with the benefits bereft of any time and space barrier. As this distance between time and space became faint, it distorted classical and Keynesian constructs. The classical construct proposes that the aggregate supply creates its own demand, and the Keynesian proposition revolves around the importance of the aggregate order to guide the economy towards equilibrium. The difference can be seen from many angles, one of which might be asymmetrical information. The classical construct considers that consumers are blind and will grab anything suppliers provide. Keynes modified this particular hypothesis with the lagged response on behalf of the consumer, who is not entirely blind in nature.

However, this time and space-less exchange scenario leads to the ancient paradox of the chicken and egg. There is less asymmetric information between producer and consumer, which means real-time demand, would be met by real-time supply. This much less asymmetrical information leads to a lower moral hazard volume and promotes competition. Such competition encourages fair play among the economic entities involved, especially on the producers' part. Among the other boons of the digital economy, the innovative pricing plan and sound refund policy deserve special mention; together, they have fostered a real-time global competitive market that runs 24 X 7 hours a day. This digital revolution in the worldwide market boosted global trade. A little data crunching will make this proposition even more convincing. From 2018 to 2020, the world trade volume declined by almost 11.9%, whereas "digitally deliverable services went from below 52% of services exports in 2019 to almost 64% in 2020, while ICT services grew from 10% to almost 14%, a marked acceleration of the long-term trend" (UNCTAD, 2021). This certainly depicts that throughout the COVID-19-time digital trade has rescued the global trade from further decline.

Again, digital trade is a directly related with meaningful digital penetration and meaningful digital penetration and literacy go hand in hand. This is for two reasons: first, digital penetration and COVID-19 preventive apps would be of no use bereft of a certain level of literacy; and second, the mass-level approach of disseminating information regarding lockdown and social distancing will also be less effective owing to less concoction of information, excluding literacy. However, a question about the need for such consideration for a chapter chiefly related to international trade is also looming.

Humans are the main stakeholders in international trade. International trade can't move involuntarily, ignoring its stakeholders. This particular aspect makes the safety of human beings a prime concern for uninterrupted trade flow. Moreover, the function of digital penetration to sustain trade in rough times is the theme of the present chapter. Here, literacy, anti-covid apps, digital access, and business relationships are far from water-tight compartments.

To deal this meticulous cross disciplinary method, the present chapter emphasizes the influence of literacy on COVID-19 endurance in India, and it resorts to a detailed dialogue on different apps that turned into the shield in opposition to the concerning pandemic in India. In these two aspects, consideration of only India has kept the scale of discussion under check; otherwise, the vastness of the data would have overwhelmed the whole chapter. On the other hand, while considering the impact of digital penetration on ease of doing business, it goes global. This perfect blend makes this chapter novel and unique.

It was beyond the worst nightmare the world would witness something such as COVID-19 in a life span. The world has seen Severe Acute Respiratory Syndrome (SARS) before and has moved to comprehend the history of Yersinia Pestis, Vibrio Cholerae, Varicella Zoster Virus, Salmonella Typhi, and so forth. The human genome has boasted of these victories, which eventually strengthened the foundation of self-belief and reliance of the present generation. At the time, the thought of being ready to counterattack any such pandemic was almost engraved in the human mind; the COVID-19 catastrophe came in the form of the first COVID patient in the last days of December 2019 in the Wuhan province in China. Since China and India are in close proximity, the first COVID case in India was detected in the last days of January 2020. Seventy-two hours later, the World Health Organization (WHO) affirmed the COVID-19 epidemic as a PHEIC (Public Health Emergency of International Concern).

Furthermore, regarding its brisk spread disregarding the geological landscapes and the soaring rate of mortality, WHO confirmed COVID-19 as a pandemic by the second week of March, 2020. However, almost one month ahead of such declaration, almost two hundred countries in the world fell prey to this destructive pandemic (Attia et al., 2021). Spreading awareness and timely approaching people was the major problem. The mismatch between the speed of the government and the swelling of COVID-19, with the former falling miles behind, required innovative ways and ideas to bridge the gap between the two paces. This milieu initiated numerous applications considering the already established conjugation of the Internet and mobile smart phones.

The Indian government, like others, paid attention to technological advancement and interventions and opted for APPs like the AarogyaSetu, CoWIN, Chatbot, Corona Kavach, e-Sanjeevani Teleconsultation Services, etc. Different states and union territories have furthermore invented their own APPs as Chhattisgarh opted for CGTEEKA, Goa selected Test Yourself, Karnataka chose Quarantine Watch, Punjab opted for COVA, Kerala set GoK Direct, Maharashtra resorted to Mahakavach (Maharasthra), etc. Such applications emerged as vital paraphernalia in combating the CORONA pandemic. They were effective in taming the surge of COVID-19 and extended help in locating, restricting, early identification, and inoculating related to the infection.

The installation of web portals devoted to the CORONA pandemic also facilitated accurate real-time quantitative nuances on the pandemic. It is not an embellishment that this is a digital reprisal by India against one of the most outrageous pandemics so far. In addition, this digital interference gave people their safety in their own hands. An initially top-down approach eventually seems bottom-up due to the substantial trickledown effect. Such empowering of the mass through digital interference is exceptional in history.

It is beyond any doubt that in developing digital tools, a particular level of literacy is required. The concerned chapter has been partly committed to determining the influence of literacy on the COVID-19 pandemic in India. In this backdrop, undertaking an exhaustive discussion on the impact of literacy on COVID-19 is needed. Furthermore, the present chapter is novel, considering data crunching to comprehend the relationship amid successes in opposition to COVID-19 through literacy. This kind of empirical investigation was long-awaited and eradicated a vital shortcoming of previous research.

It is appealing to mention that smart lockdown also has proved very effectual fighting COVID-19 (Loh et al., 2021; Wang et al., 2021).Adhering to and conformity to this lockdown is another facet strongly related to literacy. Throughout these lockdowns, digitalisation, as defined before, has helped to continue nearly a normal life (Maqableh & Alia, 2021; Pandey et al., 2022; Srivastava et al., 2021; Ullah & Ali, 2021).

Furthermore, courting a pecuniary and worldwide economic debacle, the whole of humankind has been profoundly in debt to the digital markets that somehow drove the economic and pecuniary deeds. An example might be share markets (Alola et al., 2021; Barua, 2021). Without satisfactory literacy that will facilitate the population to harvest the fruits of digital conjugation and the COVID-related applications, the world would have faced a much more complex situation. In this background the present chapter seeks answer to two related research questions does literacy worked as a shield against COVID-19? And, whether digitalization has any positive impact on business? The first objective of the chapter is to empirically verify the impact of literacy on COVID-19. The second objective of the chapter is to investigate whether digitalization has any impact on business paradigm.

EDUCATION AND HEALTH

It has been stated that for the United Kingdom (U.K.), education and health are directly proportional and statistically significant (Johnston et al., 2015). Fletcher (2015) emphasized that education has a positive impact on self-reporting, cardiovascular and weight outcomes. Hahn and Truman (2015)elaborated that education elevates health and health equity. Kim (2016) opined that higher education reduces the Bio Mass Index of American population. Masoudiyekta *et al.* (2018) highlighted that paucity of knowledge among female population considering their crucial health issues can be reduced through formal education. Cannonier and Mocan (2018) highlighted that increased schooling within Sierra Leone has improved women's perception regarding health.

Hejazi *et al.* (2017) mentioned that educational interference augments health literacy, self-care behaviour and self-efficacy. Davies *et al.* (2018)concluded educated people have higher life expectancy and less co-morbidity. Lutz and Kebede (2018) asserted that women literacy is positively correlated with empowerment and better health of women belonging to developing countries. Mensch *et al.*(2019) mentioned following their systematic literature review that education is positively correlated with maternal and child health.

COVID-19: Social Distancing, Lockdown, Social Media and Infodemics

The vivid increase of the novel corona virus has buzzed immense alarm around the world; countries struggled to deal with the exponential rise in confirmed cases. Naturally uncertainty driven rise in fear and anxiety among people became a common phenomenon. The first preventive measure against this panic was to empower the people with factual information. Shaking hands and hugging was very usual among people but COVID taught us to restrain from such common social interaction. However, small it may look like but it is a big change and people find hard to maintain (Ali & Gatiti, 2020).

Before initiating the actions against COVID such as lockdown, the government resorted to media channels, and social media for dissemination regarding the danger of the virus (Alqutob et al., 2020). Over this time period, the religious and opinion leader, public figures, and educators all joined hand in informing people, regarding the significance of lock down and social distancing (Liu et al., 2020).

Awareness generation regarding social distancing came to be directly proportional in reducing spread of the concerned pandemic (Al-Dmour et al., 2020).The WHO understood the accessibility of accurate scientific information is vital to keep the public informed and instructed all the governments to do the needful (Mheidly & Fares, 2020). Following such instruction the COVID-19 also initiated the phase of infodemic that made the spread of information wide (Mheidly & Fares, 2020).

However, the half-truths have infested the social media, and people often shared the fact without proof (Jammal et al., 2020).Curbing such tsunami of flawed information was the foremost challenge for the government and authorities (Ros & Neuwirth, 2020).It has also been discussed that in these stages of critical time the inclination of awareness has acted as an important ingredient in building the prevention process, down grading the rate of transmission by disseminating genuine and efficient information (Alahdal et al., 2020).They have been supported by other researchers (Nazir et al., 2020).Apart from the cross checking of information received through different platforms, expecting an affirmative impact and considering the information as genuine as it is received by an individual, will become hard to evaluate with passing time (Shacham et al., 2021).

Health Literacy

Crucial health literacy is most vital now, when a communicable and rapidly spreading covid-19 pandemic comes in the presence of abundant knowledge and lofty hope regarding health control. In such a context, it is hard for the people to understand the messages delivered by public health professionals along with politicians.

Nutbeam (1998) illustrated health literacy like "the cognitive and social skills which determine the motivation and ability of individuals to gain access understand and use information in ways which promote and maintain good health." An inadequate level of health literacy is linked to a variety of negative health results(Berkman et al., 2011; Sørensen et al., 2015)as well as greater health-care expenses in the past(Eichler et al., 2009; Palumbo, 2017). Critical health literacy is vital when faced with such challenges.

As a result, health literacy is needed more than ever now to combat the infodemic as well as empower individuals to belief and proceed upon dependable information and advice. It requires people to use different abilities to interpret health information and services that are available, especially in situations that are fast-changing (Sørensen et al., 2012). In general, health literacy is described as the ability to obtain, interpret, assess, and utilise health information to take health-related decisions (Sørensen et al., 2012).

In another study, it was found that almost 50 percent of the population have inadequate health literacy and it may be challenging for them to obtain, comprehend, evaluate, and utilize information to improve or preserve their health (Sørensen et al., 2015). Duong et al.(2017) revealed a large proportion of Asian populations have difficulty handling health-related information. Furthermore, multiple researches have shown that inadequate health literacy has a social gradient, with financial disadvantage, education, and social standing being the biggest indicators (Levin-Zamir et al., 2016; Stormacq et al., 2019). Due to the soaring level of asymmetric information, it is mostly hard to deduce news and official recommendations related with Covid-19 (Abel & McQueen, 2020).

There is a major challenge in how each individual can incorporate this ocean of information into their own behaviours. Other studies done by few researchers revealed that increase in health literacy may reduce the level of anxiety(H. T. Nguyen et al., 2020)and safeguard covid-19 related depression (Nguyen et al., 2020). Inadequate health literacy is linked to a lower quality of life, minimum or no self-care, higher health spending, and higher mortality. COVID-19 consciousness and deterrence behaviour are significantly influenced by health literacy(Bailey et al., 2020).In the Indian perspective, Gautam *et al.*(2021) discovered that 65.8% of the population lacks adequate health literacy, and that health literacy can help avert the COVID 19 pandemic.

Apart from the aforementioned literature lots of other academicians have considered COVID 19, literacy and various applications (Ahammad et al., 2021; Alanzi, 2021; Anthony Jnr, 2021; Bassi et al., 2020; Basu, 2021; Dadaczynski et al., 2021; Gunasekeran et al., 2021; Gupta et al., 2020; Huang et al., 2021; Iyengar et al., 2020; Jaju & Thakkar, 2021; Jhunjhunwala, 2020; Kodali et al., 2020; Kumar &

Veer, 2021; Kundu et al., 2021; Li et al., 2021; Mahasuar, 2021; Majhi et al., 2021; Mudgal et al., 2021; Mukherjee et al., 2021; Pham et al., 2020; Robishaw et al., 2021; Rout & Sahu, 2020; Sahoo et al., 2021; Singh, 2020; Tilahun et al., 2021) incidentally their focus was also on India.

It is apparent from the literature review that no study has been made so far to judge the impact of literacy on this dreadful pandemic. Specially, quantification of that impact can be a novel addition to the existing literature. In this background the present chapter has chosen India to find the impact of literacy on COVID-19 pandemic. However, it is also true that with the current status of statistics carrying such analysis is arduous and will require carefully selected proxy variables. Apart from that the chapter has also considered measuring the impact of digitalization on international trade at global level.

METHODOLOGY

The methodology has been divided into two parts part one reflects on the interaction between Literacy and COVID-19 focusing on India and the second part reflects globally that what might happen to international trade if digital penetration is enhanced. For the first analysis cross sectional analysis has been deployed and for the second analyses opt for pulled regression with ease of doing business as dependent variable and per 100 mobile connections along with per 100 fixed broad band connection as independent variable over 137 countries of the world.

The first analysis resorts to two separate regressions with robust standard errors. In the two regression equations ratio of population recovered to population tested and fully vaccinated to total population have been taken as two dependent variables respectively and in both the equations population density and rate of literacy have been taken as two independent variables. The population density has been considered as the mentioned pandemic has a tendency to spread faster in densely populated areas.

Furthermore, it will also help to overcome the endogeneity problem that arises out of omitted variable bias. However, a test for endogeneity has been avoided as "handling endogeneity due to simultaneity is virtually impossible with cross-sectional data because all variables are measured simultaneously. Ultimately, results of analyses using such data rested on theoretical arguments about the temporal priority of variables and the theoretical plausibility of reciprocal effects"(Lynch & Brown, 2011, p.112).

Considering the nature of the data first a test for multicollinearity through variable inflation factors (VIF) has been undertaken. The two econometric equations might be represented as:

$$PRPT_i = a + b.\ LR_i + c.\ PDS_i + u_i \text{ where } i = 1,2,3,4.....29 \quad (1)$$

$$PTV_j = d + e.\ LR_j + f.\ PDS_j + v_j \text{ where } j = 1,2,3,4,......29 \quad (2)$$

In the above equations $PRPT_i$Þ% of people recovered among people tested in different Indian States and PTV_j Þ% of population fully vaccinated in different Indian states, $LR_{i/j}$Þliteracy rates of different Indian states, $PDS_{i/j}$Þpopulation density of different Indian states. a and d are constant, b, c, e and f are coefficients and u_i along with v_j are stochastic error terms. i and j refers to the 29 Indian states.

The second econometric analysis considers data of 137 countries over the world on ease of doing business ranking (edb_{it}), per 100 broadband penetrations (pcb_{it}), per 100 mobile subscriptions ($pmss_{it}$) for the year 2019 and 2020. Data on $pmss_{it}$ and pcb_{it} have been acquired from the World Development

Indicators of World Bank; and data related with edb_{it} has been collected from doingbusiness.com. The study aspires to guesstimate the below mentioned regression equation through pooled regression analysis. If any statistically significant relationship exists between the regression and the regressor variables, then it might be said that pcb_{it} and $pmss_{it}$, impact the edb_{it}.

The robust standard errors have been considered disregarding the homo or heteroskedastic nature of the error terms (Angrist & Jorn-Steffen, 2009; Imbens & Kolesar, 2015, Banerjee, Sar, & Pandey, 2020). For the second econometric analysis the equation has been framed as $edb_{it} = a + b.pcb_{it} + c.pmss_{it} + y_{it}$, where; $i = 1, 2, 3 \ldots 137$ and $t = 2019$ and 2020. In the above equation, 'a' is the constant term, b, c, are the coefficients of pcb_{it} and, $pmss_{it}$ respectively. y_{it} is the stochastic error term.

The analysis starts with impact of literacy (measured through as previously mentioned) on COVID-19 pandemic and ends with the impact of digital penetration on ease of doing business ranking.

Econometric Analysis

Table 1. Regression test results for PRPTi

Independent Variables	Coefficients	t Statistics	Probability	R^2	Adjusted R^2	F (2,26)	Probability	VIF
LR_i	0.25	4	0.000	0.417	0.3722	8.3	0.0016	1
PDS_i	-0.0006	-0.41	0.684					

Source: Computed

It is apparent from Table 1 that there is no multicollinearity considering the VIF value. The model is rightly set considering probability associated with the F statistics. Moreover, literacy rate exerts a positive impact on the percentage of recovered person out of the tested population. The population density impacts the percentage of recovered person out of the tested population in a negative way; however, it is statistically insignificant.

Table 2. Regression test results for PTV_j

Independent Variables	Coefficients	t Statistics	Probability	R^2	Adjusted R^2	F (2,26)	Probability	VIF
LR_j	0.61	3.33	0.003	0.3456	0.2952	6.96	0.0038	1
PDS_j	-0.01	1.8	0.083					

Source: Computed

It is apparent from Table 2 there is no multicollinearity considering the VIF value. The model is rightly set considering probability associated with the F statistics. Moreover, literacy rate exerts a positive impact on the percentage of fully vaccinated people out of total population. The population density impacts the percentage of fully vaccinated people out of total population in a negative way; however, it is statistically insignificant.

Table 3. Econometric test results

edb_{it}(Dependent Variable)	pcb_{it}, $pmss_{it}$(Independent Variables)	
Econometric tests	**Results**	
Multicollinearity: Variance inflation factors (vif)	Statistics	Probability
	1.25<2	NA

Source: Computed

As illustrated in Table 3, there is no multicollinearity.

Table 4. Regression results (dependent variable edb_{it})

List of Independent Variables	Coefficient	t Statistics	Probability	R^2	Adjusted R^2	F Statistics (2, 271)	Probability
$Pmss_{it}$	-0.34	-4.97	0.000				
Pcbit	-2.25	-15.40	0.000	0.55	0.54	180.34	0.000
Constant	159.37	20.91	0.000				

Source: Computed

As depicted in Table 4, the coefficients of $Pmss_{it}$ and Pbc_{it} are negative and statistically significant. Moreover, the model as a whole is significant, as represented by the F statistics. It implies that augmented digital connectivity might have led to the business facilitation. As with the increase in both the independent variables namely mobile subscription per hundred people and fixed broadband connection per hundred people the rank in ease of doing business declines which is good as lesser rank is better. Today, business over the Internet is a usual practice. Applications like Amazon and Flipkart are gaining popularity over time; both of them are devoted to digital business, irrespective of indigenous or international.

The augmented reimbursement policy following customer dissatisfaction has heightened their assurance to choose digital over physical as far as market is concerned. The demanding timetable and hasty life have contributed to the aforementioned aspect. Bandwagon effect and possibility of considerable peer pressure should never be ignored as well.

CONCLUSION

The present chapter aspires to assess the impact of digitalization and digital literacy on post COVID-19, as the anti-COVID-19 apps that have been launched requires basic education to use, for this purpose India has been chosen and it has been successfully proven that literacy acts as a deterrent to COVID-19. The third wave of COVID-19 is in progress, though not as vicious as the first and the second wave but there is no scope to lower the guard.

What have been discussed so far portrays how common people might be empowered through simple mobile apps and can stand against a pandemic. It has also been illustrated that a certain level of literacy is required to use these applications and increased literacy will improve the chances of survival against

COVID-19. Not only the applications; courting COVID-19 the educational institutes have resorted to online teaching mode. Such quick transformation from offline to online teaching mode was made possible through introduction of online meeting platforms like ZOOM, Cisco WebEx, and Google meet, Microsoft teams etc. Moreover, these platforms have also helped to maintain social distancing but maintain social connections. The economy would have stumbled if these platforms would not have made work from home possible. The transformation from individual behaviour to collective behaviour is one of the lessons that the concerned pandemic taught us.

This chapter cannot opt for the luxury to fall the drape here as the main objective of the chapter is to investigate the relevance of digital economy as a buffer facing similar catastrophe in future. In this backdrop, the stress of the current chapter is on digitalization and its relationship with business as might be undergone by 137 countries of the world. The pooled regression approach that considered pertinent data on 137 countries for the years 2019 and 2020 illustrates that broadband access and mobile subscription negatively and statistically significantly impact the ease of doing business rank. This implies if these two mentioned independent variables increase then ease of doing business rank will decrease, which is better. Moreover, overtime, the consumer-friendly policies like; strict refund, free offers, discounts, special festival bonanza has established consumer faith in digital merchants. The advantage to the producer is zero advertisement cost.

In a corporate world, time is money; moreover, there is less asymmetric information to the consumer than before. These two aspects together led to the evolution of a market where the consumer can compare products and take a quick decision. The internationalization of the market through digitalization explains the vitality between digitalization and international business as felt by the selected one hundred and thirty-seven countries of the world. Countries all over the world might look after added access to broadband and mobile to enjoy prosperity in a digitalized world.

A competitive and symmetric business environment benefitting both the producers and consumers rapped within the cocoon of ease of doing business might define the future paradigm of the business world and waiting behind the veil of digital duo. It is obvious that considering any future catastrophe similar to COVID-19 that may leave us homebound and make physical distancing mandatory. The aforementioned digital intervention might act as a shield and carry-on business and therefore international trade in a normal order.

REFERENCES

Abel, T., & McQueen, D. (2020). Critical health literacy and the COVID-19 crisis. *Health Promotion International*, *35*(6), 1612–1613. doi:10.1093/heapro/daaa040 PMID:32239213

Ahammad, I., Hossain, M. U., Rahman, A., Chowdhury, Z. M., Bhattacharjee, A., Das, K. C., Keya, C. A., & Salimullah, M. (2021). Wave-wise comparative genomic study for revealing the complete scenario and dynamic nature of COVID-19 pandemic in Bangladesh. *PLoS One*, *16*(9), 1–21. doi:10.1371/journal.pone.0258019 PMID:34587212

Al-Dmour, H., Masa'deh, R., Salman, A., Abuhashesh, M., & Al-Dmour, R. (2020). Influence of Social Media Platforms on Public Health Protection Against the COVID-19 Pandemic via the Mediating Effects of Public Health Awareness and Behavioral Changes: Integrated Model. *Journal of Medical Internet Research*, *22*(8), 1–15. doi:10.2196/19996 PMID:32750004

Alahdal, H., Basingab, F., & Alotaibi, R. (2020). An analytical study on the awareness, attitude and practice during the COVID-19 pandemic in Riyadh, Saudi Arabia. *Journal of Infection and Public Health, 13*(10), 1446–1452. doi:10.1016/j.jiph.2020.06.015 PMID:32563674

Alanzi, T. (2021). A Review of Mobile Applications Available in the App and Google Play Stores Used During the COVID-19 Outbreak. *Journal of Multidisciplinary Healthcare, 14*, 45–57. doi:10.2147/JMDH.S285014 PMID:33469298

Ali, M. Y., & Gatiti, P. (2020). The COVID-19 (Coronavirus) pandemic: Reflections on the roles of librarians and information professionals. *Health Information and Libraries Journal, 37*(2), 158–162. doi:10.1111/hir.12307 PMID:32251543

Alola, A. A., Alola, U. V., & Sarkodie, S. A. (2021). The COVID-19 and financial stress in the USA: Health is wealth. *Environment, Development and Sustainability, 23*(6), 9367–9378. doi:10.100710668-020-01029-w PMID:33052193

Alqutob, R., Al Nsour, M., Tarawneh, M. R., Ajlouni, M., Khader, Y., Aqel, I., Kharabsheh, S., & Obeidat, N. (2020). COVID-19 Crisis in Jordan: Response, Scenarios, Strategies, and Recommendations. *JMIR Public Health and Surveillance, 6*(3), 1–6. doi:10.2196/19332 PMID:32407289

Anthony, B. Jr. (2021). Integrating telemedicine to support digital health care for the management of COVID-19 pandemic. *International Journal of Healthcare Management, 14*(1), 280–289. doi:10.1080/20479700.2020.1870354

Attia, Y. A., El-Saadony, M. T., Swelum, A. A., Qattan, S. Y. A., Al-qurashi, A. D., Asiry, K. A., Shafi, M. E., Elbestawy, A. R., Gado, A. R., Khafaga, A. F., Hussein, E. O. S., Ba-Awadh, H., Tiwari, R., Dhama, K., Alhussaini, B., Alyileili, S. R., El-Tarabily, K. A., & Abd El-Hack, M. E. (2021). COVID-19: pathogenesis, advances in treatment and vaccine development and environmental impact—an updated review. *Environmental Science and Pollution Research, 28*(18), 22241–22264. doi:10.1007/S11356-021-13018-1

Bailey, S. C., Serper, M., Opsasnick, L., Persell, S. D., O'Conor, R., Curtis, L. M., Benavente, J. Y., Wismer, G., Batio, S., Eifler, M., Zheng, P., Russell, A., Arvanitis, M., Ladner, D. P., Kwasny, M. J., Rowe, T., Linder, J. A., & Wolf, M. S. (2020). Changes in COVID-19 Knowledge, Beliefs, Behaviors, and Preparedness Among High-Risk Adults from the Onset to the Acceleration Phase of the US Outbreak. *Journal of General Internal Medicine, 35*(11), 3285–3292. doi:10.100711606-020-05980-2 PMID:32875509

Barua, S. (2021). Understanding Coronanomics: The Economic Implications of the Covid-19 Pandemic. *Journal of Developing Areas, 55*(3), 435–450. doi:10.1353/jda.2021.0073

Bassi, A., Arfin, S., John, O., & Jha, V. (2020). An overview of mobile applications (apps) to support the coronavirus disease 2019 response in India. *The Indian Journal of Medical Research, 151*(5), 473. doi:10.4103/IJMR.IJMR_1200_20 PMID:32474557

Basu, S. (2021). Effective Contact Tracing for COVID-19 Using Mobile Phones: An Ethical Analysis of the Mandatory Use of the Aarogya Setu Application in India. *Cambridge Quarterly of Healthcare Ethics, 30*(2), 262–271. doi:10.1017/S0963180120000821 PMID:32993842

Berkman, N. D., Sheridan, S. L., Donahue, K. E., Halpern, D. J., & Crotty, K. (2011). Low health literacy and health outcomes: An updated systematic review. *Annals of Internal Medicine, 155*(2), 97–107. doi:10.7326/0003-4819-155-2-201107190-00005 PMID:21768583

Cannonier, C., & Mocan, N. (2018). The impact of education on women's preferences for gender equality: Evidence from Sierra Leone. *Journal of Demographic Economics, 84*(1), 3–40. doi:10.1017/dem.2016.12

Dadaczynski, K., Okan, O., Messer, M., Leung, A. Y. M., Rosário, R., Darlington, E., & Rathmann, K. (2021). Digital Health Literacy and Web-Based Information-Seeking Behaviors of University Students in Germany During the COVID-19 Pandemic: Cross-sectional Survey Study. *Journal of Medical Internet Research, 23*(1), 1–17. doi:10.2196/24097 PMID:33395396

Davies, N. M., Dickson, M., Smith, G. D., Van Den Berg, G. J., & Windmeijer, F. (2018). The causal effects of education on health outcomes in the UK Biobank. *Nature Human Behaviour, 2*(2), 117–125. doi:10.103841562-017-0279-y PMID:30406209

Duong, T. V., Aringazina, A., Baisunova, G., Nurjanah, Pham, T. V., Pham, K. M., Truong, T. Q., Nguyen, K. T., Oo, W. M., Mohamad, E., Su, T. T., Huang, H.-L., Sørensen, K., Pelikan, J. M., Van den Broucke, S., & Chang, P. W. (2017). Measuring health literacy in Asia: Validation of the HLS-EU-Q47 survey tool in six Asian countries. *Journal of Epidemiology, 27*(2), 80–86. doi:10.1016/j.je.2016.09.005 PMID:28142016

Eichler, K., Wieser, S., & Brügger, U. (2009). The costs of limited health literacy: A systematic review. *International Journal of Public Health, 54*(5), 313–324. doi:10.100700038-009-0058-2 PMID:19644651

Fletcher, J. M. (2015). New evidence of the effects of education on health in the US: Compulsory schooling laws revisited. *Social Science & Medicine, 127*, 101–107. doi:10.1016/j.socscimed.2014.09.052 PMID:25311783

Gautam, V. S. D., Rustagi, N., Mittal, A., Patel, M., Shafi, S., Thirunavukkarasu, P., & Raghav, P. (2021). Health literacy, preventive COVID 19 behaviour and adherence to chronic disease treatment during lockdown among patients registered at primary health facility in urban Jodhpur, Rajasthan. *Diabetes & Metabolic Syndrome, 15*(1), 205–211. doi:10.1016/j.dsx.2020.12.023 PMID:33387854

Gunasekeran, D. V., Tham, Y. C., Ting, D. S. W., Tan, G. S. W., & Wong, T. Y. (2021). Digital health during COVID-19: Lessons from operationalising new models of care in ophthalmology. *The Lancet Digital Health, 3*(2), e124–e134. doi:10.1016/S2589-7500(20)30287-9 PMID:33509383

Gupta, R., Bedi, M., Goyal, P., Wadhera, S., & Verma, V. (2020). Analysis of COVID-19 Tracking Tool in India. *Digital Government: Research and Practice, 1*(4), 1–8. doi:10.1145/3416088

Hahn, R. A., & Truman, B. I. (2015). Education improves public health and promotes health equity. *International Journal of Health Services, 45*(4), 657–678. doi:10.1177/0020731415585986 PMID:25995305

Hejazi, S., Peyman, N., Tajfard, M., & Esmaily, H. (2017). The Impact of Education Based on Self-efficacy Theory on Health Literacy, Self-efficacy and Self-care Behaviors in Patients With Type 2 Diabetes. *Iranian Journal of Health Education and Health Promotion, 5*(4), 296–303. doi:10.30699/acadpub.ijhehp.5.4.296

Huang, S., Yang, J., Fong, S., & Zhao, Q. (2021). Artificial intelligence in the diagnosis of COVID-19: Challenges and perspectives. *International Journal of Biological Sciences, 17*(6), 1587. doi:10.7150/ijbs.58855 PMID:33907522

Iyengar, K., Upadhyaya, G. K., Vaishya, R., & Jain, V. (2020). COVID-19 and applications of smartphone technology in the current pandemic. *Diabetes & Metabolic Syndrome, 14*(5), 733–737. doi:10.1016/j.dsx.2020.05.033 PMID:32497963

Jaju, K., & Thakkar, H. (2021). Impact of Artificial Intelligence and Internet of Things in Effective Handling of Coronavirus Crisis. In S. Mishra, P. K. Mallick, H. K. Tripathy, & G. M. Chae (Eds.), Impact of AI and Data Science in Response to Coronavirus Pandemic (pp. 235–251). Springer. doi:10.1007/978-981-16-2786-6_12

Jammal, H. M., Alqudah, N. M., & Khader, Y. (2020). Awareness, Perceptions, and Attitude Regarding Coronavirus Disease 2019 (COVID-19) Among Ophthalmologists in Jordan: Cross-Sectional Online Survey. *Clinical Ophthalmology (Auckland, N.Z.), 14*(1), 2202. doi:10.2147/OPTH.S260460 PMID:32801630

Jhunjhunwala, A. (2020). Role of Telecom Network to Manage COVID-19 in India: Aarogya Setu. *Transactions of the Indian National Academy of Engineering, 5*(2), 157–161. doi:10.1007/S41403-020-00109-7

Johnston, D. W., Lordan, G., Shields, M. A., & Suziedelyte, A. (2015). Education and health knowledge: Evidence from UK compulsory schooling reform. *Social Science & Medicine, 127*, 92–100. doi:10.1016/j.socscimed.2014.10.026 PMID:25459203

Kim, Y. J. (2016). The long-run effect of education on obesity in the US. *Economics and Human Biology, 21*, 100–109. doi:10.1016/j.ehb.2015.12.003 PMID:26828291

Kodali, P. B., Hense, S., Kopparty, S., Kalapala, G. R., & Haloi, B. (2020). How Indians responded to the Arogya Setu app? *Indian Journal of Public Health, 64*(6), S228–S230. doi:10.4103/ijph.IJPH_499_20 PMID:32496261

Kumar, R., & Veer, K. (2021). How artificial intelligence and internet of things can aid in the distribution of COVID-19 vaccines. *Diabetes & Metabolic Syndrome, 15*(3), 1050. doi:10.1016/j.dsx.2021.04.021 PMID:33941496

Kundu, S., Al Banna, M. H., Sayeed, A., Akter, S., Aktar, A., Islam, M. A., Proshad, R., & Khan, M. S. I. (2021). *Effect of vendors' socio-demography and other factors on hygienic practices of street food shops.* doi:10.1080/15378020.2020.1870785

Levin-Zamir, D., Baron-Epel, O. B., Cohen, V., & Elhayany, A. (2016). The Association of Health Literacy with Health Behavior, Socioeconomic Indicators, and Self-Assessed Health From a National Adult Survey in Israel. *Journal of Health Communication, 21*(sup2), 61–68. doi:10.1080/10810730.2016.1207115 PMID:27669363

Li, X., Chang, J., Chen, S., Wang, L., Yau, T. O., Zhao, Q., Hong, Z., Ruan, J., Duan, G., & Gao, S. (2021). Genomic Feature Analysis of Betacoronavirus Provides Insights Into SARS and COVID-19 Pandemics. *Frontiers in Microbiology, 12*, 1–10. doi:10.3389/fmicb.2021.614494 PMID:33815307

Liu, Y., Cao, L., Li, X., Jia, Y., & Xia, H. (2020). Awareness of mental health problems in patients with coronavirus disease 19 (COVID-19): A lesson from an adult man attempting suicide. *Asian Journal of Psychiatry*, *51*, 1–3. doi:10.1016/j.ajp.2020.102106 PMID:32334411

Loh, H. C., Looi, I., Ch'ng, A. S. H., Goh, K. W., Ming, L. C., & Ang, K. H. (2021). Positive global environmental impacts of the COVID-19 pandemic lockdown: A review. *GeoJournal*, 1–13. doi:10.1007/S10708-021-10475-6 PMID:34316088

Lutz, W., & Kebede, E. (2018). Education and Health: Redrawing the Preston Curve. *Population and Development Review*, *44*(2), 361. doi:10.1111/padr.12141 PMID:29937609

Lynch, S. M., & Brown, J. S. (2011). Stratification and Inequality Over the Life Course. Handbook of Aging and the Social Sciences, 105–117. doi:10.1016/B978-0-12-380880-6.00008-3

Mahasuar, K. (2021). Lies, damned lies, and statistics: The uncertainty over COVID-19 numbers in India. *Knowledge and Process Management*. Advance online publication. doi:10.1002/kpm.1685

Majhi, S., Verma, M., Chauhan, I., Kumari, R., & Sharma, M. (2021). A field survey after covid-19 immunization programme at Ghaziabad, India: Highlighting adverse events. *Journal of Applied Pharmaceutical Sciences and Research*, *4*(2), 10–14. doi:10.31069/japsr.v4i2.3

Maqableh, M., & Alia, M. (2021). Evaluation online learning of undergraduate students under lockdown amidst COVID-19 Pandemic: The online learning experience and students' satisfaction. *Children and Youth Services Review*, *128*, 1–11. doi:10.1016/j.childyouth.2021.106160

Masoudiyekta, L., Rezaei-Bayatiyani, H., Dashtbozorgi, B., Gheibizadeh, M., Malehi, A., & Moradi, M. (2018). Effect of education based on health belief model on the behavior of breast cancer screening in women. *Asia-Pacific Journal of Oncology Nursing*, *5*(1), 114–120. doi:10.4103/apjon.apjon_36_17 PMID:29379843

Mensch, B. S., Chuang, E. K., Melnikas, A. J., & Psaki, S. R. (2019). Evidence for causal links between education and maternal and child health: Systematic review. *Tropical Medicine & International Health*, *24*(5), 504–522. doi:10.1111/tmi.13218 PMID:30767343

Mheidly, N., & Fares, J. (2020). Leveraging media and health communication strategies to overcome the COVID-19 infodemic. *Journal of Public Health Policy*, *41*(4), 410–420. doi:10.105741271-020-00247-w PMID:32826935

Mudgal, S., Yadav, R., Haokip, H. R., Pandit, A., & Mary, Y. S. (2021). Genomic variation and point mutations analysis of Indian COVID-19 patient samples submitted in GISAID database. *Journal of the Indian Chemical Society*, *98*(10), 1–7. doi:10.1016/j.jics.2021.100156

Mukherjee, D., Maskey, U., Ishak, A., Sarfraz, Z., Sarfraz, A., & Jaiswal, V. (2021). Fake COVID-19 vaccination in India: an emerging dilemma? *Postgraduate Medical Journal*. doi:10.1136/postgradmedj-2021-141003

Nazir, M., Hussain, I., Tian, J., Akram, S., Tshiaba, S. M., Mushtaq, S., & Shad, M. A. (2020). A Multidimensional Model of Public Health Approaches Against COVID-19. *International Journal of Environmental Research and Public Health*, *17*(11), 1–11. doi:10.3390/ijerph17113780 PMID:32466581

Nguyen, H. C., Nguyen, M. H., Do, B. N., Tran, C. Q., Nguyen, T. T. P., Pham, K. M., Pham, L. V., Tran, K. V., Duong, T. T., Tran, T. V., Duong, T. H., Nguyen, T. T., Nguyen, Q. H., Hoang, T. M., Nguyen, K. T., Pham, T. T. M., Yang, S. H., Chao, J. C. J., & Van Duong, T. (2020). People with Suspected COVID-19 Symptoms Were More Likely Depressed and Had Lower Health-Related Quality of Life: The Potential Benefit of Health Literacy. *Journal of Clinical Medicine*, *9*(4), 1–18. doi:10.3390/jcm9040965 PMID:32244415

Nguyen, H. T., Do, B. N., Pham, K. M., Kim, G. B., Dam, H. T. B., Nguyen, T. T., Nguyen, T. T. P., Nguyen, Y. H., Sørensen, K., Pleasant, A., & Van Duong, T. (2020). Fear of COVID-19 Scale—Associations of Its Scores with Health Literacy and Health-Related Behaviors among Medical Students. *International Journal of Environmental Research and Public Health*, *17*(11), 1–14. doi:10.3390/ijerph17114164 PMID:32545240

Nutbeam, D. (1998). Health promotion glossary. *Health Promotion International*, *13*(4), 349–364. https://www.jstor.org/stable/45152457. doi:10.1093/heapro/13.4.349

Palumbo, R. (2017). Examining the impacts of health literacy on healthcare costs. An evidence synthesis. *Health Services Management Research*, *30*(4), 197–212. doi:10.1177/0951484817733366 PMID:29034727

Pandey, D., Ogunmola, G. A., Enbeyle, W., Abdullahi, M., Pandey, B. K., & Pramanik, S. (2022). COVID-19: A Framework for Effective Delivering of Online Classes During Lockdown. *Human Arenas*, *5*(2), 322–336. doi:10.100742087-020-00175-x

Pham, Q. V., Nguyen, D. C., Huynh-The, T., Hwang, W. J., & Pathirana, P. N. (2020). Artificial Intelligence (AI) and Big Data for Coronavirus (COVID-19) Pandemic: A Survey on the State-of-the-Arts. *IEEE Access: Practical Innovations, Open Solutions*, *8*, 130839. doi:10.1109/ACCESS.2020.3009328 PMID:34812339

Robishaw, J. D., Alter, S. M., Solano, J. J., Shih, R. D., DeMets, D. L., Maki, D. G., & Hennekens, C. H. (2021). Genomic surveillance to combat COVID-19: Challenges and opportunities. *The Lancet Microbe*, *2*(9), e481–e484. doi:10.1016/S2666-5247(21)00121-X PMID:34337584

Ros, M., & Neuwirth, L. S. (2020). Increasing global awareness of timely COVID-19 healthcare guidelines through FPV training tutorials: Portable public health crises teaching method. *Nurse Education Today*, *91*, 1–6. doi:10.1016/j.nedt.2020.104479 PMID:32473497

Rout, K., & Sahu, S. (2020). Exploring Factors Influencing the Users' Intention to Use Aarogya Setu Contact Tracing Mobile Health Application during COVID-19 Pandemic Article history. *Journal of Humanities and Social Sciences Research*, *2*(S), 29–36. doi:10.37534/bp.jhssr.2020.v2.nS.id1068.p29

Sahoo, J. P., Nath, S., Ghosh, L., & Samal, K. C. (2021). Concepts of Immunity and Recent Immunization Programme against COVID-19 in India. *Biotica Research Today*, *3*(2), 103–106. https://biospub.com/index.php/biorestoday/article/view/728

Shacham, M., Greenblatt-Kimron, L., Hamama-Raz, Y., Martin, L. R., Peleg, O., Ben-Ezra, M., & Mijiritsky, E. (2021). Increased COVID-19 Vaccination Hesitancy and Health Awareness amid COVID-19 Vaccinations Programs in Israel. *International Journal of Environmental Research and Public Health*, *18*(7), 1–11. doi:10.3390/ijerph18073804 PMID:33917327

Singh, V. (2020). The Effect of COVID-19 Pandemic on Immunization Services in India - Possible Challenges and way forward. *Epidemiology International*, *05*(02), 53–60. doi:10.24321/2455.7048.202018

Sørensen, K., Pelikan, J. M., Röthlin, F., Ganahl, K., Slonska, Z., Doyle, G., Fullam, J., Kondilis, B., Agrafiotis, D., Uiters, E., Falcon, M., Mensing, M., Tchamov, K., Broucke, S., & Brand, H. (2015). Health literacy in Europe: Comparative results of the European health literacy survey (HLS-EU). *European Journal of Public Health*, *25*(6), 1053–1058. doi:10.1093/eurpub/ckv043 PMID:25843827

Sørensen, K., Van Den Broucke, S., Fullam, J., Doyle, G., Pelikan, J., Slonska, Z., & Brand, H. (2012). Health literacy and public health: A systematic review and integration of definitions and models. *BMC Public Health*, *12*(1), 1–13. doi:10.1186/1471-2458-12-80 PMID:22276600

Srivastava, K. C., Shrivastava, D., Alam, M. K., & Al-Mahmood, A. K. (2021). Is SARS CoV-2 viral mutation leading us to a virtual world? *Bangladesh Journal of Medical Science*, *20*, 185–187. doi:10.3329/bjms.v20i5.55559

Stormacq, C., Van Den Broucke, S., & Wosinski, J. (2019). Does health literacy mediate the relationship between socioeconomic status and health disparities? Integrative review. *Health Promotion International*, *34*(5), e1–e17. doi:10.1093/heapro/day062 PMID:30107564

Tilahun, B., Gashu, K. D., Mekonnen, Z. A., Endehabtu, B. F., & Angaw, D. A. (2021). Mapping the Role of Digital Health Technologies in Prevention and Control of COVID-19 Pandemic: Review of the Literature. *Yearbook of Medical Informatics*, *30*(1), 26–37. doi:10.1055-0041-1726505 PMID:34479378

Ullah, H., & Ali, J. (2021). Impact of COVID-19 pandemic on the schooling of public and private school students in Pakistan. *Education 3-13*, 1–10. doi:10.1080/03004279.2021.1931917

UNCTAD. (2021, October 27). *Trade data for 2020 confirm growing importance of digital technologies during COVID-19*. https://unctad.org/news/trade-data-2020-confirm-growing-importance-digital-technologies-during-covid-19

Wang, C., Wang, D., Abbas, J., Duan, K., & Mubeen, R. (2021). Global Financial Crisis, Smart Lockdown Strategies, and the COVID-19 Spillover Impacts: A Global Perspective Implications From Southeast Asia. *Frontiers in Psychiatry*, *12*, 1–16. doi:10.3389/fpsyt.2021.643783 PMID:34539457

Chapter 11
Sustainability and Urban Innovation by Smart City Implementation

Aldo Alvarez-Risco
Universidad de Lima, Peru

Patricia V. Tapia-Meza
Leibniz University Hannover, Germany

Shyla Del-Aguila-Arcentales
Escuela de Posgrado, Universidad San Ignacio de Loyola, Lima, Peru

ABSTRACT

Sustainability is a global need, both for companies and people. It is not only a matter of convenience to achieve more excellent business benefits, but it is also accompanied by the concept of a smart city, which is of fundamental importance since it also goes in parallel with Industry 4.0. This chapter describes the technologies associated with the implementation of smart cities, benefits, limitations, and contribution to sustainability. Different examples of smart cities are described, highlighting the requirements for implementation and the associated risks. The amount and type of specific technologies available in implementing a smart city are striking. Sustainable cities and smart cities undoubtedly share many characteristics, so the interconnection of concepts facilitates implementation, knowing all the technological requirements necessary for development.

INTRODUCTION

The planet has experienced more severe and rapid climate change in the last years, with significant consequences for humanity. Many authors argue that we live in the Anthropocene era, where human activities have led to vast ecological and geological consequences (CrutzenWill Steffen, 2003). International organizations and governments worldwide have joined efforts to face these current and future problems. Similarly, more people are worried about working on new movements and campaigns to spread

DOI: 10.4018/978-1-6684-3749-0.ch011

environmental awareness in society. Global climate change has shown us our vulnerabilities as human beings more closely, and it has exacerbated injustice and inequality around the world. Accordingly, many issues arise that are related to responsibilities and sustainability. The development of fair environmental policies should be sought to address the uncertainties of climate projections and the risks they entail. The increasing concentration of the world population in urban megalopolises has created several challenges, particularly in the growth of resources and the environmental challenges that city planners face (Ershova & Orlovskaya, 2020; Qingsong et al., 2019).

Greenhouse emissions and carbon dioxide are the most significant cause of increasing earth's temperature (Yigitcanlar & Dizdaroglu, 2015). The global energy consumption and the production of gases responsible for the greenhouse effect in cities are 75% and 80%, respectively. In 1959, 30% of people worldwide lived in metropolises; this percentage is likely growth by 66% in 2050 (United Nations, 2019). Furthermore, the urban population growth is one of the leading causes of the Anthropocene era, which currently contributes globally to 75% of $CO2$ production, 80% of energy consumption, and 75% of natural resources (Perveen et al., 2017). According to (United Nations, 2016), the world has 7450 million inhabitants, approximately 83 million people are being added to the population each year. Even if fertility levels continue to decline, the world population reach approximately 8600 million in 2030 and 9800 million in 2050. Therefore, cities represent platforms for the consumption of resources in which companies and individuals face activities and services with a high effect on the economy and society.

Rapid population growth, urbanization, scarcity of resources, and global warming have highlighted sustainable cities as a new framework of vital importance (United Nations, 2016). These challenges have given rise to the new term "smart city". The smart city model drives sustainable progress based on energy and environmental policies to reduce, improve, and manage fossil fuel effects and climate change hazards (Arbolino et al., 2017).

Different approaches are known about a smart city, but all are mainly oriented towards innovation and the city's administration and infrastructure. Accordingly, a smart city comprises people, processes, and data connected via information and communication technologies (ICT) to solve urban habitability, viability, and sustainability. They are implementing technology advancement within smart city infrastructure results in a place that always remains connected using real-time information. So, the infrastructure represents the nucleus of a city, where the unification and combination of all the metropolis systems make it a smart city (Nam & Pardo, 2011). In this context, the population and the city are interconnected via different ICTs. Hence, all public services are interactive, such as mobility, education, health, and achieve a comprehensive approach to government by raising the quality of life of each inhabitant of the city (Orecchini et al., 2019).

Smart is a term linked directly to innovative solutions for attaining sustainability. Smart cities are expected to solve all urban issues by integrating new technology into the management and operation of cities (Soyata et al., 2019). Thus, smart urban technologies are vital in the smart city agenda for rolling out an intelligent infrastructure along with the cities (Komninos et al., 2019). Furthermore, the rise of digital social media offers different interfaces to facilitate the activities of citizens by adopting them in their daily lives (White & Marchet, 2021)

Governments and organizations have made significant investments in new technologies to pursue social, economic, political, and environmental development, enhance people's lives, and save our planet (European Parliament, 2014; Yigitcanlar, 2016). Then, smart city discourse leads to public policy speech encouraging environmental concerns through big innovative projects (Cowley & Caprotti, 2018). Policy makers acknowledge the potential of smart advances for achieving effectiveness (Giffinger et al., 2007;

Kramers et al., 2014). Besides, researchers evaluate the most suitable procedures and sustainability tools as Lee and Wu (2014). Furthermore, several studies highlight the benefits of achieving the urban challenges such as reducing emissions, more energy efficiency, competitiveness, and enhancing people's lives.

We are following up that the smart cities' application is linked to achieving the current significant challenges of a sustainable world. According to the smart city framework and assessment model (Giffinger et al., 2007), smart cities are composed of six dimensions: smart economy, smart governance, smart mobility, smart environment, smart people, and smart living. However, this chapter focuses on examining only four dimensions: smart governance, smart mobility, smart environment, and smart people. We do not try to diminish the importance of the other two dimensions (smart economy and smart living); instead, we believe that they complement a successful system.

The main aim is to show how the implementation of smart cities can lead to attaining sustainability. Therefore, the four dimensions are displayed as the core for accomplishing sustainability in significant cities. First, it is explained how each dimension of a smart city is a reason to face the current challenges through innovation and management. Second, it is offered a review about how smart and innovative technology has contributed to sustainability in the last years and possible constraints. Finally, it concludes that the smart city model can lead to sustainable cities. However, citizens are the main protagonists of smart cities' progress where technology and innovation become the fuel they use to drive production, environmental and social processes that lead to sustainability.

SUSTAINABILITY AND SMART CITIES DIMENSIONS

The most influential and widespread concept of a smart city framework and assessment model was provided by Giffinger et al. (2007), in their report entitled Smart Cities: Ranking of medium-sized European cities, where they evaluate 90 medium-sized European cities based on 6 characteristics and 90 indicators. Since then, researchers have cited the model in numerous works seeking to refine the smart city notion (Anthopoulos, 2015). Giffinger et al. (2007) encompass the following six dimensions: smart economy, smart governance, smart mobility, smart environment, smart people, and smart living:

Smart Economy and Smart Government

Smart economy and smart government work complementary in creating and promoting appropriate policies for an efficient operation of intelligent systems in the city. On the one hand, smart governance offers public information about the city that fosters civic engagement and collaboration. Public information enables citizens to learn and adapt quickly to new digital technologies. Furthermore, an intelligent government is transparent in all city's procedures, activities, and services because it uses public and reliable data (Chourabi et al., 2012).

Then, citizen engagement, collaboration, and reliable public information allow successful city management. The smart city is concerned primarily with citizens' needs. The first step of a good government is setting up policies and programs that encourage the participation and collaboration of the population. Then, policy makers can gather important information and determine appropriate indicators for solving social problems. In addition, individuals can receive efficient public services that are required (Caragliu et al., 2011). Another important aspect is the alliances and collaboration with internal and external partnerships that can support democracy and transparency in political subjects (Rida Khatoun, 2016).

On the other hand, a smart economy promotes the creation of enterprises and innovation that allows economic growth. In the same way, an intelligent economy maintains a strong relationship with international economies. Besides, it works with local and external connections for boosting creativity and knowledge. Furthermore, the interaction between research and technology permits smart cities to improve productivity and increase prospects for their inhabitants (Angelidou, 2017). In the same way, it creates training programs for improving residents' competencies, such as entrepreneurship programs, digital learning programs. Therefore, flexibility for adopting innovations, labor relations, and interconnectivity can be easily conceivable by ICT tools (Anttiroiko et al., 2014).

The overconsumption in the last years spotlights the change from a pursuing economy to sharing economy. The smart city prefers a sharing economy model to accomplish sustainability goals. Then, if Individuals prefer sharing things rather than purchasing, the city produces less trash, and all its processes are efficient. As well, new digital sustainable e-commerce models can be established. However, an intelligent infrastructure rolling out technology along the city can only work appropriately and lead to sustainability with a smart government. Following that, smart government and smart economy complement building an intelligent infrastructure and setting up a package of sound policies. These policies regulate the deployment of new technologies and encourage new sustainable, efficient services around the cities.

Data-driven City as Sustainable Development

Many authors underline the ability of government and citizens ability to manage big data through technological innovation. For instance, adopting innovative products and services would reduce waiting times and deliver quality and eco-friendly products. Big Data has become a significant source for supporting and boosting services function. Notorious results of the employment of information technology in the efficiency of the processes and services of the metropolises highlight the value of big data. Likewise, it increases the application and proliferation of other Artificial Intelligence (AI), Internet of Things (IoT), and data mining technologies (Soomro et al., 2019).

The objective of analyzing gigantic amounts of information is to discern and find relationships between consumer favoritism. For instance, the correlations between patterns and characteristics of the general public are advantageous and lucrative for companies in their decision-making based on truthful and processed information in real-time (Rouse, 2017). From a more technical point of view (Stephenson, 2013), the Big Data analysis lies on a chain of techniques that handle to examine the data, and it includes machine learning and different types of algorithm analysis, among others.

Extensive data analysis has been applied in climate science, such as analyzing patterns and variables to manage vital resources better, reduce energy consumption, etc. (Barkham et al., 2018). Furthermore, its large amount of diverse information can be processed through intelligent processing techniques that can be carried out using artificial intelligence (Mohanty, 2015).

Sustainable development relies on information produced by human and technology interaction from the urban city. Bibri (2020) argues that a smart sustainable city needs constant monitoring of omnipresent technologies displayed in the infrastructure. The generated data is stored, processed, analyzed, and used to choose the best environmental effectiveness options depending on the city's problems.

Many authors refer that the big production and operation of data through technology is the primary source for improving and optimizing operation and services in the cities. Therefore, many institutions support using and exploiting these advanced technologies, such as operation centers, investigation hubs, and so forth. Though solutions' employment always depends on each city's different characteristics.

Furthermore, the data produced about the urban environment and citizens is vital information to address different issues such as sustainability, urbanization, and the scarceness of natural resources issues in urban cities (Bibri, 2020).

Principal Disruptive Technologies in Smart Cities

Internet of Things (IoT)

The Internet of Things is a wireless network between smart products or things connected to the Internet. It is a crucial element for building an intelligent infrastructure in metropolises. IoT is all artifacts linked to the Internet within a smart city with information technology that allows automated decision-making without human intervention. Bibri (2020) considers that IoT rapid progress enables the connectivity between smart components and not only things and individuals. Therefore, the IoT products market is expected to grow (Rahman & Shah, 2016). According to Ahmed et al. (2017), various reports showed an increasing variation in internet thing connectivity between 2016 and 2020 from 22.9 billion to 50 billion, respectively.

One example easy to follow is the representation of a smart home that contains other smart components as mobile phones, energy services, security cameras, air-conditioning, etc. All these devices interact to maintain a sustainable household, such as suitable temperature in winter, convenient illumination in the evenings, security, energy efficiency, etc. Furthermore, these interactions provide effectiveness, affordability, and productivity to create a more sustainable and resilient future city. In short, IoT makes fluid communication possible without interferences among individuals, smart objects, and the context.

Artificial Intelligence (AI)

The implementation of artificial intelligence (AI) in almost all industries has benefited the worldwide economies. AI is defined as the study of intelligent components that perceive their environment and make correct decisions. It transforms complex problems into efficient and practical innovative solutions using learning algorithms (Hernández-Orallo, 2017). It works with a program that automates machine learning through examples and guidelines. Then, computers can provide different solutions to various and complex problems. One may say that CPUs are trained by these learning programs to act and react as human beings with the capacity to make decisions following behavioral patterns (Tecuci, 2012).

This technology offers specific computational procedures that gather information from everywhere that help makes the best choices based on reliable data (Teece, 2018). Likewise, in a smart city, collective intelligence is the community's cooperation in exchanging knowledge, learn and inventing. Hence, it may lead to creating an intelligent environment (Nowicka, 2014). For instance, extensive data analysis is done by artificial intelligence. The accuracy of the outcomes depends on the amount of information collected and examined. Therefore, big data production in the real-time permit that technologies give rapid and efficient solutions in all areas (Aguilera et al., 2017). In general, AI implications are beyond the scope of technological changes. Accordingly, some authors compare AI to the industrial revolution that transformed humankind (Moutselos et al., 2018; Teece, 2018). Accordingly, artificial intelligence applications transform how we interact with each other and our environment. Artificial intelligence offers new insights into the human mind and reveals new forms that the mindset can take (Huang et al., 2019).

Within the ecosystem of innovation and problem-solving in the transformation of smart cities, artificial intelligence offers solutions in digital spaces and smart environments. For instance, data centers alone consume about 3% of global energy each year; massive factory operations consume a lot of energy. Google using DeepMind technology, achieved 40% less energy by cooling its data centers, which is a breakthrough and demonstrates how AI can be used to make manufacturing plants, power grids, power plants, and data centers more efficient. AI deployment within smart cities is essential in applications for efficient energy management, considering the tendency for population growth in metropolises in the coming years.

There are currently many examples of the use of AI to solve environmental problems. Such as the application of climate impact models based on machine learning developed by IBM Research allows Deep Learning to evaluate the effect of the climate in a given area, taking into account historical forecasts and environmental data, such as vegetation and soil conditions that resulted in Deep Thunder providing custom local forecasts (White et al., 2019). Furthermore, it can also combat air pollution; IBM Research China works on an innovative product capable of forecasting the time in advance that pollution could occur in the country's capital.

A system prototype capable of generating air quality forecasts has been built 72 hours in advance. Furthermore, it gives the variations of levels upon them such as dangerous or tolerable level of pollution (Kadlec et al., 2000). As well as in cases of earthquakes and seismic phenomena, data is exanimated through algorithms that determine the safest and most dangerous locations of the city. Then, this program is used for planning, building, and prioritizing emergencies in an eventual natural disaster (Baraniuk, 2013). These are just a few examples of how AI positively impacts the environment. Johnston et al. (2021) indicate that IBM's machine learning crystal ball can predict the availability of renewable energy. Technology can predict how much energy solar and wind power sources can generate by predicting the weather.

In addition, the conservation of species thanks to artificial intelligence in applications such as eBird, allows ordinary people to enter data about any bird they see around them, allowing the institute to predict where certain species change their habitat and move during migration. They can then share those predictions with conservationists and policymakers who use them to decide how to protect bird habitats.

Blockchain Technology

Moreover, blockchain is one of the world's emerging technologies and is acknowledged as a distributed technology. Chatterjee and Chatterjee (2017) define the blockchain as a distributed technology because the information does not include storage only in one server; rather, the data is dispersed along with all participants that interact in the current network. As a result, everyone has access to the distributed record, which contains all product information such as the complete process of the product since its creation time or modifications. Each blockchain refers to the previous one and cannot alter other blocks

In contrast, individuals can alter or modify the product's information in a standard database system, but no participants would disclose it. The information is kept in different records, which is more vulnerable to falsifications. Therefore, the value of this distributed technology stands out above all others for offering transparent and trustworthy processes (Al-Khateeb et al., 2019).

The features of blockchain technology guarantee a high level of security since the transactions carried out are completely anonymous. Every transaction or digital event on a blockchain network is verified, only if so, agreed via a mutual agreement of most participants in this process. For instance, Bitcoin has been the most popular cryptocurrency since it was invented and is the best example using blockchain technology.

Similarly, blockchain technologies are used in different areas, such as pharmaceutical products. In this context, blockchain technology warrant drugs authenticity because it is tracked during all steps of its production process. Nevertheless, it confirms prescription medicines' quality, legitimacy, transparency, and process. Furthermore, it contributes to the pharmaceutical industry reducing the distribution and production of forged medical products.

Smart Infrastructure Implementation and Sustainability

In the first place, ICTs operate as the framework for adding and incorporating information and data which better understand the city's functioning, including citizen services, resources, lifestyles, and standards that govern the inhabitants. At the same time, thanks to the integration and complementation of the ubiquitous sensors installed throughout the city, the connection of the IoT, open data, and mobile broadband, it is possible to obtain predictions of behaviors and patterns from the analysis of large amounts of information, all of them based on a solid ICT infrastructure. Within the enabling of technologies for services and applications, smart mobile devices are rapidly becoming the daily life of the inhabitants. All smart devices are composed of smart subcomponents such as sensors in cars, mobile phones, iPad, etc. The integration of these smart components makes it possible to deliver plenty of services with only a tiny device.

Consequently, new markets are emerging, generating more advanced products and services that exploit the value of this connectivity. In addition, it brings new opportunities and improvements for society in general (Balakrishna, 2012). For instance, as Figure 1 displays, the supply chain could have a sustainable effect in leading business operations by the traceability of products.

Figure 1.

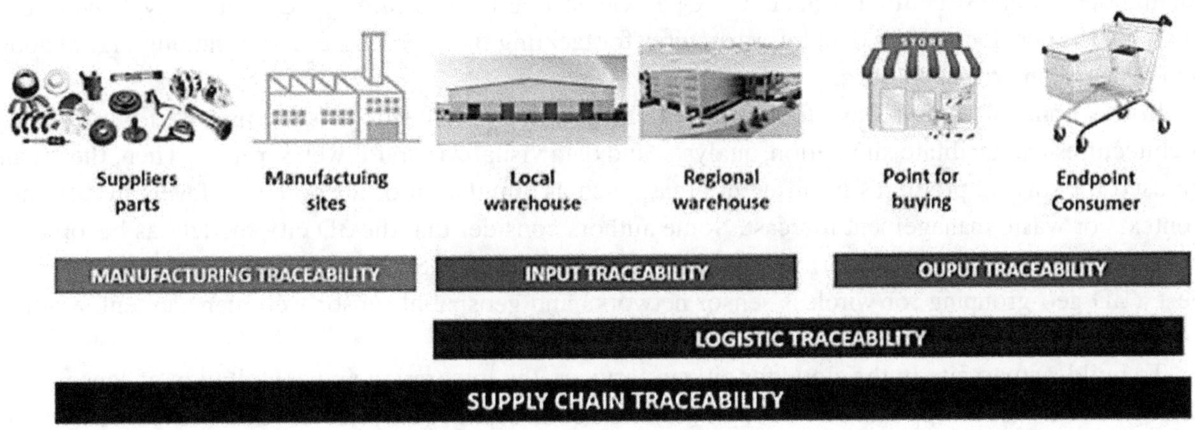

The most challenging subject in the Mobil operator industry is rolling out 5G networks and perfectly covering the different demands that it represents. Rolling out this network and the whole city demand a proficient infrastructure that succeeds with the alienation of old and new services and interoperability issues (Oproiu et al., 2018). Likewise, different 5G-ready applications continue to be developed that are implemented around its ability to integrate and support different areas of the industry (health, manufacturing, media, automotive, IoT, smart cities), thus becoming a key facilitator for new business opportunities and digital transformation (Okumura et al., 2019). IoT has also been the subject of increasing use in implementing the circular economy, as illustrated in Figure 2.

Figure 2.

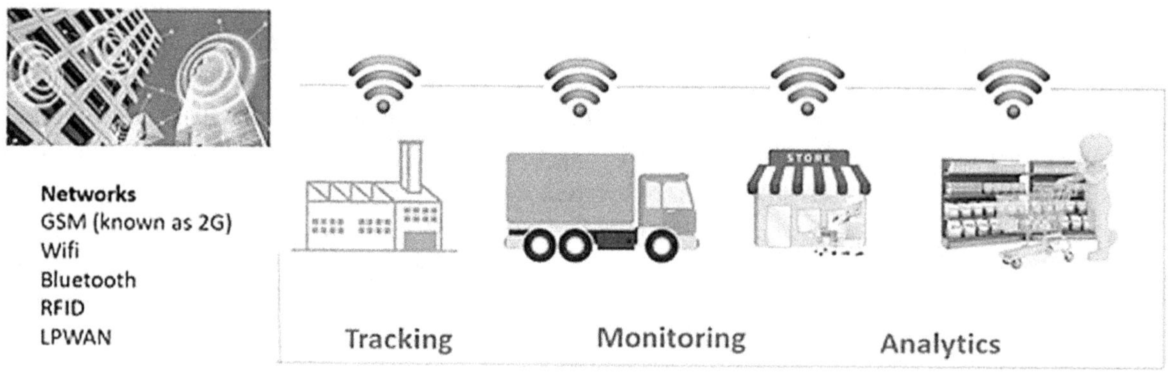

Urban infrastructure plays a relevant and determining role in being intelligent. Traditionally there have been two types of infrastructure: physical (buildings, roads, transport, power plants) and digital (IT and communications infrastructure). However, the intelligent management of both provides a multiplier effect in the operation of a smart city (Quer et al., 2019). For instance, Smart District Data Infrastructure (SDDI) can implant various sensors, connect IoT devices, and three-dimension drawings of the city in a mutual operational structure thanks to the Open Geospatial Consortium (OGC). Similarly, Chaturvedi et al. (2019) consider spatial data infrastructures for tackling interoperability issues among digital apps and different interfaces in the city.

In this context, authors have found that offering various platforms or systems based on different architectures can facilitate simulation, analysis, and data visualization for web services. Then, these can be used for solving problems in different areas, such as simulation of air pollution levels in different contexts or waste management forecast. Some authors consider that the 3D city model has become an essential part of the modern information infrastructure of the city (Spatial Data Infrastructure) and suggest a 3D geo-grouping for wireless sensor networks and geospatial sensor web management systems (Ahmad et al., 2020).

To build a smart city in the cloud for citizen services, the integration and exploitation of sensor data through events-based applications through the Internet of Things (IoT) devices allow awareness of the situation and context (Garcia Alvarez et al., 2019; Zou et al., 2018). For example, OpenStack is a platform that gathers raw data of different private and public clouds for further examination and processing using IoT (Belahsen et al., 2019). However, it can threaten the privacy of personal and sensitive data because it is distributed and have free access to everyone (Chaturvedi et al., 2019).

In short, smart cities infrastructure is folded with technology that allows obtaining large amounts of data from the city. The integration of networks through intelligent technologies makes it possible. An intelligent government uses this technology to identify the weaknesses and main problems of the city, such as pollution, traffic, insecurity, etc. Then, we can more accurately identify environmental problems such as levels of air pollution or whether the city uses too much energy. City problems are easier to identify, improve and monitor if the city infrastructure is working correctly. In this way, implementing a smart city with exceptional technological infrastructure and a smart government that accurately manages the city's big data lead to achieving sustainability objectives.

This chapter is the case of smart city infrastructure in London, England. The UK government considers that the availability of high-quality infrastructure is critical for development. The government has improved coverage for digital infrastructure; it is estimated that 95% of the premises have had access to ultra-fast broadband since 2017 and 96% have 4G data coverage (Oughton et al., 2018). UK cities embrace new technology, instructed by Swansea to explore the potential for 5G technology as part of its city deal.

Challenges and Opportunities in the Smart Government Dimension

Network security is a contemporary challenge in digital cities, their infrastructures that have integrated intelligence elements, together with their real-time monitoring systems, generate enormous volumes of data every day. On the one hand, information may potentially improve health services, enhance transport efficiency, and reduce carbon dioxide emissions through the proper analysis of big data. On the other hand, it could also represent a confidentiality threat to not-trusted or unauthorized entities. Furthermore, the large number of devices connected in real-time causes network traffic for which new sensor services are being developed, mechanisms for classifying IoT traffic assisted by a capsule network, both to guarantee network security and to improve service quality (Wang et al., 2020; Yao et al., 2019).

However, there are plenty of innovative solutions for network traffic problems. For instance, Pan et al. (2019) proposes a network traffic prediction mechanism based on the DE-B neural network. This innovative product aims to relieve the network traffic by obtaining the network traffic's predicted value. Cui et al. (2019) suggest the Inter Sensor Service that creates a balance of the traffic network via smart cities' wireless sensor system infrastructure. Similarly, de Godoi et al. (2018) and Xiao et al. (2018) emphasize optimizing the service quality of the wireless sensor network.

Nevertheless, the importance of data security and privacy has increased worldwide. However, smart city infrastructure is more capable and flexible to adopt innovative solutions than other cities. In this regard, among the types of security technologies and services based on self-identification in data review, the following categories have been representatively found:

Privacy Preservation Authentication Protocols (PPA) for mobile services (Li et al., 2019). Audit service for information security and privacy through artificial intelligence and cognitive services in smart metropolises (Huerta & Salazar, 2018). Other options include portable sensors on mobile phones for self-identification, single sign-on authentication, digital identity service (Chaturvedi et al., 2019; Malik et al., 2019). Furthermore, the digital identity service in a smart city is created by information from public services as an ontology to be stored on the user's device and provided to services on demand. Hence, this identification would reduce privacy issues with sensitive data because it does not need storage (Teslya et al., 2019).

Likewise, user identification applications are based on the registration center for intelligent electronic government applications and blockchain technology for data security (Alotaibi, 2019). As well as biometric systems for identification used by global mobility networks could help with the security and vulnerability of denials in the smart city.

SMART MOBILITY

Smart cities must remain at the forefront of advanced and cutting-edge technology infrastructure to offer citizens smart mobility. First, transport organization for the total city capacity requires planning and adequate technology. Second, transport integration of all city's roads demands an adequate infrastructure. Third, according to individuals' requirements, such as notable routes for disabled people, cycle routes, emergency routes, and so forth. To achieve intelligent mobility, the planning of transport integration in cities should cover all the possible needs of the citizens.

In addition, within planning, the scope of sustainability, accessibility, and costs are considered essential. In this context, the different modes of transport must be evaluated and prioritized, the most environmentally friendly ones such as bicycles, public transport, etc. Citizens who are satisfied with public services in their city reduce their use of private transportation, bringing significant benefits to the environment, such as reducing carbon emissions (Battarra et al., 2018; Ning et al., 2017).

Consequently, a sound system for managing and monitoring all the logistics operation of integration and communication in real-time in the city is needed (Benevolo et al., 2016). In this way, it is possible to have safe, fast, ecological, and reliable transportation for all inhabitants. Furthermore, the transport implementation must consider not only the inhabitants of the city scepter but also those in the suburbs. Regardless of the location, everyone should feel part of the city, and then individuals are more committed to the city's issues (Ben Letaifa, 2015; Zygiaris, 2013). Social cohesion encourages inclusivity that reduces problems of separation or inaccessibility, creating a balance between all citizens and fair transport distribution (Currie & Stanley, 2008).

Mobility Challenges and Sustainability

According to the extant literature, global transport has increased due to the development of urban cities. World Business Council for Sustainable Development (WBCSD) (2004) point out that in 2000, the travel distance covered approximately 32 trillion passenger-km in the world but only 2.8 trillion passenger-km 50 years ago. As well as the mode of transport most used for travelers is by car and plane (Moriarty & Honnery, 2004). Most modes of transport produce air pollution from the combustion of liquid fossil fuel in different quantities and depend on the combustion conditions.

The most crucial transport emissions to the atmosphere are carbon dioxide (CO_2) and water vapor (H_2O) caused by the complete combustion of the fuel. Furthermore, all fuel sources contain different impurities, and it varies according to the combustion temperatures (Colvile et al., 2001). Vehicles stuck in traffic have a high level of combustion more than an average or quick trip. Another factor is consumerism, mainly in big cities where the delivery services burden the environment. The excessive use of private transport in big cities produces traffic most of the time, and it abruptly increases air pollution.

Consequently, the air quality has deteriorated in the cities threatening the health of the citizens. According to the Health World Organization, exposure to air pollution can lead to many diseases such as stroke, asthma, respiratory infections and pulmonary difficulties, and lung cancers. Furthermore, cities' traffic is responsible for more combustion linked to the local transportation and waiting time.

In the last years, the effects of global warming have been more severe than ever. Governments acknowledged the importance of the depletion of fossil fuels and environmental protection as a priority subject in the agenda. As a result, it has increased fuel prices in the market to accomplish international environmental agreements. Likewise, policymakers have faced issues about innovating in sustainable transport and urban modeling in the cities. Some authors underline the need for new policies that prioritize initiatives promoting low carbon total efficiency via clean, innovative technology.

According to Wegener (2013), one of the significant challenges of urban transportation and mobility, in general, require a decrease in the level of emission carbon produced by fossil fuels and energy effectiveness. Therefore, it involves new policies within inner-city transport and regulation of land uses. Furthermore, the infrastructure must roll out charging stations for new electric vehicles along with the city. Then, the promotion and adaptability to new sustainable transport options more energy-efficient and alternative fuels. Hence, improvement of public transport and other modes of transport as cycling, walking infrastructure.

Complementary, it is crucial to enforce citizens' behavior by increasing fuel taxation, congestion road penalties, irregularities in speed limits penalties. Implementing this set of policies enforces better individuals' behavior and essential services maintenance. Although, it also requires time and investment. Furthermore, it needs a close examination of the distribution and adequate supervision of the impacts and effectiveness to avoid future ethical, social conflicts. Most of the problems about mobility and transport in urban cities mentioned in the paragraph above are addressed in the dimension of smart mobility.

Implementation of Smart Mobility

Smart cities join efforts for increasing environmentally friendly transport systems replacing regular transport progressively with electric cars and other modes of ecological transport. Then, the rates of harmful gases to the environment would be decreased more and more through incorporating new ecological units. Such as a study by Ruggieri et al. (2021) explains how Hamburg has replaced its transport units following environmental plans and future production goals. Public and private acquisitions for new electric units are expected to increase by 50% by 2020 (Flämig et al., 2020). Hamburg, Helsinki, and Nantes have been incorporating smart technology pursuing sustainable mobility, and they won the acknowledging as lighthouse cities to fulfill the mySMARTLife European project requirements (Lange & Knieling, 2020).

In the same way, there are many technologies used by smart cities in the dimension of mobility and transport. Kumar et al. (2018) highlight the demand for renewable resources in a mobility context grounded on the global proliferation of population growth, traffic, health problems, and urbanization. New markets have emerged for producing, developing, and selling cleantech products and improving transport services. Likewise, there are more studies about how development and facing the problems regarding cities with digital infrastructure.

Public transport involves many problems because it is the most popular service in the city. Maintaining and continuously improving this service is essential in modern cities. However, implementing a simple function that extends the essential functions of the service can be expensive but sustainable. For example, making efforts to cover all problems of interoperability and the use of different interfaces in real-time would be impossible without a cutting-edge infrastructure that may require an expensive investment.

The multiple functionalities of Tafficlnfo rely on the dispersed smart technologies around the city, such as sensors embedded in mobile phones, computers, and all connected devices (Farkas et al., 2015).

However, there is a range of possibilities, such as TrafficInfo. It is a mobile app that collects information from Google maps and updates data in real-time. Furthermore, it displays the last incidents or traffic areas by tracking systems. This kind of tracking apps with information in real-time avoids the unnecessary use of transport for finding places and makes efficient mobility possible.

Similarly, innovative ideas using crowdsourced public transport systems are developed and employed in smart cities. The demand for package delivery services has increased significantly in recent years; online shopping has caused e-commerce proliferation and digitalization in all imageable areas. As a result, delivery companies increase unit transport in the city, making traffic hours worse. However, using crowdsourced public transport for delivering packages can relieve traffic congestion.

Cheng et al. (2019) present a city-wide package distribution service using crowdsourced public transport systems. The packets are delivered carefully by public transport through the city. Public transport transports packages throughout the city, taking advantage of the free storage capacity. Packages are collected at various stations according to the delivery route schedule. All products have a tracking system to avoid losses and see the travel time.

Geospatial mapping services allow calculating the mobility of users with special needs. This service aims to offer adequate roads and vias to disabled people, older adults, and special needs people using public information in real-time. The Open Street Map gathers information from citizens' insights about the accessibility to places of the city. It contributes to finding better alternatives when people with disabilities and older adults move from one place to another, such as finding ramps, signposted paths, and reducing mobility time (Mirri et al., 2014).

Dynamic public transport service through multi-agent systems. Multi-agent systems based on different data sources. The input parameters of the sensor network represent the online demand for public transport. The public transport operator's best understanding of the public transport demand is offered to the citizens. The dynamic public transport offer is calculated using a multi-agent system that continuously processes all available online data and proposes dynamic routes and schedules of different means of public transport (Horažďovský et al., 2019). Augmented reality apps for public transport exploiting the benefits of connectivity of IoT infrastructure can access data, location, and images storage in different cloud interfaces ensuring safe procedures (Pokrić et al., 2014).

Intelligent Services and Products for Traffic Management

Mobility is impregnated mainly by ICT. Therefore, it is used not only for gathering data but also to facilitate emergency services. Many people die in ambulances on their way to hospitals because rush-hour traffic does not let to arrive on time. Products for traffic management are required in these cases for saving individuals' lives. Each city service collects multidimensional data from abundant IoT nodes; therefore, centralized traffic management has become fundamentally tricky for a large volume of smart city network data, requiring innovative products and systems to help achieve an efficient traffic management system (Amer et al., 2018; Gohar et al., 2018; Khanna et al., 2019).

Different proposals have been found for the solution of vehicular traffic using automatic learning with the internet of things between software and sensors. It allows examination and integration of possible complex possibilities for evading rush-hour traffic. Furthermore, it improves the configuration of these options by AI analytics, such as Sii-Mobility (Badii et al., 2019; Reid et al., 2018). Vehicles routinely navigate the city streets can have onboard sensors and offer a dynamic network that monitors the urban environment in a comprehensive and efficient system (Anjomshoaa et al., 2018; Rego et al., 2018).

Vehicles with onboard computer equipment can facilitate delay-sensitive applications (Shah et al., 2019). Data transmission through IoT in vehicular Ad Hoc networks (VANET) can help traffic congestion in smart cities (Saleem et al., 2019). These cars use the connection of car to car to exchange information in real (Quer et al., 2019). Likewise, Arshad et al. (2019) propose an intelligent signaling system in a VANET (Vehicular Ad Hoc Networks) that uses its algorithm system to evade redundant circulation and avoid rush-hour traffic in urban cities. Lai et al. (2019) suggest an architecture of microservices for multi-mobility available on the Web such as App Smart Mobility that can help reduce the unnecessary circulation of transport units within the city because they can track free traffic flow.

In this context, thanks to the exploitation of mobile edge computing, it is possible to improve and develop new vehicle applications within smart cities. The main idea is to collect the current vehicle locations, and similar to App Smart Mobility, it shows a range of routes options with less traffic congestion, but this system uses AI algorithms and provides advice during all trajectories (Trombin et al., 2020).

Driving around the city searching for available spaces causes carbon emissions to the environment. Therefore, the high level of contamination causes inhabitants health issues. It would signify higher healthcare costs for society, then seeking available spaces is a matter that goes beyond getting a parking space (Vakula & Kolli, 2017). Different applications have been developed to achieve the optimal allocation of parking spaces through algorithms based on the IoT for the Internet of Things in smart cities (Arellano-Verdejo et al., 2019; Sotres et al., 2018). For instance, Pawłowicz et al. (2019) focus on taking advantage of 5G communication; electric cars can easily find a parking spot and check the battery level capacity via the cloud system of the metropolises service area.

Services and Products for Connected and Autonomous Vehicles (CAV)

In smart cities, all the major automakers and leading technology companies pursue the development of connected and autonomous vehicles (CAV). However, given that cities are more affected by CAVs. Big Data analysis and network calculation allow the intelligent management of autonomous vehicles; for this, assisted AI by the network allows an efficient smart transport paradigm in smart cities while achieving substantial energy savings (Ahmed Khan et al., 2019).

Moreover, drones and uncrewed aerial vehicles have gained incredible popularity due to their diverse uses and practical applications. These are currently employed in different activities. Drones can be used to deliver packages, surveillance, and citizen security and at the same time collect information with internet access. (Garge & Balakrishna, 2018) explore the potential of UAVs that could help to improve the streaming quality of most multimedia applications, such as online games, streaming. Typically, the transmissions use the broadband infrastructure, but if this is combined with UAV, they have a better connection quality, security, and higher performance.

Smart urban routing service called SURF 'for pedestrians and cyclists. This device uses information from the IoT test benches installed around the world. Using this application, all city dwellers can take long walks, choosing the route with the highest clean air quality. In addition, it can also be used by cyclists and skaters. Furthermore, using this app could reduce illnesses caused by breathing polluted air. (Pimpinella et al., 2019).

SMART ENVIRONMENT

An intelligent environment is achieved through three critical factors. In the first place, promote sustainability through sustainable energy use and preservation of the planet's resources. It needs education and public campaigns that help raise awareness about global warming, its effects, and the daily responsibility (Khansari et al., 2014; Zygiaris, 2013).

Second is the extensive use of cutting-edge technologies to improve city processes, provide eco-friendly solutions to current environmental problems, and tackle urbanization effects via innovative cleantech products and systems. Third, a legal framework and policies are needed to enforce the inhabitants' behavior. For example, companies apply laws to contribute to the sustainable production of products. The behavior of citizens and the flexibility to adopt habits in their daily lives are vital to achieving a sustainable city.

Furthermore, citizens can enjoy large green areas, better air quality, and an ecological environment in smart cities (Chu et al., 2021; Khatibi et al., 2021; Simonofski et al., 2021). For instance, smart city -London prioritizes investments in clean energy infrastructure that have helped to reduce carbon emissions by 42% since, while the economy grew by 2.3% (Albanito et al., 2019). As well as all partners in each nation collaborate in synchronize. Decentralized administrations in Scotland, Wales, and Northern Ireland are responsible for their regional infrastructure development water, waste, flood defenses, and road transportation. The UK government is responsible for digital infrastructure and telecommunications across the country.

Environmental Challenges and Smart Technology

The main challenges in big cities are the enormous waste production and resource management. In the first place, population growth and consumption have increased in the last two decades, aggravating current environmental problems. In the second place, governments around the world set up environmental agreements for attaining the reduction of global warming effects. In this regard, smart cities are presented as a potential model for solving ecological complications, especially waste organization, through state-of-the-art technology and new innovative practices.

For instance, the overall EU recycling varied from 53% in 2010 to 55% by 2016. Similarly, the packaging waste recycling percentage varied from 64% in 2010 to 67% by 2016, while the packaging waste percentage of plastic varies only by 18% from 2010 to 2016, respectively (BEIS, 2018).

Smart cities such as London address waste and resource management in the following way. First, the behavior of the citizens depends on a good investment in education. Hence, the strategy of applying best practices in education, compliance, and infrastructure to deliver a substantial reduction in litter and littering behavior improves over time. Second, natural capital is considered valuable assets such as air, water, the land. Therefore, it is essential to establish conserved resources guidelines, minimize waste, and promote efficiency.

Smart cities are focused on sustainable production. According to Gong et al. (2020), during the first stage of the life cycle of resources, natural and material resources are converted into the goods and services on which modern life depends. Some authors highlight the stage of production of waste as the most crucial consideration. For example, England introduced a legal environment procedure for holding accountability. It appeals to the "polluter pays" individuals must pay for using plastic bags the value of 5 pence. This kind of policy encourages a change in people's behavior and habits. According to UK reports, this initiative reduced plastic bag use considerably to 15.6 billion (Wüstemann et al., 2017).

A Community Initiative That Supports the Circular Economy Goals in the United Kingdom Introducing Plastics Pact

There is a foundation promoting the elimination of plastic from the natural environment. All collaborators encourage recycling and reusing activities during the whole plastics value chain. Similarly, the demand for recycled plastic is stimulated by introducing a tax on plastic packaging. It aims to obtain 100% of plastic packing reusable by 2025 and gradually progress recycling packing (van Beukering et al., 2007). Another strategy used by smart cities is promoting sustainability.

First, overconsumption that would result in garbage dumps is avoided (Hanson & Mitchell, 2017). Therefore, consumers adopt changes in their purchasing behavior. The intention is to buy long-lasting products instead of cheap but short-lived products. In this way, pollution from cheap and low-quality products is significantly reduced. Furthermore, it needs precise information about long-lasting ecological products, extending the useful life of products through repair, reuse, and remanufacture. Additionally, it promotes better quantity and quality in recycling, and encourage sustainable businesses.

Smart cities promote environmental policies and innovative practices for accomplishing sustainability. They are mainly supported by technology that makes possible innovative solutions such as systems for optimal solid waste management using the Internet of Things. Different systems models have been presented for waste collection, wireless garbage management, waste generation prediction based on IoT (Anagnostopoulos et al., 2015; Chaudhari & Bhole, 2018; Rajaprabha et al., 2018; Talha et al., 2017). Camero et al. (2019) suggest a waste generation prediction system in smart cities based on recurrent neural networks used to automate in a deep network that encapsulates the behavior of all city's garbage dumpsters. These containers can correctly separate organic and recyclable waste both indoors and outdoors, presenting low response times, which leads to a good quality of experience for users of the system (Idwan et al., 2020; Mahmood & Zubairi, 2019).

For example, Renescience from Orsted Renescience is a unique technology that facilitates the separation and classification of waste. Waste is collected and mixed in water; then, it is decomposed and separated according to the classification of the type of material. In addition, the bioliquid is used to convert it into biomethane.

Systems for Optimal Energy Management Using the Internet of Things

According to the revised bibliography, in the scenario of software, platforms, and services that satisfy energy demand efficiently, it can be inferred that the smart grid offers the supply of energy in an efficient, sustainable, and economical way with a minimum environmental effect and pursuing necessary energy demands. Smart power supplies are a great prospect for energy savings; however, which also demand high requirements such as fluid communication between all actors to obtain a high-quality service. (Omarov & Altayeva, 2018). Faheem et al. (2019) Likewise, the supply operation's administration, control, and maintenance are necessary. Some systems assess similar products' performance by simulating results like EstiNet9.0.

Khan et al. (2018) suggest microgrids boost energy efficiency through AI in this context. The application of these microgrids is increasing mainly in construction projects and public lighting services in cities. This technology can automate energy systems so it is not fully utilized.

In addition to the famous Smart Grids, another component of smart cities is solar energy implemented through photovoltaic technologies. This technology has been implemented in infrastructures, transforming carefully designed buildings into power generation systems. In this field, it is possible to take advantage of the multifunctional use in the endowment of the building to offer advanced services to improve efficiency and participation in city processes (Scognamiglio et al., 2014). On the other hand, wireless sensor networks (WSN) systems can gather energy from all intelligent systems connected to the internet thanks to the nanosensors dispersed along with the city. Furthermore, these nanosensors can collect data for environmental protection, urban planning, and risk prevention of smart cities.

Ayala-Ruiz et al. (2019) present a technology developed to monitor crucial environmental information and the variability of gases such as ozone and carbon dioxide. This energy collecting device is embedded in plants in a microbial fuel cell plant (PMFC), allowing works without batteries operation only through sensors. In turn, all the information provided is published in an application for investigation and flora preservation uses.

Systems for the Management of Environmental Pollution

The main objective of smart cities is to offer solutions to urban air pollution, taking advantage of the great possibilities offered by ICT. Emissions from the automobile fleet, industrial factories, and homes, the absence of rain for prolonged periods are the causes of the impoverishment of the air in recent years. Consequently, the population's health has been affected, and cardiovascular and respiratory diseases are increasing. Different solutions have been created for the optimal management of solid waste, air, water, and soil pollution and intelligent systems that manage the demand for energy and resources to face the different pollution problems

Therefore, studies focused on innovative products and services for the optimization, development, and prevention of intelligent sensors, intelligent software for the monitoring of air quality, indoors and outdoors, have been increased since they have the potential to provide information on the air pollution at higher spatial resolutions than traditional monitoring, promoting pollution-free routes in smart cities through the IoT (Duangsuwan et al., 2018; Ramos et al., 2018). Likewise, Chung and Jeng (2018) propose an information extraction methodology by extracting data from the web using machine learning to train air quality monitors. Furthermore, the origin and means of the information recompilation are essential.

Garzon and Louis (2020) suggest a context-aware urban air pollution alert and monitoring service. The idea is to be informed about the variations of the air pollution within the city. There are pick hours of high concentration of contaminant particles in the air that could affect inhabitants' health. Therefore, this app sends notifications about these variations and regularly compares a citizen's position with the areas of poor air quality.

Liu and Peng (2014) present a unique device that can detect variations and accurately forecast. It contains a humidity sensor, pressure sensor, temperature sensor, GPS module, and GPRS module. This device also uses the data harvested and simulate different possibilities for preventing natural disaster or forecasting extreme weather.

Nowadays, extensive green areas in the cities give fresh air and create a harmonious ecosystem. Furthermore, plans are used as bioindicators and participate in creating a sustainable green city and collecting valuable information. For instance, RFID plants for urban green management are radiofrequency identification devices for protecting flora and diverse natural species with a tag that works as identification. Research and scientists can determine changes and find ways to preserve these species. According to the label, they can monitor their production, grow, and eliminate all risks of loss (Luvisi & Lorenzini, 2014).

SMART PEOPLE AND SMART LIVING

Giffinger et al. (2007) argue that a smart city depends on smart citizens, so one does not exist without the other part. Individuals are givers and creators of the information within the city. Accordingly, the quality of information generated by the population is relative to their level of education, abilities, creativity, and skills. Education is based on smart cities because educated people collaborate and participate in the community. Furthermore, they will be more flexible and capable of creating innovations and adopting them. Individuals must be capable of making good decisions and suggesting solutions to the community problems, such as active participation in social and political matters (Echebarria et al., 2021). In addition, citizens should have an active, participative role in society, taking advantage of the new innovative technology of the city.

A smart society benefits from knowledge and innovation, leading to general city progress (Nam & Pardo, 2011). Smart living is reflected in the success of quality, efficiency, affordability, accessibility of town's services, and the appropriate use of intelligent systems. (Zygiaris, 2013). Therefore, these conditions help people live with less stress, illnesses, and better life expectancy (Lombardi et al., 2012). Therefore, intelligent living is the perception related to the standard of living of all individuals in society. The standard of living can be measured by governmental services such as education programs, healthcare system, security, employment rate, tourism, art programs, sports facilities, and others (Ben Letaifa, 2015; Giffinger et al., 2007). The pleasure and satisfaction of living in their city increase the communal unity and feeling of membership.

CONCLUSION

According to the literature reviewed, the implementation of smart cities is aligned with sustainability objectives. In the first place, its infrastructure equipped with state-of-the-art technology allows fluid communication between all city systems and citizens. Second, large amounts of information can be collected in real-time thanks to this technology. This information is one pillar together ICT applied is examined to provide solutions to the city's problems. Additionally, improve the efficiency of processes and services. The main problems of the cities are related to the deterioration of the environment and the extinction of resources. However, one smart city has great potential to solve environmental problems.

Therefore, smart technologies developed in smart cities mitigate or solve resource management, air pollution, water, and so forth. However, the relevant aspects for innovation are ICT applied to the development of public services such as the government and private ones such as companies and mainly the different clean technology industries. The main protagonists of the change towards sustainability are smart citizens and smart government. On the one hand, the policies applied to promote sustainability, information, and innovative business practices. On the other hand, citizens' adaptability results in more sustainable and intelligent behavior.

REFERENCES

Aguilera, U., Peña, O., Belmonte, O., & López-de-Ipiña, D. (2017). Citizen-centric data services for smarter cities. *Future Generation Computer Systems*, *76*, 234–247. doi:10.1016/j.future.2016.10.031

Ahmad, T., Li, X. J., Seet, B.-C., & Cano, J.-C. (2020). Social Network Analysis Based Localization Technique with Clustered Closeness Centrality for 3D Wireless Sensor Networks. *Electronics (Basel), 9*(5), 738. Advance online publication. doi:10.3390/electronics9050738

Ahmed, E., Yaqoob, I., Hashem, I. A. T., Khan, I., Ahmed, A. I. A., Imran, M., & Vasilakos, A. V. (2017). The role of big data analytics in Internet of Things. *Computer Networks, 129*, 459–471. doi:10.1016/j.comnet.2017.06.013

Ahmed Khan, J., Wang, L., Jacobs, E., Talebian, A., Mishra, S., Santo, C. A., . . . Astorne-Figari, C. (2019). Smart Cities Connected and Autonomous Vehicles Readiness Index. *Proceedings of the 2nd ACM/EIGSCC Symposium on Smart Cities and Communities.* doi:10.1145/3357492.335863110.1145/3357492.3358631

Al-Khateeb, H., Epiphaniou, G., & Daly, H. (2019). Blockchain for Modern Digital Forensics: The Chain-of-Custody as a Distributed Ledger. In H. Jahankhani, S. Kendzierskyj, A. Jamal, G. Epiphaniou, & H. Al-Khateeb (Eds.), *Blockchain and Clinical Trial: Securing Patient Data* (pp. 149–168). Springer International Publishing. doi:10.1007/978-3-030-11289-9_7

Albanito, F., Hastings, A., Fitton, N., Richards, M., Martin, M., Mac Dowell, N., . . . Smith, P. (2019). Mitigation potential and environmental impact of centralized versus distributed BECCS with domestic biomass production in Great Britain. *GCB Bioenergy, 11*(10), 1234-1252.

Alotaibi, S. S. (2019). Registration Center Based User Authentication Scheme for Smart E-Governance Applications in Smart Cities. *IEEE Access: Practical Innovations, Open Solutions, 7*, 5819–5833. doi:10.1109/ACCESS.2018.2884541

Amer, H. M., Al-Kashoash, H. A. A., Kemp, A., Mihaylova, L., & Mayfield, M. (2018). Coalition Game for Emergency Vehicles Re-Routing in Smart Cities. *2018 IEEE 10th Sensor Array and Multichannel Signal Processing Workshop (SAM).*

Anagnostopoulos, T., Zaslavsy, A., Medvedev, A., & Khoruzhnicov, S. (2015, June 15-18). Top — k Query Based Dynamic Scheduling for IoT-enabled Smart City Waste Collection. *2015 16th IEEE International Conference on Mobile Data Management.*

Angelidou, M. (2017). The Role of Smart City Characteristics in the Plans of Fifteen Cities. *Journal of Urban Technology, 24*(4), 3–28. doi:10.1080/10630732.2017.1348880

Anjomshoaa, A., Duarte, F., Rennings, D., Matarazzo, T. J., deSouza, P., & Ratti, C. (2018). City Scanner: Building and Scheduling a Mobile Sensing Platform for Smart City Services. *IEEE Internet of Things Journal, 5*(6), 4567–4579. doi:10.1109/JIOT.2018.2839058

Anthopoulos, L. G. (2015). Understanding the Smart City Domain: A Literature Review. In M. P. Rodríguez-Bolívar (Ed.), *Transforming City Governments for Successful Smart Cities* (pp. 9–21). Springer International Publishing. doi:10.1007/978-3-319-03167-5_2

Anttiroiko, A.-V., Valkama, P., & Bailey, S. J. (2014). Smart cities in the new service economy: Building platforms for smart services. *AI & Society, 29*(3), 323–334. doi:10.100700146-013-0464-0

Arellano-Verdejo, J., Alonso-Pecina, F., Alba, E., & Guzmán Arenas, A. (2019). Optimal allocation of public parking spots in a smart city: Problem characterisation and first algorithms. *Journal of Experimental & Theoretical Artificial Intelligence, 31*(4), 575–597. doi:10.1080/0952813X.2019.1591522

Arshad, S., Raza, Q., & Hussain, M. (2019). VANETs Embedded Novel Traffic Management Paradigm for Smart City Milieu. *Proceedings of the 3rd International Conference on Future Networks and Distributed Systems.* doi:10.1145/3341325.334203810.1145/3341325.3342038

Ayala-Ruiz, D., Castillo Atoche, A., Ruiz-Ibarra, E., Osorio de la Rosa, E., & Vázquez Castillo, J. (2019). A Self-Powered PMFC-Based Wireless Sensor Node for Smart City Applications. *Wireless Communications and Mobile Computing, 8986302*, 1–10. Advance online publication. doi:10.1155/2019/8986302

Badii, C., Bellini, P., Difino, A., & Nesi, P. (2019). Sii-Mobility: An IoT/IoE Architecture to Enhance Smart City Mobility and Transportation Services. *Sensors (Basel), 19*(1), 1. Advance online publication. doi:10.339019010001 PMID:30577434

Balakrishna, C. (2012, September 12-14). Enabling Technologies for Smart City Services and Applications. *2012 Sixth International Conference on Next Generation Mobile Applications, Services and Technologies.*

Baraniuk, C. (2013). The civic hackers reshaping your government. *New Scientist, 218*(2923), 36–39.

Barkham, R., Bokhari, S., & Saiz, A. (2018). *Urban big data: City management and real estate markets.* Retrieved 11/30/2021 from https://mitcre.mit.edu/wp-content/uploads/2018/01/URBAN-DATA-AND-REAL-ESTATE-JAN-2018-1.pdf

Battarra, R., Gargiulo, C., Tremiterra, M. R., & Zucaro, F. (2018). Smart mobility in Italian metropolitan cities: A comparative analysis through indicators and actions. *Sustainable Cities and Society, 41*, 556–567. doi:10.1016/j.scs.2018.06.006

BEIS. (2018). *UK greenhouse gas emissions, Final figures.* https://assets.publishing.service.gov.uk/government/uploads/system/uploads/attachment_data/file/862887/2018_Final_greenh ouse_gas_emissions_statistical_release.pdf

Belahsen, C. A., Lyhyaoui, A., & Boufardi, N. (2019). IoT Data-Based Architecture on OpenStack for Smart City. Advanced Intelligent Systems for Sustainable Development (AI2SD'2018), Cham, Switzerland.

Ben Letaifa, S. (2015). How to strategize smart cities: Revealing the SMART model. *Journal of Business Research, 68*(7), 1414–1419. doi:10.1016/j.jbusres.2015.01.024

Benevolo, C., Dameri, R. P., & D'Auria, B. (2016). *Smart Mobility in Smart City.* Empowering Organizations.

Bibri, S. E. (2020). *Advances in the leading paradigms of urbanism and their amalgamation: compact cities, eco–cities, and data-driven smart cities.* Springer. doi:10.1007/978-3-030-41746-8

Caragliu, A., Del Bo, C., & Nijkamp, P. (2011). Smart Cities in Europe. *Journal of Urban Technology, 18*(2), 65–82. doi:10.1080/10630732.2011.601117

Chatterjee, R., & Chatterjee, R. (2017). An Overview of the Emerging Technology: Blockchain. *2017 3rd International Conference on Computational Intelligence and Networks (CINE).*

Chaturvedi, K., Matheus, A., Nguyen, S. H., & Kolbe, T. H. (2019). Securing Spatial Data Infrastructures for Distributed Smart City applications and services. *Future Generation Computer Systems, 101*, 723–736. doi:10.1016/j.future.2019.07.002

Chaudhari, S. S., & Bhole, V. Y. (2018). Solid Waste Collection as a Service using IoT-Solution for Smart Cities. *2018 International Conference on Smart City and Emerging Technology (ICSCET).* 10.1109/ICSCET.2018.8537326

Cheng, G., Guo, D., Shi, J., & Qin, Y. (2019). Smart City-Wide Package Distribution Using Crowdsourced Public Transportation Systems. *IEEE Internet of Things Journal, 6*(5), 7584–7594. doi:10.1109/JIOT.2019.2901116

Chourabi, H., Nam, T., Walker, S., Gil-Garcia, J. R., Mellouli, S., Nahon, K., . . . Scholl, H. J. (2012). Understanding Smart Cities: An Integrative Framework. *2012 45th Hawaii International Conference on System Sciences.*

Chu, Z., Cheng, M., & Yu, N. N. (2021). A smart city is a less polluted city. *Technological Forecasting and Social Change, 172*, 121037. doi:10.1016/j.techfore.2021.121037

Chung, C. C., & Jeng, T. (2018). *Information Extraction Methodology by Web Scraping for Smart Cities - Using Machine Learning to Train Air Quality Monitor for Smart Cities.* Academic Press.

Colvile, R. N., Hutchinson, E. J., Mindell, J. S., & Warren, R. F. (2001). The transport sector is a source of air pollution. *Atmospheric Environment, 35*(9), 1537–1565. doi:10.1016/S1352-2310(00)00551-3

Cowley, R., & Caprotti, F. (2018). Smart city as anti-planning in the UK. *Environment and Planning. D, Society & Space, 37*(3), 428–448. doi:10.1177/0263775818787506

Crutzen, W., & Steffen, P. J. (2003). How Long Have We Been in the Anthropocene Era? *Climatic Change, 61*(3), 251-257.

Cui, X., Huang, X., Ma, Y., & Meng, Q. (2019). A Load Balancing Routing Mechanism Based on SDWSN in Smart City. *Electronics (Basel), 8*(3), 273. Advance online publication. doi:10.3390/electronics8030273

Currie, G., & Stanley, J. (2008). Investigating Links between Social Capital and Public Transport. *Transport Reviews, 28*(4), 529–547. doi:10.1080/01441640701817197

de Godoi, F. N., Denardin, G. W., Barriquello, C. H., & do Prado, R. N. (2018). Wireless sensor network quality of service optimization for smart cities. *2018 IEEE International Conference on Industrial Technology (ICIT).* 10.1109/ICIT.2018.8352485

Duangsuwan, S., Takarn, A., & Jamjareegulgarn, P. (2018). A Development on Air Pollution Detection Sensors based on NB-IoT Network for Smart Cities. *2018 18th International Symposium on Communications and Information Technologies (ISCIT).*

Echebarria, C., Barrutia, J. M., & Aguado-Moralejo, I. (2021). The Smart City journey: A systematic review and future research agenda. *Innovation (Abingdon), 34*(2), 159–201. doi:10.1080/13511610.2020.1785277

Ershova, S. A., & Orlovskaya, T. N. (2020). Differentiation of Russian megalopolises by the level of urban environment quality and the standard needs of the population. *IOP Conference Series. Materials Science and Engineering, 962*(3), 032066. doi:10.1088/1757-899X/962/3/032066

European Parliament. (2014). *Mapping smart cities in the EU.* Retrieved 11/30/2021 from https://www.europarl.europa.eu/RegData/etudes/etudes/join/2014/507480/IPOL-ITRE_ET(2014)507480_EN.pdf

Faheem, M., Butt, R. A., Raza, B., Ashraf, M. W., Ngadi, M. A., & Gungor, V. C. (2019). Energy efficient and reliable data gathering using internet of software-defined mobile sinks for WSNs-based smart grid applications. *Computer Standards & Interfaces, 66*, 103341. doi:10.1016/j.csi.2019.03.009

Flämig, H., Lunkeit, S., Rosenberger, K., & Wolff, J. (2020). Enlarging the scale of BEVs through environmental zoning to reduce GHG emissions: A case study for the city of Hamburg. *Research in Transportation Business & Management, 36*, 100418. doi:10.1016/j.rtbm.2019.100418

Garcia Alvarez, M., Morales, J., & Kraak, M.-J. (2019). Integration and Exploitation of Sensor Data in Smart Cities through Event-Driven Applications. *Sensors (Basel), 19*(6), 1372. Advance online publication. doi:10.339019061372 PMID:30893843

Garge, G. K., & Balakrishna, C. (2018). Unmanned Aerial Vehicles (UAVs) as on-demand QoS enabler for Multimedia Applications in Smart Cities. *2018 International Conference on Innovation and Intelligence for Informatics, Computing, and Technologies (3ICT).*

Garzon, S. R., & Louis, B. (2020). Context Flow Graphs: Situation Modeling for Rule-Based Proactive Context-Aware Systems. *IEEE Access: Practical Innovations, Open Solutions, 8*, 212939–212960. doi:10.1109/ACCESS.2020.3040060

Giffinger, R., Fertner, C., Kramar, H., Kalasek, R., Pichler-Milanovic, N., & Meijers, E. (2007). *Smart cities ranking of European medium-sized cities.* Retrieved on November 30, 2021, from: http://www.smart-cities.eu/download/smart_cities_final_report.pdf

Gohar, M., Muzammal, M., & Ur Rahman, A. (2018). SMART TSS: Defining transportation system behavior using big data analytics in smart cities. *Sustainable Cities and Society, 41*, 114–119. doi:10.1016/j.scs.2018.05.008

Gong, Y., Putnam, E., You, W., & Zhao, C. (2020). Investigation into circular economy of plastics: The case of the UK fast moving consumer goods industry. *Journal of Cleaner Production, 244*, 118941. doi:10.1016/j.jclepro.2019.118941

Horažďovský, P., & Kozhevnikov, S., & Svítek, M. (2019). Dynamic Public Transport in Smart City using Multi-agent system. *2019 Smart City Symposium Prague (SCSP).* 10.1109/SCSP.2019.8805716

Huang, M.-H., Rust, R., & Maksimovic, V. (2019). The Feeling Economy: Managing in the Next Generation of Artificial Intelligence (AI). *California Management Review, 61*(4), 43–65. doi:10.1177/0008125619863436

Huerta, J., & Salazar, P. (2018). Audit Process Framework for Data Protection and Privacy Compliance Using Artificial Intelligence and Cognitive Services in Smart Cities. *2018 IEEE International Smart Cities Conference (ISC2).*

Johnston, A., Hochachka, W. M., Strimas-Mackey, M. E., Ruiz Gutierrez, V., Robinson, O. J., Miller, E. T., . . . Fink, D. (2021). Analytical guidelines to increase the value of community science data: An example using eBird data to estimate species distributions. *Diversity and Distributions, 27*(7), 1265-1277.

Kadlec, R., Knight, R., Vymazal, J., Brix, H., Cooper, P., & Haberl, R. (2000). *Constructed wetlands for pollution control: processes, performance, design and operation.* IWA Publishing.

Khanna, A., Goyal, R., Verma, M., & Joshi, D. (2019). Intelligent Traffic Management System for Smart Cities. Futuristic Trends in Network and Communication Technologies, Singapore.

Khansari, N., Mostashari, A., & Mansouri, M. (2014). Impacting Sustainable Behavior and Planning in Smart City. *International Journal of Sustainable Built Environment, 1.*

Khatibi, H., Wilkinson, S., Baghersad, M., Dianat, H., Ramli, H., Suhatril, M., Javanmardi, A., & Ghaedi, K. (2021). The resilient – smart city development: A literature review and novel frameworks exploration. *Built Environment Project and Asset Management, 11*(4), 493–510. doi:10.1108/BEPAM-03-2020-0049

Komninos, N., Kakderi, C., Panori, A., & Tsarchopoulos, P. (2019). Smart City Planning from an Evolutionary Perspective. *Journal of Urban Technology, 26*(2), 3–20. doi:10.1080/10630732.2018.1485368

Kramers, A., Höjer, M., Lövehagen, N., & Wangel, J. (2014). Smart sustainable cities – Exploring ICT solutions for reduced energy use in cities. *Environmental Modelling & Software, 56*, 52–62. doi:10.1016/j.envsoft.2013.12.019

Kumar, H., Singh, M. K., & Gupta, M. P. (2018). Smart mobility: Crowdsourcing solutions for smart transport system in smart cities context. *Proceedings of the 11th International Conference on Theory and Practice of Electronic Governance.* 10.1145/3209415.3209417

Lai, C., Boi, F., Buschettu, A., & Caboni, R. (2019). SmartMobility, an Application for Multiple Integrated Transportation Services in a Smart City. *Proceedings of the 15th International Conference on Web Information Systems and Technologies.* 10.5220/0008066600002366

Lange, K., & Knieling, J. (2020). EU Smart City Lighthouse Projects between Top-Down Strategies and Local Legitimation: The Case of Hamburg. *Urban Plan, 5*(1), 107–115. doi:10.17645/up.v5i1.2531

Lee, K.-H., & Wu, Y. (2014). Integrating sustainability performance measurement into logistics and supply networks: A multi-methodological approach. *The British Accounting Review, 46*(4), 361–378. doi:10.1016/j.bar.2014.10.005

Li, C., Liu, X., Dai, Z., & Zhao, Z. (2019). Smart City: A Shareable Framework and Its Applications in China. *Sustainability, 11*(16), 4346. Advance online publication. doi:10.3390u11164346

Liu, P., & Peng, Z. (2014). China's Smart City Pilots: A Progress Report. *Computer*, *47*(10), 72–81. doi:10.1109/MC.2013.149

Lombardi, P., Giordano, S., Farouh, H., & Yousef, W. (2012). Modelling the smart city performance. *Innovation (Abingdon)*, *25*(2), 137–149. doi:10.1080/13511610.2012.660325

Luvisi, A., & Lorenzini, G. (2014). RFID-plants in the smart city: Applications and outlook for urban green management. *Urban Forestry & Urban Greening*, *13*(4), 630–637. doi:10.1016/j.ufug.2014.07.003

Malik, M. N., Azam, M. A., Ehatisham-Ul-Haq, M., Ejaz, W., & Khalid, A. (2019). ADLAuth: Passive Authentication Based on Activity of Daily Living Using Heterogeneous Sensing in Smart Cities. *Sensors (Basel)*, *19*(11), 2466. Advance online publication. doi:10.339019112466 PMID:31146477

Mirri, S., Prandi, C., Salomoni, P., Callegati, F., & Campi, A. (2014). On Combining Crowdsourcing, Sensing and Open Data for an Accessible Smart City. *2014 Eighth International Conference on Next Generation Mobile Apps, Services and Technologies*. 10.1109/NGMAST.2014.59

Mohanty, S. (2015). *The four essential V's for a big data analytics platform*. Retrieved on November 30, 2021, from: https://dataconomy.com/2015/06/the-four-essentials-vs-for-a-big-data-analytics-platform

Moriarty, P., & Honnery, D. (2004). Forecasting world transport in the year 2050. *International Journal of Vehicle Design*, *35*(1-2), 151–165. doi:10.1504/IJVD.2004.004053

Moutselos, K., Kyriazis, D., & Maglogiannis, I. (2018). A Web Based Modular Environment for Assisting Health Policy Making Utilizing Big Data Analytics. *2018 9th International Conference on Information, Intelligence, Systems and Applications (IISA)*.

Nam, T., & Pardo, T. A. (2011). Conceptualizing smart city with dimensions of technology, people, and institutions. *Proceedings of the 12th Annual International Digital Government Research Conference: Digital Government Innovation in Challenging Times*. 10.1145/2037556.2037602

Ning, Z., Xia, F., Ullah, N., Kong, X., & Hu, X. (2017). Vehicular Social Networks: Enabling Smart Mobility. *IEEE Communications Magazine*, *55*(5), 16–55. doi:10.1109/MCOM.2017.1600263

Nowicka, K. (2014). Smart City Logistics on Cloud Computing Model. *Procedia: Social and Behavioral Sciences*, *151*, 266–281. doi:10.1016/j.sbspro.2014.10.025

Okumura, Y., Suyama, S., Ishii, N., Maruta, Y., Okazaki, A., Okamura, A., . . . Onizawa, T. (2019). 5G R&D Achievements for High-Data-Rate and Low-Power-Consumption Radio Access Technologies with Higher-Frequency-Band and Wider-Bandwidth Massive MIMO. *2019 IEEE 89th Vehicular Technology Conference (VTC2019-Spring)*.

Omarov, B., & Altayeva, A. (2018). Towards Intelligent IoT Smart City platform Based on OneM2M Guideline: Smart Grid Case Study. *2018 IEEE International Conference on Big Data and Smart Computing (BigComp)*. 10.1109/BigComp.2018.00130

Oproiu, E., Iordache, M., Costea, C. X., Brezeanu, C., & Patachia, C. (2018). 5G Network Architecture, Functional Model and Business Role for 5G Smart City Use Case: Mobile Operator Perspective. *2018 International Conference on Communications (COMM)*. 10.1109/ICComm.2018.8484747

Orecchini, F., Santiangeli, A., Zuccari, F., Pieroni, A., & Suppa, T. (2019). Blockchain Technology in Smart City: A New Opportunity for Smart Environment and Smart Mobility. Intelligent Computing & Optimization.

Oughton, E. J., Frias, Z., Dohler, M., Whalley, J., Sicker, D., Hall, J. W., Crowcroft, J., & Cleevely, D. D. (2018). The strategic national infrastructure assessment of digital communications. *Digital Policy, Regulation & Governance*, *20*(3), 197–210. doi:10.1108/DPRG-02-2018-0004

Pawłowicz, B., Salach, M., & Trybus, B. (2019). Smart City Traffic Monitoring System Based on 5G Cellular Network, RFID and Machine Learning. Engineering Software Systems: Research and Praxis.

Perveen, S., Yigitcanlar, T., Kamruzzaman, M., & Hayes, J. (2017). Evaluating transport externalities of urban growth: A critical review of scenario-based planning methods. *International Journal of Environmental Science and Technology*, *14*(3), 663–678. doi:10.100713762-016-1144-7

Pimpinella, A., Redondi, A. E. C., & Cesana, M. (2019). Walk this way! An IoT-based urban routing system for smart cities. *Computer Networks*, *162*, 106857. doi:10.1016/j.comnet.2019.07.013

Pokrić, B., Krčo, S., & Pokrić, M. (2014). Augmented Reality Based Smart City Services Using Secure IoT Infrastructure. *2014 28th International Conference on Advanced Information Networking and Applications Workshops.*

Qingsong, H., Chen, Z., Peng, X., Shukui, T., & Jiayu, W. (2019). Comparison of urban growth patterns and changes between three urban agglomerations in China and three metropolises in the USA from 1995 to 2015. *Sustainable Cities and Society*, *50*, 101649. doi:10.1016/j.scs.2019.101649

Quer, G., Aktas, T., Librino, F., Javidi, T., & Rao, R. R. (2019). A Wireless Vehicle-based mobile network infrastructure designed for smarter cities. *Ad Hoc Networks*, *85*, 160–169. doi:10.1016/j.adhoc.2018.10.014

Rahman, R. A., & Shah, B. (2016). Security analysis of IoT protocols: A focus in CoAP. *2016 3rd MEC International Conference on Big Data and Smart City (ICBDSC).*

Rajaprabha, M. N., Jayalakshmi, P., & Anand, R. V. (2018). *IoT based smart garbage collector for smart cities*. Academic Press.

Ramos, F., Trilles, S., Muñoz, A., & Huerta, J. (2018). Promoting Pollution-Free Routes in Smart Cities Using Air Quality Sensor Networks. *Sensors (Basel)*, *18*(8), 2507. Advance online publication. doi:10.339018082507 PMID:30071647

Rego, A., Garcia, L., Sendra, S., & Lloret, J. (2018). Software Defined Network-based control system for an efficient traffic management for emergency situations in smart cities. *Future Generation Computer Systems*, *88*, 243–253. doi:10.1016/j.future.2018.05.054

Reid, A. R., Pérez, C. R. C., & Rodríguez, D. M. (2018). Inference of vehicular traffic in smart cities using machine learning with the internet of things. *International Journal on Interactive Design and Manufacturing*, *12*(2), 459–472. doi:10.100712008-017-0404-1

Rida Khatoun, S. Z. (2016). Smart cities: Concepts, architectures, research opportunities. *Communications of the ACM*, *59*(8), 46–57. doi:10.1145/2858789

Rouse, M. (2017). *Big data analytics*. Retrieved on November 30, 2021, from: https://searchbusinessanalytics.techtarget.com/definition/big-data-analytics

Ruggieri, R., Ruggeri, M., Vinci, G., & Poponi, S. (2021). Electric Mobility in a Smart City: European Overview. *Energies, 14*(2), 315. Advance online publication. doi:10.3390/en14020315

Saleem, M. A., Shijie, Z., & Sharif, A. (2019). Data Transmission Using IoT in Vehicular Ad-Hoc Networks in Smart City Congestion. *Mobile Networks and Applications, 24*(1), 248–258. doi:10.100711036-018-1205-x

Scognamiglio, A., Adinolfi, G., Graditi, G., & Saretta, E. (2014). Photovoltaics in Net Zero Energy Buildings and Clusters: Enabling the Smart City Operation. *Energy Procedia, 61*, 1171–1174. doi:10.1016/j.egypro.2014.11.1046

Shah, S. S., Ali, M., Malik, A. W., Khan, M. A., & Ravana, S. D. (2019). vFog: A Vehicle-Assisted Computing Framework for Delay-Sensitive Applications in Smart Cities. *IEEE Access: Practical Innovations, Open Solutions, 7*, 34900–34909. doi:10.1109/ACCESS.2019.2903302

Simonofski, A., Hertoghe, E., Steegmans, M., Snoeck, M., & Wautelet, Y. (2021). Engaging citizens in the smart city through participation platforms: A framework for public servants and developers. *Computers in Human Behavior, 124*, 106901. doi:10.1016/j.chb.2021.106901

Soomro, K., Bhutta, M. N. M., Khan, Z., & Tahir, M. A. (2019). Smart city big data analytics: An advanced review. *WIREs Data Mining and Knowledge Discovery, 9*(5), e1319.

Sotres, P., López de la Torre, C., Sánchez, L., Jeong, S. M., & Kim, J. (2018). Smart City Services Over a Global Interoperable Internet-of-Things System: The Smart Parking Case. *2018 Global Internet of Things Summit (GIoTS).*

Soyata, T., Habibzadeh, H., Ekenna, C., Nussbaum, B., & Lozano, J. (2019). Smart city in crisis: Technology and policy concerns. *Sustainable Cities and Society, 50*, 101566. doi:10.1016/j.scs.2019.101566

Stephenson, D. (2013). *7 big data techniques that create business value*. Retrieved on November 30, 2021, from: https://www.firmex.com/thedealroom/7-big-data-techniques-that-create-business-value

Talha, M., Upadhyay, A., Shamim, R., & Beg, M. S. (2017). A cloud integrated wireless garbage management system for smart cities. *2017 International Conference on Multimedia, Signal Processing and Communication Technologies (IMPACT).* 10.1109/MSPCT.2017.8363999

Tecuci, G. (2012). Artificial intelligence. *WIREs Computational Statistics, 4*(2), 168-180.

Teece, D. J. (2018). Profiting from innovation in the digital economy: Enabling technologies, standards, and licensing models in the wireless world. *Research Policy, 47*(8), 1367–1387. doi:10.1016/j.respol.2017.01.015

Teslya, N., Ryabchikov, I., & Mikhailov, S. (2019). Forming of Smart City Resident Digital Identity Based On the City Sources Analysis. *2019 IEEE International Black Sea Conference on Communications and Networking (BlackSeaCom).* 10.1109/BlackSeaCom.2019.8812838

Trombin, M., Pinna, R., Musso, M., Magnaghi, E., & De Marco, M. (2020). Mobility Management: From Traditional to People-Centric Approach in the Smart City. In M. Elhoseny & A. E. Hassanien (Eds.), *Emerging Technologies for Connected Internet of Vehicles and Intelligent Transportation System Networks: Emerging Technologies for Connected and Smart Vehicles* (pp. 165–182). Springer International Publishing., doi:10.1007/978-3-030-22773-9_11

United Nations. (2016). *UN data: A world of information.* United Nations Statistics Division. Retrieved on November 30, 2021, from: http://data.un.org

United Nations. D. o. E. a. S. A., Population Division. (2019). *World Population Prospects 2019: Highlights. ST/ESA/SER.A/423.* Retrieved on November 30, 2021, from: https://population.un.org/wpp/Publications/Files/WPP2019_Highlights.pdf

Vakula, D., & Kolli, Y. K. (2017). Low cost smart parking system for smart cities. *2017 International Conference on Intelligent Sustainable Systems (ICISS).* 10.1109/ISS1.2017.8389415

van Beukering, P., Brander, L., Tompkins, E., & Mackenzie, E. (2007). Valuing the Environment in Small Islands: An Environmental Economics Toolkit. Joint Nature Conservation Committee.

Wang, T., Luo, H., Jia, W., Liu, A., & Xie, M. (2020). MTES: An Intelligent Trust Evaluation Scheme in Sensor-Cloud-Enabled Industrial Internet of Things. *IEEE Transactions on Industrial Informatics, 16*(3), 2054–2062. doi:10.1109/TII.2019.2930286

Wegener, M. (2013). The future of mobility in cities: Challenges for urban modelling. *Transport Policy, 29*, 275–282. doi:10.1016/j.tranpol.2012.07.004

White, S., Moore-Colyer, M., Marti, E., Coüetil, L., Hannant, D., Richard, E. A., & Alcocer, M. (2019). Development of a comprehensive protein microarray for immunoglobulin E profiling in horses with severe asthma. *Journal of Veterinary Internal Medicine, 33*(5), 2327-2335.

White, T., & Marchet, F. (2021). Digital Social Markets: Exploring the Opportunities and Impacts of Gamification and Reward Mechanisms in Citizen Engagement and Smart City Services. In M. I. Aldinhas Ferreira (Ed.), *How Smart Is Your City? Technological Innovation, Ethics and Inclusiveness* (pp. 103–125). Springer International Publishing. doi:10.1007/978-3-030-56926-6_9

World Business Council for Sustainable Development (WBCSD). (2004). *Mobility 2030: Meeting the challenges to sustainability.* https://www.wbcsd.org/Programs/Cities-and-Mobility/Sustainable-Cities/City-Business-Collaboration/SiMPlify/Resources/Mobility-2030-Meeting-the-challenges-to-sustainability-Executive-Summary-2004

Wüstemann, H., Kalisch, D., & Kolbe, J. (2017). Access to urban green space and environmental inequalities in Germany. *Landscape and Urban Planning, 164*, 124–131. doi:10.1016/j.landurbplan.2017.04.002

Xiao, F., Xie, X., Li, Z., Deng, Q., Liu, A., & Sun, L. (2018). Wireless Network Optimization via Physical Layer Information for Smart Cities. *IEEE Network, 32*(4), 88–93. doi:10.1109/MNET.2018.1700281

Yao, H., Gao, P., Wang, J., Zhang, P., Jiang, C., & Han, Z. (2019). Capsule Network Assisted IoT Traffic Classification Mechanism for Smart Cities. *IEEE Internet of Things Journal, 6*(5), 7515–7525. doi:10.1109/JIOT.2019.2901348

Yigitcanlar, T. (2016). *Technology and the city: Systems, applications and implications*. Routledge. doi:10.4324/9781315739090

Yigitcanlar, T., & Dizdaroglu, D. (2015). Ecological approaches in planning for sustainable cities: A review of the literature. *Global Journal of Environmental Science and Management, 1*(12), 159–188. doi:10.7508/GJESM.2015.02.008

Zou, H., Zhou, Y., Yang, J., Gu, W., Xie, L., & Spanos, C. (2018). WiFi-Based Human Identification via Convex Tensor Shapelet Learning. *Proceedings of the AAAI Conference on Artificial Intelligence, 32*(1). Advance online publication. doi:10.1609/aaai.v32i1.11497

Zygiaris, S. (2013). Smart City Reference Model: Assisting Planners to Conceptualize the Building of Smart City Innovation Ecosystems. *Journal of the Knowledge Economy, 4*(2), 217–231. doi:10.100713132-012-0089-4

Compilation of References

Aalto-yliopisto, A. (2011). *Investigating the relationship of inward foreign direct investment and poverty in developing countries* [Master's dissertation]. Aalto University School of Economics.

Abel, T., & McQueen, D. (2020). Critical health literacy and the COVID-19 crisis. *Health Promotion International, 35*(6), 1612–1613. doi:10.1093/heapro/daaa040 PMID:32239213

Abi-Rached, J. M. (2021). The Covid-19 caesura and the post-pandemic future. *Biosocieties, 16*(1), 142–156. doi:10.105741292-020-00212-6

Acedo, F. J., & Casillas, J. C. (2005). Current paradigms in the international management field: An author co-citation analysis. *International Business Review, 14*(5), 619–639. doi:10.1016/j.ibusrev.2005.05.003

Addison, T., & Heshmati, A. (2003). *The New Global Determinants of FDI Flows to Developing Countries: he Importance of ICT and Democratization.* World Institute for Development Economics Research.

Adekoya, F. (2020, Dec. 8). $140bn yearly loss to corruption can address Africa's power challenge. *The Guardian*. Retrieved on May 4, 2021, from: https://guardian.ng/business-services/140bn-yearly-loss-to-corruption-can-address-africas-power-challenge/

Adesina, J. O. (2016). *Inequality in Sub-Saharan Africa: Dimensions & drivers. World Social Science Report, 2016.* Retrieved on September 22, 2021, from: https://en.unesco.org/inclusivepolicylab/sites/default/files/analytics/document/2019/7/Adesina_wssr_2016_chap_18.pdf

Adler, N. J., Brody, L. W., & Osland, J. S. (2001). Going beyond twentieth century leadership: A CEO develops his company's global competitiveness. *Cross Cultural Management, 8*(3/4), 11–34. doi:10.1108/13527600110797263

Adler, N. J., & Graham, J. L. (1989). Cross-Cultural Interaction: The International Comparison Fallacy? *Journal of International Business Studies, 20*(3), 515–537. doi:10.1057/palgrave.jibs.8490367

Adner, R., & Kapoor, R. (2010). Value creation in innovation ecosystems: How the structure of technological interdependence affects firm performance in new technology generations. *Strategic Management Journal, 31*(3), 306–333. doi:10.1002mj.821

AETNA. (2020). Expat Family Wellness Survey. *AETNA*. https://www.aetnainternational.com/en/about-us/explore/living-abroad/expatriate-life/expat-family-wellness-survey-2020.html

African Development Bank Group. (2021). Retrieved on December 22, 2021, from: https://www.afdb.org/en/topics-and-sectors/topics/quality-assurance-results/gender-equality-index

Agarwal, P., Swami, S., & Malhotra, S. K. (2022). Artificial Intelligence Adoption in the Post COVID-19 New-Normal and Role of Smart Technologies in Transforming Business: a Review. *Journal of Science and Technology Policy Management*.

Agarwal, S., & Ramaswami, S. (1992). Choice of Foreign Market Entry Mode: Impact of Ownership, Location and Internalization Factors. *Journal of International Business Studies*, *23*(1), 1–27. doi:10.1057/palgrave.jibs.8490257

Ağraş, S., Atba, F., & Şeyba, E. (2017). Mavi Okyanus Stratejisi: Dünyadan ve Türkiye'den Örnekler. [Blue Ocean Strategy: Examples from the World and Turkey.]. *Yönetim, Ekonomi, Edebiyat, İslami ve Politik Bilimler Dergisi*, *2*(2), 126–144.

Aguilera, U., Peña, O., Belmonte, O., & López-de-Ipiña, D. (2017). Citizen-centric data services for smarter cities. *Future Generation Computer Systems*, *76*, 234–247. doi:10.1016/j.future.2016.10.031

Ahammad, I., Hossain, M. U., Rahman, A., Chowdhury, Z. M., Bhattacharjee, A., Das, K. C., Keya, C. A., & Salimullah, M. (2021). Wave-wise comparative genomic study for revealing the complete scenario and dynamic nature of COVID-19 pandemic in Bangladesh. *PLoS One*, *16*(9), 1–21. doi:10.1371/journal.pone.0258019 PMID:34587212

Ahlstrom, D., Arregle, J., Hitt, M. A., Qian, G., Ma, X., & Faems, D. (2020). Managing Technological, Sociopolitical, and Institutional Change in the New Normal. *Journal of Management Studies*, *57*(3), 411–437. doi:10.1111/joms.12569

Ahmad, T., Li, X. J., Seet, B.-C., & Cano, J.-C. (2020). Social Network Analysis Based Localization Technique with Clustered Closeness Centrality for 3D Wireless Sensor Networks. *Electronics (Basel)*, *9*(5), 738. Advance online publication. doi:10.3390/electronics9050738

Ahmed Khan, J., Wang, L., Jacobs, E., Talebian, A., Mishra, S., Santo, C. A., ... Astorne-Figari, C. (2019). Smart Cities Connected and Autonomous Vehicles Readiness Index. *Proceedings of the 2nd ACM/EIGSCC Symposium on Smart Cities and Communities*. 10.1145/3357492.3358631

Ahmed, E., Yaqoob, I., Hashem, I. A. T., Khan, I., Ahmed, A. I. A., Imran, M., & Vasilakos, A. V. (2017). The role of big data analytics in Internet of Things. *Computer Networks*, *129*, 459–471. doi:10.1016/j.comnet.2017.06.013

Ahuja, G., & Katila, R. (2001). Technological acquisitions and the innovation performance of acquiring firms: A longitudinal study. *Strategic Management Journal*, *22*(3), 197–220. doi:10.1002mj.157

Ajide, F. M., & Osinubi, T. T. (2020). Covid-19 pandemic and outward foreign direct investment: A preliminary note. *ECONOMICS*, *8*(2), 79–88. doi:10.2478/eoik-2020-0019

Alahdal, H., Basingab, F., & Alotaibi, R. (2020). An analytical study on the awareness, attitude and practice during the COVID-19 pandemic in Riyadh, Saudi Arabia. *Journal of Infection and Public Health*, *13*(10), 1446–1452. doi:10.1016/j.jiph.2020.06.015 PMID:32563674

Alanzi, T. (2021). A Review of Mobile Applications Available in the App and Google Play Stores Used During the COVID-19 Outbreak. *Journal of Multidisciplinary Healthcare*, *14*, 45–57. doi:10.2147/JMDH.S285014 PMID:33469298

Albanito, F., Hastings, A., Fitton, N., Richards, M., Martin, M., Mac Dowell, N., . . . Smith, P. (2019). Mitigation potential and environmental impact of centralized versus distributed BECCS with domestic biomass production in Great Britain. *GCB Bioenergy*, *11*(10), 1234-1252.

Al-Dmour, H., Masa'deh, R., Salman, A., Abuhashesh, M., & Al-Dmour, R. (2020). Influence of Social Media Platforms on Public Health Protection Against the COVID-19 Pandemic via the Mediating Effects of Public Health Awareness and Behavioral Changes: Integrated Model. *Journal of Medical Internet Research*, *22*(8), 1–15. doi:10.2196/19996 PMID:32750004

Alexander, A., Mysore, M., Cracknell, R., De Smet, A., Langstaff, A., & Ravid, D. (2021). What executives are saying about the future of hybrid work. *McKinsey.* https://www.mckinsey.com/business-functions/organization/our-insights/what-executives-are-saying-about-the-future-of-hyb rid- work

Alicke, K., Barriball, E., & Trautwein, V. (2021, November). *How COVID-19 is Reshaping Supply Chains.* McKinsey and Company.

Ali, M. Y., & Gatiti, P. (2020). The COVID-19 (Coronavirus) pandemic: Reflections on the roles of librarians and information professionals. *Health Information and Libraries Journal, 37*(2), 158–162. doi:10.1111/hir.12307 PMID:32251543

Al-Khateeb, H., Epiphaniou, G., & Daly, H. (2019). Blockchain for Modern Digital Forensics: The Chain-of-Custody as a Distributed Ledger. In H. Jahankhani, S. Kendzierskyj, A. Jamal, G. Epiphaniou, & H. Al-Khateeb (Eds.), *Blockchain and Clinical Trial: Securing Patient Data* (pp. 149–168). Springer International Publishing. doi:10.1007/978-3-030-11289-9_7

Alola, A. A., Alola, U. V., & Sarkodie, S. A. (2021). The COVID-19 and financial stress in the USA: Health is wealth. *Environment, Development and Sustainability, 23*(6), 9367–9378. doi:10.100710668-020-01029-w PMID:33052193

Alon, I. (2020). COVID-19 and international business: A viewpoint. *FIIB Business Review, 9*(2), 75–77. doi:10.1177/2319714520923579

Alotaibi, S. S. (2019). Registration Center Based User Authentication Scheme for Smart E-Governance Applications in Smart Cities. *IEEE Access: Practical Innovations, Open Solutions, 7*, 5819–5833. doi:10.1109/ACCESS.2018.2884541

Alqutob, R., Al Nsour, M., Tarawneh, M. R., Ajlouni, M., Khader, Y., Aqel, I., Kharabsheh, S., & Obeidat, N. (2020). COVID-19 Crisis in Jordan: Response, Scenarios, Strategies, and Recommendations. *JMIR Public Health and Surveillance, 6*(3), 1–6. doi:10.2196/19332 PMID:32407289

Altuntuğ, N. (2007). Rekabet Sürecinin Dinamik Boyutu, Bileşenleri ve Dinamizmi Sürdürebilme Yolları. [The Dynamic Dimension of the Competitive Process, Its Components and Ways of Sustaining Dynamism.]. *Süleyman Demirel Üniversitesi Sosyal Bilimler Enstitüsü Dergisi, 5*, 29–15.

Amah, O. E. (2017). Leadership styles and relational energy in high quality mentoring Relationship. *Indian Journal of Industrial Relations, 53*(1), 59–71.

Amah, O. E. (2019). *Globalization and leadership in Africa: Developments and challenges for the future.* New York Palgrave Macmillan. doi:10.1007/978-3-319-98764-4

Amann, E., & Virmani, S. (2015). Foreign direct investment and reverse technology spillovers. *OECD Journal: Economic Studies, 2014*(1), 129–153.

Amaral, J. (2013). Index of Foreign Direct Investment Attractiveness of Groh & Wich: Robustness Analysis and Reconstruction [Master's thesis]. Instituto Superior Técnico, Lisboa.

Amer, H. M., Al-Kashoash, H. A. A., Kemp, A., Mihaylova, L., & Mayfield, M. (2018). Coalition Game for Emergency Vehicles Re-Routing in Smart Cities. *2018 IEEE 10th Sensor Array and Multichannel Signal Processing Workshop (SAM).*

Amesse, F., & Cohendet, P. (2001). Technology transfer revisited from the perspective of the knowledge-based economy. *Research Policy, 30*(9), 1459–1478. doi:10.1016/S0048-7333(01)00162-7

Anagnostopoulos, T., Zaslavsy, A., Medvedev, A., & Khoruzhnicov, S. (2015, June 15-18). Top — k Query Based Dynamic Scheduling for IoT-enabled Smart City Waste Collection. *2015 16th IEEE International Conference on Mobile Data Management.*

Anderson, D., & Kelliher, C. (2020). Enforced remote working and the work-life interface during lockdown. *Gender in Management, 35*(7), 677–683. doi:10.1108/GM-07-2020-0224

Anderson, E., & Gatignon, H. (1986). Modes of Foreign Entry: A Transaction Cost Analysis and Propositions. *Journal of International Business Studies, 17*(3), 1–26. doi:10.1057/palgrave.jibs.8490432

Andresen, M., & Bergdolt, F. (2017). A systematic literature review on the definitions of global mindset and cultural intelligence–merging two different research streams. *International Journal of Human Resource Management, 28*(1), 170–195. doi:10.1080/09585192.2016.1243568

Angelidou, M. (2017). The Role of Smart City Characteristics in the Plans of Fifteen Cities. *Journal of Urban Technology, 24*(4), 3–28. doi:10.1080/10630732.2017.1348880

Ang, S., Van Dyne, L., Koh, C., Ng, K. Y., Templer, K. J., Tay, C., & Chandrasekar, N. A. (2007). Cultural intelligence: Its measurement and effects on cultural judgment and decision making, cultural adaptation and task performance. *Management and Organization Review, 3*(3), 335–371. doi:10.1111/j.1740-8784.2007.00082.x

Anjomshoaa, A., Duarte, F., Rennings, D., Matarazzo, T. J., deSouza, P., & Ratti, C. (2018). City Scanner: Building and Scheduling a Mobile Sensing Platform for Smart City Services. *IEEE Internet of Things Journal, 5*(6), 4567–4579. doi:10.1109/JIOT.2018.2839058

Anthony, B. Jr. (2021). Integrating telemedicine to support digital health care for the management of COVID-19 pandemic. *International Journal of Healthcare Management, 14*(1), 280–289. doi:10.1080/20479700.2020.1870354

Anthopoulos, L. G. (2015). Understanding the Smart City Domain: A Literature Review. In M. P. Rodríguez-Bolívar (Ed.), *Transforming City Governments for Successful Smart Cities* (pp. 9–21). Springer International Publishing. doi:10.1007/978-3-319-03167-5_2

Anttiroiko, A.-V., Valkama, P., & Bailey, S. J. (2014). Smart cities in the new service economy: Building platforms for smart services. *AI & Society, 29*(3), 323–334. doi:10.100700146-013-0464-0

Ar, A. Y., & Abbas, A. (2021). Corporate response against COVID-19: Manufacturing shift by Ford-Otosan. *Annals of Global Health, 87*(1), 1–5. doi:10.5334/aogh.3434 PMID:34277362

Archibugi, D., & Coco, A. (2004). A New Indicator of Technological Capabilities for Developed and Developing Countries (ArCo). *World Development, 32*(4), 629–654. doi:10.1016/j.worlddev.2003.10.008

Arellano-Verdejo, J., Alonso-Pecina, F., Alba, E., & Guzmán Arenas, A. (2019). Optimal allocation of public parking spots in a smart city: Problem characterisation and first algorithms. *Journal of Experimental & Theoretical Artificial Intelligence, 31*(4), 575–597. doi:10.1080/0952813X.2019.1591522

Arita, S., Grant, J., Sydow, S., & Beckman, J. (2022). Has global agricultural trade been resilient under coronavirus (COVID-19)? Findings from an econometric assessment of 2020. *Food Policy, 107*, 102204. doi:10.1016/j.foodpol.2021.102204 PMID:34903907

Arshad, S., Raza, Q., & Hussain, M. (2019). VANETs Embedded Novel Traffic Management Paradigm for Smart City Milieu. *Proceedings of the 3rd International Conference on Future Networks and Distributed Systems*. 10.1145/3341325.3342038

Atkinson, R., & Flint, J. (2001). Accessing hidden and hard-to-reach populations: Snowball research strategies. *Social Research Update, 33*(1), 1–4. doi:10.4135/9780857020024.n94

Attia, Y. A., El-Saadony, M. T., Swelum, A. A., Qattan, S. Y. A., Al-qurashi, A. D., Asiry, K. A., Shafi, M. E., Elbestawy, A. R., Gado, A. R., Khafaga, A. F., Hussein, E. O. S., Ba-Awadh, H., Tiwari, R., Dhama, K., Alhussaini, B., Alyileili, S. R., El-Tarabily, K. A., & Abd El-Hack, M. E. (2021). COVID-19: pathogenesis, advances in treatment and vaccine development and environmental impact—an updated review. *Environmental Science and Pollution Research, 28*(18), 22241–22264. doi:10.1007/S11356-021-13018-1

Aulakh, P. S., & Kotabe, M. (1997). Antecedents and Performance Implications of Channel Integration in Foreign Markets. *Journal of International Business Studies, 28*(1), 145–175. doi:10.1057/palgrave.jibs.8490096

Aulakh, P. S., Kotabe, M., & Sahay, A. (1996). Trust and Performance in Cross-Border Marketing Partnerships: A Behavioral Approach. *Journal of International Business Studies, 27*(5), 1005–1032. doi:10.1057/palgrave.jibs.8490161

Autio, E., Pathak, S., & Wennberg, K. (2013). Consequences of cultural practices for entrepreneurial behaviors. *Journal of International Business Studies, 44*(4), 334–362. doi:10.1057/jibs.2013.15

Ayala-Ruiz, D., Castillo Atoche, A., Ruiz-Ibarra, E., Osorio de la Rosa, E., & Vázquez Castillo, J. (2019). A Self-Powered PMFC-Based Wireless Sensor Node for Smart City Applications. *Wireless Communications and Mobile Computing, 8986302*, 1–10. Advance online publication. doi:10.1155/2019/8986302

Aytug, Z. G., Kern, M. C., & Dilchert, S. (2018). Multicultural experience: Development and validation of a multidimensional scale. *International Journal of Intercultural Relations, 65*, 1–16. doi:10.1016/j.ijintrel.2018.04.004

Badii, C., Bellini, P., Difino, A., & Nesi, P. (2019). Sii-Mobility: An IoT/IoE Architecture to Enhance Smart City Mobility and Transportation Services. *Sensors (Basel), 19*(1), 1. Advance online publication. doi:10.339019010001 PMID:30577434

Bailey, S. C., Serper, M., Opsasnick, L., Persell, S. D., O'Conor, R., Curtis, L. M., Benavente, J. Y., Wismer, G., Batio, S., Eifler, M., Zheng, P., Russell, A., Arvanitis, M., Ladner, D. P., Kwasny, M. J., Rowe, T., Linder, J. A., & Wolf, M. S. (2020). Changes in COVID-19 Knowledge, Beliefs, Behaviors, and Preparedness Among High-Risk Adults from the Onset to the Acceleration Phase of the US Outbreak. *Journal of General Internal Medicine, 35*(11), 3285–3292. doi:10.100711606-020-05980-2 PMID:32875509

Bain, J. S. (1964). The impact on industrial organization. *The American Economic Review, 54*(3), 28–32.

Bait, S., Lauria, S. M., & Schiraldi, M. M. (2021). Multi-criteria decision-making model for supporting manufacturing settlements location in Africa after COVID-19. *International Journal of Engineering Business Management, 13*, 1–15. doi:10.1177/18479790211023348

Balakrishna, C. (2012, September 12-14). Enabling Technologies for Smart City Services and Applications. *2012 Sixth International Conference on Next Generation Mobile Applications, Services and Technologies.*

Baldassar, L. (2016). De-demonizing distance in mobile family lives: Co-presence, care circulation and polymedia as vibrant matter. *Global Networks, 16*(2), 145–163. doi:10.1111/glob.12109

Baldwin, R. (2016). *The Great Convergence: Information Technology and the New Globalization.* Harvard University Press. doi:10.2307/j.ctv24w655w

Baldwin, R., & Tomiura, E. (2020). Thinking ahead about the trade impact of COVID-19. *Economics in the Time of COVID, 19*(59), 59–71.

Balkir, C., & Kirkulak, B. (2007). Turkey as a new destination for retirement migration. *International migration, multi-local livelihoods and human security: perspectives from Europe, Asia and Africa.* doi:10.4337/9781849802017.00015

Banalieva, E. R., & Dhanaraj, C. (2013). Home-region orientation in international expansion strategies. *Journal of International Business Studies, 44*(2), 89–116. doi:10.1057/jibs.2012.33

Bandura, R. (2005). *Measuring Country Performance and State Behavior: A Survey of Composite Indices*. Office of Development Studies United Nations Development Programme.

Baraniuk, C. (2013). The civic hackers reshaping your government. *New Scientist, 218*(2923), 36–39.

Barbero, J., de Lucio, J. J., & Rodríguez-Crespo, E. (2021). Effects of COVID-19 on trade flows: Measuring their impact through government policy responses. *PLoS One, 16*(10), 1–20. doi:10.1371/journal.pone.0258356 PMID:34644312

Barkema, H. G., & Vemeulen, F. (1998). International Expansion through Start up or Acquistion: A Learning Perspective. *Academy of Management Journal, 41*(1), 7–26. doi:10.2307/256894

Barkham, R., Bokhari, S., & Saiz, A. (2018). *Urban big data: City management and real estate markets*. Retrieved 11/30/2021 from https://mitcre.mit.edu/wp-content/uploads/2018/01/URBAN-DATA-AND-REAL-ESTATE-JAN-2018-1.pdf

Barney, B. (1991). Firm resources and sustained competitive advantage. *Journal of Management, 17*(1), 99–120. doi:10.1177/014920639101700108

Barney, J. B. (1995). Looking inside for Competitive Advantage. *The Academy of Management Executive, 9*(4), 49–61. doi:10.5465/ame.1995.9512032192

Barney, J. B., & Clark, D. N. (2007). *Resource-based Theory: Creating and Sustaining Competitive Advantage*. Oxford University Press.

Barrell, R., & Pain, N. (1997). *Foreign Direct Investment, Technological Change, and Economic Growth within Europe* (107th ed.). The Economic Journal. doi:10.1111/j.1468-0297.1997.tb00081.x

Bartel, A. P., Lach, S., & Sicherman, N. (2012). Technological change and the make-or-by decision. *Journal of Law Economics and Organization, 30*(1), 165–192. doi:10.1093/jleo/ews035

Bartol, K. M., & David, C. M. (1994). Management, Second Edition. New York.

Barua, S. (2021). Understanding Coronanomics: The Economic Implications of the Covid-19 Pandemic. *Journal of Developing Areas, 55*(3), 435–450. doi:10.1353/jda.2021.0073

Bassi, A., Arfin, S., John, O., & Jha, V. (2020). An overview of mobile applications (apps) to support the coronavirus disease 2019 response in India. *The Indian Journal of Medical Research, 151*(5), 473. doi:10.4103/IJMR.IJMR_1200_20 PMID:32474557

Basu, S. (2021). Effective Contact Tracing for COVID-19 Using Mobile Phones: An Ethical Analysis of the Mandatory Use of the Aarogya Setu Application in India. *Cambridge Quarterly of Healthcare Ethics, 30*(2), 262–271. doi:10.1017/S0963180120000821 PMID:32993842

Battarra, R., Gargiulo, C., Tremiterra, M. R., & Zucaro, F. (2018). Smart mobility in Italian metropolitan cities: A comparative analysis through indicators and actions. *Sustainable Cities and Society, 41*, 556–567. doi:10.1016/j.scs.2018.06.006

BBC. (2020). Coronavirus: Immigration to US to be suspended amid pandemic, Trump says. 21 April. *BBC*. .https://www.bbc.com/news/world-us-canada-52363852

Beamish, P. W., & Banks, J. C. (1987). Equity Joint Ventures and the Theory of the Multinational Enterprise. *Journal of International Business Studies, 18*(2), 1–16. doi:10.1057/palgrave.jibs.8490403

Bebenroth, R. (2022). *Adjustment of Expatriates' Work Practices during the Covid-19 Pandemic*. Discussion paper Series. Research Institute for Economics & Business Administration (RIEB)

Beechler. S., & Javidan, M. (2007). Leading with a global mindset. In The global mindset. Emerald Group Publishing Limited. doi:10.10161571-5027(07)19006-9

BEIS. (2018). *UK greenhouse gas emissions, Final figures.* https://assets.publishing.service.gov.uk/government/uploads/system/uploads/attachment_data/file/862887/2018_Final_greenh ouse_gas_emissions_statistical_release.pdf

Bekkers, E., & Koopman, R. B. (2020). Simulating the trade effects of the COVID-19 pandemic. *World Economy, 45*(2), 445–467. doi:10.1111/twec.13063 PMID:33362334

Belahsen, C. A., Lyhyaoui, A., & Boufardi, N. (2019). IoT Data-Based Architecture on OpenStack for Smart City. Advanced Intelligent Systems for Sustainable Development (AI2SD'2018), Cham, Switzerland.

Bellow, W. (2008). *Deglobalization: Ideas for a New World Economy.* Zed Books.

Belohlav, J. A. (1996). The Evolving Competitive Paradigm. *Business Horizons, 39*(2), 11–19. doi:10.1016/S0007-6813(96)90018-X

Belu, M. G. (2021). COVID-19 Pandemic Impact on the Exports and Imports. *The Romanian Economic Journal, 82*(82), 31–46. doi:10.24818/REJ/2021/82/03

Ben Letaifa, S. (2015). How to strategize smart cities: Revealing the SMART model. *Journal of Business Research, 68*(7), 1414–1419. doi:10.1016/j.jbusres.2015.01.024

Benacek, V., Miroslaw, G., & Holland, D. (2000). The Determinants and Impact of Foreign Direct Investment in Central and Eastern Europe: A comparison of survey and econometric evidence. *Journal of United Nations, 9*, 163–212.

Bénassy-Quéré, A., Coupet, M., & Mayer, T. (2007). *Institutional Determinants of Foreign Direct Investment* (35th ed., Vol. 30). World Economy.

Benevolo, C., Dameri, R. P., & D'Auria, B. (2016). *Smart Mobility in Smart City.* Empowering Organizations.

Berkman, N. D., Sheridan, S. L., Donahue, K. E., Halpern, D. J., & Crotty, K. (2011). Low health literacy and health outcomes: An updated systematic review. *Annals of Internal Medicine, 155*(2), 97–107. doi:10.7326/0003-4819-155-2-201107190-00005 PMID:21768583

Berlingieri, G. (2013). *Outsourcing and the rise in services.* CEP Discussion Paper DP1199, Centre for Economic Performance, London School of Economics (LSE), London.

Berry, D. P., & Bell, M. P. (2012). 'Expatriates': Gender, race and class distinctions in international management. *Gender, Work and Organization, 19*(1), 10–28. doi:10.1111/j.1468-0432.2011.00577.x

Bessant, J., & Tidd, J. (2007). *Innovation and Entrepreneurship.* John Wiley & Sons.

BGRS. (2021) Growth opportunity for employee mobility in the next normal. *BGRS.* https://www.bgrs.com/tmts_article/growth-opportunity-for-employee-mobility-in-the-next-normal/

BGRS. (2021) Virtual mobility. Evolving mobility for the future of work. *BGRS.* https://www.bgrs.com/tmts_article/virtual-mobility-evolving-mobility-for-the-future-of-work/

Bibri, S. E. (2020). *Advances in the leading paradigms of urbanism and their amalgamation: compact cities, eco–cities, and data-driven smart cities.* Springer. doi:10.1007/978-3-030-41746-8

Bilkey, W. J. (1978). An Attempted Integration of the Literature on the Export Behavior of Firms. *Journal of International Business Studies*, *9*(1), 33–46. doi:10.1057/palgrave.jibs.8490649

Bilkey, W. J. (1982). Variables Associated with Export Profitability. *Journal of International Business Studies*, *13*(2), 39–55. doi:10.1057/palgrave.jibs.8490549

Bilkey, W. J., & Tesar, G. (1977). The Export Behavior of Smaller-Sized Wisconsin Manufacturing Firms. *Journal of International Business Studies*, *8*(1), 93–98. doi:10.1057/palgrave.jibs.8490783

Birkinshaw, J. M., & Morrison, A. J. (1995). Configurations of Strategy and Structure in Subsidiaries of Multinational Corporations. *Journal of International Business Studies*, *26*(4), 729–753. doi:10.1057/palgrave.jibs.8490818

Black, J. S. (1988). Work Role Transitions: A Study of American Expatriate Managers in Japan. *Journal of International Business Studies*, *19*(2), 277–294. doi:10.1057/palgrave.jibs.8490383

Blomström, M., & Kokko, A. (1999). *How Foreingn Investment Affects Hose Countries*. World Bank Publications. doi:10.1596/1813-9450-1745

Boddewyn, J. J. (1981). B Comparative Marketing: The First Twenty-Five Years. *Journal of International Business Studies*, *12*(1), 61–79. doi:10.1057/palgrave.jibs.8490571

Boddewyn, J. J. (1999). The domain of international management. *Journal of International Management*, *5*(1), 3–14. doi:10.1016/S1075-4253(99)00003-4

Boddewyn, J. J., Halbrich, M. B., & Perry, A. C. (1986). Service Multinationals: Conceptualization, Measurement and Theory. *Journal of International Business Studies*, *17*(3), 41–57. doi:10.1057/palgrave.jibs.8490860

Bodomo, A. (2017). The globalization of foreign investment in Africa: The Role of Europe, China, and India. Emerald Publishing. doi:10.1108/9781787433571

Borensztein, E., De Gregorio, J., & Lee, J. W. (1998). How does foreign direct investment affect economic growth? *Journal of International Economics*, *45*(1), 115–135. doi:10.1016/S0022-1996(97)00033-0

Brainard, S. L. (1997). An Empirical Assessment of the Proximity-Concentration Trade-off Between Multinational Sales and Trade. *The American Economic Review*, *87*, 520–544.

Braun, V., & Clarke, V. (2006). Using thematic analysis in psychology. *Qualitative Research in Psychology*, *3*(2), 77–101. doi:10.1191/1478088706qp063oa

Bresman, H., Birkinshaw, J., & Nobel, R. (1999). Knowledge Transfer in International Acquisitions. *Journal of International Business Studies*, *30*(3), 439–462. doi:10.1057/palgrave.jibs.8490078

Bridgland, V., Moeck, E., Green, D., Swain, T., Nayda, D., Matson, L., Hutchinson, N., & Takarangi, M. (2021). Why the COVID-19 Pandemic is a Traumatic Stressor. *PLoS One*, *16*(1), e0240146. doi:10.1371/journal.pone.0240146 PMID:33428630

Bucher, J., & Deller, J. (2021). *Digital Technologies and Expatriation*. A systematic literature review. *Academy of Management Proceedings*, (1), 11027

Buckley, P. J. (1989). Foreign direct investment by small-and medium-sized enterprises: the theoretical background. In *The multinational enterprise* (pp. 24–45). Palgrave Macmillan. doi:10.1007/978-1-349-11026-1_2

Buckley, P. J. (2002). Is the International Business Research Agenda Running out of Steam? *Journal of International Business Studies*, *33*(2), 365–373. doi:10.1057/palgrave.jibs.8491021

Buckley, P. J. (2020). The theory and empirics of the structural reshaping of globalization. *Journal of International Business Studies*, *51*(9), 1580–1592. doi:10.105741267-020-00355-5 PMID:32836503

Buckley, P. J., & Casson, M. C. (1998). Analyzing Foreign Market Entry Strategies: Extending the Internalization Approach. *Journal of International Business Studies*, *29*(3), 539–561. doi:10.1057/palgrave.jibs.8490006

Buckley, P. J., Clegg, L. J., Cross, A. R., Liu, X., Voss, H., & Zheng, P. (2007). The determinants of Chinese outward foreign direct investment. *Journal of International Business Studies*, *38*(4), 499–518. doi:10.1057/palgrave.jibs.8400277

Buckley, P. J., & Pearce, R. D. (1979). Overseas Production and Exporting by the World's Largest Enterprises: A Study in Sourcing Policy. *Journal of International Business Studies*, *10*(1), 9–20. doi:10.1057/palgrave.jibs.8490626

Buuren, S. V. (2012). *Flexible Imputation of Missing Data*. CRC Press. doi:10.1201/b11826

Cairns, D. (2014). Becoming Mobile. In Youth Transitions, International Student Mobility and Spatial Reflexivity (pp. 41-93). London: Palgrave Macmillan. doi:10.1057/9781137388513_3

Cairns, D., Cuzzocrea, V., Briggs, D., & Veloso, L. (2017). *The consequences of mobility: Reflexivity, social inequality and the reproduction of precariousness in highly qualified migration*. Springer., doi:10.1007/978-3-319-46741-2

Calamur, K. (2017, August 22). High traffic, high risk in the Strait of Malacca. *Atlantic (Boston, Mass.)*.

Caligiuri, P., De Cieri, H., Minbaeva, D., Verbeke, A., & Zimmermann, A. (2020). International HRM insights for navigating the COVID-19 pandemic: Implications for future research and practice. *Journal of International Business Studies*, *51*(5), 697–713. doi:10.105741267-020-00335-9 PMID:32836500

Callaghan, C. W. (2021). Consequences of deindustrialisation for globalisation: Insights for international business. *International Business Review*, *30*(3), 101804. doi:10.1016/j.ibusrev.2021.101804

Calvet, A. L. (1981). A Synthesis of Foreign Direct Investment Theories and Theories of the Multinational Firm. *Journal of International Business Studies*, *12*(1), 43–59. doi:10.1057/palgrave.jibs.8490570

Cannonier, C., & Mocan, N. (2018). The impact of education on women's preferences for gender equality: Evidence from Sierra Leone. *Journal of Demographic Economics*, *84*(1), 3–40. doi:10.1017/dem.2016.12

Cantwell, J. (1989). *Technological innovation and multinational corporations*. Blackwell.

Cantwell, J., Dunning, J. H., & Lundan, S. M. (2010). An evolutionary approach to understanding international business activity: The co-evolution of MNEs and the institutional environment. *Journal of International Business Studies*, *41*(4), 567–586. doi:10.1057/jibs.2009.95

Cantwell, J., & Janne, O. (1999). Technological globalisation and innovative centres: The role of corporate technological leadership and locational hierarchy. *Research Policy*, *28*(2-3), 119–144. doi:10.1016/S0048-7333(98)00118-8

Caragliu, A., Del Bo, C., & Nijkamp, P. (2011). Smart Cities in Europe. *Journal of Urban Technology*, *18*(2), 65–82. doi:10.1080/10630732.2011.601117

Carter, C. R. (2008). Knowledge production and knowledge transfer: Closing the research – practice gap. *The Journal of Supply Chain Management*, *44*(2), 78–82. doi:10.1111/j.1745-493X.2008.00059.x

Cascio, W. F., & Aguinis, H. (2008). 3 Staffing Twenty-first-century Organizations. *The Academy of Management Annals*, *2*(1), 133–165. doi:10.5465/19416520802211461

Casseres, B. G. (1990). Firm Ownership Preferences and Host Government Restrictions: An Integrated Approach. *Journal of International Business Studies*, *21*(1), 1–22. doi:10.1057/palgrave.jibs.8490324

Cassiman, B., & Golovko, E. (2011). Innovation and internationalization through exports. *Journal of International Business Studies*, *42*(1), 56–75. doi:10.1057/jibs.2010.36

Castaneda-Navarrete, J., Hauge, J., & López-Gómez, C. (2021). COVID-19's impacts on global value chains, as seen in the apparel industry. *Development Policy Review*, *39*(6), 953–970. doi:10.1111/dpr.12539

Caves, R. E., & Caves, R. E. (1996). *Multinational enterprise and economic analysis*. Cambridge University Press.

Cavusgil, S. T., & Knight, G. (2015). The born global firm: An entrepreneurial and capabilities perspective on early and rapid internationalization. *Journal of International Business Studies*, *46*(1), 3–16. doi:10.1057/jibs.2014.62

Cavusgil, T., Bilkey, W. J., & Tesar, G. (1979). A Note on the Export Behavior of Firms: Exporter Profiles. *Journal of International Business Studies*, *10*(1), 91–97. doi:10.1057/palgrave.jibs.8490633

Cernicky, J. (n.d.). *What is the good of ECOWAS?* Retrieved on January 3, 2022, from: https://www.kas.de/documents/252038/253252/7_dokument_dok_pdf_11781_2.pdf/75ef6c30-4f45-bd72-73f3-19b78fec8cf9?version=1.0&t=1539664207887

Chandy, P. R., & Williams, T. G. E. (1994). The impact of journals and authors on international business research: A citation analysis of JIBS articles. *Journal of International Business Studies*, *25*(4), 715–728. doi:10.1057/palgrave.jibs.8490221

Chatterjee, R., & Chatterjee, R. (2017). An Overview of the Emerging Technology: Blockchain. *2017 3rd International Conference on Computational Intelligence and Networks (CINE).*

Chaturvedi, K., Matheus, A., Nguyen, S. H., & Kolbe, T. H. (2019). Securing Spatial Data Infrastructures for Distributed Smart City applications and services. *Future Generation Computer Systems*, *101*, 723–736. doi:10.1016/j.future.2019.07.002

Chaudhari, S. S., & Bhole, V. Y. (2018). Solid Waste Collection as a Service using IoT-Solution for Smart Cities. *2018 International Conference on Smart City and Emerging Technology (ICSCET).* 10.1109/ICSCET.2018.8537326

Cheng, J. L., Henisz, W. J., Roth, K., & Swaminathan, A. (2009). From the Editors: Advancing interdisciplinary research in the field of international business: Prospects, issues and challenges. Journal of International Business Studies, 40(7), 1070-1074.

Cheng, G., Guo, D., Shi, J., & Qin, Y. (2019). Smart City-Wide Package Distribution Using Crowdsourced Public Transportation Systems. *IEEE Internet of Things Journal*, *6*(5), 7584–7594. doi:10.1109/JIOT.2019.2901116

Cheung, M. S., & Myers, M. B. (2008). Managing knowledge sharing networks in global supply chains. *International Journal of Management and Decision Making*, *9*(6), 581–599. doi:10.1504/IJMDM.2008.021216

Choudhury, P. (2021). Geographic Mobility, Immobility, and Geographic Flexibility–A Review and Agenda for Research on the Changing Geography of Work. *Academy of Management Annals*, (ja). https://journals.aom.org/doi/pdf/10.5465/annals.2020.0242?casa_token=BFsejbgQCzgAAAAA:BmKRU-N8Ep9uItdgqem0bN8eMj-bBZ1hTGvr0Wb01s4ChPoGAC1TWkPBH7Iuh_0OgCiq7Ku_doM

Chourabi, H., Nam, T., Walker, S., Gil-Garcia, J. R., Mellouli, S., Nahon, K., . . . Scholl, H. J. (2012). Understanding Smart Cities: An Integrative Framework. *2012 45th Hawaii International Conference on System Sciences.*

Christensen, C. H., Rocha, A., & Gertner, R. K. (1987). An Empirical Investigation of the Factors Influencing Exporting Success of Brazilian Firms. *Journal of International Business Studies*, *18*(3), 61–77. doi:10.1057/palgrave.jibs.8490412

Christmann, P., & Taylor, G. (2001). Globalization and the Environment: Determinants of Firm Self-Regulation in China. *Journal of International Business Studies*, *32*(3), 439–458. doi:10.1057/palgrave.jibs.8490976

Christopher, M., & Peck, H. (2004). Building the resilient supply chain. *International Journal of Logistics Management*, *15*(2), 1–13. doi:10.1108/09574090410700275

Chui, M., Edin, P., & Manyika, J. (2009). Time to Raise the CIO's Game. *McKinsey on Business Technology, 17*, (4-9).

Chung, C. C., & Jeng, T. (2018). *Information Extraction Methodology by Web Scraping for Smart Cities - Using Machine Learning to Train Air Quality Monitor for Smart Cities*. Academic Press.

Chung, W., & Alcácer, J. (2002). Knowledge seeking and location choice of foreign direct investment in the United States. *Management Science*, *48*(12), 1534–1554. doi:10.1287/mnsc.48.12.1534.440

Chu, Z., Cheng, M., & Yu, N. N. (2021). A smart city is a less polluted city. *Technological Forecasting and Social Change*, *172*, 121037. doi:10.1016/j.techfore.2021.121037

Coase, R. H. (1937). The nature of the firm. *Economica*, *4*(16), 386–405. doi:10.1111/j.1468-0335.1937.tb00002.x

Cohen, W. M. (2010). Fifty years of empirical studies of innovative activity and performance. Handbook of the Economics of Innovation, 1, 129-213. doi:10.10160169-7218(10)01004-x

Cohen, W. M., & Levinthal, D. A. (1990). Absorptive capacity: A new perspective on learning and innovation. *Administrative Science Quarterly*, *35*(1), 128–152. doi:10.2307/2393553

Collings, D. G., McMackin, J., Nyberg, A. J., & Wright, P. M. (2021). Strategic human resource management and COVID-19: Emerging challenges and research opportunities. *Journal of Management Studies*, *58*(5), 1378–1382. doi:10.1111/joms.12695

Collings, D. G., & Sheeran, R. (2020). Research insights: Global mobility in a post-covid world1. *Irish Journal of Management*, *39*(2), 77–84. doi:10.2478/ijm-2020-0002

Collis, D. J. (1994). Research Note: How Valuable Are Organizational Capabilities? *Strategic Management Journal, 15,* 143-152.

Collis, D. J., & Montgomery, C. A. (1999). Competing on Resources: Strategy in the 1990s. *Harvard Business Review*, 33–62. doi:10.1016/B978-0-7506-7088-3.50005-X

Colvile, R. N., Hutchinson, E. J., Mindell, J. S., & Warren, R. F. (2001). The transport sector is a source of air pollution. *Atmospheric Environment*, *35*(9), 1537–1565. doi:10.1016/S1352-2310(00)00551-3

Contractor, F. J. (2000). The raisons d'être for international management as a field of study. *Journal of International Management*, *6*(1), 3–10. doi:10.1016/S1075-4253(00)00017-X

Contractor, F. J. (2022). The world economy will need even more globalization in the post-pandemic 2021 decade. *Journal of International Business Studies*, *53*(1), 156–171. doi:10.105741267-020-00394-y PMID:33551513

Contractor, F. J., Kundu, S. K., & Hsu, C. C. (2003). A Three-Stage Theory of International Expansion: The Link between Multinationality and Performance in the Service Sector. *Journal of International Business Studies*, *34*(1), 5–18. doi:10.1057/palgrave.jibs.8400003

Coombs, W. T. (2010). Sustainability: a new and complex 'challenge' for crisis managers. *International Journal Sustainable Strategic Management*, *2*(1), 4-17.

Cooper, W. (2022). COVID-19 & Mental Health For Expats Research. *William Russell.* https://www.william-russell.com/blog/how-has-covid-affected-mental-health-awareness-for-expats-research/

Cooper, R. G., & Kleinschmidt, E. J. (1985). The Impact of Export Strategy on Export Sales Performance. *Journal of International Business Studies, 16*(1), 37–55. doi:10.1057/palgrave.jibs.8490441

Coquidé, C., Lages, J., Ermann, L., & Shepelyansky, D. L. (2022). COVID-19's impact on international trade. *Entropy (Basel, Switzerland), 24*(3), 327. doi:10.3390/e24030327 PMID:35327838

Cortina, J. (1993). What is coefficient alpha? An examination of theory and applications. *Journal of Applied Psychology, 78*(1), 98-104.

Cowley, R., & Caprotti, F. (2018). Smart city as anti-planning in the UK. *Environment and Planning. D, Society & Space, 37*(3), 428–448. doi:10.1177/0263775818787506

Cronbach, L. J. (1954). Coefficient Alpha and the Internal Structure of Tests. Psychometrik, 16(3).

Crutzen, W., & Steffen, P. J. (2003). How Long Have We Been in the Anthropocene Era? *Climatic Change, 61*(3), 251-257.

Cui, L., & Jiang, F. (2012). State ownership effect on firms' FDI ownership decisions under institutional pressure: A study of Chinese outward-investing firms. *Journal of International Business Studies, 43*(3), 264–284. doi:10.1057/jibs.2012.1

Cui, L., Meyer, K. E., & Hu, H. W. (2014). What drives firms' intent to seek strategic assets by foreign direct investment? A study of emerging economy firms. *Journal of World Business, 49*(4), 488–501. doi:10.1016/j.jwb.2013.12.003

Cui, X., Huang, X., Ma, Y., & Meng, Q. (2019). A Load Balancing Routing Mechanism Based on SDWSN in Smart City. *Electronics (Basel), 8*(3), 273. Advance online publication. doi:10.3390/electronics8030273

Cumberland, D. M., Herd, A., Alagaraja, M., & Kerrick, S. A. (2016). Assessment and development of global leadership competencies in the workplace: A review of literature. *Advances in Developing Human Resources, 18*(3), 301–317. doi:10.1177/1523422316645883

Curran, L., Eckhardt, J., & Lee, J. (2021). The trade policy response to COVID-19 and its implications for international business. *Critical Perspectives on International Business, 17*(2), 252–320. doi:10.1108/cpoib-05-2020-0041

Currie, G., & Stanley, J. (2008). Investigating Links between Social Capital and Public Transport. *Transport Reviews, 28*(4), 529–547. doi:10.1080/01441640701817197

Cutler, D. M., & Summers, L. H. (2020). The COVID-19 pandemic and the $16 trillion virus. *Journal of the American Medical Association, 324*(15), 1495–1496. doi:10.1001/jama.2020.19759 PMID:33044484

Dadaczynski, K., Okan, O., Messer, M., Leung, A. Y. M., Rosário, R., Darlington, E., & Rathmann, K. (2021). Digital Health Literacy and Web-Based Information-Seeking Behaviors of University Students in Germany During the COVID-19 Pandemic: Cross-sectional Survey Study. *Journal of Medical Internet Research, 23*(1), 1–17. doi:10.2196/24097 PMID:33395396

Dallas, M. P., Horner, R., & Li, L. (2021). The mutual constraints of states and global value chains during COVID-19: The case of personal protective equipment. *World Development, 139*, 105324. doi:10.1016/j.worlddev.2020.105324 PMID:33293754

Daniels, J. D. (1970). Recent Foreign Direct Manufacturing Investment in the United States. *Journal of International Business Studies, 1*(1), 125–132. doi:10.1057/palgrave.jibs.8490725

Daniels, J. D. (1991). Relevance in international business research: A need for more linkages. *Journal of International Business Studies*, *22*(2), 177–186. doi:10.1057/palgrave.jibs.8490298

Daniels, J. P., & von der Ruhr, M. (2005). God and the global economy: Religion and attitudes towards trade and immigration in the United States. *Socio-economic Review*, *3*(3), 467–489. doi:10.1093/SER/mwi020

Davidson, W. H. (1980). The location of foreign direct investment activity: Country characteristics and experience effects. *Journal of International Business Studies*, *11*(2), 9–22. doi:10.1057/palgrave.jibs.8490602

Davidson, W. H., & McFetridge, D. G. (1985). Key characteristics in the choice of international technology transfer mode. *Journal of International Business Studies*, *16*(2), 5–21. doi:10.1057/palgrave.jibs.8490448

Davies, N. M., Dickson, M., Smith, G. D., Van Den Berg, G. J., & Windmeijer, F. (2018). The causal effects of education on health outcomes in the UK Biobank. *Nature Human Behaviour*, *2*(2), 117–125. doi:10.103841562-017-0279-y PMID:30406209

Davis, I. (2009, March). The New Normal. *The McKinsey Quarterly*.

de Godoi, F. N., Denardin, G. W., Barriquello, C. H., & do Prado, R. N. (2018). Wireless sensor network quality of service optimization for smart cities. *2018 IEEE International Conference on Industrial Technology (ICIT)*. 10.1109/ICIT.2018.8352485

De Vos, J. (2020). The effect of COVID-19 and subsequent social distancing on travel behavior. *Transportation Research Interdisciplinary Perspectives*, *5*, 100121. doi:10.1016/j.trip.2020.100121 PMID:34171016

Delios, A., Perchtold, G., & Capri, A. (2021). Cohesion, COVID-19 and contemporary challenges to globalization. (2021). *Journal of World Business*, *56*(3), 101197. doi:10.1016/j.jwb.2021.101197

Deloitte. (2020). *Understanding the COVID-19 impact for Global Mobility*. Turning the dial towards recovery https://www2.deloitte.com/content/dam/Deloitte/uk/Documents/energy-resources/deloitte-uk-er-covid-19-global-mobility.pdf

Deng, P. (2008). Resources, capability, and outbound FDI from Chinese companies. *Globalization of Chinese Enterprises*, 17-30.

Devinney, T. M., & Hartwell, C. A. (2020). Varieties of populism. *Global Strategy Journal*, *10*(1), 32–66. doi:10.1002/gsj.1373

Dhanaraj, C., Lyles, M. A., Steensma, H. K., & Tihanyi, L. (2004). Managing Tacit and Explicit Knowledge Transfer in IJVs: The Role of Relational Embeddedness and the Impact on Performance. *Journal of International Business Studies*, *35*(5), 428–442. doi:10.1057/palgrave.jibs.8400098

Diagnostic and Statistical Manual of Mental Disorders (DSM-5-TR). (2022). Retrieved 01 May 2022. https://psychiatry.org/psychiatrists/practice/dsm

Dickmann, M., & Oleškevičiūtė, E. (August 2021). Do expatriates want this new normal? Covid, flexible work and embeddedness. *GLOMO*. https://www.relocatemagazine.com/articles/do-expatriates-want-this-new-normal-covid-flexible-work-and-embeddedness-healt
h-wellbeing-dickmann-olekeviit-0821

Dierickx, I., & Cool, K. (1989). Asset Stock Accumulation and Sustainability of Competitive Advantage. *Management Science*, *35*(12), 1504–1511. doi:10.1287/mnsc.35.12.1504

Djulius, H. (2017). Foreign Direct Investment and Technology Transfer: Knowledge Spillover in the Manufacturing Sector in Indonesia. *Global Business Review*, *18*(1), 57–70. doi:10.1177/0972150916666878

Dockery, M., & Bawa, S. (2020). Working from Home in the COVID-19 Lockdown. Bentley: Bankwest Curtin Economics Centre.

Dorfman, P., Javidan, M., Hanges, P., Dastmalchian, A., & House, R. (2012). GLOBE: A twenty year journey into the intriguing world of culture and leadership. *Journal of World Business*, *47*(4), 504–518. doi:10.1016/j.jwb.2012.01.004

Dörrenbacher, C., Sinkovics, R. R., Becker-Ritterspach, F., Boussebaa, M., Curran, L., de Jonge, A., & Khan, Z. (2021). The Covid-19 pandemic: Towards a societally engaged IB perspective. *Critical Perspectives on International Business*, *17*(2), 149–164. doi:10.1108/cpoib-02-2021-0021

Dow, D., & Karunaratna, A. (2006). Developing a multidimensional instrument to measure psychic distance stimuli. *Journal of International Business Studies*, *37*(5), 578–602. doi:10.1057/palgrave.jibs.8400221

Doyle, O., & Fidrmuc, J. (2006). Who favors enlargement?: Determinants of support for EU membership referenda. *European Journal of Political Economy*, *22*, 520–543. doi:10.1016/j.ejpoleco.2005.09.008

Drucker, P. (2000). Buluşçuluk Disiplini. [The Discipline of Inventiveness.] [Çığır Açıcı Düşünme,] [Çev. Ahmet Gürsel] [MESS Yayınları, İstanbul.]. *Harvard Business Review*, 143–158.

DSM history. (2022). Retrieved May 3, 2022, from: https://www.psychiatry.org/psychiatrists/practice/dsm/history-of-the-dsm#section_0

DSM. (2022). Retrieved on May 4, 2022, from: https://psychiatry.org/psychiatrists/practice/dsm

Duangsuwan, S., Takarn, A., & Jamjareegulgarn, P. (2018). A Development on Air Pollution Detection Sensors based on NB-IoT Network for Smart Cities. *2018 18th International Symposium on Communications and Information Technologies (ISCIT)*.

DuBois, F. L., & Reeb, D. (2000). Ranking the international business journals. *Journal of International Business Studies*, *31*(4), 689–704. doi:10.1057/palgrave.jibs.8490929

Dunning, J. H. (1980). Toward an ecletic Theory of International Production: Some Empirical Tests. *Journal of International Business Studies*, *11*(1), 9–31. doi:10.1057/palgrave.jibs.8490593

Dunning, J. H. (1982). Explaining the international direct investment position of countries: towards a dynamic or developmental approach. In *International Capital Movements* (pp. 84–121). Palgrave Macmillan. doi:10.1007/978-1-349-05989-8_4

Dunning, J. H. (1988). The Eclectic Paradigm of International Production: A Restatement and Some Possible Extensions. *Journal of International Business Studies*, *19*(1), 1–31. doi:10.1057/palgrave.jibs.8490372

Dunning, J. H. (1989). The study of international business: A plea for a more interdisciplinary approach. *Journal of International Business Studies*, *20*(3), 411–436. doi:10.1057/palgrave.jibs.8490371

Dunning, J. H. (1993). *Multinational Enterprises and the Global Economy*. Addison-Wesley.

Dunning, J. H. (1995). Reaprising the Eclectic Paradigm in an Age of Alliance Capitalism. *Journal of International Business Studies*, *26*(3), 461–491. doi:10.1057/palgrave.jibs.8490183

Dunning, J. H. (2001). The eclectic (OLI) paradigm of international production: Past, present and future. *International Journal of the Economics of Business*, *8*(2), 173–190. doi:10.1080/13571510110051441

Dunning, J. H., & Lundan, S. M. (2008). *Multinational enterprises and the global economy.* Edward Elgar Publishing.

Duong, T. V., Aringazina, A., Baisunova, G., Nurjanah, Pham, T. V., Pham, K. M., Truong, T. Q., Nguyen, K. T., Oo, W. M., Mohamad, E., Su, T. T., Huang, H.-L., Sørensen, K., Pelikan, J. M., Van den Broucke, S., & Chang, P. W. (2017). Measuring health literacy in Asia: Validation of the HLS-EU-Q47 survey tool in six Asian countries. *Journal of Epidemiology, 27*(2), 80–86. doi:10.1016/j.je.2016.09.005 PMID:28142016

Dyer, J. H., & Chu, W. (2000). The Determinants of Trust in Supplier-Automaker Relationships in the U.S., Japan, and Korea. *Journal of International Business Studies, 31*(2), 259–285. doi:10.1057/palgrave.jibs.8490905

Earley, P. C., & Ang, S. (2003). *Cultural intelligence: Individual interactions across cultures.*

Earley, P. C., & Peterson, R. S. (2004). The elusive cultural chameleon: Cultural intelligence as a new approach to intercultural training for the global manager. *Academy of Management Learning & Education, 3*(1), 100–115. doi:10.5465/amle.2004.12436826

Ebert, U., & Welsch, H. (2004). Meaningful environmental indices: A social choice approach. *Journal of Environmental Economics and Management, 47*(2), 270–283. doi:10.1016/j.jeem.2003.09.001

ECA. (2020). How Covid-19 has affected Global Mobility. Retrieved on October 4, 2021, from: https://www.forum-expat-management.com/posts/how-covid-19-has-affected-global-mobility

Echebarria, C., Barrutia, J. M., & Aguado-Moralejo, I. (2021). The Smart City journey: A systematic review and future research agenda. *Innovation (Abingdon), 34*(2), 159–201. doi:10.1080/13511610.2020.1785277

Egelhoff, W. G. (1984). Patterns of Control in U. S., UK, and European Multinational Corporations. *Journal of International Business Studies, 15*(2), 73–83. doi:10.1057/palgrave.jibs.8490866

Eichler, K., Wieser, S., & Brügger, U. (2009). The costs of limited health literacy: A systematic review. *International Journal of Public Health, 54*(5), 313–324. doi:10.100700038-009-0058-2 PMID:19644651

El-Erian, M. A. (2010). Sovereign Wealth Funds in the New Normal. *Finance & Development*, 44–48.

Emiroğlu, A. (2017). *Çekişmesiz Pazar Alanı Yaratmak: Mavi Okyanus Stratejisi ve Uygulama Örnekleri.* [*Creating a Non-Contentious Market Area: Blue Ocean Strategy and Implementation Examples.*] Uluslararası Yönetim İktisat ve İşletme Kongresi, Zonguldak, Türkiye.

Enderwick, P., & Buckley, P. J. (2020). Rising regionalization: will the post-COVID-19 world see a retreat from globalization? *Transnational Corporations Journal, 27*(2).

Enderwick, P. (2006). Managing the new global threats. *University of Auckland Business Review, 8*(2), 63–72.

Enderwick, P. (2011). A 'China-Plus-One' strategy: The best of both worlds? *Human Systems Management, 30*(1-2), 85–96. doi:10.3233/HSM-2011-0735

Enderwick, P. (2017). International investment by state-controlled enterprises: A source for concern? *Strategic Change, 26*(3), 261–271. doi:10.1002/jsc.2127

Enderwick, P. (2020). *The Competitive Challenge of Emerging Markets: China and India.* Cambridge Scholars Publishing.

Enderwick, P., & Buckley, P. J. (2020). Rising regionalization: Will the post-COVID-19 world see a retreat from globalization? *Transnational Corporations, 27*(2), 99–112. doi:10.18356/8008753a-en

Eriksson, K., Johanson, J., Majkgard, A., & Sharma, D. D. (1997). Experiential Knowledge and Cost in the Internationalization Process. *Journal of International Business Studies, 28*(2), 337–360. doi:10.1057/palgrave.jibs.8490104

Ershova, S. A., & Orlovskaya, T. N. (2020). Differentiation of Russian megalopolises by the level of urban environment quality and the standard needs of the population. *IOP Conference Series. Materials Science and Engineering, 962*(3), 032066. doi:10.1088/1757-899X/962/3/032066

European Parliament. (2014). *Mapping smart cities in the EU.* Retrieved 11/30/2021 from https://www.europarl.europa.eu/RegData/etudes/etudes/join/2014/507480/IPOL-ITRE_ET(2014)507480_EN.pdf

Eurostat. (2022a). *Health Main Tables.* Retrieved on January 31, 2022, from: https://ec.europa.eu/eurostat/web/health/data/main-tables

Eurostat. (2022b). *Glossary: Free on board (FOB).* Retrieved on January 29, 2022, from: https://ec.europa.eu/eurostat/statistics-explained/index.php?title=Category:International_trade_glossary

Evenett, S. J. (2020). Chinese whispers: COVID-19, global supply chains in essential goods and public policy. *Journal of International Business Policy, 3*(4), 408–429. doi:10.105742214-020-00075-5

EViews. (2022). *Innovative Solutions for econometric analysis, forecasting & simulation.* Retrieved on December 19, 2021, from: https://www.eviews.com/home.html

EY. (2020). Global board risk survey, EY. https://www.ey.com/en_us/news/2020/04/nearly-80-percent-of-board-members-felt-unprepared-for-a-major-risk-event-like-covid-19-ey-survey (April 20, 2020)

Fagre, N., & Wells, L. T. Jr. (1982). Bargaining power of multinationals and host governments. *Journal of International Business Studies, 13*(2), 9–23. doi:10.1057/palgrave.jibs.8490547

Faheem, M., Butt, R. A., Raza, B., Ashraf, M. W., Ngadi, M. A., & Gungor, V. C. (2019). Energy efficient and reliable data gathering using internet of software-defined mobile sinks for WSNs-based smart grid applications. *Computer Standards & Interfaces, 66*, 103341. doi:10.1016/j.csi.2019.03.009

Fajgelbaum, P. D., Goldberg, P. K., Kennedy, P. J., & Khandelwal, A. K. (2020). The return of protectionism. *The Quarterly Journal of Economics*, 1–55. https://doi. doi:10.1093/qje/qjz036

Fang, J., Collins, A., & Yao, S. (2021). On the global COVID-19 pandemic and China's FDI. *Journal of Asian Economics, 74*, 101300. doi:10.1016/j.asieco.2021.101300 PMID:35702564

Farrell, H., & Newman, A. L. (2020). *Chained to globalization*: Why it's too late to decouple. *Foreign Affairs, 99*, 70–80.

Farrer, J. (2010). New Shanghailanders or New Shanghainese? Narratives of emplacement of Western expatriate settlers in shanghai. *Journal of Ethnic and Migration Studies, 36*(8), 1211–1228. doi:10.1080/13691831003687675

Fechter, A. M., & Walsh, K. (2010). Examining 'expatriate' continuities: Postcolonial approaches to mobile professionals. *Journal of Ethnic and Migration Studies, 36*(8), 1197–1210. doi:10.1080/13691831003687667

Fee, A., McGrath-Champ, S., & Liu, H. (2013). Human resources and expatriate evacuation: A conceptual model. *Journal of Global Mobility, 1*(3), 246–263. doi:10.1108/JGM-01-2013-0007

Feldman, D. C., & Thomas, D. C. (1992). Career Management Issues Facing Expatriates. *Journal of International Business Studies, 23*(2), 271–293. doi:10.1057/palgrave.jibs.8490268

Fernandes, N. (2020). Economic effects of coronavirus outbreak (COVID-19) on the world economy. Retrieved on August 22, 2021, from: https://papers.ssrn.com/sol3/papers.cfm?abstract_id=3557504

Ferragina, A. M., & Mazzotta, F. (2014). FDI spillovers on firm survival in Italy: Absorptive capacity matters! *The Journal of Technology Transfer*, *39*(6), 859–897. doi:10.100710961-013-9321-z

Finaccord (2017). *Global Expatriates: Size, Segmentation and Forecast for the World-wide Market*. https://www.finaccord.com/Home/About-Us/Press-Releases/Global-Expatriates-Size,-Segmentation-and-Forecast

Firey, T. A. (2020). Government in a Pandemic Policy Analysis 902. CATO Institute.

Flämig, H., Lunkeit, S., Rosenberger, K., & Wolff, J. (2020). Enlarging the scale of BEVs through environmental zoning to reduce GHG emissions: A case study for the city of Hamburg. *Research in Transportation Business & Management*, *36*, 100418. doi:10.1016/j.rtbm.2019.100418

Fletcher, J. M. (2015). New evidence of the effects of education on health in the US: Compulsory schooling laws revisited. *Social Science & Medicine*, *127*, 101–107. doi:10.1016/j.socscimed.2014.09.052 PMID:25311783

Flowers, E. B. (1976). Oligopolistic Reactions in European and Canadian Direct Investment in the United States. *Journal of International Business Studies*, *7*(2), 43–55. doi:10.1057/palgrave.jibs.8490700

Fonseca, L., & Azevedo, A. (2020). COVID- 19: Outcomes for global supply chains. *Management and Marketing: Challenges for the Knowledge Society*, *15*(Special Issue), 424–438. doi:10.2478/mmcks-2020-0025

Fontaine, R. (2020, April 17). Globalization will look very different after the coronavirus pandemic. In: *Foreign policy*. Retrieved on June 2, 2021, from: https://foreignpolicy.com/2020/04/17/globalization-trade-war-after-coronavirus-pandemic/

Forsgren, M. (2017). *Theories of the multinational firm: A multidimensional creature in the global economy*. Edward Elgar Publishing.

Friedman, T. L. (2005, Apr. 3). It is a Flat World, After All. *NY Times Magazine*.

Fung, K. C., Iizaka, H., Lee, J., & Parker, S. (2002). Determinants of U.S. and Japanese Foreign Direct Investment in China. *Journal of Comparative Economics*, *30-3*(3), 567–578. doi:10.1006/jcec.2002.1788

Fu, Y., Alleyne, A., & Mu, Y. (2021). Does lockdown bring shutdown? Impact of the COVID-19 pandemic on foreign direct investment. *Emerging Markets Finance & Trade*, *57*(10), 2792–2811. doi:10.1080/1540496X.2020.1865150

Gabel, M. (1998). *Interests and Integration: Market Liberalization, Public Opinion, and the European Union*. University of Michigan Press. doi:10.3998/mpub.15828

Gang, D. (2021, June 2). Decoupling from China will see US globally detached. *Global Times*.

Gapar, V., Medas, P., & Perrelli, R. (2021). *IMFBlog: Global Economy/ Global Debt Reaches a Record $226 Trillion*. Retrieved on January 23, 2022, from: https://blogs.imf.org/2021/12/15/global-debt-reaches-a-record-226-trillion/#:~:text=Policymakers%20must%20strike%20the%2
0right,crisis%20and%20a%20deep%20recession

Garcia Alvarez, M., Morales, J., & Kraak, M.-J. (2019). Integration and Exploitation of Sensor Data in Smart Cities through Event-Driven Applications. *Sensors (Basel)*, *19*(6), 1372. Advance online publication. doi:10.339019061372 PMID:30893843

Garcia-Herrero, A. (2020, February 3) From globalization to deglobalization: Zooming into trade. *Bruegel Report*. https://www.bruegel.org/2020/02/from-globalization-to-deglobalization-zooming-into-trade

Garge, G. K., & Balakrishna, C. (2018). Unmanned Aerial Vehicles (UAVs) as on-demand QoS enabler for Multimedia Applications in Smart Cities. *2018 International Conference on Innovation and Intelligence for Informatics, Computing, and Technologies (3ICT).*

Garzon, S. R., & Louis, B. (2020). Context Flow Graphs: Situation Modeling for Rule-Based Proactive Context-Aware Systems. *IEEE Access: Practical Innovations, Open Solutions*, *8*, 212939–212960. doi:10.1109/ACCESS.2020.3040060

Gautam, V. S. D., Rustagi, N., Mittal, A., Patel, M., Shafi, S., Thirunavukkarasu, P., & Raghav, P. (2021). Health literacy, preventive COVID 19 behaviour and adherence to chronic disease treatment during lockdown among patients registered at primary health facility in urban Jodhpur, Rajasthan. *Diabetes & Metabolic Syndrome*, *15*(1), 205–211. doi:10.1016/j.dsx.2020.12.023 PMID:33387854

Gereffi, G. (2020). What does the COVID-19 pandemic teach us about global value chains? The case of medical supplies. *Journal of International Business Policy*, *3*(3), 287–301. doi:10.105742214-020-00062-w

Gereffi, G., Humphrey, J., & Sturgeon, T. (2005). The governance of global value chains. *Review of International Political Economy*, *12*(1), 78–104. doi:10.1080/09692290500049805

Geringer, J. M. (1991). Strategic Determinants of Partner Selection Criteria in International Joint Ventures. *Journal of International Business Studies*, *22*(1), 41–62. doi:10.1057/palgrave.jibs.8490291

Geuens, M. (2011). Where does business research go from here? Food-for-thought on academic papers in business research. *Journal of Business Research*, *64*(10), 1104–1107. doi:10.1016/j.jbusres.2010.11.005

Ghauri, P., Strange, R., & Cooke, F. L. (2021). Research on international business: The new realities. *International Business Review*, *30*(2), 101794. doi:10.1016/j.ibusrev.2021.101794

Ghoshal, S., & Bartlett, C. A. (1988). Creation, Adoption, and Diffusion of Innovations by Subsidiaries of Multinational Corporations. *Journal of International Business Studies*, *19*(3), 365–388. doi:10.1057/palgrave.jibs.8490388

Gibler, K. M., Casado-Díaz, J. M., Casado-Díaz, M. A., Rodríguez, V., & Taltavull, P. (2009). *Late life second move housing choices of international retiree migrants*. International Journal of Housing Markets and Analysis., doi:10.1108/17538270910963117

Gibson, R., & Singh, J. P. (2018). *China RX: Exposing the Risks of America's Dependence on China for Medicines*. Prometheus Books.

Giddy, I. H., & Dufey, G. (1975). The Random Behavior of Flexible Exchange Rates Implications for Forecasting. *Journal of International Business Studies*, *6*(1), 1–32. doi:10.1057/palgrave.jibs.8490765

Giffinger, R., Fertner, C., Kramar, H., Kalasek, R., Pichler-Milanovic, N., & Meijers, E. (2007). *Smart cities ranking of European medium-sized cities*. Retrieved on November 30, 2021, from: http://www.smart-cities.eu/download/smart_cities_final_report.pdf

Gilson, R. J., Sabel, C. F., & Scott, R. E. (2009). Contracting for innovation: Vertical disintegration and interfirm collaboration. *Columbia Law Journal*, *109*(3), 431–502.

Gohar, M., Muzammal, M., & Ur Rahman, A. (2018). SMART TSS: Defining transportation system behavior using big data analytics in smart cities. *Sustainable Cities and Society*, *41*, 114–119. doi:10.1016/j.scs.2018.05.008

Golgeci, I., Yildiz, H.E., & Andersson, U. (2020). The rising tensions between efficiency and resilience in global value chains in the post-COVID-19 world. *Transnational Corporations, 27*(2), 127-141.

Gong, Y., Putnam, E., You, W., & Zhao, C. (2020). Investigation into circular economy of plastics: The case of the UK fast moving consumer goods industry. *Journal of Cleaner Production, 244*, 118941. doi:10.1016/j.jclepro.2019.118941

Goodnow, J. D., & Hansz, J. E. (1972). Environmental Determinants of Overseas Market Entry Strategies. *Journal of International Business Studies, 3*(1), 33–50. doi:10.1057/palgrave.jibs.8490740

Gopinath, C., & Hoffman, R. C. (1995). The relevance of strategy research; practitioners and academic viewpoints. *Journal of Management Studies, 32*(5), 575–594. doi:10.1111/j.1467-6486.1995.tb00789.x

Grandin, J. M., & Hedderich, N. (2009). Global competence for engineers. The SAGE handbook of intercultural competence, 362-373. doi:10.4135/9781452218397.n16

Grant, R. M. (1987). Multinationality and Performance among British Manufacturing Companies. *Journal of International Business Studies, 18*(3), 79–89. doi:10.1057/palgrave.jibs.8490413

Green, R. T., & White, P. D. (1976). Methodological Considerations in Cross-National Consumer Research. *Journal of International Business Studies, 7*(2), 81–87. doi:10.1057/palgrave.jibs.8490703

Groh, A. P., & Wich, M. (2009). *A Composite Measure to Determine a Host Country's Attractivenessfor Foreign Direct Investement*. IESE Business School.

Grosse, R., Gamso, J., & Nelson, R. C. (2021). China's rise, world order, and the implications for international business. *Management International Review, 61*(1), 1–26. doi:10.100711575-020-00433-8 PMID:33679004

Grossman, G. M., & Helpman, E. (1993). *Innovation and growth in the global economy*. MIT press.

Groves, J. M., & O'Connor, P. (2018). Negotiating global citizenship, protecting privilege: Western expatriates choosing local schools in Hong Kong. *British Journal of Sociology of Education, 39*(3), 381–395. doi:10.1080/01425692.2017.1351866

Guillén, M. F., & García-Canal, E. (2009). The American model of the multinational firm and the "new" multinationals from emerging economies. *The Academy of Management Perspectives, 23*(2), 23–35. doi:10.5465/amp.2009.39985538

Gulati, R. (2007). Tent poles, tribalism, and boundary spanning: The rigor-relevance debate in management research. *Academy of Management Journal, 50*(4), 775–782. doi:10.5465/amj.2007.26279170

Gunasekeran, D. V., Tham, Y. C., Ting, D. S. W., Tan, G. S. W., & Wong, T. Y. (2021). Digital health during COVID-19: Lessons from operationalising new models of care in ophthalmology. *The Lancet Digital Health, 3*(2), e124–e134. doi:10.1016/S2589-7500(20)30287-9 PMID:33509383

Gupta, R., Bedi, M., Goyal, P., Wadhera, S., & Verma, V. (2020). Analysis of COVID-19 Tracking Tool in India. *Digital Government: Research and Practice, 1*(4), 1–8. doi:10.1145/3416088

Gürler, M., & Özsoy, Ö. (2019). Exploring the relationship between life expectancy at birth and economic growth in 56 developing countries. *Journal of Global Health Reports, 3*, e2019001. doi:10.29392/joghr.3.e2019001

Gürler, M., & Özsoy, Ö. (2020). Benchmarking the Devastating Effects of COVID-19 on Economies and Social Life in the EU and In Selected Countries Mostly Affected By the Pandemic. *Diversity and Equality in Health and Care, 17*(4), 136–145. doi:10.36648/2049-5471.17.4.204

Gürler, M., & Özsoy, Ö. (2021a). The Health System Infrastructure and Economic Effects of COVID-19 in OECD Countries, the Policy Responses of Nations and international Organizations against Pandemic. *Diversity and Equality in Health and Care, 18*(4), 258–275.

Gürler, M., & Özsoy, Ö. (2021b). Schooling Effect in Economic Growth: Benchmarking Turkey vs High Income Countries. *Acta Scientific Nutritional Health, 5*(2), 67–79. doi:10.31080/ASNH.2020.05.0812

Hahn, R. A., & Truman, B. I. (2015). Education improves public health and promotes health equity. *International Journal of Health Services, 45*(4), 657–678. doi:10.1177/0020731415585986 PMID:25995305

Hair, J., Anderson, R., Tatham, R., & Black, W. (1998). Multivariate Data Analysis. Academic Press.

Hampden-Turner, C., & Trompenaars, F. (2020). Riding the waves of culture: Understanding diversity in global business. Hachette UK.

Handfield, R. B., Graham, G., & Burns, L. (2020). Corona virus, tariffs, trade wars and supply chain evolutionary design. *International Journal of Operations & Production Management, 40*(10), 1649–1660. doi:10.1108/IJOPM-03-2020-0171

Hausmann, R., Hidalgo, C. A., Bustos, S., Coscia, M., Simoes, A., & Yildirim, M. A. (2014). *The atlas of economic complexity: Mapping paths to prosperity*. MIT Press. doi:10.7551/mitpress/9647.001.0001

Hava, H. T. (2020). An analysis of the effects of Covid-19 Outbreak on global supply chain and international trade. *Turkish Studies-Economics, Finance. Politics, 15*(4), 2083–2100.

Hayakawa, K., & Mukunoki, H. (2021). The impact of COVID-19 on international trade: Evidence from the first shock. *Journal of the Japanese and International Economies, 60*, 101135. doi:10.1016/j.jjie.2021.101135

Hejazi, S., Peyman, N., Tajfard, M., & Esmaily, H. (2017). The Impact of Education Based on Self-efficacy Theory on Health Literacy, Self-efficacy and Self-care Behaviors in Patients With Type 2 Diabetes. *Iranian Journal of Health Education and Health Promotion, 5*(4), 296–303. doi:10.30699/acadpub.ijhehp.5.4.296

Helpman, E., Melitz, M. J., & Yeaple, S. R. (2004). Export Versus FDI with Heterogeneous Firms. *The American Economic Review, 94*(1), 300–316. doi:10.1257/000282804322970814

Herjanto, H., Erickson, E., & Calleja, N. F. (2017). Antecedents of business travelers' satisfaction. *Journal of Hospitality Marketing & Management, 26*(3), 259–275. doi:10.1080/19368623.2017.1234954

Herrero, A. C. (2020). *From globalization to deglobalization: Zooming into trade*. Retrieved on November 11, 2021, from: https://www.bruegel.org/2020/02/from-globalization-to-deglobalization-zooming-into-trade/

Hertel, T., Hummels, D., & Walmsley, T. L. (2014). The vulnerability of the Asian supply chain to localised disasters. In B. Ferrarini & D. Hummels (Eds.), *Asia and Global Production Networks: Implications for Trade, Incomes and Economic Vulnerability* (pp. 81–111). Edward Elgar.

Hillebrand, E. E. (2010). Deglobalization scenarios: Who wins? who loses? *Global Economy Journal, 10*(2), 1850197. doi:10.2202/1524-5861.1611

History of the DSM. (2022). Retrieved May 2, 2022, from: https://www.psychdb.com/teaching/1-history-of-dsm

Hitt, M. A., Holmes, R. M. Jr, & Arregle, J. L. (2021). The (COVID-19) pandemic and the new world (dis) order. *Journal of World Business, 56*(4), 101210. doi:10.1016/j.jwb.2021.101210

Hitt, M. A., Javidan, M., & Steers, R. M. (2007). *The global mindset: An introduction*. Emerald Group Publishing Limited. doi:10.10161571-5027(07)19001-x

Hoch, J. E., Bommer, W. H., Dulebohn, J. H., & Wu, D. (2018). Do ethical, authentic, and servant leadership explain variance above and beyond transformational leadership? *Journal of Management*, *44*(2), 501–529. doi:10.1177/0149206316665461

Hofbauer, G. C., & Elliot, K. A. (1994). *Measuring the costs of protectionism in the United States*. Institute of International Economic.

Hoffman, P. N. (2000). An Examination of the "Sustainable Competitive Advantage Concept: Past, Present, and Future. *Academy of Marketing Science Review*, 4.

Hofmann, P. (2013). *The impact of international trade and FDI on economic growth and technological change*. Springer Science & Business Media. doi:10.1007/978-3-642-34581-4

Hofstede, G. (2006). What did GLOB really measure? Researchers' minds versus respondents' minds. *Journal of International Business Studies*, *37*(6), 882–896. doi:10.1057/palgrave.jibs.8400233

Holliday, C. (2001, September). Sustainable Growth, the DuPont. *Harvard Business Review*, •••, 129–136. PMID:11550629

Hong, P. C., Singh, N. P., Elangovan, N., & Yeon, G. (2022). Responding to pandemic challenges: Leadership lessons from multinational enterprises (MNEs) in India. *Journal of Management Development*, *41*(4), 205–222. doi:10.1108/JMD-11-2021-0309

Hora, H., Monteiro, G., & Arica, J. (2010). Confiabilidade em Questionários para Qualidade: Um Estudo com o Coeficiente Alfa de Cronbach. *Produto & Produção*, *11*(2), 85–103. doi:10.22456/1983-8026.9321

Horak, S., Farndale, E., Brannen, M. Y., & Collings, D. G. (2019). International human resource management in an era of political nationalism. *Thunderbird International Business Review*, *61*(3), 471–480. doi:10.1002/tie.21959

Horažďovský, P., & Kozhevnikov, S., & Svítek, M. (2019). Dynamic Public Transport in Smart City using Multi-agent system. *2019 Smart City Symposium Prague (SCSP)*. 10.1109/SCSP.2019.8805716

Huang, Y. (2021). *The U.S.-China Trade War Has Become a Cold War*. Retrieved on December 2, 2021, from: https://carnegieendowment.org/2021/09/16/u.s.-china-trade-war-has-become-cold-war-pub-85352

Huang, M.-H., Rust, R., & Maksimovic, V. (2019). The Feeling Economy: Managing in the Next Generation of Artificial Intelligence (AI). *California Management Review*, *61*(4), 43–65. doi:10.1177/0008125619863436

Huang, S., Yang, J., Fong, S., & Zhao, Q. (2021). Artificial intelligence in the diagnosis of COVID-19: Challenges and perspectives. *International Journal of Biological Sciences*, *17*(6), 1587. doi:10.7150/ijbs.58855 PMID:33907522

Huerta, J., & Salazar, P. (2018). Audit Process Framework for Data Protection and Privacy Compliance Using Artificial Intelligence and Cognitive Services in Smart Cities. *2018 IEEE International Smart Cities Conference (ISC2)*.

Hymer, S. H. (1960). The international operations of national firms: A study of direct foreign investment.

Iammarino, S., & McCann, P. (2006). The structure and evolution of industrial clusters: Transactions, technology and knowledge spillovers. *Research Policy*, *35*(7), 1018–1036. doi:10.1016/j.respol.2006.05.004

IBM-SPSS. (2022). *IBM SPSS Statistics*. Retrieved on January 30, 2022, from: https://www.ibm.com/products/spss-statistics

IFC (2020, June). *The Impact of COVID-19 on Logistics*. International Finance Corporation.

ILO. (2022a). *ILOSTAT data: Unemployment rate by sex and age -- ILO modelled estimates, Nov. 2021 (%)*. Retrieved on January 25, 2022, from: https://www.ilo.org/ilostat-files/WEB_bulk_download/indicator/UNE_2UNE_SEX_AGE_NB_A.csv.gz

ILO. (2022b). *ILOSTAT data: Working hours lost due to the COVID-19 crisis -- ILO modelled estimates (%).* Retrieved on January 25, 2022, from: https://www.ilo.org/shinyapps/bulkexplorer30/?lang=en&segment=indicator&id=HOW_2LSS_NOC_RT_A

ILO. (2022c). *ILOSTAT data: Labour force participation rate by sex and age -- ILO modelled estimates, Nov. 2021 (%).* Retrieved on January 25, 2022, from: https://www.ilo.org/shinyapps/bulkexplorer3/?lang=en&segment=indicator&id=EAP_2WAP_SEX_AGE_RT_A

IMF. (2012). World Economic Outlook. *Coping with High Debt and Sluggish Growth*, p. 151.

IMF. (2020). IMF annual report 2020: a crisis like no other. Washington DC, USA.

International Monetary Fund World Economic Outlook Database. (2016). Retrieved on December 22, 2021, from: https://www.imf.org/external/pubs/2016

International Trade Centre (ITC). (2022a). *COVID-19 Temporary Trade Measures.* Retrieved on January 25, 2022, from: https://www.macmap.org/covid19

International Trade Centre (ITC). (2022b). *TradeMap.* Retrieved on January 29, 2022, from: https://www.trademap.org/Country_SelProduct_TS.aspx?nvpm=1%7c%7c%7c%7c%7c%7cTOTAL%7c%7c%7c2%7c1%7c1%7c1%7c2%7c1%7c2%7c1%7c1%7c1

Irwin, D. A. (2005). *Free trade is under fire.* Princeton University Press.

Ivanov, D., & Dolgui, A. (2020). Viability of intertwined supply networks: Extending the supply chain resilience angles towards survivability. A position paper motivated by COVID-19 outbreak. *International Journal of Production Research, 58*(10), 2904–2915. doi:10.1080/00207543.2020.1750727

Iyengar, K., Upadhyaya, G. K., Vaishya, R., & Jain, V. (2020). COVID-19 and applications of smartphone technology in the current pandemic. *Diabetes & Metabolic Syndrome, 14*(5), 733–737. doi:10.1016/j.dsx.2020.05.033 PMID:32497963

Iyer, A. V., Seshandri, S., & Vasher, R. (2009). *Toyota Supply Chain Management: A Strategic Approach to Toyota's Renowned System.* McGraw Hill.

Jaeger, A. M. (1983). The Transfer of Organizational Culture Overseas: An Approach to Control in the Multinational Corporation. *Journal of International Business Studies, 14*(2), 91–114. doi:10.1057/palgrave.jibs.8490520

Jaju, K., & Thakkar, H. (2021). Impact of Artificial Intelligence and Internet of Things in Effective Handling of Coronavirus Crisis. In S. Mishra, P. K. Mallick, H. K. Tripathy, & G. M. Chae (Eds.), Impact of AI and Data Science in Response to Coronavirus Pandemic (pp. 235–251). Springer. doi:10.1007/978-981-16-2786-6_12

Jammal, H. M., Alqudah, N. M., & Khader, Y. (2020). Awareness, Perceptions, and Attitude Regarding Coronavirus Disease 2019 (COVID-19) Among Ophthalmologists in Jordan: Cross-Sectional Online Survey. *Clinical Ophthalmology (Auckland, N.Z.), 14*(1), 2202. doi:10.2147/OPTH.S260460 PMID:32801630

Javidan, M. (May 19, 2010) *Bringing the Global Mindset to Leadership* https://hbr.org/2010/05/bringing-the-global-mindset-to.html

Javidan, M. (2007). Forward-thinking cultures. *Harvard Business Review, 85*(7-8), 20.

Javidan, M. (2013). Comments on the interview: Competencies required for working across borders and managing multicultural teams. *Academy of Management Learning & Education, 12*(3), 506–508. doi:10.5465/amle.2012.0246b

Javidan, M., House, R. J., Dorfman, P. W., Hanges, P. J., & Luque, M. S. (2006). Conceptualizing and measuring cultures and their consequences: A comparative view of GLOBE's and Hofstede's approaches. *Journal of International Business Studies, 37*(6), 897–914. doi:10.1057/palgrave.jibs.8400234

Javidan, M., Teagarden, M., & Bowen, D. (2010). Making it overseas. *Harvard Business Review, 88*(4), 109–113.

Javorcik, B. (2020). Global supply chains will not be the same in the post-COVID-19 world. In R. Baldwin & S. J. Evenett (Eds.), *COVID-19 and Trade Policy: Why Turning Inward Won't Work* (pp. 111–117). CEPR Press.

Jenkins, J. (2019). *Is living abroad the key to developing a global mindset and skillset?* If so-is there a 'golden age' at which to do so? [Unpublished master's thesis, Birkbeck, University of London, England].

Jenkins, J. (2020, September 21) The Future of Global Work. *People Matters Global.* https://www.peoplematters.in/article/life-at-work/the-future-of-global-work-27026

Jesuthasan, R., Malcolm, T., & Cantrel, S. (2020). How the Coronavirus Crisis Is Redefining Jobs. *Harvard Business Review, 2020*(4). https://hbr.org/2020/04/how-the-coronavirus-crisis-is-redefining-jobs

Jhunjhunwala, A. (2020). Role of Telecom Network to Manage COVID-19 in India: Aarogya Setu. *Transactions of the Indian National Academy of Engineering, 5*(2), 157–161. doi:10.1007/S41403-020-00109-7

Johanson, J., & Vahlne, J. E. (2002). The internationalization process of the firm. *International Business: Theory of the multinational enterprise, 1*(1), 47.

Johanson, J., & Vahlne, J.E. (1977). The Internationalization Process of the Firm-A Model of Knowledge Development and Increasing Foreign Market Commitments. *Journal of International Business Studies, 8*(1).23-32.

Johanson, J., & Vahlne, J. E. (1977). The internationalization process of the firm—A model of knowledge development and increasing foreign market commitments. *Journal of International Business Studies, 8*(1), 23–32. doi:10.1057/palgrave.jibs.8490676

Johanson, J., & Vahlne, J. E. (2009). The Uppsala internationalization process model revisited: From liability of foreignness to liability of outsidership. *Journal of International Business Studies, 40*(9), 1411–1431. doi:10.1057/jibs.2009.24

Johnson, A. (2006). The Effects of FDI Inflows on Host Country Economic Growth. *CESIS Working Paper Series in Economics and Institutions of Innovation, 58*, 1-57.

Johnston, A., Hochachka, W. M., Strimas-Mackey, M. E., Ruiz Gutierrez, V., Robinson, O. J., Miller, E. T., . . . Fink, D. (2021). Analytical guidelines to increase the value of community science data: An example using eBird data to estimate species distributions. *Diversity and Distributions, 27*(7), 1265-1277.

Johnston, D. W., Lordan, G., Shields, M. A., & Suziedelyte, A. (2015). Education and health knowledge: Evidence from UK compulsory schooling reform. *Social Science & Medicine, 127*, 92–100. doi:10.1016/j.socscimed.2014.10.026 PMID:25459203

Jones, M. V., & Coviello, N. E. (2005). Internationalisation: Conceptualising an Entrepreneurial Process of Behaviour in Time. *Journal of International Business Studies, 36*(3), 284–303. doi:10.1057/palgrave.jibs.8400138

Jordaan, J. A. (2012). Foreign Direct Investment and Technology Transfers to Local Suppliers: Identifying the effects of type of ownership and the technology gap.

Kadaster, P. (2017). The Founder: Patates Kızartmasından Franchise Restoranlara Uzanan Dönüşüm. *Harvard Business Review*.

Kadlec, R., Knight, R., Vymazal, J., Brix, H., Cooper, P., & Haberl, R. (2000). *Constructed wetlands for pollution control: processes, performance, design and operation*. IWA Publishing.

Kaiser, H. (1958). The varimax criterion for analytic rotation in factor analysis. *Psychometrika*, *23*(3), 187–200. doi:10.1007/BF02289233

Kano, L. (2018). Global value chain governance: A relational perspective. *Journal of International Business Studies*, *49*(6), 684–705. doi:10.105741267-017-0086-8

Karunaratne, N. D. (2012). The globalization-deglobalization policy conundrum. *Modern Economy*, *3*, 373-383. https:// doi. doi:10.4236/me.2012.34048

Keller, W. (2010). International trade, foreign direct investment, and technology spillovers. Handbook of the Economics of Innovation, 2, 793-829.

Keller, W. (2004). International technology diffusion. *Journal of Economic Literature*, *42*(3), 752–782. doi:10.1257/0022051042177685

Kelley, L., Whatley, A., & Worthley, R. (1987). Assessing the Effects of Culture on Managerial Attitudes: A Three-Culture Test. *Journal of International Business Studies*, *18*(2), 17–31. doi:10.1057/palgrave.jibs.8490404

Kennedy, S., & Tan, S. (2020, June 10). *Decoupling between Washington and Western industry*. Center for Strategic and International Studies.

Kersan-Škabić, I. (2021). The COVID-19 pandemic and the internationalization of production: A review of the literature. *Development Policy Review*, *40*(2), 12560. PMID:34219988

Khanna, A., Goyal, R., Verma, M., & Joshi, D. (2019). Intelligent Traffic Management System for Smart Cities. Futuristic Trends in Network and Communication Technologies, Singapore.

Khansari, N., Mostashari, A., & Mansouri, M. (2014). Impacting Sustainable Behavior and Planning in Smart City. *International Journal of Sustainable Built Environment, 1*.

Khatibi, H., Wilkinson, S., Baghersad, M., Dianat, H., Ramli, H., Suhatril, M., Javanmardi, A., & Ghaedi, K. (2021). The resilient – smart city development: A literature review and novel frameworks exploration. *Built Environment Project and Asset Management*, *11*(4), 493–510. doi:10.1108/BEPAM-03-2020-0049

Kim, W. C., & Mauborgne, R. (2005). Mavi Okyanus Stratejisi, 9. Baskı. [Blue Ocean Strategy, 9. Printing.] CSA Global Publishing.

Kim, H. (2013). Regionalism, globalization, and economic development of the world. *Journal of Globalization Studies*, *4*(2), 21–31.

Kim, H., Li, P., & Lee, Y. R. (2020). Observations of deglobalization against globalization and impacts on global business. *International Trade, Politics and Development*, *4*(2), 83–103.

Kim, W. C., & Hwang, P. (1992). Global strategy and multinationals' entry mode choice. *Journal of International Business Studies*, *23*(1), 29–53. doi:10.1057/palgrave.jibs.8490258

Kim, Y. J. (2016). The long-run effect of education on obesity in the US. *Economics and Human Biology*, *21*, 100–109. doi:10.1016/j.ehb.2015.12.003 PMID:26828291

King, N. (2004). *Using Templates in the Thematic Analysis of Text*. Essential guide to qualitative methods in organizational research, 256. doi:10.4135/9781446280119.n21

Kirkman, B. L., Lowe, K. B., & Gibson, C. B. (2006). A quarter century of culture's consequences: A review of empirical research incorporating Hofstede's cultural values framework. *Journal of International Business Studies*, *37*(3), 285–320. doi:10.1057/palgrave.jibs.8400202

Kıyan, Ş. S., & Özer, A. (2011). İşletme Sınırlarının Girişimci Faaliyetle Yeniden Yapılandırılması: Yeni Pazar Oluşturma. [Restructuring Business Boundaries Through Entrepreneurial Activity: Creating a New Market.]. *Ankara Üniversitesi SBF Dergisi*, *66*(2), 93–120. doi:10.1501/SBFder_0000002205

Klein, L. K. (2009). Measurement of Shift in the World's Canter of Economic Gravity. *Journal of Policy Modelling*, *31*(4), 489-492. https://doi. doi:10.1016/j.jpolmod.2009.05.005

Knight, F. H. (1921). *Risk, Uncertainty and Profit*. University of Chicago Press.

Knight, G., & Cavusgil, S. (2004). Innovation, Organizational Capabilities, and the Born-Global Firm. *Journal of International Business Studies*, *35*(2), 124–141. doi:10.1057/palgrave.jibs.8400071

Knoerich, J. (2017). How does outward foreign direct investment contribute to economic development in less advanced home countries? *Oxford Development Studies*, *45*(4), 443–459. doi:10.1080/13600818.2017.1283009

Kobrin, S. J. (1976). The Environmental Determinants of Foreign Direct Manufacturing Investment: An Ex-Post Empirical Analysis. *Journal of International Business Studies*, *7*(2), 29–42. doi:10.1057/palgrave.jibs.8490699

Kobrin, S. J. (1979). Political Risk: A Review and Reconsideration. *Journal of International Business Studies*, *10*(1), 67–80. doi:10.1057/palgrave.jibs.8490631

Kodali, P. B., Hense, S., Kopparty, S., Kalapala, G. R., & Haloi, B. (2020). How Indians responded to the Arogya Setu app? *Indian Journal of Public Health*, *64*(6), S228–S230. doi:10.4103/ijph.IJPH_499_20 PMID:32496261

Kogut, B. (1988). Joint Ventures: Theoretical and Empirical Perspectives. *Strategic Management Journal*, *9*(4), 319–332. doi:10.1002mj.4250090403

Kogut, B., & Singh, H. (1988). The Effect of National Culture on the Choice of Entry Mode. *Journal of International Business Studies*, *19*(3), 411–432. doi:10.1057/palgrave.jibs.8490394

Kogut, B., & Zander, U. (1992). Knowledge of the firm, combinative capabilities, and the replication of technology. *Organization Science*, *3*(3), 383–397. doi:10.1287/orsc.3.3.383

Kogut, B., & Zander, U. (1993). Knowledge of the Firm and the Evolutionary Theory of the Multinational Corporation. *Journal of International Business Studies*, *24*(4), 625–645. doi:10.1057/palgrave.jibs.8490248

Komninos, N., Kakderi, C., Panori, A., & Tsarchopoulos, P. (2019). Smart City Planning from an Evolutionary Perspective. *Journal of Urban Technology*, *26*(2), 3–20. doi:10.1080/10630732.2018.1485368

Kramers, A., Höjer, M., Lövehagen, N., & Wangel, J. (2014). Smart sustainable cities – Exploring ICT solutions for reduced energy use in cities. *Environmental Modelling & Software*, *56*, 52–62. doi:10.1016/j.envsoft.2013.12.019

Kropp, B. (2021). Trends that will shape work in 2021 and beyond. *Harvard Business Review*. https://hbr. org/2021/01/9-trends-that-will-shape-work-in-2021-and-beyond. https://hbr.org/2021/01/9-trends-that-will-shape-work-in-2021-and-beyond

Krugman, P. R. (1979). Increasing returns, monopolistic competition, and international trade. *Journal of International Economics*, *9*(4), 469–479. doi:10.1016/0022-1996(79)90017-5

Kuemmerle, W. (1999). The Drivers of Foreign Direct Investment into Research and Development: An Empirical Investigation. *Journal of International Business Studies*, *30*(1), 1–24. doi:10.1057/palgrave.jibs.8490058

Kumar, H., Singh, M. K., & Gupta, M. P. (2018). Smart mobility: Crowdsourcing solutions for smart transport system in smart cities context. *Proceedings of the 11th International Conference on Theory and Practice of Electronic Governance*. 10.1145/3209415.3209417

Kumari, M., & Bharti, N. (2021). Estimating the impact of COVID-19 on South Asia's exports: Does trade facilitation matter now more than ever? *Transnational Corporations Review*, *13*(4), 406–421. doi:10.1080/19186444.2021.1911280

Kumar, R., & Veer, K. (2021). How artificial intelligence and internet of things can aid in the distribution of COVID-19 vaccines. *Diabetes & Metabolic Syndrome*, *15*(3), 1050. doi:10.1016/j.dsx.2021.04.021 PMID:33941496

Kundu, S., Al Banna, M. H., Sayeed, A., Akter, S., Aktar, A., Islam, M. A., Proshad, R., & Khan, M. S. I. (2021). *Effect of vendors' socio-demography and other factors on hygienic practices of street food shops.* doi:10.1080/15378020.2020.1870785

Lai, C., Boi, F., Buschettu, A., & Caboni, R. (2019). SmartMobility, an Application for Multiple Integrated Transportation Services in a Smart City. *Proceedings of the 15th International Conference on Web Information Systems and Technologies*. 10.5220/0008066600002366

Lall, S., & Narula, R. (2004). Foreign direct investment and its role in economic development: Do we need a new agenda? *European Journal of Development Research*, *16*(3), 447–464. doi:10.1080/0957881042000266589

Land, K. C., Michalos, A. C., & Sirgy, M. J. (2012). *Handbook of Social Indicators and Quality-Of-Life Research.* Springer. doi:10.1007/978-94-007-2421-1

Lange, K., & Knieling, J. (2020). EU Smart City Lighthouse Projects between Top-Down Strategies and Local Legitimation: The Case of Hamburg. *Urban Plan*, *5*(1), 107–115. doi:10.17645/up.v5i1.2531

Langlois, C. C., & Schlegelmilch, B. B. (1990). Do Corporate Codes of Ethics Reflect National Character? Evidence from Europe and the United States. *Journal of International Business Studies*, *21*(4), 519–539. doi:10.1057/palgrave.jibs.8490340

Leblang, D., & Peters, M. E. (2022). Immigration and Globalization (and Deglobalization). *Annual Review of Political Science*, *25*(1), 377–399. doi:10.1146/annurev-polisci-051120-105059

Lecraw, D. J. (1984). Bargaining Power, Ownership, and Profitability of Transnational Corporations in Developing Countries. *Journal of International Business Studies*, *15*(1), 27–43. doi:10.1057/palgrave.jibs.8490469

Lee, K.-H., & Wu, Y. (2014). Integrating sustainability performance measurement into logistics and supply networks: A multi-methodological approach. *The British Accounting Review*, *46*(4), 361–378. doi:10.1016/j.bar.2014.10.005

Leonard, P. (2010). Work, identity and change? Post/colonial encounters in Hong Kong. *Journal of Ethnic and Migration Studies*, *36*(8), 1247–1263. doi:10.1080/13691831003687691

Levin-Zamir, D., Baron-Epel, O. B., Cohen, V., & Elhayany, A. (2016). The Association of Health Literacy with Health Behavior, Socioeconomic Indicators, and Self-Assessed Health From a National Adult Survey in Israel. *Journal of Health Communication*, *21*(sup2), 61–68. doi:10.1080/10810730.2016.1207115 PMID:27669363

Levy, O., Beechler, S., Taylor, S., & Boyacigiller, N. A. (2007). What we talk about when we talk about 'global mindset': Managerial cognition in multinational corporations. *Journal of International Business Studies, 38*(2), 231–258. doi:10.1057/palgrave.jibs.8400265

Levy, O., Lee, H. J., Jonsen, K., & Peiperl, M. A. (2019). Transcultural brokerage: The role of cosmopolitans in bridging structural and cultural holes. *Journal of Management, 45*(2), 417–450. doi:10.1177/0149206318773404

Lewin, A. Y. (2004). Letter from the Editor. *Journal of International Business Studies, 35*(1), 79–80. doi:10.1057/palgrave.jibs.8400079

Lewin, A. Y., Massini, S., & Peeters, C. (2009). Why are companies offshoring innovation? The emerging global race for talent. *Journal of International Business Studies, 40*(6), 901–925. doi:10.1057/jibs.2008.92

Li, C., Liu, X., Dai, Z., & Zhao, Z. (2019). Smart City: A Shareable Framework and Its Applications in China. *Sustainability, 11*(16), 4346. Advance online publication. doi:10.3390u11164346

Liesch, P. W., Buckley, P. J., Simonin, B. L., & Knight, G. (2012). Organizing the modern firm in the worldwide market for market transactions. *Management International Review, 52*(1), 3–21. doi:10.100711575-011-0096-x

Liu, F., & Chan-Olmsted, S. M. (2002). Partnerships Between the Old and the New: Examining the Strategic Alliances Between Broadcast Television Networks and Internet Firms in the Context of Convergence. *The International Journal on Media Management, 5*(1), 47–56. doi:10.1080/14241270309390018

Liu, P., & Peng, Z. (2014). China's Smart City Pilots: A Progress Report. *Computer, 47*(10), 72–81. doi:10.1109/MC.2013.149

Liu, Y., Cao, L., Li, X., Jia, Y., & Xia, H. (2020). Awareness of mental health problems in patients with coronavirus disease 19 (COVID-19): A lesson from an adult man attempting suicide. *Asian Journal of Psychiatry, 51*, 1–3. doi:10.1016/j.ajp.2020.102106 PMID:32334411

Liu, Z. (2008). Foreign direct investment and technology spillovers: Theory and evidence. *Journal of Development Economics, 85*(1-2), 176–193. doi:10.1016/j.jdeveco.2006.07.001

Livermore, D. (2011). The cultural intelligence difference-special eBook edition: Master the one skill you can't do without in today's global economy. *Amacom.*

Li, X., Chang, J., Chen, S., Wang, L., Yau, T. O., Zhao, Q., Hong, Z., Ruan, J., Duan, G., & Gao, S. (2021). Genomic Feature Analysis of Betacoronavirus Provides Insights Into SARS and COVID-19 Pandemics. *Frontiers in Microbiology, 12*, 1–10. doi:10.3389/fmicb.2021.614494 PMID:33815307

Loh, H. C., Looi, I., Ch'ng, A. S. H., Goh, K. W., Ming, L. C., & Ang, K. H. (2021). Positive global environmental impacts of the COVID-19 pandemic lockdown: A review. *GeoJournal*, 1–13. doi:10.1007/S10708-021-10475-6 PMID:34316088

Lombardi, P., Giordano, S., Farouh, H., & Yousef, W. (2012). Modelling the smart city performance. *Innovation (Abingdon), 25*(2), 137–149. doi:10.1080/13511610.2012.660325

Longley, R. (2018). *Understanding the pros and cons of protectionism*. https://www.thoughtco.com/protectionism-definition-and-examples-4571027?print

Lorenzen, M., Mudambi, R., & Schotter, A. (2020). International connectedness and local disconnectedness: MNE strategy, city-regions and disruption. *Journal of International Business Studies, 51*(8), 1199–1222. doi:10.105741267-020-00339-5 PMID:32836501

Lu, J. W. (2003). The evolving contributions in international strategic management research. *Journal of International Management, 9*(2), 193–213. doi:10.1016/S1075-4253(03)00006-1

Luo, Y., & Tung, R. L. (2007). International expansion of emerging market enterprises: A springboard perspective.

Luo, Y. (2021). Illustrations of techno-nationalism. *Journal of International Business Studies.* doi:10.105741267-021-00468-5 PMID:34511654

Luo, Y., & Peng, M. W. (1999). Learning to Compete in a Transition Economy: Experience, Environment, and Performance. *Journal of International Business Studies, 30*(2), 269–295. doi:10.1057/palgrave.jibs.8490070

Luo, Y., & Tung, R. L. (2007). International expansion of emerging market enterprises: A springboard perspective. *Journal of International Business Studies, 38*(4), 481–498. doi:10.1057/palgrave.jibs.8400275

Lutz, W., & Kebede, E. (2018). Education and Health: Redrawing the Preston Curve. *Population and Development Review, 44*(2), 361. doi:10.1111/padr.12141 PMID:29937609

Luvisi, A., & Lorenzini, G. (2014). RFID-plants in the smart city: Applications and outlook for urban green management. *Urban Forestry & Urban Greening, 13*(4), 630–637. doi:10.1016/j.ufug.2014.07.003

Lyles, M. A., & Salk, J. E. (1996). Knowledge Acquisition from Foreign Parents in International Joint Ventures: An Empirical Examination in the Hungarian Context. *Journal of International Business Studies, 27*(5), 877–903. doi:10.1057/palgrave.jibs.8490155

Lynch, D. J. (2021, November 15). As supply lines strain, some corporations rewrite production playbook. *The Washington Post.*

Lynch, S. M., & Brown, J. S. (2011). Stratification and Inequality Over the Life Course. Handbook of Aging and the Social Sciences, 105–117. doi:10.1016/B978-0-12-380880-6.00008-3

Maddux, W. W., & Galinsky, A. D. (2009). Cultural borders and mental barriers: The relationship between living abroad and creativity. *Journal of Personality and Social Psychology, 96*(5), 1047–1061. doi:10.1037/a0014861 PMID:19379035

Madhok, A. (1995). Revisiting Multinational Firms' Tolerance for Joint Ventures: A Trust-Based Approach. *Journal of International Business Studies, 26*(1), 117–137. doi:10.1057/palgrave.jibs.8490168

Mahasuar, K. (2021). Lies, damned lies, and statistics: The uncertainty over COVID-19 numbers in India. *Knowledge and Process Management.* Advance online publication. doi:10.1002/kpm.1685

Maignan, I., & Ralston, D. A. (2002). Corporate Social Responsibility in Europe and the U.S.: Insights from Businesses' Self- Presentations. *Journal of International Business Studies, 33*(3), 497–514. doi:10.1057/palgrave.jibs.8491028

Majhi, S., Verma, M., Chauhan, I., Kumari, R., & Sharma, M. (2021). A field survey after covid-19 immunization programme at Ghaziabad, India: Highlighting adverse events. *Journal of Applied Pharmaceutical Sciences and Research, 4*(2), 10–14. doi:10.31069/japsr.v4i2.3

Makki, S., & Somwaru, A. (2004). Impact of Foreign Direct Investment and Trade on Economic Growth. *American Journal of Agricultural Economics, 86*(3), 795–801. doi:10.1111/j.0002-9092.2004.00627.x

Malik, M. N., Azam, M. A., Ehatisham-Ul-Haq, M., Ejaz, W., & Khalid, A. (2019). ADLAuth: Passive Authentication Based on Activity of Daily Living Using Heterogeneous Sensing in Smart Cities. *Sensors (Basel), 19*(11), 2466. Advance online publication. doi:10.339019112466 PMID:31146477

Mani, S. (2013). Outward foreign direct investment from India and knowledge flows, the case of three automotive firms. *Asian Journal of Technology Innovation, 21*(sup1), 25-38.

Maqableh, M., & Alia, M. (2021). Evaluation online learning of undergraduate students under lockdown amidst COVID-19 Pandemic: The online learning experience and students' satisfaction. *Children and Youth Services Review*, *128*, 1–11. doi:10.1016/j.childyouth.2021.106160

Mariani, P. (2021). The EU market in times of a global state of emergency: Internal and external trade barriers in the age of pandemics. *Legal Issues of Economic Integration*, *48*(1), 5–18. doi:10.54648/LEIE2021002

Marinov, T. T., & Marinova, R. S. (2020). Dynamics of COVID-19 using inverse problem for coefficient identification in SIR epidemic models. Chaos. *Solitons & Fractals: X*, *5*, 100041. doi:10.1016/j.csfx.2020.100041

Marjanović, D., & Domazet, I. S. (2021). Foreign Direct Investments: A Key Factor for Business Globalization. In *Handbook of Research on Institutional, Economic, and Social Impacts of Globalization and Liberalization* (pp. 96–116). IGI Global. doi:10.4018/978-1-7998-4459-4.ch006

Maroco, J., & Garcia-Marques, T. (2006). *Qual a fiabilidade do alfa de Cronbach? Questões antigas e soluções modernas?* (Vol. 4-1). ISPA Laboratório de Psicologia.

Martinez, J. I., & Jarillo, J. C. (1989). The Evolution of Research on Coordination Mechanisms in Multinational Corporations. *Journal of International Business Studies*, *20*(3), 489–514. doi:10.1057/palgrave.jibs.8490370

Martínez, Z. L., & Toyne, B. (2000). What is international management, and what is its domain? *Journal of International Management*, *6*(1), 11–28. doi:10.1016/S1075-4253(00)00018-1

Mason, E. S. (1939). Price and Production Policies of Large-Scale Enterprise. Papers and Proceedings of the Fifty-first Annual Meeting of the American Economic Association. *The American Economic Review*, *29*(1), Supplement,, 61-74.

Masoudiyekta, L., Rezaei-Bayatiyani, H., Dashtbozorgi, B., Gheibizadeh, M., Malehi, A., & Moradi, M. (2018). Effect of education based on health belief model on the behavior of breast cancer screening in women. *Asia-Pacific Journal of Oncology Nursing*, *5*(1), 114–120. doi:10.4103/apjon.apjon_36_17 PMID:29379843

Mata, F. J., Fuerst, W. L., & Barney, J. B. (1995). Information Technology and Sustained Competitive Advantage: A Resource-Based Analysis. *Management Information Systems Quarterly*, *19*(4), 487–505. doi:10.2307/249630

Ma, X., Tong, T. W., & Fitza, M. (2013). How much does subnational region matter to foreign subsidiary performance? Evidence from Fortune Global 500 Corporations' investment in China. *Journal of International Business Studies*, *44*(1), 66–87. doi:10.1057/jibs.2012.32

McDonald, J. (2022). *China's Trade Surplus Hit Record in 2021—With Exports Jumping 30% Amid Pandemic Demand.* Retrieved on January 23, 2022, from: https://time.com/6139334/china-record-trade-surplus-2021/

McNally, C. A. (2012). Sino-capitalism: China's re-emergence and the international political economy. *World Politics*, *64*(4), 741–776. doi:10.1017/S0043887112000202

McNulty, Y. (2014). *Women as female breadwinners in non-traditional expatriate families*: Status-reversal marriages, single parents, split families, and lesbian partnerships. In *Research Handbook on Women in International Management.* Edward Elgar Publishing. doi:10.4337/9781781955031.00025

McNulty, Y., & Selmer, J. (Eds.). (2017). *Research handbook of expatriates.* Edward Elgar Publishing. doi:10.4337/9781784718183

McWilliam, S. E., Kim, J. K., Mudambi, R., & Nielsen, B. B. (2020). Global value chain governance: Intersections with international business. *Journal of World Business*, *55*(4), 101067. doi:10.1016/j.jwb.2019.101067

Mehreen, H., Rammal, H. G., Pereira, V., & Del Giudice, M. (2021). Investigating the influence of absorptive capacity of recipients within cross-border transfer of knowledge: Evidence from emerging markets. *International Marketing Review*.

Meier, O. (2021) *Managing international employees working from anywhere, part 1: Redefining mobility.*

Meier, O., & Traber, Y. (2021). The impact of the COVID-19 crisis on talent mobility. *Mercer.* https://www.mercer.com/events/webcasts/the-impact-of-the-covid-19-crisis-on-talent-mobility-cost-of-living-survey.html

Melgar, N., Milgram-Baleix, J., & Rossi, M. (2013). *Explaining protectionism support: The role of economic factors.* Hindawi Publishing Corporation. . doi:10.1155/2013/954071

Mello, S. F., & Tomei, P. A. (2021). The impact of the COVID-19 pandemic on expatriates: A pathway to work-life harmony? *Global Business and Organizational Excellence*, *40*(5), 6–22. doi:10.1002/joe.22088

Mena, C., Karatzas, A., & Hansen, C. (2022). International trade resilience and the Covid-19 pandemic. *Journal of Business Research*, *138*, 77–91. doi:10.1016/j.jbusres.2021.08.064 PMID:34538982

Mensch, B. S., Chuang, E. K., Melnikas, A. J., & Psaki, S. R. (2019). Evidence for causal links between education and maternal and child health: Systematic review. *Tropical Medicine & International Health*, *24*(5), 504–522. doi:10.1111/tmi.13218 PMID:30767343

Merz, M., Hiete, M., Comes, T., & Schultmann, F. (2013). A composite indicator model to assess natural disaster risks in industry on a spatial level. *Journal of Risk Research*, *16*(9), 1077–1099. doi:10.1080/13669877.2012.737820

Meyer, K. E. (2004). Perspectives on Multinational Enterprises in Emerging Economies. *Journal of International Business Studies*, *35*(4), 259–276. doi:10.1057/palgrave.jibs.8400084

Meyer, K. E., & Peng, M. W. (2016). Theoretical foundations of emerging economy business research. *Journal of International Business Studies*, *47*(1), 3–22. doi:10.1057/jibs.2015.34

Meyer, K. E., & Sinani, E. (2009). When and where does foreign direct investment generate positive spillovers? A meta-analysis. *Journal of International Business Studies*, *40*(7), 1075–1094. doi:10.1057/jibs.2008.111

MGI. (2019). *The Future of Asia*. McKinsey Global Institute.

MGI. (2020). *Risk, Resilience and Rebalancing in Global Value Chains*. McKinsey Global Institute.

Mheidly, N., & Fares, J. (2020). Leveraging media and health communication strategies to overcome the COVID-19 infodemic. *Journal of Public Health Policy*, *41*(4), 410–420. doi:10.105741271-020-00247-w PMID:32826935

Michalopoulos, S., & Papaioannou, E. (2013). Pre-colonial ethnic institutions and contemporary African development. *Econometrica*, *81*(1), 113–152. doi:10.3982/ECTA9613 PMID:25089052

Mihaylova, M. (2021). The impact of global trends and Covid-19 on international new ventures. *Economic Archive*, *3*, 46–58.

Milani, G. S., & Dickman, M. (2021). *Is global work losing its attractiveness?* https://www.relocatemagazine.com/articles/international-assignments-is-global-work-losing-its-attractiveness-giovanna-silveira-milani-michael-dickmann-glomo-su21

Mingoti, S. (2005). *Análise de dados através de métodos de estatística multivariada.* Ed. UFMG.

Mintzberg, H., Ahlstrand, B., & Lampel, J. (1998). Chapter 1, And over here, ladies and gentlemen: the strategic management beast, pp 1-21. In Strategy Safari. The Free Press.

Miroudot, S. (2020). Resilience versus robustness in global value chains: Some policy implications. In R. E. Baldwin & S. J. Evenett (Eds.), *COVID-19 and Trade Policy: Why Turning Inward Won't Work* (pp. 117–130). CEPR Press.

Miroudot, S., & Nordstrom, H. (2020). Made in the world? global value chains in the midst of rising protectionism. *Review of Industrial Organization*, *57*(2), 195–222. doi:10.100711151-020-09781-z

Mirri, S., Prandi, C., Salomoni, P., Callegati, F., & Campi, A. (2014). On Combining Crowdsourcing, Sensing and Open Data for an Accessible Smart City. *2014 Eighth International Conference on Next Generation Mobile Apps, Services and Technologies*. 10.1109/NGMAST.2014.59

Modgil, S. (2021, April 08) With a distributed workforce, companies need to be even more aware of compliances: Charles Ferguson, Globalization Partners. *People Matters Global*. https://www.peoplemattersglobal.com/article/strategic-hr/with-a-distributed-workforce-companies-need-to-be-even-more-aware-of-compliances-charles-ferguson-globalization-partners-28956

Mohanty, S. (2015). *The four essential V's for a big data analytics platform*. Retrieved on November 30, 2021, from: https://dataconomy.com/2015/06/the-four-essentials-vs-for-a-big-data-analytics-platform

Montano, S., & Savitt, A. (2020) *Not All Disasters Are Disasters: Pandemic Categorization and Its Consequences*. https://items.ssrc.org/covid-19-and-the-social-sciences/disaster-studies/not-all-disasters-are-disasters-pandemic-categorization-and-its-consequences/

Moosa, I. A., & Cardak, B. A. (2006). The Determinants of Foreign Direct Investment: An Extrexeme Bounds Analysis. *Journal of Multinational Financial Management*, *16*(2), 199–211. doi:10.1016/j.mulfin.2005.07.002

Moosa, I. A., & Merza, E. (2022). The effect of COVID-19 on foreign direct investment inflows: Stylised facts and some explanations. *Future Business Journal*, *8*(1), 1–12. doi:10.118643093-022-00129-5

Morgan, S. (2020, May 27.) Macron demands carmakers turn to "Made in France" for €8bn virus aid. *Euractiv*.

Moriarty, P., & Honnery, D. (2004). Forecasting world transport in the year 2050. *International Journal of Vehicle Design*, *35*(1-2), 151–165. doi:10.1504/IJVD.2004.004053

Moutselos, K., Kyriazis, D., & Maglogiannis, I. (2018). A Web Based Modular Environment for Assisting Health Policy Making Utilizing Big Data Analytics. *2018 9th International Conference on Information, Intelligence, Systems and Applications (IISA)*.

Mudgal, S., Yadav, R., Haokip, H. R., Pandit, A., & Mary, Y. S. (2021). Genomic variation and point mutations analysis of Indian COVID-19 patient samples submitted in GISAID database. *Journal of the Indian Chemical Society*, *98*(10), 1–7. doi:10.1016/j.jics.2021.100156

Mukherjee, D., Maskey, U., Ishak, A., Sarfraz, Z., Sarfraz, A., & Jaiswal, V. (2021). Fake COVID-19 vaccination in India: an emerging dilemma? *Postgraduate Medical Journal*. doi:10.1136/postgradmedj-2021-141003

Mukherjee, S., Baral, M. M., & Venkataiah, C. (2022). Supply Chain Strategies for Achieving Resilience in the MSMEs: An Empirical Study. In H. Webb & H. Al Numairy (Eds.), *External Events and Crises That Impact Firms and Other Entities* (pp. 158–183). IGI Global. doi:10.4018/978-1-7998-8346-3.ch004

Mukherjee, S., Baral, M. M., Venkataiah, C., Pal, S. K., & Nagariya, R. (2021). Service robots are an option for contactless services due to the COVID-19 pandemic in the hotels. *Decision (Washington, D.C.)*, *48*, 445–460. doi:10.100740622-021-00300-x

Mukherji, R. (2009). The state, economic growth, and development in India. *India Review*, *8*(1), 81–106. doi:10.1080/14736480802665238

Mullen, M. R. (1995). Diagnosing Measurement Equivalence in Cross-National Research. *Journal of International Business Studies*, *26*(3), 573–596. doi:10.1057/palgrave.jibs.8490187

Mullins, R. (2020). COVID-19 is reshaping the pharmaceutical supply chain. *Chemical and Engineering News*, *98*(16), 30–45.

Muralidharan, E., & Pathak, S. (2017). Informal institutions and international entrepreneurship. *International Business Review*, *26*(2), 288–302. doi:10.1016/j.ibusrev.2016.07.006

Muralidharan, E., & Pathak, S. (2020). Home Country Institutions and International Entrepreneurship: A Multi-Level Framework–Institutions and International Entrepreneurship. In J. G. L. Dantas & L. G. Carvalho (Eds.), *Handbook of Research on Approaches to Alternative Entrepreneurship Opportunities: 291-314*. IGI Global. doi:10.4018/978-1-7998-1981-3.ch014

Muralidharan, E., Wei, W., & Liu, X. (2017). Integration by emerging economy multinationals: Perspectives from Chinese mergers and acquisitions. *Thunderbird International Business Review*, *59*(4), 503–518. doi:10.1002/tie.21850

Najmi, M., Sepehri, M., & Hashemi, S. (2010). *The evaluation of Business Intelligence maturity level in Iranian banking industry*. Paper presented at the Industrial Engineering and Engineering Management (IE&EM), 2010 IEEE 17Th International Conference.

Nambar, J., Li, X., Sawhney, R., & Pradhan, N. (2018). Supply chain resilience for single and multiple sourcing in the presence of disruptive risks. *International Journal of Production Research*, *56*(6), 2339–2360. doi:10.1080/00207543.2017.1370149

Nam, T., & Pardo, T. A. (2011). Conceptualizing smart city with dimensions of technology, people, and institutions. *Proceedings of the 12th Annual International Digital Government Research Conference: Digital Government Innovation in Challenging Times*. 10.1145/2037556.2037602

Nardo, M., Saisana, M., Saltelli, A., & Tarantola, S. (2005). *Tools for Composite Indicators Building*. European Commission Joint Research Centre.

Nardo, M., Saisana, M., Saltelli, A., Tarantola, S., Hoffmann, A., & Giovannini, E. (2008). *Handbook on Constructing Composite Indicators: Methodology and User Guide*. OECD Publications.

Nasser, O. M. (2007). The Determinants of the U.S. Foreign Direct Investment: Does the Region Matter? *Global Economic Review*, *36*(1), 37–51. doi:10.1080/12265080701217181

Nazir, M., Hussain, I., Tian, J., Akram, S., Tshiaba, S. M., Mushtaq, S., & Shad, M. A. (2020). A Multidimensional Model of Public Health Approaches Against COVID-19. *International Journal of Environmental Research and Public Health*, *17*(11), 1–11. doi:10.3390/ijerph17113780 PMID:32466581

Nee, V., & Opper, L. (2009). *Bureaucracy and Financial Markets*. Academic Press.

Nelaeva, A., & Nilssen, F. (2022). Contrasting knowledge development for internationalization among emerging and advanced economy firms: A review and future research. *Journal of Business Research*, *139*, 232–256. doi:10.1016/j.jbusres.2021.09.053

Newman, K. L., & Nollen, S. D. (1996). Culture and Congruence: The Fit between Management Practices and National Culture. *Journal of International Business Studies*, *27*(4), 753–779. doi:10.1057/palgrave.jibs.8490152

News, U. N. (2020, May 4). None of us is safe until we all are, says UN chief at EU push to end COVID-19 pandemic. https://news.un.org/en/story/2020/05/1063132

Nguyen, H. C., Nguyen, M. H., Do, B. N., Tran, C. Q., Nguyen, T. T. P., Pham, K. M., Pham, L. V., Tran, K. V., Duong, T. T., Tran, T. V., Duong, T. H., Nguyen, T. T., Nguyen, Q. H., Hoang, T. M., Nguyen, K. T., Pham, T. T. M., Yang, S. H., Chao, J. C. J., & Van Duong, T. (2020). People with Suspected COVID-19 Symptoms Were More Likely Depressed and Had Lower Health-Related Quality of Life: The Potential Benefit of Health Literacy. *Journal of Clinical Medicine*, *9*(4), 1–18. doi:10.3390/jcm9040965 PMID:32244415

Nguyen, H. T., Do, B. N., Pham, K. M., Kim, G. B., Dam, H. T. B., Nguyen, T. T., Nguyen, T. T. P., Nguyen, Y. H., Sørensen, K., Pleasant, A., & Van Duong, T. (2020). Fear of COVID-19 Scale—Associations of Its Scores with Health Literacy and Health-Related Behaviors among Medical Students. *International Journal of Environmental Research and Public Health*, *17*(11), 1–14. doi:10.3390/ijerph17114164 PMID:32545240

Ngwane, M. G. (2001). *Going Global*. Retrieved on December 3, 2021, from: https://www.accord.org.za/publications/ct-2001/global.htm

Nicoletti, G., Scarpetta, S., & Boylaud, O. (2000). Summary Indicators of Product market Regulation With an Extension to Employment Protection Legislation. *OECD, Economic Department Working Papers 226*.

Nigh, D. (1985). The Effect of Political Events on United States Direct Foreign Investment: A Pooled Time- Series Cross-Sectional Analysis. *Journal of International Business Studies*, *16*(1), 1–17. doi:10.1057/palgrave.jibs.8490439

Ning, Z., Xia, F., Ullah, N., Kong, X., & Hu, X. (2017). Vehicular Social Networks: Enabling Smart Mobility. *IEEE Communications Magazine*, *55*(5), 16–55. doi:10.1109/MCOM.2017.1600263

Nitsch, V. (2022). Covid-19 and international trade: Evidence from New Zealand. *Economics Letters*, *217*, 110627. doi:10.1016/j.econlet.2022.110627 PMID:35645436

Noorbakhsh, F., Paloni, A., & Youssef, A. (2001). Human Capital and FDI Inflows to Developing Countries: New Empirical Evidence. *World Development*, *29*(9), 1593–1610. doi:10.1016/S0305-750X(01)00054-7

Norrlof, C. (2021). Is COVID-19 the end of US hegemony? Public bads, leadership failure and monetary hegemony. *International Affairs*, *96*(5), 1281–1303. doi:10.1093/ia/iiaa134 PMID:34191870

Nowicka, K. (2014). Smart City Logistics on Cloud Computing Model. *Procedia: Social and Behavioral Sciences*, *151*, 266–281. doi:10.1016/j.sbspro.2014.10.025

Nunnally, J. C. (1978). *Psychometric theory*. McGraw Hill.

Nutbeam, D. (1998). Health promotion glossary. *Health Promotion International*, *13*(4), 349–364. https://www.jstor.org/stable/45152457. doi:10.1093/heapro/13.4.349

Nwoke, N. (2019). (In)Effective business responsibility engagements in areas of limited statehood: Nigeria's oil sector as a case study. *Business & Society*, 1–37.

OECD Statistics. (2022a). *Health expenditure and financing*. Retrieved on January 31, 2022, from: https://stats.oecd.org/

OECD Statistics. (2022b). *Health Status: Life expectancy*. Retrieved on January 31, 2022, from: https://stats.oecd.org/

OECD. (2021a). *Health at a Glance 2021: OECD Indicators*. OECD Publishing. doi:10.1787/ae3016b9-en

OECD. (2021b). *Economic Outlook, 2021*. Retrieved January 23, 2022, from https://www.oecd-ilibrary.org/sites/66c5ac2c-en/index.html?itemId=/content/publication/66c5ac2c-en

OECD. (2022c). *Statistics/Globalisation: FDI main aggregates – Summary*. Retrieved on January 23, 2022, from: https://stats.oecd.org/

OECD. (2022d). *Definition of Inflation (CPI)*. Retrieved on January 29, 2022, from: https://data.oecd.org/price/inflation-cpi.htm/

Oesterle, M. J., & Laudien, S. (2007). The future of international business research and the relevance gap: A German perspective. *European Journal of International Management*, *1*(1/2), 39–55. doi:10.1504/EJIM.2007.012916

Öge, S. (2005). Düzen mi Düzensizlik (Kaos) mi? Örgütsel Varlığın Sürdürülebilirliği Açısından Bir Değerlendirme. [Order or Chaos? An Assessment in terms of the Sustainability of Organizational Existence.]. *Selçuk Üniversitesi Sosyal Bilimler Enstitüsü Dergisi*, *13*, 285–303.

Okumura, Y., Suyama, S., Ishii, N., Maruta, Y., Okazaki, A., Okamura, A., . . . Onizawa, T. (2019). 5G R&D Achievements for High-Data-Rate and Low-Power-Consumption Radio Access Technologies with Higher-Frequency-Band and Wider-Bandwidth Massive MIMO. *2019 IEEE 89th Vehicular Technology Conference (VTC2019-Spring)*.

Olsen, K. B. (2006). *Productivity Impacts of Offshoring and Outsourcing: A Review*. STI Working Paper 2006/1. Paris: OECD.

Omarov, B., & Altayeva, A. (2018). Towards Intelligent IoT Smart City platform Based on OneM2M Guideline: Smart Grid Case Study. *2018 IEEE International Conference on Big Data and Smart Computing (BigComp)*. 10.1109/BigComp.2018.00130

Oproiu, E., Iordache, M., Costea, C. X., Brezeanu, C., & Patachia, C. (2018). 5G Network Architecture, Functional Model and Business Role for 5G Smart City Use Case: Mobile Operator Perspective. *2018 International Conference on Communications (COMM)*. 10.1109/ICComm.2018.8484747

Orecchini, F., Santiangeli, A., Zuccari, F., Pieroni, A., & Suppa, T. (2019). Blockchain Technology in Smart City: A New Opportunity for Smart Environment and Smart Mobility. Intelligent Computing & Optimization.

Oughton, E. J., Frias, Z., Dohler, M., Whalley, J., Sicker, D., Hall, J. W., Crowcroft, J., & Cleevely, D. D. (2018). The strategic national infrastructure assessment of digital communications. *Digital Policy, Regulation & Governance*, *20*(3), 197–210. doi:10.1108/DPRG-02-2018-0004

Our World in Data. (2022a). *Dataset*. Retrieved on January 7, 2022, from: https://covid.ourworldindata.org/data/owid-covid-data.csv

Our World in Data. (2022b). *Excess mortality during the Coronavirus pandemic (COVID-19)*. Retrieved on January 23, 2022, from: https://ourworldindata.org/excess-mortality-covid

Oviatt, B. M., & McDougall, P. P. (1994). Toward a Theory of International New Ventures. *Journal of International Business Studies*, *25*(1), 45–64. doi:10.1057/palgrave.jibs.8490193

Özlem, Ö., & Gürler, M. (2020). The Analysis of Health Expenditure as a Determinant of Economic Growth in 37 High Income Countries. *Acta Scientific Nutritional Health*, *4*(9), 19–33.

Özsoy, Ö. (2021). Dilemma in Health during Pandemic in OECD Countries: Increasing Health Expenditures for Preventing against the Pandemic Will Cause a Crowding-out in Increasing the Employment in Nursing Service or not? *European Journal of Science and Technology*, (32), 1094-1102.

Özsoy, Ö., & Gürler, M. (2021a). *Poverty and social exclusion of older people in ageing European Union and Turkey. J Public Health.* doi:10.100710389-021-01525-x

Özsoy, Ö., & Gürler, M. (2021b). The Negative Effects of COVID-19 on the Sustainable Development Goals, Economic Growth, Foreign Trade, and Social Life. *Advances in Human Services and Public Health*, 105–155. doi:10.4018/978-1-7998-8202-2.CH007

Palumbo, R. (2017). Examining the impacts of health literacy on healthcare costs. An evidence synthesis. *Health Services Management Research*, *30*(4), 197–212. doi:10.1177/0951484817733366 PMID:29034727

Pandey, D., Ogunmola, G. A., Enbeyle, W., Abdullahi, M., Pandey, B. K., & Pramanik, S. (2022). COVID-19: A Framework for Effective Delivering of Online Classes During Lockdown. *Human Arenas*, *5*(2), 322–336. doi:10.100742087-020-00175-x

Parameswaran, R., & Yaprak, A. (1987). A Cross-National Comparison of Consumer Research Measures. *Journal of International Business Studies*, *18*(1), 35–49. doi:10.1057/palgrave.jibs.8490398

Parmigiani, A., & Rivera-Santos, M. (2011). Clearing a path through the forest: A meta-review of interorganizational relationships. *Journal of Management*, *37*(4), 1108–1136. doi:10.1177/0149206311407507

Pathak, S., Muralidharan, E., & Laplume, A. (2014). Home country factors and the decision to internationalize technology-based new ventures: A multi-level study of early-stage entrepreneurs. *Frontiers of Entrepreneurship Research*, *34*(19), 1.

Pathak, S., & Muralidharan, E. (2020a). The Role of Emotional Intelligence in the Culture-Entrepreneurship Fit Perspective. In *Cultural Factors and Performance in 21st Century Businesses* (pp. 90–120). IGI Global. doi:10.4018/978-1-7998-3744-2.ch005

Pathak, S., & Muralidharan, E. (2020b). Implications of culturally implicit perspective of emotional intelligence. *Cross-Cultural Research*, *54*(5), 502–533. doi:10.1177/1069397120938690

Pavitt, K. (1985). Patent statistics as indicators of innovative activities: Possibilities and problems. *Scientometrics*, *7*(1-2), 77–99. doi:10.1007/BF02020142

Pawłowicz, B., Salach, M., & Trybus, B. (2019). Smart City Traffic Monitoring System Based on 5G Cellular Network, RFID and Machine Learning. Engineering Software Systems: Research and Praxis.

Pearce, J. A., & Robinson, R. B. (2015). Stratejik Yönetim: Geliştirme, Uygulama ve Kontrol. [Strategic Management: Development, Implementation and Control.] (Çev: M. Barca), Nobel Yayınları, Ankara.

Pearson, A. E. (2003). Yenilikçilikte Kararlı Olma Yolları. [Ways to Be Committed to Innovate.] [Yenilikçilik,] [Çev. Ahmet Kardam] [MESS Yayınları, İstanbul.]. *Harvard Business Review*, 37–58.

Pedersen, J., & Dobbin, F. (2006). In search of identity and legitimation. *The American Behavioral Scientist*, *49*(7), 897–907. doi:10.1177/0002764205284798

Peeples, E. (2003). Yeniliği Esinlendirmek. [Inspiring Innovation.] [Yenilikçilik,] [Çev. Ahmet Kardam] [, MESS Yayınları, İstanbul.]. *Harvard Business Review*, 97–118.

Peerally, J. A., De Fuentes, C., Santiago, F., & Zhao, S. (2022). The sustainability of multinational enterprises' pandemic-induced social innovation approaches. *Thunderbird International Business Review*, *64*(2), 115–124. doi:10.1002/tie.22256

Pellegrini, G. (2006). Measures of Competitiveness and Attractiveness: a Critical appraisal focused on Italy. *Proceedings of the Scientific Meeting of the Italian Statistical Society*, 1, 355-364.

Peng, M. W. (2004). Identifying the big question in international business research. *Journal of International Business Research, 35*(2), 99–18. doi:10.1057/palgrave.jibs.8400077

Perveen, S., Yigitcanlar, T., Kamruzzaman, M., & Hayes, J. (2017). Evaluating transport externalities of urban growth: A critical review of scenario-based planning methods. *International Journal of Environmental Science and Technology, 14*(3), 663–678. doi:10.100713762-016-1144-7

Peterson, R. B., & Schwind, H. F. (1977). A Comparative Study of Personnel Problems in International Companies and Joint Ventures in Japan. *Journal of International Business Studies, 8*(1), 45–55. doi:10.1057/palgrave.jibs.8490678

Petricevic, O., & Teece, D. J. (2019). The structural reshaping of globalization: Implications for strategic sectors, profiting from innovation, and the multinational enterprise. *Journal of International Business Studies, 50*(9), 1487–1512. doi:10.105741267-019-00269-x

Pham, Q. V., Nguyen, D. C., Huynh-The, T., Hwang, W. J., & Pathirana, P. N. (2020). Artificial Intelligence (AI) and Big Data for Coronavirus (COVID-19) Pandemic: A Survey on the State-of-the-Arts. *IEEE Access: Practical Innovations, Open Solutions, 8*, 130839. doi:10.1109/ACCESS.2020.3009328 PMID:34812339

Pilloni, M., Kádár, J., & Abu Hamed, T. (2022). The impact of COVID-19 on energy start-up companies: The use of global financial crisis (GFC) as a lesson for future recovery. *Energies, 15*(10), 3530. doi:10.3390/en15103530

Pimpinella, A., Redondi, A. E. C., & Cesana, M. (2019). Walk this way! An IoT-based urban routing system for smart cities. *Computer Networks, 162*, 106857. doi:10.1016/j.comnet.2019.07.013

Pinheiro-Alves, R., & Zambujal-Oliveira, J. (2012). The Ease of Doing Business Index as a tool for investment location decicions. *Economics Letters, 117*(1), 66–70. doi:10.1016/j.econlet.2012.04.026

Pisani, N. (2009). International management research: Investigating its recent diffusion in top management journals. *Journal of Management, 35*(2), 199–218. doi:10.1177/0149206308321552

Pittaway, L., Robertson, M., Munir, K., Denyer, D., & Neely, A. (2004). Networking and innovation: A systematic review of the evidence. *International Journal of Management Reviews, 5/6*(3&4), 137–168. doi:10.1111/j.1460-8545.2004.00101.x

Pokrić, B., Krčo, S., & Pokrić, M. (2014). Augmented Reality Based Smart City Services Using Secure IoT Infrastructure. *2014 28th International Conference on Advanced Information Networking and Applications Workshops.*

Porter, M. E. (2007). Rekabet Stratejisi: Sektör ve Rakip Analizi Teknikleri. [Competitive Strategy: Sector and Competitor Analysis Techniques.] (Çev. Gülen Ulubilgen), Sistem Yayıncılık, İzmir.

Porter, M. E. (1980). *Competitive Strategy: Techniques for Analyzing Industries and Competitors.* Free Press.

Porter, M. E. (1981). The Contributions of Industrial Organization To Strategic Management. *Academy of Management Review, 6*(4), 609–620. doi:10.2307/257639

Porter, M. E. (1985). *Competitive Advantage: Creating and Sustaining Superior Performance.* Free Press.

Porter, M. E. (1990, March-April). The competitive advantage of nations. *Harvard Business Review.*

Porter, M. E. (1991). Competitive Advantage and Global Trade in the 1990's. *Harvard International Review, 13*(4), 12–15.

Portes, A., & Smith, L. D. (2010). Institutions and national development in Latin America: A comparative study. *Socio-economic Review, 8*(4), mwq018. doi:10.1093er/mwq018 PMID:26543407

Prah, K. K. (2000). *African Unity, Pan-Africanism and the Dilemmas of Regional Integration.* Paper presented to the Southern African Regional Institute for Policy Studies (SARIPS) Annual Colloquium, Harare.

Prahalad, C. K., & Hamel, G. (1990). The core competence of the corporation. *Harvard Business Review*, *69*(3), 275–292.

Premium Times. (2021, December). *Nigerian govt says ban on rice import stays*. Retrieved on May 3, 2022, from: https://www.premiumtimesng.com/news/more-news/435082-nigerian-govt-says-ban-on-rice-import-stays.html

Qingsong, H., Chen, Z., Peng, X., Shukui, T., & Jiayu, W. (2019). Comparison of urban growth patterns and changes between three urban agglomerations in China and three metropolises in the USA from 1995 to 2015. *Sustainable Cities and Society*, *50*, 101649. doi:10.1016/j.scs.2019.101649

Qin, M., Liu, X., & Zhou, X. (2020). COVID-19 shock and global value chains: Is there a substitute for China? *Emerging Markets Finance & Trade*, *56*(15), 3588–3598. doi:10.1080/1540496X.2020.1855137

Quer, G., Aktas, T., Librino, F., Javidi, T., & Rao, R. R. (2019). A Wireless Vehicle-based mobile network infrastructure designed for smarter cities. *Ad Hoc Networks*, *85*, 160–169. doi:10.1016/j.adhoc.2018.10.014

Radjou, N., Prabhu, J., & Ahuja, S. (2012). Jugaad innovation: Think frugal, be flexible, generate breakthrough growth. In J. Bessant & J. Tidd (Eds.), *Innovation and Entrepreneurship*. John Wiley & Sons.

Radosevic, S. (1999). *International technology transfer and catch-up in economic development*. Edward Elgar Publishing.

Rahman, R. A., & Shah, B. (2016). Security analysis of IoT protocols: A focus in CoAP. *2016 3rd MEC International Conference on Big Data and Smart City (ICBDSC).*

Rajaprabha, M. N., Jayalakshmi, P., & Anand, R. V. (2018). *IoT based smart garbage collector for smart cities*. Academic Press.

Ralston, D. A., Gustason, D. J., Cheung, F. M., & Terpstra, R. H. (1993). Differences in Managerial Values: A Study of U.S., Hong Kong and PRC Managers. *Journal of International Business Studies*, *24*(2), 249–275. doi:10.1057/palgrave.jibs.8490232

Ralston, D. A., Holt, D. H., Terpstra, R. H., & Cheng, Y. K. (1997). The Impact of National Culture and Economic Ideology on Managerial Work Values: A Study of the United States, Russia, Japan, and China. *Journal of International Business Studies*, *28*(1), 177–207. doi:10.1057/palgrave.jibs.8490097

Ramos, F., Trilles, S., Muñoz, A., & Huerta, J. (2018). Promoting Pollution-Free Routes in Smart Cities Using Air Quality Sensor Networks. *Sensors (Basel)*, *18*(8), 2507. Advance online publication. doi:10.339018082507 PMID:30071647

Rapoza, K. (2020). Is Apple slowly moving out of China? Its supplier is. *Forbes*, (August), 14.

Ratten, V. (2020). Coronavirus and international business: An entrepreneurial ecosystem perspective. *Thunderbird International Business Review*, *62*(5), 629–634. doi:10.1002/tie.22161

Reeves, M., & Varadarajan, R. (2020). *When Resilience is More Important than Efficiency*. BCG/Henderson Institute.

Rego, A., Garcia, L., Sendra, S., & Lloret, J. (2018). Software Defined Network-based control system for an efficient traffic management for emergency situations in smart cities. *Future Generation Computer Systems*, *88*, 243–253. doi:10.1016/j.future.2018.05.054

Reid, A. R., Pérez, C. R. C., & Rodríguez, D. M. (2018). Inference of vehicular traffic in smart cities using machine learning with the internet of things. *International Journal on Interactive Design and Manufacturing*, *12*(2), 459–472. doi:10.100712008-017-0404-1

Reyes, J. A. P., & Rajagopal, A. (2022). The Secondary Economic Sector's Role in Post-pandemic Recovery: Analysis in the Neoliberal Capitalism Context. In A. M. López-Fernández & A. Terán-Bustamante (Eds.), *Business Recovery in Emerging Markets. Palgrave Studies in Democracy, Innovation, and Entrepreneurship for Growth*. Palgrave Macmillan. doi:10.1007/978-3-030-91532-2_2

Richardson, J. (2006). Self-directed expatriation: Family matters. *Personnel Review*, *35*(4), 469–486. doi:10.1108/00483480610670616

Richter, A. (2020). Locked-down digital work. *International Journal of Information Management*, *55*, 102–157. doi:10.1016/j.ijinfomgt.2020.102157 PMID:32836629

Rida Khatoun, S. Z. (2016). Smart cities: Concepts, architectures, research opportunities. *Communications of the ACM*, *59*(8), 46–57. doi:10.1145/2858789

Ritchie, B. K. (2002). Foreign direct investment and intellectual capital formation in Southeast Asia.

Roach, S. (2020, January 3). The myth of global decoupling. *Project Syndicate*.

Roberts, M. J., & Muralidharan, E. (2022). Internationalization of service SMEs: Perspectives from Canadian SMEs internationalizing in Asia. *Global Business Review*, *23*(4), 890–910. doi:10.1177/0972150919887250

Robishaw, J. D., Alter, S. M., Solano, J. J., Shih, R. D., DeMets, D. L., Maki, D. G., & Hennekens, C. H. (2021). Genomic surveillance to combat COVID-19: Challenges and opportunities. *The Lancet Microbe*, *2*(9), e481–e484. doi:10.1016/S2666-5247(21)00121-X PMID:34337584

Rodrik, D. (2018). Populism and the economics of globalization. *Journal of International Business Policy*, *1*(1), 12–33. doi:10.105742214-018-0001-4

Rogoff, K. (2009). The "New Normal" for Growth. *Project Syndicate*, 1-2.

Ronen, S., & Shenkar, O. (2013). Mapping world cultures: Cluster formation, sources and implications. *Journal of International Business Studies*, *44*(9), 867–897. doi:10.1057/jibs.2013.42

Ronstadt, R. C. (1978). International R&D: The Establishment and Evolution of Research and Development Abroad by Seven U. S. Multinationals. *Journal of International Business Studies*, *9*(1), 7–24. doi:10.1057/palgrave.jibs.8490647

Root, F. R., & Ahmed, A. A. (1978). The Influence of Policy Instruments on Manufacturing Direct Foreign Investment in Developing Countries. *Journal of International Business Studies*, *9*(3), 81–93. doi:10.1057/palgrave.jibs.8490670

Rosenberg, C. E. (1992). *Explaining epidemics*. Cambridge University Press. doi:10.1017/CBO9780511666865.015

Rosenbusch, K., & Cseh, M. (2012). The cross-cultural adjustment process of expatriate families in a multinational organization: A family system theory perspective. *Human Resource Development International*, *15*(1), 61–77. doi:10.1080/13678868.2011.646895

Rosenzweig, P. M., & Nohria, N. (1994). Influences on Human Resource Management Practices in Multinational Corporations. *Journal of International Business Studies*, *25*(2), 229–251. doi:10.1057/palgrave.jibs.8490199

Ros, M., & Neuwirth, L. S. (2020). Increasing global awareness of timely COVID-19 healthcare guidelines through FPV training tutorials: Portable public health crises teaching method. *Nurse Education Today*, *91*, 1–6. doi:10.1016/j.nedt.2020.104479 PMID:32473497

Rosson, P. J., & Ford, D. (1982). Manufacturer-Overseas Distributor Relations and Export Performance. *Journal of International Business Studies*, *13*(2), 57–72. doi:10.1057/palgrave.jibs.8490550

Roth, K., & Morrison, A. J. (1990). An Empirical Analysis of the Integration-Responsiveness Framework in Global Industries. *Journal of International Business Studies, 21*(4), 541–564. doi:10.1057/palgrave.jibs.8490341

Rouse, M. (2017). *Big data analytics.* Retrieved on November 30, 2021, from: https://searchbusinessanalytics.techtarget.com/definition/big-data-analytics

Rout, K., & Sahu, S. (2020). Exploring Factors Influencing the Users' Intention to Use Aarogya Setu Contact Tracing Mobile Health Application during COVID-19 Pandemic Article history. *Journal of Humanities and Social Sciences Research, 2*(S), 29–36. doi:10.37534/bp.jhssr.2020.v2.nS.id1068.p29

Ruggieri, R., Ruggeri, M., Vinci, G., & Poponi, S. (2021). Electric Mobility in a Smart City: European Overview. *Energies, 14*(2), 315. Advance online publication. doi:10.3390/en14020315

Rugman, A. M. (1976). Risk Reduction by International Diversification. *Journal of International Business Studies, 7*(2), 75–80. doi:10.1057/palgrave.jibs.8490702

Rugman, A. M., & Verbeke, A. (2004). A Perspective on Regional and Global Strategies of Multinational Enterprises. *Journal of International Business Studies, 35*(1), 3–18. doi:10.1057/palgrave.jibs.8400073

Rugman, A. M., & Verbeke, A. (2008). Internalization theory and its impact on the field of international business. In *International business scholarship: AIB fellows on the first 50 years and beyond.* Emerald Group Publishing Limited. doi:10.1016/S1064-4857(08)00003-X

Rugman, A., & Oh, C. H. (2008). Friedman's follies: Insights on the globalization/regionalization debate. *Business and Politics, 10*(2), 1–14. doi:10.2202/1469-3569.1222

Rynes, S. L., Bartunek, J. M., & Daft, R. L. (2001). Across the great divide: Knowledge creation and transfer between practitioners and academics. *Academy of Management Journal, 44*(2), 340–355. doi:10.2307/3069460

Saggi, K. (2002). Trade, foreign direct investment, and international technology transfer: A survey. *The World Bank Research Observer, 17*(2), 191–235. doi:10.1093/wbro/17.2.191

Sahoo, J. P., Nath, S., Ghosh, L., & Samal, K. C. (2021). Concepts of Immunity and Recent Immunization Programme against COVID-19 in India. *Biotica Research Today, 3*(2), 103–106. https://biospub.com/index.php/biorestoday/article/view/728

Saisana, M., & Tarantola, S. (2002). *State-of-the-art Report on Current Methodologies and Practices for Composite Indicator Development.* European Commission-JRC.

Saleem, M. A., Shijie, Z., & Sharif, A. (2019). Data Transmission Using IoT in Vehicular Ad-Hoc Networks in Smart City Congestion. *Mobile Networks and Applications, 24*(1), 248–258. doi:10.100711036-018-1205-x

Salvatore, D. (2004). Growth and Poverty in a Globalizing World. *Journal of Policy Modeling, 26*(4), 543-551. https://doi. doi:10.1016/j.jpolmod.2004.04.009

Santa Fe Relocations. (2018). *Transformation in The Age of Uncertainty: The Global Mobility Survey 2018.* https://www.aon.es/site/ipm-club/2018/11/15/santafe-survey/

Santos, E., Oliveira, M., Ratten, V., Tavares, F. O., & Tavares, V. C. (2020). A reflection on explanatory factors for Covid -19: A comparative study between countries. *Thunderbird International Business Review, 63*(3), 285–301. doi:10.1002/tie.22188

Sarıkaya, M., & Kara, F.Z. (2007). Sürdürülebilir Kalkınmada İşletmenin Rolü: Kurumsal Vatandaşlık. [The Role of Business in Sustainable Development: Corporate Citizenship.] *Yönetim ve Ekonomi, 14*(2), (221-233).

Sarıkaya, M., Erdoğan, M., & Kara, F.Z. (2010). Internet Ekonomisi ve Kurumsal Sürdürülebilirlik. [Internet Economics and Corporate Sustainability.] Eskişehir Osmangazi Üniversitesi *İİBF Dergisi, 5*(2), (31-50).

Schieman, S., Badawy, P. J. A., Milkie, M., & Bierman, A. (2021). Work-life conflict during the COVID-19 pandemic. *Socius, 7*, 2378023120982856. doi:10.1177/2378023120982856

Schmidt, J., & Keil, T. (2013). What makes a resource valuable? Identifying the drivers of firm-idiosyncratic resource value. *Academy of Management Review, 38*(2), 206–228. doi:10.5465/amr.2010.0404

Schooler, R. (1971). Bias Phenomena Attendant to the Marketing of Foreign Goods in the U. S. *Journal of International Business Studies, 2*(1), 71–80. doi:10.1057/palgrave.jibs.8490732

Scognamiglio, A., Adinolfi, G., Graditi, G., & Saretta, E. (2014). Photovoltaics in Net Zero Energy Buildings and Clusters: Enabling the Smart City Operation. *Energy Procedia, 61*, 1171–1174. doi:10.1016/j.egypro.2014.11.1046

Scott, A. D., Cobban, P., Nair, R., & Painchaud, N. (2019). İnovasyonun Önündeki Engelleri Kaldırmak. [Removing Barriers to Innovation.]. *Harvard Business Review.*

Segal, A. (2020). The coming tech cold war with China. *Foreign Affairs*, 99.

Sekaran, U. (1983). Methodological and Theoretical Issues and Advancements in Cross-Cultural Research. *Journal of International Business Studies, 14*(2), 61–73. doi:10.1057/palgrave.jibs.8490519

Shacham, M., Greenblatt-Kimron, L., Hamama-Raz, Y., Martin, L. R., Peleg, O., Ben-Ezra, M., & Mijiritsky, E. (2021). Increased COVID-19 Vaccination Hesitancy and Health Awareness amid COVID-19 Vaccinations Programs in Israel. *International Journal of Environmental Research and Public Health, 18*(7), 1–11. doi:10.3390/ijerph18073804 PMID:33917327

Shaffer, M. A., Harrison, D. A., & Gilley, K. M. (1999). Dimensions, Determinants, and Differences in the Expatriate Adjustment Process. *Journal of International Business Studies, 30*(3), 557–581. doi:10.1057/palgrave.jibs.8490083

Shah, A. (2008). Poverty Facts and Stats. *Global Issues.*

Shah, S. S., Ali, M., Malik, A. W., Khan, M. A., & Ravana, S. D. (2019). vFog: A Vehicle-Assisted Computing Framework for Delay-Sensitive Applications in Smart Cities. *IEEE Access: Practical Innovations, Open Solutions, 7*, 34900–34909. doi:10.1109/ACCESS.2019.2903302

Sharma, B., & Gani, A. (2004). The effects of foreign direct investment on human Development. *Global Economy Journal, 4*(2), 1–18. doi:10.2202/1524-5861.1049

Shatz, H. J., & Venables, A. J. (2000). The Geography of International Investment. *The World Bank, Policy Research Working Paper 2338.*

Shenkar, O. (2001). Cultural Distance Revisited: Towards a More Rigorous Conceptualization and Measurement of Cultural Differences. *Journal of International Business Studies, 32*(3), 519–535. doi:10.1057/palgrave.jibs.8490982

Shenkar, O. (2004). One more time: International business in a global economy. *Journal of International Business Studies, 35*(2), 161–171. doi:10.1057/palgrave.jibs.8400074

Sherer, P., & Lee, K. (2002). Institutional change in large law firms: A resource dependency and institutional perspective. *Academy of Management Journal, 45*(1), 102–120. doi:10.2307/3069287

Sherman, E. (2020). 94% of the Fortune 1000 are seeing coronavirus supply chain disruptions. *Fortune*. https://fortune.com/2020/02/21/fortune-1000-coronavirus-china-supply-chain-impact/

Simonofski, A., Hertoghe, E., Steegmans, M., Snoeck, M., & Wautelet, Y. (2021). Engaging citizens in the smart city through participation platforms: A framework for public servants and developers. *Computers in Human Behavior, 124*, 106901. doi:10.1016/j.chb.2021.106901

Sinani, E., & Meyer, K. E. (2004). Spillovers of technology transfer from FDI: The case of Estonia. *Journal of Comparative Economics, 32*(3), 445–466. doi:10.1016/j.jce.2004.03.002

Singh, J. (1995). Measurement Issues in Cross-National Research. *Journal of International Business Studies, 26*(3), 597–619. doi:10.1057/palgrave.jibs.8490188

Singh, V. (2020). The Effect of COVID-19 Pandemic on Immunization Services in India - Possible Challenges and way forward. *Epidemiology International, 05*(02), 53–60. doi:10.24321/2455.7048.202018

Şirin, E. F., & Yetim, A. A. (2009). Beden Eğitimi Ve Spor Yüksekokulu Yöneticilerinin Dönüşümcü Liderlik Stiline İlişkin Yönetici Algıları. [Executive Perceptions of School of Physical Education and Sports Administrators on Transformational Leadership Style.]. *Niğde Üniversitesi Beden Eğitimi ve Spor Bilimleri Dergisi, 3*(1), 69–85.

Snedecor, G., & Cochran, W. (1967). *Statistical Methods* (6th ed.). Iowa State University Press.

Snyder, H. (2019). Literature review as a research methodology: An overview and guidelines. *Journal of Business Research, 104*, 333–339. doi:10.1016/j.jbusres.2019.07.039

Song, L., & Zhou, Y. (2020). The COVID-19 pandemic and its impact on the global economy: What does it take to turn crisis into opportunity? *China & World Economy, 28*(4), 1–25. doi:10.1111/cwe.12349

Song, P., Zhang, X., Zhao, Y., & Xu, L. (2020). Exogenous shocks on the dual-country industrial network: A simulation based on the policies during the COVID-19 pandemic. *Emerging Markets Finance & Trade, 56*(15), 3554–3561. doi:10.1080/1540496X.2020.1854723

Sönmez, R., Düzgün, A., & Öz, E. (2019). Firmanın İş Modeli Değişiminin Rekabetçiliğine Etkisi: Atlasjet'ten Atlasglobal'e", 27. [The Impact of Business Model Change on Competitiveness: From Atlasjet to Atlasglobal", 27.] Ulusal Yönetim ve Organizasyon Kongresi, İstanbul Üniversitesi, 18-20 Nisan, Antalya.

Soomro, K., Bhutta, M. N. M., Khan, Z., & Tahir, M. A. (2019). Smart city big data analytics: An advanced review. *WIREs Data Mining and Knowledge Discovery, 9*(5), e1319.

Sørensen, K., Pelikan, J. M., Röthlin, F., Ganahl, K., Slonska, Z., Doyle, G., Fullam, J., Kondilis, B., Agrafiotis, D., Uiters, E., Falcon, M., Mensing, M., Tchamov, K., Broucke, S., & Brand, H. (2015). Health literacy in Europe: Comparative results of the European health literacy survey (HLS-EU). *European Journal of Public Health, 25*(6), 1053–1058. doi:10.1093/eurpub/ckv043 PMID:25843827

Sørensen, K., Van Den Broucke, S., Fullam, J., Doyle, G., Pelikan, J., Slonska, Z., & Brand, H. (2012). Health literacy and public health: A systematic review and integration of definitions and models. *BMC Public Health, 12*(1), 1–13. doi:10.1186/1471-2458-12-80 PMID:22276600

Sotres, P., López de la Torre, C., Sánchez, L., Jeong, S. M., & Kim, J. (2018). Smart City Services Over a Global Interoperable Internet-of-Things System: The Smart Parking Case. *2018 Global Internet of Things Summit (GIoTS).*

Soundararajan, V., Sahasranamam, S., Khan, Z., & Jain, T. (2021). Multinational enterprises and the governance of sustainability practices in emerging market supply chains: An agile governance perspective. *Journal of World Business, 56*(2), 101149. doi:10.1016/j.jwb.2020.101149

Soyata, T., Habibzadeh, H., Ekenna, C., Nussbaum, B., & Lozano, J. (2019). Smart city in crisis: Technology and policy concerns. *Sustainable Cities and Society, 50*, 101566. doi:10.1016/j.scs.2019.101566

Spencer-Oatey, H., & Franklin, P. (2009). *Intercultural interaction: A multidisciplinary approach to intercultural communication*. Springer. doi:10.1057/9780230244511

Srivastava, K. C., Shrivastava, D., Alam, M. K., & Al-Mahmood, A. K. (2021). Is SARS CoV-2 viral mutation leading us to a virtual world? *Bangladesh Journal of Medical Science, 20*, 185–187. doi:10.3329/bjms.v20i5.55559

Stahl, G. K., Maznevski, M. L., Voigt, A., & Jonsen, K. (2009). Unraveling the effects of cultural diversity in teams: A meta-analysis of research on multicultural work groups. *Journal of International Business Studies, 41*(4), 690–709. doi:10.1057/jibs.2009.85

Stahl, G. K., & Tung, R. L. (2015). Towards a more balanced treatment of culture in international business studies: The need for positive cross-cultural scholarship. *Journal of International Business Studies, 46*(4), 391–414. doi:10.1057/jibs.2014.68

Steenkamp, J. E. M., Batra, R., & Alden, D. L. (2003). How Perceived Brand Globalness Creates Brand Value. *Journal of International Business Studies, 34*(1), 53–65. doi:10.1057/palgrave.jibs.8400002

Stephan, U., Uhlaner, L. M., & Stride, C. (2015). Institutions and social entrepreneurship: The role of institutional voids, institutional support, and institutional configurations. *Journal of International Business Studies, 46*(3), 308–331. doi:10.1057/jibs.2014.38

Stephenson, D. (2013). *7 big data techniques that create business value*. Retrieved on November 30, 2021, from: https://www.firmex.com/thedealroom/7-big-data-techniques-that-create-business-value

Stormacq, C., Van Den Broucke, S., & Wosinski, J. (2019). Does health literacy mediate the relationship between socioeconomic status and health disparities? Integrative review. *Health Promotion International, 34*(5), e1–e17. doi:10.1093/heapro/day062 PMID:30107564

Sullivan, D. (1994). Measuring the Degree of Internationalization of a Firm. *Journal of International Business Studies, 25*(2), 325–342. doi:10.1057/palgrave.jibs.8490203

Suutari, V., & Brewster, C. (2000). Making their own way: International experience through self-initiated foreign assignments. *Journal of World Business, 35*(4), 417–436. doi:10.1016/S1090-9516(00)00046-8

Talha, M., Upadhyay, A., Shamim, R., & Beg, M. S. (2017). A cloud integrated wireless garbage management system for smart cities. *2017 International Conference on Multimedia, Signal Processing and Communication Technologies (IMPACT)*. 10.1109/MSPCT.2017.8363999

Tecuci, G. (2012). Artificial intelligence. *WIREs Computational Statistics, 4*(2), 168-180.

Teddlie, C., & Tashakkori, A. (2011). Mixed methods research. The Sage Handbook of Qualitative Research, 4, 285-300.

Teece, D. (2019). A capability theory of the firm: An exonomics and (Strategic) management perspective. *New Zealand Economic Papers., 53*(1), 1–43. doi:10.1080/00779954.2017.1371208

Teece, D. J. (1977). Technology transfer by multinational firms: The resource cost of transferring technological know-how. *Economic Journal (London)*, *87*(346), 242–261. doi:10.2307/2232084

Teece, D. J. (2007). Explicating dynamic capabilities: The nature and microfoundations of (sustainable) enterprise performance. *Strategic Management Journal*, *28*(13), 1319–1350. doi:10.1002mj.640

Teece, D. J. (2014). A dynamic capabilities-based entrepreneurial theory of the multinational enterprise. *Journal of International Business Studies*, *45*(1), 8–37. doi:10.1057/jibs.2013.54

Teece, D. J. (2018). Profiting from innovation in the digital economy: Enabling technologies, standards, and licensing models in the wireless world. *Research Policy*, *47*(8), 1367–1387. doi:10.1016/j.respol.2017.01.015

Tenzer, H., Pudelko, M., & Harzing, A. (2014). The impact of language barriers on trust formation in multinational teams. *Journal of International Business Studies*, *45*(5), 508–535. doi:10.1057/jibs.2013.64

Terpstra, V., & Yu, C. M. (1988). Determinants of Foreign Investment of U.S. Advertising Agencies. *Journal of International Business Studies*, *19*(1), 33–46. doi:10.1057/palgrave.jibs.8490373

Teslya, N., Ryabchikov, I., & Mikhailov, S. (2019). Forming of Smart City Resident Digital Identity Based On the City Sources Analysis. *2019 IEEE International Black Sea Conference on Communications and Networking (BlackSeaCom)*. 10.1109/BlackSeaCom.2019.8812838

The Bank for International Settlements (BIS). (2022). *Central Bank Policy rates (End of period)*. Retrieved on January 25, 202, from: https://stats.bis.org/statx/srs/table/l1

The International Civil Aviation Organization (ICAO). (2022). *Economic Impacts of COVID-19 on Civil Aviation*. Retrieved on January 25, 2022, from: https://www.icao.int/sustainability/Documents/COVID-19/ICAO_Coronavirus_Econ_Impact.pdf

The International Monetary Fund (IMF). (2020). *Gross Domestic Product: An Economy's All*. Retrieved on January 29, 2022, from: https://www.imf.org/external/pubs/ft/fandd/basics/gdp.htm

The International Monetary Fund (IMF). (2021a). *World Economic Outlook databases*. Retrieved on January 23, 2022, from: https://www.imf.org/en/Publications/WEO/weo-database/2021/October

The International Monetary Fund (IMF). (2021b). *Datasets. Fiscal Monitor October 2021. Gross Debt Position*. Retrieved on January 25, 2022, from: https://www.imf.org/external/datamapper/G_XWDG_G01_GDP_PT@FM/ADVEC/FM_EMG/FM_LIDC

The International Monetary Fund (IMF). (2022). *World Economic Outlook International Monetary Fund: Rising Caseloads, a Disrupted Recovery, and Higher Inflation*. Retrieved on January 27, 2022, from: https://www.imf.org/-/media/Files/Publications/WEO/2022/Update/January/English/text.ashx

The PwC Global Mobility Pulse Survey (2020, April). What does COVID-19 mean for global mobility. *PWC*. https://www.pwc.com/gx/en/services/tax/publications/covid-19-mean-for-globalmobility.html

The U.S. Centers for Medicare & Medicaid Services. (n.d.). *The National Health Expenditure Accounts (NHEA) data.* Retrieved on January 31, 2022, from: https://www.cms.gov/Research-Statistics-Data-and-Systems/Statistics-Trends-and-Reports/NationalHealthExpendData/National HealthAccountsHistorical#:~:text=U.S.%20health%20care%20spending%20grew,spending%20accounted%20for%2019.7%20percent

The World Bank. (2020). *Global Economic Prospects June 2020: HIGHLIGHTS from Box 1.1: How Deep Will the COVID-19 Recession Be?* Retrieved on January 31, 2022, from: https://thedocs.worldbank.org/en/doc/395721588788243295-0050022020/original/GlobalEconomicProspectsJune2020TopicalIssue3 highlights.pdf

The World Bank. (2021a). *Updated estimates of the impact of COVID-19 on global poverty: Turning the corner on the pandemic in 2021?* Retrieved on March 24, 2022, from: https://blogs.worldbank.org/opendata/updated-estimates-impact-covid-19-global-poverty-turning-corner-pandemic-2021#:~:text=In%20January%202021%2C%20we%20estimated,around%20the%20globe%20in%202020

The World Bank. (2021b). *International Debt Statistics 2022.* Retrieved on January 24, 2022, from: https://openknowledge.worldbank.org/bitstream/handle/10986/36289/9781464818004.pdf?sequence=4&isAllowed=y

The World Bank. (2022a). *Dataset.* Retrieved on January 24, 2022, from: https://data.worldbank.org

The World Bank. (2022b). *Global Economic Prospects.* Retrieved on January 23, 2022, from: https://openknowledge.worldbank.org/bitstream/handle/10986/36519/9781464817601.pdf

The World Bank. (2022c). *Metadata Glossary.* Retrieved on January 29, 2022, from: https://databank.worldbank.org/metadataglossary/jobs/series/BX.KLT.DINV.WD.GD.ZS

Thomas, D. C., & Inkson, K. (2005). People skills for a global workplace. *Consulting to Management, 16*(1), 5.

Thompson, E. R. (2002). Clustering of foreign direct investment and enhanced technology transfer: Evidence from Hong Kong garment firms in China. *World Development, 30*(5), 873–889. doi:10.1016/S0305-750X(02)00009-8

Tilahun, B., Gashu, K. D., Mekonnen, Z. A., Endehabtu, B. F., & Angaw, D. A. (2021). Mapping the Role of Digital Health Technologies in Prevention and Control of COVID-19 Pandemic: Review of the Literature. *Yearbook of Medical Informatics, 30*(1), 26–37. doi:10.1055-0041-1726505 PMID:34479378

Tokgöz, N., & Önce, S. (2009). Şirket Sürdürülebilirliği: Geleneksel Yönetim Anlayışına Alternatif. [Company Sustainability: Alternative to Traditional Management Approach.] Afyon Kocatepe Üniversitesi *İ.İ.B.F. Dergisi.*

Torsello, M., & Winkler, M. M. (2020). Coronavirus-infected international business transactions: A preliminary diagnosis. *European Journal of Risk Regulation, 11*(2), 396–401. doi:10.1017/err.2020.30

Toyne, B., & Nigh, D. (1998). A more expansive view of international business. *Journal of International Business Studies, 29*(4), 863–876. doi:10.1057/palgrave.jibs.8490056

Trauma & Stressor Related Disorders That Are Not PTSD. (2022). Retrieved May 4, 2022, from: https://familypsychnj.com/2020/09/trauma-stressor-related-disorders-that-are-not-ptsd/

Tripathi, C. M., & Singh, T. (2021). Sailing through the COVID-19 pandemic: managing expatriates' psychological well-being and performance during natural crises. *Journal of Global Mobility: The Home of Expatriate Management Research.*

Trombin, M., Pinna, R., Musso, M., Magnaghi, E., & De Marco, M. (2020). Mobility Management: From Traditional to People-Centric Approach in the Smart City. In M. Elhoseny & A. E. Hassanien (Eds.), *Emerging Technologies for Connected Internet of Vehicles and Intelligent Transportation System Networks: Emerging Technologies for Connected and Smart Vehicles* (pp. 165–182). Springer International Publishing., doi:10.1007/978-3-030-22773-9_11

Tucker & Czapla. (2021, January 8). Post-COVID Stress Disorder: Another Emerging Consequence of the Global Pandemic. *Psychiatric Times, 38*(1).

TURKSTAT. (2021). *Health Expenditure Statistics, 2020.* Retrieved on January 31, 2022, from: https://data.tuik.gov.tr/Bulten/Index?p=Health-Expenditure-Statistics-2020-37192

U.S. Chamber of Commerce. (2021). *U.S.-China Decoupling: Macro-Trends and Industry Impacts.* U.S. Chamber of Commerce/Rhodium Group.

Ullah, H., & Ali, J. (2021). Impact of COVID-19 pandemic on the schooling of public and private school students in Pakistan. *Education 3-13*, 1–10. doi:10.1080/03004279.2021.1931917

Umiński, S., & Borowicz, A. (2021). Will multinational enterprises contribute to Poland's economic resilience and recovery during and post COVID-19 pandemic. *Transnational Corporations Review, 13*(1), 74–87. doi:10.1080/19186444.2021.1888638

UNCTAD World Investment Report. (2016). Retrieved on August 14, 2021, from: https://www.unctad,org,en/pages

UNCTAD. (2013). *World investment report 207 3: Global value chains: Investment and trade for development.* United Nations.

UNCTAD. (2020). *World investment report 2020: International production beyond the pandemic.* United Nations.

UNCTAD. (2020). *World Investment Report 2020: International Production Beyond the Pandemic.* United Nations.

UNCTAD. (2021, October 27). *Trade data for 2020 confirm growing importance of digital technologies during COVID-19.* https://unctad.org/news/trade-data-2020-confirm-growing-importance-digital-technologies-during-covid-19

UNCTAD. (2021c). *COVID-19 and Tourism an Update.* Retrieved on January 25, 2022, from: https://unctad.org/system/files/official-document/ditcinf2021d3_en_0.pdf

UNIDO. (2018). *Global Value Chains and Industrial Development: Lessons from China, South-East and South Asia.* UNIDO.

United Nations Conference on Trade and Development. (2021a). *World Investment Report 2021.* Retrieved on January 24, 2022, from: https://unctad.org/system/files/non-official-document/WIR2021_tab01.xlsx

United Nations Conference on Trade and Development. (2021b). *Trade and Development Report 2021.* Retrieved on January 23, 2022, from: https://unctad.org/system/files/official-document/tdr2021_en.pdf

United Nations Industrial Development Organization (UNIDO). (2022). Retrieved on January 25, 2022, from: https://stat.unido.org/database/MVA%202021,%20Manufacturing

United Nations. (2016). *UN data: A world of information.* United Nations Statistics Division. Retrieved on November 30, 2021, from: http://data.un.org

United Nations. D. o. E. a. S. A., Population Division. (2019). *World Population Prospects 2019: Highlights. ST/ESA/SER.A/423.* Retrieved on November 30, 2021, from: https://population.un.org/wpp/Publications/Files/WPP2019_Highlights.pdf

United States Census Bureau. (2022). Census.gov/ *Business & Industry/ Foreign Trade/ Definitions.* Retrieved on January 29, 2022, from: https://www.census.gov/foreign-trade/reference/definitions/index.html

Vakula, D., & Kolli, Y. K. (2017). Low cost smart parking system for smart cities. *2017 International Conference on Intelligent Sustainable Systems (ICISS).* 10.1109/ISS1.2017.8389415

van Beukering, P., Brander, L., Tompkins, E., & Mackenzie, E. (2007). Valuing the Environment in Small Islands: An Environmental Economics Toolkit. Joint Nature Conservation Committee.

van Hoek, R. (2020). Research opportunities for a more resilient post-COVID-19 supply chain – closing the gap between research findings and industry practice. *International Journal of Operations & Production Management, 40*(4), 341–355. doi:10.1108/IJOPM-03-2020-0165

Vargas-Hernández, J. G. (2022). Sustainable Green Resilience and Globalization or De-Globalization in a Post-COVID World. In *Economic and Societal Transformation in Pandemic-Trapped India* (pp. 33–51). Springer. doi:10.1007/978-981-16-5755-9_2

Varrela, S. (2021). Petrol import in Nigeria 2018-2021. *Statista.* Retrieved on October 7, 2021, from: https://www.statista.com/statistics/1165962/petrol-import-in-nigeria/

Verbeke, A. (2020). Will the COVID-19 pandemic really change the governance of global value chains? *British Journal of Management, 31*(3), 444–446. doi:10.1111/1467-8551.12422

Verbeke, A., & Yuan, W. (2021). A few implications of the COVID-19 pandemic for international business strategy research. *Journal of Management Studies, 58*(2), 597–601. doi:10.1111/joms.12665

Vidya, C. T., & Prabheesh, K. P. (2020). Implications of COVID-19 pandemic on the global trade networks. *Emerging Markets Finance & Trade, 56*(10), 2408–2421. doi:10.1080/1540496X.2020.1785426

Volberda, H. W., Foss, N. J., & Lyles, M. A. (2010). Perspective—Absorbing the concept of absorptive capacity: How to realize its potential in the organization field. *Organization Science, 21*(4), 931–951. doi:10.1287/orsc.1090.0503

Waizenegger, L., McKenna, B., Cai, W., & Bendz, T. (2020). An affordance perspective of team collaboration and enforced working from home during COVID-19. *European Journal of Information Systems, 29*(4), 429–442. doi:10.1080/0960085X.2020.1800417

Wang, C., Wang, D., Abbas, J., Duan, K., & Mubeen, R. (2021). Global Financial Crisis, Smart Lockdown Strategies, and the COVID-19 Spillover Impacts: A Global Perspective Implications From Southeast Asia. *Frontiers in Psychiatry, 12*, 1–16. doi:10.3389/fpsyt.2021.643783 PMID:34539457

Wang, T., Luo, H., Jia, W., Liu, A., & Xie, M. (2020). MTES: An Intelligent Trust Evaluation Scheme in Sensor-Cloud-Enabled Industrial Internet of Things. *IEEE Transactions on Industrial Informatics, 16*(3), 2054–2062. doi:10.1109/TII.2019.2930286

Webb, A. (2009). Navigating the New Normal: A Conversation with Four Chief Strategy Officers. *The McKinsey Quarterly*, 1–6.

Wegener, M. (2013). The future of mobility in cities: Challenges for urban modelling. *Transport Policy, 29*, 275–282. doi:10.1016/j.tranpol.2012.07.004

Weinstein, A. K. (1977). Foreign Investments by Service Firms: The Case of Multinational Advertising Agencies. *Journal of International Business Studies, 8*(1), 83–91. doi:10.1057/palgrave.jibs.8490681

Wernerfelt, B. (1984). A Resource-Based View of the Firm. *Strategic Management Journal, 5*(2), 171–180. doi:10.1002mj.4250050207

Werner, S. (2002). Recent Developments in International Management Research: A Review of 20 Top Management Journals. *Journal of Management, 28*(3), 277–305. doi:10.1177/014920630202800303

Werner, S., & Brouthers, L. E. (2002). How International is Management? *Journal of International Business Studies, 33*(3), 583–591. doi:10.1057/palgrave.jibs.8491033

Westman, M., Etzion, D., & Chen, S. (2009). Crossover of positive experiences from business travelers to their spouses. *Journal of Managerial Psychology, 24*(3), 269–284. doi:10.1108/02683940910939340

Wheelen, T. L., & Hunger, J. D. (2011). Strategic Management and Business Policy, (5th ed.). Addison – Wesley Publishing Firm.

White, S., Moore-Colyer, M., Marti, E., Coüetil, L., Hannant, D., Richard, E. A., & Alcocer, M. (2019). Development of a comprehensive protein microarray for immunoglobulin E profiling in horses with severe asthma. *Journal of Veterinary Internal Medicine, 33*(5), 2327-2335.

White, T., & Marchet, F. (2021). Digital Social Markets: Exploring the Opportunities and Impacts of Gamification and Reward Mechanisms in Citizen Engagement and Smart City Services. In M. I. Aldinhas Ferreira (Ed.), *How Smart Is Your City? Technological Innovation, Ethics and Inclusiveness* (pp. 103–125). Springer International Publishing. doi:10.1007/978-3-030-56926-6_9

WHO. (2020a). *State of the world's nursing 2020: investing in education, jobs and leadership*. Retrieved on January 19, 2021, from: https://apps.who.int/iris/rest/bitstreams/1274201/retrieve

WHO. (2020b). *Home/Newsroom/Fact sheets/Detail/Nursing and midwifery/ Key facts*. Retrieved on January https://www.who.int/news-room/fact-sheets/detail/nursing-and-midwifery

WHO. (2021a). *Global expenditure on health: public spending on the rise?* World Health Organization. https://apps.who.int/iris/bitstream/handle/10665/350560/9789240041219-eng.pdf

WHO. (2021b). *Home/Multimedia/Multimedia item/Extending Life Expectancy*. https://www.who.int/multi-media/details/extending-life-expectancy-SDGs

WHO. (2021c). *Home/Newsroom/Questions and answers/Global excess deaths associated with the COVID-19 pandemic.* https://www.who.int/news-room/questions-and-answers/item/global-excess-deaths-associated-with-the-COVID-19-pandemic

WHO. (2022a). *COVID-19 Weekly Epidemiological Update. Edition 73, published 6 January 2022* https://www.who.int/docs/default-source/coronaviruse/situation-reports/20220106_weekly_epi_update_73.pdf?sfvrsn=c731e59b_3&download=true

WHO. (2022b). *The true death toll of COVID-19: Estimating global excess mortality.* https://www.who.int/data/stories/the-true-death-toll-of-covid-19-estimating-global-excess-mortality

WHO. (2022c). *The Global Health Observatory Data:* https://www.who.int/data/gho/data/indicators

WHO. (2022d). *The Global Health Observatory: Indicator Metadata Registry List.* https://www.who.int/data/gho/indicator-metadata-registry

Williamson, O. (1991). Strategizing, economizing and economic organization. *Strategic Management Journal, 12*(Special issue), 75–94. doi:10.1002mj.4250121007

Williamson, P. (2021). De-globalisation and decoupling: Post COVID-19 myths versus realities. *Management and Organization Review, 17*(1), 29–34. doi:10.1017/mor.2020.80

Wilson, R., & Dewaele, J. M. (2010). The use of web questionnaires in second language acquisition and bilingualism research. *Second Language Research, 26*(1), 103–123. doi:10.1177/0267658309337640

WIR (World Investment Report). (2020). International Production beyond the Pandemic. *UNCTAD.*

Witt, M. A. (2019). De-globalization: Theories, predictions, and opportunities for international business research. *Journal of International Business Studies, 50*(7), 1053–1077. doi:10.105741267-019-00219-7

Witt, M., Li, P., Valikangas, L., & Lewin, A. (2021). De-globalisation and decoupling: Game changing consequences? *Management and Organization Review, 17*(1), 6–15. doi:10.1017/mor.2021.9

Worbey, L. (2020) *Flexibility and agility post COVID-19.* KPMG Insights. https://home.kpmg/xx/en/home/insights/2020/08/flexibility-and-agiliity-post-covid-19.html

World Bank. (2021). *World Bank and African Union team up to support rapid vaccination for up to 400 million people in Africa.* Retrieved on June 2, 2022, from: https://www.worldbank.org/en/news/press-release/2021/06/21/world-bank-and-african-union-team-up-to-support-rapid-vaccination-for-up-to-400-million-people-in-africa

World Business Council for Sustainable Development (WBCSD). (2004). *Mobility 2030: Meeting the challenges to sustainability.* https://www.wbcsd.org/Programs/Cities-and-Mobility/Sustainable-Cities/City-Business-Collaboration/SiMPlify/Resources/Mobility-2030-Meeting-the-challenges-to-sustainability-Executive-Summary-2004

World Economic Forum (WEF). (2014). *The Global Competitiveness Report 2014–2015.* Retrieved on January 24, 2022, from: https://www3.weforum.org/docs/WEF_GlobalCompetitivenessReport_2014-15.pdf

World Tourism Organization. (2021, November). *UNWTO World Tourism Barometer and Statistical Annex, November 2021*. Retrieved on January 25, 2022, from: https://www.e-unwto.org/doi/epdf/10.18111/wtobarometereng.2021.19.1.6

World Tourism Organization. (2022a). *Secretary-General's Policy Brief on Tourism and COVID-19: Tourism and Covid-19 – Unprecedented Economic Impacts*. Retrieved on January 25, 2022, from: https://www.e- https://www.unwto.org/tourism-and-covid-19-unprecedented-economic-impacts

World Tourism Organization. (2022b). *UNWTO Tourism Data Dashboard*. Retrieved on January 25, 2022, from: https://www.unwto.org/unwto-tourism-dashboard

WTO. (2020a). Trade set to plunge as COVID-19 pandemic upends global economy. *WTO*. www.wto.org/english/news_e/pres20_e/pr855_e.pdf

WTO. (2020b). The Covid-19 pandemic and trade-related developments in LDCS. *WTO*. www.wto.org/english/tratop_e/covid19_e/ldcs_report_e.pdf

WTO. (2021). *World Trade Statistical Review 2021*. https://www.wto.org/english/res_e/statis_e/wts2021_e/wts2021_e.pdf

WTO. (2022). *Documents, data and resources/WTO data portal*. https://data.wto.org/

Wüstemann, H., Kalisch, D., & Kolbe, J. (2017). Access to urban green space and environmental inequalities in Germany. *Landscape and Urban Planning*, *164*, 124–131. doi:10.1016/j.landurbplan.2017.04.002

Xiao, F., Xie, X., Li, Z., Deng, Q., Liu, A., & Sun, L. (2018). Wireless Network Optimization via Physical Layer Information for Smart Cities. *IEEE Network*, *32*(4), 88–93. doi:10.1109/MNET.2018.1700281

Yao, H., Gao, P., Wang, J., Zhang, P., Jiang, C., & Han, Z. (2019). Capsule Network Assisted IoT Traffic Classification Mechanism for Smart Cities. *IEEE Internet of Things Journal*, *6*(5), 7515–7525. doi:10.1109/JIOT.2019.2901348

Yew, L. K. (2000). *From third world to first world: The Singapore story:1965-2000*. HarperCollins Publishers.

Yigitcanlar, T. (2016). *Technology and the city: Systems, applications and implications*. Routledge. doi:10.4324/9781315739090

Yigitcanlar, T., & Dizdaroglu, D. (2015). Ecological approaches in planning for sustainable cities: A review of the literature. *Global Journal of Environmental Science and Management*, *1*(12), 159–188. doi:10.7508/GJESM.2015.02.008

Yılmam, M. (2011). *Yeni Normal"de Rekabet II* [Competition in the New Normal II.]. KobiEfor, Nisan.

Yiu, D. W., Lau, C., & Bruton, G. D. (2007). International venturing by emerging economy firms: The effects of firm capabilities, home country networks, and corporate entrepreneurship. *Journal of International Business Studies*, *38*(4), 519–540. doi:10.1057/palgrave.jibs.8400278

Yu, C.-h. (2014). *Using SAS for Item Analysis and Test Construction*. Retrieved on August 22, 2021, from: http://www.creative-wisdom.com/teaching/assessment/alpha.html

Zaheer, S., Schomaker, M. S., & Nachum, L. (2012). Distance without direction: Restoring credibility to a much-loved construct. *Journal of International Business Studies*, *43*(1), 18–27. doi:10.1057/jibs.2011.43

Zahra, S. A. (2005). A Theory of International New Ventures: A Decade of Research. *Journal of International Business Studies*, *36*(1), 20–28. doi:10.1057/palgrave.jibs.8400118

Zaman, U., Barnes, S. J., Abbasi, S., Anjam, M., Aktan, M., & Khwaja, M. G. (2022). The Bridge at the End of the World: Linking Expat's Pandemic Fatigue, Travel FOMO, Destination Crisis Marketing, and Vaxication for "Greatest of All Trips". *Sustainability*, *14*(4), 2312. doi:10.3390u14042312

Zeshan, M. (2020). Double-hit scenario of Covid-19 and global value chains. *Environment, Development and Sustainability*, *23*(6), 8559–8572. doi:10.100710668-020-00982-w PMID:32982574

Zhang, J., & Vortherms, S. (2021, August 10). Unstoppable force meets an immovable object: US-China supply chains in the age of decoupling. *Asia Dispatches*.

Zhang, C., & Houghlin, K. (2006). Does international investment help poverty reduction in China. *Chinese Economy*, *34*(3), 79–70. doi:10.2753/CES1097-1475390306

Zhao, M. (2006). Conducting R&D in countries with weak intellectual property rights protection. *Management Science*, *52*(8), 1185–1199. doi:10.1287/mnsc.1060.0516

Zhou, L., Wu, W., & Luo, X. (2007). Internationalization and the performance of born-global SMEs: The mediating role of social networks. *Journal of International Business Studies*, *38*(4), 673–690. doi:10.1057/palgrave.jibs.8400282

Zou, C., Zhao, W., & Siau, K. (2020), COVID-19 calls for remote reskilling and retraining. Cutter Business Technology, 33(7).

Zou, H., Zhou, Y., Yang, J., Gu, W., Xie, L., & Spanos, C. (2018). WiFi-Based Human Identification via Convex Tensor Shapelet Learning. *Proceedings of the AAAI Conference on Artificial Intelligence*, *32*(1). Advance online publication. doi:10.1609/aaai.v32i1.11497

Zygiaris, S. (2013). Smart City Reference Model: Assisting Planners to Conceptualize the Building of Smart City Innovation Ecosystems. *Journal of the Knowledge Economy*, *4*(2), 217–231. doi:10.100713132-012-0089-4

About the Contributors

Bryan Christiansen is the Executive Director and Founder of Colorado-based The Christiansen Foundation that provides training for economically and socially disadvantaged adults to meet the challenges of the 21st century. Christiansen has published 36 Reference books for university libraries that are mostly Scopus- and/or Web of Science-indexed. A former business professor in Kazakhstan, Russia, Turkey, and the USA, he is fluent in Chinese, Japanese, and Spanish with extensive exposure to Russian and Turkish. He is currently working with professors in the United Kingdom and Russia to develop new social sciences models based on his published cultural indoctrination theoretical framework.

John D. Branch currently teaches a variety of marketing and international business courses at the undergraduate, MBA, and executive levels at the Stephen M Ross School of Business at the University of Michigan (USA), and serves as Co-Director of the Yaffe Digital Media Initiative. Previously, he was Academic Director of the School's weekend and evening MBA programmes; earlier, he was also Director of Educational Outreach at the University's William Davidson Institute. John also holds an appointment at the University's Center for Russian, East European, & Eurasian Studies, and maintains a Research Fellowship at the William Davidson Institute. John is originally from Canada. He holds a Bachelor of Engineering Science in electronics from the University of Western Ontario (Canada), a Master of Business Administration from the University of New Brunswick (Canada), a Master of Arts in education from Washington University in Saint Louis (USA), a Doctor of Philosophy in marketing from the University of Cambridge (England), a Doctor of Education from the University of Michigan (USA), and a Doctor of Professional Studies from Middlesex University (England).

* * *

Aldo Alvarez-Risco has experience in carrying out and publishing research studies in sustainability and business. Author of articles, chapters of books and books. Speaker at academic events in 22 countries.

Okechukwu Ethelbert Amah is a full-time faculty at Lagos Business School, Pan Atlantic University where he facilitates sessions in organizational behavior and human resources management. He is the author of the book "Globalization and Leadership in Africa: Developments and Challenges for the Future.

Subhanil Banerjee is an Economist currently working as Associate Professor and Head of the Economics Department, School of Humanities and Social Science, K.R. Mangalam University, Gurgaon. Doctor Banerjee has 19 years of experience in Core Social Science Research. His Research interests are International Trade, Foreign Direct Investment, Health Economics, Digital Economy, Sustainable Development, Environmental Economics, Econometrics, History of economics, Gender Studies and others. So far he has 17 publications 9 of them are SCOPUS indexed Journal Articles, 4 of them are International book chapters, 1 Conference proceeding and 3 other peer reviewed publications.

Marie-Therese Claes is Head of the Institute for Gender and Diversity at the WU Vienna University of Economics and Business. Previously she was CEMS professor Cross-Cultural Management and Leader of the CEMS interfaculty group for many years, and director of the Executive MBA program at the Louvain School of Management (UCLouvain, Belgium). She was also Dean of the Faculty of Business at Asian University in Thailand, and has been visiting professor at several universities in Europe, Asia and the USA, as well as consultant for international organizations. She is past president of SIETAR Europa (and of EWMD (European Women Management Development Network). She is a co-founder and board member of SIETAR Southeast Asia. She is also committee member of IACCM and Fulbright and Japan Foundation alumna.

Metin Gürler has completed his undergraduate study at İhsan Doğramacı Bilkent University, Department of Economics in 1994. He has completed his master education at Marmara University, Department of Economics. He completed his PhD studies in the same department and worked in various manufacturing and service sectors as a professional and entrepreneur at different levels while he has been working as a consultant in many competitiveness, strategy, innovation and cluster projects. He gave undergraduate and graduate level courses at İstinye University in 2016–2017. He is teaching "International Competitiveness Policy", "Current Issues in Foreign Trade" and “”International Retail Management" courses at Medipol University since 2018. Competitiveness of sectors, cities, provinces and nations, clusters, middle income trap, growth economy, economic policy, education, health tourism, health economy and human capital are his main study areas.

Joyce Jenkins is a leadership development facilitator, coach, and consultant, with extensive international business and management experience and specialist expertise in the intercultural management field. She is a co-founder and board member of SIETAR (Society for Intercultural Education, Training and Research) Southeast Asia and a past-president of SIETAR Europa. She has coached and facilitated programmes for senior leaders and teams in some of the world's leading businesses and organisations including as an adjunct faculty member at the Center for Creative Leadership (CCL) Asia-Pacific, as a Research Associate at INSEAD in Singapore and France and as a member of the Asia Pacific and European Alliance of Leadership Facilitators and Global Executive Coaches. She also teaches Intercultural Coaching and Development at the University of Warwick, UK. She has a MA in Chinese and Japanese studies, an MA in Intercultural Communication and is a Fellow of the RSA.

Souren Koner (B.Sc., MBA, Ph.D.) has been acting as an Assistant Professor at the Amity University, Raipur, Chhattisgarh since Aug 2019. He has more than 15 years of experience teaching in different management institutions all over India. His area of specialization is Marketing. He has been teaching in the areas of Marketing Management, Advertising, Sales Management, Service Marketing, etc. So far, he has 15 publications. 2 of them are SCOPUS indexed Journal Articles, 1 of them is in UGC care, 3 of them are international book chapters, 2 Conference proceedings, and 7 other peer-reviewed publications.

Etayankara Muralidharan is an Associate Professor at MacEwan University, School of Business in Canada. He received his PhD from the University of Manitoba in Canada. His research interests are in organizational crisis management, emerging market multinationals, and entrepreneurship. His research has been published in leading management journals (e.g., Journal Business Ethics, Journal of Business Research, International Business Review, Journal of Small Business Management, Thunderbird International Business Review, Cross-Cultural Research, Sustainability) and has been presented at the Academy of Management, Academy of International Business, Babson Entrepreneurship Conference (BCERC), and the Administrative Sciences Association of Canada.

Özlem Özsoy has completed his undergraduate study Ege University, Nursing Faculty, Department of Nursing in 1999. She has completed her master education at Ege University, Institute of Health Sciences, Department of Public Health Nursing. She completed her PhD studies in the same department and worked as an academic staff and in various hospitals in health sector as a professional at different levels (last one is a nursing director of a hospital). She gave graduate level courses at İstinye University in 2016–2017. Public health, nursing management, geriatrics, intensive care, pandemics, health education, health tourism, health economy and human capital are her main study areas.

Rukiye Sönmez graduated from the Department of Business Administration, Faculty of Economics and Administrative Sciences at Adnan Menderes University. She completed her master's degree in Business Administration from the Graduate School of Social Sciences at Canakkale Onsekiz Mart University with a thesis titled, "The Role of Strategic Alliances in Gaining Sustainable Competitive Advantage". She received her doctoral degrees in the department of Business Administration, Faculty of Economics and Administrative Science at Canakkale Onsekiz Mart University, Turkey. With the dissertation of "Collaboration and Competition Dilemma: The Impact of Co-Opetition on Firms Competitive Behaviors in Turkish Airline Industry" she received PhD at the Social Science Institute of Canakkale Onsekiz Mart University. Her research focused on the dilemma between competition and collaboration simultaneously, also known as 'coopetition' in the network settings. She became Assistant Professor at the Banking and Finance of Faculty of Applied Sciences at Biga. Her research interests and publications in academic journals include strategic management issues such as strategic alliances, value creation, competitive dynamics, competitive action and response, competitive behavior, competitive interaction, business model, and social networks.

Aytug Sozuer is Associate Professor at Yalova University, International Trade and Finance Department. He has a doctoral degree in Business Management and Organization from Istanbul University. Previously, he worked at several multinational companies as a specialist in sales and exporting for over five years. His academic research fields of interest include international business, entrepreneurship, and inter-firm relationships.

Nasrin Sultana's research interests include social network analysis, knowledge and technology transfer, management of innovation, innovation ecosystem, sustainability, foreign direct investment, and international business. She wants to study how different organizations are linked and understand the impact of such linkages on organizations, industries, and ecosystems at both local and global levels. She has published in refereed journals including the International Business Review and the Competitiveness

Review. Currently, she is studying the emergence of innovation ecosystems and investigating the role of intermediaries in connecting actors across ecosystems and building sustainable ecosystems.

Patricia V. Tapia-Meza holds a double Master's Licentiate degree in International Business Management from Furtwangen University in Germany and San Martin de Porres University in Peru. She is currently continuing her studies at the Institute of Philosophy of Science, Leibniz University Hannover. Her research revolves around the nexus between the ethics of Artificial Intelligence, smart cities, and strategic management.

Sejal Tiwari is a Master's student at the University of Ottawa. Her research interests are in the area of international business and development.

Ekaterina Turkina holds a PhD in Public and International Affairs from the University of Pittsburgh, USA. She is associate professor at HEC Montreal and a holder of Research Chair in Global Innovation Networks. Ekaterina is also an associate editor of Journal of Small Business and Entrepreneurship, as well as a member of International Advisory Board of International Journal of Productivity Management and Assessment Technologies. Her main research areas are social network analysis, innovation and inter-firm networks, industrial clustering, international business and international entrepreneurship. She has published in Journal of Business Venturing, Economic Geography Journal, Journal of Common Market Studies, Journal of Business Research, Applied Energy, Physica A: Statistical Mechanics and its Applications, International Journal of Computer Science and Network and other journals. She has written four books and was a recipient of several awards, including the Highly Commended Paper Award from the Journal of Enterprising Communities, Best Paper from the European Community Studies Association, and other. She was also the finalist for Alan Rugman Award that is given to most talented researchers in international business under 40 years old.

Judit Végh is a PhD Candidate at the Doctoral School of Psychology, ELTE Eötvös Loránd University, Budapest, Hungary (Institute of Intercultural Psychology and Education and Institute of People-Environment Transaction). She is a co-founder and board member of SIETAR (Society for Intercultural Education, Training and Research) Southeast Asia. She supports global families as a PEaCH Ambassador in Hong Kong (Preserving and promoting Europe's cultural and linguistic heritage through empowerment of bilingual children and families). She is an Intercultural Psychology and Education Expert (MA) and works with transnational families.

Index

I

K

L

M

N

P

R

S

T

U

V

www.ingramcontent.com/pod-product-compliance
Lightning Source LLC
LaVergne TN
LVHW062144300926
849161LV00010B/2621